Reconstructing Keynesian Macroeconomics Volume 2

This book represents the second of three volumes offering a complete reinterpretation and restructuring of Keynesian macroeconomics and a detailed investigation of the disequilibrium adjustment processes characterizing the financial, the goods and the labor markets and their interaction.

In this second volume the authors present a detailed analysis and comparison of two competing types of approaches to Keynesian macroeconomics, one that integrates goods, labor and financial markets, and another from the perspective of a conventional type of labor market analysis or interest rate policy of the central bank. The authors employ rigorous dynamic macro-models of a descriptive and applicable nature, which will be of interest to all macroeconomists who use formal model building in their investigations.

The research in this book with its focus on Keynesian propagation mechanisms provides a unique alternative to the black-box shock-absorber approaches that dominate modern macroeconomics. The main conclusion of the work is that policy-makers need to reconsider Keynesian ideas, but in the modern form in which they are expressed in this volume.

Reconstructing Keynesian Macroeconomics, Volume 2 will be of interest to students and researchers who want to look at alternatives to the mainstream macrodynamics that emerged from the monetarist critique of Keynesianism. This book will also engage central bankers and macroeconomic policy-makers.

Carl Chiarella is Professor of Quantitative Finance at the University of Technology, Sydney, Australia.

Peter Flaschel is Professor of Economics at Bielefeld University, Germany.

Willi Semmler is Professor of Economics at The New School for Social Research, New York, USA.

Routledge frontiers of political economy

1 **Equilibrium Versus Understanding**
Towards the rehumanization of economics within social theory
Mark Addleson

2 **Evolution, Order and Complexity**
Edited by Elias L. Khalil and Kenneth E. Boulding

3 **Interactions in Political Economy**
Malvern after ten years
Edited by Steven Pressman

4 **The End of Economics**
Michael Perelman

5 **Probability in Economics**
Omar F. Hamouda and Robin Rowley

6 **Capital Controversy, Post Keynesian Economics and the History of Economics**
Essays in honour of Geoff Harcourt, Volume one
Edited by Philip Arestis, Gabriel Palma and Malcolm Sawyer

7 **Markets, Unemployment and Economic Policy**
Essays in honour of Geoff Harcourt, Volume two
Edited by Philip Arestis, Gabriel Palma and Malcolm Sawyer

8 **Social Economy**
The logic of capitalist development
Clark Everling

9 **New Keynesian Economics/Post Keynesian Alternatives**
Edited by Roy J. Rotheim

10 **The Representative Agent in Macroeconomics**
James E. Hartley

11 **Borderlands of Economics**
Essays in honour of Daniel R. Fusfeld
Edited by Nahid Aslanbeigui and Young Back Choi

12 **Value, Distribution and Capital**
Essays in Honour of Pierangelo Garegnani
Edited by Gary Mongiovi and Fabio Petri

13 **The Economics of Science**
Methodology and epistemology as if economics really mattered
James R. Wible

14 **Competitiveness, Localised Learning and Regional Development**
Specialisation and prosperity in small open economies
Peter Maskell, Heikki Eskelinen, Ingjaldur Hannibalsson, Anders Malmberg and Eirik Vatne

15 **Labour Market Theory**
A constructive reassessment
Ben J. Fine

16 **Women and European Employment**
Jill Rubery, Mark Smith, Colette Fagan, Damian Grimshaw

17 **Explorations in Economic Methodology**
From Lakatos to empirical philosophy of science
Roger Backhouse

18 **Subjectivity in Political Economy**
Essays on wanting and choosing
David P. Levine

19 **The Political Economy of Middle East Peace**
The impact of competing trade agendas
Edited by J.W. Wright, Jnr.

20 **The Active Consumer**
Novelty and surprise in consumer choice
Edited by Marina Bianchi

21 **Subjectivism and Economic Analysis**
Essays in memory of Ludwig Lachmann
Edited by Roger Koppl and Gary Mongiovi

22 **Themes in Post-Keynesian Economics**
Essays in honour of Geoff Harcourt, Volume three
Edited by Claudio Sardoni and Peter Kriesler

23 **The Dynamics of Technological Knowledge**
Cristiano Antonelli

24 **The Political Economy of Diet, Health and Food Policy**
Ben J. Fine

25 **The End of Finance**
Capital market inflation, financial derivatives and pension fund capitalism
Jan Toporowski

26 **Political Economy and the New Capitalism**
Edited by Jan Toporowski

27 **Growth Theory**
A philosophical perspective
Patricia Northover

28 **The Political Economy of the Small Firm**
Edited by Charlie Dannreuther

29 **Hahn and Economic Methodology**
Edited by Thomas Boylan and Paschal F. O'Gorman

30 **Gender, Growth and Trade**
The miracle economies of the postwar years
David Kucera

31 **Normative Political Economy**
Subjective freedom, the market and the state
David Levine

32 **Economist with a Public Purpose**
Essays in honour of John Kenneth Galbraith
Edited by Michael Keaney

33 **Involuntary Unemployment**
The elusive quest for a theory
Michel De Vroey

34 **The Fundamental Institutions of Capitalism**
Ernesto Screpanti

35 Transcending Transaction
The search for self-generating markets
Alan Shipman

36 Power in Business and the State
An historical analysis of its concentration
Frank Bealey

37 Editing Economics
Essays in honour of Mark Perlman
Hank Lim, Ungsuh K. Park and Geoff Harcourt

38 Money, Macroeconomics and Keynes
Essays in honour of Victoria Chick, Volume 1
Philip Arestis, Meghnad Desai and Sheila Dow

39 Methodology, Microeconomics and Keynes
Essays in honour of Victoria Chick, Volume Two
Philip Arestis, Meghnad Desai and Sheila Dow

40 Market Drive and Governance
Reexamining the rules for economic and commercial contest
Ralf Boscheck

41 The Value of Marx
Political economy for contemporary capitalism
Alfredo Saad-Filho

42 Issues in Positive Political Economy
S. Mansoob Murshed

43 The Enigma of Globalisation
A journey to a new stage of capitalism
Robert Went

44 The Market
Equilibrium, stability, mythology
S. N. Afriat

45 The Political Economy of Rule Evasion and Policy Reform
Jim Leitzel

46 Unpaid Work and the Economy
Edited by Antonella Picchio

47 Distributional Justice
Theory and measurement
Hilde Bojer

48 Cognitive Developments in Economics
Edited by Salvatore Rizzello

49 Social Foundations of Markets, Money and Credit
Costas Lapavitsas

50 Rethinking Capitalist Development
Essays on the economics of Josef Steindl
Edited by Tracy Mott and Nina Shapiro

51 An Evolutionary Approach to Social Welfare
Christian Sartorius

52 Kalecki's Economics Today
Edited by Zdzislaw L. Sadowski and Adam Szeworski

53 Fiscal Policy from Reagan to Blair
The left veers right
Ravi K. Roy and Arthur T. Denzau

54 The Cognitive Mechanics of Economic Development and Institutional Change
Bertin Martens

55 **Individualism and the Social Order**
The social element in liberal thought
Charles R. McCann Jnr.

56 **Affirmative Action in the United States and India**
A comparative perspective
Thomas E. Weisskopf

57 **Global Political Economy and the Wealth of Nations**
Performance, institutions, problems and policies
Edited by Phillip Anthony O'Hara

58 **Structural Economics**
Thijs ten Raa

59 **Macroeconomic Theory and Economic Policy**
Essays in honour of Jean-Paul Fitoussi
Edited by K. Vela Velupillai

60 **The Struggle Over Work**
The "end of work" and employment alternatives in post-industrial societies
Shaun Wilson

61 **The Political Economy of Global Sporting Organisations**
John Forster and Nigel Pope

62 **The Flawed Foundations of General Equilibrium Theory**
Critical essays on economic theory
Frank Ackerman and Alejandro Nadal

63 **Uncertainty in Economic Theory**
Essays in honor of David Schmeidler's 65th birthday
Edited by Itzhak Gilboa

64 **The New Institutional Economics of Corruption**
Edited by Johann Graf Lambsdorff, Markus Taube and Matthias Schramm

65 **The Price Index and its Extension**
A chapter in economic measurement
S.N. Afriat

66 **Reduction, Rationality and Game Theory in Marxian Economics**
Bruce Philp

67 **Culture and Politics in Economic Development**
Volker Bornschier

68 **Modern Applications of Austrian Thought**
Edited by Jürgen G. Backhaus

69 **Ordinary Choices**
Individuals, incommensurability, and democracy
Robert Urquhart

70 **Labour Theory of Value**
Peter C. Dooley

71 **Capitalism**
Victor D. Lippit

72 **Macroeconomic Foundations of Macroeconomics**
Alvaro Cencini

73 **Marx for the 21st Century**
Edited by Hiroshi Uchida

74 **Growth and Development in the Global Political Economy**
Social structures of accumulation and modes of regulation
Phillip Anthony O'Hara

75 **The New Economy and Macroeconomic Stability**
A neo-modern perspective drawing on the complexity approach and Keynesian economics
Teodoro Dario Togati

76 **The Future of Social Security Policy**
Women, work and a citizen's basic income
Ailsa McKay

77 **Clinton and Blair**
The political economy of the third way
Flavio Romano

78 **Marxian Reproduction Schema**
Money and aggregate demand in a capitalist economy
A.B. Trigg

79 **The Core Theory in Economics**
Problems and solutions
Lester G. Telser

80 **Economics, Ethics and the Market**
Introduction and applications
Johan J. Graafland

81 **Social Costs and Public Action in Modern Capitalism**
Essays inspired by Karl William Kapp's Theory of Social Costs
Edited by Wolfram Elsner, Pietro Frigato and Paolo Ramazzotti

82 **Globalization and the Myths of Free Trade**
History, theory and empirical evidence
Edited by Anwar Shaikh

83 **Equilibrium in Economics: Scope and Limits**
Edited by Valeria Mosini

84 **Globalization**
State of the art and perspectives
Edited by Stefan A. Schirm

85 **Neoliberalism**
National and regional experiments with global ideas
Edited by Ravi K. Roy, Arthur T. Denzau, Thomas D. Willett

86 **Post-Keynesian Macroeconomics Economics**
Essays in honour of Ingrid Rima
Edited by Mathew Forstater, Gary Mongiovi and Steven Pressman

87 **Consumer Capitalism**
Anastasios S. Korkotsides

88 **Remapping Gender in the New Global Order**
Edited Marjorie Griffin Cohen and Janine Brodie

89 **Hayek and Natural Law**
Erik Angner

90 **Race and Economic Opportunity in the Twenty-First Century**
Edited by Marlene Kim

91 **Renaissance in Behavioural Economics**
Harvey Leibenstein's impact on contemporary economic analysis
Edited by Roger Frantz

92 **Human Ecology Economics**
A new framework for global sustainability
Edited by Roy E. Allen

93 **Imagining Economics Otherwise**
Encounters with identity/difference
Nitasha Kaul

94 **Reigniting the Labor Movement**
Restoring means to ends in a democratic labor movement
Gerald Friedman

95 **The Spatial Model of Politics**
Norman Schofield

96 **The Economics of American Judaism**
Carmel Ullman Chiswick

97 **Critical Political Economy**
Christian Arnsperger

98 **Culture and Economic Explanation**
Economics in the US and Japan
Donald W. Katzner

99 **Feminism, Economics and Utopia**
Time travelling through paradigms
Karin Schönpflug

100 **Risk in International Finance**
Vikash Yadav

101 **Economic Policy and Performance in Industrial Democracies**
Party governments, central banks and the fiscal-monetary policy mix
Takayuki Sakamoto

102 **Advances on Income Inequality and Concentration Measures**
Edited by Gianni Betti and Achille Lemmi

103 **Economic Representations**
Academic and everyday
Edited by David F. Ruccio

104 **Mathematical Economics and the Dynamics of Capitalism**
Goodwin's legacy continued
Edited by Peter Flaschel and Michael Landesmann

105 **The Keynesian Multiplier**
Edited by Claude Gnos and Louis-Philippe Rochon

106 **Money, Enterprise and Income Distribution**
Towards a macroeconomic theory of capitalism
John Smithin

107 **Fiscal Decentralization and Local Public Finance in Japan**
Nobuki Mochida

108 **The 'Uncertain' Foundations of Post-Keynesian Economics**
Essays in exploration
Stephen P. Dunn

109 **Karl Marx's Grundrisse**
Foundations of the critique of political economy 150 years later
Edited by Marcello Musto

110 **Economics and the Price Index**
S.N. Afriat and Carlo Milana

111 **Sublime Economy**
On the intersection of art and economics
Edited by Jack Amariglio, Joseph W. Childers and Stephen E. Cullenberg

112 **Popper, Hayek and the Open Society**
Calvin Hayes

113 **The Political Economy of Work**
David Spencer

114 **Institutional Economics**
Bernard Chavance

115 **Religion, Economics and Demography**
The effects of religion on education, work, and the family
Evelyn L. Lehrer

116 **Economics, Rational Choice and Normative Philosophy**
Edited by Thomas A. Boylan and Ruvin Gekker

117 **Economics Versus Human Rights**
Manuel Couret Branco

118 **Hayek Versus Marx and Today's Challenges**
Eric Aarons

119 **Work Time Regulation as Sustainable Full Employment Policy**
Robert LaJeunesse

120 **Equilibrium, Welfare and Uncertainty**
Mukul Majumdar

121 **Capitalism, Institutions and Economic Development**
Michael Heller

122 **Economic Pluralism**
Robert Garnett, Erik Olsen and Martha Starr

123 **Dialectics of Class Struggle in the Global Economy**
Clark Everling

124 **Political Economy and Globalization**
Richard Westra

125 **Full-Spectrum Economics**
Toward an inclusive and emancipatory social science
Christian Arnsperger

126 **Computable, Constructive and Behavioural Economic Dynamics**
Essays in honour of Kumaraswamy (Vela) Velupillai
Stefano Zambelli

127 **Monetary Macrodynamics**
Toichiro Asada, Carl Chiarella, Peter Flaschel and Reiner Franke

128 **Rationality and Explanation in Economics**
Maurice Lagueux

129 **The Market, Happiness and Solidarity**
A Christian perspective
Johan J. Graafland

130 **Economic Complexity and Equilibrium Illusion**
Essays on market instability and macro vitality
Ping Chen

131 **Economic Theory and Social Change**
Problems and revisions
Hasse Ekstedt and Angelo Fusari

132 **The Practices of Happiness**
Political economy, religion and wellbeing
Edited by John Atherton, Elaine Graham and Ian Steedman

133 **The Measurement of Individual Well-Being and Group Inequalities**
Essays in memory of Z. M. Berrebi
Edited by Joseph Deutsch and Jacques Silber

134 **Wage Policy, Income Distribution, and Democratic Theory**
Oren M. Levin-Waldman

135 **The Political Economy of Bureaucracy**
Steven O. Richardson

136 **The Moral Rhetoric of Political Economy: Justice and Modern Economic**
Thought
Paul Turpin

137 **Macroeconomic Regimes in Western Industrial Countries**
Hansjörg Herr and Milka Kazandziska

138 **Business Ethics and the Austrian Tradition in Economics**
Hardy Bouillon

139 **Inequality and Power: The Economics of Class**
Eric A. Schutz

140 **Capital as a Social Kind: Definitions and Transformations in the Critique of Political economy**
Howard Engelskirchen

141 **Happiness, Ethics and Economics**
Johannes Hirata

142 **Capital, Exploitation and Economic Crisis**
John Weeks

143 **The Global Economic Crisis**
New perspectives on the critique of economic theory and policy
Edited by Emiliano Brancaccio and Giuseppe Fontana

144 **Economics and Diversity**
Carlo D'Ippoliti

145 **Political Economy of Human Rights**
Rights, realities and realization
Bas de Gaay Fortman

146 **Robinson Crusoe's Economic Man**
A construction and deconstruction
Edited by Ulla Grapard and Gillian Hewitson

147 **Freedom and Happiness in Economic Thought and Philosophy**
From clash to reconciliation
Edited by Ragip Ege and Herrade Igersheim

148 **Political Economy After Economics**
David Laibman

149 **Reconstructing Keynesian Macroeconomics Volume 1**
Partial perspectives
Carl Chiarella, Peter Flaschel and Willi Semmler

150 **Institutional Economics and National Competitiveness**
Edited by Young Back Choi

151 **Capitalist Diversity and Diversity within Capitalism**
Edited by Geoffrey T. Wood and Christel Lane

152 **The Consumer, Credit and Neoliberalism**
Governing the modern economy
Christopher Payne

153 **Order and Control in American Socio-Economic Thought**
U.S. social scientists and progressive-era reform
Charles McCann

154 **The Irreconcilable Inconsistencies of Neoclassical Macroeconomics**
A false paradigm
John Weeks

155 **The Political Economy of Putin's Russia**
Pekka Sutela

156 **Facts, Values and Objectivity in Economics**
José Castro Caldas and Vítor Neves

157 **Economic Growth and the High Wage Economy: Choices, Constraints and Opportunities in the market economy**
Morris Altman

158 **Social Costs Today: Institutional Analyses of the Present Crises**
Edited by Wolfram Elsner, Pietro Frigato and Paolo Ramazzotti

159 **Economics, Sustainability and Democracy**
Economics in the era of climate change
Christopher Nobbs

160 **Organizations, Individualism and Economic Theory**
Maria Brouwer

161 **Economic Models for Policy Making**
Principles and designs revisited
S. I. Cohen

162 **Reconstructing Keynesian Macroeconomics Volume 2**
Integrated approaches
Carl Chiarella, Peter Flaschel and Willi Semmler

Reconstructing Keynesian Macroeconomics Volume 2

Integrated approaches

Carl Chiarella, Peter Flaschel and Willi Semmler

Routledge
Taylor & Francis Group
LONDON AND NEW YORK

First published 2013
by Routledge
2 Park Square, Milton Park, Abingdon, Oxfordshire OX14 4RN

Simultaneously published in the USA and Canada
by Routledge
711 Third Avenue, New York, NY 10017

First issued in paperback 2014

Routledge is an imprint of the Taylor and Francis Group, an informa business

British Library Cataloguing in Publication Data
A catalogue record for this book is available from the British Library

Library of Congress Cataloging in Publication Data
Chiarella, Carl, Reconstructing Keynesian macroeconomics: partial perspectives/
Carl Chiarella, Peter Flaschel, and Willi Semmler.
p. cm.
Includes bibliographical references and index.
1. Keynesian economics. 2. Macroeconomics.
I. Flaschel, Peter, 1943- II. Semmler, Willi. III. Title.
HB99.7.C53 2011
339.5–dc22 2011014501

ISBN 978-0-415-66857-6 (hbk)
ISBN 978-1-138-90133-9 (pbk)
ISBN 978-0-203-08509-7 (ebk)

Typeset in Times New Roman
by Sunrise Setting Ltd, Paignton, UK

Contents

Figures

Tables

Notation

Steady-state or trend values are indicated by a sub- or superscript "0" (sometimes also by "o" or "$*$"). When no confusion arises, letters F, G, H may also define certain functional expressions in a specific context. A dot over a variable $x = x(t)$ denotes the time derivative, a caret its growth rate: $\dot{x} = dx/dt$, $\hat{x} = \dot{x}/x$. In the numerical simulations, flow variables are measured at annual rates.

As far as possible, the notation tries to follow the logic of using capital letters for level variables and lower-case letters for variables in intensive form, or for constant (steady-state) ratios. Greek letters are most often constant coefficients in behavioral equations (with, however, the notable exceptions being the inflation climate π^c and the real wage ω). We use the abbreviation "NAIRE" for the nonaccelerating inflation rate of employment and "NAIRU" for the nonaccelerating inflation rate of unemployment but use this acronym also in the case "utilization" (of labor or capital) in place of "unemployment." The acronym "RE(S)" stands for the "rational expectations (school)." Further acronyms are of a local nature only and will be explained in the sections where they are used. There will also be some chapter-specific (local) notation in some of the chapters.

B	outstanding government fixed-price bonds (priced at $p_b = 1$)
C	real private consumption (demand is generally realized)
E	number of equities
F	neoclassical production function
	otherwise a generic symbol for functions defined in a local context
G	real government expenditure (demand is always realized)
I	real net investment of fixed capital (demand is always realized)
$\mathcal{I}$	desired real inventory investment
J	Jacobian matrix in the mathematical analysis
K	stock of fixed capital
L^d	total working hours (labor demand is always realized)
L^w	employed workforce, i.e. number of employed people
L or N	labor supply, i.e. supply of total working hours per year
M	stock of money supply
N	inventories of finished goods
N^d	desired stock of inventories

S_f	real saving of firms
S_g	real government saving
S_p	real saving of private households
S	total real saving
T	total real tax collections
$T_w(t_w)$	real taxes of workers (per unit of capital)
$T_c(t_c)$	real taxes of asset-holders (per unit of capital)
W	real wealth of private households
Y	real output
Y^p	potential real output
Y^f	full employment real output
Y^d	real aggregate demand
Y^e	expected real aggregate demand
c	marginal propensity to consume
e	employment rate
$U = 1 - e$	unemployment rate
$f_x = f_1$, etc.	partial derivative
r, i	nominal rate of interest on government bonds;
k	capital intensity K/L (also used as a parameter in money demand)
$\sigma = 1/y$	capital coefficient K/Y
l	labor intensity (in efficiency units)
m	real balances relative to the capital stock; $m = M/pK$
ν	inventory/capital ratio; $\nu = N/K$
p	price level
p_e	price of equities
q	return differential; $q = r - (i - \pi)$ or Tobin's q
r, ρ	rate of return on fixed capital, specified as $r = (pY - wL - \delta pK)/pK$
s_c	propensity to save out of capital income on the part of asset-owners
u, u^w, e^w	rate of capacity utilization; of capital $u = Y/Y^n = y/y^n$ and of labor
v	wage share (in gross product); $v = wL/pY$
w	nominal wage rate per hour
y	output/capital ratio; $y = Y/K$;
y^d	ratio of aggregate demand to capital stock; $y^d = Y^d/K$
y^e	ratio of expected demand to capital stock; $y^e = Y^e/K$
z or x	labor productivity, i.e. output per worker; $z = Y/L^d$
α	symbol for policy parameters in Taylor rule
α_i	coefficient measuring interest rate smoothing in the Taylor rule
α_p	coefficient on inflation gap in the Taylor rule
α_u	coefficient on output gap in the Taylor rule

β_x	generically, reaction coefficient in an equation determining $x, \dot{x}$ or $\hat{x}$
β_y	adjustment speed in adaptive sales expectations
β_π	general adjustment speed in revisions of the inflation climate
β_{xy}	generically, reaction coefficient related to the determination of variable x, $\dot{x}$ or $\hat{x}$ with respect to changes in the exogenous variable y
α_q	responsiveness of investment (capital growth rate) to changes in q
α_u	responsiveness of investment to changes in u
β_n	stock adjustment speed
α_{n^d}	desired ratio of inventories over expected sales
β_{pu}	reaction coefficient of u in the price Phillips curve
β_{pv}	reaction coefficient of $(1+\mu)v-1$ in the price Phillips curve
β_{we}	reaction coefficient of e in the wage Phillips curve
β_{wv}	reaction coefficient of $(v-v^0)/v^0$ in the wage Phillips curve
γ	government expenditures per unit of fixed capital; $\gamma = G/K$ (a constant)
τ	lump sum taxes per unit of fixed capital; $\tau = T/K$ (a constant)
δ	rate of depreciation of fixed capital (a constant)
$\eta_{m,i}$	interest elasticity of money demand (a positive number)
κ	coefficient in reduced-form wage–price equations; $\kappa = 1/(1-\kappa_p\kappa_w)$
κ_p	parameter weighting $\widehat{w}$ vs. π in the price Phillips curve
κ_w	parameter weighting $\hat{p}$ vs. π in the wage Phillips curve
κ_{wp}	same as κ_w
κ_{wz}	parameter weighting $\hat{z}$ vs. $\hat{z}^0$ in the wage Phillips curve
κ_π	parameter weighting adaptive expectations vs. regressive expectations in revisions of the inflation climate
π^c	general inflation climate;
θ	log of real wages
$\tau_c = T_c/K$	tax parameter for T^c (net of interest and per unit of capital); $T^c - iB/p$
ω	real wage rate w/p

Preface

This book is the second in the trilogy *Reconstructing Keynesian Macroeconomics*. The general introduction of the first volume still holds for the current volume as well. This book continues the message of reinterpreting and restructuring Keynesian macroeconomics by giving a detailed investigation of the disequilibrium adjustment processes that characterize the financial, the goods and the labor markets and their interaction. It remains critical of the rational expectations school and stresses the feedback channels in the traditional Tobin model and focuses on theories of the wage–price spiral.

The current book focuses on competing approaches to Keynesian macroeconomics, demand-driven inflation and the distributive cycle, the semistructural aggregate demand–aggregate supply (AD–AS) model, the structural Keynes–Metzler–Goodwin (KMG) model and finally some extensions and a discussion of the role of financial markets.

Carl Chiarella, Peter Flaschel and Willi Semmler
Sydney, Bielefeld and New York
February 21st, 2012

Part I

Competing approaches to Keynesian macroeconomics

1 Representative households or principal-agent capitalism?

1.1 Introduction

In this chapter we will question the assumption of a representative household for the whole economy commonly made in the macroeconomics literature. This assumption is completely at odds with what we observe as the real outcomes of capitalist economies, particularly in the more advanced ones. In reality there is conflict over income distribution between the owners of the capital stock and labor. Firms may be assumed to be profit-maximizing and interacting with the unions of workers in the wage bargaining process, the latter also holding in the representative agent framework that we will discuss in this chapter.

But the assumption that workers get all the profits from firms in addition to their wages should simply change their behavior away from – possibly inefficient – real wage claims to the maximization of the output of firms, since this is the income they will get at the end of the day. But this would mean that they would indeed gain from real wage decreases, since this increases output, until the level of full employment has been reached. This is a kind of people's capitalism as it flows from the assumption that workers are the owners of firms in a capitalist economy, a view that we do not pursue.

The view we adopt in this chapter is that microfoundations are of course desirable, but they need to take into consideration what it is that one needs to model. Perhaps many of the different viewpoints in economics can be traced back to disagreement over this issue.

1.2 The role and scope of microfoundations

In our view the basic objection to traditional mainstream microfoundations, namely, the Ramsey "representative agent" approach, is given by the simple observation that capitalism is at the absolute minimum based on the interaction of two representative agents (Robinson as the principal and Friday as the agent), plus entrepreneurs and their management from a Schumpeterian perspective. We believe that capitalism cannot be sensibly modeled under the assumption that a *ceteris paribus* reduction in wages simply reappears as profits in the income statement of the single representative agent of orthodox macroeconomics, who therefore may benefit in fact from lowering his or her wages. In the representative agent framework workers act as workers on the labor market, while the firms are acting against them (as Goethe wrote in Faust: "Two souls alas! are dwelling in my breast").

The conflict over income distribution (and changes in the techniques of production) is a very fundamental conflict in a capitalist economy, one that is not at all only a subject of Marxian economics. It may even be claimed that it is the core element in the explanation of the dynamics of capitalism, shaping Keynesian goods market dynamics (based on the wage-led profit-led distinction) as well as Schumpeterian cycles in the economic and the social structure of accumulation, and all this in very significant ways. The long-run nature of this conflict is exemplified with respect to the short- and long-phase cycles it implies for the case of the US economy, as discussed in Tavani *et al.* (2011) and Proaño *et al.* (2011). The representative agent straitjacket is not removed from macroeconomic model building by making use of overlapping generations (OLG) models, since the distinction between capitalists and workers is not a matter of age. Instead, if this distinction were made, we would get four distinct types of economic agents in our view, since social affiliations tend to be stable in time and are thus quite the opposite of the case considered in the single-agent OLG framework where everybody becomes a capitalist when old.

There are of course more than just the two considered social classes, but our argument is not directed toward finding the most appropriate representation for a capitalist economy, but to establish what should be assumed as a minimum in the investigation of its dynamics. On the basis of such a minimum framework, one should then however formulate a situation that is more general than the case of classical saving habits where only savings out of profits are allowed for. In a modern capitalist economy both capitalists and workers save so that personal income distribution will be different from functional income distribution and there will be wealth accumulation also on the side of workers, the long-run effects of which have to be investigated.

There will then be the evolution of unions, pension funds and more, and workers' preferences may also change in the course of wealth accumulation. Yet, these are secondary issues that should be kept apart from the baseline version of the model that attempts to investigate the dynamics of wages, profits and wealth in a society where interests differ about the evolution of these magnitudes.

There is however a second argument which questions the validity of the arguments put forth by those who insist on the representative agent approach. Households in this approach are often modeled in a Walrasian manner, not only as price takers, but also as seeing no (income) restrictions for the supply they are offering through their optimizing procedures. With respect to the Walrasian framework we know however from the theorem proved by Sonnenschein, Mantel and Debreu (see Debreu 1974; Mantel 1977; Sonnenschein 1973; Rizvi 2006)[1] that nearly everything can be microfounded, once enough heterogeneity is assumed among economic agents. What therefore is the value of a Robinson Crusoe type of microfoundation of certain demand and supply schedules? The answer is that nothing can really be proved in this way to be superior to a well-specified supply and demand relationship (formulated within well-specified budget restrictions), at least from the viewpoint of the Sonnenschein, Mantel and Debreu theorems.

The argument can only be a methodological one, namely to avoid situations where this type of well-specified behavior is neglected by assuming supply and demand relationships that are inconsistent with the stock-flow interactions generated by the budget restrictions of the various types of agents. This implies that these latter restrictions should always be carefully specified, but that the matter of what agents actually optimize within these constraints should at the very least be a matter of dispute, if not even a matter of empirical investigation that cannot be subjected to theoretical analysis alone. All this also holds outside the counterfactual general equilibrium analysis of Walrasian production economies. Such an approach should be used to demand rigor on the side of stock–flow specifications of the considered economy, but – in the interests of scientific pluralism – not be used to just refuse coherent modeling of this type simply because they are not based on the representative agent assumption or related modeling devices.

1.3 Representative agent macrodynamics

In this section we discuss a simple model of the representative agent approach of neoclassical macroeconomics (one household and one firm) and will focus here in particular on the assumed behavior of the household sector of the economy. We will allow for real wage rigidity, based on a standard real wage Phillips curve as it can be obtained from its standard expectations-augmented form by assuming myopic perfect foresight with respect to price inflation. Assuming that a gradual adjustment of the real wage is based on the existence of unemployed members of the workforce, giving rise here to a Solovian type of less than full employment dynamics with microfounded consumption (and investment behavior). The point of this section is to highlight the conceptual difficulties of the representative agent approach.

The household sector

The household sector is represented by one household, which maximizes the discounted stream of utility arising from per-capita consumption, $C(t)$, over an infinite time horizon subject to its budget constraint, taking factor prices as given. The utility function is assumed to be logarithmic, $U(C) = \ln C$, and the household inelastically supplies L units of labor, of which L^d is demanded by the productive sector at the real wage rate ω. We assume that households are characterized by an extended family structure, so that its older members hold and control the capital stock and they employ as workers (or if unemployed, support) the younger ones. Optimized consumption is distributed uniformly across the extended family. Total labor supply L is assumed to be constant over time.[2]

The maximization problem of the household sector can be written as

$$\max_{C} \int_0^\infty e^{-\rho t} \ln C \, dt, \tag{1.1}$$

subject to

$$\omega L^d + rK = C + \delta K + \dot{K}. \tag{1.2}$$

The coefficient ρ is the household's rate of time preference, r is the rate of return to capital K and the capital stock depreciates at the rate δ.

To solve the optimization problem we formulate the current-value Hamiltonian which is written as

$$\mathcal{H} = \ln C + \gamma\left(\omega L^d + rK - C - \delta K\right), \tag{1.3}$$

where γ is the co-state variable. Necessary optimality conditions are given by

$$C^{-1} = \gamma, \tag{1.4}$$

$$\dot{\gamma} = (\rho + \delta)\gamma - \gamma r. \tag{1.5}$$

If the transversality condition $\lim_{t\to\infty} e^{-\rho t} K/C = 0$ holds, which is fulfilled for a time path on which assets grow at the same rate as consumption, the necessary conditions are also sufficient.

The productive sector and the labor market

The productive sector is represented by one firm which behaves competitively and which maximizes static profits. The production function of the firm is assumed to be given by a constant returns to scale Cobb–Douglas production function

$$Y = K^{1-\alpha}\left(L^d\right)^{\alpha}. \tag{1.6}$$

Here Y is output and $\alpha \in (0, 1)$ gives the elasticity of output with respect to labor input and $(1-\alpha)$ is the capital share. Profit maximization gives the profit rate, r, as

$$r = (1-\alpha)Y/K \equiv (1-\alpha)y. \tag{1.7}$$

Labor demand is obtained from the firm maximizing profits leading to

$$l^d \equiv L^d/K = (\omega/\alpha)^{1/(\alpha-1)} \quad \text{and} \quad y = Y/K = (l^d)^{\alpha}. \tag{1.8}$$

The reason for rigid wages are labor market imperfections due to trade unions setting the nominal wage rate. We here follow Blanchard and Katz (1999)[3] and assume as real wage dynamics

$$\widehat{\omega} = \dot{\omega}/\omega = \beta_{w1}(e-\bar{e}) - \beta_{w2}(\omega-\omega_0)l^d/y, \quad e = L^d/L = l^d/l,$$

where e denotes the current rate of employment and $\bar{e}$ the given NAIRE (nonaccelerating inflation rate of employment) level of this rate (L the stationary labor supply). Note here that the assumption of myopic perfect foresight allows us to ignore the way the price inflation rate is determined in the model.

Hence, given the unions' wage setting behavior, the evolution of the real wage rate can be described by a relationship where the change in the real wage rate negatively depends on the rate of unemployment and also negatively on the level of real wages, viewed as an error correction term in this Phillips curve. This approach to a real wage Phillips curve is an interesting one, since it derives a NAIRE rate of employment from the parameters of the model.

In the present framework however it raises the question as to why workers (and their unions) do not simply opt for full employment, since this would maximize their family's income[4] as well as improve their employment position.[5] In the Solow (1956) approach, full employment was achieved by assuming perfectly flexible wages and such a scenario should also be a plausible one for the workers and their unions within the present model.

Analysis of the model

In order to analyze the economy around its stationary steady state we consider the variables $c \equiv C/K, l \equiv L/K$ and ω. Differentiating these variables with respect to time gives a three-dimensional (3D) system of differential equations that can be written as

$$\widehat{\omega} = \beta_{w1}\left(\frac{l^d}{l} - \bar{e}\right) - \beta_{w2}(\omega - \omega_0)l^d/y, \tag{1.9}$$

$$\hat{l} = \delta + c - y, \tag{1.10}$$

$$\hat{c} = r - (\rho + \delta) - (y - \delta - c) = -\alpha y - \rho + c, \tag{1.11}$$

with $l^d = (\omega/\alpha)^{1/\alpha - 1}$ and $y = (l^d)^\alpha = (\omega/\alpha)^{\alpha/(\alpha-1)}$.

The stationary state for our economy is obtained when the left hand side of the equation system (1.9)–(1.11) equals zero, which gives

$$y_0 = \frac{\rho + \delta}{1 - \alpha}, \quad l_0^d = y_0^{1/\alpha}, \quad l_0 = \frac{l_0^d}{\bar{e}}, \quad c_0 = y_0 - \delta, \quad \omega_0 = \alpha(l_0^d)^{\alpha - 1}. \tag{1.12}$$

Note that the economy is not a growing one, since $\hat{l} = -\widehat{K} = 0$ holds true.

The Jacobian matrix of the dynamics evaluated at the steady state is characterized by

$$J = \begin{pmatrix} - & - & 0 \\ + & 0 & + \\ + & 0 & + \end{pmatrix}.$$

The interaction of the state variables ω, l is of cross-dual Goodwin (1967) growth cycle type, augmented by smooth factor substitution (and a Blanchard and Katz error correction mechanism) which makes these center type dynamics convergent (since a negative trace is added to the expanding/contracting mechanism of this Lotka–Volterra system $J_{21} > 0,\ J_{11} < 0$). So far the model synthesizes the classical and the neoclassical approach to the process of capital accumulation. The theory of consumption is however a strictly neoclassical one. This microfounded determination of consumption per unit of capital introduces a cumulative process into the Solow–Goodwin framework, since increasing consumption per unit of capital reduces the growth rate of the capital stock whereby the time rate of change of consumption per unit of capital is further increased and so on. The same positive self-reference mechanism works also in the downward direction.

The determinant of the Jacobian matrix is characterized by

$$J = \begin{vmatrix} - & - & 0 \\ + & 0 & + \\ - & 0 & 0 \end{vmatrix},$$

since a multiple of its second row can be deducted from its third one without changing its value. The determinant is therefore obviously positive in its sign. Since the determinant is the product of the eigenvalues of the matrix J, it follows that these eigenvalues have either all positive real parts or one of them is positive while the real parts of the other two are negative. Since the first case represents a purely explosive situation we exclude it here from consideration. A sufficient condition for the second case is given by a choice of the parameter β_{w1} that is chosen sufficiently large, such that the trace of J becomes positive. In this case there must exist a negative eigenvalue, since the trace of J is given by the sum of the three eigenvalues.

The stable manifold around the steady state of J is therefore of dimension two and the unstable one of dimension one. The variables ω, l are clearly predetermined ones, while the consumption ratio c is capable of jumping since it is not predetermined. The model is then solved for any shock hitting the economy by jumps of the variable c for each given initial values $\omega(0)$, $l(0)$ onto the stable manifold.

We do not go into the details of this jump variable technique here however (which in fact is here a microfounded one), since we are only interested in an investigation of the household behavior within such an economy. From a purely macroeconomic point of view we would however have the case that the above dynamical system is stabilized by assumption, a result that is typical for models of the myopic perfect foresight variety.

Evaluation of the model

The maximization problem of the household sector has been assumed in the above model to be of the form

$$\max_{C} \int_{0}^{\infty} e^{-\rho t} \ln C \, dt, \tag{1.13}$$

subject to

$$\omega L^d + rK = C + \delta K + \dot{K}. \tag{1.14}$$

Such a description just assumes that this sector is acting like an extended family, where grandparents own the capital stock, while parents do the work (or are unemployed) and raise their children. There is no conflict in this family, since all of its members pool their income, also with the unemployed members of the parent generation. This would be an easy life for grandparents, as firms just maximize profits at each moment of time (for a given value of the capital stock). The only disturbing element is that the generation of the parents insists on real wage negotiations which create unemployment at a NAIRE level on average. Grandparents could however just tell them not to do this any more, since these actions reduce the family's income. Instead parents should accept the Solovian full employment real wage as remuneration, avoiding thereby time consuming arguments with firms. Their labor supply decision would then be realized, family income would be maximized and the whole family would thus be better off.

Why do grandparents not communicate this to their children? We consider this to be the major interpretation problem of the Ramsey approach to the investigation of actual capitalist economies.

1.4 Principal/agent capitalism and the distribution of income and wealth

In this section we build a very simple macromodel which is microfounded, and considers disequilibrium by way of real wage rigidity (in the form of a conventional real wage Phillips curve, based on myopic perfect foresight with respect to the price inflation rate). The model also assumes heterogeneous agents, in fact two, the representative worker and the pure capitalist, both with their own utility function[6] and with differing degrees of ownership in the total capital stock of the economy (which can change over time).

Household behavior: workers and asset-holders

We use a continuous-time framework with a stationary population of both types of agents, the first normalized to unity and the second to a (small) fraction of unity.[7] Workers maximize a Cobb–Douglas utility function

$$C_w^{\alpha_w} I_w^{1-\alpha_w},$$

with C_w their planned consumption and I_w their planned investment into the capital stock they own (all capital items depreciate at the rate δ).[8] The temporary budget restriction of workers is given by

$$C_w + I_w = \omega L^d + \rho K_w, \quad \rho = (Y - \delta K - \omega L^d)/K = y - \delta - \omega l^d,$$

where Y, L^d are gross output and employment, K_w the capital stock owned by workers and ρ the rate of profit of the economy ($\omega = w/p$ the real wage).[9] We assume fixed proportions in production, so that y, l^d are given magnitudes here for reasons of simplicity.[10] Utility maximization then implies for workers the gross savings equals gross investment relationship that can be written

$$I_w = (1-\alpha_w)[\omega l^d + \rho k_w]K, \quad k_w = K_w/K. \tag{1.15}$$

Pure capitalists also maximize a Cobb–Douglas utility function

$$C_c^{\alpha_c} I_c^{1-\alpha_c},$$

with C_c their planned consumption and I_c their planned investment into the capital stock that they own. We assume that $\alpha_w > \alpha_c$ holds true with respect to the utility generated by consumption and that capitalists do not work, but consume on the basis of their profit income solely. The temporary budget restriction of capitalists is therefore given by

$$C_c + I_c = \rho K_c, \quad \rho = y - \delta - \omega l^d, \quad K_c = K - K_w,$$

where K_c is the capital stock owned by capitalists.

Utility maximization then implies for capitalists the gross savings equals gross investment relationship

$$I_c = (1-\alpha_c)\rho k_c K, \quad k_c = K_c/K.$$

This completes the description of the household sector of the economy. The interaction of workers and the managers of firms is considered next. Since we have assumed fixed proportions in production, the conventional approach to profit-maximizing firms is not of importance, since profits are here determined through the dynamics of wages and prices.

Wage formation: workers vs. firms

This subsection builds on the paper by Blanchard and Katz (1999) and briefly summarizes their theoretical motivation of a money wage Phillips curve which is closely related to our dynamic equation (1.19) considered below.[11] Blanchard and Katz assume (following the suggestions of standard models of wage setting) that real wage expectations of workers, $\omega^e = w_t - p_t^e$, are basically determined by the reservation wage, $\bar{\omega}_t$, current labor productivity, $y_t - l_t^d$, and the rate of unemployment, e_t, according to

$$\omega_t^e = \theta\bar{\omega}_t + (1-\theta)(y_t - l_t^d) - \beta_w e_t. \tag{1.16}$$

Expected real wages are thus a Cobb–Douglas average of the reservation wage and output per worker, but depart from this normal level of expectations in their dependence on the state of the demand pressure on the labor market measured by the employment rate e_t.

The reservation wage in turn is determined as a Cobb–Douglas average of past real wages, $\omega_{t-1} = w_{t-1} - p_{t-1}$, and current labor productivity, augmented by a factor $a < 0$; thus we have

$$\bar{\omega}_t = a + \lambda\omega_{t-1} + (1-\lambda)(y_t - l_t^d). \tag{1.17}$$

Inserting equation (1.16) into equation (1.17) results in

$$\omega_t^e = \theta a + \theta\lambda\omega_{t-1} + (1-\theta\lambda)(y_t - l_t^d) - \beta_w e_t,$$

which after some rearrangement gives

$$\begin{aligned}\Delta w_t &= p_t^e - p_{t-1} + \theta a - (1-\theta\lambda)[(w_{t-1} - p_{t-1}) - (y_{t-1} - l_{t-1}^d)] \\ &\quad + (1-\theta\lambda)(\Delta y_t - \Delta l_t^d) - \beta_w e_t \\ &= \Delta p_t^e + \theta a - (1-\theta\lambda)v_{t-1} + (1-\theta\lambda)(\Delta y_t - \Delta l_t^d) - \beta_w e_t,\end{aligned} \tag{1.18}$$

where Δp_t^e denotes the expected rate of inflation, v_{t-1} the past (log) wage share and $\Delta y_t - \Delta l_t^d$ the current growth rate of labor productivity. Equation (1.18) is the growth law for nominal wages that flows from the theoretical models referred to in Blanchard and Katz (1999).

We use this approach – which is supplemented in Blanchard and Katz (1999) by a markup pricing rule – in place of the new Keynesian formulation of a staggered wage and price setting and ignore as in these baseline models what money (as a stock) is doing in the background of the assumed nominal wage and nominal price adjustment processes.

The implied integrated dynamics

Assuming myopic perfect foresight with respect to price inflation, from what has been shown in the preceding subsection, gives as law of motion for the real wage a fairly conventional type of real wage Phillips curve, namely (in continuous time)

$$\widehat{\omega} = \dot{\omega}/\omega = \beta_w(e - \bar{e}) - (1-\theta\lambda)(\omega - \omega_0)l^d/y, \quad e = L^d/L = l^d/l, \tag{1.19}$$

where e denotes the current rate of employment and $\bar{e}$ the given NAIRE level of this rate (L is the stationary labor supply). Note here that the assumption of myopic perfect foresight allows us to ignore the way the price inflation rate is determined in the model.

Since $l^d = L^d/K$ and L are given magnitudes we have two state variables ω, e (or l) and their laws of motion in this model so far, which are given by

$$\widehat{\omega} = \beta_w(e - \bar{e}) - (1-\theta\lambda)(\omega - \omega_0)l^d/y, \quad \hat{e} = \widehat{K} = I_w/K + I_c/K - \delta.$$

The latter law of motion gives (when investment behavior equation (1.15) is inserted)

$$\hat{e} = (1-\alpha_w)[\omega l^d + \rho k_w] + (1-\alpha_c)\rho k_c - \delta.$$

We therefore have to make use of a third state variable in order to close the model, which is given by $k_c = K_c/K$, the percentage of the capital stock that is owned by capitalists. This finally gives

$$\hat{e} = (1-\alpha_w)[\omega l^d + \rho(1-k_c)] + (1-\alpha_c)\rho k_c - \delta,$$

and for the new state variable the law of motion

$$\hat{k}_c = \widehat{K}_c - \widehat{K} = (1-\alpha_c)\rho - (1-\alpha_w)[\omega l^d + \rho(1-k_c)] - (1-\alpha_c)\rho k_c.$$

This completes the description of the dynamical model to be analyzed below.

Balanced reproduction and stability issues

The dynamical system implied by our simple model therefore reads

$$\widehat{\omega} = \beta_w(e-\bar{e}) - (1-\theta\lambda)(\omega-\omega_0)l^d/y, \tag{1.20}$$

$$\begin{aligned}\hat{e} &= (1-\alpha_w)(y-\delta) + (\alpha_w-\alpha_c)\rho k_c - \delta \\ &= g(\omega, k_c), \quad g_\omega < 0, \quad g_{k_c} > 0,\end{aligned} \tag{1.21}$$

$$\hat{k}_c = (1-\alpha_c)\rho - g(\omega, k_c), \tag{1.22}$$

with all parametric expressions in front of the state variables ω, e, k_c being positive.

The interior steady state solution of these dynamics (where $I_w = \delta K_w$, $I_c = \delta K_c$ holds) are given by

$$e_0 = \bar{e}, \tag{1.23}$$

$$\rho_0 = \delta/(1-\alpha_c), \tag{1.24}$$

$$\omega_0 = \frac{y-\delta-\rho_0}{l^d} = \frac{(1-\alpha_c)(y-\delta)-\delta}{(1-\alpha_c)l^d}, \tag{1.25}$$

$$k_c^0 = \frac{\delta-(1-\alpha_w)(y-\delta)}{(\alpha_w-\alpha_c)\rho_0}. \tag{1.26}$$

The steady state values of the real wage and the percentage of the capital stock of capitalist are positive if and only if there holds

$$\alpha_w > (y-2\delta)/(y-\delta) > \alpha_c.$$

If the left-hand inequality holds as an equality it would imply that $\omega_0 = 0$, and the right-hand one holding as an equality would imply the relationship $k_c^0 = 0$. Workers' propensity to consume must therefore be sufficiently large and capitalists' consumption propensity sufficiently low in order to guarantee in the first case the existence of capitalists at the steady state and in the second case that workers in fact get remunerated for their work.

The matrix of partial derivatives of the dynamical system (1.20)–(1.22) at the steady state is given by

$$J = \begin{pmatrix} -(1-\theta\lambda)\omega_o l^d/y & \beta_w\omega_0 & 0 \\ g_\omega e_0 & 0 & g_{k_c}e_0 \\ -(1-\alpha_c)l^d k_c^0 - g_\omega k_c^0 & 0 & -g_{k_c}k_c^0 \end{pmatrix}.$$

It is easy to show that the trace and the determinant of this Jacobian matrix are both negative and that the sum a_2 of the principal minors of order two is positive. The Routh–Hurwitz stability conditions (see **??**) are therefore fulfilled if also the expression $-\text{trace}\,J \cdot a_2 + \det J$ can be shown to be positive. For this expression we get from the above Jacobian that

$$\begin{aligned} & g_{k_c}k_c^0\beta_w\omega_0(-g_\omega e_0) - \beta_w\omega_0 g_{k_c}e_0 - (1-\alpha_c)l^d k_c^0 \\ & \quad = c[(\alpha_w - \alpha_c)k_c^0 - (1-\alpha_c)] < 0. \end{aligned}$$

We thus have the somewhat astonishing result that the steady state of this economy is nearly stable, but that the fourth Routh–Hurwitz stability condition is in fact working against stability, implying that there must be eigenvalues with positive real parts so that the dynamics becomes divergent sooner or later. These locally unstable dynamics can however be made convergent, for example in the following simple manner. Assume that the propensity to consume α_c of capitalists depends positively on the rate of employment e, meaning that they invest less in situations of increasing employment, since they consider such a situation as undermining their bargaining position on the labor market. This implies as modified Jacobian the matrix

$$J = \begin{pmatrix} 0 & \beta_w\omega_0 & 0 \\ g_\omega e_0 & -\alpha_c'(\bar{e})\rho_0 k_c^0 & g_{k_c}e_0 \\ -(1-\alpha_c)l^d k_c^0 - g_\omega k_c^0 & -\alpha_c'(\bar{e})\rho_0(k_c^0+1) & -g_{k_c}k_c^0 \end{pmatrix}.$$

This extension of the model increases the term $-\text{trace}\,J \cdot a_2 + \det J$ without altering the determinant component. Choosing $\alpha_c'(\bar{e})$ sufficiently large will therefore make this expression positive. This happens by way of a Hopf bifurcation, leading to Goodwin (1967) type, yet damped, not persistent oscillations around the steady state, since the form of the determinant of the matrix J prevents the occurrence of zero eigenvalues.

Inflation

Another extension of the model could be approached by including price inflation dynamics explicitly into its representation, for example by way of the delayed markup pricing rule. In this case the price dynamics would become

$$\hat{p} = \beta_p \left((1+m)\frac{\omega L^d}{Y} - 1 \right) = \beta_p \left((1+m)\frac{\omega}{Y/L^d} - 1 \right),$$

where m is a given markup. In its current form, the model does not alter anything. However if one departs from the myopic perfect foresight condition and assumes for example an adaptive expectations mechanism, so that

$$\dot{\pi} = \beta_\pi (\hat{p} - \pi),$$

where π denotes the expected rate of inflation, we would get revised real wage dynamics. This is a form that is now to be augmented by the dynamics of inflationary expectations, so that the dynamical system becomes

$$\begin{aligned} \widehat{\omega} &= \pi + \beta_w (e - \bar{e}) - \frac{(1-\theta\lambda)(\omega - \omega_0) l^d}{y} \\ &\quad - \beta_p \left((1+m)\frac{\omega}{y/l^d} - 1 \right), && (1.27) \\ \hat{e} &= (1-\alpha_w)(y - \delta) + (\alpha_w - \alpha_c)\rho k_c - \delta, && (1.28) \\ \hat{k}_c &= (1-\alpha_c)\rho - g(\omega, k_c), && (1.29) \\ \dot{\pi} &= \beta_\pi \left(\beta_p \left((1+m)\frac{\omega}{y/l^d} - 1 \right) - \pi \right). && (1.30) \end{aligned}$$

This extension of the model indicates the need to add money explicitly and to provide an anchor by which inflation can be controlled. This is suggested by the observation that the determinant of the dynamics at the steady state has a zero root, since the last equation can be used to make the first three independent of the variable π. The inflation rate level is therefore subject to zero root hysteresis and thus needs an additional influence (perhaps from a monetary authority), in particular if a constant price level is desirable in the steady state.

1.5 Conclusions

In this chapter we have built what in our view is the simplest type of continuous-time model of capitalism with a microfounded principal-agent structure (and thus not two souls in just one breast, to quote Goethe), with conflict and disequilibrium on the labor market and gradually adjusting real wages that are derived from a conventional type of expectations-augmented Phillips curve coupled with myopic perfect foresight on price inflation. Furthermore all budget equations are specified and there is an implied coherent stock–flow interaction. This structure can give rise to damped oscillations around the model's interior steady-state position where capitalists coexist with workers and thus own part of the capital stock.

Given this situation we therefore do not develop a model where pure capitalists would disappear and where some sort of peoples' capitalism would come about with workers as the representative agent. Of course, one may ask how the economy and with it the model would change if workers' share of the capital stock is run under other conditions than the one of pure capitalism, since workers not only get income from firms (through firm bonds), but may also be able to decide on the way these firms are run (through equities). Moreover Keynesian demand problems may be encountered when investment projects financed through credit markets are added to the model. Schumpeterian long-phase waves may also be added through a microprocess of creative destruction that may create continuing increases in labor productivity Y/L^d and bounded fluctuations in the actual output/capital ratio y.

Such model extensions are however not the topic of this conclusion, which is solely seeking to show the minimal type of structure one should allow for in the theoretical as well as the empirical investigation of the fundamental forces that drive capitalism. This in our view is the sometimes more, sometimes less, intensive conflict over income distribution between two types of agent (and about the conditions of capitalist production), with long-phase cycles in the evolution of social structures of accumulation, as they were classified in **??** work on business cycles and long-phased waves.

Using the model strategies proposed here, this volume will provide the elements for a synthesis of Marx's reserve army mechanism with Keynes's trade cycle analysis, but will not go into the microdetails of the Schumpeterian view on the cyclical evolution of capitalism ranging from his characterization of the restless dynamic entrepreneur (and his imitators) to the bureaucratic megacorporation with its routinized R&D work.

2 The two-class Pasinetti model from a neoclassical perspective

2.1 Introduction

With the emergence of the "new" growth theory, economic growth has again become a major issue in macroeconomics. With the renewed interest in the determinants of economic growth, the connection between income distribution and economic growth has also received new attention and become a topic of interest in economics.

The new literature on distribution and economic growth has emphasized three ways through which distributional aspects may affect the growth performance of economies – voting on fiscal policy, sociopolitical conflicts and imperfect capital markets.

In the first class of models, greater inequality makes the median voter choose that party which is more favorable to income redistribution. Income redistribution, however, raises tax rates, which discourages investment and leads to lower economic growth (cf. Alesina and Rodrick 1994; Persson and Tabellini 1996).

The second approach goes back to Hibbs (1973) and Veniers and Gupta (1986) and states that income inequality due to sociopolitical instability reduces aggregate investment. The mechanism in that class of models works as follows. A highly unequal distribution of wealth and income makes the poor susceptible to illegal and violent actions. Sociopolitical instability, however, discourages investment by creating an uncertain environment and by disrupting market activities directly. A formal model which contains that idea has been presented by Benhabib and Rustichini (1996).

The third class of models, finally, focuses on capital market imperfections. One approach within that theory starts with Loury (1981). If poor people are subject to credit constraints they cannot realize the efficient amount of investment. Redistribution of income then can raise economic growth because the marginal product of poor people's capital is relatively high. Another line of research underlines intergenerational aspects and credit constraints. If individuals cannot borrow freely at a given interest rate, the inherited wealth plays the dominant role in determining their investment in capital. As a consequence, a less unequal distribution implies that more households have enough resources to invest (cf. Bénabou 2000; Saint-Paul and Verdier 1993). In a related line of research, income distribution shows macroeconomic effects due to the sorting of agents into homogeneous communities (see e.g. Durlauf 1996; Fernandez and Rogerson 1996).[1]

An early approach which differs from the models mentioned above are the contributions by Pasinetti (1962) and Samuelson and Modigliani (1966). Those models also consider the connection between economic growth and income distribution but assume that there are two classes – workers who receive income from their savings and work, and capitalists who do not work but get income solely from their stock of capital. In this chapter[2] we consider a variant of the growth models by Pasinetti and by Samuelson and Modigliani. In contrast to these authors, we allow for optimizing agents and we suppose that positive sustained per-capita growth occurs in our economy.

As to the mechanisms which generate sustained per-capita growth, we assume that externalities of investment and education together build up knowledge capital which positively affects the marginal product of private capital. Thus, our approach is based on the endogenous growth models by Romer (1986), Lucas (1988) and Uzawa (1965). In contrast to Romer, however, we assume that physical and knowledge capital cannot be merged into one variable but are rather treated as two distinct variables. In addition, we suppose that the positive externalities of investment can only be obtained if workers devote time to education. So, we do not posit that education shows immediate growth effects but only indirectly by affecting the workers' ability to use new machines efficiently. In that respect our model differs from the Lucas–Uzawa approach, as these authors posit that education directly affects the formation of human capital and, as a consequence, the growth rate.

The rest of the chapter is organized as follows. In the next section (Section 2.2), we introduce our model and derive the balanced growth path. In Section 2.3 we discuss the model and point out its implications. Section 2.4, finally, concludes the chapter.

2.2 The model

We consider a decentralized economy that consists of a household sector and a representative firm. The firm chooses labor and capital input in order to maximize profits. The household sector consists of two different classes – the workers who work and save, and the capitalists who receive capital income. Further, there is a positive externality associated with investment that brings about constant returns to scale on the aggregate level.

The productive sector

The productive sector is represented by a firm which produces a homogeneous good Y with a Cobb–Douglas production function[3]

$$Y = (uAL)^{\alpha} K^{1-\alpha} \equiv (uA)^{\alpha} K^{1-\alpha}.$$

Here α denotes the labor share in the production function and labor L is constant over time and normalized to unity; K and A denote the stock of physical and knowledge capital respectively, where A raises labor productivity and is taken as given by the firm in solving its optimization problem. The quantity $u \in (0, 1]$ is the time devoted to production and is assumed to be given exogenously. The total amount of time available to the household is normalized to unity and $1 - u$ is the fraction of time devoted to education.

The firm behaves competitively, yielding

$$r = (1 - \alpha) K^{-\alpha} (uA)^{\alpha}, \tag{2.1}$$

$$w = \alpha\, u^{\alpha - 1} A^{\alpha} K^{1-\alpha}. \tag{2.2}$$

The external effect

The stock of knowledge capital A is assumed to be a by-product of cumulated past gross investment (cf. Arrow 1962; Levhari 1966; Romer 1986), but in our economy it is also affected by the educational effort.

As in Levhari (1966) and Romer (1986) we suppose that the stock of knowledge capital equals cumulated past gross investment. However, in contrast to Levhari and Romer we posit that investment only shows positive externalities if workers devote time to education. The quantity $\varphi(u)$ determines the magnitude of the external effect and gives the contribution of one unit of investment to the formation of the stock of knowledge capital. It is assumed that $\varphi(u)$ is a positive function of the time devoted to education, or, equivalently, that $1 - u$ is a negative function of the time used for production, so that $\varphi'(u) < 0$. The larger the fraction of time devoted to education, the stronger the external effect of investment on the formation of knowledge. From the economic point of view we can state that any new machine is operated more efficiently the more education workers undergo. In our framework, the increase in efficiency then is reflected by a rise in the stock of knowledge.

Further, we suppose that $\varphi(u) \to 0$ for $u \to 1$, stating that without education no learning effect takes place and individuals are not capable of building up knowledge as a by-product of investment in new machines. In that case, investment does not show any externalities. That assumption can be justified by requiring that workers must undergo a minimum level of education, for example be able to read and write, in order to be able to increase their skills, and thus labor productivity, as a by-product of investment in new machines. However, in the industrialized or newly industrializing countries the case $u = 1$ will not be observed for the average individual because governmental regulations prescribe that any citizen has to take a minimum of education.

Formally, the stock of knowledge capital can be expressed as

$$A(t) = \varphi(u) \int_{-\infty}^{t} I(s)\, ds,$$

with I gross investment and $\varphi(\cdot) \geq 0$ the contribution of one unit of investment to the formation of knowledge capital. This becomes clearer by differentiating A with respect to time, leading to

$$\dot{A} = \varphi(u)I, \tag{2.3}$$

with u being time-invariant. For simplicity we assume that there is no depreciation of knowledge.

The household sector

The household sector consists of two classes, a working class and a capitalistic class, which are each represented by one household respectively. The capitalist maximizes the discounted stream of utility resulting from consumption $C_p(t)$ over an infinite time horizon

$$\max_{C_p(t)} \int_0^\infty e^{-\rho_p t} U(C_p(t))\, dt, \tag{2.4}$$

where $\rho_p > 0$ is the rate of time preference and $U(\cdot)$ is the utility function, with $U'(\cdot) > 0$ and $U''(\cdot) < 0$. Moreover, we assume a constant relative risk aversion (CRRA) utility function so that the intertemporal elasticity of substitution of consumption, $1/\sigma_p$, is constant. The capitalist's budget constraint is written as

$$C_p + \dot{K}_p + \delta K_p = r K_p, \tag{2.5}$$

where δ is the depreciation rate, r gives the return to physical capital and K_p is the capitalist's stock of physical capital. Forming the current-value Hamiltonian

$$H(\cdot) = U(C_p) + \gamma_p(-C_p - \delta K_p + r K_p),$$

with γ_p the current-value co-state variable, the necessary conditions give the growth rate of the capitalist's consumption as

$$\frac{\dot{C}_p}{C_p} = -\frac{\rho_p + \delta}{\sigma_p} + \frac{r}{\sigma_p}. \tag{2.6}$$

The necessary conditions are also sufficient if the transversality condition at infinity, $\lim_{t\to\infty} e^{-\rho_p t} \gamma_p(t) K_p(t) = 0$, holds, which is automatically fulfilled for $g < \rho_p$, with g denoting the growth rate.[4]

The worker also maximizes the discounted stream of utility resulting from consumption $C_w(t)$ over an infinite time horizon

$$\max_{C_w(t)} \int_0^\infty e^{-\rho_w t} \bar{U}(C_w(t))\, dt, \tag{2.7}$$

with $\rho_w > 0$ being the worker's rate of time preference and $\bar{U}(\cdot)$ the utility function, with $\bar{U}'(\cdot) > 0$ and $\bar{U}''(\cdot) < 0$. Again we suppose that the intertemporal elasticity of substitution of consumption, $1/\sigma_w$, is constant. The workers's budget constraint is written as

$$C_w + \dot{K}_w + \delta K_w = (wu + rK_w). \tag{2.8}$$

Here C_w and K_w are, respectively, the level of consumption and the capital stock of the working household. Recall that the labor supply is assumed to be constant and normalized to unity so that all variables give per-capita quantities. Furthermore r is the return to physical capital, which is the same as for the capitalist, and w denotes the wage rate, which the household takes as given in solving its optimization problem.

The symbol u gives the time devoted to production and so $1-u$ is the time spent for education. As to the fraction of time used for education, we assume that it is the result of governmental regulations which primarily determine the level of basic education in an economy. So, we postulate that it is not so much higher education that is of importance as concerns the formation of knowledge (as a by-product of investment) but basic knowledge, which is the result of primary education of a large part of the population. That sort of education seems of particular relevance especially for less developed countries which intend to catch up with highly developed ones. For those countries it is more important to adopt existing technologies and to be able to produce with them than to develop new products or methods of production. So, it is often argued that the increase in basic education in the fast growing economies of South East Asia was a major reason for their high per-capita growth rates in recent decades.

To derive necessary conditions for a maximum of (2.7) subject to (2.8) we formulate the current-value Hamiltonian

$$H(\cdot) = \bar{U}(C_w) + \gamma_w(-C_w - \delta K_w + wu + rK_w),$$

with γ_w the current-value co-state variable of the worker's capital stock. The growth rate of consumption is derived as

$$\frac{\dot{C}_w}{C_w} = -\frac{\rho_w + \delta}{\sigma_w} + \frac{r}{\sigma_w}. \tag{2.9}$$

Furthermore, we need the limiting transversality condition, $\lim_{t\to\infty} e^{-\rho_w t} \gamma_w(t) K_w(t) = 0$, to hold – which again makes the necessary conditions also sufficient.

Equilibrium conditions and the balanced growth path

In equilibrium, the aggregate capital stock K equals the capital stocks of the worker and the capitalist, i.e. $K = K_p + K_w$. From that identity we get the economy-wide resource constraint as $C_p + C_w + \dot{K} + \delta K = wu + rK_p + rK_w$. Using (2.1) and (2.2) the last equation is equivalent to

$$\frac{\dot{K}}{K} = (uA)^{\alpha} K^{-\alpha} - \frac{C}{K} - \delta, \quad K(0) = K_0 > 0, \tag{2.10}$$

with $C_p + C_w = C$, aggregate consumption.

Taking into account that $C_p + C_w = C$, the evolution of the stock of knowledge is assumed to be given by

$$\frac{\dot{A}}{A} = \varphi(uA)^{\alpha-1} K^{1-\alpha} - \varphi\frac{C}{A}, \quad A(0) = A_0 > 0. \tag{2.11}$$

The growth rates of the capitalist's and worker's consumption, finally, are given by (2.6) and (2.9) respectively, with r determined by (2.1).

A balanced growth path then is defined as a path on which all variables grow at the same constant rate, i.e. as a path for which $\dot{K}/K = \dot{A}/A = \dot{C}_p/C_p = \dot{C}_w/C_w =$ const. holds. It should be noted that $\dot{C}_p/C_p = \dot{C}_w/C_w = g^{\star}$ implies $\dot{C}/C = g^{\star}$ and vice versa, with $g^{\star}$ denoting the balanced growth rate. That is, a balanced growth path where the consumption levels of the worker and capitalist grow at a constant rate implies that aggregate consumption also grows at the same rate. That follows immediately from differentiating C with respect to time and using $\dot{C}_p/C_p = \dot{C}_w/C_w = g^{\star} =$ const. On the other hand, the existence of a balanced growth path with $\dot{K}/K = \dot{A}/A = \dot{C}/C =$ const. implies that consumption of the worker and capitalist grows at the same rate because $r =$ const. on such a path.

In the next section we will analyze the structure of our model in more detail.

2.3 Discussion of the model

The dynamic behavior

To get further insight into the dynamics of our aggregate model we first derive the differential equations describing the aggregate economy. Those are given by (2.10), (2.11) and

$$\frac{\dot{C}}{C} = \frac{\dot{C}_p}{C_p}\frac{C_p}{C} + \frac{\dot{C}_w}{C_w}\frac{C_w}{C}.$$

On a balanced growth path we have $\dot{C}_p/C_p = \dot{C}_w/C_w = g^{\star}$ implying $\dot{C}/C = g^{\star}$. Consequently, the growth rate of aggregate consumption locally around a balanced growth path is given by

$$\frac{\dot{C}}{C} = -\frac{\rho_i + \delta}{\sigma_i} + (1-\alpha)(u)^{\alpha} k^{-\alpha} (\sigma_i)^{-1}, \quad i = p, w, \tag{2.12}$$

with $k \equiv K/A$. Thus, the balanced growth rate depends on the ratio of K to A on the balanced growth path, which are endogenous variables. In general, this ratio cannot be determined explicitly but is only implicitly given. So, it is not possible to give the balanced growth rate as an explicit function of exogenous parameters. For more details, see the appendix to this chapter. It should also be noted that the existence of a balanced growth path implies that subjective discount rates and the intertemporal elasticity of substitution cannot take arbitrary values although they do not have to be equal. The following equation must hold: $\sigma_p/\sigma_w = (\rho_p + \delta - r)/(\rho_w + \delta - r)$.

To analyze the structure of a balanced growth path we make use of the fact that the growth rates of C, K and A are constant on such a path implying that the ratios $c = C/A$ and $k = K/A$ are also constant. Differentiating c and k with respect to time yields

$$\frac{\dot{c}}{c} = -\frac{\rho_i}{\sigma_i} - \frac{\delta}{\sigma_i} + (1-\alpha)u^{\alpha}k^{-\alpha}(\sigma_i)^{-1} + c\,\varphi(u) - \varphi(u)u^{\alpha}k^{1-\alpha}, \tag{2.13}$$

$$\frac{\dot{k}}{k} = -\delta - \frac{c}{k} + u^{\alpha}k^{-\alpha} + c\,\varphi(u) - \varphi(u)u^{\alpha}k^{1-\alpha}. \tag{2.14}$$

Equations (2.13) and (2.14) completely describe our model around a balanced growth path and a rest point of this system gives a balanced growth path for the economy. Note that we write (2.13) and (2.14) in terms of rates of growth. We can do so because k is raised to a negative power in (2.13) and $c = 0$ does not makes sense from the economic point of view. Therefore, a balanced growth path with $k^\star = 0$ and/or $c^\star = 0$ can be excluded a priori.

To further analyze our system we set $\dot{k}/k = 0$ and solve for $c^\star$ which gives the ratio of consumption per knowledge capital on the balanced growth path. Doing so gives

$$c^\star = (k^\star)^{1-\alpha}u^{\alpha} - \frac{\delta k^\star}{1-\varphi(u)k^\star}. \tag{2.15}$$

It is immediately clear that $1 - \varphi(u)k^\star > 0$ must hold because otherwise C would be larger than aggregate production, $K^{1-\alpha}(uA)^{\alpha}$, which is not possible. Inserting $c^\star$ in $\dot{k}/k$ leads to

$$q(k) = -\frac{\rho_i}{\sigma_i} - \frac{\delta}{\sigma_i} + (1-\alpha)u^{\alpha}k^{-\alpha}(\sigma_i)^{-1} - \frac{\delta\varphi(u)k}{1-\varphi(u)k}. \tag{2.16}$$

A value $k^\star$ such that $q(k)$ equals zero gives a rest point for (2.13) and (2.14) and, consequently, a balanced growth path for our growth model. Proposition 2.1 characterizes the dynamics of the economy.

PROPOSITION 2.1 *For the economy described by equations (2.10)–(2.12), there exists a unique balanced growth path which is a saddle-point.*

Proof: See the appendix to this chapter. □

That proposition demonstrates that sustained per-capita growth can be observed in the economy. From the economic point of view, a prerequisite for long-run growth is a constant return to capital, r, which implies a constant incentive to invest. In our model, that is assured by the assumption that investment is associated with positive externalities that build up a stock of knowledge capital. However, such an effect only takes place if workers spend time on education. Thus, investment without education will not generate much growth. In our view, investment and education are complementary in the sense that neither of these activities is capable of increasing the stock of knowledge capital, and thus economic growth, unless it is accompanied by the other.

An additional result of Proposition 2.1 is that the balanced growth path is a saddle-point. That is, there exists a unique initial value $c(0) = C(0)/A_0$ such that the economy converges to the balanced growth path in the long run. Thus, our model is determinate just as is the basic neoclassical growth model with exogenous growth.[5]

In the next section we will analyze how variations in the time spent for education affect the wage rate, the return to capital and the balanced growth rate.

Distributional aspects on the balanced growth path

Before we study how a variation in u affects the distribution of income, we analyze its effect on the return to capital r, which is given by (2.1), and on the balanced growth rate $g^{\star}$, which is given by (2.12). Before we proceed we want to mention that a decrease or increase in the return to capital, brought about by variations in u, is equivalent to a decrease or increase in the balanced growth rate $g^{\star}$, which is immediately seen by differentiating (2.12) with respect to u. From the economic point of view that is obvious because the time spent for education does not affect the balanced growth rate directly but only indirectly by affecting the return to capital. Thus, if more education is undertaken, a decrease in u raises (lowers) the incentive to invest, i.e. the marginal product of physical capital, the balanced growth rate also rises (declines) because the savings rate takes on a higher (lower) value.

From the expression $r = (1-\alpha)u^{\alpha}(k^{\star})^{-\alpha}$ we immediately see that an increase in the time spent on education, i.e. a decrease in u, has a negative direct effect on the return to capital. That is seen by partial differentiation of r with respect to u, which gives $\partial r/\partial u = (1-\alpha)\alpha u^{\alpha-1}(k^{\star})^{-\alpha} > 0$. That result states that more time spent on education, or, equivalently, less time spent on production, shows a negative partial effect on the return to capital and, thus, on the incentive to invest. That seems obvious from the economic point of view because the less people work, the lower is the return of an additional unit of capital.

On the other hand, however, more education exerts a positive indirect effect on the return to capital. That holds because workers are more efficient the more education they enjoy. In our framework, that means that the external effect of investment is larger, i.e. with any unit of investment the stock of knowledge rises to a greater degree in comparison to a situation where education is lower. That is a consequence of our assumption $\varphi'(u) < 0$. As a consequence, the ratio $K^\star/A^\star = k^\star$ takes on a lower value and, thus, raises r. Which of those two effects dominates depends on the elasticity of $\varphi(u)$ with respect to u. That is seen in more detail in Proposition 2.2.

PROPOSITION 2.2 *An increase in the time spent on education (a decrease in u) raises (leaves unchanged, lowers) the balanced growth if and only if*

$$-\frac{\partial\varphi}{\partial u}\frac{u}{\varphi} > (=, <)\, 1.$$

Proof: See the appendix to this chapter. □

The result demonstrates that the elasticity of $\varphi(\cdot)$ with respect to the time used for education is decisive as to the growth effects of a decrease in u. If the elasticity of $\varphi(\cdot)$ with respect to the time spent on education is larger than one, that is, if $(\partial\varphi/(-\partial u))(u/\varphi) > 1$, more education raises economic growth. That condition states that a 1% increase in the time spent on education must raise the positive external effect associated with investment by more than 1%. Then, the negative direct growth effect of a decrease in the time spent on production (=increase in the time spent on education) is compensated, and devoting more time to education raises the balanced growth rate.

From our considerations at the beginning of Section 2.3 we also know that education is a prerequisite for sustained per-capita growth in our economy. Further, on the balanced growth path the wage rate is given by $w = \alpha u^{\alpha-1}(k^\star)^{-\alpha} K_0 e^{g^\star t}$, which immediately shows that w is monotonically increasing on the balanced growth path. That is, the worker is better off if he/she spends time on education compared to a situation without education because in the latter case the long-run wage rate would be constant. Further, education also shows a direct positive effect on the wage rate because any value $u < 1$ gives a higher wage rate than $u = 1$, that is, in comparison to a situation where the worker spends all of his/her time on production. Therefore, we can state that education is not only a prerequisite for long-run growth but it also leads to a higher equilibrium wage rate w.

However, those considerations do not imply that an increase in the time spent on education raises the wage rate once education is positive. It is true that more education, a lower u, has a positive direct effect on the equilibrium wage rate because of

$$\partial w/\partial u = \alpha(\alpha-1)u^{\alpha-2}(k^\star)^{-\alpha} K_0 e^{g^\star t} < 0.$$

However, variations in u also affect the wage rate by influencing the balanced growth rate $g^\star$ and the ratio $k^\star = K^\star/A^\star$.[6] But, as we have shown in Proposition 2.2, the latter effect is ambiguous.

Only if more education raises the balanced growth rate are both the direct effect and the indirect effect positive. Then, increasing the time spent on education has an unequivocal positive effect on the wage rate. But it should be stressed that there is always a positive direct growth effect on the wage rate, which goes along with more education, even if more education reduces the balanced growth rate.

Next, we want to study how variations in the time spent on education affect the workers' income relative to the income of the capitalists. To do so we first state that the workers' and the capitalists' incomes are given by $Y_w = wu + rK_w$ and $Y_p = rK_p$, respectively. Along the balanced growth rate the incomes $Y_w(t)$ and $Y_p(t)$ then are

$$Y_w(t) = \alpha u^{\alpha}(k^{\star})^{-\alpha} K(0)e^{g^{\star}t} + (1-\alpha)u^{\alpha}(k^{\star})^{-\alpha} K_w(0)e^{g^{\star}t},$$

$$Y_p = (1-\alpha)u^{\alpha}(k^{\star})^{-\alpha} K_p(0)e^{g^{\star}t}.$$

This implies that the relative income of workers to capitalists is given by

$$\frac{Y_w}{Y_p} = \frac{\alpha K(0) + (1-\alpha)K_w(0)}{(1-\alpha)K_p(0)}.$$

From this last expression we immediately realize that the time spent on education does not affect the relative income of workers. This is the content of Proposition 2.3.

PROPOSITION 2.3 *Along the balanced growth path variations in the time spent on education do not affect the workers' income relative to the capitalists' income.*

Proof: Follows immediately from the expression for Y_w/Y_p. □

As demonstrated in Proposition 2.2, varying the time spent on education has an influence on the workers' income by affecting the balanced growth rate. However, the relative income is not affected because on the balanced growth path the capitalists' income rises in the same proportion as the workers' income so that the ratio remains unchanged. With a constant capital and labor share, a rise in this ratio can only be obtained by a redistribution of capital from capitalists to workers and/or by an increase in the overall capital stock, $K(t)$, at time $t = 0$.

2.4 Conclusions

In this chapter we have generalized the two-class Pasinetti model to allow for sustained per-capita growth. A prerequisite for long-run growth was that workers spend time on education, which increases their stock of knowledge as a by-product of investment. It was demonstrated that there exists a unique balanced growth path for the model that is a saddle-point.

Further, we have seen that raising the time spent on education influences the return to capital, the growth rate and the wage rate. So, we could show that education exerts a positive direct effect on the wage rate and an indirect effect that depends on the effect of education on the balanced growth rate. As to the return to capital, we have derived the result that education exerts a negative direct effect but a positive indirect one by raising the positive externalities associated with investment. If the first effect dominates the latter, more education lowers the return to capital and, consequently, economic growth and vice versa.

We have also shown that variation in the time spent on education does not affect the workers' income relative to the income of the capitalists along the balanced growth path. This is due to the fact that on the balanced growth path variations in the time spent on education affect the workers' income in the same proportion as the capitalists' income so that the ratio remains unchanged. An increase in this ratio can only be obtained by redistributing capital from capitalists to workers and/or if the economy-wide capital stock $K(0)$ rises.

We should also point out that all of our results remain valid in the case that the worker has no savings, namely for $K_w = 0$. Then the aggregate capital stock is owned by the capitalist alone and the balanced growth rate is given by (2.12) with $i = p$.

Appendix: proof of propositions

The balanced growth rate is given by

$$\frac{\dot{C}}{C} = -\frac{\rho_i + \delta}{\sigma_i} + (1-\alpha)(u)^{\alpha} k^{-\alpha} (\sigma_i)^{-1}, \qquad i = p, w,$$

with k the solution to

$$q(k) = -\frac{\rho_i}{\sigma_i} - \frac{\delta}{\sigma_i} + (1-\alpha) u^{\alpha} k^{-\alpha} (\sigma_i)^{-1} - \frac{\delta \varphi(\cdot) k}{1 - \varphi(\cdot) k}.$$

In general, this equation cannot be solved explicitly with respect to k. Therefore, the effects of changes in exogenous parameters on the balanced growth rate are calculated by differentiating $\dot{C}/C$ with respect to the parameter under consideration where the effect of this parameter on k along the balanced growth path can only be obtained by implicit differentiation from $q(k) = 0$.

Proof of Proposition 2.1

From our considerations in Section 2.1 we know that a $k^{\star}$ so that $q(k^{\star}) = 0$ gives a balanced growth path. Further, we also know that $k^{\star} < \varphi(\cdot)^{-1}$ must hold. Otherwise, $c^{\star} > (k^{\star})^{1-\alpha} u^{\alpha}$, which would imply that aggregate consumption exceeds aggregate production, which is not feasible. Therefore, it is sufficient to consider $k \in (0, \varphi(\cdot)^{-1})$. Recalling that $q(k)$ is given by

$$q(k) = -\frac{\rho_i}{\sigma_i} - \frac{\delta}{\sigma_i} + (1-\alpha) u^{\alpha} k^{-\alpha} (\sigma_i)^{-1} - \frac{\delta \varphi(\cdot) k}{1 - \varphi(\cdot) k},$$

it is immediately seen that there holds

$$\lim_{k\to 0} q(k) = +\infty \quad \text{and} \quad \lim_{k\nearrow\varphi^{-1}} q(k) = -\infty,$$

where $\nearrow$ means that k approaches $\varphi(u)^{-1}$ from below. Further, the derivative of $q(k)$ is calculated as

$$\frac{\partial q(k)}{\partial k} = -\alpha k^{-\alpha-1}\frac{1-\alpha}{\sigma_i}u^{\alpha} - \frac{\delta\varphi(\cdot)}{(1-k\varphi(\cdot))^2}.$$

It is immediately seen that this derivative is continuous for $k \in (0, \varphi(\cdot)^{-1})$ and negative so that there exists a unique $k^\star$ in the range $(0, \varphi(\cdot)^{-1})$ that solves $q(k) = 0$.

To show saddle-point stability we compute the Jacobian at a rest point of system (2.13)–(2.14), which is given by

$$J = \begin{bmatrix} \varphi(\cdot) & (-\alpha)(k^\star)^{(-\alpha-1)}\left(\dfrac{1-\alpha}{\sigma_i}\right)u^{\alpha} - (1-\alpha)(k^\star)^{-\alpha}\varphi(\cdot)u^{\alpha} \\ \varphi(\cdot) - \dfrac{1}{k^\star} & \dfrac{c^\star}{(k^\star)^2} - \alpha(k^\star)^{-\alpha-1}u^{\alpha} - (1-\alpha)(k^\star)^{-\alpha}\varphi(\cdot)u^{\alpha} \end{bmatrix}.$$

A necessary and sufficient condition for saddle-path stability is $\det J < 0$. Knowing that $c^\star = (k^\star)^{1-\alpha}u^{\alpha} - k^\star\delta/(1-\varphi(\cdot)k^\star)$ holds on the balanced growth path we can easily calculate $\det J$ as

$$\det J = (1-k^\star\varphi(\cdot))(k^\star)^{-1}\left(-\alpha(k^\star)^{-\alpha-1}\frac{1-\alpha}{\sigma_i}u^{\alpha} - \frac{\delta\varphi(\cdot)}{(1-k^\star\varphi(\cdot))^2}\right).$$

From above we know that $1-\varphi(\cdot)k^\star > 0$, which shows that $\det J < 0$ and the rest point is a saddle-point. Thus, Proposition 2.1 is proved. □

Proof of Proposition 2.2

To prove Proposition 2.2, we differentiate the balanced growth rate $g^\star$, which is given by (2.12), with respect to $-u$. This gives

$$\frac{\partial g^\star}{-\partial u} = -\frac{\partial g^\star}{\partial u} = -\frac{\alpha(1-\alpha)u^{\alpha}}{\sigma_i k^{\alpha}}\left(\frac{1}{u} - \frac{1}{k}\frac{\partial k}{\partial u}\right).$$

This demonstrates that

$$-\frac{\partial g^\star}{\partial u}\begin{Bmatrix} > \\ = \\ < \end{Bmatrix} 0 \iff -\frac{\partial k}{\partial u}\frac{u}{k}\begin{Bmatrix} < \\ = \\ > \end{Bmatrix} -1.$$

To get the expression $-(\partial k/\partial u)(u/k)$ we first state that $q(k,\cdot)=0$ must hold on the balanced growth path. Implicit differentiation of $q(k,\cdot)$ gives

$$-\frac{\partial k}{\partial u}\frac{u}{k}=(-1)\left(\frac{\alpha k^{-\alpha}((1-\alpha)/\sigma_i)u^{\alpha}+\delta(-\varphi'(\cdot)uk)/(1-k\varphi(\cdot))^2}{\alpha k^{-\alpha}((1-\alpha)/\sigma_i)u^{\alpha}+\delta(\varphi(\cdot)k)/(1-k\varphi(\cdot))^2}\right).$$

For $-\varphi'(\cdot)u=\varphi(\cdot)$ the numerator just equals the denominator and $-(\partial k/\partial u)(u/k)=-1$. If $-\varphi'(\cdot)u>(<)\,\varphi(\cdot)$ the numerator is larger (smaller) than the denominator. Thus, Proposition 2.2 is proved. □

3 Expectations and the (Un-)importance of the real-wage feedback channel

3.1 Introduction

Despite the popularity of rational expectations dynamic stochastic general equilibrium (DSGE) models in academic and policy-oriented institutions, the new Keynesian approach (that is built upon this framework) features a variety of known theoretical and empirical shortcomings such as dynamic inconsistencies (Estrella and Fuhrer 2002) of rational expectations models as well as the ambiguous empirical evidence on the rational expectations forward-looking term in the Phillips curve (Rudd and Whelan 2005; Galí *et al.* 2005), which raises the question whether it indeed should be used as the standard workhorse in macroeconometric policy analysis.

In this chapter[1] we address a further open issue of the new Keynesian modeling of the macroeconomy that concerns the equivalence of continuous-time or discrete-time modeling or rather period vs. continuous-time analysis. Our considerations start from the empirical fact that while the actual data-generating process (DGP) at the macrolevel, even in the real markets, is by and large a daily one (concerning averages over the day), the corresponding data-collection process (DCP) on the economy-wide goods and labor markets is (due to technological and suitability issues) often at a much lower frequency (on a monthly or quarterly basis). Under the premise that the dynamical properties of both modeling approaches should not depend on the choice of the period length, and taking into account the fact that the behavior of the macroeconomy is in fact of a quasi-continuous-time nature, implies that empirically applicable period macromodels (using annualized data) should be iterated approximately with a step size between 1/365 and 1/52 of a year in order to assure that they generate qualitative results that are equivalent to the ones of their continuous-time analogs. Such empirically applicable period macromodels will then (for example) typically not be able to give rise to chaotic dynamics in one and two dimensions, suggesting that the literature on such chaotic dynamics is of no empirical relevance; see Flaschel and Proaño (2009) for details.

In the majority of theoretical new Keynesian models, however, this issue has not been addressed properly, leaving the underlying length of the "one-period delay" unspecified or assuming that the DGP and the DCP are equivalent, with the DGP being set equal to the DCP. This modeling strategy leads to the highly questionable implication that all wage and price changes occur in clustered or completely synchronized fashion at the beginning and the end of each considered period (the beginning of the next one). Though in reality micro price and wage changes may be staggered with considerable period lengths in between (at the firm level), this surely does not hold at the macrolevel, where due to the aggregation of overlapping staggered wage and price decisions, the assumption of a quasi-continuous-time-like behavior is more realistic for the macroeconomic time series.

From this perspective we reconsider in this chapter the baseline four-dimensional (4D) new Keynesian period model as discussed in Erceg *et al.* (2000), Woodford (2003, ch. 4) and Galí (2008). We suggest that changes in the qualitative eigenvalue structure with respect to their position inside or outside the unit circle (left or right), if they occur when the period length is for example increased from one month to one quarter, put a question mark over the relevance of the larger step size, but not necessarily one over the shorter period. This leads to the conclusion that shorter periods provide the better approach to determinacy analysis as far as empirical applications are concerned.

Using a sufficiently high frequency which allows us to reformulate the 4D new Keynesian model featuring both staggered wage and price setting in continuous time, we will show in Section 3.3 that these models can then be analyzed very easily (despite their seemingly analytical intractability in their original period formulation), showing especially that the continuous-time analog of the 4D new Keynesian period model gives rise to determinacy along the lines suggested by the numerical examples in Galí (2008, ch. 6).

By contrast, a closely related reformulation of the 4D new Keynesian baseline model in terms of a wage–price spiral with only model-consistent expectations (not rational expectations) is shown in Section 3.4 to be globally asymptotically stable for conventional types of interest rate policy rules and much more attractive in its deterministic properties than the purely forward-looking 4D baseline new Keynesian approach with its fairly trivial deterministic core (in the case of determinacy). Our alternative Keynesian dynamics overcomes the trivial explanation of turning points in economic activity of earlier monetarist-type baseline models (see Flaschel *et al.* 2008c, ch. 1), and it remains – as these models – globally asymptotically stable in a setup which integrates real interest rate effects, real wage effects and a nominal interest rate policy rule.

The remainder of this chapter is organized as follows. In Section 3.2 we briefly discuss the issue of (non)equivalence of period and continuous-time analysis on the basis of some observations made by Foley (1975) and Sims (1998) and suggest that period models that do not mirror the properties of their continuous-time analog should be questioned as to their relevance. We then show in Section 3.3 that 4D new Keynesian models with both staggered wage and price setting can be analyzed under such equivalence very easily (as compared to their discrete-time analog) and shown to be determinate in the way suggested in Galí (2008) by way of numerical examples. We then derive in Section 3.4 a reformulation of this model type, in terms of a wage–price spiral with model-consistent expectations (and only predetermined variables), which can be shown to be globally asymptotically stable and much more attractive in its deterministic properties than the new Keynesian approach with its fairly trivial deterministic core. We show in Section 3.5 that this model type performs well when estimated empirically and that it gives the real wage feedback channel a dominant role to play in comparison to the conventional real interest rate channel. Section 3.6 concludes.

3.2 The limitations of perfectly synchronized period analysis

Continuous vs. discrete-time modeling in macroeconomics was discussed extensively in the 1970s and 1980s, sometimes in very confusing ways and often by means of highly sophisticated, but also by an unnecessarily complicated, mathematical apparatus. There are some statements in the literature, old and new, which suggested that period analysis in macroeconomics, that is, discrete-time analysis where all economic agents are forced to act in a synchronized manner (with a time unit that is usually left unspecified), can be misleading from the formal as well as from the economic point of view. Foley (1975, p. 310) in particular states:

> The arguments of this section are based on a methodological precept concerning macroeconomic period models *No substantive prediction or explanation in a well-defined macroeconomic period model should depend on the real time length of the period.*

Such a statement has however been completely ignored in the numerous analytical and numerical investigations of complex or chaotic macrodynamics. Furthermore, from the viewpoint of economic modeling, Sims (1998, p. 318) states that:

> The next several sections examine the behavior of a variety of models that differ mainly in how they model real and nominal stickiness... They are formulated in continuous time to avoid the need to use the uninterpretable "one period" delays that plague the discrete-time models in this literature.

Our view concerning these issues is that a macrodynamic analysis that is intended to consider sooner or later real and financial markets simultaneously must consider period analysis with a very short time unit ("1 day"), if a uniform and synchronized period length is assumed. But then real markets cannot be considered in equilibrium all of the time. Instead, gradual adjustment of wages, prices and quantities occurs in view of labor and goods markets imbalances for which, moreover, convergence to real market equilibria cannot automatically be assumed. Real market behavior is therefore to be based on gradual adjustment processes and it can be discussed whether, on this basis, financial markets should be modeled by equilibrium conditions or also by somewhat delayed responses as well, both in short-period analysis as well as in continuous time.

The above suggests that period analysis and continuous-time modeling should provide qualitatively the same results. In the linear case this can be motivated further by the following type of argument. Consider the mathematically equivalent discrete- and continuous-time models[2]

$$x_{t+1} = Ax_t \quad \text{and} \quad \dot{x} = (A - I)x = Jx,$$

which follow the literature by assuming an unspecified time unit of one period.

The above arguments suggest that we should generalize such an approach and rewrite it with a variable period length as

$$x_{t+h} - x_t = hJx_t \quad \text{and} \quad \dot{x} = Jx.$$

This gives for the system matrices the relationship

$$A = hJ + I.$$

According to Foley's postulate both J and A should be stable matrices if period as well as continuous-time analysis is used for macroeconomic analysis in such a linear framework. That is, all eigenvalues of J should have negative real parts, while the eigenvalues of A should all lie within the unit circle. Graphically this implies the situation shown in Figure 3.1, which shows that if the eigenvalues of J do not lie inside the unit circle shown then they have to be moved into it by a proper choice of the time unit and thus the matrix hJ.

If the eigenvalues of the matrix J of the continuous-time case are such that they lie outside the solid circle shown, but for example within a circle of radius 2, the discrete-time matrix $J + I$ would, in contrast to the continuous-time case, have unstable roots (on the basis of a period length $h = 1$ that generally is left implicit

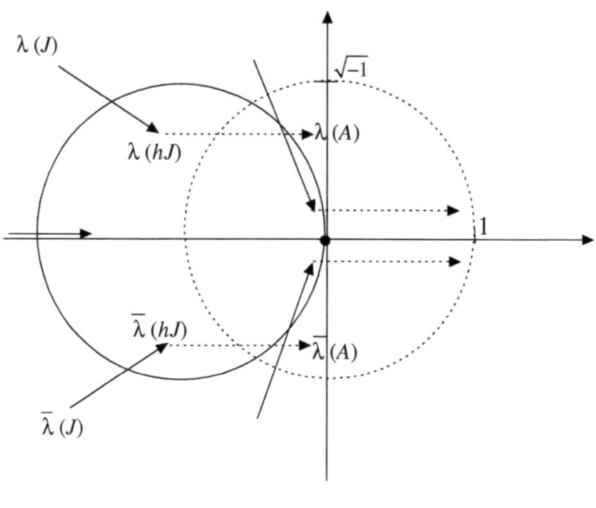

Figure 3.1 A choice of the period length that guarantees equivalence of continuous- and discrete-time analysis.

in such approaches). The system $x_{t+1} = Ax_t$, $A = J + I$, then has eigenvalues outside the unit circle (obtained by shifting the solid unit circle shown by one unit to the right (into the dotted one)). Choosing $h = 1/2$ would however be sufficient to move all eigenvalues $\lambda(A) = h\lambda(J) + 1$ of $A = hJ + I$ into this unit circle, since all eigenvalues of hJ are moved by this change in period length into the solid unit circle shown in Figure 3.1, since the eigenvalues of J have all been assumed to have negative real parts and are thus moved toward the origin of the space of complex numbers when the period length h is reduced.

In view of this we claim that sensible macrodynamic period models $x_{t+h} = (hJ + I)x_t = Ax_t$ should all be based on a choice of the period length h such that $\|\lambda(A)\| < 1$ can be achieved (if the matrix J is stable).[3] Since models of the real-financial interaction suggest very small period lengths and since the macroeconomy is updated at the least on a daily basis in reality, such a choice should always be available for the model-builder. In this way it is guaranteed that linear period and continuous-time models give qualitatively the same answer.

We also note here (in view of the new Keynesian approach to be considered next) that matrices J with eigenvalues with only positive real parts will always give rise to totally unstable matrices $A = hJ + I$, since the real parts are augmented by "1" in such a situation. We will however show in the next section that the simple h dependence of the eigenvalues of the matrix A, $\lambda(A) = h\lambda(J) + 1$, considered here (in this linear setup) does not apply to baseline new Keynesian models, since they (though linear) depend nonlinearly on their period length h and are only directly comparable to the above in the special case $h = 1$. Comparisons for larger period lengths h are therefore not so easy and demand other means of analysis in order to compare determinacy in both continuous and discrete time.

As a general statement and conclusion, related to Foley (1975) observation, we however would assert that new Keynesian period models with stable/unstable eigenvalue structures that differ from their continuous-time analog should be questioned with respect to their relevance from the theoretical and (even more) from the empirical point of view. Period models, if meaningful, thus depend on their continuous-time analogs in the validity of their results.

3.3 New Keynesian macrodynamics

In this section we provide some succinct propositions on equilibrium determinacy of the 4D new Keynesian model with both staggered prices and wages from the continuous-time perspective, but also review the relevance of this type of approach from a critical perspective. We start directly from the presentation of Galí (2008, ch. 6) of the log-linearly reduced-form of the new Keynesian model with both staggered wages and prices in order to discuss analytically the determinacy properties of this model type.

The deterministic "Skeleton" of new Keynesian AD–AS model

In the literature on new Keynesian baseline models one often encounters the treatment of the case of a price Phillips curve, a dynamic investment–saving (IS) curve and a Taylor rule (TR) as the point of departure for new Keynesian and dynamic stochastic general equilibrium (DSGE) model-building. A modern model of the Keynesian variety, but also older ones, should however in our view accept the proposition that both wage levels and price levels are only gradually adjusting at each moment in time, since they are macrovariables and do not perform noticeable jumps on a daily timescale, which we consider as the relevant time unit for the macrodata-*generating* process.

The above assertion rests on the idea that individual wage and price movements may be occurring in a staggered fashion, but that these staggered movements are not clustered in time, as is generally assumed, especially in the empirically oriented new Keynesian approaches. The data-collection process in contrast may be a staggered as well as a clustered one, but this does not imply that models that have been estimated, say on a quarterly data basis, should then also be iterated and analyzed with such a crude period length, as far as the rhythm of the data-generating process (which is much finer) is concerned. Bunching or synchronizing staggered actions, as period models do, may lead in fact to illegitimate results as in particular the one-dimensional (1D) chaotic macromodels make clear, since they generate trajectories that are totally impossible in continuous time (or even for small period lengths).

The foregoing statements in our view suggest that macromodels should be formulated, analyzed and simulated as continuous processes (or quasi-continuous ones, with step size 1/365 with respect to their annualized data framework). This is indeed the perspective that we pursue in this section, which allows us to use continuous-time methods to analyze models which are normally formulated strictly as period models in the new Keynesian tradition, which we will briefly reconsider from the continuous-time perspective in this section.

In our own model, treated in Section 3.4, we use continuous time as the modeling strategy, since that allows for stability proofs even in high-order dynamical systems (which nevertheless can be simulated adequately with a step length of 1/365). In these models, also built on the assumptions of gradually adjusting wages and prices, we can of course consider limit cases where wages, prices or expectations adjust with infinite speed, but in our view these are more a matter of theoretical curiosity than of fundamental importance. Consequently, the natural starting point of the Keynesian version of the new neoclassical synthesis and our matured approach to "old" Keynesian model-building should be staggered wage and price setting as the baseline situation rather than one of its two limit cases (with which it may nevertheless be compared).

The need to have a theoretical baseline model of new Keynesian type that is investigated thoroughly from the theoretical perspective concerning feedback channels and related stability issues (such as our Keynesian reformulation and extension of the old neoclassical synthesis later on) has not been carried out in the literature so far, despite the fact that such model types are now heavily used in empirical applications – see Smets and Wouters (2003) for a prominent example.

The log-linear new Keynesian model employed in Galí (2008, ch. 6) reads

$$\pi_t^w \overset{\text{wage Phillips curve}}{=} \beta(h)\pi_{t+h}^w + h\kappa_w\tilde{y}_t - h\lambda_w\tilde{\omega}_t, \quad \pi_t^w = (w_t - w_{t-h})/h, \tag{3.1}$$

$$\pi_t^p \overset{\text{price Phillips curve}}{=} \beta(h)\pi_{t+h}^p + h\kappa_p\tilde{y}_t + h\lambda_p\tilde{\omega}_t, \quad \pi_t^p = (p_t - p_{t-h})/h, \tag{3.2}$$

$$\tilde{y}_t \overset{\text{IS}}{=} \tilde{y}_{t+h} - h\sigma^{-1}(i_t - \pi_{t+h}^p - r^n), \tag{3.3}$$

$$i_t \overset{\text{TR}}{=} r^n + \phi_p\pi_t^p + \phi_w\pi_t^w + \phi_y\tilde{y}_t, \tag{3.4}$$

with

$$\tilde{\omega}_t \equiv \tilde{\omega}_{t-h} + h(\pi_t^w - \pi_t^p) - \Delta\omega_{t+h}^n$$

as the identity relating the changes in the real wage gap $\tilde{\omega}_t = \omega_t - \omega_t^n$ (ω_t^n being the natural real wage) to wage inflation, price inflation and the change in the natural real wage $\Delta\omega_t^n$. Note here also that $\beta(h) := 1/(1 + h\rho)$ is the discount factor that applies to the period length h, and that there holds $[1 - \beta(h)]/\beta(h) = h\rho$, or $\beta(h) = 1/(1 + h\rho)$, when solved for the discount rate ρ of the new Keynesian model, which will be of importance below.

Equation (3.1) describes a new Keynesian wage Phillips curve, and equation (3.2), analogously, describes a new Keynesian price Phillips curve, all parameters being positive – see Galí (2008) for their derivation. We assume as in Galí (2008, p. 128) that the conditions stated there for the existence of a zero steady-state solution are fulfilled, namely that (a) $\Delta\omega_t^n = 0$ for all t, and (b) the intercept in the nominal interest rate rule adjusts always in a one-to-one fashion to variations in the natural rate of interest. The dynamic IS equation (derived by combining the goods markets clearing condition $y_t = c_t$ with the Euler equation of the households) is given by equation (3.3), with $\tilde{y}_t \equiv y_t - y_t^n$ being the output gap (y_t^n being the equilibrium level of output attainable in the absence of both wage and price rigidities) and r^n being the natural rate of interest. Finally, equation (3.4) describes a generalized type of contemporaneous Taylor interest rate policy rule (TR), where the nominal interest rate is assumed to be a function of the natural rate of interest, of wage inflation, of price inflation as well as of the output gap – see Galí (2008, ch. 6.2) for details.

Note that in this formulation of the model we have three forward-looking variables and one equation that is updating the historically given real wage. We thus need for the determinacy of the model the existence of three unstable eigenvalues (three variables that can jump to the 1D stable submanifold) and one eigenvalue that is negative (corresponding to the stable submanifold). In contrast to Galí (2008, footnote 6) we use annualized rates, obtained by dividing the corresponding period differences through the period length h (usually a quarter year in the literature). We thereby show which parameters change with the data frequency or just the iteration step size h when the model is simulated. We thus use conventional scaling for the rates under consideration here, but allow for changes in the data-collection frequency or iteration frequency.[4] We consequently consider the equations (3.1)–(3.4) from an applied perspective, that is, we take them as the starting point for an empirically motivated study of the influence of the data frequency (quarterly, monthly or weekly) on the size of the parameter values to be estimated.

The new Keynesian model completed in this way represents an implicitly formulated system of difference equations, where all variables with index $t+h$ are expected variables or should be interpreted as representing perfect foresight in the deterministic skeleton of the considered dynamics. Making use again of the Taylor rule and the price Phillips curve (see equations (3.17) and (3.19) below) and using the above representation of $\tilde{\omega}_t$, it can be made an explicit system of difference equations that may be written (with $\eta = \sigma^{-1}$)

$$\pi_{t+h}^w = \frac{\pi_t^w - h\kappa_w \tilde{y}_t + h\lambda_w \tilde{\omega}_t}{\beta(h)}$$

$$= \pi_t^w + h\rho\pi_t^w - h\frac{\kappa_w \tilde{y}_t - \lambda_w \tilde{\omega}_{t-h} - h\lambda_w(\pi_t^w - \pi_t^p)}{\beta(h)}, \tag{3.5}$$

$$\pi_{t+h}^p = \frac{\pi_t^p - h\kappa_p \tilde{y}_t - h\lambda_p \tilde{\omega}_t}{\beta(h)}$$

$$= \pi_t^p + h\rho\pi_t^p - h\frac{\kappa_p \tilde{y}_t + \lambda_p \tilde{\omega}_{t-h} + h\lambda_p(\pi_t^w - \pi_t^p)}{\beta(h)}, \tag{3.6}$$

$$\tilde{y}_{t+h} = \tilde{y}_t + h\eta\left[\phi_w \pi_t^w + \left(\phi_p - \frac{1}{\beta(h)}\right)\pi_t^p + \phi_y \tilde{y}_t + h\frac{\kappa_p \tilde{y}_t + \lambda_p \tilde{\omega}_{t-h} + h\lambda_p(\pi_t^w - \pi_t^p)}{\beta(h)}\right], \tag{3.7}$$

$$\tilde{\omega}_t = \tilde{\omega}_{t-h} + h(\pi_t^w - \pi_t^p), \tag{3.8}$$

which we can represent succinctly through the matrix equation

$$x_{t+h} = x_t + h(J_0 + hJ_1(h))x_t = x_t + hA(h)x_t = (I + hA(h))x_t,$$

where $x_t = (\pi_t^w, \pi_t^p, \tilde{y}_t, \tilde{\omega}_t)$ and J_0 collects the terms that are linear in h, which therefore will characterize the continuous-time limit case.

As already discussed, the model should not depend in its fundamental qualitative properties on the length of the period h, in particular when frequencies of empirical relevance are considered. We therefore expect that it reflects the properties of its continuous-time analog, abbreviated by $\dot{x} = J_0 x$. The new Keynesian baseline model with both staggered wage and price setting (the Keynesian version of the new neoclassical synthesis) reads in its log-linearly approximated form

(see Erceg *et al.* 2000; Woodford 2003, p. 225ff.; Galí 2008, ch. 6)

$$\dot{\pi}^w = \rho\pi^w - \kappa_w\tilde{y} + \lambda_w\tilde{\omega}, \tag{3.9}$$

$$\dot{\pi}^p = \rho\pi^p - \kappa_p\tilde{y} - \lambda_p\tilde{\omega}, \tag{3.10}$$

$$\dot{\tilde{y}} = \eta\phi_w\pi^w + \eta(\phi_p - 1)\pi^p + \eta\phi_y\tilde{y}, \tag{3.11}$$

$$\dot{\tilde{\omega}} = \pi^w - \pi^p, \tag{3.12}$$

where we note that there holds $1/\beta(h) = 1 + h\rho$, which tends to 1 in the limit as $h \to 0$.

Determinacy analysis

The above representation of the model implies for the system matrix of the considered dynamics the structure

$$J_0 = \begin{pmatrix} 0 & 0 & -\kappa_w & \lambda_w \\ 0 & 0 & -\kappa_p & -\lambda_p \\ \phi_w\eta & (\phi_p - 1)\eta & \phi_y\eta & 0 \\ 1 & -1 & 0 & 0 \end{pmatrix}.$$

With respect to this model type, it is asserted in Galí (2008, p. 128) (and illustrated numerically in his figure 6.1) that the new Keynesian model is, in the case $\phi_y = 0$ considered below, determinate (exhibits three unstable and one stable root) for all policy parameters ϕ_p, ϕ_w when $\phi_w + \phi_p > 1$ holds in the Taylor rule. We show in this section that this determinacy condition is in fact necessary and sufficient for the 4D new Keynesian model for all positive values of the parameter ϕ_y provided that $\rho = 0$ holds. To investigate this assertion we have to consider the eigenvalues of the system matrix J_0 of our system of differential equations for $\rho = 0$. Doing so we can derive the following two propositions[5]

PROPOSITION 3.1 *Assume that $\rho = 0$ and that $\phi_y > 0$. Then, the characteristic equation $|\lambda I - J_0| = 0$ has three roots with positive real parts and one negative root if and only if the generalized Taylor principle $\phi_p + \phi_w > 1$ holds true.*

Proof: See Asada *et al.* (2010a, ch. 5) and Flaschel *et al.* (2008a, proposition 1). □

PROPOSITION 3.2 *Consider $\rho > 0$ and assume that*

$$\phi_y > \rho\frac{[-(\lambda_w + \lambda_p) + \eta(\kappa_w\phi_w + \kappa_p(\phi_p - 1))]}{\eta[\lambda_w + \lambda_p - \rho^2]}$$

holds true. Then, the characteristic equation $|\lambda I - J_0| = 0$ *has three roots with positive real parts and one negative root if and only if*

$$\phi_w + \phi_p > 1 - \frac{\rho(\lambda_w + \lambda_p)}{\kappa_w \lambda_p + \lambda_w \kappa_p} \phi_y.$$

Proof: See Flaschel *et al.* (1997, proposition 2). □

These propositions state conditions – in particular for monetary policy – such that equilibrium determinacy is given, in which case the resulting dynamics do not need to be ignored.

The proofs of these two propositions show how a thorough analytical analysis of the determinacy properties of the new Keynesian model with staggered wages and prices is to be conducted by using a continuous-time representation of the model. This strategy allows us to circumvent the calculation of the significantly more complicated conditions that hold for the corresponding discrete-time case – see for example the mathematical appendices in Woodford (2003) for the difficulties that exist just in the 3D case.

However, these considerations concern a log-linear approximation of the true nonlinear model (where rational expectations must be of a global nature), which need not be mirrored through the rational expectations paths generated by the log-linear approximation. It may therefore well be that the paths that are generated through computer algorithms in the log-linearized version do not have much in common with the corresponding ones of the true model.

Our approach to determinacy analysis has made use of the view that the intrinsic dynamics and determinacy properties of a dynamic model should not depend on whether such a model is formulated in continuous or discrete time. In other words, the dynamical properties of a model are (or should be) invariant to the assumed frequency of the decision-making of the economic agents in the discrete-time version of the model.[6] On this basis the approach pursued here makes determinacy analysis of new Keynesian models, studied for example in Woodford (2003), much easier and represents a valid (though indirect) strategy for the analytical determinacy analysis for high-dimensional rational expectations models.

A critical evaluation of new Keynesian macrodynamics

A first set of questions concerning the validity of the new Keynesian approach to macrodynamics is its use of the word Keynesian as a label. There is in fact no IS-curve, representing Keynesian demand rationing on the market for goods, as the model is formulated, but simply a Walrasian type of notional goods demand and the assumption of goods market equilibrium. The theory of rational expectations (RE) has also very little to do with Keynes (1936) views on the difficulties of expectations formation, in particular for the evaluation of long-term investment projects. By contrast, RE expectations formation represents an approach that can be handled by a computer routine (often simply used as a black box) that by construction will deliver, at most, only damped oscillations. Finally, Keynes' liquidity preference theory is no longer a subject to which attention is paid, because of the disappearance (due to its irrelevance) of the liquidity preference–money supply (LM) schedule, which is at best present in the background of a simple-to-handle Taylor interest rate policy rule. But, liquidity preference is now back on the research agenda, as the recent crises in financial markets show.

Therefore, when compared with Keynes's (1936, ch. 22) 'Notes on the trade cycle' and its important constituent parts, the marginal propensity to consume out of rationed income, the marginal efficiency of investment (and the expected cash flow that underlies it) and the parameters that shape liquidity preference, not much of this is left in the new Keynesian approach to macrodynamics, in particular concerning the systematic forces within the business cycle and its turning points as they are discussed in Keynes (1936, ch. 22).

Moreover, further important feedback channels, in particular the real wage channel, as they have been discussed in Chiarella and Flaschel (2000a) and later work, cannot carry out their roles in the shaping of cyclical adjustment processes and their inflationary consequences. Rather such feedback channels are revised in their structure in the search for a Taylor rule until they imply the three/one combination of unstable/stable roots for the Jacobian matrix of the dynamics for a reasonable range of policy parameters, when stability becomes enforceable. This latter result then ensures that real wages (the pre-determined variable) are always adjusting monotonically along a 1D stable manifold toward the steady state and are thus capable of behaving only in a very simple manner. This picture is changed in significant ways in our competing matured Keynesian dynamical model that we will consider in the next section.

The construction and the implications of this new Keynesian approach to macrodynamics are therefore heavily dependent on the addition of stochastic processes and are consequently governed literally by the Frisch–Slutzky stochastic shock absorber paradigm and are thus based on socalled "ad-shockeries." Its rational expectations solutions are nothing but, in a sense, specifically iterated types of suitably chosen stochastic processes, with the iteration being based on the inverse matrix of the Jacobian of the system we considered above.

We conclude from this discussion[7] that the new Keynesian approach to macrodynamics creates more theoretical problems than it helps to solve. Reasons for this may be given by its following indispensable ingredients

(a) Microfoundations, which are stressed by the rational expectations school, are per se an important desideratum to be reflected also by behaviorally oriented macrodynamics, but agents are heterogeneous, form heterogeneous expectations along other lines than suggested by the rational expectations school and have short-term as well as long-term views about the economy. The straitjacket postulated by the supporters of the representative agent approach is just too narrow to allow a treatment of what is known as interesting behavior of economic agents and it is also not detailed enough to discuss the various feedback channels of the macroeconomics literature.

(b) Market clearing, the next ingredient of such approaches, is a questionable device to study the macroeconomy in particular on its real side. The data-generating process is too fast to allow for period models with a uniform period length of a quarter or more. So period models of this type, which deviate from their continuous-time analogs, should be replaced by the latter modeling approach. In continuous time however it is much too heroic to assume market clearing at all moments in time, but real markets can then only adjust toward moving equilibria in such a framework (as for example in the modeling approach that we outline later).

(c) Yet, neither microfoundations per se nor market clearing assumptions are the true dividing line between the approaches we are advocating and the ones considered in this section. It is the *ad hoc* assumption, that is, the not behaviorally microfounded assumption of rational expectations, that by the chosen analytical method makes the world in general log-linear (by construction) and the generated dynamics convergent (by assumption) to its unique steady state which is the root of the problem that this chapter seeks to make explicit.

The basic argument here is that the chosen starting point of the new Keynesian approach, purely forward-looking rational expectations, is axiomatically seen to be a wrong one so that complicated additional constructions (epicycles) become necessary in order to reconcile this approach with the facts. In the words of Fuhrer:[8]

> Are we adding "epicycles" to a dead model?

By epicycles Fuhrer means habits, indexing, adding lags and high-order adjustment costs, which are the examples he mentions on the slides from which the above quotation has been taken.

Compared to the disequilibrium AD–AS model that we will formulate in Section 3.4, we find (despite this criticism) many common elements in the structure of the two AD–AS approaches, in particular as far as the formal structure of the wage Phillips curve and the price Phillips curve are concerned. In addition, our model of Section 3.4 also has a dynamic IS curve and a specific type of Taylor rule. However we will employ four gaps in place of only two (concerning various activity measures and real wages) and use Okun's law to link the labor market gaps to the one on the goods market. In addition, by its origin, our model type will always use hybrid expectations formation right from the start (see Chiarella and Flaschel 1996b), based on short-run crossover and model-consistent expectations and the concept of an inflationary climate within which the short run is embedded that is updated adaptively. We use simultaneous dating and crossover wage and price expectations in the formulated wage–price spiral, in place of the forward-looking self-reference that characterizes the new Keynesian approach on both the labor and the goods market, and (as stated) in addition hybrid ones that give inertia to our formulation of wage-price dynamics.

We will show stability of the steady state under quite meaningful assumptions on the parameters of our model and can expand our baseline scenario easily in many directions. By contrast, the new Keynesian baseline model faces difficulties when one tries to generalize it (for example to the case where there is steady-state inflation). It is moreover not easily extended beyond the nonrationed Walrasian approach concerning theory of aggregate demand that it employs.

We conclude that the new Keynesian approach does not represent a theoretically and empirically convincing strategy for the study of the fluctuating growth that we observe in capitalist economies. It gives the features of the deterministic core of the considered dynamics (if determinate) a by and large trivial outlook. It reduces the nonlinear growth dynamics of capitalist market economies to log-linear approximations (within which routinized expectations are formed that are convergent by construction) and suggests that such systems when driven by certain stochastic processes are all that one needs to have for a good model of the real-financial market interaction. Altogether, the new Keynesian approach to macrodynamics is too narrowly oriented concerning methodological restrictions and too inflexible concerning substantial generalizations so that there are sometimes huge efforts needed for only limited generalizations or improvements of the model's structure.

There is thus a need for alternative baseline scenarios which can be communicated across scientific approaches, can be investigated in detail with respect to their theoretical properties in their original nonlinear format, and which, when applied to actual economies, remain controllable from the theoretical point of view as far as the basic feedback chains they contain are concerned. The happy incidence here is that such an alternative indeed exists and does not deny the validity of the old neoclassical synthesis. This synthesis now appears as a special case of this larger framework, a special case that is however problematic when one attempts to apply it to the study of actual economies. Nevertheless, there is thus continuity in the development of Keynesian macrodynamic models from this perspective, and thus not the total denial of the usefulness of past evolutions in Keynesian macrotheory that the new Keynesian approach is implicitly suggesting.

3.4 Matured Keynesian macrodynamics

In this section we provide our alternative to the new Keynesian scenario we have investigated in the preceding section. Quoting again from Fuhrer:[9]

> In a way, this takes us back to the very old models
> – With decent long-run, theory-grounded properties
> – But dynamics from a-theoretic sources.

We approach this task by way of an extension of the AD–AS model of the old neoclassical synthesis that primarily improves the AS side, the nominal side, of this traditional integrated Keynesian AD–AS approach, and which in addition allows for the impact of wage-price dynamics on the AD side of the model. We call this model type DAD–DAS where the additional "D" stands for "disequilibrium." We attempt to show that this matured Keynesian approach can compete with the new neoclassical synthesis with respect to an understanding of the basic feedback mechanisms that characterize the working of the macroeconomy, their stability properties and their empirical validity.

In this section we thus propose a traditionally oriented alternative to the new Keynesian model of the preceding section,[10] in the spirit of Chen *et al.* (2006) which, though being based on a quite different philosophy, shares significant similarities with the 4D new Keynesian models previously discussed. We in particular also assume that in a properly formulated Keynesian model, both the nominal wage level and the price level should react in a sluggish manner to the state of economic activity.

We do not base our theoretical formulation however on utility/profit maximization under monopolistic competition and (as in Calvo 1983) staggered wage and price setting schemes as is done in new Keynesian models. Instead, we postulate that due to the sluggishness of wages and prices the goods and labor markets *cannot* be in equilibrium at every point in time, so that wage and price inflation gradually react to disequilibrium situations in both markets, here represented only by the output gap. As in the new Keynesian approach of Section 3.3, the output gap and the wage share also enter our wage and price Phillips curve equations, the latter variable however not as a result of a monopolistic utility/profit maximization of households and firms, respectively (see for instance Woodford 2003), but rather due to wage bargaining and price setting situations as they are discussed for example in Blanchard and Katz (1999) in their microfoundation of the wage Phillips curve – see also Flaschel and Krolzig (2006) in this regard.

Concerning the modeling of inflationary expectations and the "rationality" of the agents of our theoretical framework, we assume that the economic agents form their expectations in our model in a model-consistent, but crossover manner, meaning that agents incorporate the perfectly foreseen wage inflation rate in the equation for the price inflation rate, and the perfectly foreseen price inflation rate in the equation for the wage inflation rate. Additionally, as also done now in new Keynesian models featuring "hybrid" Phillips curves such as Galí and Gertler (1999) and Galí *et al.* (2001), and following Chiarella and Flaschel (2000a) and later work based on this book, we incorporate an inflation inertia or better still an inflation climate term into both the wage and the price Phillips curves of our model. Under these modifications, with the inclusion of a conventional IS equation and a standard monetary policy rule, the deterministic part of the model of the preceding section reads (now with a neoclassical dating of inflationary expectations and thus without the need to put an h in front of the terms that drive wage and price inflation)[11]

$$\pi^w_{t+h} \equiv (w_{t+h} - w_t)/(w_t h) = \tilde{\pi}^p_{t+h} + \beta_{wy} y_t - \beta_{w\omega}\theta_t, \tag{3.13}$$

$$\pi^p_{t+h} \equiv (p_{t+h} - p_t)/(p_t h) = \tilde{\pi}^w_{t+h} + \beta_{py} y_t + \beta_{p\omega}\theta_t, \tag{3.14}$$

$$y_{t+h} = y_t - h\alpha_{yi}(i_t - \pi^p_{t+h} - i_0), \tag{3.15}$$

$$i_t = i_0 + \beta_{ip}\pi^p_t + \beta_{iy}y_t. \tag{3.16}$$

As just discussed, for the impact of price inflation on wage inflation (and vice versa) we assume in addition that it is not only of a temporary nature, but subject also to some inertia, here measured by an index for the inflation climate in which the economy is currently operating. It is natural to assume that such a medium-run climate expression (π^c) is updated in an adaptive fashion, i.e. in the simplest approach that it satisfies a law of motion of the type

$$\pi^c_{t+h} = \pi^c_t + h\beta_{\pi^c}(\pi^p_t - \pi^c_t). \tag{3.17}$$

We define on this basis the still undefined variables $\tilde{\pi}^p_{t+h}$ and $\tilde{\pi}^w_{t+h}$ by the expressions

$$\begin{aligned} \tilde{\pi}^p_{t+h} &= \alpha_p\pi^p_{t+h} + (1-\alpha_p)\pi^c_{t+h}, \\ \tilde{\pi}^w_{t+h} &= \alpha_w\pi^w_{t+h} + (1-\alpha_w)\pi^c_{t+h}, \end{aligned} \tag{3.18}$$

with $\alpha_p, \alpha_w \in (0, 1)$.

In continuous time the system can then be summarized as

$$\begin{aligned} \pi^w &= \alpha_w\pi^p + (1-\alpha_w)\pi^c + \beta_{wy}y - \beta_{w\omega}\theta, \\ \pi^p &= \alpha_p\pi^w + (1-\alpha_p)\pi^c + \beta_{py}y + \beta_{p\omega}\theta, \\ \dot{y} &= -\alpha_{yi}((\beta_{ip}-1)\pi^p + \beta_{iy}y), \\ \dot{\pi}^c &= \beta_{\pi c}(\pi^p - \pi^c), \\ \dot{\theta} &= \pi^w - \pi^p, \end{aligned}$$

if π^w and π^p are used to denote the forward rate of inflation of wages and prices, that is, the right-hand derivatives of $\ln w$ and $\ln p$.

The first two equations in this system can be solved with respect to the unknowns $\pi^w - \pi^c$, $\pi^p - \pi^c$ and (setting $\alpha = 1/(1-\alpha_p\alpha_w)$) give rise to

$$\begin{aligned} \pi^w - \pi^c &= \alpha[\beta_{wy}y - \beta_{w\omega}\theta + \alpha_w(\beta_{py}y + \beta_{p\omega}\theta)], \\ \pi^p - \pi^c &= \alpha[\beta_{py}y + \beta_{p\omega}\theta + \alpha_p(\beta_{wy}y - \beta_{w\omega}\theta)], \\ \pi^w - \pi^p &= \alpha[(1-\alpha_p)(\beta_{wy}y - \beta_{w\omega}\theta) - (1-\alpha_w)(\beta_{py}y + \beta_{p\omega}\theta)]. \end{aligned}$$

We thus get

$$\pi^w = \pi^w(y,\theta) + \pi^c \qquad (\pi^w_y > 0,\ \pi^w_\theta \gtreqless 0),$$

$$\pi^p = \pi^p(y,\theta) + \pi^c \qquad (\pi^p_y > 0,\ \pi^p_\theta \gtreqless 0),$$

$$\pi^w - \pi^p = \dot{\theta}(y,\theta) \qquad (\dot{\theta}_y \gtreqless 0, \dot{\theta}_\theta < 0).$$

With respect to $\dot{\theta}_y$, the dependence of real wage growth on economic activity, we assume (in line with what is known on the pro-cyclicity of real wages (see e.g. Chen *et al.* 2006)) that this partial derivative is positive.

The dynamical system to be investigated on the basis of this assumption is

$$\dot{y} = -\alpha_{yi}[(\beta_{ip} - 1)(\pi^p(y,\theta) + \pi^c) + \beta_{iy} y], \tag{3.19}$$

$$\dot{\pi}^c = \beta_{\pi^c}\pi^p(y,\theta), \tag{3.20}$$

$$\dot{\theta} = \dot{\theta}(y,\theta), \tag{3.21}$$

and it exhibits (as the one in the preceding section) the origin as the steady state. For the Jacobian J of these dynamics we get for an active monetary policy rule ($\beta_{ip} > 1$) that the Jacobian J of the 3D system has the form

$$J = \begin{pmatrix} - & - & ? \\ + & 0 & ? \\ + & 0 & - \end{pmatrix}. \tag{3.22}$$

Exploiting the linear dependences within the considered dynamics and the Jacobian, one can show that the characteristic polynomial of the matrix J is given by

$$\lambda^3 + b_1\lambda^2 + b_2\lambda + b_3,$$

with the conditions $b_1 > 0$ and $b_3 > 0$. Furthermore the parameter β_{iy} only appears in the entry J_{11} of the matrix J. Making it sufficiently large therefore will obviously ensure that $b_2 > 0$ and $b_1 b_2 - b_3 > 0$ hold true in addition.

We therefore obtain from these Routh-Hurwitz stability conditions the following result.

PROPOSITION 3.3 *The interior steady state of the dynamical system (3.19)–(3.21) is globally asymptotically stable if the growth rate of real wages depends positively on economic activity, if monetary policy is active with respect to the inflation gap (which overcomes the destabilizing Mundell effect in this model type) and if the state of the business cycle operates on the interest rate setting policy of the central bank with sufficient strength.*

Proof: See Asada *et al.* (2010a, proposition 2). □

Should this stability result not hold (in the situation where the growth rate of real wages depends negatively on economic activity and where the dynamics of real wages is therefore goods market-led), Asada *et al.* (2010a) show that this can happen only in a range for the parameter $\beta_{\pi c}$ that is in general fairly negligible. In this conceivable, but limited, situation strong monetary policy reactions with respect to the parameter β_{iy} or meaningful behavioral nonlinearities off the steady state may in addition be needed in order to make the dynamics bounded or viable if it departs by too much from the steady state.[12]

3.5 Real wage channel dominance

In this section, we provide a brief empirical consideration of the baseline model of traditional type. In order to obtain a good fit we have extended this model type (as represented by equations (3.13)–(3.16)) slightly as far as the goods market dynamics and the interest rate policy rule are concerned. Since this Keynesian approach is centered around wage-price dynamics of a wage-price spiral type and thus integrates the dynamics of income distribution we include the real wage, or better the wage share $v = w/(pz)$,[13] into the goods market dynamics (since both the price Phillips curve ($d \ln p$) and the wage Phillips curve ($d \ln w$) are here augmented by the growth rate of labor productivity ($d \ln z$) in a way that is compatible with steady state calculations; see the estimated equations below). Moreover, in the tradition of the Keynesian dynamic multiplier story we include a term that makes the time rate of change of output Y dependent on its level. The goods market dynamics are therefore extended in a way that integrates the dynamic multiplier and the fact that economic activity will depend on income distribution, a commonly assumed fact in the debate on real wage policies. In the Taylor interest rate policy rule we moreover have added interest rate smoothing, since this improves the estimate significantly. The estimated equations and the estimation results are given in Table 3.1.

In deriving Table 3.1 we use π^{12} as a moving average of past consumer price index (CPI) inflation rate over the last 12 quarters with linearly declining weights,

Table 3.1 UK data set

Variable	*Description of the original series*
e	Employment rate
u	Industrial production Hodrick–Prescott cyclical term (calculated with a smoothing factor of $\lambda = 1600$)
w	Average earning in industrial production, seasonally adjusted (index: 2000 = 100)
p	Gross domestic product: implicit price deflator, 2000 = 100
p_c	CPI index, all items, 2000 = 100
z	Labor productivity, 1996 = 100
v	Real unit wage costs (deflated by the GDP deflator), 2003 = 100
i	Treasury bill rate

as a particularly simple expression for the current inflation climate in which the economy is operating. The formulation of such a moving average of course slightly reduces the number of observations to be used in the estimate. The benchmark rates for output and the wage share are given simply by their averages over the considered timespan. Since the wage and price Phillips curves are based on the approach of Blanchard and Katz (1999), see Flaschel and Krolzig (2006) for details, we have to use the log of the wage share in these two Phillips curves (but we do not use logs otherwise). Note here finally that the coefficient ϕ_i measures the degree of interest rate smoothing in the reduced-form interest rate policy rule of the central bank

$$i_t = \phi_i i_{t-1} + (1-\phi_i)\alpha_{ip}\hat{p}_t + (1-\phi_i)\alpha_{iy}y_t,$$

which can be derived from its usual two-stage formulation in continuous time, namely

$$i^* = (i_0 - \bar{\pi}) + \hat{p} + \alpha_p \hat{p} + \alpha_y y,$$
$$\frac{di}{dt} = \alpha_i (i^* - i),$$

by inserting the first into the second equation and discretizing the resulting expression. The parameter estimates for this extended traditional Keynesian models are given in Table 3.1.

For the econometric estimation of the model for the UK (Table 3.2 and Figure 3.2), we use the aggregate time series available from the International Financial Statistics database and the National Statistics database (www.statistics.gov.uk). The data is quarterly, seasonally adjusted and concerns the period from 1980:1 to 2003:4.

The logarithms of wages and prices are denoted now by $\ln(w_t)$ and $\ln(p_t)$, respectively. Their first differences (backwardly dated), that is, the current rate of wage and price inflation, are denoted $\hat{w}_t$ and $\hat{p}_t$. The inflationary climate π^c of the theoretical part of this chapter is approximated here in a very simple way by a linearly declining moving average of CPI price inflation rates with linearly decreasing weights over the past 12 quarters, denoted π_t^{12}.

Our estimates show for the considered wage–price spiral that Blanchard and Katz (1999) error correction terms are present in the Phillips curves of a degree expected in general for European economies. Demand pressure in the market for labor, measured by the output gap as a measure of the utilization of the workforce employed by firms (the insiders), is present to a significant degree in the British economy. The same holds for the goods market to a lesser degree. In combination with the degree of forward-looking behavior as measured by the parameters α_w, α_p, which in both Phillips curves are approximately given by

Table 3.2 GMM parameter estimates

Estimation sample: 1980:1 to 2003:4
Kernel: Bartlett; Bandwidth: variable Newey-West (6)

	β_{wy}	$\beta_{w\omega}$	α_w		$\bar{R}^2$	DW
$\widehat{w}_t$	1.067 [10.085]	−0.245 [4.930]	0.382 [5.764]		0.469	1.672
	β_{py}	$\beta_{p\omega}$	α_p		$\bar{R}^2$	DW
$\hat{p}_t$	0.366 [2.318]	0.238 [3.633]	0.416 [6.685]		0.354	2.331
$\dot{y}_t$	β_{yy}	β_{yi}	β_{yv}		$\bar{R}^2$	DW
	−0.409 [12.243]	−0.029 [2.677]	−0.115 [4.449]		0.435	1.917
	ϕ_i	$(1-\phi)\alpha_{ip}$	$(1-\phi_i)\alpha_{iu}$	c_i	$\bar{R}^2$	DW
$d(i_t)$	−0.075 [5.274]	0.043 [4.014]	0.077 [3.111]	0.003 [3.083]	0.937	1.785
Determinant residual covariance					1.87×10^{-19}	
J statistic					0.156	

0.4, we get from all these coefficients that the growth rate of the real wage (the wage share) depends positively on the output gap, i.e. it is dominated by the labor market and not by the market for goods. This growth rate depends moreover negatively on its level, since the Blanchard and Katz (1999) error correction terms have the signs expected by our theoretical approach. We thus have a wage-price spiral that is labor market led and controlled by error adjustment mechanisms.

Concerning the output dynamics we find that they depend negatively on the output level, as suggested by the Keynesian dynamic multiplier, and that they also depend negatively on the real rate of interest and the wage share. The latter dependence suggests that aggregate demand is profit led (cost effects dominate purchasing power effects), but it may also include aspects of the openness of the British economy. As we can see from the estimated coefficients in Table 3.1, the conventional interest rate channel of Keynesian macrodynamics is a weak one, while the real wage channel, that is seldom considered in the macroeconomics literature, is quite strong, leading from real wage increases to decreases in economic activity and from there to decreases in the growth rate of real wages. As it is measured it is therefore a stabilizing mechanism in the British economy.

If we in fact remove the interest rate channel from the dynamics (by setting $\alpha_{yi} = 0$) we get a core dynamical system where only the activity level Y and the real wage $\omega = w/p$ are interacting with each other (ignoring productivity growth again), so that

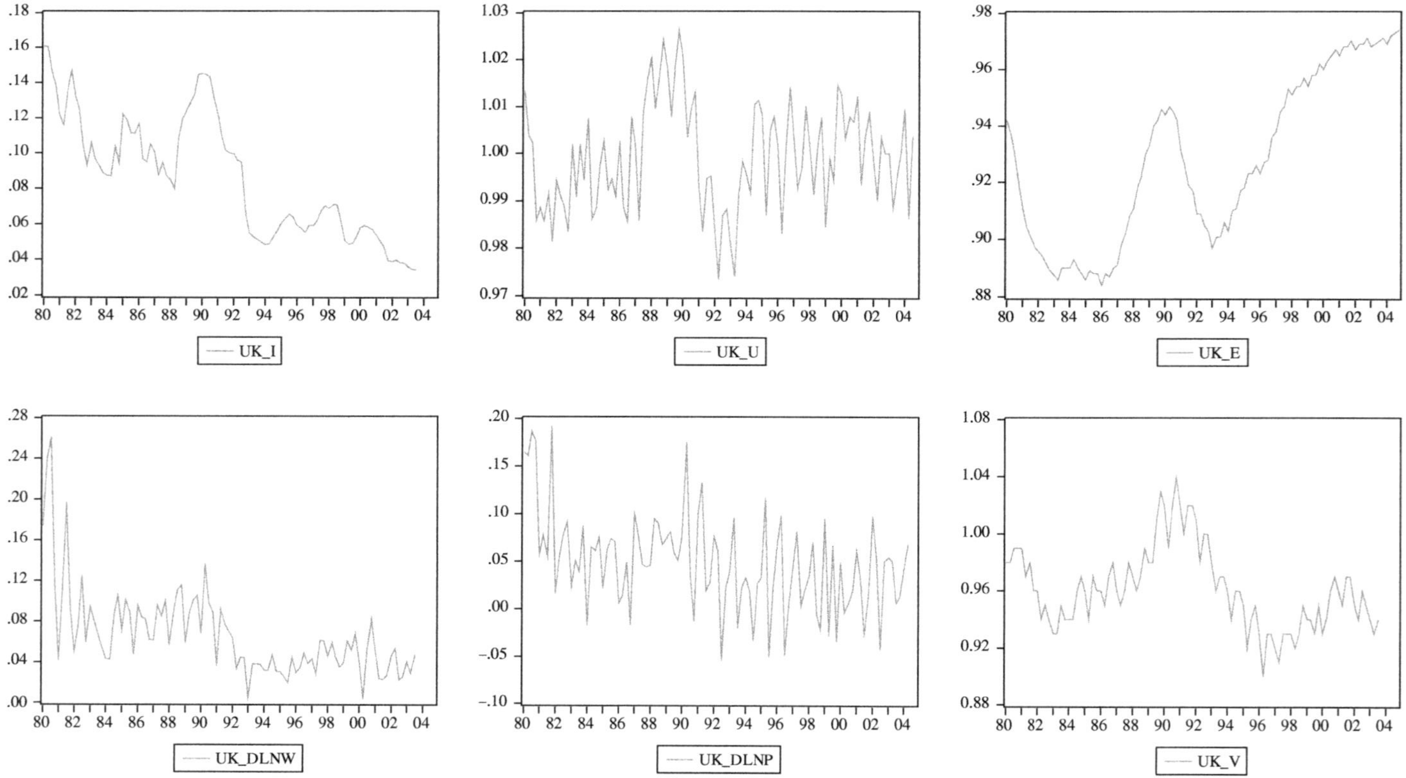

Figure 3.2 UK aggregate time series.

$$\begin{aligned}\widehat{\omega} &= \pi^w - \pi^p \\ &= \alpha\Bigg[((1-\alpha_p)\beta_{wy} - (1-\alpha_w)\beta_{py})\left(\frac{Y}{\bar{Y}} - 1\right) \\ &\qquad - ((1-\alpha_p)\beta_{w\omega} + (1-\alpha_w)\beta_{p\omega})\ln\left(\frac{\omega}{\bar{\omega}}\right)\Bigg], \\ \dot{Y} &= -\alpha_{yy}(Y/\bar{Y} - 1) + \alpha_{y\omega}(\omega - \bar{\omega}).\end{aligned}$$

For the Jacobian J of this basically linear system we get on the basis of the estimated parameter values the approximate values

$$J = \begin{pmatrix} -0.35 & 0.46 \\ -0.11 & -0.41 \end{pmatrix},$$

which obviously is a stable matrix, the eigenvalues of which are approximately given by $\lambda_{1,2} \approx -0.4 \pm 0.2\sqrt{-1}$. So this is a stable adjustment process that is only slightly modified if the real rate of interest rate channel and the Taylor rule is added again on the basis of the estimated coefficients (which adds the state variables π^c and i to the dynamics) unless the adjustment of the inflationary climate is made sufficiently fast and the Taylor rule is still weak in its operation. From the (2D) core dynamics we get in addition that increasing price flexibility β_{py} will eventually make the steady state of the dynamics unstable. By contrast, decreasing the Blanchard and Katz error correction terms and the strength of the dynamic multiplier process will make the dynamics more cyclical – approaching in fact a Goodwin (1967) growth cycle plot in this way – as shown in Figure 3.3 (where Blanchard and Katz error terms have been set to zero and where $\alpha_{yy} = 0.1$ holds).

We conclude that there exist a structurally fairly similar, but with respect to model-consistent expectations nevertheless quite different (and in our view superior), model alternative to the new Keynesian approach with both staggered wage and price setting. In its deterministic setup this model allows for a meaningful theory of the business cycle with monotonic convergence or damped fluctuations in economic activity toward its steady state, in contrast to the indeterminate new Keynesian model with both staggered wage and price setting. Our alternative, traditional, Keynesian dynamics also overcomes the trivial explanation of turning points in economic activity of the monetarist baseline models (with its narrow quantity theory driven inflation ceiling[14]) and remains (just as these simpler models) under certain mild assumptions globally asymptotically stable in a setup that integrates real interest rate effects and a nominal interest rate policy rule with the real wage feedback channel of our Keynesian approach to the wage-price spiral. This real wage channel allows in principle for the four cases, $\eta = (1-\alpha_p)\beta_{wy} - (1-\alpha_w)\beta_{py}$, displayed in Table 3.3.

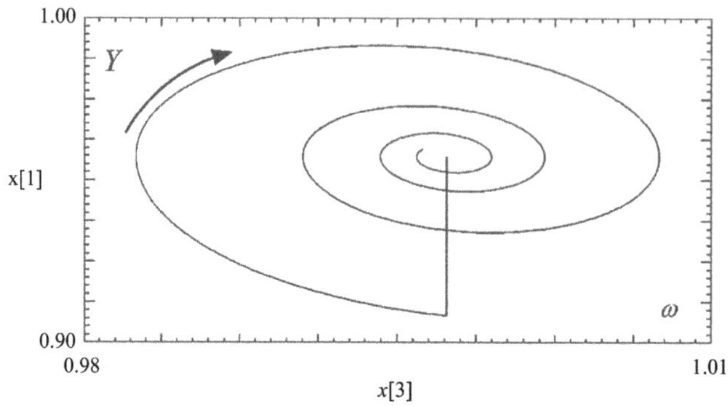

Figure 3.3 Impulse–response reaction of the distributive output/real wage cycle.

Table 3.3 The four types of real wage feedback channel

	Wage-led goods market, $\alpha_{y\omega} < 0$	*Profit-led goods market,* $\alpha_{y\omega} > 0$
Labor market-led real wage adjustment, $\eta > 0$	adverse (divergent)	normal (convergent)
Goods market-led real wage adjustment, $\eta < 0$	normal (convergent)	adverse (divergent)

Our traditional Keynesian model therefore exhibits an interesting feedback structure that is rarely considered in the literature from the theoretical or the empirical point of view. For the UK economy we have found in our brief empirical investigation that the case of interacting stable profit-led goods market dynamics and a labor market led wage-price spiral is the relevant one, in line with earlier investigations of the US economy and the Eurozone (see Proaño *et al.* 2007). Our model moreover allows modern issues of monetary policy to be addressed, as they are typical for the new Keynesian approaches, though such issues may be dominated by the distributive cycle and should therefore be reconsidered from this perspective.

3.6 Conclusions

In this chapter, we have reconsidered the issue of the (non-)equivalence of period and continuous time model building. We have argued that the data generating process in macroeconomics is of much higher frequency than the data collection process, at least in the real markets of the economy. This implies that period models calibrated with parameter values obtained from estimates based on annualized data should be iterated approximately with step size between 1/365 and 1/52 of a year in order to provide economically sensible dynamics which will thus generally give rise to results that are equivalent to the ones of their continuous time limit.

This issue has to our knowledge been ignored by and large by the new Keynesian literature. Erceg *et al.* (2000, sec. 5.3), for example, consider numerically the implications of varying contract durations both for wages and prices in their new Keynesian model with staggered wage and price settings. They allow for contract length variations of one quarter up to ten quarters in a period model of the usual type. This however, in view of the analysis of the present chapter, is an empirically completely meaningless exercise if this staggered process is assumed to occur for all agents at one and the same time, that is assumed to be completely synchronized. There may be contracts of such length in certain sectors of the economy, but they definitely do not occur in the radically synchronized fashion of uniform quarters or even ten quarters synchronized actions, as assumed in such "uninterpretable" period models of new Keynesian and other variety. This is particularly obvious for price setting behavior, but should also be the case for factual money wage movements where we should also find daily (slight) changes of the aggregate effective money wage level in real macroeconomies like the US or the UK economy.

Based upon the (also empirically motivated) methodological precept of the equivalence of discrete and continuous time macro-models concerning their dynamical properties, we have reformulated the 4D baseline new Keynesian model in continuous time and shown that this reformulation can be analyzed very easily under the premise of such equivalence (as compared to their discrete time analogs). Furthermore, we have proved that the 4D new Keynesian model with both staggered wage and price setting is determinate for Taylor rules of the conventional type in the continuous time case in the way that is suggested by the numerical examples in Galí (2008, ch. 6).

In contrast to this, we have discussed in Section 3.4 a reformulation of the 4D new Keynesian model in terms of a wage-price spiral with forward-looking model-consistent crossover expectations (but not rational expectations), which can be solved through standard iteration methods by the use of predetermined variables solely (as long as anticipated events are excluded from consideration). Under certain assumptions, this model can be shown to be globally asymptotically stable and thus much more attractive in its deterministic properties than the new Keynesian approach with its fairly trivial deterministic core.

Our macromodel was obtained from Blanchard and Katz (1999) type microfoundations of the wage and the price Phillips curves, see Flaschel and Krolzig (2006) and Chiarella *et al.* (2005) in this regard. We use economically motivated hybrid expectations formation as an integral part of the wage-price spiral since its first formulation in Chiarella and Flaschel (1996b), economically motivated as inertia generating inflationary climate expressions; see Chiarella and Flaschel (2000a) in particular. Finally, we use gradual adjustments of wages, prices and quantities in a non market-clearing framework as is adequate in a model that is formulated in (quasi-)continuous time (where the assumption of continuous market-clearing would stretch economic imagination too much). Estimates (in Section 3.5) of the parameters of the model showed that it is in line with and also significantly extends the results that are stated in Blanchard and Katz (1999) and that the real wage feedback channel of this model type is of much more relevance than the real rate of interest channel that is the focus of interest in the new Keynesian literature.

This chapter therefore proposes that (quasi-)continuous time modeling (using small period lengths) is the better choice to approach macrodynamic issues, since it avoids the empirically uninterpretable situation of a uniform period with an unspecified, possibly too large length of artificially synchronized or clustered economic decision making (and since it simplifies qualitative analysis considerably). Moreover, our reformulation of the 4D new Keynesian baseline model in terms of a wage-price spiral with only predetermined variables overcomes the trivial nature of the deterministic core of the new Keynesian approach, where Keynes (1936) analysis of turning points in economic activity is completely meaningless. It can (if locally unstable and globally bounded via appropriate nonlinearities such as downward wage rigidities) open up the route to the analysis of complex attractors in continuous time, since it exemplifies that modern baseline models of the business cycle and inflation are necessarily of a dimension higher than two and thus capable of generating complex dynamics and complex attractors; see Chiarella and Flaschel (2000a, ch. 6). They avoid in such findings empirically implausible overshooting processes that are generated by a too stiff behavior of a period model with a choice of period lengths that is too large to represent the behavior of actual economies on the macro level.

If discrete-time formulations (not period analysis) are considered for macroeconomic model building, they should represent averages over the day as the relevant time unit for models of the real-financial interaction (which are the relevant perspective for all partial macrodynamic models). There may however be reasons to add specific delays into such models, like gestation lags, but this is a complicated matter that is outside the scope of the present chapter.

Part II

Supply dynamics, demand-driven inflation and the distributive cycle

4 Viability and corridor stability in Keynesian supply driven growth

4.1 Introduction

In this chapter[1] we reconsider and generalize a 2D growth cycle model of Skott (1989a, b, 1991) which is based on supply-side adjustment processes and a Kaldorian theory of income distribution. This model is of the Keynes–Wicksell variety,[2] but does not assume full capacity growth, which was a characteristic of the Keynes–Wicksell approach to macrodynamics. Instead, there is the assumption of a (microfounded) output expansion function of firms, which depends on profitability and the state of the labor market. This function immediately implies the first law of motion of the model, for the rate of employment, when labor productivity is assumed as given (or growing at a constant rate). Capital stock growth furthermore depends on income distribution, which in turn depends on Keynesian effective demand and goods market equilibrium in a Kaldorian way, via the assumption of a price level that is completely flexible and that clears the market for goods. Combined with the output expansion function, this provides us with the second law of motion, for the actual output/capital ratio, of our version of Skott's growth cycle model.

We show in Section 4.2 that this 2D dynamical model produces local convergence to the steady state for sluggish output adjustment (with respect to profitability) and gives rise to degenerate Hopf bifurcations thereafter if behavior is linear (in terms of rates of growth) close to the steady state. This conclusion indeed applies to all such linear growth rate systems which therefore cannot exhibit isolated periodic orbits.[3] After the bifurcation point has been passed, the dynamics become purely explosive and are thus not yet completely specified. Full capacity limits are therefore added and lead (in Section 4.3) to meaningfully bounded economic behavior that converges globally to the steady-state solution for adjustment speeds below the Hopf bifurcation point and to persistent fluctuations in a certain "corridor" or compact domain around the steady state for adjustment speeds above this point, where the dynamics are not asymptotically stable. There is thus always an economically meaningful subdomain in the positive part of the phase space $\Re^2$, determined by global arguments, that is closed and invariant under the flow generated by the dynamics and is thus "viable" from the economic point of view, so that the state variables of the dynamics always stay in this domain and cannot approach zero.[4]

The 2D dynamics are generalized in Section 4.4 to a 3D growth cycle extension of the Skott model, based on sluggish real wage dynamics deriving from sluggish money wage as well as price level adjustments as in **??** full capacity employment cycle model. This extension provides a synthesis of the growth cycle model of Goodwin (1967) with the consideration of less than full capacity growth according to Skott's output expansion function.[5] Employing the output expansion function in such a framework gives rise again to Hopf bifurcations and local instability when the profitability component in this function becomes sufficiently pronounced. The resulting locally explosive dynamics can again be made viable, leading to persistent fluctuations in a certain corridor, by means of appropriate nonlinearities in the output expansion function and the rule that governs the adjustment of the price level.

4.2 A Keynesian model of supply-driven growth

The dynamic model of cyclical growth of Skott (1989a, b, 1991) is based on output dynamics on the one hand and on fluctuating capital stock growth on the other. These dynamics are interrelated through Keynesian IS equilibrium, whereby the rate of profit (or the profit share) is determined through price level adjustments that clear the market for goods. Goods supply, the fundamental innovation of the Skott model, is determined by a dynamic output expansion function, depending positively on profitability and negatively on the state of the labor market, which combined with the savings out of profits provides us with two laws of motion, one for the rate of employment and one for the output/capital ratio (a measure of the rate of capacity utilization of firms in the case of fixed proportions in production). There are no monetary dynamics involved and there is also no explicit treatment of real wage dynamics, since income distribution and the real wage are determined as statically endogenous variables through goods market equilibrium solely. Adding money wage dynamics by means of a standard Phillips curve and assuming, as is typical for models of Keynes–Wicksell type, a sluggish adjustment of the price level, based on goods market disequilibrium in place of Skott's perfectly flexible prices, make the dynamics 3D, with the real wage as the third state variable. This extension of the model, which in a basic way integrates labor market effects on income distribution, will be considered in Section 4.4.[6]

In terms of the variables $V = L^d/L$, the rate of employment, and $y = Y/K$, the output/capital ratio, a linear version (in terms of rates of growth) of the dynamic model of Skott (1989a, b, 1991) can be reformulated as

$$\widehat{V} = \widehat{Y} - n = y_1(\rho - \rho_0) - y_2(V - \bar{V}), \tag{4.1}$$

$$\hat{y} = \widehat{Y} - \widehat{K} = y_1(\rho - \rho_0) - y_2(V - \bar{V}) + n - s_c\rho. \tag{4.2}$$

These equations assume a fixed relationship between output Y and employment L^d (constant labor productivity $x = Y/L^d$) and a constant growth rate $n = \widehat{L}$ of labor supply L. The central element of these two laws of motion is Skott's output expansion function, given by

$$\widehat{Y} = y_1(\rho - \rho_0) - y_2(V - \bar{V}) + n, \quad y_1, y_2 > 0,$$

which states that firms plan output growth (or decline) on the basis of two signals: first, the deviation of the actual rate of profit ρ from the steady one, ρ_0, and second, the deviation of the actual rate of employment V from the "natural" or long-run one, $\bar{V}$. These two benchmarks for output expansion or contraction are not explicitly shown in Skott's presentation of the model, but appear here due to our assumption that behavior around the steady state should at first be assumed to be as linear as possible in order to investigate the dynamics first on the basis of intrinsic or unavoidable nonlinearities solely, that is, as linear growth rate dynamics. Note that there must be a trend term in output expansion which is set equal to n here for simplicity. Note also that the output expansion function is justified from the microeconomic perspective in Skott (1989b).

We have not yet determined the rate of profit ρ underlying the dynamics. It is determined in Skott (1989a, b, 1991) through goods market or IS equilibrium, expressed relative to the capital stock K, in other words in terms of accumulation rates, so that we have

$$s(\cdot) = s_c\rho = i(\cdot) = i_1(\rho - \rho_0) + i_2(y - \bar{U}y^p) + n, \quad \rho_0 = n/s_c. \tag{4.3}$$

Again we have linearized the behavioral assumptions of Skott around ρ_0, the steady state-rate of profit, and $\bar{U}$, the desired rate of capacity utilization of firms – see Skott (1989b) for microeconomic considerations that justify this target rate of capacity utilization. – In view of this representation of goods market equilibrium, it should be obvious that the model is based on differential saving habits, $s_w = 0 < s_c \leq 1$, of workers and capitalists. The investment behavior of firms differs from the savings behavior of households and depends on relative profitability, $\rho - \rho_0$, and relative capacity utilization, $y - \bar{U}y^p$, where y^p denotes the maximal output capital ratio, and on a trend term which is given by the natural rate of growth for simplicity ($i_1, i_2 > 0$). Such an investment function is a natural extension of the one assumed in full capacity growth Keynes–Wicksell models if one takes into account the fact that output can deviate from full capacity output y^pK. The growth rate of the capital stock is, of course, given by $\widehat{K} = s(\cdot) = i(\cdot)$ and it provides the link between changes in the employment rate $V = L^d/L$ and the capacity ratio of firms, $y = Y/K$, as shown in equations (4.1) and (4.2). Note that we have not only linearized the Skott model of cyclical growth with respect to the economic behavior around its interior steady state, but have also used profit rates in place of profit shares to represent this behavior. This makes the growth laws of the model completely linear, in contrast to the approach that is used by Skott.

On the basis of a temporarily given level of output per unit of capital, y, equation (4.3) can be solved for the rate of profit ρ, and thus also for income shares and the real wage, if one wants to refer to these magnitudes. For the purposes of the following dynamical investigations, the expression for ρ is, however, all that is needed from among these magnitudes and it is immediately determined from (4.3) as

$$\rho = \rho(y) = \frac{i_2(y - \bar{U}y^p) + n - i_1\rho_0}{s_c - i_1} = \frac{n}{s_c} + \frac{i_2(y - \bar{U}y^p)}{s_c - i_1}.$$

Note here that it is assumed in Skott (1989a, b, 1991) and also in this chapter that the assumption $s_c > i_1$ holds true, which implies that the rate of profit ρ is a strictly increasing function of the output capital ratio y.

This dynamical system corresponds to real growth cycle dynamics of Skott (1989a, b, 1991), but is here formulated without the extrinsic nonlinearities that Skott uses in the case of the local instability of the steady state in order to get bounded dynamics. It determines the price level and with it income distribution in a way that equilibrates aggregate demand with aggregate supply, and the resulting income distribution then determines (in conjunction with the state of employment and of output levels) the expansion of output and the growth rate of the capital stock and with them the growth rate of the rate of employment and of the output/capital ratio. These dynamics will now be investigated from the local point of view.

PROPOSITION 4.1 *The following hold.*

1 *The dynamical system (4.1)–(4.2) has a unique interior steady state given by*

$$V_0 = \bar{V}, \quad y_0 = \bar{U}y^p, \quad \rho_0 = n/s_c.$$

2 *This steady state is locally asymptotically stable if and only if*

$$y_1 < y_1^H = s_c + \frac{(s_c - i_1)y_2 V_0}{i_2 y_0}.$$

3 *At the value y_1^H of the parameter y_1 there occurs a Hopf bifurcation of a degenerate type. The system thus passes through the well-known center dynamics of Lotka–Volterra–Goodwin type at this bifurcation value y_1^H and becomes purely explosive thereafter.*

Proof:

1 This is obvious.
2 Making use of the steady-state expressions, the dynamics (4.1)–(4.2) can be rewritten as an autonomous system in the state variables V and y as

$$\widehat{V} = -y_2(V - V_0) + y_1 q(y - y_0), \tag{4.4}$$

$$\hat{y} = -y_2(V - V_0) + (y_1 - s_c)q(y - y_0), \tag{4.5}$$

where $q = i_2/(s_c - i_1)$. It easy to show for this system that its Jacobian J at the steady state has a positive determinant throughout, while trace J becomes zero (and thereafter positive) at y_1^H given by $y_2 V_0 = (y_1^H - s_c) q y_0$ which implies the expression y_1^H given in assertion 2 of the proposition and also its implications for (the loss of) asymptotic stability.

3 Frauenthal (1980, p. 111ff.) shows by an application of Green's theorem to double integrals for planar systems that linear growth rate systems of dimension two (with $\det J \neq 0$) cannot have a periodic solution unless a certain number composed of the parameters of the dynamics is equal to zero. It is easy to show that this number is zero for the special case of a quadratic two-species population model corresponding to our model of economic growth if and only if $y_1 = y_1^H$ holds true. This implies that nondegenerate Hopf bifurcations (which imply periodic orbits to the left or right of the bifurcation point) are not possible in our (as well as all other) linear models of economic growth of dimension two.

□

The proof of assertion 3 of Proposition 4.1 basically rests on the construction of a nonconstant first integral H for the planar dynamical system (4.4)–(4.5), that is, of a function H that is non trivial, real-valued and constant along the orbits of these dynamics. This function is here of the Cobb–Douglas type $V^\alpha y^\beta$ with appropriately chosen parameters α and β – see Frauenthal (1980, p. 112) for details, and also Hirsch and Smale (1974, p. 252) for the proposition on first integrals that excludes the possibility of periodic orbits.

Applying formula (3′) in Perko (1991, p. 317) implies for the dynamics (4.1)–(4.2) the occurrence of a Hopf bifurcation of subcritical type (the case of local corridor stability below the bifurcation point) which obviously contradicts assertion 3 of the proposition. Perko's formula is applicable to all 2D dynamical systems where the steady state has been transformed to the origin of $\Re^2$, which is easily done. It thus allows one to avoid the much more complicated so-called standard transformation used for proving the Hopf bifurcation theorem. Transforming our system to this standard form – see Lux (1992, p. 189) for the further transformations that are then necessary – it can be shown that the Liapunov coefficient (whose sign discriminates between sub-, super- and degenerate Hopf bifurcations) is indeed zero for the dynamical systems considered in this section. This implies that the Perko formula needs correction in order to provide proper results in the untransformed case. Indeed, closer inspection of the formula shows that the last expression in its first line, $a_{11}b_{02}$, should read $a_{11}b_{20}$. This gives the result of a zero Liapunov coefficient and thus of a degenerate Hopf bifurcation also in the case of systems not transformed to standard form, for the one in Lux (1995a) as well as for all quadratic two-species population models such as our dynamical system (4.1)–(4.2).[7]

Remark There is a simple modification of the output expansion function which leads to an interesting alternative to the dynamic model (4.1)–(4.2) and

Proposition 4.1. It is of the form

$$\widehat{Y} = y_1(\rho - \rho_0) - y_2(V - \bar{V}) + \widehat{K}, \quad y_1, y_2 > 0.$$

In this equation, the trend component n has been replaced by the measure $\widehat{K}$ which makes no difference with respect to steady state analysis. Outside the steady-state we now have that capacity utilization Y/K is increased when expansion is dominant and decreased in the opposite situation. The laws of motion of the dynamics then read

$$\widehat{V} = \widehat{Y} - n = y_1(\rho - \rho_0) - y_2(V - \bar{V}) + s_c\rho - n, \tag{4.6}$$

$$\hat{y} = \widehat{Y} - \widehat{K} = y_1(\rho - \rho_0) - y_2(V - \bar{V}). \tag{4.7}$$

These dynamics give rise to the same proposition as the system (4.1)–(4.2), with the Hopf bifurcation now occurring at $y_1 = y_1^H = (s_c - i_1)y_2 V_0/(i_2 y_0)$.

The results of this section, and the underlying theory of quadratic two-species population models, are of use only when the local asymptotic stability of the steady state is guaranteed. Indeed it is only admissible to formulate the model as a linear growth rate system in a certain neighborhood of the steady state. Far off the steady state, however, extrinsic nonlinearities come into being, in particular in the form of supply bottlenecks during the boom phase of our growth cycle dynamics. The laws of motion (4.1)–(4.2) therefore must be modified when global aspects are to be investigated. This modification is the subject of the next section.

4.3 Global viability, corridor stability and persistent business fluctuations

The isoclines of the linear growth rate system (4.1)–(4.2) considered in Section 4.2 are given by

$$\dot{V} = 0 \implies V = \bar{V} + \frac{y_1(\rho(y) - \rho_0)}{y_2} \equiv g_1(y), \tag{4.8}$$

$$\dot{y} = 0 \implies V = \bar{V} + \frac{(y_1 - i_1)(\rho(y) - \rho_0) - i_2(y - \bar{U}y^p)}{y_2}$$

$$= \bar{V} + \frac{(y_1 - s_c)(\rho(y) - \rho_0)}{y_2} \equiv g_2(y). \tag{4.9}$$

These are straight lines and imply a phase diagram that does not ensure economically bounded dynamics (meaning $V \leq 1, y \leq y^p$) in general and economic viability (boundedness and positivity of the state variables, even in the limit). In order to obtain these features we now introduce the following basic nonlinearity.

ASSUMPTION 4.1 *Assume that the parameter y_1 of the system (4.1)–(4.2) is no longer constant to the right of the steady-state value for y, but is rather determined there by a continuously differentiable function of the form*[8]

$$y_1(y) = \begin{cases} y_1(y) = \bar{y}_1 = const., & y \leq \bar{U} y^p, \\ y_1(y),\ y_1' < 0,\ y_1(y^p) = 0, & y > \bar{U} y^p. \end{cases}$$

Thus profitability determined output expansion is reduced to zero when the value of y approaches the capacity limit y^p. This is a meaningful assumption as firms cannot expand output any further at the capacity limit y^p.

ASSUMPTION 4.2 *Assume that $y_2 \bar{V} + n - s_c \rho(y^p) < 0$ holds with respect to the parameters of the dynamics (4.1)–(4.2).*

As we shall see below, these assumptions keep y below the limiting value y^p. Furthermore, the first assumption also guarantees that the rate of employment V stays below the absolute limit $V = 1$, if the function y_1 approaches zero sufficiently rapidly once the steady-state value $\bar{U} y^p$ has been crossed by y from below (see Figure 4.1). Note also that the interior steady state and the isoclines, to the left of y^p, are unaffected by the assumptions 1 and 2.

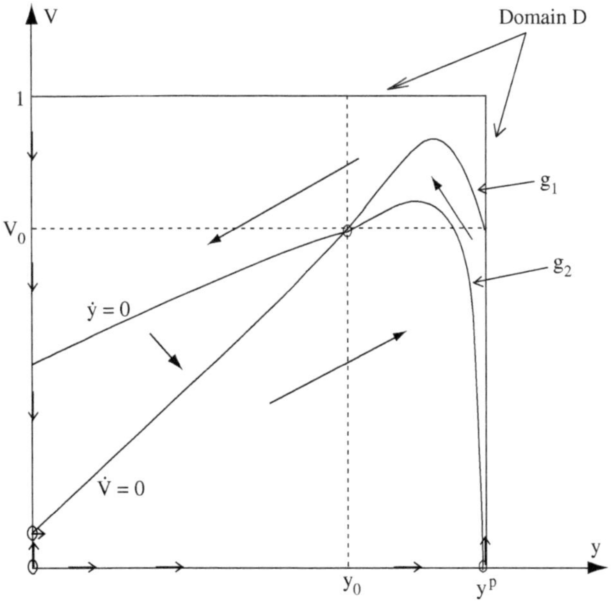

Figure 4.1 The phase portrait of the dynamics (4.1)–(4.2) with one extrinsic nonlinearity.

LEMMA 4.1 *The function g_2 in (4.9) satisfies $g_2(0) > 0$ if and only if $\bar{y}_1 < y_1^H$.*

Proof: At zero output level we have

$$\rho(0) - \rho_0 = -\frac{i_2 \bar{U} y^p}{s_c - i_1}.$$

This gives

$$g_2(0) = \bar{V} + \frac{(s_c - \bar{y}_1) i_2 \bar{U} y^p}{y_2(s_c - i_1)},$$

which is positive if and only if

$$s_c i_2 \bar{U} y^p + \bar{V} y_2 (s_c - i_1) > \bar{y}_1 i_2 \bar{U} y^p$$

holds. This latter inequality in turn holds if and only if $\bar{y}_1 < y_1^H$ holds true due to the expression obtained for y_1^H in Proposition 4.1. □

LEMMA 4.2 *Assumptions 1 and 2 imply for the isoclines of the dynamics $g_1(y^p) = \bar{V}$ and $g_2(y^p) < 0$; see (4.8) and (4.9).*

Proof: This is obvious from the expressions that define the $\dot{y} = 0$ and $\dot{V} = 0$ isoclines. □

PROPOSITION 4.2 *Assume in addition to assumptions 1 and 2 that $\bar{y}_1 < y_1^H$ holds true. Then the dynamical system (4.1)–(4.2) is viable in the domain D shown in Figure 4.1, i.e. no trajectory that starts in the interior of D will approach the boundary of D.*

Proof: In the case with $\bar{y}_1 > s_c$ and $g_1(0) > 0$ we have, using Lemmas 1 and 2, that $g_2(0) > 0$ and $g_2(y^p) < 0$ hold simultaneously. We thus get the phase portrait shown in Figure 4.1. As the figure shows, there are then three further equilibria (indicated by small circles) on the boundary of the positive orthant of $\Re^2$, none of which can however be approached by the trajectories that start in the interior of D due to the direction of the dynamics in the areas of D separated by the shown isoclines and on the boundary of $\Re^2$. Note that this boundary is an invariant set of the dynamics, that is, all trajectories that start there must remain there.

Not shown in Figure 4.1 is the case where the $\dot{V} = 0$ isocline intersects the horizontal axis at a positive value of y, namely the case $g_1(0) < 0$. In this case there are only two relevant steady-state solutions on the boundary (due to the positivity of y at the intersection). Their properties (again obtained by graphical inspection of the phase portrait of the dynamics) also imply that no trajectory of the dynamics that starts inside D can approach the horizontal axis (nor the vertical axis, since there is no steady-state solution on the vertical axis in this case). This guarantees the existence of positive lower turning points of V (and y) even in the situation where the origin is the only point of rest of the dynamics on the nonnegative part of the vertical axis.

Assuming that $\bar{y}_1 < s_c$ holds, finally, would imply a falling $\dot{y}=0$ isocline to the left of the steady state which allows for the same assertion on the domain D as in the case $\bar{y}_1 > s_c$.[9] □

Note that the value of y where the rate of profit $\rho(y)$ becomes zero is given by

$$\underline{y} = \bar{U} y^p - \frac{n(1 - i_1/s_c)}{i_2}.$$

This value can be made negative (and thus removed from the domain D) by choosing i_2 sufficiently small (which need not be assumed however).

We observe that Proposition 4.2 also applies to situations where Assumption 4.2 is not fulfilled if it is assumed that y becomes stationary at $y = y^p$ (and beyond) by making use of differential inequalities in place of equalities in this border situation. The y dynamics are therefore suspended at this border until V has increased by so much that $\dot{y}$ points inwards again.

PROPOSITION 4.3 *Assume that $\bar{y}_1 > y_1^H$ holds. Then we have the following.*

1 *There is a uniquely determined value $y_{oo} \in (0, y_0)$ of the variable y where $\dot{y} = g_2(y) = 0$ holds.*[10]
2 *All economically meaningful trajectories that start to the left of y_{oo} converge to $(0, 0)$ and thus lead to economic breakdown.*[11]
3 *There may exist a corridor around the unstable interior steady state of the dynamics (4.1)–(4.2) in which all orbits are attracted by a periodic motion surrounding the interior steady state.*[12]

Proof: Assertions 1 and 2 of Proposition 4.3 are obvious from Figure 4.2 which shows that the $\dot{y} = 0$ isocline (and thus also the other isocline) now cut the horizontal axis at a positive value for y. Figure 4.2 however does not establish the existence of a viability corridor (with persistent fluctuations inside this domain). This conclusion can only be obtained by means of numerical simulations, an example of which is given below. □

We close this section with a numerical simulation of the extrinsically nonlinear version of Skott's employment cycle for a value of $\bar{y}_1$ $(=6)$, much beyond the Hopf bifurcation value of $y_1^H = 3.9\bar{6}$, where the linear growth model would be extremely explosive in the absence of the extrinsic nonlinearity in the output adjustment function.[13] Note again that the $\dot{y} = 0$ isocline cuts the horizontal axis at a positive value creating a point of rest at this intersection as shown in Figure 4.2 and that all initial conditions for y to the left of this intersection imply convergence to the origin of $\Re^2$. Yet, as the numerical example in Figure 4.3 shows, the dynamics can be viable in a certain domain around the steady state.

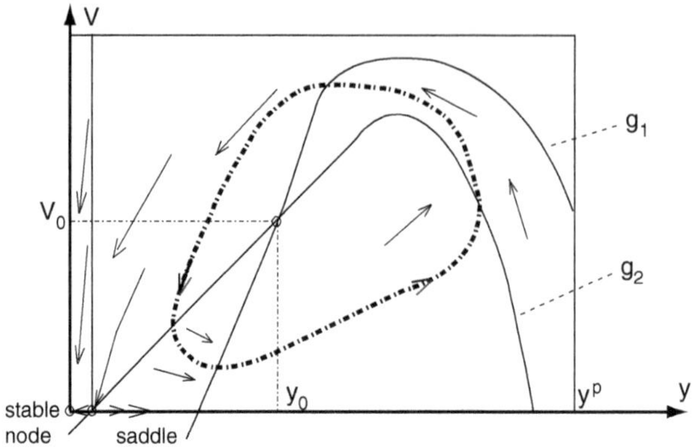

Figure 4.2 Strong local explosiveness with extinction or persistent fluctuations.

We have applied here only Assumption 4.1 on the function y_1 and have obtained already a limit cycle that is economically viable ($0 < V \leq 1$, $0 < y \leq y^p = 1$) for all reasonably large shocks out of the steady state. Note the asymmetric shape of the cycle, with phases of decline being much longer than phases of recovery. Note also that the two 2D cycles shown are basically of the same shape, since the rate of profit ρ is solely dependent on, and a strictly increasing function of, the output/capital ratio y. This will change in the 3D dynamics considered in the next section.

REMARK In the case of system (4.6)–(4.7) the isoclines are

$$\dot{V} = 0: \qquad V = \bar{V} + \frac{y_1(\rho(y) - \rho_0) + s_c\rho(y) - n}{y_2}, \tag{4.10}$$

$$\dot{y} = 0: \qquad V = \bar{V} + \frac{y_1(\rho(y) - \rho_0)}{y_2}. \tag{4.11}$$

They give rise to the phase portrait shown in Figure 4.4 when Assumption 4.1 and the condition $\bar{y}_1 < y_1^H$ are again valid, now to be combined with the additional assumptions

$$\widehat{Y} = 0 \quad \text{for } y = y^p,\ V \leq \bar{V} \quad \text{and} \quad 1 > V^{\max} = \bar{V} + \frac{s_c\rho(y^p) - n}{y_2}.$$

These assumptions now make use of a hard constraint at the $y = y^p$ border line (below $\bar{V}$ where $\hat{V}$ is positive) and they restrict the intersection of the $\dot{V} = 0$ isocline with this border line to a value of V that is less than 1.

Output expansion thus comes to a halt here by a hard constraint and $V \leq 1$ is ensured by assuming y_2 is sufficiently large. The system (4.6)–(4.7) needs more

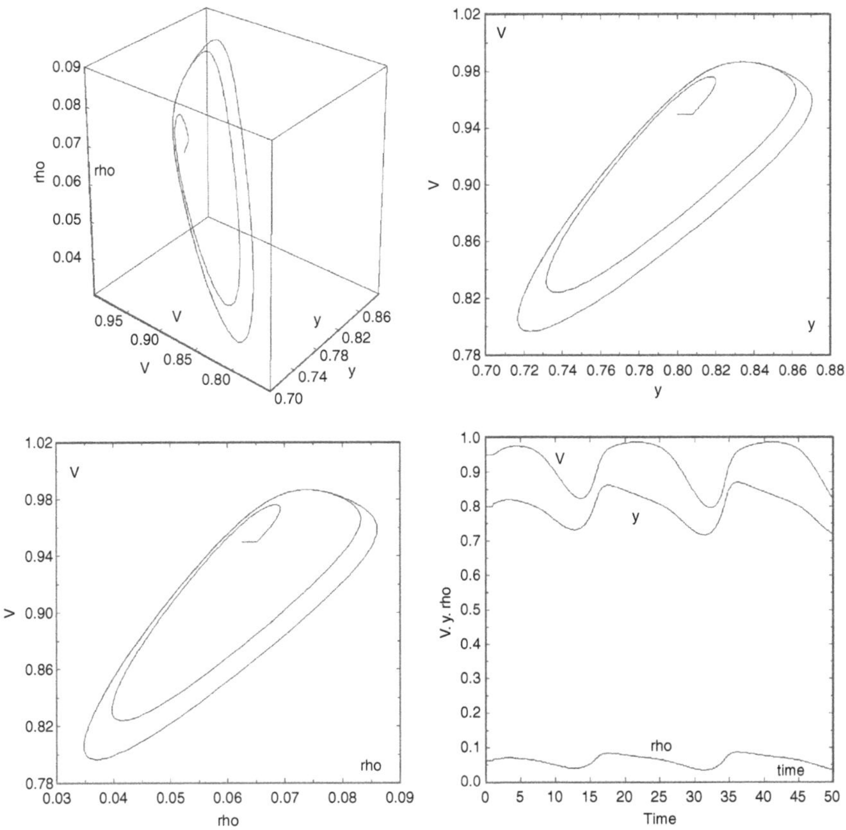

Figure 4.3 Stable limit cycles in the case of strong local instability: a numerical example.[14]

constraints in order to stay in the domain $D = [0, y^p] \times [0, 1]$, since we now have an accelerator term $\widehat{K}$ in the output expansion function $\widehat{Y}$. We shall extend these 2D dynamics in the next section by assuming sluggish wage and price level adjustment processes which will ensure positive profitability in a less restrictive way than was found above.

4.4 Sluggish wage and price adjustment

This section extends the model of the preceding section by adding real wage dynamics as in Rose (1967), thereby considering explicitly the interaction of the employment rate and nominal wage dynamics, combined now with sluggish price level adjustment in place of Skott's assumption of a price level that is completely

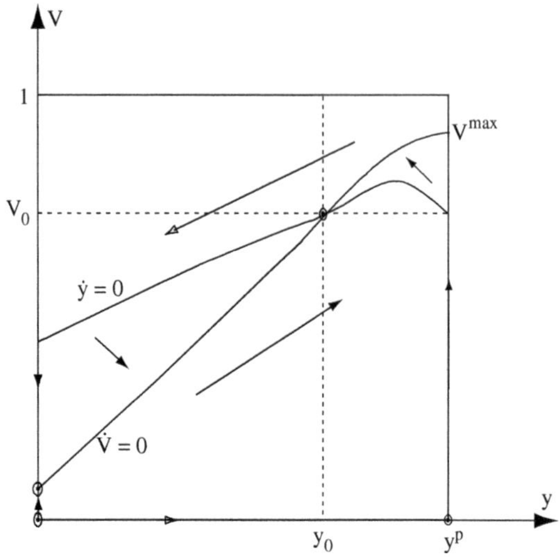

Figure 4.4 The phase portrait of the modified dynamics (4.6)–(4.7).

flexible. We now assume as output expansion function

$$\widehat{Y} = y_1(\rho - \rho_0) - y_2(V - \bar{V}) + \widehat{K}, \quad y_1, y_2 > 0,$$

which is the alternative formulation considered briefly in Sections 4.2 and 4.3. This formulation has the advantage that it allows us to obtain Skott's model (with sluggish real wage adjustment) as a natural extension of the Rose (1967) employment cycle model, here without smooth factor substitution however and with Skott's stability condition $s_c > i_1$ throughout. In the Rose model, the steady state was made locally unstable by choosing wage flexibility sufficiently low at the steady state, which gave rise there to an adverse real wage adjustment due to a price level that reacted more strongly than the level of wages close to the steady state. Rose then assumed in addition that nominal wages reacted more strongly than the price level far off the steady state in order to get economic boundedness of the dynamics through an appropriate application of the Poincaré–Bendixson theorem.

We thus assume that the adjustment equations for money wages w and the price level p are given by[15]

$$\widehat{w} = \beta_w(V - \bar{V}) + \kappa_w \hat{p} + (1 - \kappa_w)\pi, \tag{4.12}$$

$$\hat{p} = \beta_p((I - S)/K) + \kappa_p \widehat{w} + (1 - \kappa_p)\pi. \tag{4.13}$$

Money wages react to the state of the labor market $(V - \bar{V})$ and to the level of current price inflation $\hat{p}$, with weight κ_w, as well as to an expected medium-run inflation rate π, with weight $1 - \kappa_w$. Similarly prices react, now sluggishly, to disequilibrium on the market for goods, as measured by $(I - S)/K$, and to wage inflation $\widehat{w}$ as a cost-push term coupled again (in the form of a weighted average) with the medium-run rate of inflation π. These equations are conventional demand-pull and cost-push characterizations of the wage–price spiral. We assume that both weights κ_w and κ_p are between zero and one and that expected inflation π is zero here as there is no steady-state inflation in the present model.[16] The above two equations can then be reduced to a single law of motion for the real wage ω or the share of wages $u = \omega/x$, $x = Y/L^d$ = const., of the type[17]

$$\hat{u} = \widehat{\omega} = \frac{(1-\kappa_p)\beta_w(V-\bar{V}) - (1-\kappa_w)\beta_p(i(\cdot) - s(\cdot))}{1-\kappa_w\kappa_p}, \tag{4.14}$$

where we now have

$$\begin{aligned} s(\cdot) &= s_c\rho \neq i(\cdot) = i_1(\rho - \rho_0) + i_2(y - \bar{U}y^p) + n, \\ \rho_0 &= n/s_c, \end{aligned} \tag{4.15}$$

as ingredients of the demand-pull component in the price level adjustment equation. Note that the rate of profit is now given by $\rho = \rho(y,\omega) = y(1 - \omega/x) = y(1 - u)$ with $x = Y/L^d$ the given output/labor ratio of the model.

If investment differs from saving we have to state which of the two magnitudes determines capital stock growth. We here stay in a supply-side-oriented framework and assume that saving determines the growth rate $\widehat{K}$ of the capital stock. The alternative assumption as well as intermediate cases give rise to similar conclusions as the ones that follow here for $\widehat{K} = s_c\rho$, and will not be treated due to space limitations – see Chiarella and Flaschel (2000a, ch. 3) for their treatment in the context of Keynes–Wicksell models of full capacity growth. –

The dynamical system to be investigated in this section consequently reads

$$\widehat{V} = y_1(\rho - \rho_0) - y_2(V - \bar{V}) + s_c\rho - n, \tag{4.16}$$

$$\hat{y} = y_1(\rho - \rho_0) - y_2(V - \bar{V}), \quad y_1, y_2 = \text{const.}, \tag{4.17}$$

$$\hat{u} = \kappa[(1-\kappa_p)\beta_w(V-\bar{V}) - (1-\kappa_w)\beta_p(i(\cdot) - s(\cdot))], \tag{4.18}$$

with the expressions $s(\cdot)$, $i(\cdot)$, $\rho(\cdot,\cdot)$ as defined above in equations (4.15) and three lines below. With respect to this dynamical system we can prove the local results in Propositions 4.4 and 4.5.

PROPOSITION 4.4 *The following hold.*

1 *The dynamical system (4.16)–(4.18) has a unique interior steady state given by*

$$V_0 = \bar{V}, \quad y_0 = \bar{U} y^p, \quad \rho_0 = n/s_c, \quad \omega_0 = (y_0 - \rho_0)/(y_0/x), \quad u_0 = 1 - \rho_0/y_0,$$

which is the same as the one under the 2D dynamics.

2 *This steady state is asymptotically stable if* γ_1, γ_2 *are sufficiently small.*

3 *There is a unique value* γ_1^H *of the parameter* γ_1 *where there occurs a Hopf bifurcation (of generally subcritical or supercritical type). This bifurcation parameter is strictly smaller than*

$$\gamma_1^u = \frac{\gamma_2 V_0 + \kappa(1-\kappa_w)\beta_p(s_c - i_1) y_0 u_0}{(1-u_0) y_0}.$$

Proof:

1 The proof is similar to the reasoning in the assertion of Proposition 4.1.

2 Consider first the 2D dynamics $\hat{V}$, $\hat{u}$ for $\gamma_1 = \gamma_2 = 0$, $y \equiv y^p$. We obtain at the steady state that

$$\det J = \begin{vmatrix} 0 & - \\ + & - \end{vmatrix} > 0,$$

as well as trace $J < 0$, indicating that the steady state of the dynamics is asymptotically stable, as both eigenvalues of the Jacobian J must have negative real part. Furthermore, we get for the 3D dynamical system at the steady state the result

$$\det J = -s_c \gamma_2 (1-\kappa_w) \kappa i_2 \beta_p y_0^2 V_0 u_0 < 0,$$

indicating that the product of all three eigenvalues of J must always be negative. If there are two eigenvalues with negative real parts, the third one must always be real and negative in such a situation. Since eigenvalues depend contiguously on the parameters of the model (see Sontag 1998), we therefore get that all three eigenvalues of the 3D matrix J must exhibit negative real parts if γ_1, γ_2 are sufficiently close to zero.

3 The trace of J at the steady state of the 3D dynamics is given by

$$\begin{aligned} \text{trace } J &= \gamma_1(1-u_0) y_0 - \gamma_2 V_0 - \kappa(1-\kappa_w)\beta_p(s_c - i_1) y_0 u_0 \\ &= \beta_1 \gamma_1 + \beta_0, \quad \beta_1 > 0, \beta_0 < 0. \end{aligned}$$

The steady state is unstable for all y_1 where trace $J > 0$ holds true, that is, for all y_1 satisfying

$$y_1 > \frac{y_2 V_0 + \kappa(1-\kappa_w)\beta_p(s_c - i_1)y_0 u_0}{(1-u_0)y_0}.$$

Furthermore, the coefficient a_2 of the Routh–Hurwitz conditions ($a_1 = -\text{trace } J$, $a_3 = -\det J$, $a_2 =$ the sum of principal minors of order two; see Gantmacher 1998)

$$a_1, a_2, a_3 > 0, \quad b = a_1 a_2 - a_3 > 0,$$

is a linear function of y_1 of the form

$$a_2(y_1) = \alpha_1 y_1 + \alpha_0, \quad \alpha_1 > 0$$

(note that we already assume that $\alpha_0 > 0$) while a_3 does not depend on y_1. We thus get that $b = b(y_1)$ is a quadratic function of y_1 of the form

$$b(y_1) = \gamma_2 y_1^2 + \gamma_1 y_1 + \gamma_0, \quad \gamma_2 < 0,$$

with $b(0) > 0$ due to part 2 of the proposition. There is thus exactly one positive root y_1^H of this function, beyond which the steady state must be locally unstable, since $b(y_1) < 0$ holds from there on, while b and a_1, a_2 must be positive to the left of y_1^H for all $y_1 > 0$, since $a_3 > 0$ holds at all times.

Finally, the pair of eigenvalues of the Jacobian J at the steady state (that corresponds to y_1^H) crosses the imaginary axis with positive speed if y_1 crosses the value y_1^H (where b becomes zero), since $b'(y_1) < 0$ holds true according to the above. This is a consequence of Orlando's formula (see Gantmacher 1998), which reads

$$b(y_1) = (\lambda_1(y_1) + \lambda_2(y_1))(\lambda_1(y_1) + \lambda_3(y_1))(\lambda_2(y_1) + \lambda_3(y_1)),$$

where the λ are the eigenvalues of the matrix J at the steady state (corresponding to the parameter value y_1). Owing to the above we know that the derivative on the left-hand side of this equation is negative, which immediately implies the above speed assertion. See also the appendix in Benhabib and Miyao (1981) in this regard. □

Remark For $y_1 = y_2 = 0$, i.e. for full capacity growth $y \equiv y^p$, the system (4.16)–(4.18) reduces to a classical growth cycle model with the state variables V, u as in Goodwin (1967) and with employment growth equal to capital stock growth, so that

$$\widehat{V} = s_c \rho - n,$$

but now with extended Rose (1967) real wage dynamics. This system can be shown to be always locally asymptotically stable around its interior steady-state solution.

Proposition 4.5 *Assume for the adjustment parameter y_1 the functional form:*

$$y_1(y)=\begin{cases} y_1(y)=\bar{y}_1=const., & y\le \bar{U}y^p,\\ y_1(y),\, y_1'\le 0,\, y_1(y^p)=0, & y>\bar{U}y^p.\end{cases}$$

We furthermore impose the hard constraints $V\le 1$ and $y\le y^p$ on the rate of employment and the output/capital ratio.[18] *Finally,*

$$\beta_p=\begin{cases} const., & u\le u_0,\\ \beta_p(u),\, \beta_p'(u)>0,\, \beta_p(1)=\infty, & u>u_0,\end{cases}$$

meaning that the negative auto-feedback of real wages onto themselves – via the positive (partial) dependence of the price inflation rate on income distribution and the real wage – becomes infinitely strong as the wage share $u=\omega/x$ approaches 1. Then the following hold.

1 *The dynamical system (4.16)–(4.18) with the ceilings just described has a unique interior steady state which is the same as the one of the 3D dynamics without ceilings.*
2 *The trajectories of the dynamics (4.16)–(4.18) are bounded from above by $V=1$, $y=y^p$, $u=1$ and thus always exhibit upper turning points when these limits are approached, if i_2 is sufficiently small.*

Proof:

1 This is obvious.
2 This assertion is fulfilled by assumption as far as $V\le 1$ is concerned. Furthermore, the inequality

$$\hat{y}=-y_2(V-\bar{V})<0, \quad \text{for} \quad y_1(y^p)=0,\ V>\bar{V},$$

is generally sufficient to induce upper turning points of the capital/output ratio y below y^p. If this not the case, the hard constraint $y\le y^p$ will apply and imply the assertion directly by assumption. Finally we have that $\hat{u}$ is dominated in its sign by the term

$$-(1-\kappa_w)\beta_p(u)[(1-i_1/s_c)n+i_2(-\bar{U}y^p)]$$

if u is close to 1, a term which is negative for i_2 sufficiently small. □

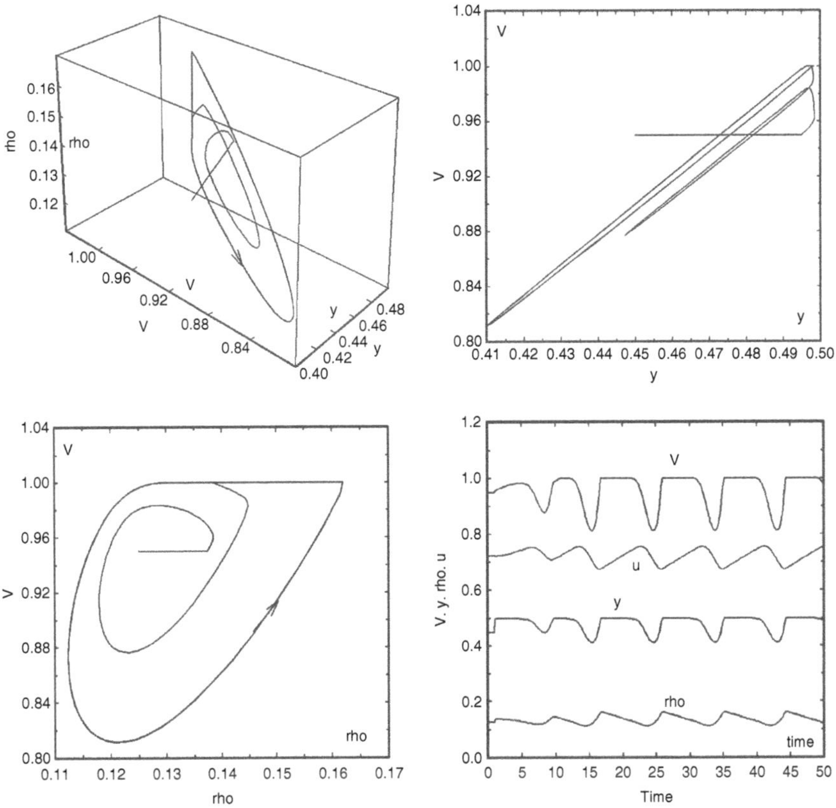

Figure 4.5 Ceilings and boundedness of the 3D dynamics.[20]

REMARK The trajectories of the dynamics (4.16)–(4.18) need not exhibit a lower turning point, but may converge to the equilibrium $(0, 0, 0)$ in the case of large parameter values $\bar{y}_1$ when sufficiently below $\bar{U}y^p$ (as in the 2D case). We therefore have economic boundedness, but not necessarily economic viability,[19] over the whole range of admissible parameter values. We stress that the assumptions of the proposition are much stronger than needed, since there generally is a strong co-movement between the state variables V and y. Simulating the dynamics has however shown that downturns in its fluctuations may become more and more pronounced and can lead to economic collapse if $\bar{y}_1$ is sufficiently large. In order to avoid such an occurrence one has to impose lower limits on the output expansion function in those phases where it would imply output contractions.

Figure 4.5 shows the effects of the upper bounds (assumed in Proposition 4.5) on economic boundedness of the dynamics which here lead to an attracting limit cycle (and again corridor stability) as the attractor of the trajectories in the domain

$(0, 1) \times (0, y^p) \times (0, 1)$. The truly 3D orbits of the dynamics projected into the y–V plane (top right) and the ρ–V plane (bottom left) are now clearly differentiated from each other, the first showing a strict co-movement between output and the rate of employment, and the second one showing the growth cycle mechanism of Goodwin (1967) and Rose (1967) of the conflict over income distribution. Note that the asymmetric shape of output and employment rate fluctuations is much more pronounced in Figure 4.5 bottom right than it was in the corresponding Figure 4.3 of the 2D cycle mechanism. The time series generated by the model (Figure 4.5, bottom right) in fact now have a shape that was considered as typical for the business cycle in the 1950s and 1960s.

4.5 Conclusions

We have arrived in Section 4.4 at a 3D dynamical system which can give rise either to convergence to its interior steady state or to persistent fluctuations around it that stay within the capacity limits of firms and the supply limitations on the labor market. These dynamics are basically driven by supply side considerations, but they also rely on a Keynesian description of goods market behavior and a Wicksellian theory of price inflation. This represents a significant growth cycle extension of the models of Goodwin (1967) and Rose (1967), and one that now exhibits less than full capacity growth both on the market for labor as well as within firms. It is not difficult to extend this model even further, to four dimensions, by incorporating an LM curve as theory of the rate of interest, which adds a stabilizing Keynes effect to the dynamics. A further extension to five dimensions would be achieved by the addition of inflationary expectations (for the medium run) and real rate of interest effects, which are generally destabilizing. These monetary extensions of the dynamics considered in this chapter are investigated in Flaschel (2001a) from the local perspective, but are difficult to handle from the global point of view of this chapter.

5 Wicksellian inflation pressure in Keynesian models of monetary growth

5.1 Introduction

In this chapter,[1] we shall make use of a general model of Keynes–Wicksell type[2] to show that these and other well-known models of cycles and growth can all be considered as *special cases* of this prototype model, so that they all belong to one particular theory, which despite its "Keynes–Wicksell" origin is fairly (neo)classical or supply-side oriented in nature. Such a statement does not, in our view, devalue this model type from a Keynesian perspective, but it leads us instead to a general and unifying framework of Keynes–Wicksell models[3] with which models that attempt to be of a (more) Keynesian type[4] can be usefully compared.

Since our general Keynes–Wicksell prototype model synthesizes Goodwin's classical growth cycle and Rose's "Keynesian employment cycle" (based on sluggish wages and prices and smooth factor substitution), it must inherit the dynamic features of these real models to some extent. This result will in fact be shown in the following sections on the basis of a fixed proportions technology. Smooth factor substitution can be easily added to our model (see Chiarella and Flaschel 2000a, ch. 5), but we will not investigate here its (often obvious) implications.[5] We stress that such an extension does not introduce a new theory of real wages into the model since the marginal productivity postulate does not represent a theory of real wages in this context, as it is often incorrectly believed. Real wage changes are instead determined by demand pressures on the market for labor *and* for goods, and they determine employment in a classical fashion if smooth factor substitution is allowed for.

The classical nature of the model on this basis primarily arises from the fact that output is determined through supply-side conditions, so that we have full capacity growth throughout. The Keynesian IS–LM–(dis)equilibrium block here only serves to determine the rate of inflation and it is fed back into the real part of the model via the real wage dynamics, expectations and the real rate of interest as one determinant of investment behavior. This is the Keynes–Wicksell portion of this predominantly (neo)classical approach to monetary growth and cycles.

In the next section, we present the general model. In Section 5.3 we present it in intensive form and the five laws of motion to which it gives rise. We then focus on the central 4D subcase obtained when lump sum taxes net of interest payments are held constant per unit of capital, which allows us to ignore the government budget constraint (GBR). This 4D subcase is the standard general reference for all of our investigations of the considered prototype models. The remaining fifth dynamic law, the dynamics of the government budget constraint, will seldom be explicitly treated in this chapter as well as in the subsequent chapters of the book.

It is our intention to build the analysis of the most general model on a systematic and detailed investigation of its important 2D, 3D and 4D subcases representing the private sector of the economy. From the viewpoint of completeness of such models, the GBR is nevertheless necessarily involved in their complete formulation and will thus always be included in the initial presentation and explanation of the general case (here of dimension five). In later work we intend to study the role of the GBR and also various feedback policy rules that can be built upon it in a systematic fashion.

Two-dimensional subcases of Goodwin and Rose growth cycle type based on a number of simplifying assumptions are investigated in Sections 5.4 and 5.5 by means of Liapunov functions and the Poincaré–Bendixson theorem, respectively. One-dimensional discrete-time versions of these models which can give rise to chaotic dynamics are also briefly considered as well as Ito's regime switching model which (in our reinterpretation of it) adds boundary conditions (ceilings) to the Goodwin growth cycle. In Section 5.6, interest rate flexibility is added to the Rose employment limit cycle via a less extreme formulation of money market equilibrium, and is found to imply that the limit cycle of the 2D case disappears if the flexibility of the interest rate becomes sufficiently large. This section, however, still makes use of an extreme type of "asymptotically rational expectations" in its treatment of inflationary expectations, in order that the implied dynamical system remain of dimension three. This allows for typical applications of the Routh–Hurwitz and the Hopf bifurcation theorems in the characterization of the stability features and the cyclical properties of the system near the steady state.

Sections 5.7 and 5.8 finally, consider various types of inflationary expectations, the pure monetary cycle to which they can give rise and the general 4D dynamics when this cycle is integrated with the real cycle considered previously. This 4D case is investigated by means of computer simulations and from the perspective of the various submodels we have treated analytically in the preceding sections. Section 5.9 also briefly introduces the limit case model where product prices adjust with an infinite speed, a case which has been very central in the literature on Keynesian dynamics and which has been taken up at the end of chapter 4 of the Keynesian prototype model in Chiarella and Flaschel (2000a).

5.2 A general prototype model of Keynes–Wicksell type

The following model type is derived by way of a systematic variation of the general Tobin prototype model discussed at the end of chapter 2 in Chiarella and Flaschel (2000a). These variations concern the assumed investment behavior of firms and their financing, asset market equilibrium conditions and the description of goods market disequilibrium on which the theory of price inflation is now based. On the other hand we now disregard for reasons of simplicity the fundamental distinction made in the Tobin models between actual and perceived disposable income of the household sector.

The equations of the model are as follows.[6]

1. *Definitions (remunerations and wealth):*

$$\omega = w/p, \quad u = \omega/x, \quad \rho = (Y - \delta K - \omega L^d)/K, \tag{5.1}$$

$$W = (M + B + p_e E)/p, \quad p_b = 1. \tag{5.2}$$

2. *Households (workers and asset-holders):*

$$W = (M^d + B^d + p_e E^d)/p, \tag{5.3}$$

$$M^d = h_1 pY + h_2 pK(1-\tau)(\bar{r} - r),$$

$$C = \omega L^d + (1 - s_c)[\rho K + rB/p - T], \quad s_w = 0, \tag{5.4}$$

$$\begin{aligned} S_p &= \omega L^d + Y_c^D - C = Y - \delta K + rB/p - T - C \\ &= s_c[\rho K + rB/p - T] = s_c Y_c^D \\ &= (\dot{M}^d + \dot{B}^d + p_e \dot{E}^d)/p, \end{aligned} \tag{5.5}$$

$$\widehat{L} = n = \text{const.} \tag{5.6}$$

3. *Firms (production units and investors):*

$$Y = yK \; (= Y^p = y^p K), \quad L^d = Y/x, \tag{5.7}$$

$$y, x = \text{const.}, \quad V = L^d/L,$$

$$I = i(\rho - (r - \pi))K + \gamma K, \quad \gamma = n, \tag{5.8}$$

$$p_e \dot{E}/p = I + (S - I) = S = S_p + S_g = Y - \delta K - C - G, \tag{5.9}$$

$$\begin{aligned} \widehat{K} &= \beta_k I/K + (1 - \beta_k)S/K \\ &= I/K + (1 - \beta_k)(S/K - I/K), \quad \beta_k \in [0, 1], \end{aligned} \tag{5.10}$$

$$\dot{N} = \delta_2 K + \beta_k(S - I). \tag{5.11}$$

4. *Government (fiscal and monetary authority):*

$$T = \tau(\rho K + rB/p) \quad [\text{or } t^n = (T - rB/p)/K = \text{const.}], \tag{5.12}$$

$$G = T - rB/p + \mu_2 M/p, \tag{5.13}$$

$$S_g = T - rB/p - G \quad [= -(\dot{M} + \dot{B})/p, \text{ see below}], \tag{5.14}$$

$$\hat{M} = \mu_0, \tag{5.15}$$

$$\dot{B} = pG + rB - pT - \dot{M} \quad [= (\mu_2 - \mu_0)M]. \tag{5.16}$$

5. *Equilibrium conditions (asset markets):*

$$M = M^d = h_1 pY + h_2 pK(1-\tau)(\bar{r} - r) \tag{5.17}$$

$$[B = B^d, E = E^d],$$

$$p_e E = (1-\tau)\rho pK/((1-\tau)r - \pi), \tag{5.18}$$

$$\dot{M} = \dot{M}^d, \quad \dot{B} = \dot{B}^d \quad [\dot{E} = \dot{E}^d]. \tag{5.19}$$

6. *Disequilibrium situation (goods market):*

$$S = S_p + S_g = Y - \delta K - C - G, \tag{5.20}$$

$$I = i(\rho - r + \pi)K + nK, \tag{5.21}$$

$$S \neq I.$$

7. *Wage–price sector (adjustment equations):*

$$\widehat{w} = \beta_w(V - \bar{V}) + \kappa_w \hat{p} + (1-\kappa_w)\pi, \tag{5.22}$$

$$\hat{p} = \beta_p((I-S)/K) + \kappa_p \widehat{w} + (1-\kappa_p)\pi, \tag{5.23}$$

$$\dot{\pi} = \beta_{\pi_1}(\hat{p} - \pi) + \beta_{\pi_2}(\mu_0 - n - \pi). \tag{5.24}$$

The important innovation of this general Keynes–Wicksell prototype model is the assumption that investment plans (of firms) are made independently of the savings decisions of asset-owners, up to the fact that they will be confronted and in some way or another be coordinated with these saving plans through market interactions. This new fact, in conjunction with the assumed LM equation (5.17), can be viewed as being responsible for the label "Keynes" in the name of this model type. The particular form of the investment function (5.8) and the particular determination of the inflation rate (5.23) is responsible for the name "Wicksell" in this type of literature.

The foregoing are the obvious and generally documented characteristics of models of Keynes–Wicksell type, while further necessary consequences of these changes in comparison to models of Tobinian type (see e.g. Chiarella and Flaschel 2000a, ch. 2) have been by and large ignored in the literature. This is in particular due to the fact there did not exist a general model of the Tobinian type from which this new model could be obtained through systematic variations of its structural equations and with which the Keynes–Wicksell model could be compared in detail. Our following discussion of the new equations of this Keynes–Wicksell model (in comparison to those of the model of Chiarella and Flaschel (2000a, sec. 2.5)) will indeed show that it represents a very systematic variation of this former model which improves it considerably with respect to plausibility, completeness and consistency.

The newly added investment function (5.8) assumes that investment per unit of capital is determined in a natural, and here linear, way by the differential that is now allowed to exist between the rate of return ρ on capital and the real rate of return $r - \pi$ on government bonds.[7] This differential was zero in the Tobin models of monetary growth in which capital, held by households, and bonds were perfect substitutes. There is a further trend term γ in this investment function which is here for simplicity set equal to n (see Chiarella and Flaschel (1998) for an endogenization of this term).

Investment is assumed in this model to be entirely financed by equities issued by firms. The asset structure that is available to capitalists (or pure asset-holders) therefore now consists of outside money, government bonds and equities (see Sargent (1987, p. 12) for the same starting point). Equities and bonds are assumed to be perfect substitutes in the eyes of asset-holders which represents the most basic assumption that can be made in this context. We assume in this model that there are no planned retained earnings of firms, which means that all expected profits ρpK are paid out to equity-owners in each period. The after-tax return per unit of equity to equity-owners is therefore $(1-\tau)\rho pK/E$. The price of equities (determined by the above perfect substitute assumption) is denoted by p_e (p_b, the price of bonds, is not equal to one). Thus the actual rate of return on equities per unit of money is given by $(1-\tau)\rho pK/(p_eE)$. Under the perfect substitute assumption this must be equal to $(1-\tau)r-\pi$, the real rate of interest after taxes, which is the context of the equation (5.18).[8]

Wealth-owners now hold equities in place of real capital, which is under the command of firms with regard to its use for production as well as with regard to its intended rate of change in time. Thus we have to replace the real wealth component K in asset-owners' portfolio by p_eE/p with respect to actual holdings as well as with respect to stock demand (giving rise to a new form of Walras's law of stocks). Furthermore, the savings decision of capitalist households now, of course, includes besides money and bonds the term $p_e\dot{E}^d/p$, i.e. that part of private savings that is intended to go into equities. These aspects are reflected in equations (5.2)–(5.6).

Note here that we stick to the assumption that all taxes are paid by capitalists. Note furthermore that we no longer distinguish between the actual and the perceived disposable income of capitalist households. This distinction has been extensively treated in Chiarella and Flaschel (2000a, ch. 2), so here we use the simple income concept $Y-\delta K-T$ as perceived disposable income for the private sector as in the rest of this chapter. Note finally that this income is based on production plans and not on actual sales, just as in the models of Tobin type. Of course, the discussion of more elaborate concepts of perceived disposable income needs to be pursued in future investigations.

Firms issue equities in order to finance investment and they have by assumption no retained earnings with respect to their planned production and planned proceeds. Investment may and will differ from total savings in models of Keynes–Wicksell type in general which means that planned production and proceeds ρpK and actual sales and proceeds will be different from each other. The amount of production that is not sold is given by $S-I=Y-\delta K-C-I-G$.[9] Yet, this additional production has already (by assumption) been paid out to equity-holders which means that firms have to issue new equities as described in (5.9) not only in order to finance their investment, but also to finance any difference between expected and actual proceeds. Newly issued equities are therefore equal in amount to total savings, which implies that private savers will be just content with the supply of new equities by firms.

Since we have independent investment behavior with $I \neq S$ in general, there is now the choice between investment goods supplied or demanded in the determination of actual capital accumulation $\dot{K}$. These two polar cases are described in (5.10) by means of the parameter β_k $(=0, 1)$ and are to be discussed briefly with respect to their consistency in the light of the other equations of the model.

Let us consider the case $\beta_k = 0$ first which is identical with the $\dot{K}$ assumption of the Tobin type models derived in Chiarella and Flaschel (2000a, ch. 2). In this case, we assume that firms involuntarily invest their extra supply of goods in new machinery and finance this extra investment as described above by issuing further equities, if supply Y exceeds aggregate demand $C + I + \delta K + G$. In the opposite case where $I - S > 0$ holds, they are forced to cancel this amount of their investment plans and orders by assumption. In the present model the only consequence of these actions of firms is therefore given by the price adjustment equation (5.23), which states that any discrepancy between demand and supply $C + I + \delta K + G - Y = I - S$ gives rise to corresponding price movements according to the so-called law of demand. The immediate consequences of goods market disequilibrium are thus purely nominal in the present model. In comparison to the model of Chiarella and Flaschel (2000a, sec. 2.5) this nevertheless represents a significant improvement, since the price level is here no longer driven by an imbalance in the market for the stock of money (an imbalance which does not exist in the present model; see (5.17)), but in a Wicksellian fashion by relative imbalances in the market for goods. The picture that emerges from this discussion of the case $\beta_k = 0$ is that of a supply-driven economy, but one with a Keynes–Wicksell goods and money market demand block which determines the rate of inflation $\hat{p}$ and the nominal rate of interest r. Since all goods produced are used for consumption or investment purposes in the present case there is no need to consider inventory changes $\dot{N}$ explicitly. This is obtained from equation (5.11) by setting $\delta_2 = 0$ in addition to the assumption $\beta_k = 0$, so that equation (5.11) can be ignored in this case.

The latter remark is not true for the alternative case $\beta_k = 1$ where capital accumulation is assumed to be driven by investment plans and not by intended savings. In this case there must be corresponding movements in inventories N which are determined by the imbalance in the market for goods as described in equation (5.11). Inventories increase when output exceeds aggregate demand $(S > I)$ and they decrease in the opposite case $(S < I)$. Note here also that we are considering a growing economy which means that there is a further reason for ongoing inventory changes, namely that inventories have to grow in order to stay in line with the permanent growth in production and the capital stock. For simplicity we assume here that a certain portion of output (and thus of the capital stock) is retained by firms for this purpose so that these inventory changes can be treated just as capital depreciation and simply be aggregated with it $(\delta = \delta_1 + \delta_2)$, just representing a portion of actual production that (generally) does not leave the sphere of production. The case $\beta_k = 1$ thus can be characterized as being more demand-oriented than the case $\beta_k = 0$ and thereby perhaps somewhat more in line with Keynesian concepts of monetary growth. Note that equation (5.9) is also valid in this case, meaning again that firms have to finance new investment and dividends that are not yet backed up by sales, but represented only by an increase in inventories (if $S > I$ holds; in the opposite case we instead have that part of the new investment is financed by unexpected sales from inventories). Again the immediate effects of goods market disequilibrium are purely nominal ones.

The description of these two polar cases shows that intermediate cases are also conceivable, so that $\beta_k \in (0, 1)$, where part of any nonsold production goes into unplanned inventory changes and part of it into unintended real capital formation[10] with obvious changes in this description if investment demand exceeds currents savings.[11] We shall however ignore this intermediate case in the analysis of this chapter, but simply state that its stability properties will in fact be intermediate with respect to the ones we shall establish for the two polar cases.

We thus end up with a significantly revised description of the behavior of firms (which induces only minor changes in the description of household behavior as we have seen above). By contrast there is no change necessary in the formulation of the government sector when going from the general Tobin model to this general version of a model of Keynes–Wicksell type.

As already stated we are no longer dependent here on money market disequilibrium in the formulation of an explicit (demand-pull) theory of the rate of inflation $\hat{p}$; see again (5.23) and note its use of a relative expression for the state of goods market disequilibrium. Otherwise the description of the wage–price module is the same as in the general Tobin model of Chiarella and Flaschel (2000a, sec. 2.5). We thus have in this model the usual LM equilibrium of Keynesian models which by the wealth constraint of asset-holders and the perfect substitute assumption for bonds and equities implies that the other asset markets must be cleared as well; see (5.17). The perfect substitute assumption (5.18) has already been explained above, while (5.19) again states that asset-holders will voluntarily accept the additional supply of money and bonds and adjust their resulting changed portfolios only in the "subsequent period." Owing to the implied equality $S = S_p + S_g = p_e\dot{E}^d/p$ (see (5.5) and (5.14)), we obtain from (5.9) the equation $\dot{E} = \dot{E}^d$ (see (5.19)), so that there is general consistency with respect to flows[12] (besides the general consistency for stocks (5.17)).

This concludes our description of the general Keynes–Wicksell model of this section (which besides labor market disequilibrium now also exhibits goods market disequilibrium as the explanation of price inflation). We stress once again that it is mainly the sector of firms which has received an extensive reformulation here accompanied by a new arrangement of equilibrium and disequilibrium conditions and their implication for the formulation of the wage–price module. In our view this model type is much more convincing than the general Tobin model of (Chiarella and Flaschel 2000a, ch. 2). Nevertheless, in discussing this model we shall find that it is still fairly neoclassical in its structure and its implications due to some definite weaknesses it contains. These weaknesses concern the description of goods market disequilibrium and the treatment of unplanned inventory changes. In most treatments these weaknesses are generally simply removed from view by the assumption of an infinite adjustment speed of prices, as we discuss it in a later section of this chapter. Better ways to overcome these weaknesses (and the differences that this implies for the working of such a model) will be the theme of subsequent work.

As far as the mathematical investigation of this general Keynes–Wicksell model is concerned we will confine ourselves here mainly to the case $t^n = t - rb = \text{const.}$ where lump sum taxes are varied in such a way that the ratio of taxes net of interest to the value of the capital stock remains constant over time. This assumption will allow us to disregard the GBR and the evolution of government debt in the following, at least from a local point of view. In making use of this simplifying device we here follow a similar assumption of Sargent (1987, ch. 5) "Dynamic analysis of a Keynesian model," which is the basic reference with respect to the models we shall investigate in this chapter.

5.3 The laws of motion of the model

Before we now start with the step-by-step investigation of the 4D case with $t^n = t - rb = \text{const.}$, let us first rewrite the general dynamical model (5.1)–(5.24) without any simplifying assumption as an autonomous dynamical system in the five variables $\omega = w/p, l = L/K, m = M/(pK), \pi, b = B/(pK)$.[13]

By calculations similar to those in Chiarella and Flaschel (2000a, ch. 2) (see in particular sec. 2.3) we obtain from (5.1)–(5.24) the intensive form equations

$$\widehat{\omega} = \kappa[(1-\kappa_p)\beta_w X^w + (\kappa_w - 1)\beta_p X^p], \tag{5.25}$$

$$\hat{l} = n - s(\cdot) \text{ or } -i(\cdot) \quad (\beta_k = 0 \text{ or} 1), \tag{5.26}$$

$$\widehat{m} = \mu - n - \pi - \kappa[\beta_p X^p + \kappa_p \beta_w X^w] + \hat{l}, \tag{5.27}$$

$$\dot{\pi} = \beta_{\pi_1}\kappa[\beta_p X^p + \kappa_p \beta_w X^w] + \beta_{\pi_2}(\mu_0 - n - \pi), \tag{5.28}$$

$$\dot{b} = (\mu_2 - \mu_0)m - (\pi + n)b - (\kappa(\beta_p X^p + \kappa_p \beta_w X^w) - \hat{l})b, \tag{5.29}$$

where we employ the abbreviations

$$\begin{aligned}
\rho &= y - \delta - \omega l^d, \quad l^d = L^d/K = y/x = \text{const.},\\
X^w &= l^d/l - \bar{V} = y/(xl) - \bar{V},\\
X^p &= i(\cdot) + n - s(\cdot),\\
r &= \bar{r} + (h_1 y - m)/(h_2(1-\tau))\\
&\qquad [h(y,r) = h_1 y + h_2(1-\tau)(\bar{r} - r), \text{ see } (5.3)],\\
t &= T/K = \tau(\rho + rb), \quad t^n = t - rb,\\
g &= t^n + \mu_2 m,
\end{aligned}$$

$$s(\cdot) = s_c(\rho - t^n) - (g - t^n),$$
$$i(\cdot) = i(\rho - r + \pi).$$

Note here that in the above presentation of the dynamics we have made use of the formula

$$\hat{p} - \pi = \kappa[\beta_p X^p + \kappa_p \beta_w X^w]$$

for the deviation of the actual rate of inflation from the expected one and that the $s(\cdot)$ equation can be easily obtained from $s(\cdot) = \widehat{K} = y - \delta - C/K - G/K$ by inserting into it the consumption function and the government expenditure rule.

In the following determination of steady-state solutions of the above dynamics we again disregard the boundary solutions $\omega, l, m = 0$ which arise from the growth rate formulation of certain laws of motion. These values of the variables ω, l, m are economically meaningless and will not appear as relevant attractors in the stability investigations to be performed. A general and global analysis of the system should of course take into account the stability properties of such boundary points of rest of the dynamics (5.25)–(5.29). For simplicity we also assume here that the parameter $\bar{r}$ in the above model is equal to the steady-state value r_0. This assumption simplifies the calculation of the steady-state values without loss in generality, but it should be kept in mind or dispensed with if steady-state comparisons are being made.

Proposition 5.1 *There is* a unique steady-state solution *or point of rest of the dynamics (5.25)–(5.29) fulfilling $\omega_0, l_0, m_0 \neq 0$.*[14] *This steady state is determined by*[15]

$$y_0 = y^p, \tag{5.30}$$
$$l_0 = y_0/(x\bar{V}), \quad l_0^d = y_0/x, \tag{5.31}$$
$$m_0 = h_1 y_0, \tag{5.32}$$
$$\pi_0 = \mu_0 - n, \tag{5.33}$$
$$b_0 = (\mu_2 - \mu_0)m_0/\mu_0, \tag{5.34}$$
$$\rho_0 = \frac{n + \mu_2 m_0 - s_c \pi_0 b_0}{s_c(1-\tau)(1+b_0)},$$
$$r_0 = \rho_0 + \pi_0,$$
$$\omega_0 = (y_0 - \delta - \rho_0)/l_0^d. \tag{5.35}$$

Proof: The equations (5.26) and (5.27) (set equal to zero) imply that $\mu_0 - n - \pi = \kappa[\beta_p X^p + \kappa_p \beta_w X^w]$ must hold in the steady state. Inserting this into (5.28) then gives that $\pi_0 = \mu_0 - n$ must hold. This in turn implies by (5.27) the equality of $\hat{p}$ and π_0. From the equations (5.25) and (5.27) we then obtain for the variables X^p, X^w the simultaneous equation system

$$0 = (1 - \kappa_p)\beta_w X^w + (\kappa_w - 1)\beta_p X^p,$$
$$0 = \beta_p X^p + \kappa_p \beta_w X^w.$$

It is easily shown for $\kappa_w \kappa_p < 1$ that this linear equation system can be uniquely solved for X^w, X^p, which must then both be zero. This implies the first two of our steady-state equations (5.30) and (5.32). Equation (5.32) then immediately follows from our assumption $\bar{r} = r_0$ and (5.33) has already been shown above. Next one gets (5.34) by solving the $\dot{b} = 0$ equation for the steady-state value of b ($X^w, X^p = 0$). The equation for ρ_0 is then obtained from (5.26), i.e. $n = s(\cdot)$ by solving this equation for ρ_0, since we have $\rho_0 - t_0^n = (1-\tau)(1+b_0)\rho_0 + \pi_0 b_0$ and $g_0 - t_0^n = \mu_2 m_0$ in the steady state. The calculation of ω_0 and r_0 is then straightforward ($i(\cdot) = 0$). □

We assume with respect to this steady-state solution first of all that the parameters of the model are chosen such that $\rho_0 > 0$ holds true. This is obviously the case if the growth rate of the money supply μ_0 and the parameter μ_2 are set equal to the natural rate of growth n, since the tax parameter τ must satisfy $\tau \in (0, 1)$. The case just described can be regarded as the basic steady-state configuration of the general model, since the government then just supplies the correct monetary frame for the growth path of the real part of the model and it injects this necessary amount of new money by buying goods (in addition to the ones that are financed by taxes), so that there is no need for government debt or credit in this situation ($b_0 = 0$). The steady-state rate of profit is in this case simply given by $(n + \mu_0 m_0)/(s_c(1-\tau)) > 0, m_0 = h_1 y$. Second, we must here also assume that this expression for the rate of profit is less than $y - \delta$ so that there is associated with it a positive steady-state level of the real wage ω_0. This condition should always be fulfilled since the magnitudes of n, h_1, μ_0 are all small from an empirical point of view. On the basis of these assumptions we thus have a unique and meaningful interior solution to the steady-state equations. It is assumed that the parameters of the model in general do not depart by so much from those of this basic steady-state configuration that the conditions $\rho_0, \omega_0 > 0$ will be violated. Note finally that $\pi_0 = \mu_0 - n$ should not be chosen so negative that $r_0 > 0$ will not hold true.

Let us now start with the investigation of the case $t^n = t - rb = \text{const}$. We simplify the notation of the 4D case by setting the value of $\bar{V}$ equal to 1. Since the variable b only enters equations (5.25)–(5.28) via the $s(\cdot)$ equation (which only depends on t^n) we immediately see that the first four dynamical laws and their components do not depend on the variable b. Furthermore, the entry J_{55} in the Jacobian J of the dynamics (5.25)–(5.29) is in this case simply given by $-(\pi_0 + n)$ at the steady state of this system. The eigenvalue structure ($\lambda_{1,\ldots,4}$) of the dynamics at the steady state is therefore given by that of the system shown below plus the eigenvalue $\lambda_5 = -(\pi_0 + n)$. Stability assertions on the subsystem (5.25)–(5.28) therefore immediately also hold for the complete model (5.25)–(5.29), at least from a local point of view.

In light of the foregoing discussion we are led to consider the 4D system

$$\widehat{\omega} = \kappa[(1-\kappa_p)\beta_w(y/(xl)-1) + (\kappa_w - 1)\beta_p(i(\cdot)+n-s(\cdot))], \tag{5.36}$$

$$\hat{l} = n - s(\cdot) \text{ or } -i(\cdot) \quad (\beta_k = 0 \text{ or } 1), \tag{5.37}$$

$$\begin{aligned}\widehat{m} = &\mu_0 - \pi - n \\ &- \kappa[\beta_p(i(\cdot)+n-s(\cdot)) + \kappa_p\beta_w(y/(xl)-1)] + \hat{l},\end{aligned} \tag{5.38}$$

$$\begin{aligned}\dot{\pi} = &\beta_{\pi_1}\kappa[\beta_p(i(\cdot)+n-s(\cdot)) + \kappa_p\beta_w(y/(xl)-1)] \\ &+ \beta_{\pi_2}(\mu_0 - n - \pi),\end{aligned} \tag{5.39}$$

where

$$s(\cdot) = s_c(y - \delta - \omega y/x - t^n) - \mu_2 m,$$
$$i(\cdot) = i(y - \delta - \omega y/x - (r_0 + (h_1 y - m)/h_2) + \pi).$$

Note that $y, x = \text{const.}$ holds in the context of the Keynes–Wicksell model of this chapter and that the parameter τ is no longer present in this model variant. Note furthermore that the steady-state solution of the 4D system is now based on the expression $\rho_0 = (n + \mu_2 m_0)/s_c + t^n$. All other expressions for the steady state remain unchanged under the above modification.[16] The above dynamic system will now be investigated by starting from an appropriate 2D subcase.

5.4 The Goodwin (1967) growth cycle case

This section starts from a set of simplifying assumptions which imply that the real part of the Keynes–Wicksell model of this chapter gives rise to dynamics of the Goodwin (1967) growth cycle type. The overshooting profit squeeze mechanism of that model is thus an integral part of our general Keynes–Wicksell model.[17]

In order to obtain the simple 2D center type dynamics of this growth cycle model from the above 4D model we make the following four assumptions:

$\kappa_w = 1$. The real wage dynamics is independent of the goods market.
$r = r_0$. Infinite interest elasticity of money demand at the steady state ($h_2 = \infty$).
$\pi = \mu_0 - n$. Extreme asymptotically rational expectations ($\beta_{\pi_2} = \infty, \beta_{\pi_1} < \infty$).
$\mu_2 = 0$. Government is a creditor in the steady state: $b_0 = -m_0$.

In the case $\widehat{K} = i(\cdot) + n$ (i.e. $\beta_k = 1$), the first three of the above assumptions are in fact already sufficient to imply the cross-dual growth cycle dynamics of the Goodwin model for the *real part of the model* (5.1)–(5.24), since we then get from equations (5.36) and (5.37) the following special dynamic equations ($y, x =$ const., $l^d = y/x$):

$$\widehat{\omega} = \beta_w(l^d/l - 1), \tag{5.40}$$

$$\hat{l} = -i(y - \delta - \omega l^d - r_0 + \mu_0 - n). \tag{5.41}$$

It is obvious from these equations that $r = r_0$ removes the influence of the money market on the real part of the model ($r_0 = \rho_0 + \mu_0 - n$), that $\pi = \mu_0 - n$ removes the dynamics of expectations formation and that $\kappa_w = 1$ suppresses the impact of the goods market disequilibrium on the dynamics of the real wage.

Since l^d and y are given magnitudes in the model (5.1)–(5.24), the above two equations are easily reformulated in terms of Goodwin's original dynamic variables $u = \omega l^d/y = \omega/x$ (the share of wages) and $V = l^d/l$ (the rate of employment) to yield

$$\hat{u} = \beta_w(V - 1) \equiv h^1(V), \tag{5.42}$$

$$\widehat{V} = i(y - \delta - uy - r_0 + \mu_0 - n) \equiv h^2(u). \tag{5.43}$$

Proposition 5.2 *The trajectories of the dynamical system (5.42) and (5.43) stay positive if they start in the positive domain of $\mathbb{R}^2$ and are all closed orbits.*

Proof: It is easily shown that all orbits that start in the positive orthant must stay in it, since the boundary of this domain is an invariant subset of the above dynamics. The proof that all trajectories of this dynamical system are closed orbits is also straightforward if one makes use of the function

$$H(u, V) = -\int_{u_0}^{u} (h^2(\widetilde{u})/\widetilde{u})\, d\widetilde{u} + \int_{V_0}^{V} (h^1(\widetilde{V})/\widetilde{V})\, d\widetilde{V}.$$

This function is zero at the steady-state values u_0, V_0 and positive elsewhere. Furthermore, one easily gets

$$\dot{H} = H_u \cdot \dot{u} + H_V \cdot \dot{V} = (-h^2(u))\hat{u} + h^1(V)\widehat{V} \equiv 0,$$

so that the function H is a Liapunov function.[18] Owing to the shape of this function, it follows that all orbits must be closed – see Flaschel (1993, ch. 4) for the details of such reasoning. The resulting phase portrait of this dynamical system is well known – see again Flaschel (1993, ch. 4) for the graphical details. □

All observations in the preceding proof can be reformulated in a straightforward way for the original presentation of the dynamical system (5.40)–(5.41) in the variables ω, l and they also hold for all nonlinear labor market reaction functions $\beta_w(l^d/l)$ with $\beta_w(0) = 1$, $\beta_w' > 0$ (see the next section for the introduction of such nonlinear Phillips curves.)

The remaining dynamical equations of this growth cycle case are

$$\widehat{m} = -\kappa(\beta_p(i(\cdot) + n - s(\cdot)) + \kappa_p\beta_w(V - 1)) - i(\cdot) = f^1(u, V),$$
$$\dot{b} = -\mu_0 m - (\hat{p}(\cdot) + \widehat{K}(\cdot))b = f^2(u, V, m, b).$$

Since we only want to show here that Goodwin's growth cycle is part of the fully interdependent dynamics of the general model we do not discuss this appended dynamical system in the special case we are considering in the present section. Of course, Goodwin's type of dynamics will also be present and tend to dominate if $r \approx r_0$ (high-interest elasticity of money demand) and $\kappa_w \approx 1$, $\beta_{\pi_2} \approx \infty$ holds, but may be modified significantly in its overshooting feature when less extreme parameter values are given.

The Goodwin model is even more closely mirrored if the alternative case $\widehat{K} = s(\cdot)$ (i.e. $\beta_k = 0$) is considered. In this case, the further above assumption $\mu_2 = 0$ on government behavior is needed, if one wants the dynamics of ω, l (i.e. u, V) to be fully independent of the rest of the system. This is due here to the form of the savings per capital function

$$s(\cdot) = s_c(y - \delta - \omega l^d - t^n) - \mu_2 m.$$

The belief that (real) wage flexibility will give rise to full employment steady growth at least in the long run is supported most when Kuh's (1967) version of the Phillips curve is used in the Goodwin context – see Akerlof and Stiglitz (1969, pp. 272–274) for such an application. This version of the Phillips curve can be formulated as follows (see Ferri and Greenberg 1989, p. 75). Set[19]

$$\omega = \beta_w(V)y/l^d, \quad \text{i.e.} \quad u = \beta_w(V).$$

With respect to the model (5.42)–(5.43), this latter equation replaces equation (5.42) and gives in conjunction with (5.43)

$$\dot{V} = iy(\beta_w(V_0) - \beta_w(V))V = H(V),$$

where V_0 is defined by $\beta_w(V_0) = 1 - (\rho_0 + \delta)/y$, $\rho_0 = r_0 - (\mu_0 - n)$ (and $u_0 = \beta_w(V_0)$). These values characterize the steady state of the model and we assume here that an economically meaningful solution $V_0 > 0$ exists. This steady state is obviously globally asymptotically stable, since we have $\dot{V} > 0$ to the left of V_0 and $\dot{V} < 0$ to its right. Employment decreases to the right of V_0 and with it the real wage until income redistribution induces a growth rate of the capital stock that is equal to the growth rate of the labor force n (the opposite occurs to the left of V_0). It has become common usage to call $1 - V_0$ the natural rate of unemployment and to consider V_0 as the "full" employment rate – see Akerlof and Stiglitz (1969, p. 271) for an early example of this. The model therefore gives the most straightforward demonstration of the long-run stability of the full employment situation.

Note, however, that the present explanation of "natural" employment

$$V_0 = \beta_w^{-1}((y - \delta - r_0 + \mu_0 - n)/y),$$

assumed to lie between 0 and 1, is far from being "natural," as its dependence in particular on β_w and μ_0 shows.

Furthermore, even this simple model of growth and (un)employment can give rise to complex dynamics if it is reformulated in discrete time, even if $\beta_w(V)$ is assumed to be a linear function of V. In this latter case it gives rise to the following well-known difference equation that allows for "chaos" at appropriate parameter values for i, y and β_w, namely

$$V_{t+1} = V_t(1 + iy\beta_w(V_0 - V_t))$$

(see Pohjola (1981) and Ferri and Greenberg (1989) for its treatment in this context). We thus can associate even chaotic behavior with this most basic form of a full employment "adjustment" mechanism if the parameter β_w becomes sufficiently large (V_0 sufficiently small) – see again Pohjola (1981) for details.

Ferri and Greenberg (1989, sec. 4.8) consider another approach to labor market dynamics which they call a neoclassical disequilibrium approach. This approach, which is based on neo-Keynesian regime switching methods, takes account of the fact that the employment rate V cannot increase beyond 1 if 1 stands for the ceiling of absolute full employment.[20] The Goodwin model (5.40)–(5.41), for example, has then to be modified to (l^d a given magnitude),

$$\widehat{\omega} = \beta_w(l^d/l - 1), \tag{5.44}$$

$$\hat{l} = \begin{cases} -i(xl^d - \delta - \omega l^d - r_0 + \mu_0 - n), & \text{if } l \geq l^d, \\ -i(xl - \delta - \omega l - r_0 + \mu_0 - n), & \text{if } l \leq l^d, \end{cases} \tag{5.45}$$

to take account of the fact that employment and production cannot increase beyond the full employment level $l^d \leq l$, $y \leq xl$. This model is considered in Ito (1980) in full detail and analyzes the mathematical complexities to which such a regime switching approach can give rise.

There is, however, one fundamental shortcoming of such regime switching approaches which lies in the fact that they usually identify the steady-state rate of employment with the maximum rate of employment. Such a view is not shared by many macroeconomists, quite independently of the particular justification they may give for the assumption (or derivation) of a positive magnitude V_0 or $1 - V_0$, often called the natural rate of (un)employment (or the NAIRU if a broader definition is given to this positive steady-state concept of (un)employment). We here use the value 1 for V_0 for simplicity to denote the "natural" level of the employment rate and thus have to use $V_{max} > 1$ if we want to refer to some sort of absolute full employment ceiling.

Introducing such a full employment ceiling into the equations (5.40) and (5.41) gives instead of (5.44) and (5.45) the equations ($l^d = y/x = \text{const.}$)

$$\widehat{\omega} = \beta_w(l^d/l - 1), \tag{5.46}$$

$$\hat{l} = \begin{cases} -i(xl^d - \delta - \omega l^d - r_0 + \mu_0 - n), & \text{if } l \geq l^d/V_{\max}, \\ -i(xlV_{\max} - \delta - \omega l V_{\max} - r_0 + \mu_0 - n), & \text{if } l \leq l^d/V_{\max}. \end{cases} \tag{5.47}$$

This implies that the dynamics are of the same type as those of (5.40) and (5.41) as long as l stays within $(l^d/V_{\max}, +\infty)$, that is, within a certain neighborhood of the steady-state value $l_0 = l^d \in (l^d/V_{\max}, +\infty)$. Only if l falls below $l^d/V_{\max}$ is there such a shortage of the labor supply that output must fall below the potential output $Y^p = yK$ and will thus modify the path of capital accumulation (and that of l). Of course, the Phillips curve may have kinks in addition as in Ferri and Greenberg (1989, p. 62) at various levels of the employment rate. This, however, only modifies the shape of the closed orbits of the Goodwin model, but not its qualitative features.

The phase portrait shown in Figure 5.1 summarizes the above findings on labor supply bottlenecks in the Goodwin model.

Leaving aside such bottlenecks from the side of labor supply and (by the use of equations (5.11) and (5.23)) also certain bottlenecks from the side of capacity output including inventories therefore simply means that the dynamics of system (5.1)–(5.24) is restricted to such a domain of economically meaningful values where neither productive capacity plus inventories nor natural capacity ($L_{\max} = L \cdot V_{\max}$) become a binding constraint for the growth path $\widehat{K} = i(\cdot)$ of the economy.[21] Important as such switches in economic regimes may be from a global

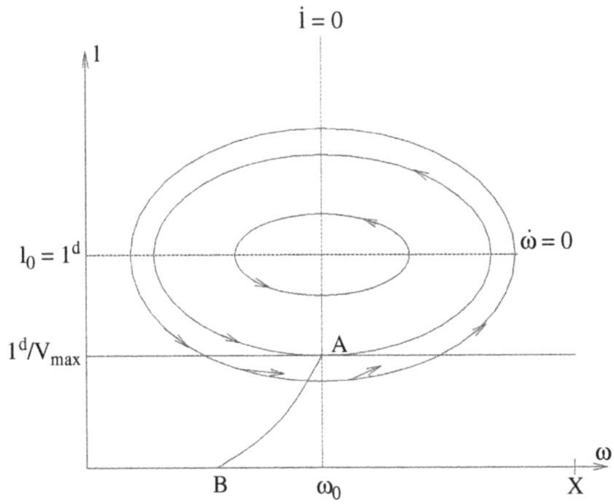

Figure 5.1 Ceilings to the validity of the Goodwin growth cycle approach.

point of view, they can at first be safely neglected in the study of the fundamental properties of the dynamic system (5.1)–(5.24) and its special cases. Ceilings to economic activity (caused by the existing supply of goods including inventories)[22] and the present volume of maximum labor supply are of no importance for the economic evolution near the steady state.

Of course, they have to be added eventually to any global treatment of the Keynes–Wicksell model, but will then not give rise to a *new theory* of labor market dynamics. Instead, there is only a switch in the determination of the isocline $\dot{l}=0$ below l^d/V_{max} as shown in Figure 5.1 by the curve AB,[23] given by

$$\omega = (x - (\delta + r_0 - (\mu_0 - n)))/(l V_{max}),$$

which should lead to it having a positive slope with respect to empirically plausible values of the parameters δ, r_0, n and μ_0. This is, of course, no significant modification of the dynamics of the Goodwin model.

This last statement can be further substantiated by means of the Liapunov function

$$H(\omega, l) = \int_{\omega_0}^{\omega} \frac{h^2(\tilde{\omega})}{\tilde{\omega}} d\tilde{\omega} - \int_{l_0}^{l} \frac{h^1(\tilde{l})}{\tilde{l}} d\tilde{l},$$

for the dynamical system (5.46) and (5.47) where $h^1(l)$ is given by $\beta_w(l^d/l - 1)$ and $h^2(\omega)$ by $-i(xl^d - \delta - \omega l^d - r_0 + \mu_0 - n)$. This function is of the same type as the Liapunov function we used before and it gives rise to[24]

$$\dot{H} = \begin{cases} 0, & \text{if } l \geq l^d/V_{max}, \\ h^1(l)[h^2(\omega) & \text{if } l \leq l^d/V_{max}, \\ \quad + i(xlV_{max} - \delta - \omega l V_{max} - r_0 + \mu_0 - n)], & \end{cases}$$
$$\leq h^1(l)[h^2(\omega) - h^2(\omega)] = 0.$$

This implies that the original closed orbits of the Goodwin model are crossed inwards by the trajectories of this new dynamical system in the region below l^d/V_{max} (see Figure 5.1) so that the closed orbit of Figure 5.1 that runs through A becomes a limit cycle for all trajectories that start at points outside of it. The closed orbits of the Goodwin model thus characterize this dynamical system in the long run also in the cases where regime switching takes place.

5.5 Rose (1967) employment cycle extension

In this section we remove one of the simplifying assumptions of the preceding section. We show that the limit cycle result of Rose (1967) can then be obtained through the interaction of the Goodwin profit squeeze mechanism (of the preceding section) and locally destabilizing but globally stabilizing relative adjustment speeds of wages and prices. These latter forces were the basic ingredients of Rose's nonlinear theory of the employment cycle.[25]

We have considered in the preceding section four variants of Goodwin's growth cycle model and have argued in particular that it is far from obvious that the real wage mechanism

$$\widehat{\omega} = \beta_w(l^d/l - 1),$$

or even a simplification of it, will guarantee full employment equilibrium in the long run. Smooth factor substitution with a sufficiently high elasticity of factor substitution may alter this conclusion to some extent, but only insofar as it thereby becomes an empirical question as to whether "Goodwin" or "Solow" provides the more convincing approach to the supply-side-determined path of capital accumulation.

In the present section we shall demonstrate that the Solovian outcome (of a monotonic convergence to the full employment growth path) becomes even more unlikely if it is realized, as in Rose's (1967) model of the employment cycle, that even in a supply-side-driven economy the evolution of real wages is driven not only by the disequilibrium on the labor market but also by disequilibrium on the market for goods. This proposition also extends to the case of smooth factor substitution as Rose (1967) has already shown with a similar real growth model. The essential ideas behind his employment limit cycle are, however, also more easily grasped in the context of a fixed proportions technology as we shall show in this section.

In order to obtain a Rose type model as a special case of our general framework (5.1)–(5.24) we have only to assume[26] $\kappa_w < 1$ as modification of the assumptions of Section 5.4 (all other assumptions of that section remain intact). The Goodwinian dynamical system (5.40)–(5.41) is thereby extended to the dynamical system (see also equations (5.22) and (5.23))

$$\widehat{\omega} = \kappa[(1-\kappa_p)\beta_w(l^d/l - 1) + (\kappa_w - 1)\beta_p(i(\cdot) + n - s(\cdot))], \tag{5.48}$$

$$\hat{l} = -i(\cdot), \quad [\text{or } n - s(\cdot)], \tag{5.49}$$

where $i(\cdot) = i(y - \delta - \omega l^d - r_0 + \mu_0 - n)$ and $s(\cdot) = s_c(y - \delta - \omega l^d - t^n)$ as in Section 5.4.

In order to study the dynamics of this extended model let us again consider the case $\dot{K} = I$ (i.e. $\beta_k = 1$). First we make use again of the Liapunov function

$$H(\omega, l) = \int_{\omega_0}^{\omega} \frac{h^2(\widetilde{\omega})}{\widetilde{\omega}}\, d\widetilde{\omega} - \int_{l_0}^{l} \frac{h^1(\tilde{l})}{\tilde{l}}\, d\tilde{l},$$

where $h^1(l) = \kappa(1-\kappa_p)\beta_w(l^d/l - 1)$ and $h^2 = -i(\omega)$. This Liapunov function is of the type we have considered for the system (5.40) and (5.41) in the preceding section. Here we obtain the following result.

PROPOSITION 5.3 *The steady state of the dynamical system (5.48)–(5.49) is globally asymptotically stable (totally unstable) if $i < s_c$ ($i > s_c$).*[27]

Proof: Calculating the time derivative of H along the trajectories of (5.48) and (5.49) yields

$$\begin{aligned}\dot{H} &= -h^1(l)\hat{l} + h^2(\omega)\widehat{\omega} \\ &= h^2(\omega)\kappa(\kappa_w - 1)\beta_p(i(\cdot) + n - s(\cdot)).\end{aligned}$$

If $i < s_c$ holds, we get that the slope of $i(\cdot) + n - s(\cdot)$ is positive $(= (-i + s_c)l^d)$. Furthermore $i(\cdot) + n - s(\cdot) = 0$ at $\omega = \omega_0$, implying that this expression is negative to the left of ω_0 and positive to its right. The same holds true for the function $h^2(\omega) = -i(\cdot)$ which taken together with the previous result implies $\dot{H} < 0$ for $\omega \neq \omega_0$. The assertion then follows from the usual theorems on Liapunov functions, for which we refer the reader to Hirsch and Smale (1974, pp. 196ff.), and Brock and Malliaris (1989, pp. 89ff.). In the same way one can show $\dot{H} > 0$ if $i > s_c$. □

Up to now we have made use of linear relationships in the market for labor as well as for goods to investigate Rose's (1967) broader view on real wage dynamics. We have obtained a result similar to his, namely that the steady state will be locally unstable if investment reacts more sensitively to real wage changes than total savings. In this case a drop in real wages will create extra goods demand pressure and thus extra inflation which will induce a further fall in real wages and thus destabilizes the neutral closed orbit structure of the Goodwin model. This locally explosive dynamical behavior is turned into global stability in Rose (1967) by means of an appropriate nonlinearity in the excess demand function of the labor market and by making use of neoclassical smooth factor substitution. In Flaschel and Sethi (1996) it is shown how this strategy can be applied to the present context. Here, however, we want to stick to fixed proportions in production and thus will have to introduce at least one further nonlinearity in order to obtain Rose's limit cycle result for a system of type (5.48) and (5.49).

The nonlinearity that Rose uses in the labor market is a very natural one if one takes into account the classical nature of our general model and its special cases. It is of the form[28] displayed in Figure 5.2. It assumes a nonlinear relation between β_w and V, the fraction of labor demanded. This relation is shallow close to the steady state and very steep as one moves to either the left or right of the steady state.

According to this form the money wage will become very flexible farther off the steady state (by way of a rising adjustment speed for larger deviations of the employment rate from its "natural" level 1). The proof of Proposition 5.3 immediately shows that this nonlinearity alone is insufficient in successfully overcoming the total instability of the case where $i > s_c$ holds. In fact, $\dot{H} > 0$ holds quite independently of the form of the Phillips curve, as long as $\kappa_w < 1$ is true – while the case $\kappa_w = 1$ brings us back to the closed orbit structure of the Goodwin model. The phase portrait of (5.48)–(5.49) for $i > s_c$ is then easily shown to be of the type[30] displayed in Figure 5.3.

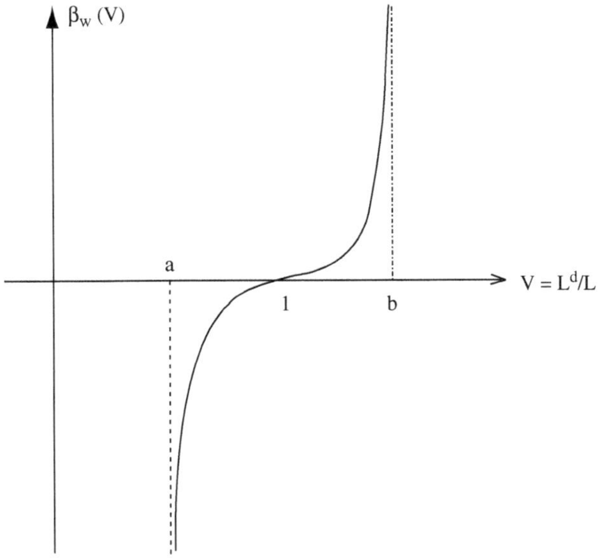

Figure 5.2 The nonlinear law of demand in the labor market.[29]

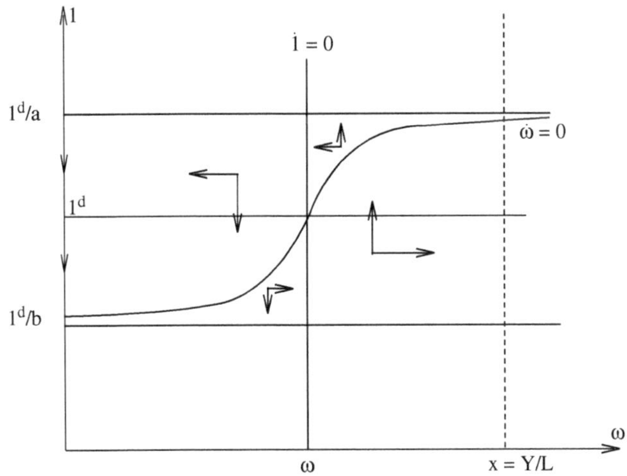

Figure 5.3 Implications of nonlinearity in the labor market.[31]

In the case $\kappa_w = 1$ the above restricted phase diagram is again filled with closed orbits as in the Goodwin model, while $\kappa_w < 1$ yields trajectories which point inwards with respect to these closed orbits for $s_c > i$ and outwards in the case $s_c < i$. Though the dynamical motion is thus now restricted to a corridor around the steady-state value $l_0 = l^d(V = 1)$, it is not viable, as we have just seen.

In view of the shape of the $\dot{\omega} = 0$ isocline[32] and the mathematical equation underlying it, it is natural to introduce a further nonlinearity, now in the market for goods in order to obtain global viability for the considered dynamics, namely by means of investment behavior. Here we assume the type of nonlinearity[33] displayed in Figure 5.4(a).

Thus though investment is more sensitive than savings with respect to real wage changes around the steady state, the opposite is the case for larger deviations of the real wage from its steady-state level ω_0. The phase portrait in Figure 5.3 is changed by these assumptions as shown in Figure 5.4(b).

We have added to this phase portrait one cycle of the closed orbit structure of the Goodwin subcase ($\kappa_w = 1$) of this 2D dynamical system and will now show

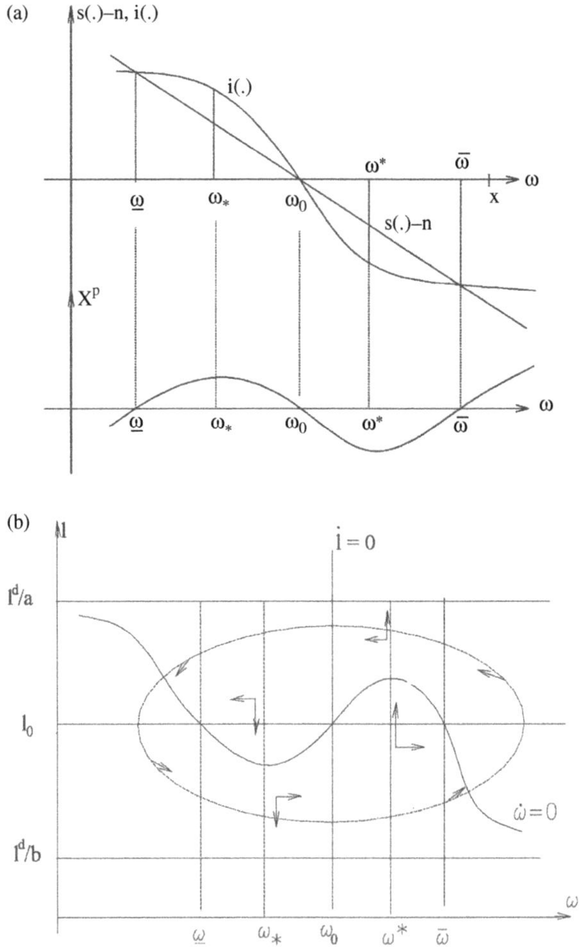

Figure 5.4 (a) A nonlinear investment–savings relationship. (b) A Rose limit cycle in the fixed proportions case.[34]

that the trajectories in the case $\kappa_w < 1$ point inwards with respect to each of these Goodwin cycles in the regions to the left of $\underline{\omega}$ and to the right of $\overline{\omega}$. By contrast, they point outwards within these two values of ω.

PROPOSITION 5.4 *Consider the Liapunov function of Proposition 5.3,*

$$H(\omega, l) = \int_{\omega_0}^{\omega} \frac{h^2(\widetilde{\omega})}{\widetilde{\omega}} d\widetilde{\omega} - \int_{l_0}^{l} \frac{h^1(\tilde{l})}{\tilde{l}} d\tilde{l},$$

$$h^1(l) = \kappa(1-\kappa_p)\beta_w(l^d/l - 1), \quad h^2 = -i(\omega),$$

but now augmented by the two nonlinearities just considered. In the present situation it is the case that

$$\dot{H} < 0 \quad \textit{for all } \omega < \underline{\omega} \textit{ or } \omega > \overline{\omega},$$

and

$$\dot{H} > 0 \quad \textit{for } \underline{\omega} < \omega < \overline{\omega}.$$

Proof: For $\omega < \underline{\omega}$ we have $0 < i(\cdot) < s(\cdot) - n$ and $-i(\cdot) < 0$ while for $\omega > \overline{\omega}$ we have $s(\cdot) - n < i(\cdot) < 0$ and $-i(\cdot) > 0$ by assumption. The function H therefore fulfills the condition

$$\dot{H} = \kappa(1-\kappa_w)\beta_p(i(\cdot) + n - s(\cdot))i(\cdot) < 0 \quad \text{for all } \omega < \underline{\omega} \text{ and all } \omega > \overline{\omega}$$

(and it is positive in between these bounds on ω). Since we know that $\dot{H} = 0$ along the closed orbits of the Goodwin case $\kappa_w = 1$, we thus get the result that the trajectories of the dynamical system (5.48)–(5.49) modified by the above two nonlinearities must point inwards along those segments of the Goodwin cycle that lie outside of the interval $(\underline{\omega}, \overline{\omega})$. □

Any trajectory off the steady state consequently must cycle around it (since it has to stay inside of an appropriate Goodwin cycle when it leaves the above depicted domain on its right-hand side). It is, however, not yet excluded that this occurs in an explosive fashion toward the boundaries of the domain depicted in Figure 5.3.

Assume now in addition that $\kappa_p \to 1$ if $\omega/x \to (y - \delta - t^n)/y$, so that there is a full cost-push effect of nominal wages with respect to the formation of the price rate of inflation if real wages tend to eliminate profit income. The $\dot{\omega} = 0$ isocline then tends to the horizontal line l^d/b as ω tends to this limit. In this case we furthermore can state the following result.

PROPOSITION 5.5 *The ω limit sets*[35] *of trajectories starting to the left of $(y - \delta - t^n)/yx$ are all compact, nonempty and do not contain the steady state (ω_0, l_0), so that by the Poincaré–Bendixson theorem*[36] *they must be closed orbits.*

Table 5.1 The set of parameters used for the simulations in Figure 5.5

$s_c = 0.8$	$\delta = 0.1$	$y = 1$	$x = 2$	$l^d = 0.5$	$n = 0.05$
$h_1 = 0.1$	$h_2 = \infty$	$i = 1$	$\beta_k = 1$		
$\beta_w = 1$	$\beta_p = 1$	$\kappa_w = \kappa_p = 0.5$		$\beta_{\pi_1} = 0$	$\beta_{\pi_2} = 0$
$\mu_0 = 0.05$	$\mu_2 = 0$	$t^n = 0.35$			

All trajectories that start to the left of $(y - \delta - t^n)/yx$ are thus attracted by some limit cycle within this set or are closed orbits themselves. This is illustrated by the simulation of the real cycle model displayed in Figure 5.5 and which is based on nonlinearities in the investment function and the Phillips curve mechanism of the type

$$i(\cdot) = \text{atan}(10\pi(\rho - r + \pi))/(10\pi),$$

$$X^w = \tan(1.25\pi(V-1))/(1.25\pi) \quad \text{for } V \geq 1,$$

$$X^w = \tan(2.5\pi(V-1))/(2.5\pi) \quad \text{for } V \leq 1,$$

and on the set of parameters displayed in Table 5.1.

The steady state of this real cycle model is disturbed at time $t = 1$ by a supply-side shock. Note here that the depicted limit cycle is based on the variables u, V of the Goodwin growth cycle model and that the range covered by the variation of goods market excess demand allows for four different states. Note furthermore that the loop showing up in the Phillips curve in the lower right-hand panel is clockwise and not counterclockwise as empirical observations have suggested.

Note that in the above we have not provided a complete proof of Proposition 5.5, since we have only conjectured in the present situation that all trajectories of this dynamical system can be continued without bound (and that they and their limit sets stay in the interior of the economically motivated rectangle depicted in Figure 5.3). The application of the Poincaré–Bendixson theorem is therefore not straightforward in the present situation. Such ambiguities can be avoided when the l^d/a curve can be shown to be (slightly) negatively sloped (as it is when we allow smooth factor substitution – see Chiarella and Flaschel (2000a, ch. 5)).

The limit cycle approach of Rose's (1967) employment cycle model thus also applies to the present context and could be further investigated as in Rose (1967). An important property of the above assumptions is that the dynamical behavior is thereby restricted to economically meaningful values of ω. Observe also that the problem encountered in Section 5.3 with respect to labor supply bottlenecks can now be completely avoided just by choosing the parameter b in the Phillips curve of Figure 5.2 such that $l^d / V_{\max} \leq l^d / b$ holds true.

We have so far treated only the case $\dot{K} = I$ (or $\hat{l} = -i(\cdot)$). The alternative case $\dot{K} = S$ (or $\hat{l} = n - s(\cdot)$) is similar and will give rise to the same results as $\hat{l} = -i(\cdot)$, since $n - s(\omega) = n - s_c(y - \delta - \omega l - t^n)$ is then of the same qualitative form as the function $-i(\omega)$. Of course, an appropriately chosen nonlinear $s(\cdot)$ function can also be used to investigate the dynamical behavior of (5.48) and (5.49) under such a modification.

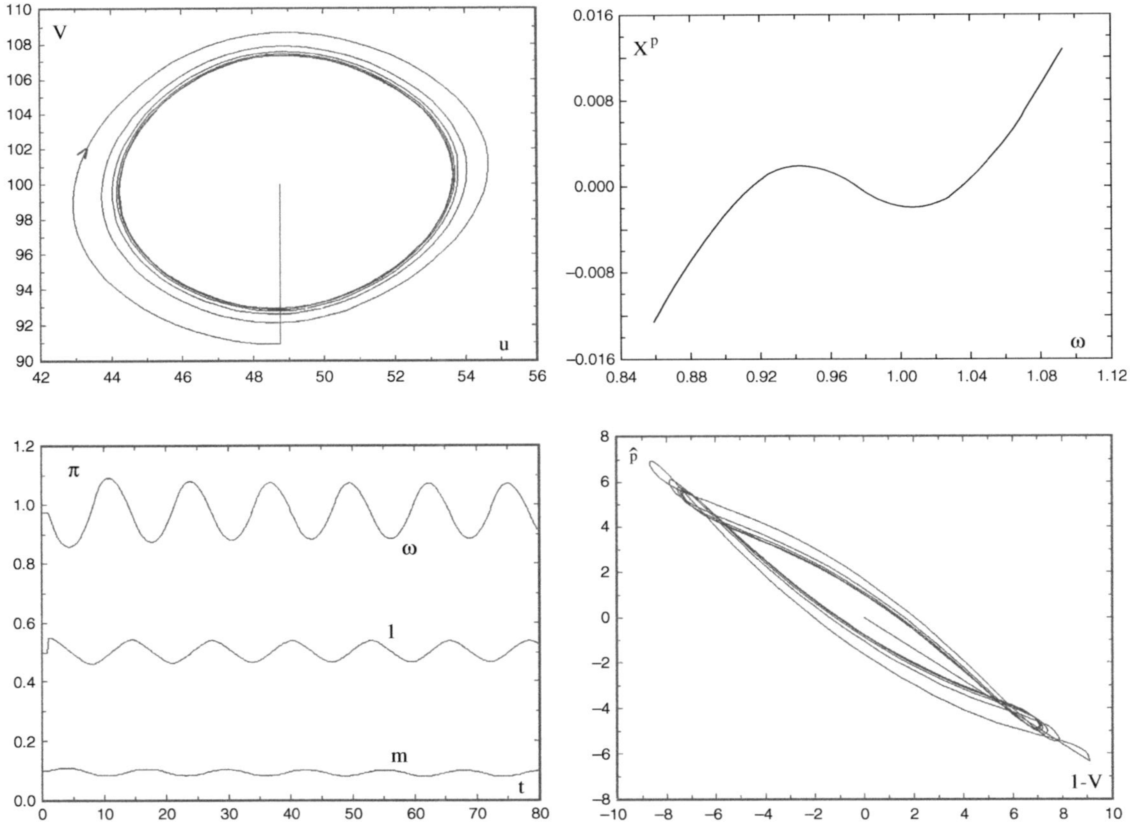

Figure 5.5 The real cycle of the Keynes–Wicksell model.

To sum up, we can conclude that the Rose extension introduces local instability into the Goodwin labor market dynamics, but also provides the means of establishing global stability, giving rise to a limit cycle result instead of the structurally unstable closed orbit structure of the Goodwin model. This is definitely an improvement over Goodwin's growth cycle result. The robustness of Rose's employment cycle will be further investigated in the following section.

5.6 Monetary growth cycles: a point of departure

Removing one further assumption, namely that concerning interest rate inflexibility in the real Goodwin/Rose growth cycle dynamics, we show in this section that the now integrated real and monetary dynamics will suppress the Rose employment (limit) cycle result with its instability of the steady state, if the flexibility of nominal interest rates becomes sufficiently high. This is mainly due to the Keynes effect, which, as has often been emphasized in static analysis, also fulfills its supposed stabilizing role in a 3D dynamic growth context. The resulting asymptotic stability of the steady state will, however, often rest nevertheless on cyclical adjustment patterns.

So far, we have only studied the cyclical properties of the real part of the model by making it independent of money market phenomena and expectations through appropriate assumptions on the interest rate elasticity of money demand, on the adjustment of expectations and on one further secondary assumption which taken together removed the influence of money and bonds (expressed per unit of capital value), that is, of the variables m, b from real wage dynamics and capital accumulation. In this section, we will now integrate the impact of the evolution of m on the real dynamics by allowing the interest rate r to fluctuate and by allowing to be positive the parameter μ_2, which describes the extent by which government expenditures are money-financed.

The assumptions $\beta_{\pi_2}=\infty$ ($\beta_{\pi_1}<\infty$) and $t^n=(T-rB)/K=$const. will, however, still be made in order to allow inflationary expectations to remain static at the steady-state value $\pi=\mu_0-n$ and, as always, for a treatment of the model where bonds can remain implicit. Medium-run adjustments in expectations will be considered in the next section.

The model to be investigated in this section is thus given by the 3D dynamical system[37]

$$\widehat{\omega}=\kappa[(1-\kappa_p)\beta_w(V-1)+(\kappa_w-1)\beta_p(i(\cdot)+n-s(\cdot))], \tag{5.50}$$

$$\widehat{V}=\widehat{K}(\cdot)-n, \tag{5.51}$$

$$\widehat{m}=\mu_0-\hat{p}(\cdot)-\widehat{K}(\cdot), \tag{5.52}$$

where

$$\widehat{K}(\cdot)=i(\cdot)+n \text{ or } s(\cdot),$$

$$i(\cdot)=i(y-\delta-\omega l^d-r+\mu_0-n),$$

$$
\begin{aligned}
s(\cdot) &= s_c(y - \delta - \omega l^d - t^n) - (g - t^n), \\
g &= t^n + \mu_2 m, \quad t^n = \text{const.}, \\
r &= r(m) = r_0 + (h_1 y - m)/h_2, \quad r' < 0, \\
\hat{p}(\cdot) &= \mu_0 - n + \kappa[\beta_p(i(\cdot) + n - s(\cdot)) + \kappa_p \beta_w (V - 1)].
\end{aligned}
$$

With respect to this model we are able to prove the following proposition, which asserts that flexibility of the nominal rate of interest of a sufficiently high degree will remove the Rose-type local instability from the real part of the model and thus also the possibility of it generating an employment limit cycle.

Proposition 5.6 *The steady state of the dynamical system (5.50)–(5.52) is locally asymptotically stable if* $-r'(m_0) = 1/h_2$ *is set sufficiently large.*

Proof: (For the case $\widehat{K} = i(\cdot) + n$.) For the Jacobian J of the dynamical system (5.50)–(5.52) at the steady state we obtain

$$
J = \begin{pmatrix}
\kappa(\kappa_w - 1)\beta_p l^d (s_c - i)\omega_0 & \kappa(1 - \kappa_p)\beta_w \omega_0 & \kappa(\kappa_w - 1)\beta_p(-ir' + \mu_2)\omega_0 \\
-il^d V_0 & 0 & -ir' V_0 \\
il^d V_0 - \kappa\beta_p(s_c - i)l^d m_0 & -\kappa\kappa_p\beta_w m_0 & ir' V_0 - \kappa\beta_p(-ir' + \mu_2)m_0
\end{pmatrix}.
$$

By means of the standard rules for the calculation of determinants, the determinant of J is easily shown to be equal to

$$
|J| = \begin{vmatrix}
\kappa(\kappa_w - 1)\beta_p(s_c - i)l^d \omega_0 & \kappa(1 - \kappa_p)\beta_w \omega_0 & \kappa(\kappa_w - 1)\beta_p(-ir' + \mu_2)\omega_0 \\
-il^d V_0 & 0 & -ir' V_0 \\
0 & -\kappa\kappa_p\beta_w m_0 - \dfrac{1 - \kappa_p}{1 - \kappa_w}\beta_w m_0 & 0
\end{vmatrix}
$$

$$
= \left(\kappa\kappa_p\beta_w m_0 + \kappa\frac{1 - \kappa_p}{1 - \kappa_w}\beta_w m_0\right)
\times \begin{vmatrix}
\kappa(\kappa_w - 1)\beta_p(s_c - i)l^d \omega_0 & \kappa(\kappa_w - 1)\beta_p(-ir' + \mu_2)\omega_0 \\
-il^d V_0 & -ir' V_0
\end{vmatrix}
$$

$$
= + \begin{vmatrix} - & - \\ - & + \end{vmatrix} < 0.
$$

This result also holds for $\mu_2 = 0$ and it is independent of the size of r'. This is the first of the four Routh–Hurwitz conditions (see Brock and Malliaris 1989,

p. 75ff.) which are necessary and sufficient for the local asymptotic stability of the steady state.

The next condition demands that the sum of the leading principal minors, $J_1 + J_2 + J_3$, of the above Jacobian must be positive. Owing to the 0 in the middle of the Jacobian J this positivity is obviously true for J_1 and J_3. For

$$J_2 = \begin{vmatrix} J_{11} & J_{13} \\ J_{31} & J_{33} \end{vmatrix}$$

we obtain

$$\begin{aligned} J_2 &= \begin{vmatrix} \kappa(\kappa_w - 1)\beta_p l^d (s_c - i)\omega_0 & \kappa(\kappa_w - 1)\beta_p(-ir' + \mu_2)\omega_0 \\ i l^d V_0 & i r' V_0 \end{vmatrix} \\ &= \begin{vmatrix} \kappa(\kappa_w - 1)\beta_p l^d \omega_0 & \kappa(\kappa_w - 1)\beta_p \mu_2 \omega_0 \\ i l^d V_0 & i r' V_0 \end{vmatrix} \\ &= \begin{vmatrix} - & - \\ + & - \end{vmatrix} > 0. \end{aligned}$$

This result also holds for $\mu_2 = 0$ and it is independent of the size of r'.

The third condition is trace $J < 0$. We calculate

$$\text{trace}\, J = \kappa(\kappa_w - 1)\beta_p l^d (s_c - i)\omega_0 + i r' V_0 - \kappa\beta_p(-ir' + \mu_2)m_0.$$

The condition trace $J < 0$ is obviously fulfilled when the Rose model is locally asymptotically stable ($i < s_c$) and it will always be fulfilled in the opposite case ($i > s_c$) if r' is chosen sufficiently large.

The final Routh–Hurwitz condition is $(-\text{trace}\, J)(J_1 + J_2 + J_3) + \det J > 0$. To see that this condition can be fulfilled for derivatives $r'(m_0)$ which are chosen sufficiently large in absolute value it suffices to note that $(-\text{trace}\, J)(J_1 + J_2 + J_3)$ is a quadratic function of r', whereas $\det J$ depends only linearly on it. The sign structure of trace J and J_1, J_2, J_3 we have discussed above then implies that b must become positive for sufficiently large values of $|r'|$. □

In the following proposition we establish that a limit cycle is born as $r'(m_0)$ decreases in value.

Proposition 5.7 *There exists exactly one value of $r'(m_0)$ (denoted $r'(m_0)^H$) such that the steady state is unstable for r' in $(r'(m_0)^H, 0)$ and stable in $(-\infty, r'(m_0)^H)$. At the value $r'(m_0)^H$ a Hopf bifurcation occurs, so that the stability proven for large $|r'(m_0|$ is lost in a cyclical fashion as $r'(m_0)$ increases across this bifurcation value.*

Proof: The proof of Proposition 5.6 has shown that we have for the quantities $a_1 = -\text{trace}\, J$, $a_2 = J_1 + J_2 + J_3$ and $a_3 = -\det J$ the relationships

$$\begin{aligned} a_1 &= \alpha_1 |r'(m_0)| + \beta_1, && (\alpha_1 > 0),\\ a_2 &= \alpha_2 |r'(m_0)| + \beta_2, && (\alpha_2 > 0),\\ a_3 &= \alpha_3 |r'(m_0)|, && (\alpha_3 > 0). \end{aligned}$$

The polynomial $b(|r'(m_0)|) = a_1(|r'(m_0)|)a_2(|r'(m_0)|) - a_3(|r'(m_0)|)$ must be quadratic and bear to the linear function $a_1(|r'(m_0)|)$ the relationship shown in Figure 5.6.

We know that there exists a unique $|r'(m_0)|$ where $a_1 = -\text{trace}\, J$ will be zero. It follows that b must be negative at this value of $|r'(m_0)|$, since $a_3 = -\det J$ is positive throughout. We thus get that a_1, a_2, a_3 and b must all be positive to the right of $|r'(m_0)^H|$ in Figure 5.6. This proves the first part of the proposition, since b cannot become positive again for lower $|r'(m_0)|$ before a_1 has turned negative.

The second part of this proposition can be proved as in the proof of a Hopf bifurcation for the general Tobin model considered in Benhabib and Miyao (1981). □

This last proposition tells us that at least in a certain neighborhood of $r'(m_0)^H$ the dynamical behavior of (5.50)–(5.52) must therefore be of a cyclical nature. We know furthermore from the preceding section that it is of this same kind also for values of $r'(m_0)$ sufficiently close to 0. It can therefore be expected that the model gives rise to monotonic adjustment paths to its steady state, if at all, only if $r'(m_0)$ is sufficiently close to $-\infty$.

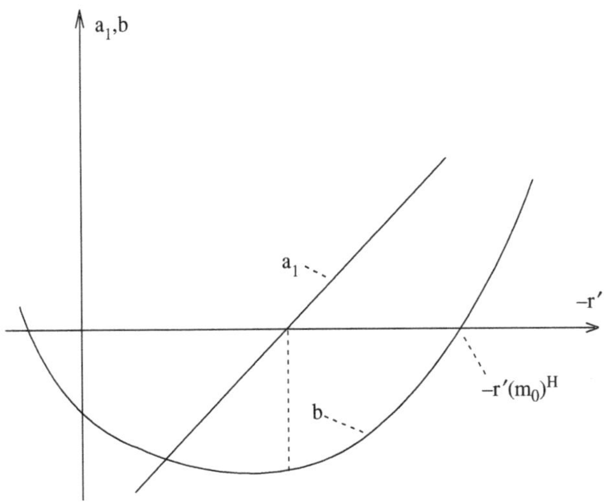

Figure 5.6 The graph of the two Routh–Hurwitz coefficients a_1 and b.

The proof of Propositions 5.6 and 5.7 for the case $\dot{K} = S$ is similar. The Hopf bifurcation theorem can furthermore also be applied to the parameters β_p, β_w and will give rise to similar propositions depending upon the influence of the real wage on excess demand in the market for goods.

In sum, we have so far found that money wage flexibility and interest rate flexibility work in favor of economic stability, while price flexibility generally works against it.

5.7 Expectations and the pure monetary cycle

Owing to our formulation of inflationary expectations (5.24) we have the choice between adaptive, regressive and myopic perfect foresight expectations (or a combination of these). As we shall see, regressive expectations preserve the stability properties of the model of the preceding section, while adaptively formed expectations when sufficiently fast can destabilize the dynamics through the working of the Mundell effect. Myopic perfect foresight expectations can be treated as the limit case of adaptive expectations and thus face the same instability problems as fast adaptive expectations. Furthermore there are economic reasons why this situation of myopic perfect foresight should be excluded from our models in their present formulation and the analysis should be restricted to situations where both forward- and backward-looking behavior prevail.

After having considered (in the following discussion) various special cases of expectations formation we shall then apply the forward- and backward-looking expectations mechanism to an investigation of the medium run. In this medium run, factor growth is ignored on the side of production and real wage changes are suppressed by means of the two assumptions $\beta_w = 0, \kappa_w = 1$, that is, nominal wages are of an extremely sluggish type with respect to demand pressure on the labor market and the actual rate of inflation has a full impact effect on nominal wage formation. These assumptions result in a monetary dynamics subsector of the Cagan type, that is, of the isolated dynamic interaction between the two variables m, π. Such a system of monetary dynamics has been often studied in the framework of pure money market adjustments under adaptive expectations as well as under perfect foresight.[38] Here however we shall consider the product market and its adjustments instead and the influence of an additional variable, the nominal rate of interest, which is determined by money market equilibrium. This situation will give rise to a pure monetary limit cycle in the above two variables if the nonlinear investment function of Section 5.4 is again assumed to apply.

Because of the applicability of the assumption for the generation of real limit cycles (see Figure 5.4) also to the generation of monetary cycles it is obvious that these two cycle models can be coupled with each other if the above two assumptions on β_w, κ_w are relaxed. This coupling of the real with monetary cycles will be briefly investigated in Section 5.8 by means of computer simulations.

Our analysis in this section proceeds by analyzing various limiting cases of the expectations mechanism and the limiting case of infinite speed of price adjustment.

We first consider regressive expectations by setting $\beta_{\pi_1} = 0, \beta_{\pi_2} < \infty$. In the case of purely regressive expectations, the 3×3 matrix J in the proof of Proposition 5.6 is augmented by a fourth column and a fourth row, the latter being represented by

$$(0 \quad 0 \quad 0 \quad -\beta_{\pi_2}),$$

since the new fourth dynamical law is here simply given by

$$\dot{\pi} = \beta_{\pi_2}(\mu_0 - n - \pi).$$

We thus can state the following result.

PROPOSITION 5.8 *The local stability properties of the 4D dynamical system under regressive expectations are the same as those of the dynamical system (5.50)–(5.52) considered in Section 5.6*

Assuming purely regressive expectations thus does not add very much to the analysis of Section 5.6, the main difference being that inflationary expectations now slowly adjust to any new steady-state value of $\mu_0 - n$, while they immediately jump to it in the cases we investigated previously.

We consider next adaptive expectations by setting $\beta_{\pi_2} = 0, \beta_{\pi_1} < \infty$. In the case of adaptive expectations the resulting 4D dynamical system becomes fully interdependent, since at least the evolution of ω and m depends on π and that of π on the evolution of all three other dynamic variables. The evolution of inflationary expectations π is now determined by

$$\dot{\pi} = \beta_{\pi_1}(\hat{p} - \pi),$$

where $\hat{p} = \pi + \kappa[\beta_p i(\cdot) + n - s(\cdot)) + \kappa_p \beta_w (V - 1)]$. This gives for the dependence of π on itself the expression

$$\frac{\partial \dot{\pi}}{\partial \pi} = \beta_{\pi_1} \kappa \beta_p i' > 0,$$

since $i(\cdot)$ (but not $s(\cdot)$) depends positively on inflationary expectations π. This expression ($= J_{44}$ of the Jacobian of this extended dynamical system) shows that the model of Section 5.6 can always be made locally unstable by choosing the parameter β_{π_1} sufficiently high. As is known from other models we here recover the result that adaptive expectations create, at least locally, explosive behavior if they become sufficiently fast. On the basis of the foregoing observations we state our next result.

PROPOSITION 5.9 *The trace of the Jacobian matrix J can be made as positive as desired by choosing the adjustment parameter β_{π_1} sufficiently large.*

We conjecture that the loss of stability that comes about by increasing β_{π_1} from 0 to $+\infty$ will occur again in a cyclical fashion by means of a Hopf bifurcation, as was the case in the previous section.[39]

Next we consider myopic perfect foresight by setting $\beta_{\pi_2}=0, \beta_{\pi_1}=\infty$. The fact that the trace of J approaches $+\infty$ for $\beta_{\pi_1}\to\infty$ in the case of adaptive expectations just considered indicates that the limit case $\beta_{\pi_1}=\infty$, that is, $\pi=\hat{p}$, may be of a problematic nature. In this case, the two Phillips-type adjustment mechanisms (5.22) and (5.23) of our general framework reduce to

$$\widehat{\omega}=\beta_w(V-1), \tag{5.53}$$

$$\kappa_p\widehat{\omega}=-\beta_p((I-S)/K), \tag{5.54}$$

and thus give rise to two different and seemingly contradictory real wage dynamics if $\kappa_p>0$ and $\beta_p<\infty$ hold true, unless labor market disequilibrium $V-1$ and goods market disequilibrium are always proportional to each other by means of the factor $-\beta_p/(\beta_w\kappa_p)$. Under this side condition the model is of the form (in the case $\dot{K}=I$)

$$\widehat{\omega}=\beta_w(V-1), \tag{5.55}$$

$$\widehat{V}=i(\rho(\omega)-r(m)+\hat{p}), \tag{5.56}$$

$$\widehat{m}=\mu_0-\hat{p}-i(\rho(\omega)-r(m)+\hat{p})-n, \tag{5.57}$$

where $\hat{p}$ has to be calculated from

$$\kappa_p\beta_w(V-1)=-\beta_p[i(\rho(\omega)-r(m)+\hat{p})+n - s_c(y-\delta-\omega l^d-t^n)+\mu_2 m].$$

This gives for $\hat{p}$ the expression

$$\hat{p}=[-\kappa_p(\beta_w/\beta_p)(V-1)+s_c(y-\delta-\omega l^d-t^n)-\mu_2 m-n]/i - \rho(\omega)+r(m). \tag{5.58}$$

In the special case $\kappa_p=0$[40] (and $\mu_2=0$) which implies $I=S$ or $i(\cdot)+n=s(\cdot)$ this determination of the rate of inflation $\hat{p}$ reduces to[41]

$$\hat{p}=[s_c(y-\delta-\omega l^d-t^n)-n]/i-\rho(\omega)+r(m). \tag{5.59}$$

We then get for the second of the above three laws of motion

$$\widehat{V}=s_c(y-\delta-\omega l^d-t^n)-n, \tag{5.60}$$

and thus again the simple growth cycle model (which we have investigated in Section 5.4) as far as the real dynamics (ω, V) is concerned. For the third law of motion, which does not feed back into the real part of the model under the circumstances assumed here, we furthermore obtain

$$\widehat{m} = \widehat{m}(\omega, V, m) \quad \text{with } \widehat{m}_m > 0, \tag{5.61}$$

which gives rise to the saddle-point instability situation to which the Sargent and Wallace (1973) jump variable methodology is then generally applied in the literature.

Yet, the question remains, whether the adaptive expectations case should not be reformulated first in such a way that it gives rise to a viable dynamics also in the case of a fast adjustment of adaptive expectations. Otherwise, there is the danger that the perfect foresight limit just formally inherits economically implausible reaction patterns of the adaptive expectations case which are in the case of myopic perfect foresight then hidden in the algebraic conditions to which the equation $\pi = \hat{p}$ gives rise. In this regard a plausible alternative to the conventional saddle-path procedure can be obtained by nonlinear modifications of the adaptive case and the consequent limit cycle and limit limit cycle results in the simple Cagan framework of Sargent and Wallace (1973) as expounded by Chiarella (1986), Chiarella (1990a) and Flaschel and Sethi (1999).

We finally consider forward- and backward-looking expectations by choosing $\beta_{\pi_1} \in (0, \infty), \beta_{\pi_2} \in (0, \infty)$. This case formally represents the summation of the case of adaptive and regressive expectations and it thus inherits the stability and instability features of its two borderline cases that we have just discussed. Note here that this combined situation can also be expressed as

$$\dot{\pi} = (\beta_{\pi_1} + \beta_{\pi_2})[\alpha\hat{p} + (1-\alpha)(\mu_0 - n) - \pi], \quad \alpha = \frac{\beta_{\pi_1}}{\beta_{\pi_1} + \beta_{\pi_2}}. \tag{5.62}$$

This form states that a certain weighted average of the currently observed rate of inflation and of the future steady-state rate is the measure according to which the expected medium-run rate of inflation is changed in an adaptive fashion.[42]

Note also that the actual rate $\hat{p}$ can be interpreted as myopically forward- as well as backward-looking as long as the adjustment speed β_p of prices p stays finite, that is, as long as prices are a differentiable function of time. This means that the above formula can also be interpreted as being forward-looking in both of its measures of the short and the long run. Again it then means that expected medium-run inflation is changed in the direction of an average of these two measures of inflation.

Stressing the present mixed case of expectation formation as the truly general one, thus means that we insist on a proper combination of short-run and long-run information in the determination of the evolution of the expected rate of inflation that is used in our expressions for the formation of planned investment, wages as well as prices. We recall that these are given by

$$i(\cdot) = i(\rho(\omega) - (r - \pi)),$$

$$\widehat{w} = \beta_w(\cdot) + \kappa_w \hat{p} + (1-\kappa_w)\pi = \pi + \beta_w(\cdot) + \kappa_w(\hat{p} - \pi),$$
$$\hat{p} = \beta_p(\cdot) + \kappa_p \widehat{w} + (1-\kappa_p)\pi = \pi + \beta_p(\cdot) + \kappa_p(\widehat{w} - \pi).$$

Myopic perfect foresight may be considered as a limiting case in the last two equations, but should not be identified with the rate π as in the one-sided myopic perfect foresight case considered above since this eliminates an important economic distinction in the present model (between the rates $\hat{p}$ and π) and also introduces strange implications as we have seen above (see equations (5.53) and (5.54)). Corresponding to the medium-run character of the rate π one has to interpret the measure M of the money supply in a broader sense in order to relate the determination of the nominal rate of interest also to the medium run.

We do not consider in this book the extension just discussed in order to ensure that the dynamical system brought about by the wage–price sector not be of too high a dimension. Improvements in the formulation of this sector would therefore still be helpful in showing that the situation where only myopic perfect foresight prevails (and nothing else) should be considered as too exceptional for a representation of the wage–price dynamics of complete models of monetary growth.

Keynes–Wicksell models have not really been considered in the literature on descriptive monetary macrodynamics, even on the textbook level. Their limit case $\beta_p = \infty$ ($I = S$), which is usually based on a neoclassical production function (see Chiarella and Flaschel 2000a, sec. 5.3), is however generally taken to represent the Keynesian variant of the neoclassical synthesis and thus viewed as underlying the widely accepted Keynesian AD–AS formulation of monetary growth dynamics as discussed by (Sargent 1987, ch. 5) for example. We here show that the resulting model is nevertheless a purely supply-side model of monetary growth and thus demonstrate that the label "Keynesian" for this type of growth dynamics is totally misleading. There in fact does not yet exist a proper formulation of "Keynesian" monetary growth dynamics in all those model variants that start from Patinkin's (1965) neoclassical synthesis in their formulation of monetary growth. Such models are generally developed by simply adding nominal wage rigidity to the Patinkin formulation of the full employment case.

As just stated, our general framework (5.1)–(5.24) of Keynes–Wicksell type has remained alive mostly through textbook presentations of the special case $\beta_p = \infty$ of AD–AS growth, that is, by the case where goods market equilibrium prevails at all moments of time. This model is usually characterized as representing "Keynesian dynamics" – see Turnovsky (1977, ch. 8), Turnovsky (1977, ch. 2) or Sargent (1987, ch. V) for example. By assuming goods market equilibrium throughout, the Wicksellian theory of inflation is only present in the background of the model and, if at all, only considered explicitly as an ultra-short-run adjustment mechanism as in Sargent (1987, ch. 2).

It is obvious from our above discussion of the case of myopic perfect foresight that the model is then (for $\mu_2 = 0$) of a purely classical Goodwin growth cycle type in the case of market clearing prices p ($\beta_p = \infty$), since we then simply get as the dynamics for the real sector the two differential equations

$$\widehat{\omega} = \beta_w(V-1),$$
$$\widehat{V} = s_c(y-\delta-\omega l^d - t^n), \quad l^d = y/x,$$

whereas for the monetary part of the model we obtain by way of the IS–LM equilibrium conditions the single nonautonomous differential equation

$$\hat{m}(t) = -r(m(t)) + f(t),$$

where $f(t)$ collects the dynamics of the predetermined real variables involved in the IS–LM equations.

An infinite adjustment speed of the price level with respect to (potential) goods market disequilibrium combined with myopic perfect foresight thus gives rise to the same situation as we obtained above for the case where the goods market was forced into equilibrium by assuming $\kappa_p = 0$ and myopic perfect foresight. In both cases we have goods market equilibrium on the basis of a full utilization of the capital stock at each moment in time so that here nothing is left from the Keynes part of this model type. This issue is discussed further in Chiarella and Flaschel (2000a, ch. 5).

This degeneracy of the model for an infinite adjustment speed of the price level p is less obvious in the model with adaptively formed expectations that in the case[43] $\kappa_w = 0$ is described by the differential equations

$$\widehat{\omega} = \beta_w(V-1) - (\hat{p} - \pi),$$
$$\widehat{V} = i(\rho(\omega) - r + \pi),$$
$$\dot{\pi} = \beta_\pi(\hat{p} - \pi),$$

where r and $\hat{p}$ have to be determined from the equations for IS–LM equilibrium. The classical nature of this particular IS–LM equilibrium version of the Keynes–Wicksell model also becomes obvious however when it is realized that such models always assume that the capital stock is fully utilized. In the present case this then gives rise to the equations (we continue to assume that $\mu_2 = 0$)

$$i(\rho(\omega) - r + \pi) + n = s_c(y - \delta - \omega l^d - t^n) \quad (y, l^d = \text{const.}),$$
$$m = h_1 y + h_2(r_0 - r) \quad (y = \text{const.}),$$

the first of which gives the rate of interest r as a function of the real wage ω and expected inflation π ($r = r(\omega, \pi)$), while the second one then determines on this basis real balances per capital m (and thus implicitly the price level p and its rate of change $\hat{p}$).

The foregoing analysis is however a very Friedmanian usage of the IS–LM block of such a monetary growth model. It makes the above dynamical system a 3D one, since both r and $\hat{p}$ can be expressed solely as functions of ω, V and π.

The general conclusion here is that the IS–LM equilibrium subcases of our general Keynes–Wicksell model do not become strictly Keynesian models simply by assuming $I = S$ in place of $I \neq S$, but instead owe their characteristic features still to the classical nature of this Keynes–Wicksell approach to economic dynamics. This topic is discussed in Chiarella and Flaschel (2000a, sec. 5.3).

For the remainder of this section we assume on the basis of the above discussion that the parameter values $\beta_p, \beta_{\pi_1}, \beta_{\pi_2}$ are all positive and finite. We thus exclude the one-sided cases we have considered above from the following discussion of the interaction of expectations first with the price dynamics and then with the real cycle of the model. We here also assume $\mu_2 = \mu_0 = n$ for reasons of simplicity.

In order to derive the pure form of the monetary cycle in this case we shall make the following two sets of assumptions:

(i) $\beta_w = 0, \kappa_w = 1$ so that the real wage is constant and set equal to its steady-state value.
(ii) $\dot{K} = n$ ($\dot{L} = n$) in which case the additional capacity effects of investment that are caused by profitability differentials (but not its trend component) are suppressed on the supply side of the model (and only there). The labor intensity $l = L/K$ thus is a constant in the following and is set equal to its steady-state value l^d in addition.

Both sets of assumptions can be justified in the usual way by stating that the intent of the present investigation is confined to some sort of pure medium-run analysis. They here simply serve to reduce the dimension of the above considered dynamical system by two to a 2D one in the variables m and π. The resulting dynamical system reads[44]

$$\hat{m} = \mu_0 - n - \pi - \kappa\beta_p(i(\cdot) + n - s(\cdot)), \tag{5.63}$$

$$\dot{\pi} = \beta_{\pi_1}\kappa\beta_p(i(\cdot) + n - s(\cdot)) + \beta_{\pi_2}(\mu_0 - n - \pi), \tag{5.64}$$

where

$$i(\cdot) + n - s(\cdot) = i(\bar{\rho} - r(m) + \pi) + n - s_c(\bar{\rho} - t^n) + nm = g(m, \pi),$$

with $g_m > 0$, $g_\pi > 0$.[45]

The isoclines $\dot{m} = 0, \dot{\pi} = 0$ of the above 2D dynamical system are implicitly defined by

$$0 = \mu_0 - n - \pi - \kappa\beta_p g(m, \pi), \tag{5.65}$$

$$0 = \beta_{\pi_1}\kappa\beta_p g(m, \pi) + \beta_{\pi_2}(\mu_0 - n - \pi). \tag{5.66}$$

Equations (5.65) and (5.66) are globally well-defined functions m of π. The function defined by (5.65) has slope

$$m'(\pi) = -\frac{\kappa\beta_p g_\pi + 1}{\kappa\beta_p g_m}.$$

On the other hand the function defined by (5.66) has slope

$$m'(\pi) = \frac{\beta_{\pi_2} - \beta_{\pi_1}\kappa\beta_p g_\pi}{\beta_{\pi_1}\kappa\beta_p g_m}.$$

These two expressions immediately show that the slope of the first isocline is always negative and smaller than the slope of the second isocline. The latter slope is positive far off the steady state (for positive values of the parameter β_{π_2}), but may become negative in a certain neighborhood of the steady state if a nonlinear shape for the investment function is assumed as in Section 5.5 (see Figure 5.4) and if the sizes of the various adjustment speeds are chosen appropriately. This follows immediately from the relationship $g_\pi = i'(\cdot)$ and the fact that the slope of the investment function becomes zero far off the steady state by assumption.

The phase portrait of the above dynamics of dimension two may therefore appear as in Figure 5.7. Such a phase portrait can be easily tailored for an application of the Poincaré–Bendixson theorem such that the nonnegativity of the

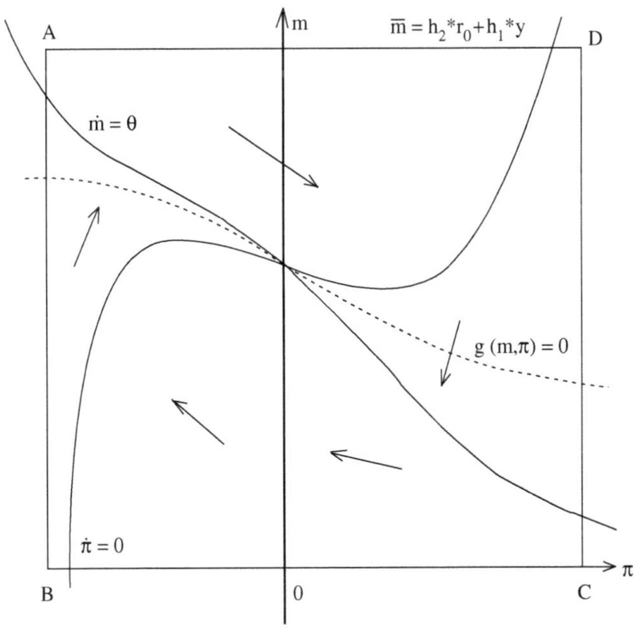

Figure 5.7 The phase diagram of the pure monetary cycle.

nominal rate of interest is assured.[46] To this end one only has to choose the parameter β_{π_2} sufficiently large so that the isocline $\dot{\pi} = 0$ cuts the horizontal parts of the box (the position of the other isocline is independent of this parameter).

The derivation of limit cycle results is therefore much easier (in the present purely monetary situation) than in the case of the real cycle considered in Section 5.4, but it obeys the same principles as were used there to obtain such a result. Figure 5.8 shows a simulation of this application of the Poincaré–Bendixson theorem. Note that the excess demand contour shown in Figure 5.8 (top right) is now strictly decreasing, since the savings component in the excess demand function is constant here. The data for this simulation are displayed in Table 5.2.

5.8 The real and the monetary cycle in interaction

We have considered in Section 5.5 the local Rose-type instability that is caused by a negative dependence of goods market disequilibrium on the real wage ($i > s_c$) which, when coupled with a sufficient strength of speed of adjustment of prices, gives rise to a positive dependence of the time rate of change of real wages on their level. Let us call this situation, in which $\hat{p}'(\omega) > 0$, a positive Rose effect for simplicity. In addition, we have investigated above the local instability of the pure monetary mechanism that is caused by the positive Mundell effect in the investment function ($\hat{p}'(\pi) > 0$). These two destabilizing mechanisms, and the ways in which we limited their potential for instability, will be integrated in this section by allowing for their full dynamic interaction in four dimensions.

Before we turn to this topic let us briefly explain why Proposition 5.6 (where we had $\beta_\pi = 0$) must also hold true for all $\beta_\pi > 0$ that are chosen sufficiently small. This result follows as a result of the following three observations: (i) the 4D situation with $\beta_\pi = 0$ applied to this proposition exhibits three eigenvalues with negative real parts and one further eigenvalue which is zero; (ii) the determinant of the Jacobian at the steady state of the dynamics (the product of the eigenvalues) is positive for all $\beta_\pi > 0$; and (iii) eigenvalues depend continuously on the parameters of the dynamics. The case $\beta_\pi > 0$ and sufficiently small is therefore characterized by at most two complex eigenvalues with negative real parts and one negative eigenvalue, as in the situation described in Proposition 5.6, and one further negative eigenvalue which is close to zero.

It is easy to show in addition that the stability just demonstrated must be lost if the parameter β_π is made sufficiently large (since $J_{44} > 0$ is thereby made the dominant expression in the trace of the matrix J). Since the determinant of the Jacobian at the steady state is always positive we in addition know that this loss of stability will occur by way of a Hopf bifurcation, that is, by way of the "death" of an unstable limit cycle or by way of the "birth" of a stable limit cycle. From the local perspective we therefore know that the 4D dynamics exhibits cyclical behavior at least for a certain range of values of the parameter β_π.

In Figures 5.5 and 5.8 we have furthermore considered the real cycle and the monetary cycle (each in two dimensions) from a global perspective by adding

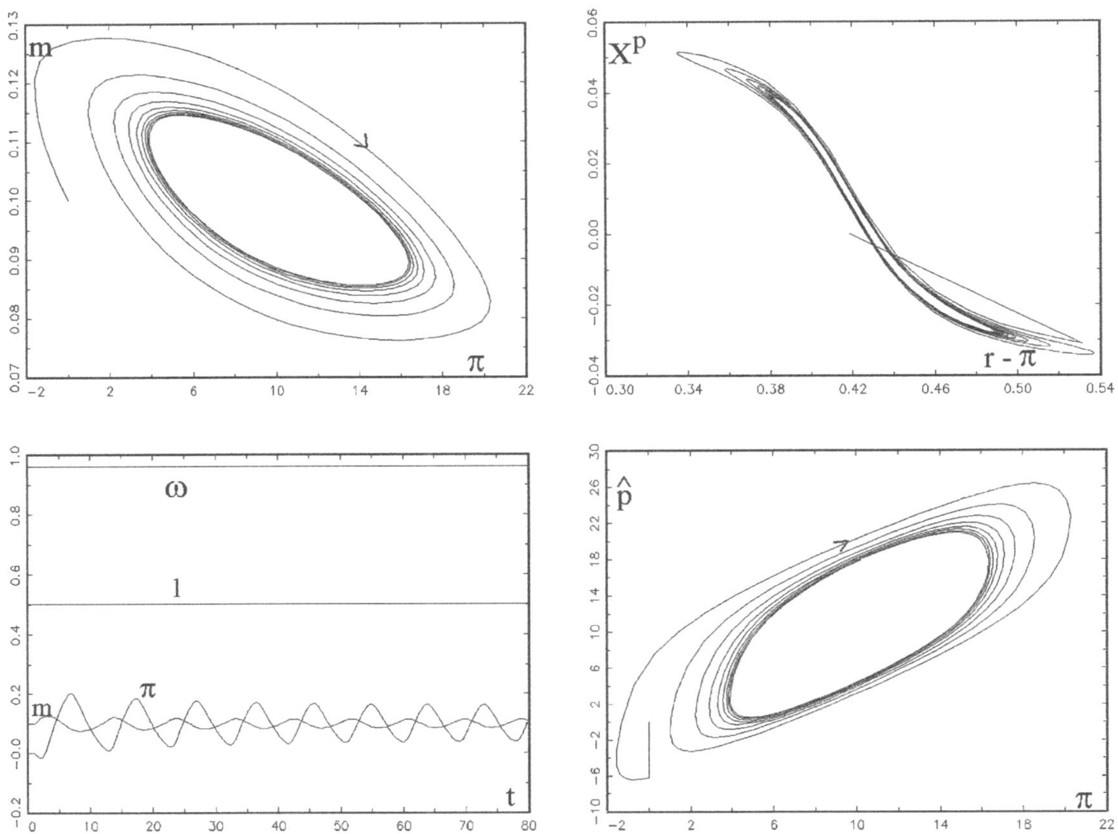

Figure 5.8 A simulation of the pure monetary limit cycle.

Table 5.2 The set of parameters used to simulate Figure 5.8

$s_c = 0.8$	$\delta = 0.1$	$y = 1$	$x = 2$	$l^d = 0.5$	$n = 0.05$
$h_1 = 0.1$	$h_2 = 0.2$	$i = 1$	$\beta_k = 1$		
$\beta_w = 0$	$\beta_p = 1$	$\kappa_w = 1$	$\kappa_p = 0.5$		
$\beta_{\pi_1} = 0.6$	$\beta_{\pi_2} = 0.15$				
$\mu_0 = \mu_2 = 0.05$	$\beta_m = \beta_g = 0$	$t^n = 0.35$			

a typical nonlinearity to the investment function of the model. This allowed us to apply the Poincaré–Bendixson theorem to these two situations and to conclude that there will be persistent fluctuations in the real and the monetary parts of the model whenever its steady state is locally unstable and that the two submodels are viable ones in a certain domain of their state variables.

Since these two cycle mechanisms have been based on the same nonlinearity (in the investment function) we are interested in studying how they interact on the basis of this viability generating nonlinearity. For the moment this can however only be answered by means of numerical investigations, an example of which is presented in what follows.[47]

The following simulation displayed in Figure 5.9 makes use of a nonlinear investment function given by

$$i(\cdot) = \text{atan}(10\pi(\rho - r + \pi))/(10\pi),$$

which has the shape discussed in Section 5.5. For the Phillips curve we take the asymmetric shape given by

$$X^w = \tan(1.25\pi(V-1))/(1.25\pi) \quad \text{for } V \geq 1,$$
$$X^w = \tan(2.5\pi(V-1))/(2.5\pi) \quad \text{for } V \leq 1.$$

The parameter values for the simulation are set out in Table 5.3.

The steady state of this economy is disturbed at time $t = 1$ by a labor supply shock. As can be seen from Figure 5.9, the real cycle and the monetary one interact with each other and generate superimposed fluctuations of a limit cycle type, with the monetary cycle being faster than the real one.

Chiarella and Flaschel (1996b) show that more complex interactions between the real and the monetary cycle of this chapter are possible. Their simulations indicate that the interaction of the two cycle generating mechanisms may produce interesting phenomena, though not yet complex dynamics.

5.9 Conclusions

This section has made use of a general model of Keynes–Wicksell type and shown how well-known models of cycles and growth can be considered as special cases of this prototype model.

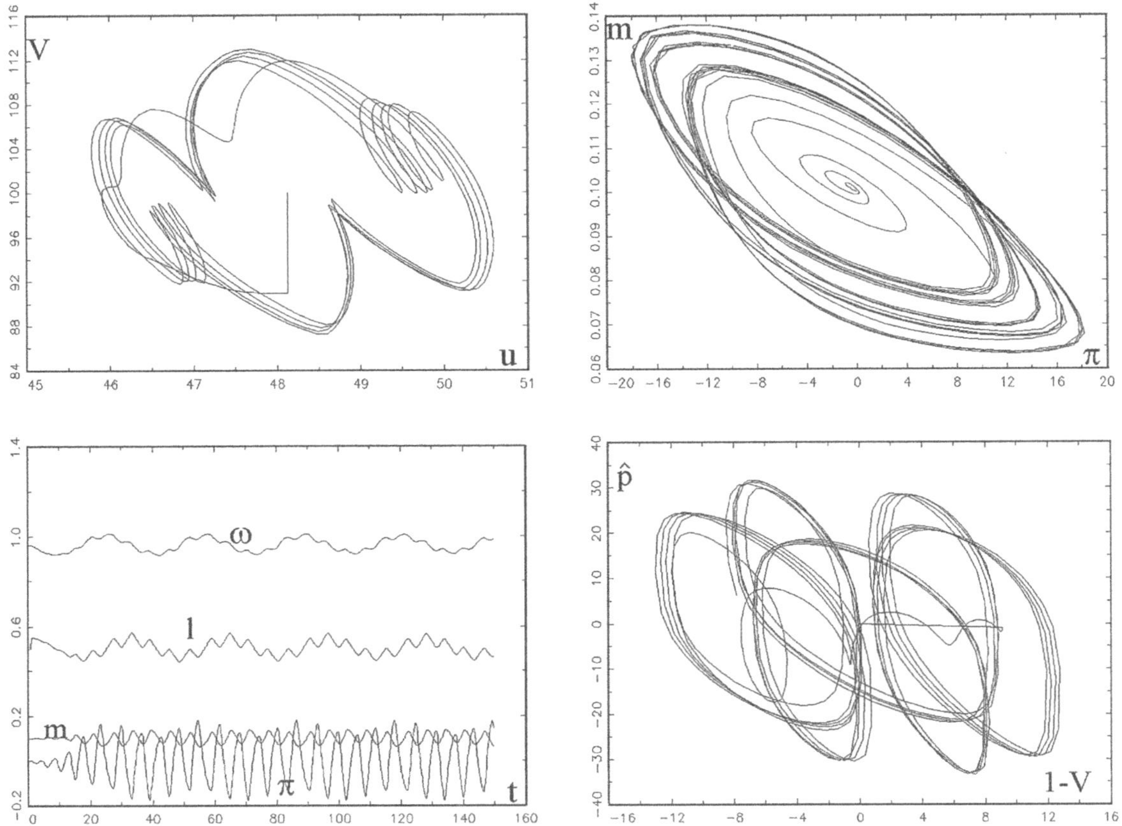

Figure 5.9 Coupled real and monetary oscillators: step length $h = 0.01$.

Table 5.3 The set of parameters used to simulate Figure 5.9

$s_c = 0.8$	$\delta = 0.1$	$y = 1$	$x = 2$	$l^d = 0.5$	$n = 0.05$
$h_1 = 0.1$	$h_2 = 0.2$	$i = 1$			
$\beta_k = 1$	$\beta_w = 0.1$	$\beta_p = 2$	$\beta_{\pi_1} = 0.9$	$\beta_{\pi_2} = 0.4$	$\beta_m = \beta_g = 0$
$\kappa_w = 0.95$	$\kappa_p = 0.5$				
$\mu_0 = \mu_2 = 0.05$	$t^n = 0.35$				

The general Keynes–Wicksell prototype model encompasses Goodwin's classical growth cycle and Rose's Keynesian employment cycle models. Here we have focused on the simple case of fixed proportions technology but have referred the reader to the book by Chiarella and Flaschel (2000a) for a more complete discussion of what is involved if one wishes to relax this assumption, but basically it is not as restrictive as one might first believe.

The classical nature of model has derived mainly from the fact that output is determined through supply-side conditions. The Keynesian IS–LM (dis)equilibrium part of the model only serves to determine the rate of inflation that feeds back to the real part of model via real wage dynamics, expectations and the real rate of interest.

6 Interacting two-country business fluctuations

6.1 Introduction

In this chapter[1] we reformulate and extend the analysis of small open economies of Asada *et al.* (2003a, chs. 8–10) toward some initial theoretical considerations and some numerical explorations of the case of two interacting large open economies like Euroland and the USA. However, we shall here reconsider the primarily simplified, compared to the 14-dimensional (14D) two-country Keynes–Metzler–Goodwin (KMG) dynamics of Asada *et al.* (2003a, ch. 10), only ten-dimensional (10D) open Keynes–Wicksell–Goodwin (KWG) growth and inflation dynamics.[2] The results obtained in this chapter still represent work in progress and thus surely need extension in order to truly judge the potential of the proposed model type for a discussion of the international transmission of the business cycle through positive or negative phase synchronization and other important topics of the literature on coupled oscillators of economic origin.[3]

Analytical propositions are indeed obtained much more easily in the KWG case than in the case of two interacting KMG economies, since in the two-country case we can indeed then economize on four laws of motion (describing the quantity adjustments in the two open KMG economies) which reduces the dimension of the considered dynamics from 14D to 10D. The economically more convincing KMG approach with its less than full capacity growth considerations is considerably more difficult to analyze analytically and is therefore excluded from consideration here. From the economic perspective we thus concentrate on the generation and transmission of international inflation by means of the KWG case and do not yet really consider Keynesian quantity driven business cycle dynamics and their transmission throughout the world economy.

This chapter first investigates the interaction of two monetary growth models of the KWG inflation dynamics type, which when assumed as closed would each generate intrinsically nonlinear dynamics of dimension four of the kind that has been investigated in detail in Chiarella and Flaschel (2000a, ch. 3) for the closed-economy case.[4] When there is trade in goods and financial assets between them, as in the Dornbusch (1976) model of overshooting exchange rate dynamics, KWG type models are coupled by way of the 2D dynamics of expected and actual exchange rate depreciation that lead to nonlinear dynamics of dimension ten. We derive local stability conditions for these dynamics and show that there exist a variety of situations where Hopf bifurcations will occur, giving rise to the local birth or death of stable or unstable limit cycles. Furthermore extrinsic nonlinearities are then introduced to limit the trajectories of the dynamics from a global point of view in the numerical analysis of this chapter. In this way limit cycles and more complex types of attractors are generated that can exhibit the co-movements typical of national business cycles (so-called 'phase locking'), but also the counter-movements typical of such cycles, in both cases primarily with respect to inflation dynamics.

It has been shown in Chiarella and Flaschel (2000a) that the supply side oriented KWG approach may be considered as a reasonable simplification of the demand side-oriented KMG approach (where prices and quantities both adjust according to demand conditions on the market for goods) if attention is restricted to topics such as income distribution and inflation, since in such situations it provides a pragmatic shortcut for the feedbacks that go from IS disequilibrium to its impact on wage and price inflation. The advantage of the KWG approach is that it reduces the number of laws of motion needed to describe a monetary growth model of the Keynesian variety, by restricting the adjustment processes considered to the dynamics of the real wage, to savings- or investment-driven capital stock growth, the law of motion for real balances (representing inflationary forces) and the one for inflationary expectations. The consideration of only these state variables simplifies the stability analysis of the closed economy case considerably. In a similar fashion it allows us to establish situations of local asymptotic stability for the case of two interacting KWG economies by first starting from a weak coupling of the two considered economies. Thereafter, a host of situations can be provided where the economies lose their asymptotic stability (by way of Hopf bifurcations, since it can in particular be shown that the system's determinant has a positive sign throughout). Of course, global stability properties have to be studied numerically since the dynamical system is of too high a dimension to allow for global analytical results.

In Section 6.2 the coupled two-country KWG dynamics is introduced and discussed on the extensive-form level, by means of a subdivision into nine modules describing the behavioral equations, the laws of motion and the identities or budget equations of the model. Section 6.3 then derives their intensive form representation on the basis of certain simplifying assumptions. In Section 6.4 we present the uniquely determined steady-state solution of the dynamics and discuss in a mathematically informal way its stability properties, concerning asymptotic stability and the loss of this stability by way of super- or subcritical Hopf bifurcations. Rigorous stability proofs that follow the methodology applied here (of starting from an appropriate 3D dynamical subsystem and enlarging it in a feedback guided and systematic way to its full dimension by making certain adjustment speeds – formerly set equal to zero – slightly positive) are provided in Asada *et al.* (2003a, ch. 10). Section 6.5 explores numerically a variety of situations of interacting real and financial cycles of the KWG type, where the steady state is locally repelling, but where the overall dynamics are bounded in an economically meaningful domain by means of a kinked money wage Phillips curve, with downward rigidity of the money wage, but with its upward flexibility of the usual type. Section 6.6 concludes.

6.2 Two interacting Keynes–Wicksell–Goodwin economies

In this section we introduce for the KWG approach to open economies, the case of two large open economies that are interacting with each other through trade in goods as well as financial assets and the resulting net interest flows. The KWG approach of this chapter to the formulation of two-country monetary macrodynamics is not yet a complete description of such a two-country world. This holds, in particular, since the allocation and accumulation of domestic and foreign bonds is not completely specified. We make some convenient technical assumptions that will ensure that the accumulation of internationally traded bonds does not feed back into the core 10D dynamics of the model and may thus be neglected for the time being. Note furthermore that the following presentations of the equations of the model involve many accounting identities that are here simply presented to ease and supplement the understanding of the model. They are however of no importance for the dynamical equations that result from this model (four for each country and two for their interconnection) that will be analyzed in this chapter from a theoretical as well as from a numerical point of view. Note finally that we use linear equations to model behavioral relationships as often as this is possible in order to have a model with only intrinsic nonlinearities as a starting point of our investigations. Extrinsic nonlinearities based for example on intertemporal constraints, changing adjustment behavior and the like will be introduced in future extensions of the model type considered here. One such extrinsic nonlinearity is discussed in Section 6.5.

In the model presented here we have chosen the units of measurement such that domestic expressions are in terms of the domestic good or the domestic currency, and foreign country expressions in terms of the commodity produced by the foreign country (or – if nominal – in the foreign currency) as far as this has been possible. For the sake of concreteness, we shall refer to the domestic and foreign economies as "Euroland" and the 'USA' with their currencies euro (EUR, e) and dollar (USD, \$) respectively. An asterisk indicates a foreign country variable while a subscript 2 on a variable indicates that the variable is sourced from the other country. For notational simplicity we use π in place of π^e in this chapter to denote the rate of inflation expected to apply over the medium run. Since both countries are modeled analogously we will focus on the domestic economy in the following presentation of the components of the model. The description and justification of the equations presented in the various modules of the model will be brief, since many of the structural equations of this two-country KWG dynamics are already well documented and explained in Chiarella and Flaschel (2000a, ch. 4).

1. *Definitions (remuneration, wealth, real exchange rate)*:

$$\omega = w/p, \quad \rho = (Y - \delta K - \omega L^d)/K, \tag{6.1}$$

$$W = (M + B_1 + eB_2 + p_e E)/p, \quad p_b = p_{b^*} = 1, \tag{6.2}$$

$$\omega^* = w^*/p^*, \quad \rho^* = (Y^* - \delta^* K^* - \omega^* L^{d*})/K^*, \tag{6.3}$$

$$W^* = (M^* + B_1^*/e + B_2^* + p_e^* E^*)/p^*, \quad p_b = p_{b^*} = 1, \tag{6.4}$$

$$\eta = p/(ep^*), \quad [\text{Goods}^*/\text{Goods}]. \tag{6.5}$$

The equations in the first module of the model provide definitions of important macroeconomic magnitudes, namely the real wage ω, the actual rate of profit ρ and real wealth W. The latter consists of real money balances, equities, bonds issued by the domestic government (B_1) and bonds issued by the foreign government (B_2). These bonds have a constant price, normalized to unity, and a variable interest rate (r and r^*, respectively). Since adding the possibility of holding foreign equities as well does not affect the main features of this model in its present formulation, we restrict ourselves to bonds as the only foreign asset that domestic residents can hold. The real exchange rate is defined by $p/(ep^*)$ and thus in the present chapter describes the exchange ratio between foreign and domestic goods.

2. *Households and asset-holders:*[5]

$$W = (M^d + B_1^d + eB_2^d + p_e E^d)/p, \tag{6.6}$$

$$M^d = h_1 pY + h_2 pW(1 - \tau_c)(r_0 - r), \tag{6.7}$$

$$Y_c^D = (1 - \tau_c)(\rho K + rB_1/p) + e(1 - \tau_c^*)r^* B_2/p, \tag{6.8}$$

$$C_1 = \gamma_w \omega L^d + \gamma_c(\eta)(1 - s_c)Y_c^D, \quad \gamma_w, \gamma_c(\eta) \in [0, 1], \tag{6.9}$$

$$C_2 = \eta[(1 - \gamma_w)\omega L^d + (1 - \gamma_c(\eta))(1 - s_c)Y_c^D], \tag{6.10}$$

$$S_p = \omega L^d + Y_c^D - C = s_c Y_c^D = (\dot{M}^d + \dot{B}_1^d + e\dot{B}_2^d + p_e \dot{E}^d)/p, \tag{6.11}$$

$$C = C_1 + C_2/\eta, \tag{6.12}$$

$$\widehat{L} = n = \text{const.}, \tag{6.13}$$

$$W^* = (M^{d*} + B_1^{d*}/e + B_2^{d*} + p_e^* E^{d*})/p^*, \tag{6.14}$$

$$M^{d*} = h_1^* p^* Y^* + h_2^* p^* W^*(1 - \tau_c^*)(r_0^* - r^*), \tag{6.15}$$

$$Y_c^{D*} = (1 - \tau_c^*)(\rho^* K^* + r^* B_2^*/p^*) + (1 - \tau_c)r B_1^*/(ep^*), \tag{6.16}$$

$$C_2^* = \gamma_w^* \omega^* L^{d*} + \gamma_c^*(\eta)(1 - s_c^*)Y_c^{D*}, \quad \gamma_w^*, \gamma_c^*(\eta) \in [0, 1], \tag{6.17}$$

$$C_1^* = [(1 - \gamma_w^*)\omega^* L^{d*} + (1 - \gamma_c^*(\eta))(1 - s_c^*)Y_c^{D*}]/\eta, \tag{6.18}$$

$$\begin{aligned} S_p^* &= \omega^* L^{d*} + Y_c^{D*} - C^* = s_c^* Y_c^{D*} \\ &= (\dot{M}^{d*} + \dot{B}_2^{d*} + \dot{B}_1^{d*}/e + p_e^* \dot{E}^{d*})/p^*, \end{aligned} \tag{6.19}$$

$$C^* = C_1^*/\eta + C_2^*, \tag{6.20}$$

$$\widehat{L}^* = n^* = \text{const.} \tag{6.21}$$

We assume two groups of households in our model that differ with respect to their savings behavior – workers who do not save (for reasons of simplicity) and asset-holders who have a constant average propensity to save, s_c, out of their disposable income. Furthermore, both groups spend a fraction ($1-\gamma_w$ and $1-\gamma_c$, respectively) of their consumption expenditures on imports (C_2). We assume that the fraction γ_c is a negative function of the real exchange rate η. This indicates that asset holders shift their consumption expenditures in favor of the commodity that becomes relatively cheaper. The disposable income Y_c^D of asset holders consists of profits, interest payments from domestic bonds and interest payments from foreign bonds – all net of taxes (which are paid in the country from where this interest income originates). Note that we have assumed – again for reasons of simplicity – that the tax rate on wage income is zero. Furthermore, the asset-holders decide how to split up their wealth between the different assets (a superscript d indicates demand). Here we assume that domestic bonds and domestic equities are perfect substitutes, which provides an equation for the price of equities. The stock demand for real money balances depends on output Y (reflecting the transaction motive), on wealth and the nominal interest rate. Equation (6.11) indicates that the asset holders have to hold their intended savings in the four assets that are available to them domestically. Finally, we assume that the labor force L grows at a constant exogenous rate n.

3. *Firms (production units and investors):*

$$Y = yK, \quad L^d = Y/x, \quad y, x = \text{const.},$$

$$V = L^d/L, \tag{6.22}$$

$$I = i(\rho - (r - \pi))K + nK, \tag{6.23}$$

$$\Delta Y = Y - \delta K - C_1 - C_1^* - I - G, \tag{6.24}$$

$$p_e\dot{E}/p = I + \Delta Y = I^a \quad (S_f = 0), \tag{6.25}$$

$$\widehat{K} = I/K + (1 - \beta_k)\Delta Y/K, \quad \beta_k \in [0, 1], \tag{6.26}$$

$$\dot{N} = \delta_2 K + \beta_k \Delta Y, \tag{6.27}$$

$$Y^* = y^* K^*, \quad L^{d*} = Y^*/x^*, \quad y^*, x^* = \text{const.},$$

$$V^* = L^{d*}/L^*, \tag{6.28}$$

$$I^* = i^*(\rho^* - (r^* - \pi^*))K^* + n^* K^*, \tag{6.29}$$

$$\Delta Y^* = Y^* - \delta^* K^* - C_2 - C_2^* - G^*, \tag{6.30}$$

$$p_e^*\dot{E}^*/p^* = I^* + \Delta Y^* = I^{a*} \quad (S_f^* = 0), \tag{6.31}$$

$$\hat{K}^* = I^*/K^* + (1 - \beta_k^*)\Delta Y^*/K^*, \quad \beta_k^* \in [0, 1], \tag{6.32}$$

$$\dot{N}^* = \delta_2^* K^* + \beta_k^* \Delta Y^*. \tag{6.33}$$

Module 3 describes the behavior of firms. Output is produced with the help of the two factors, labor and capital, using a technology with fixed input coefficients.

Capital is always fully utilized whereas demand for labor, L^d, may differ from the total workforce L. The investment per unit of capital depends on the difference between the profit rate and the real interest rate and n as a trend component. Equation (6.24) defines the excess supply, ΔY, on the domestic goods market. Since we have assumed that firms' factor payments (in the form of wages and profits) always amount to Y, they have to finance ΔY as well as their intended investment by issuing equities. This is indicated in (6.25) where actual investment, I^a, is defined as the sum of intended and involuntary investment. By equation (6.26) this involuntary investment, ΔY, can either result in unintended capital accumulation or in unintended changes in inventories. For $\beta_k = 0$, all excess supply of goods leads to involuntary capital accumulation. This implies that if output falls short of aggregate demand ($\Delta Y < 0$) investment plans are canceled by the respective amount. We see from equation (6.27) that for this value of β_k, there is no need to explicitly consider inventories. Hence in this case, δ_2 – the ratio of intended inventory holdings to the capital stock – can be set equal to zero. For $\beta_k = 1$, in contrast, intended investment will be the only force affecting the capital stock since all unsold production results in a change in the stock of inventories. This stock increases (decreases) if actual output exceeds (falls short of) aggregate demand. Moreover, a positive δ_2 indicates the assumption that firms try to hold the stock of inventories proportional to output. Because of our assumption concerning the production technology this implies a constant ratio of inventories and capital stock in the steady state.[6] Besides these polar cases, on which we will concentrate in the ensuing analysis, intermediate ones ($\beta_k \in (0, 1)$), where part of the unsold production leads to involuntary capital accumulation and part to changes in inventories, are also possible and indeed more plausible. Owing to our assumptions on firm behavior it follows finally that the savings of firms are always identically zero.

4. *Government (fiscal and monetary authority):*

$$T = \tau_c(\rho K + rB/p), \quad B = B_1 + B_1^*, \tag{6.34}$$

$$G = gK, \quad g = \text{const.}, \tag{6.35}$$

$$S_g = T - rB/p - G, \tag{6.36}$$

$$\hat{M} = \dot{M}/M = \mu, \tag{6.37}$$

$$\dot{B} = pG + rB - pT - \dot{M}, \tag{6.38}$$

$$T^* = \tau_c^*(\rho^* K^* + r^* B^*/p^*), \quad B^* = B_2^* + B_2, \tag{6.39}$$

$$G^* = g^* K^*, \quad g^* = \text{const.}, \tag{6.40}$$

$$S_g^* = T^* - r^* B^*/p^* - G^*, \tag{6.41}$$

$$\hat{M}^* = \dot{M}^*/M^* = \mu^*, \tag{6.42}$$

$$\dot{B}^* = p^* G^* + r^* B^* - p^* T^* - \dot{M}^*. \tag{6.43}$$

Module 4 describes the government. In equation (6.34) it levies a tax with a constant tax rate τ_c on profits and on interest payments from domestic bonds, i.e. only the asset holders pay taxes. Note that the interest payments going to foreigners who hold domestic bonds are also taxed. Equation (6.35) characterizes government expenditures in the simplest way possible as far as steady-state analysis is concerned, namely as being a constant fraction of the capital stock K. Equation (6.36) is simply the definition of government savings: fiscal receipts net of interest payments minus government spending. Equation (6.37) expresses the assumption that the central bank of the home country keeps the domestic money supply on a growth path with an exogenous rate μ. Consistent with this assumption, the government budget constraint then states in (6.38) that the time rate of change of the supply of government bonds (that in fact reaches the public) is determined by two items: the negative of government savings (the government deficit that must be financed) minus that part of the new money supply that is injected into the economy via open market operations (which reduces the supply of new government) and not via the foreign exchange market.[7]

5. *Equilibrium conditions and consistency (asset markets):*

$$M = M^d = h_1 pY + h_2 pW(1-\tau_c)(r_0 - r), \tag{6.44}$$

$$B = B_1^d + B_1^{d*}, \quad E = E^d, \tag{6.45}$$

$$(1-\tau_c)r = (1-\tau_c)\rho pK/(p_e E) + \hat{p}_e, \tag{6.46}$$

$$\dot{M} = \dot{M}^d, \quad \dot{B} = \dot{B}_1^d + \dot{B}_1^{d*}, \quad \dot{E} = \dot{E}^d, \tag{6.47}$$

$$M^* = M^{d*} = h_1^* p^* Y^* + h_2^* p^* W^*(1-\tau_c^*)(r_0^* - r^*), \tag{6.48}$$

$$B^* = B_2^d + B_2^{d*}, \quad E^* = E^{d*}, \tag{6.49}$$

$$p_e^* E^* = (1-\tau_c^*)\rho^* p^* K^*/((1-\tau_c^*)r^* - \pi^*), \tag{6.50}$$

$$\dot{M}^* = \dot{M}^{d*}, \quad \dot{B}^* = \dot{B}_2^d + \dot{B}_2^{d*}, \quad \dot{E}^* = \dot{E}^{d*}. \tag{6.51}$$

With regard to the asset markets we assume continuous market clearing at the end of each "trading day" (ex post). Equation (6.44) indicates the respective stock equilibria for the three domestic assets. Note that the demand for domestic bonds stems from domestic as well as from foreign asset-owners. Equation (6.46) directly follows from the assumption that domestic bonds and equities are perfect substitutes. Hence, the rate of interest net of taxes, $(1-\tau_c)r$, has to be equal to the actual rate of return on equities. This rate can be calculated as follows. In each period, all expected profits, ρpK, are paid out to equity-holders. Taking the tax and perfectly foreseen untaxed capital gains into account, the rate of return on equities, therefore, amounts to $(1-\tau_c)\rho pK/p_e E + \hat{p}_e$. Equation (6.47) then characterizes the respective flow equilibria. We assume that the government and the firms face no demand problems when issuing new bonds or equities, respectively. Note that the division of new bonds between domestic and foreign asset-holders is ambiguous.[8] Once their flow demands fulfill the condition $\dot{B} = \dot{B}_1^d + \dot{B}_1^{d*}$, however, these demands are realized ($\dot{B}_1 = \dot{B}_1^d$ and $\dot{B}_1^* = \dot{B}_1^{d*}$).

6. *Disequilibrium situation (goods markets):*

$$Y \neq C_1 + C_1^* + I + \delta K + G \quad (\Delta Y \neq 0), \tag{6.52}$$

$$Y^* \neq C_2^* + C_2 + I^* + \delta^* K^* + G^* \quad (\Delta Y^* \neq 0), \tag{6.53}$$

$$\begin{aligned} S = S_p + S_g &= I^a + (e\dot{B}_2 - \dot{B}_1^*)/p \\ &= I^a + \{C_1^* - (ep^*/p)C_2\} \\ &\quad + \{e(1-\tau_c^*)r^* B_2/p - (1-\tau_c) r B_1^*/p\}, \end{aligned} \tag{6.54}$$

$$\begin{aligned} S^* = S_p^* + S_g^* &= I^{a*} + (\dot{B}_1^*/e - \dot{B}_2)/p^* \\ &= I^{a*} + \{C_2 - (p/ep^*)C_1^*\} \\ &\quad + \{(1-\tau_c) r B_1^*/(ep^*) - (1-\tau_c^*) r^* B_2/p^*\}, \end{aligned} \tag{6.55}$$

$$S^w = S + (ep^*/p)S^* = I^a + (ep^*/p)I^{a*} = I^{aw}. \tag{6.56}$$

In module 6, the first two equations describe the disequilibrium situation on the market for the domestic and the foreign good, respectively. Then, as the first line in (6.54) shows, aggregate savings which consists of private and public savings is equal to the sum of actual investment and net private capital exports $((e\dot{B}_2 - \dot{B}_1^*)/p)$. The whole expression is equal – due to our assumptions on income, consumption and the allocation of savings – to actual investment plus net exports of goods plus the excess of foreign interest payments to domestic residents holding foreign bonds over domestic interest payments to foreigners holding home-country bonds (both net of taxes).[9] This is a direct implication of the fact that the surpluses in all accounts of the balance of payments have to sum up to zero. See also below where we explain the balance of payments in greater detail. Naturally, as shown in (6.56), for the world as a whole, aggregate savings equal aggregate actual investment.

7. *Wage–price sector (adjustment equations):*

$$\widehat{w} = \beta_w (V - \bar{V}) + \kappa_w \hat{p}_w + (1-\kappa_w)\pi_w, \tag{6.57}$$

$$\hat{p} = -\beta_p (\Delta Y/K) + \kappa_p \widehat{w} + (1-\kappa_p)\pi, \tag{6.58}$$

$$\dot{\pi} = \beta_\pi (\alpha_\pi (\hat{p} - \pi) + (1-\alpha_\pi)(\hat{p}^+ - \pi)), \tag{6.59}$$

$$\hat{p}_w = \gamma_w \hat{p} + (1-\gamma_w)(\hat{e} + \hat{p}^*), \quad p_w = p^{\gamma_w}(ep^*)^{1-\gamma_w}, \tag{6.60}$$

$$\pi_w = \gamma_w \pi + (1-\gamma_w)(\epsilon + \pi^*), \tag{6.61}$$

$$\widehat{w}^* = \beta_w^* (V^* - \bar{V}^*) + \kappa_w^* \hat{p}_w^* + (1-\kappa_w^*)\pi_w^*, \tag{6.62}$$

$$\hat{p}^* = -\beta_p^* (\Delta Y^*/K^*) + \kappa_p^* \widehat{w}^* + (1-\kappa_p^*)\pi^*, \tag{6.63}$$

$$\dot{\pi}^* = \beta_\pi^* (\alpha_\pi^* (\hat{p}^* - \pi^*) + (1-\alpha_\pi^*)((\hat{p}^+)^* - \pi^*)), \tag{6.64}$$

$$\hat{p}_w^* = \gamma_w^* \hat{p}^* + (1-\gamma_w^*)(\hat{p} - \hat{e}), \quad p_w^* = (p^*)^{\gamma_w^*}(p/e)^{1-\gamma_w^*}, \tag{6.65}$$

$$\pi_w^* = \gamma_w^* \pi^* + (1-\gamma_w^*)(\pi - \epsilon). \tag{6.66}$$

Module 7 contains the adjustment of wages, prices and inflationary expectations. Wage and price inflation are modeled analogously. In both cases, there is a combination of demand-pressure and cost-pressure factors. Wage inflation depends on the deviation of the actual rate of employment from the NAIRU rate of employment. Furthermore, it is influenced by the actual rate of change in the workers' price index, $\hat{p}_w$, and the expected future rate of change, π_w. Underlying this formulation is the assumption that not only current but also medium-run workers' price inflation is important in the wage bargaining process. From (6.60), the current rate of workers' price inflation amounts to the weighted sum of domestic price inflation and foreign price inflation (converted into domestic currency), where the weights are the proportions of the respective goods in workers' consumption expenditures. The construction of π_w is completely analogous, using only expected magnitudes. Note that the use of $\hat{p}$ and π in lieu of $\hat{p}_w$ and π_w in equation (6.57) would imply an exchange rate illusion on the part of workers. Price inflation, on the other hand, depends on the actual excess supply on the goods market as a demand-pressure factor and on wage inflation as a cost-push force. Furthermore, the expected price trend π influences today's price inflation in a similar way as today's wage inflation. Equation (6.69) describes the formation of inflationary expectations concerning the medium run. It consists of a backward-looking first term (adaptive expectations with weight α_π) and a forward-looking second term (with weight $1-\alpha_\pi$) that refers to a theoretical price forecasting method (the p-star concept of the Federal Reserve for example).

Note again with respect to the above that expected inflation variables are now no longer carrying a superscript e in order to simplify to some extent the notation of the many expressions for inflation rates now involved.

8. *Exchange rate dynamics:*

$$\hat{e} = \beta_e(\beta((1-\tau_c^*)r^* + \epsilon - (1-\tau_c)r) - NX/K) + \hat{e}_0, \tag{6.67}$$

$$\hat{e}_0 = \hat{p}_0 - \hat{p}_0^*, \tag{6.68}$$

$$\dot{\epsilon} = \beta_\epsilon(\alpha_\epsilon(\hat{e} - \epsilon) + (1-\alpha_\epsilon)(\hat{e}^+ - \epsilon)). \tag{6.69}$$

Module 8 describes the dynamics of (the rate of change of) the exchange rate and the formation of expectations about this rate of change. Here we assume as a first approach to this dynamic interaction that the interest rate differential (augmented by depreciation expectations) in the international market for bonds determines, via corresponding international capital flows, the way and the extent by which the growth rate of the exchange rate deviates from its steady-state value[10] in conjunction with the imbalance that exists in the trade account (per unit of capital) at each moment in time. Dornbusch-type models of the open economy here often assume perfect capital mobility (i.e. $\beta = \infty$) and perfect substitutability of the assets traded internationally. These assumptions are the root cause of the prevalence of the UIP (uncovered interest parity) condition as the theory that determines the exchange rate dynamics. Our formulation extends this approach and allows for (some) imperfection with respect to capital mobility and exchange rate flexibility. Furthermore, the mechanism by which exchange rate expectations are formed is – as the mechanism that determined inflationary expectations – again a weighted average of "backward"- and "forward"-looking expectations. On the one hand, we use adaptive expectations, as the simplest expression for a chartist type of behavior, and theory-based expectations,[11] using for example the relative form of purchasing power parity (PPP), on the other hand, as a simple description of a fundamentalist sort of behavior. We assume here that domestic and foreign asset-holders form the same expectations regarding the exchange rate.

9. *Balance of payments:*

$$\begin{aligned} Ex &= [(1-\gamma_w^*)\omega^* L^{d*} + (1-\gamma_c^*(\eta))(1-s_c^*)Y_c^{D*}]/\eta \\ &= C_1^* = Im^*/\eta, \end{aligned} \tag{6.70}$$

$$Im = (1-\gamma_w)\omega L^d + (1-\gamma_c(\eta))(1-s_c)Y_c^D = C_2/\eta = Ex^*/\eta, \tag{6.71}$$

$$NX/p = Ex - Im = -NX^*/\eta, \tag{6.72}$$

$$NIX = e(1-\tau_c^*)r^* B_2 - (1-\tau_c) r B_1^* = -eNIX^*, \tag{6.73}$$

$$NCX = e\dot{B}_2^d - \dot{B}_1^{*d} = -eNCX^*, \tag{6.74}$$

$$\begin{aligned} Z &= pNX + NIX - NCX \\ &= \{pC_1^* - ep^*C_2\} + \{e(1-\tau_c^*)r^*B_2 - (1-\tau_c)rB_1^*\} \\ &\quad - \{e\dot{B}_2^d - \dot{B}_1^{*d}\} = 0, \end{aligned} \tag{6.75}$$

$$\begin{aligned} Z^* &= p^*NX^* + NIX^* - NCX^* \\ &= \{p^*C_2 - pC_1^*/e\} + \{(1-\tau_c)rB_1^*/e - (1-\tau_c^*)r^*B_2\} \\ &\quad - \{\dot{B}_1^{*d}/e - \dot{B}_2^d\} \\ &= -Z/e = 0. \end{aligned} \tag{6.76}$$

Module 9 deals with the balance of payments and its components. The first three equations concern the trade balance and denote exports and imports of goods and also net exports (see also module 2). Note that domestic imports are foreign exports and vice versa. Then, equation (6.73) indicates net interest payments or exports (*NIX*) from abroad: foreign interest payments to domestic asset-holders minus domestic interest payments to foreigners (assumed to be transferred through the foreign exchange market). In the balance of payments statistics *NIP* is part of exports of services (and thus also concerns the current account) and in national income accounting it is subsumed under net factor income from abroad. Another international transaction is the change in the stock of foreign bonds that domestic residents hold. *NCX* denotes net capital exports, that is, the deficit in the private capital account: the excess of additional foreign bonds held by domestic asset-owners over additional domestic bonds held by foreigners. Note that, taking the exchange rate into account, *NIX** and *NCX** are simply mirror images of the respective domestic magnitudes. In (6.75), Z denotes the overall surplus in the balance of payments. It consists of the surplus in the current account (first and second braces) and the surplus in the private capital account (third braces). As stated in (6.75), Z is identically equal to zero on the basis of what has been assumed so far. This is the well-known accounting identity; in other words the magnitudes considered are ex post or equilibrium magnitudes. The same is true for the various terms in (6.54)–(6.56) described above, from which it immediately follows that $Z=0$ is indeed fulfilled in this model type.

6.3 The core 10D KWG growth dynamics

We now derive the intensive form representation of the two-country KWG growth dynamics on the basis of certain assumptions that simplify its structure without sacrificing too much in generality. In this way we obtain a structure that can be easily decomposed and later on reintegrated in order to allow for various stability investigations and also numerical comparisons between the closed-economy case and the case of two interacting economies. The assumptions for the somewhat restricted variant of the two-country KWG model that will be investigated in the remainder of this chapter (where the accumulation of assets other than money and real capital is still left in the background) are the following:[12]

- W, in the money demand function, is replaced by K as a narrow definition of domestic wealth (this removes feedbacks from bond and equity accumulation from part of the model).
- $t_c = (T_c - rB_1/p - er_0^* B_2/p)/K = \text{const.}$, where the variable $T_c = \tau_c(\rho K + rB_1/p) + \tau_c^* er^* B_2/p$ represents the sum of all taxes paid by domestic asset-holders worldwide. This rule of tax collection is used in place of the earlier profit tax collection rule and removes another feedback route of the accumulation of domestic and foreign bonds from the model. The question, of course, is how important such feedbacks routes are for the dynamics of the model in general.

For reasons of simplicity we also employ the following assumptions.

- $\gamma_w \equiv 1$: Wage earners consume domestic goods solely (but $\gamma_c(\eta), \gamma_c' < 0$). This simplifies the consideration of the wage/price dynamics in a way that makes it identical to that of a closed economy.
- $\rho_0^{e*} = \rho_0^e$: The domestic steady-state rate of profit is identical to that of the foreign economy. This allows the interest rate parity condition to coincide with the relative form of the PPP in the steady state or (equivalently) allows the removal of any trend from the real exchange rate in the steady state.
- $n = n^*$: In order to have a uniform real rate of growth in the world economy in the steady state for reasons of analytical simplicity.
- $\hat{p}^+ = \hat{p}_0 = \mu - n$: The simplest rule for the formation of forward-looking expectations of the rate of inflation by means of the quantity theory of money.

- $\hat{e}^+ = \hat{e}_0 = \hat{p}_0 - \hat{p}_0^* = \mu - \mu^*$: The simplest rule for the formation of forward-looking expectations of the rate of change of the exchange rate by means of the relative form of PPP theory.

We furthermore assume that the export and import of commodities is modeled in its mathematical details in the following simple way.

According to module 9 of the above presentation of our general model, and due to the assumptions just made, we have for $c_1^* = Ex/K = C_1^*/K$ and $c_2/\eta = Im/K = C_2/(\eta K)$ the expressions

$$c_1^* = (1-\gamma_c^*(\eta))(1-s_c^*)(\rho^* - t_c^*)(l/l^*)/\eta, \tag{6.77}$$

$$c_2/\eta = (1-\gamma_c(\eta))(1-s_c)(\rho - t_c). \tag{6.78}$$

These show that imports as well as exports (the first in terms of the domestic commodity and the second in terms of the foreign good) are both a linear function of the real exchange rate if, for the functions that determine the division of consumption between domestic and foreign goods in both countries, it is furthermore assumed that

$$\gamma_c(\eta) = \gamma_c + \gamma(\eta_0 - \eta), \quad \gamma > 0, \tag{6.79}$$

$$\gamma_c^*(\eta) = \gamma_c^* - \gamma^*(\eta_0 - \eta), \quad \gamma^* > 0 \tag{6.80}$$

are linear as well. This is justified in the present chapter because we want to express the model in as linear a form as possible in order to allow only for intrinsic (unavoidable) nonlinearities at the start of our considerations. Nonlinearities that rest on certain restrictions concerning the postulated behavior of agents when the economy is far off its steady state or on nonlinearities in the assumed speed of adjustment to disequilibrium far off the steady state should then be introduced step-by-step at a later stage of the analysis. With respect to the above $\gamma_c(\eta)$ function the linear relationships in (6.79) and (6.80) would then have to be replaced by, say, tanh functions in order to guarantee that $\gamma_c(\eta)$ and $\gamma_c^*(\eta)$ remain between 0 and 1 at large values of $|\eta_0 - \eta|$. The assumptions just made imply that the trade account is determined according to the way depicted in Figure 6.1.

To simplify even further our treatment of the trade that occurs between the two countries we finally assume that the parameter η_0 is given by

$$\eta_0 = \frac{l_0(1-\gamma_c^*)(1-s_c^*)(\rho_0^* - t_c^*)}{l_0^*(1-\gamma_c)(1-s_c)(\rho_0 - t_c)}. \tag{6.81}$$

The choice of this particular parameter value for η_0 guarantees (as we shall see in the following) that the steady-state value of η will be η_0 and that the trade account (per unit of capital) $nx = NX/K = (Ex - Im)/K = c_1^* - c_2/\eta$ will be balanced in the steady state.

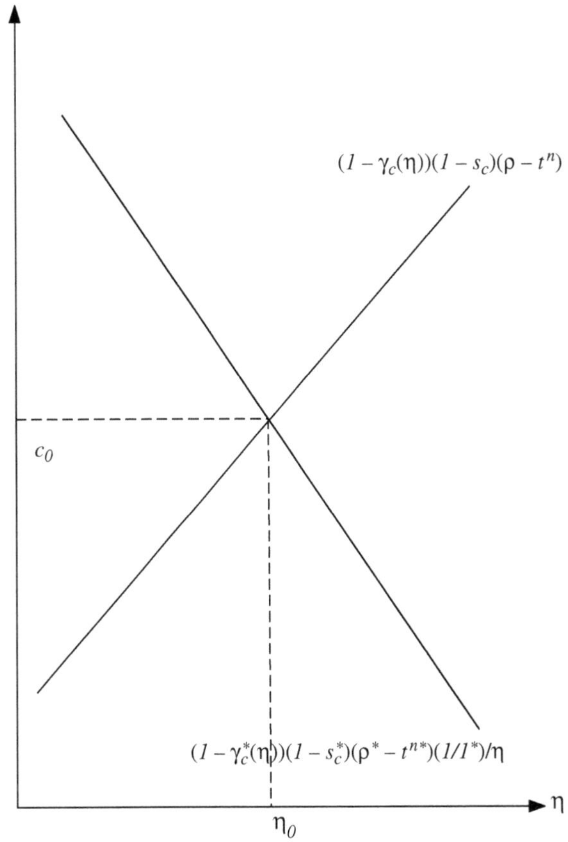

Figure 6.1 Determination of the balanced trade account ($NX = Ex - Im = 0$).

A special case that is often employed in the literature on overshooting exchange rates is recovered by making the following sequence of additional assumptions.

- $\beta_e = \infty$, $\beta = \infty$: so that $(1-\tau_c)r = (1-\tau_c^*)r_0^* + \epsilon$, uncovered interest parity (UIP), based on perfect capital mobility, is assumed to hold.
- $\beta_\epsilon = \infty$, $\alpha_\epsilon = 1$: so that $\epsilon = \hat{e}$, myopic perfect foresight (MPF), with respect to the exchange rate, is assumed to hold.

These assumptions are generally assumed in the literature for a treatment of the Dornbusch model of overshooting exchange rates. There are however also treatments of this model type that make use of adaptive expectations ($\alpha_\epsilon = 1$) in order to investigate from this point of view the MPF limit ($\alpha_\epsilon = 1$, $\beta_\epsilon = \infty$) and its properties (see Chiarella 1990a, b, 1992). Furthermore, the case $\alpha_\epsilon = 0$, in which

$\dot{\epsilon} = \beta_\epsilon(\hat{e}_0 - \epsilon)$, can be considered as a variant of Dornbusch's original choice of a regressive expectations mechanism $\epsilon = \beta_\epsilon \ln(e_0/e)$, that by differentiation implies the rule $\dot{\epsilon} = \beta_\epsilon(\hat{e}_0 - \hat{e})$.

As far as the mathematical investigation of the general two-country KWG model of the preceding section is concerned, we will confine ourselves here to the case $t_c = \text{const.}$ where lump sum taxes are varied in such a way that the ratio of real total taxes paid by domestic asset-holders (net of deflated interest payments they have received) to the capital stock remains constant over time. This assumption will allow us to disregard the GBR and the evolution of worldwide government debt in the following analysis of the model.[13] In making use of this simplifying device we employ similar assumptions to those of Sargent (1987, ch. V) and Rødseth (2000, ch. 6).

Let us now show how this model (which ignores the GBR) can be rewritten as a nonlinear autonomous dynamical system in the ten state variables $\omega = w/p$, $l = L/K$, $m = M/(pK)$, π, $\omega^* = w^*/p^*$, $l^* = L^*/K^*$, $m^* = M^*/(p^*K^*)$, π^*, $\eta = p/(ep^*)$ and ϵ.

The domestic economy:

$$\widehat{\omega} = \kappa[(1-\kappa_p)\beta_w X^w + (\kappa_w - 1)\beta_p X^p], \tag{6.82}$$

$$\hat{l} = -i(\cdot) + (1-\beta_k)X^p, \tag{6.83}$$

$$\widehat{m} = \mu - \pi - n - \kappa[\beta_p X^p + \kappa_p \beta_w X^w] + \hat{l}, \tag{6.84}$$

$$\dot{\pi} = \beta_\pi[\alpha_\pi \kappa(\beta_p X^p + \kappa_p \beta_w X^w) + (1-\alpha_\pi)(\mu - n - \pi)]. \tag{6.85}$$

Financial and trade links between the two economies:

$$\begin{aligned}\hat{\eta} &= (\hat{p} - \pi) + \pi - [(\hat{p}^* - \pi^*) + \pi^*] \\ &\quad - \beta_e(\beta(r^* + \epsilon - r) - a) - \hat{e}_0,\end{aligned} \tag{6.86}$$

$$\begin{aligned}\dot{\epsilon} &= \beta_\epsilon\{\alpha_\epsilon[(\hat{p} - \pi) + \pi - ((\hat{p}^* - \pi^*) - \pi^*) - \hat{\eta} - \epsilon] \\ &\qquad + (1-\alpha_\epsilon)(\mu - \mu^* - \epsilon)\}.\end{aligned} \tag{6.87}$$

The foreign economy:

$$\widehat{\omega}^* = \kappa^*[(1-\kappa_p^*)\beta_w^* X^{w*} + (\kappa_w^* - 1)\beta_p^* X^{p*}], \tag{6.88}$$

$$\hat{l}^* = -i^*(\cdot) + (1-\beta_k^*)X^{p*}, \tag{6.89}$$

$$\widehat{m}^* = \mu^* - \pi^* - n^* - \kappa^*[\beta_p^* X^{p*} + \kappa_p^* \beta_w^* X^{w*}] + \hat{l}^*, \tag{6.90}$$

$$\dot{\pi}^* = \beta_\pi^*[\alpha_\pi^* \kappa^*(\beta_p^* X^{p*} + \kappa_p^* \beta_w^* X^{w*}) + (1-\alpha_\pi^*)(\mu^* - n^* - \pi^*)]. \tag{6.91}$$

Here we employ the abbreviations

$$\rho = y - \delta - \omega l^d = \rho(\omega), \quad y = Y/K, \quad l^d = L^d/K = y/x = \text{const.},$$

$$
\begin{aligned}
X^w &= l^d/l - \bar{V} = y/(xl) - \bar{V}, \quad l = L/K,\\
X^p &= -\Delta Y/K = c_1 + c_1^* + i(\cdot) + n + \delta + g - y\\
&= \omega l^d + (1-s_c)(\rho - t_c) + i(\cdot) + n + \delta + g + nx(\cdot) - y,\\
i(\cdot) &= i(\rho - r + \pi),\\
r &= r_0 + (h_1 y - m)/h_2 = r(m),\\
c_1 &= C_1/K = \omega l^d + \gamma_c(\eta)(1-s_c)(\rho - t_c),\\
c_1^* &= C_1^*/K = (l/l^*)(1-\gamma_c^*(\eta))(1-s_c^*)(\rho^* - t_c^*)/\eta,\\
nx(\cdot) &= (1-\gamma_c^*(\eta))(1-s_c^*)(\rho^* - t_c^*)(l/l^*)\\
&\quad /\eta - (1-\gamma_c(\eta))(1-s_c)(\rho - t_c),\\
\hat{p} - \pi &= \kappa[\beta_p X^p + \kappa_p \beta_w X^w],\\
\hat{p}^* - \pi^* &= \kappa^*[\beta_p^* X^{p*} + \kappa_p^* \beta_w^* X^{w*}],
\end{aligned}
$$

and similarly for the other country. Here in particular we have

$$
\begin{aligned}
c_2^* &= C_2^*/K^* = \omega^* l^{d*} + \gamma_c^*(\eta)(1-s_c^*)(\rho^* - t_c^*),\\
c_2 &= C_2/K^* = (l^*/l)(1-\gamma_c(\eta))(1-s_c)(\rho - t_c)\eta.
\end{aligned}
$$

Note that the steady-state values of the domestic and the foreign economy are dependent on the above choice of the steady-state real exchange rate. Note also that the system in fact exhibits eight further laws of motion for the following two groups of variables: N/K, N^*/K^*, E/K, E^*/K^* (which do not feed back on the other laws of motion of the model by the construction of the model) and $\dot{B}_1$, $\dot{B}_2$, $\dot{B}_1^*$, $\dot{B}_2^*$ (which are not completely independent from each other and do not feed back on the other laws of motion of the model by the assumptions just made). It is of course necessary to check, for example, that both inventories per capital N/K and equities per capital E/K remain nonnegative and finite in the course of the dynamic evolution of the system. Note also that the domestic and the foreign rate of profit must be equal to each other in this formulation of a two-country model of international trade. Note again that we are using for the determination of the division of households' consumption into domestic and foreign commodities the simple linear functions

$$\gamma_c(\eta) = \gamma_c + \gamma(\eta_0 - \eta), \quad \gamma > 0, \tag{6.92}$$

$$\gamma_c^*(\eta) = \gamma_c^* - \gamma^*(\eta_0 - \eta), \quad \gamma^* > 0, \tag{6.93}$$

in order to keep the model as close as possible to a linear form. Note finally that we always have $nx_\eta < 0$ due to our assumptions on consumption behavior, so that there is no need here for the consideration of so-called Marshall–Lerner conditions to ensure a normal reaction of net exports with respect to exchange rate changes.

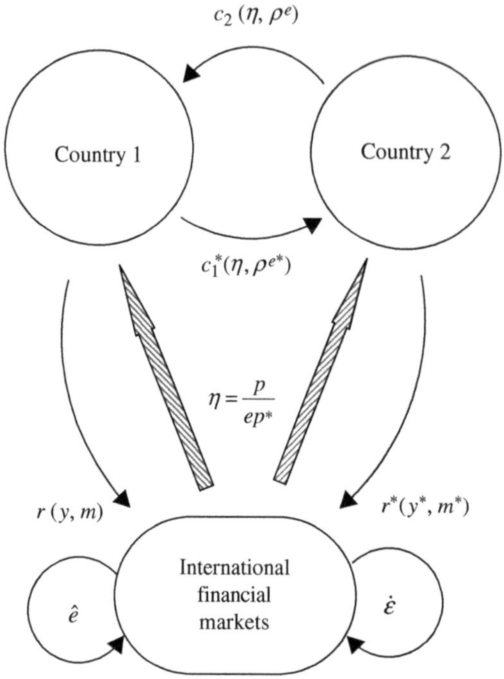

Figure 6.2 The two-country KWG framework.

In closing this section we give a brief graphical summary of the considered two-country interaction by way of the essential links for trade in commodities and in financial assets. We show in Figure 6.2 the consumption demands for foreign goods, the way the financial markets determine the real exchange via the Dornbusch exchange rate dynamics and finally the repercussions back from commodity markets to the financial markets via the interest rates implied by the transactions in the two economies.

Output and real balances per unit of capital indeed determine the domestic as well as the foreign interest rate by way of Keynesian liquidity preference theory. These in turn – together with expected currency depreciation or appreciation and the currency demand originating in the trade account – determine the actual rate of currency depreciation or appreciation (and on this basis also the change in the expected one). Given price levels in the two countries imply a certain real exchange rate whose rate of change is given by inflation at home and abroad and the just determined actual exchange rate dynamics. Inflation at home and abroad are simultaneously determined by demand and cost pressure in the markets for goods and give rise to an international transmission of inflation. Of course we have wage dynamics in addition (and behind goods price inflation) and also investment and growth, leading to a dynamic structure where two Keynes effects, two Mundell

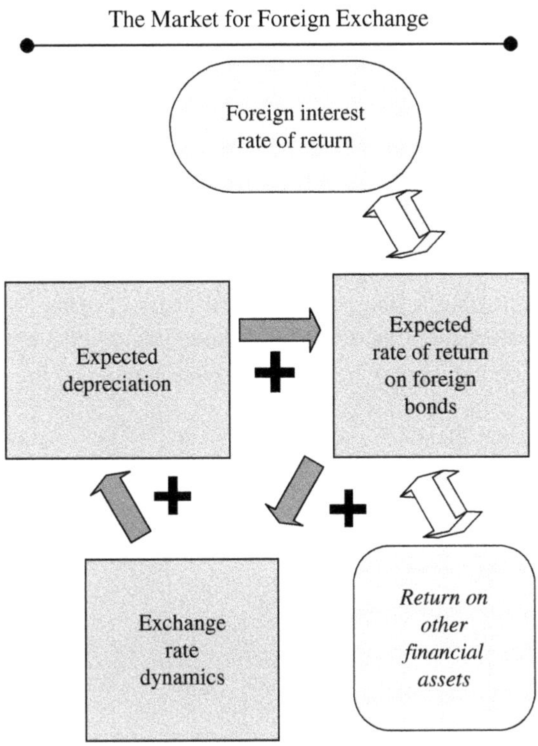

Figure 6.3 The Dornbusch exchange rate link of the model.

effects and two Rose effects interact with the Dornbusch exchange rate dynamics on the foreign exchange market (as illustrated in Figure 6.3). The overall effect of this interaction is to create a fairly complex situation of two business cycle mechanisms that interact via trade and via what happens on international financial markets.

Note again that the feedback structure in the foreign exchange market is such that a tendency toward cumulative instability is established. This instability can be overcome by the interaction with the real sectors of the two economies and by, for example, the relaxation oscillations methodology we have considered earlier. There are of course other possible mechanisms that can tame an, in principle, unstable financial accelerator of this type; however this is left for future research.

6.4 Steady-state and β-stability analysis

In this section we present in a mathematically informal way a variety of subsystem stability investigations that eventually allow us to derive the stability of the fully integrated 10D dynamics in a systematic fashion by way of our

β-stability approach to macroeconomic dynamics. We thereby again show the merits of a feedback guided stability analysis, here however from the purely local perspective.[14] Let us first however consider the uniquely determined interior steady-state solution of the 10D dynamics of the preceding section.

We thus disregard the boundary solutions $\omega,\ l,\ m = 0$, etc. – caused by the growth rate formulation of their laws of motion – in the following determination of the steady-state solutions of the above dynamics. These values of the variables $\omega,\ l,\ m$, etc. are economically meaningless and never appear as attractors in the numerical investigations to be performed later. Furthermore, the achieved theoretical results will all be constrained to a neighborhood of the unique interior steady state considered below. Of course, a general and global analysis of the system must take into account the stability properties of such boundary points of rest of the dynamics.

THEOREM 6.1 *There is* a unique steady-state solution *or point of rest of the simplified dynamics (6.82)–(6.91) fulfilling* $\omega_0, l_0, m_0 \neq 0$ *given by*[15]

$$l_0 = l^d/\bar{V} = y/(x\bar{V}), \tag{6.94}$$

$$m_0 = h_1 y, \tag{6.95}$$

$$\pi_0 = \mu - n, \tag{6.96}$$

$$\rho_0 = t_c + (n + g - t_c)/s_c, \tag{6.97}$$

$$r_0 = \rho_0 + \pi_0, \tag{6.98}$$

$$\omega_0 = (y - \delta - \rho_0)/l^d, \tag{6.99}$$

for the domestic economy and correspondingly $\omega^*,\ l^*,\ m^*,\ \pi^*,\ r^*,\ \rho^*$ *for the foreign economy, and*

$$\eta_0 = \frac{l_0(1-\gamma_c^*)(1-s_c^*)(\rho_0^* - t_c^*)}{l^*(1-\gamma_c)(1-s_c)(\rho_0 - t_c)}, \tag{6.100}$$

$$\epsilon_0 = \mu - n - (\mu^* - n) = \mu - \mu^* = \hat{e}_0. \tag{6.101}$$

We assume that the parameters of the model are chosen such that the steady-state values for $\omega,\ l,\ m,\ \rho,\ r,\ \eta$ are all positive. Note in particular that $\pi_0 = \mu_0 - n$ should not be so negative that $r_0 > 0$ will not hold true. All the following investigations will be confined to local stability considerations around such steady-state solutions.

Proof: By setting to zero the right-hand sides of (6.83)–(6.85) and (6.89)–(6.91), we have $\pi_0 = \mu - n,\ \hat{p}_0 = \pi_0$ as well as $\pi_0^* = \mu^* - n,\ \hat{p}_0^* = \pi_0^*$. From (6.86) and (6.87), also set equal to zero, we obtain $\epsilon_0 = \mu - \mu^*(= \hat{p}_0 - \hat{p}_0^* = \hat{e}_0)$ and thus $r_0^* + \epsilon_0 - r_0$ due to our assumption that $\rho_0 = \rho_0^*$ and because of $r_0 = \rho_0 + \pi_0,\ r_0^* = \rho_0^* + \pi_0^*$. From (6.86) we then get $a(\cdot) = 0$ which implies $\eta = \eta_0$, since a is nx negatively sloped function of η solely (all other variables in nx are fixed at their steady-state values by assumption). We thus have $c_1^* = c_2/\eta_0$ in the steady state and therefore a description of goods market disequilibrium as if both economies were closed, i.e. for example

$$X^p = \omega_0 l^d + (1 - s_c)(\rho_0 - t_c) + i(\cdot) + n + \delta + g - y.$$

Equations (6.82)–(6.85) and (6.88)–(6.91) can therefore now be considered in isolation from each other, as in the case of closed economies. We shall concentrate on equations (6.82)–(6.85) in the following analysis.

From the equations (6.82) and (6.84) we get for the variables X^p, X^w the equation system

$$0 = (1 - \kappa_p)\beta_w X^w + (\kappa_w - 1)\beta_p X^p,$$
$$0 = \beta_p X^p + \kappa_p \beta_w X^w.$$

It is easily shown for $\kappa_w \kappa_p < 1$ that this linear equation system can be uniquely solved for X^w, X^p, which must then both be zero. This implies the first of our steady-state equations (6.94) as well as $i(\cdot) = 0$, i.e. $r = \rho_0 - \pi_0$. Equation (6.95) then immediately follows and (6.96) has already been shown above. The equation for ρ_0 is obtained from $X^p = 0$ by solving this equation for $\rho_0 (= y - \delta - \omega_0 l^d)$. The calculation of ω_0 is then straightforward. □

We now investigate stability properties of a convenient slightly more special case of the above 10D dynamical system which can be written as a nonlinear autonomous dynamical system in the ten state variables: $\omega = w/p$, $l = L/K$, p, π, $\omega^* = w^*/p^*$, $l^* = L^*/K^*$, p^*, π^*, e and ϵ. As this list shows we now intend to neglect all trends in the nominal magnitudes, by assuming $\mu - n = \mu^* - n^* = 0$ (no steady-state inflation at home and abroad and also no steady depreciation or appreciation). Furthermore, since we have $nx_0 = 0$ in steady state we (continue to) assume that $\rho_0 = \rho_0^*$ holds in the steady state. This allows for interest rate parity $r_0 = r_0^*$ in the steady state (where $\hat{e}_0 = \epsilon_0 = 0$ holds and where interest rates coincide with the profit rates of firms). Finally, we consider only the case where capital stock growth is driven by investment demand, that is, we assume $\beta_k = 1$ in the following analysis. We then have the steady-state values of the nominal magnitudes (in addition to what has been listed in Theorem 6.1) given by

$$p_0 = \frac{m(0)l_0}{h_1 y}, \quad p_0^* = \frac{m^*(0)l_0^*}{h_1^* y^*},$$
$$m(0) = \frac{M(0)}{L(0)}, \quad m^*(0) = \frac{M^*(0)}{L^*(0)},$$
$$e_0 = \frac{\eta_0 p_0^*}{p_0},$$

and of course $w_0 = \omega_0 p_0$ and $w_0^* = \omega_0^* p_0^*$ for the level of money wages. The laws of motion of the two economies and their interaction in the situation now being considered simply read as follows, in the case $\beta_k = 1$.

The domestic economy:

$$\widehat{\omega} = \kappa[(1-\kappa_p)\beta_w X^w + (\kappa_w - 1)\beta_p X^p], \tag{6.102}$$

$$\hat{l} = -i(\rho + \pi - r), \tag{6.103}$$

$$\hat{p} = \kappa[\beta_p X^p + \kappa_p \beta_w X^w] + \pi, \tag{6.104}$$

$$\dot{\pi} = \beta_\pi[\alpha_\pi(\hat{p} - \pi) + (1-\alpha_\pi)(-\pi)]. \tag{6.105}$$

Financial and trade links between the two economies:

$$\hat{e} = \beta_e(\beta(r^* + \epsilon - r) - a(\cdot)), \tag{6.106}$$

$$\dot{\epsilon} = \beta_\epsilon[\alpha_\epsilon(\hat{e} - \epsilon) + (1-\alpha_\epsilon)(-\epsilon)]. \tag{6.107}$$

The foreign economy:

$$\widehat{\omega}^* = \kappa^*[(1-\kappa_p^*)\beta_w^* X^{w*} + (\kappa_w^* - 1)\beta_p^* X^{p*}], \tag{6.108}$$

$$\hat{l}^* = -i^*(\rho^* + \pi^* - r^*), \tag{6.109}$$

$$\hat{p}^* = \kappa^*[\beta_p^* X^{p*} + \kappa_p^* \beta_w^* X^{w*}] + \pi^*, \tag{6.110}$$

$$\dot{\pi}^* = \beta_\pi^*[\alpha_\pi^*(\hat{p}^* - \pi^*) + (1-\alpha_\pi^*)(-\pi^*)]. \tag{6.111}$$

Here for the domestic economy we employ the abbreviations

$$\begin{aligned}
\rho &= y - \delta - \omega y/x, \quad y = \text{const.},\\
X^w &= y/(xl) - \bar{V}, \quad X^p = c_1 + c_1^* + i(\cdot) + n + \delta + g - y,\\
i(\cdot) &= i(\rho + \pi - r), \quad r = r_0 + (h_1 y - m)/h_2, \quad m = m(0)l/p,\\
c_1 &= \omega y/x + \gamma_c(\eta)(1-s_c)(\rho - t_c),\\
c_1^* &= (l/l^*)(1-\gamma_c^*(\eta))(1-s_c^*)(\rho^* - t_c^*)/\eta,\\
a(\cdot) &= (1-\gamma_c^*(\eta))(1-s_c^*)(\rho^* - t_c^*)(l/l^*)/\eta\\
&\quad - (1-\gamma_c(\eta))(1-s_c)(\rho - t_c), \quad \eta = p/(ep^*),
\end{aligned}$$

and similarly for the foreign economy.[16] Note again that, for the determination of the division of household consumption into domestic and foreign commodities, we are using the simple linear functions

$$\begin{aligned}
\gamma_c(\eta) &= \gamma_c + \gamma(\eta_0 - \eta), \quad \gamma > 0, \quad \eta = p/(ep^*),\\
\gamma_c^*(\eta) &= \gamma_c^* - \gamma^*(\eta_0 - \eta), \quad \gamma^* > 0, \quad \eta = p/(ep^*),
\end{aligned}$$

in order to keep the model as close as possible to a linear form for the time being.

We now start our local stability investigations by a series of propositions and their proofs which are both concentrated on the essential issues to be dealt with and thus do not present every detail that is necessary for their final formulation. A detailed proof of the local stability of the steady state of the fully integrated 10D dynamics will be presented in the next section. In the following theorems we neglect all borderline cases where parameters other than adjustment speed parameters, such as the κ values, are set equal to zero or one.

THEOREM 6.2 *Assume that the parameters β_p, β_p^*, β_e, β_ϵ are all set equal to zero.*[17] *Then the following hold.*

1 *The dynamics of the two countries are completely decoupled from each other and the determinants of the Jacobians at the steady states of the two separate 4D dynamics at home and abroad are both zero.*
2 *These dynamics can both be reduced to two 3D systems, each with a locally asymptotically stable steady state, if β_π, β_π^* are chosen sufficiently small. Concerning the eigenvalue structure of the dynamics at the steady state, we therefore have in this case six eigenvalues with negative real parts and four that are zero.*

Proof:

1 As the KWG model is formulated it only links the two countries via excess demands X^p and X^{p*}, terms which are suppressed when price adjustment speeds with respect to demand pressure are set equal to zero. The first and the third blocks of the laws of motion are therefore then independent of each other and can be investigated separately. Furthermore, there exist positive numbers a and b such that $-a\widehat{\omega} + \hat{p} + b\dot{\pi} \equiv 0$ which implies the statement on the 4D determinants.
2 Integrating the linear dependence just shown gives (for example for country 1) with respect to the price level p that $p = +\text{const.} \times \omega^a \exp(-b\pi)$. This equation feeds into the investment equation via

$$i(\cdot) = i(\rho + \pi - r), \quad r = r_0 + (h_1 y - m)/h_2,$$
$$m = m(0)l/p, \quad p = +\text{const.} \times \omega^a \exp(-b\pi),$$

which thereby reduces the original 4D dynamics to dimension three. The Jacobian of the reduced 3D dynamics (for ω, l, π) is characterized by

$$\begin{pmatrix} J_{11} & J_{12} & J_{13} \\ J_{21} & J_{22} & J_{23} \\ J_{31} & J_{32} & J_{33} \end{pmatrix} = \begin{pmatrix} 0 & - & 0 \\ + & - & - \\ 0 & - & - \end{pmatrix}.$$

The trace is unambiguously negative in this case. For β_π sufficiently small we have that $J_{22}J_{33} - J_{23}J_{32}$ will be dominated by $J_{12}J_{21}$ which gives the local asymptotic stability result, since the Routh–Hurwitz coefficient $a_1 a_2$ will always be larger than $a_3 = -\det J$ in the considered situation, due to the fact that the determinant will be just one expression in the product $a_1 a_2$. □

As the proof has shown, we have zero root hysteresis present in each country, meaning that the price levels in both countries are not uniquely determined in their long-run position, but depend on the history of the economy and the shocks it has experienced. This is due to the fact that demand pressure in the market for goods does not matter for the dynamics of the price level. It is also due to this fact that neither Mundell effects nor Keynes effects are present in the situation currently being considered in their typical format (since there is no positive feedback of expected inflation on its time rate of change by way of the third law of motion and no negative effect of the price level onto its rate of change by the law of motion for the price level). Furthermore, a positive dependence of aggregate demand on real wages cannot be destabilizing here via the Rose effect, while a negative dependence is destabilizing, but only if the price level reacts with sufficient strength with respect to demand pressure on the market for goods.

THEOREM 6.3 *Assume that the parameters β_p^*, β_e and β_ϵ remain fixed at zero, but that the parameter β_p is made positive such that the negative real parts considered in Theorem 6.2 remain so. Then the following hold.*

1 *The dynamics of the home country now depends on what happens in the foreign economy.*
2 *There are now seven eigenvalues of the full dynamical system with negative real parts, while three remain at zero.*

The hysteresis argument can only be applied to the foreign economy and the price level there, while the price level at home now has a unique long-run position (as has been determined above). Note also that we only consider an 8D dynamical system for the moment, since e and ϵ are kept frozen at their steady-state values. We thus have an 8D system with vanishing 8D determinant ($a_8 = 0$), but with all other conditions of the Routh–Hurwitz theorem being fulfilled (i.e. for the Routh–Hurwitz coefficients $a_1, \ldots, a_7$).

Proof: We reduce the dynamics in the foreign economy to 3D according to the proof strategy of Theorem 6.2. The 8D dynamics is thereby made 7D. The Jacobian to be investigated then is of the form (with the domestic economy shown first)

$$\begin{pmatrix} J_{11} & J_{12} & J_{13} & J_{14} & ? & ? & ? \\ J_{21} & J_{22} & J_{23} & J_{24} & ? & ? & ? \\ J_{31} & J_{32} & J_{33} & J_{34} & ? & ? & ? \\ J_{41} & J_{42} & J_{43} & J_{44} & ? & ? & ? \\ 0 & 0 & 0 & 0 & J_{55} & J_{56} & J_{57} \\ 0 & 0 & 0 & 0 & J_{65} & J_{66} & J_{67} \\ 0 & 0 & 0 & 0 & J_{75} & J_{76} & J_{77} \end{pmatrix}.$$

The entries with question mark do not matter for the calculation of the eigenvalues of this Jacobian. Furthermore, the foreign country exhibits three eigenvalues with negative real parts according to what has been shown in Theorem 6.2. These eigenvalues are independent of what happens in the domestic economy. For the latter economy we have assumed that three of its eigenvalues still have negative real parts when β_p is made positive. It suffices therefore to show that

$$\det\begin{pmatrix} J_{11} & J_{12} & J_{13} & J_{14} \\ J_{21} & J_{22} & J_{23} & J_{24} \\ J_{31} & J_{32} & J_{33} & J_{34} \\ J_{41} & J_{42} & J_{43} & J_{44} \end{pmatrix}$$

is always positive in order to get the result that the eigenvalue that moves away from zero must become negative. The sign of the determinant can – as usual – be obtained by removing linear dependences from the laws of motion involved according to

$$\widehat{\omega} = X^w,$$
$$\hat{l} = -i(\cdot),$$
$$\hat{p} = X^p,$$
$$\dot{\pi} = -\pi.$$

Continuing in this way we get

$$\widehat{\omega} = -l,$$
$$\hat{l} = +\omega + p,$$
$$\hat{p} = +\omega - p,$$
$$\dot{\pi} = -\pi.$$

Note that we have to employ $m = m(0)l/p$ in the rate of interest expression in the investment function, but that the influence of l does not matter due to what is shown in the first row of the considered 4D matrix J. We thus finally get (with the usual interpretation that the equality sign only indicates that there is no change in the sign of the corresponding determinant)

$$\widehat{\omega} = -l,$$
$$\hat{l} = +\omega,$$
$$\hat{p} = -p,$$
$$\dot{\pi} = -\pi.$$

This last form of dynamic interdependence indeed implies that $\det J$ must be positive in sign. □

We have so far considered the domestic economy as – so to speak – a satellite of the foreign one (with convergence to a steady state however). We therefore next assume that the adjustment speed β_p^* is also made positive. In this case the two economies become dependent on each other, like in a monetary union, since the exchange rate is still kept fixed and can therefore be set equal to one. In this 8D case we have full interdependence though only via the excess demand channels and their influence on domestic and foreign price dynamics and thus now investigate the international price level connection. We therefore consider the first and the third block of our laws of motion in full interaction, yet still an inactive Dornbusch type of exchange rate dynamics. In this case the following theorem holds.

THEOREM 6.4 *Assume that the parameters β_e and β_ϵ remain fixed at zero, but that the parameters β_p and β_p^* are now both positive, but chosen sufficiently small (such that the negative real parts of the eigenvalues considered in Theorem 6.3 remain negative). Then the following hold.*

1. *The determinant of the Jacobian at the steady state of the 8D dynamics is always positive (independently of speed of adjustment conditions).*
2. *There are now eight eigenvalues with negative real parts, implying the steady state is locally asymptotically stable in the situation being considered.*

Proof: We proceed again by removing from the laws of motion of the 8D case (where e and ϵ are still kept fixed at their steady-state values) all expressions that are irrelevant for the sign of the determinant of their Jacobian at the steady state. This leads us again first of all to the following.

The domestic economy:

$$\widehat{\omega} = X^w,$$

$$\hat{l} = -i(\cdot),$$

$$\hat{p} = X^p,$$

$$\dot{\pi} = -\pi.$$

The foreign economy:

$$\widehat{\omega}^* = X^{w*},$$

$$\hat{l}^* = -i^*(\cdot),$$

$$\hat{p}^* = X^{p*},$$

$$\dot{\pi}^* = -\pi^*.$$

We then simplify in the same way even further (due to $nx_0 = 0$).

The domestic economy:

$$\widehat{\omega} = -l,$$

$$\hat{l} = +\omega + p,$$

$$\hat{p} = \omega y/x + (1 - s_c)\rho + nx(\cdot),$$
$$\dot{\pi} = -\pi.$$

The foreign economy:

$$\widehat{\omega}^* = -l^*,$$
$$\hat{l}^* = +\omega^* + p^*,$$
$$\hat{p}^* = \omega^* y^*/x^* + (1 - s_c^*)\rho^* - (l_0^*/l_0)\eta_0 nx(\cdot),$$
$$\dot{\pi}^* = -\pi^*.$$

From this result we finally obtain the following by continuing the employed method of reduction (since a depends negatively on η and ω^* and positively on ω).

The domestic economy:

$$\widehat{\omega} = -l,$$
$$\hat{l} = +\omega + p,$$
$$\hat{p} = +\omega + \omega^*,$$
$$\dot{\pi} = -\pi.$$

The foreign economy:

$$\widehat{\omega}^* = -l^*,$$
$$\hat{l}^* = +\omega^* + p^*,$$
$$\hat{p}^* = +\omega^* - \omega + p - p^*,$$
$$\dot{\pi}^* = -\pi^*.$$

We are now in a position to calculate the sign of the determinant under consideration. Note first of all that the laws of motion for π and π^* can be neglected in this calculation, since their two rows and columns in the Jacobian do not change the sign of its determinant. For the remaining entries of J (in the order ω, l, p, ω^*, l^*, p^*), according to what has been shown above, we have

$$\det \begin{pmatrix} 0 & - & 0 & 0 & 0 & 0 \\ + & 0 & + & 0 & 0 & 0 \\ + & 0 & 0 & + & 0 & 0 \\ 0 & 0 & 0 & 0 & - & 0 \\ 0 & 0 & 0 & + & 0 & + \\ 0 & 0 & + & 0 & 0 & - \end{pmatrix} = +\det \begin{pmatrix} + & + & 0 & 0 & 0 \\ + & 0 & + & 0 & 0 \\ 0 & 0 & 0 & - & 0 \\ 0 & 0 & + & 0 & + \\ 0 & + & 0 & 0 & - \end{pmatrix}$$

$$= +\det\begin{pmatrix} + & + & 0 & 0 \\ + & 0 & + & 0 \\ 0 & 0 & + & + \\ 0 & + & 0 & - \end{pmatrix}$$

$$= +\det\begin{pmatrix} 0 & + & 0 \\ 0 & + & + \\ + & 0 & - \end{pmatrix} - \det\begin{pmatrix} + & + & 0 \\ 0 & + & + \\ 0 & 0 & - \end{pmatrix}$$

$$= -\det\begin{pmatrix} 0 & + \\ + & - \end{pmatrix} - \det\begin{pmatrix} + & + \\ 0 & - \end{pmatrix} > 0.$$

This proves assertion 1 of Theorem 6.4. Assertion 2 then follows immediately from what has been shown for the 7D case and the fact that the positive 8D determinant enforces a negative eigenvalue if the real parts of the eigenvalues of the 7D case are all negative. □

We thus have shown the result that monetary unions of KWG type exhibit cyclical or even monotonic convergence of trajectories to their interior steady-state position if wages and in particular prices adjust sufficiently sluggishly in both countries. Though the proofs concern only the local validity of such a statement, numerical simulations suggest that such a result also holds from the global perspective, since the nonlinearities intrinsically present in the employed laws of motion are generally of a type that generate such a result. The same however generally also applies to situations of divergence which therefore demand the introduction of extrinsic nonlinearities in order to get viable dynamics.

Let us now allow for $\beta_e > 0$, but not yet for adjusting expectations of depreciation or appreciation. In this situation we leave the case of a monetary union and consider now the role of capital mobility and of adjusting nominal exchange rates, again at first with respect to asymptotic stability and with the presence of just intrinsic nonlinearities.

THEOREM 6.5 *Assume that the parameter β_ϵ remains fixed at zero, but that the parameters β_e and β are now positive, and chosen sufficiently small (such that the negative real parts of the eigenvalues considered in Theorem 6.4 remain negative). Then the following hold.*

1 *The determinant of the Jacobian at the steady state of the considered 9D dynamics is always negative (independently of speed of adjustment conditions).*[18]
2 *Assume that β, the degree of capital mobility, is chosen sufficiently small. The considered 9D dynamics then exhibits nine eigenvalues with negative real*

parts, so that their interior steady state is locally asymptotically stable in this situation.

Proof: In the case $\beta = 0$, because of

$$X^p = \omega y/x + (1 - s_c)(\rho - t_c) + i(\cdot) + n + \delta + g + nx(\cdot) - y,$$
$$X^{p*} = \omega^* y^*/x^* + (1 - s_c^*)(\rho^* - t_c^*) + i^*(\cdot) + n^* + \delta^* + g^* - (l^*/l)a(\cdot)\eta - y^*,$$

we get that the a expression can be removed from both the domestic and the foreign economy as far as the calculation of determinants is concerned, since we then simply have $\hat{e} = -\beta_e a$. The system decomposes into two 4D dynamics with positive determinants and $\hat{e} = -e$, again of course solely as far as the calculation of the determinant of the Jacobian at the steady state is concerned. This proves the first assertion, but – due to the method chosen – only for β values that are sufficiently small (all other speed of adjustment parameters can be arbitrary). We conjecture that this result holds for all positive β as well.[19] The second assertion of the theorem finally follows immediately, and in the usual way, from the continuity of eigenvalues on the parameters of the considered dynamics. □

THEOREM 6.6 *Assume finally that the parameter β_ϵ is made positive, in the situation considered in Theorem 6.5. Then the following hold.*

1 *The determinant of the Jacobian at the steady state of the considered 10D dynamics is always positive.*
2 *Assume that β_ϵ, the speed of adjustment of expectations on exchange rate depreciation, is chosen sufficiently small. The 10D dynamics then exhibits ten eigenvalues with negative real parts, so that their interior steady-state solution is locally asymptotically stable.*

Proof: This is obvious from what has been shown so far, since the $\dot{\epsilon}$ law of motion can be reduced to $\dot{\epsilon} = -\beta_\epsilon \epsilon$ by means of the $\hat{e}$ law of motion, as usual, though only as far as the calculation of determinants is concerned. □

THEOREM 6.7 *From the locally asymptotically stable situation of Theorem 6.6, the steady state must lose its local stability by way of Hopf bifurcations if one of the parameters β_π (carrying the destabilizing Mundell effect), β_ϵ (carrying the destabilizing Dornbusch effect) or β_p (carrying the destabilizing Rose effect) is made sufficiently large, the latter however only in the case where the real wage effect in investment demand dominates the real wage effect in consumption demand.*

Proof: This is straightforward, since the trace of the Jacobian J of the dynamics at the steady state can be made positive, by way of $\dot{\pi}'(\pi) > 0$, $\dot{\epsilon}'(\epsilon) > 0$ and $\widehat{\omega}'(\omega) > 0$, respectively. □

Fast adjustment of expectations and fast adjustment of prices (in the case of a negative dependence of aggregate demand on the real wage level) are thus dangerous for asymptotic stability and will lead to loss of stability which is always accompanied by business fluctuations, possibly persistent ones if a supercritical Hopf bifurcation occurs, but generally explosive ones as long as only intrinsic nonlinearities are present in the considered dynamical system. Numerical simulations have then to be used to gain insights into the global dynamics. These indicate that stable limit cycle situations or persistent cycles can be generated by the additional assumption of extrinsic nonlinearities, such as asymmetries in the money wage Phillips curve.

6.5 Numerical investigation of the KWG dynamics

In this section we provide some numerical illustrations of the dynamic features of the two-country KWG growth model that has so far only been studied from the local perspective around its unique interior steady state.[20] It is not difficult to provide numerical examples of damped oscillations or even monotonic adjustment back to the steady state based on what has been shown for the speed of adjustment parameters in the two preceding sections. Increasing such speed of adjustment parameters will then also provide examples of supercritical Hopf bifurcations where – after the loss of local stability – stable limit cycles and thus persistent economic fluctuations will be born for a certain parameter range. However there will often simply be purely explosive behavior after such loss of stability, indicating that the intrinsic nonlinearities are generally too weak to bound the dynamics within economically meaningful ranges. The addition of extrinsic or behavioral nonlinearities is thus generally unavoidable in order to arrive at an economically meaningful dynamic behavior.

In the following we will however make use of another prominent behavioral nonlinearity, already discussed in Keynes (1936), namely a kinked money wage Phillips curve, expressing in stylized form the fact that wages are much more flexible upwards than downwards. This nonlinearity is often already sufficient to limit the dynamics to economically viable domains, though in reality of course coupled with other behavioral nonlinearities, also in operation at some distance from the steady state. Downward nominal wage rigidity however can often already by itself overcome the destabilizing feedback channels of Mundell type (working through the real interest rate) or Rose type (working through the real wage rate) and thus succeed in stylizing the economy in a certain area outside the steady state. This in particular holds if wages are assumed to be completely inflexible in the downward direction and if there is zero steady-state inflation, where they can even stylize an economy toward damped oscillations that would otherwise – without this inflexibility – break down immediately as for example in the following first simulation exercise of the KWG dynamics.

We show in Figure 6.4, at the top, the time series for the inflationary climate π and π^*, when both countries are still completely decoupled from each other with country 1 exhibiting the larger fluctuations (and shorter phase length) in this

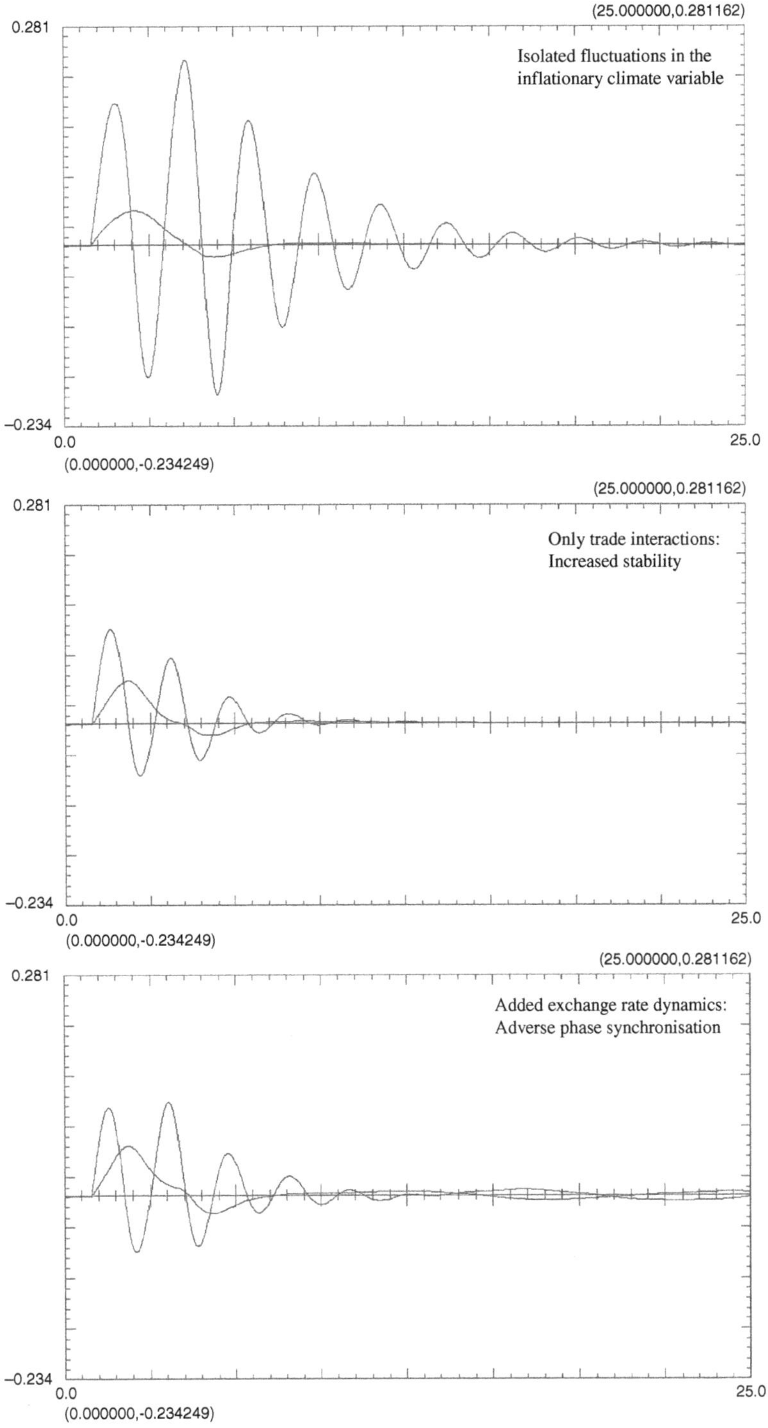

Figure 6.4 KWG cycles: isolated, with trade interactions, and finally with financial market interaction: π and π^*.[21]

state variable. Owing to the strict kink in the money wage Phillips curve we have a marked convergence to the steady state in both countries. Note here that, though wage deflation is excluded from the model, nevertheless goods price deflation occurs. Allowing now for trade in goods between the two countries (but not yet for financial links) dampens the cycle in country 1 considerably and makes that in country 2 slightly more pronounced, as shown in the middle of Figure 6.4. This change remains true if financial links are added (as shown in the parameter set). Now, however, the dynamics converge to a limit cycle and no longer to the steady state (only crudely shown at the bottom of Figure 6.4 to the right). This limit cycle exhibits nearly completely adverse phase synchronization at least in the inflationary climate of the two considered countries, since the exchange rate dynamics now dominate the outcome and produce the negative correlation in inflation dynamics shown. There is thus no positive international transmission of inflation dynamics, contrary to what is generally expected, if trade is dominated by exchange rate movements and their (always adverse) effect on one of the two countries.

In Figure 6.5 we show (again for π, π^*) with the time series in the top figure that increasing speed of adjustment of the exchange rate produces increasing volatility, here shown for the inflationary climate variable π. The final outcome shown (the lower figure) is convergence to a persistent business cycle (stable limit cycle) in both countries, yet – as the lower time series show – with nearly perfect negative correlation. This figure again demonstrates that business fluctuations need not at all be synchronized with respect to upswings and downswings, though they are clearly synchronized here with respect to phase length. Note that setting $\beta_e = 0$ (no exchange rate dynamics) is already sufficient to decouple the real dynamics from what happens in the foreign exchange market.

The top figure in Figure 6.6 shows that business fluctuations (represented here again by the two inflation climate variables) are now fairly synchronized and also somewhat damped again (with the home country the one with initially more volatility in inflation, since the expansionary monetary shock is occurring in this country solely, there lowering the interest rate and thus increasing investment and inflation directly). Wage flexibility is very high ($\beta_w = 5$) in the simulation under consideration, but is again tamed in a radical way by the assumption that there is no wage deflation possible (which is more restrictive than just the assumption $\beta_w = 0$). In the lower graph of Figure 6.6 we show in addition that there is now zero root hysteresis involved in the evolution of the nominal as well as the real variables. This is due to the fact that the relevant 9D dynamics, with its suppression of the Dornbusch nominal exchange rates, but still with changing real exchange rate dynamics due to differing inflation in the two countries considered, now exhibits a law of motion for the real exchange rate η that is "linearly dependent" on the two laws of motion for the two price levels of the investigated economies. There is thus hysteresis present in the evolution of the real exchange rate which is transmitted also to hysteresis in real wages and full employment labor intensity, as shown in Figure 6.6. We note that hysteresis can here also be partly due to the kink in the Phillips curve, which when based on this fact implies that the steady-state employment rate need no longer coincide with the given NAIRU rate $\bar{V}$, if it is

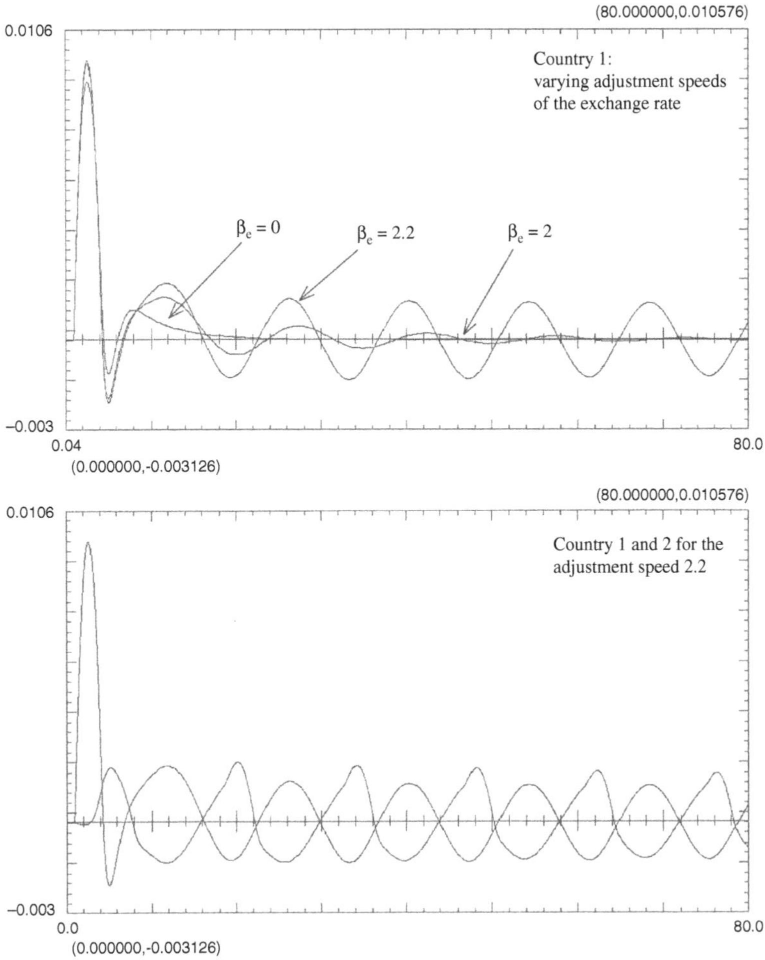

Figure 6.5 The occurrence of limit cycles and of negative transmissions of inflation.[22]

characterized by zero inflation rates in the steady state so that the kink becomes operative immediately below the steady state.[23]

Figure 6.7 shows in its lower part, and in a striking fashion (for π and π^*), that only radically damped oscillations may occur in the case where both countries pursue the policy of zero steady-state inflation. In the upper part however we show what happens if country 1 allows for 0.7% of inflation in the steady state by increasing its money supply growth rate accordingly. There are now persistent fluctuations not only occurring in the country that allows for such monetary policy, but also induced persistent fluctuations in the other country, here with a significant degree of phase synchronization, since the Dornbusch dynamics is again absent

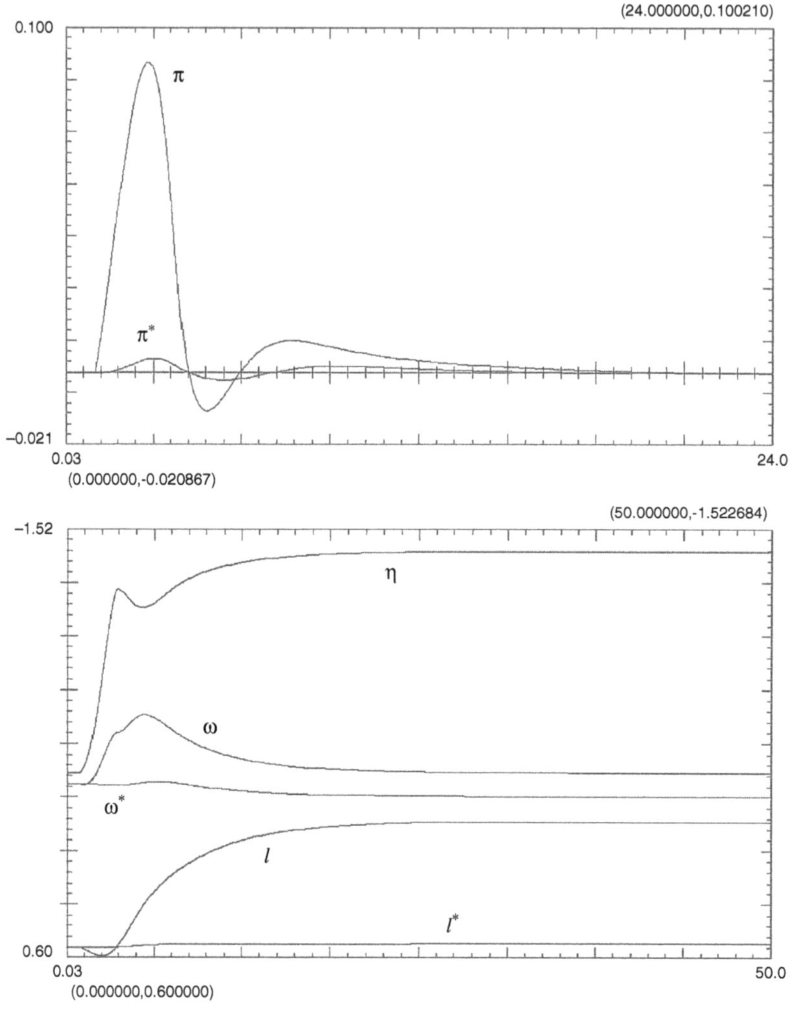

Figure 6.6 Positively correlated trade and hysteresis in a monetary union.[24]

from the considered situation. The inflationary environment in which the kinked money wage Phillips curve is operating does therefore matter very much and may give rise to situations where the economy is no longer viable (which occurs here for $\mu = 0.07$).

The time series in Figure 6.8 (as usual for the inflationary climate variable in both countries) show for varying wage adjustment speeds (and a 1% inflation rate in both countries in the steady state) how phases get synchronized in the two countries, here with respect to inflation rates. Owing to the higher wage adjustment speed in country 1 we find in the case of independent fluctuations that phase

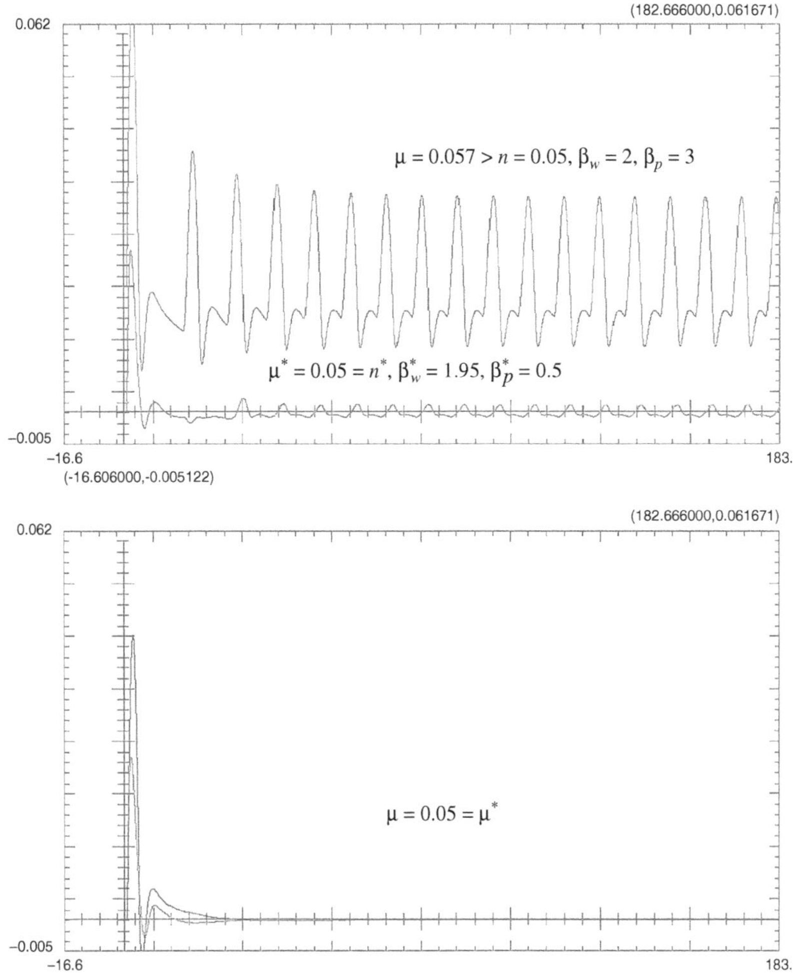

Figure 6.7 The generation of persistent economic fluctuations in the case of positive steady-state inflation in country 1.[25]

lengths differ considerably in the more volatile inflation dynamics of the home country from the ones observed abroad (with less flexible wages). Yet once the countries are coupled with each other, as indicated by the parameter set shown in endnote 26, cycle phase lengths become by and large synchronized in the upper graph (though not their amplitudes), while we can see in the lower time-series comparison that phase lengths stay in a ratio of two to each other when only the significant peaks are taken into account. There are thus various possibilities for

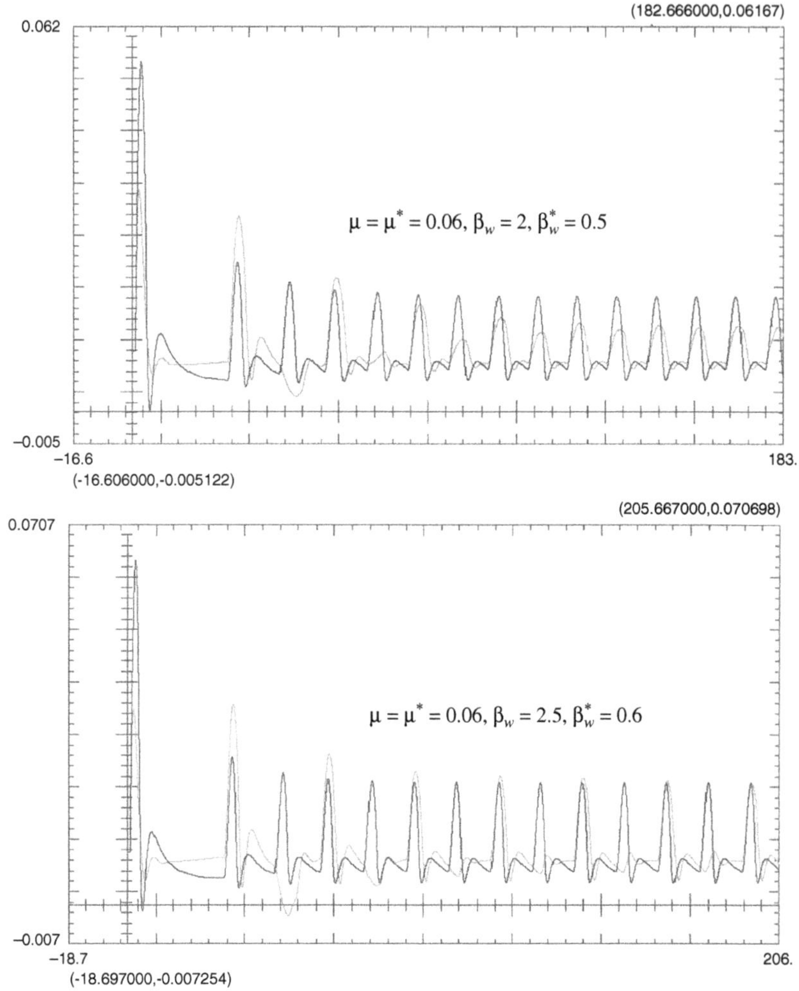

Figure 6.8 Phase synchronization in a fixed exchange rate system.[26]

phase synchronization to be taken into account and to be explored further in future studies of the considered dynamics.

In Figure 6.9 (top) we show how cycles for countries that are interacting with respect to trade (in a fixed exchange rate system) are to some extent synchronized (with respect to the longer phase length in country 2). This synchronization gets lost to some extent in the case of a flexible exchange rate system ($\beta_e = \beta = \beta_\epsilon = 0.5$), and this in a way that makes the then still occurring persistent fluctuations (bottom figure) much more pronounced than they were in the fixed exchange rate

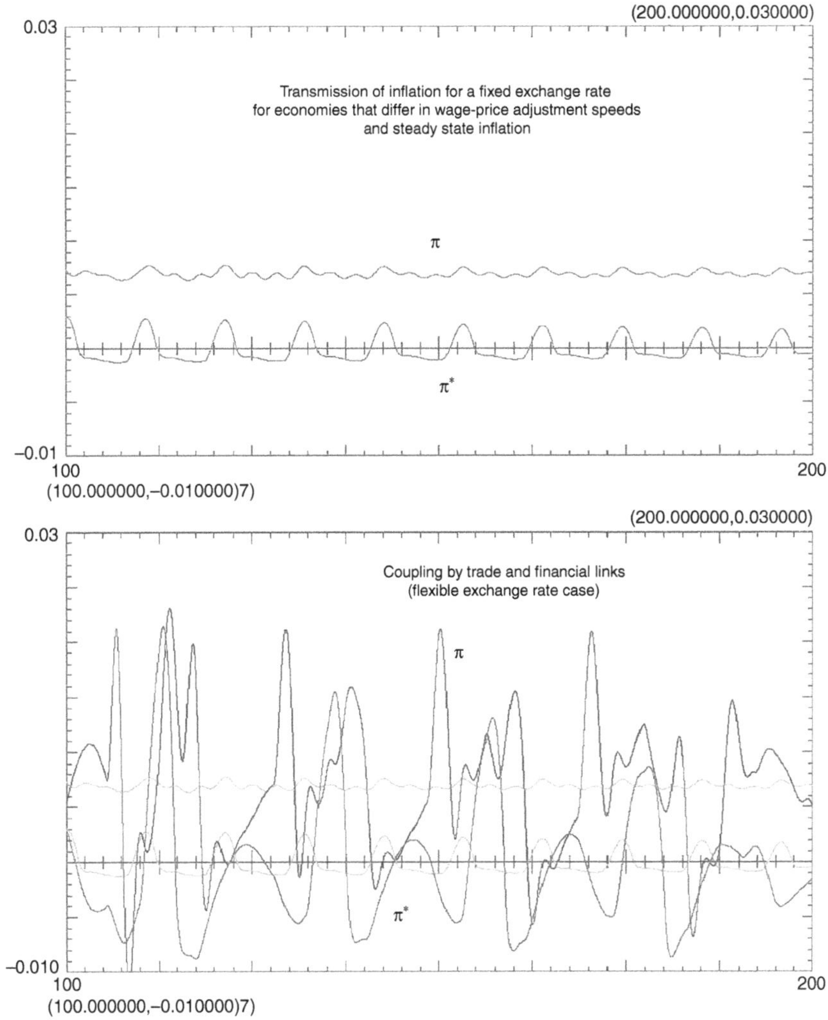

Figure 6.9 Phase synchronization in a fixed exchange rate system and its loss under flexible exchange rates.[28]

case (top figure). Cycle interaction in the real and the financial part thus may make such interacting economies fairly volatile.[27]

Note with respect to Figure 6.9 that countries are still very similar in their parameter values, both with a kink in their money wage Phillips curve which however becomes operative only in country 2 due to the fact that the steady state exhibits zero inflation there. In this country, we can observe therefore prolonged

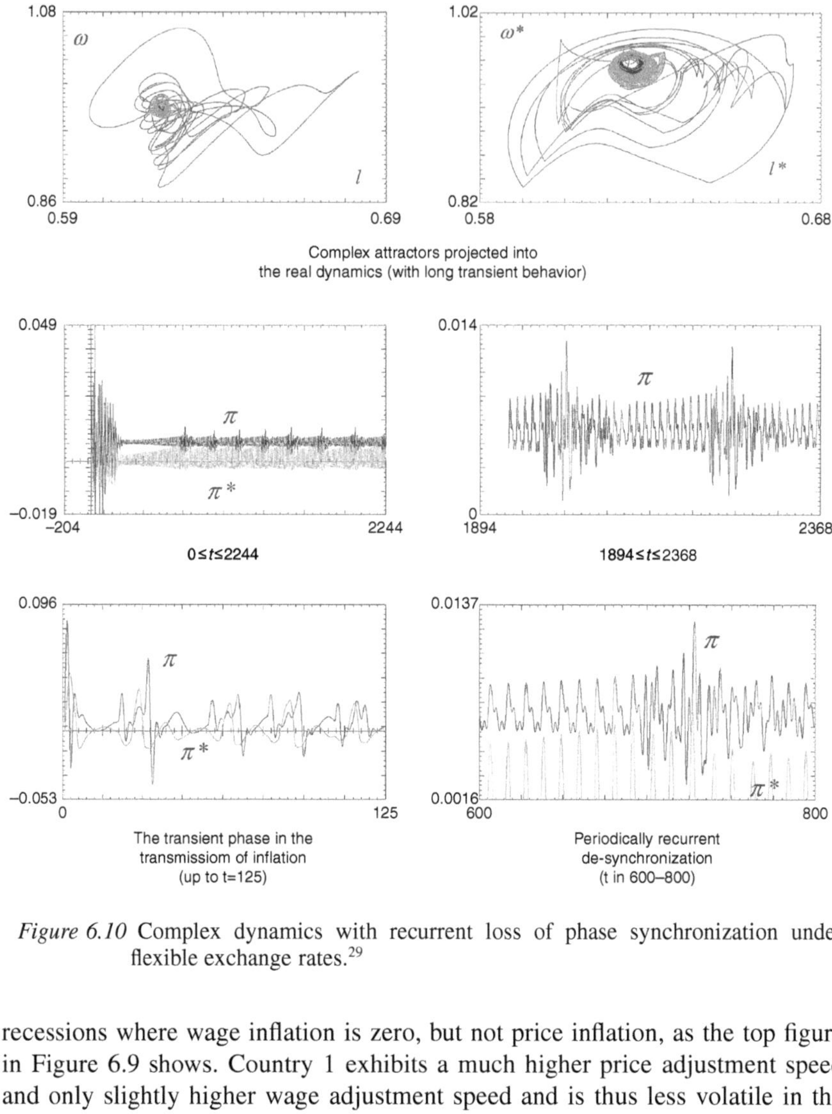

Figure 6.10 Complex dynamics with recurrent loss of phase synchronization under flexible exchange rates.[29]

recessions where wage inflation is zero, but not price inflation, as the top figure in Figure 6.9 shows. Country 1 exhibits a much higher price adjustment speed and only slightly higher wage adjustment speed and is thus less volatile in the fluctuations of the inflationary climate series shown, since price flexibility, but not wage flexibility, is stabilizing in the parameter range of the present case (as can be shown by eigenvalue diagrams). Yet, owing to the operation of the kink in country 2, fluctuations there are also much less volatile than they would have been if some wage deflation had been allowed for.

In Figure 6.10 we provide an example of a complex attractor in our two-country setup. Projected into the (l, ω) phase subspaces these attractors appear (in the top figure) – after a long transient phase – more or less as fairly simple quasi-periodic motions, a periodicity that however goes hand in hand with slight

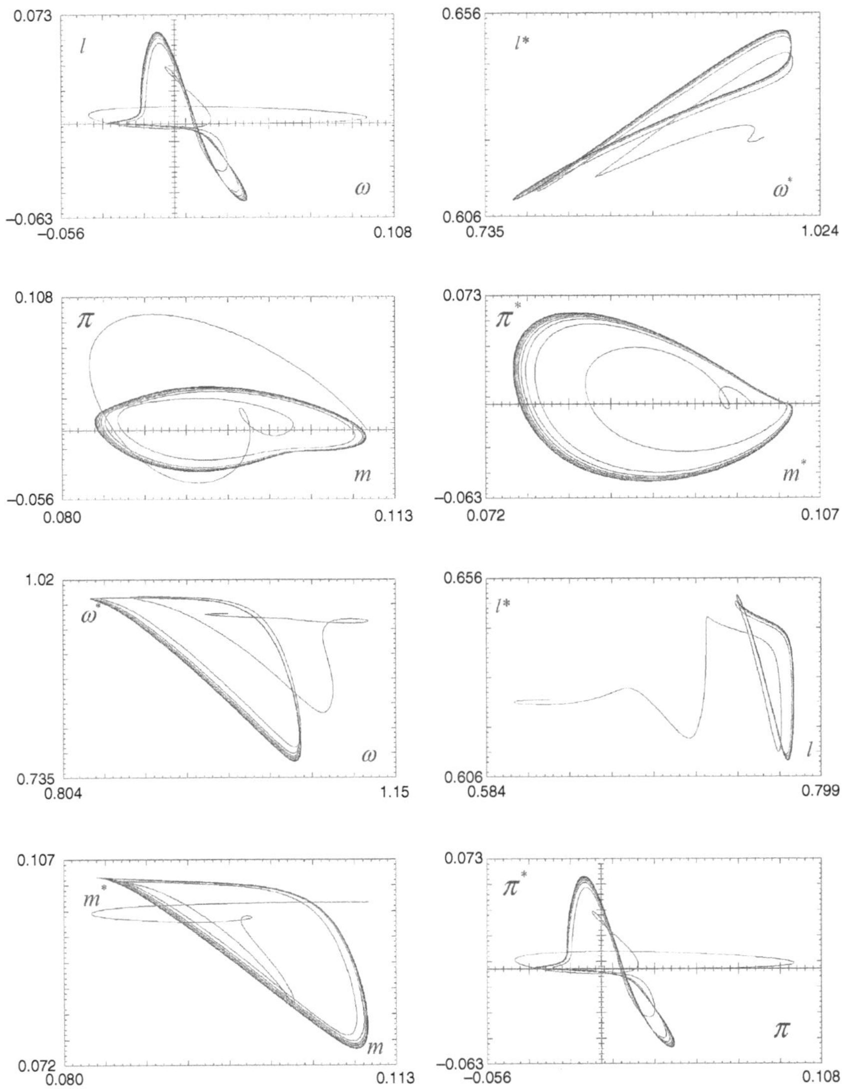

The case $\mu^* = 0.05 = \mu$: $\pi^*_o = \pi_o = 0$.

Figure 6.11 No steady-state inflation and limit cycle projections.[30]

increases in amplitude until there is an outbreak of more irregular fluctuations as shown in the middle of Figure 6.10. At the bottom in Figure 6.10 we finally show the fluctuating inflationary climates in the transient period after the expansionary monetary shock, applied in all our figures, with little phase synchronization over the first 125 years and to the right we show how phase synchronization gets lost in periods where irregularities and amplitudes increase. Note here that the figure at bottom right only shows the upswings in the foreign economy while the longer periods where there is some price, but no wage deflation, are not shown explicitly.

In Figure 6.11 we consider again the case of no steady-state inflation, now projecting the limit cycle then obtained into various subspaces of the 10D phase space. We note first of all that the steady state would be unstable in the absence of floors to money wages (here given by the assumption of complete inflexibility downwards). In the first four panels in the figure we see that real and monetary cycles are fairly different in the two countries, due to the much higher wage–price flexibility in country 1. Real wages and labor intensity are basically negatively correlated as the next two panels then show and this also holds for the monetary sector as the panels at the bottom indicate.

Yet more important than these findings are the numerical findings shown in Figure 6.12. Top left we again show that the kink in the money wage Phillips curve rapidly gives rise to stable limit cycle behavior, while the darker area in the middle of the figure shows the behavior of the dynamics without the kink. The dynamics is, on the one hand, not as volatile as the one with the kink, but, on the other, not viable over the very long horizon (roughly 1300 years in this simulation run). Really striking however is that very small variations in the growth rate of the money supply at home or abroad have dramatic consequences on the dynamic outcome of the model. In place of the limit cycle top left (just discussed) we get the recurrent fluctuations directly below it when the growth of the domestic money supply is changed from 0.05 to 0.051 while the dynamics is very close to the steady state in between the shown irregular fluctuations (shown for a time horizon of 2300 years). Eigenvalue diagrams indeed confirm a very sensitive behavior of the maximum eigenvalue close to the growth rate of the money supply where there is zero steady-state inflation.

In the opposite situation where μ^* is changed from 0.05 to 0.051 by contrast we get convergence to the steady state within the first 150 years, but finally economic breakdown (after 700 years) due to a very small positive root of the dynamics. This breakdown can be delayed a bit if also the growth rate of domestic money supply is changed to 0.051, giving rise to a second outburst as shown, but not to viability in the very long run.

Figure 6.12 supplements Figure 6.11 in the way just discussed and is of course based on the same parameter values as Figure 6.11. It shows finally in its bottom panels cases of very minor steady-state deflation. When there is steady-state deflation in the domestic economy (with its high speeds of adjustments in the wage–price module of the model) we now get convergence to the steady state, in the bottom left panel again confronted with the dark area of the dynamics when the kink is removed from them. In the case of deflationary policy in the foreign economy we however get instability both with and without the kink, though the kink makes the dynamics viable over a much longer horizon than in the case of no kink in the money wage Phillips curve. We stress finally that the cycle length in

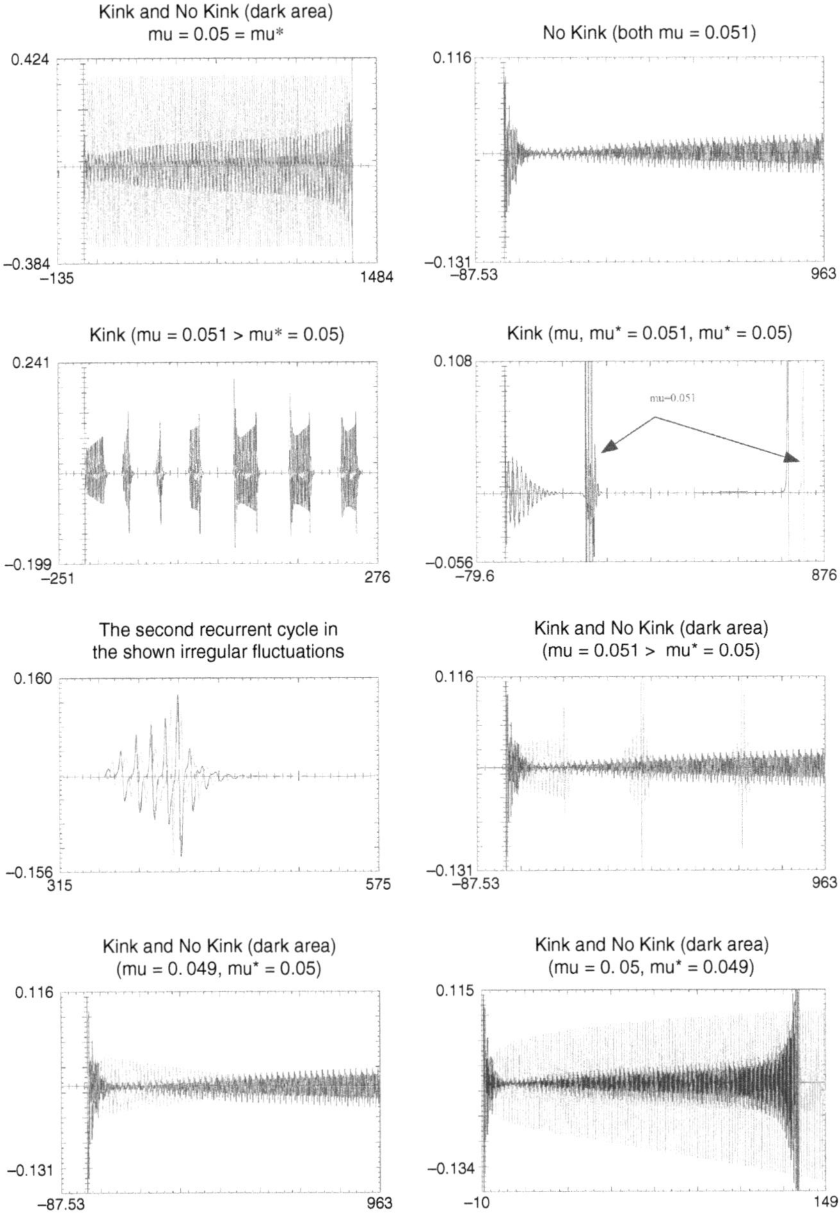

Figure 6.12 Steady-state inflation and the generation of irregular time-series patterns (here shown for the inflation rate π).[31]

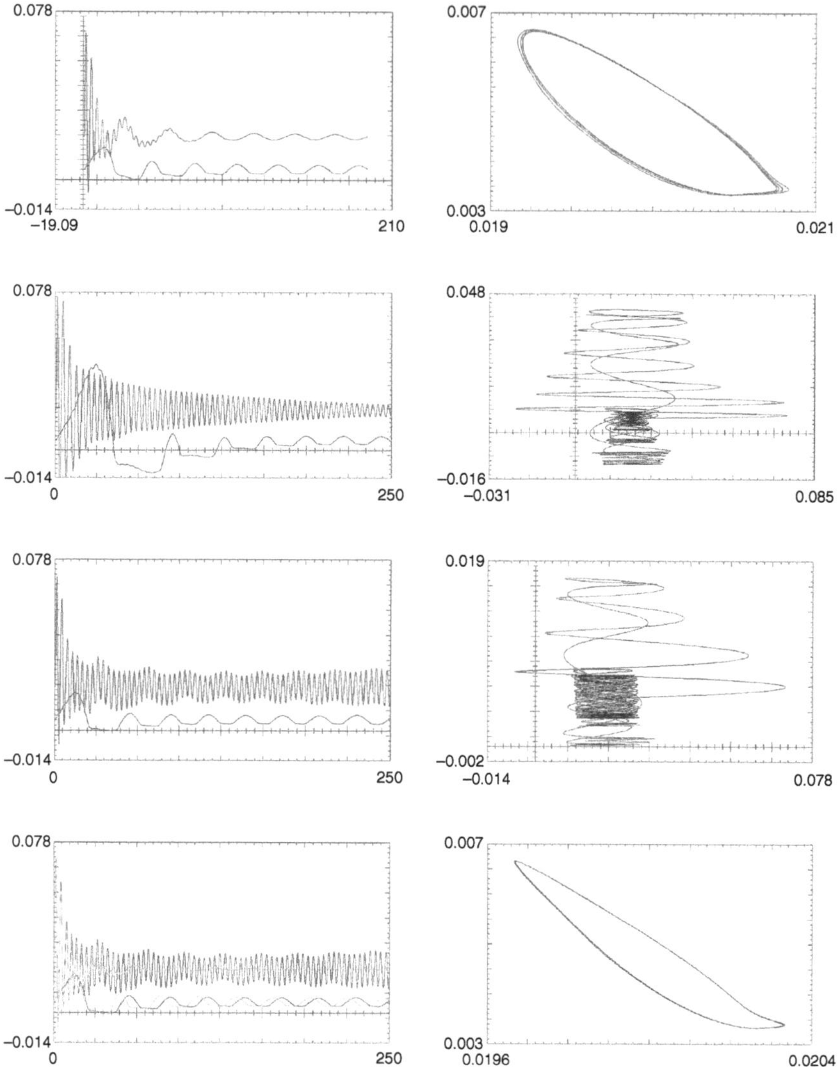

Figure 6.13 Interacting economies with fast vs. slow wage–price dynamics and further significant differences.[32]

the shown time series is approximately ten years and that this phase length tends to become longer the more sluggish wages (and prices) become.

Finally in Figure 6.13 we show a situation where countries have now been differentiated from each other in most of their parameter values, not only in the wage–price module. We indicate various types of phase synchronization, basically by the establishment of negative correlations and consider again the case of separated economies, of economies that are only linked via trade (the fixed exchange rate case) and economies that have the usual financial links in addition.

This closes the numerical illustrations of this chapter for the case of two coupled KWG economies, where wage–price dynamics is at the main focus of interest (besides income-distribution-driven accumulation dynamics), but where the quantity dynamics of the KMG modeling framework are still absent in this formulation of full capacity growth.

6.6 Conclusions

In this chapter we have extended the KWG approach to the dynamics of closed economies to the case of two interacting open economies. The model was introduced on the extensive-form level by way of nine submodules, presenting the behavioral equations, the laws of motion and the budget equations of the sectors and markets. On the basis of simplifying assumptions we then derived the 10D core dynamics implied by the model. The uniquely determined interior steady state of the dynamics, its stability and its loss stability by way of Hopf bifurcations was discussed in an economically intuitive, but mathematically informal, way. Finally, in the case of local explosiveness of the dynamics around the steady state we have bounded them by an institutionally determined kink in the money wage Phillips curve of the model (adding downward wage rigidity to it). This behavioral nonlinearity restricts the dynamics around the interior steady state to economically meaningful domains in many situations, a variety of which were investigated from the numerical point of view in the preceding section. These numerical simulations of the dynamics showed interesting features of more or less coupled oscillators and thus indicated that interesting dynamics may be obtained from the coupling of models of monetary growth of the KWG when applied to the case of two interacting open economies.

Part III

The semistructural aggregate demand–aggregate supply model

Theory and evidence

7 Distributive cycles, business fluctuations and the wage-led/profit-led debate

7.1 Introduction

The central issue in macroeconomic theory deals with the long-term sustainability of capitalist society, the interaction between the level of economic activity in a country and distribution of the income that is generated among its citizens. This still represents, nevertheless, an issue that has not yet been sufficiently investigated and understood in the macroeconomics literature.

In this context, the question is whether an increase in the real wage leads to a rise (via consumption increases) or to a decline (via lower investment) in the level of overall economic activity, or, in other words, whether the economy is primarily wage-led or profit-led. Following Bowles and Boyer (1995) and Gordon (1995), a large body of studies – see e.g. Stockhammer and Onaran (2004), Naastepad and Storm (2007), Stockhammer *et al.* (2009) and Hein and Vogel (2008) for important contributions along this line of research – has investigated this issue empirically, the majority of it by means of single-equation estimation techniques – see Hein and Vogel (2008) for a detailed overview of this literature.

The approach of this chapter is however a different one. Instead of investigating the plausibility of wage- or profit-led regimes from an empirical and partial perspective, we intend to contribute to the macroeconomics literature by focusing on the interaction of macroeconomic activity and the dynamics of the real wage at both the theoretical and empirical levels from a system macrodynamics perspective, which, as we will attempt to show below, takes more appropriately into account the macroeconomic feedback channels which determine the dynamic stability of the system analyzed. As we will show, a proper analysis of the relationship between income distribution and economic activity moreover needs to take into account the feedback influence of economic activity on income distribution in a systematic and consistent manner, because when such interactions are properly taken into account and theoretically modeled, potential instability scenarios (at least at the theoretical level) come to light. These show the need to incorporate additional stabilizing mechanisms such as monetary policy into the theoretical framework – see Galí (2008) and Flaschel *et al.* (2008a) for a discussion of the role of monetary policy in the achievement of determinacy in new Keynesian models with staggered wages and prices. For the analysis of these issues we will use a simplified version of the semistructural macroeconomic model introduced by Chen *et al.* (2006), which is closely related in spirit to the model by Barbosa-Filho and Taylor (2006).

In the following theoretical analysis the modeling of the dynamics of labor productivity and endogenous technical change will be left aside by assuming that it is exogenously given. The implications of the theoretical framework to be discussed here should thus be handled with care, since no final conclusions on the interaction of economic activity and income distribution can be drawn from models which do not fully and properly endogenize the dynamics of labor productivity. This caveat applies of course not only to our model but to many other models which also generally neglect this important feature of real capitalist economies.

The remainder of this chapter is organized as follows. In the next section we deliver some theoretical considerations on the wage-led/profit-led debate as well as empirical stylized facts on long- and short-run distributive and business cycles in the US economy. In Section 7.3 the theoretical framework is described, and in Section 7.4 the role of monetary policy in wage- and profit-led economies is analyzed. Section 7.5 concludes. In an appendix we provide the mathematical proofs of the results discussed in Section 7.4.

7.2 Theoretical considerations and stylized facts

As already acknowledged by Rose (1967), the real wage channel in Keynesian macrodynamics is characterized by an intrinsic ambiguity which arises from the opposite effect of real wage increases on the different components of aggregate demand (consumption, investment and net exports), on the one hand, and the influence of these variables on the dynamics of wage and price inflation, on the other.

Indeed, as illustrated in Figure 7.1, taken by itself, a real wage increase can act in a stabilizing or destabilizing manner, depending among other things on whether the output dynamics depend positively or negatively on the real wage (i.e. on whether consumption reacts more strongly to real wage changes than investment or vice versa) *and* on whether the reaction of price inflation is larger than the reaction of wage inflation with respect to such a development.

This interdependence can be expressed – here still in an abstract manner – in the following way:

$$\dot{y} = f(y, \omega),$$
$$\dot{\omega} = f(y, e(y) - e_0),$$

where $\omega = \ln(W/P)$ denotes the log real wage, W and P being the levels of nominal wages and prices, respectively, y is the output gap and $e - e_0$ is the employment gap, with e the employment rate (which is a function of y) and e_0 the equilibrium employment rate ($\dot{x}$ represents the time derivative of a variable x).

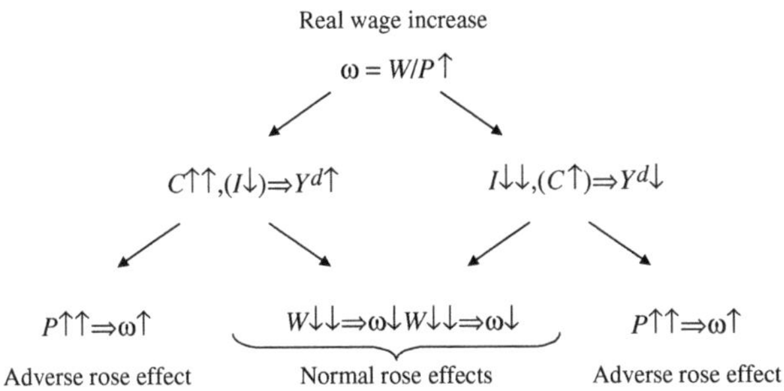

Figure 7.1 Normal (convergent) and adverse (divergent) Rose effects: the real wage channel of Keynesian macrodynamics.

Table 7.1 Four baseline real wage adjustment scenarios

	Wage-led goods market	*Profit-led goods market*
Labor market-led	$\begin{pmatrix} - & + \\ + & 0 \end{pmatrix}$	$\begin{pmatrix} - & - \\ + & 0 \end{pmatrix}$
Real wage adjustment	Divergent or convergent	Convergent
Goods market-led	$\begin{pmatrix} - & + \\ - & 0 \end{pmatrix}$	$\begin{pmatrix} - & - \\ - & 0 \end{pmatrix}$
Real wage adjustment	Convergent	Divergent or convergent

The Jacobian matrix J of this abstract 2D dynamical system evaluated at its steady state is characterized by

$$J = \begin{pmatrix} \partial\dot{y}/\partial y & \partial\dot{y}/\omega \\ \partial\dot{\omega}/\partial y & \partial\dot{\omega}/\omega \end{pmatrix} = \begin{pmatrix} - & ? \\ ? & 0 \end{pmatrix}.$$

As can easily be observed, the above Jacobian matrix allows for four different cases, indeed the four cases illustrated in Figure 7.1. These four different scenarios can be jointly summarized as in Table 7.1.

As illustrated in Table 7.1, there exist two cases where the Rose (1967) real wage channel operates in a stabilizing manner. In the first case, the goods markets (represented in our analysis by the output gap) depend negatively on the real wage ($\partial\dot{y}/\partial\omega < 0$) – a situation where the economy is usually referred to as "profit-led" – and the dynamics of the real wage are determined primarily by the nominal wage dynamics and therefore by the developments in the labor market ($\partial\dot{\omega}/\partial y > 0$). In this case, because labor market-led real wage increases ($\partial\dot{\omega}/\partial y > 0$) *receive a check* through the implied negative effect on goods markets activity levels, the interaction between these two variables is intrinsically stable. In the second case, the goods markets depend positively on the real wage ($\partial\dot{y}/\partial\omega < 0$) – in which case the economy would be categorized as "wage-led" – and the price level dynamics, and therefore the goods markets, primarily determines the behavior of the real wages, i.e. $\partial\dot{\omega}/\partial y < 0$.

The diagrammatic representation in Table 7.1 of different scenarios by the Jacobian matrices of this simple 2D dynamical system shows that an economic system characterized by wage-led goods market dynamics (in which case trace $J < 0$ holds in all cases) can only be asymptotically stable if

$$\det J = -(\partial\dot{y}/\partial\omega)(\partial\dot{\omega}/\partial y) > 0,$$

which is true if and only if $\partial\dot{\omega}/\partial y < 0$, that is, in the case of a goods market-led real wage adjustment. For a profit-led economy, in turn, the necessary condition for asymptotic stability is a labor market-led real wage adjustment, that is, $\partial\dot{\omega}/\partial y > 0$.[1]

The considered 2D dynamics thus correspond to four possible situations concerning wage and price flexibilities and the relationship between the real wage and economic activity (a strictly negative one according to Keynes (1936)), as they were already in principle considered in the seminal paper by Rose (1967) and as they are illustrated in Table 7.1 and Figure 7.1. The reader will notice that an important feature of this theoretical representation is that we have – in place of Keynes (1936) strictly negative correlation between the real wage and economic activity – now two interacting dynamic laws instead of one static relationship as in his case, a situation which nevertheless allows us to share his view on negative real wage/economic activity relationships to a certain degree if the goods market is profit-led and the wage–price dynamics labor market-led.[2]

We next show, in Figure 7.2, the local phase portraits of the four considered cases in the same order as the matrices are shown in Table 7.1, under the additional assumption that the diagonal terms in these matrices are still zero (which makes the isoclines all vertical or horizontal and the Jacobian in the diagonal of Table 7.1 only stable of center point type).[3]

As the reader might have noticed, there is an obvious connection between the isoclines sketched in the phase diagrams of Figure 7.2 and the distributive and effective demand cycles discussed by Barbosa-Filho and Taylor (2006). Indeed, as them, we analyze not only the same issue from a similar perspective but, as will become clear below, this paper could be considered as delivering an enhanced formalization and extension of their framework.[4]

Recall that in the two cases illustrated on the left-hand side of Figure 7.2 economic activity is always wage-led, and on the right-hand side it is profit-led. Real wage growth is labor market-led in the top figures and goods market-led in the bottom figures. As can clearly be observed, the combinations wage- and labor market-led and profit- and goods market-led imply in the assumed situation saddle-path dynamics. In the first case (the upper left diagram) we have the plausible dynamic features of a self-enforcing inflationary boom or a self-enforcing deflationary depression.[5] The lower right diagram (the second case), in contrast,

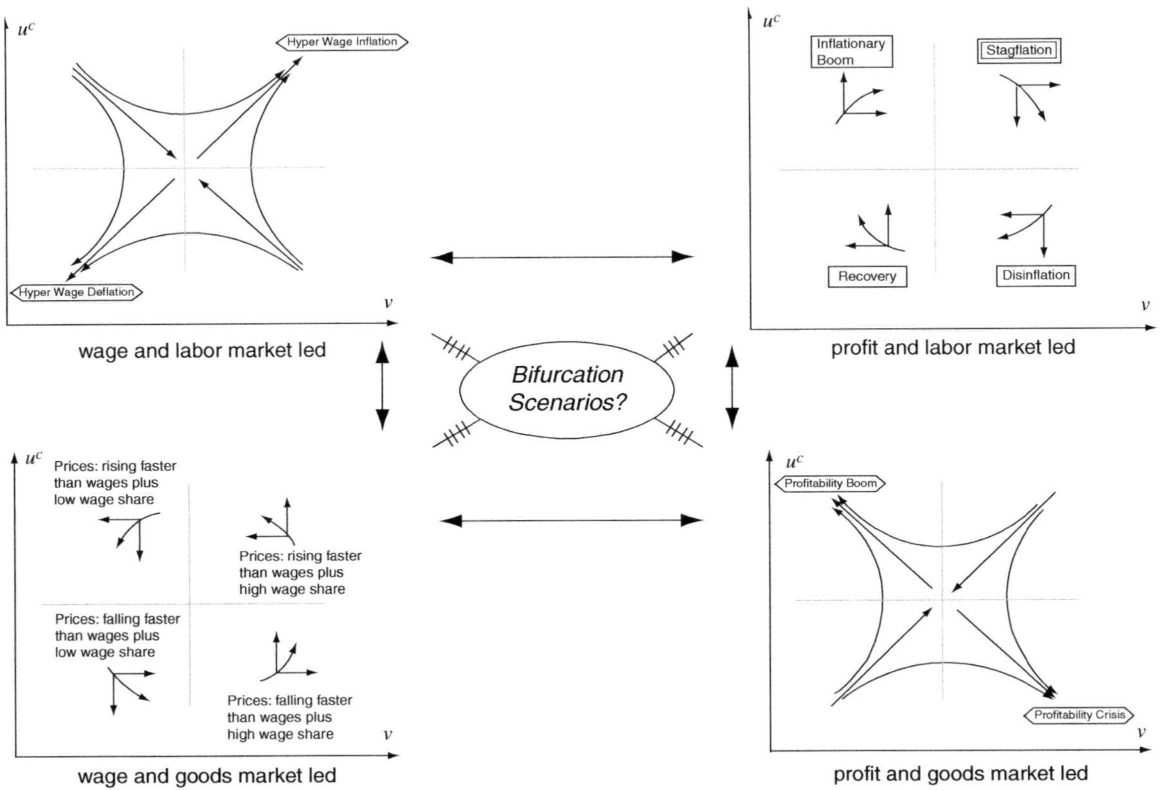

Figure 7.2 Phase portraits of the four types of real wage feedback channels of Keynesian macrodynamics.

shows on the top left profitability booms where prices outperform wages systematically and on the bottom right a profitability crisis where low activity is coupled with rising real wages, since prices fall faster then wages.[6]

The combination profit- and labor market-led (illustrated by the upper right diagram) is exactly equal to the Marx–Goodwin growth cycle model. It will produce convergent dynamics if the effects in the trace of the matrix J are added again. The typical prediction of this situation is that the distributive cycle has a clockwise orientation (if the diagonal terms in J are not too strong). In the opposite case (lower left diagram), which combines the wage- with goods market-led cases, we have the opposite orientation, i.e. a counterclockwise one. This is due to the fact that real wage changes are dominated by price level effects and not by changes in the money wage, the wage share falls in situations of high economic activity and rises in situations of low economic activity. We do not consider this a long-lasting regime, but rather would conclude, as in Flaschel *et al.* (2008b), that it may have temporarily existed during the sequence of business cycles that have characterized for example the USA economy after World War II.

From a temporary perspective however all situations shown can happen, but in view of Keynes's (1936) assumption of a strictly negative relationship between real wages and economic activity in a capitalist economy, we would expect that this distributive conflict constraint is characterizing capitalistic economies in the longer run and thus may be founded on the weaker conflicting claims assumptions that underlie the situation top right in Figure 7.2.[7]

The next graphs deliver some additional insight into this issue. On the one hand Figure 7.3 shows the decomposition obtained through penalized splines of US time series of the wage share and the employment rate in long-phase and short-phase (business cycle) components.[8] As can be clearly observed, the long-phase Goodwinian wage share/employment rate cycle exhibits by and large a pronounced clockwise orientation, showing that the long-phase dynamics in the labor markets are negatively correlated (in an overshooting fashion) with the wage share in the US economy.[9]

But this correlation is not only present in the long term. Figure 7.4 on the other hand shows the single short-run distributive cycles previously depicted jointly in the lower right panel of Figure 7.3. Having again the employment rate on the y-axis and the wage share on the x-axis, the single-phase diagrams of the wage share/employment rate business cycles around the long cycle shown in Figure 7.4 have in five of six cases by and large the same clockwise orientation as the long-phase cycle depicted in the lower left panel of Figure 7.3. This empirical observation – obtained by the nonparametric methodology of penalized splines – leads us to the preliminary conclusion that the dynamics of the wage share are by and large pro-cyclical and thus – using our characterization – labor market-led. If we consider that in reality a viable economic system cannot be intrinsically unstable – at least not over long periods of time – then Figure 7.2 would suggest that the goods market dynamics has to be of a profit-led nature for the system not to feature diverging forces.

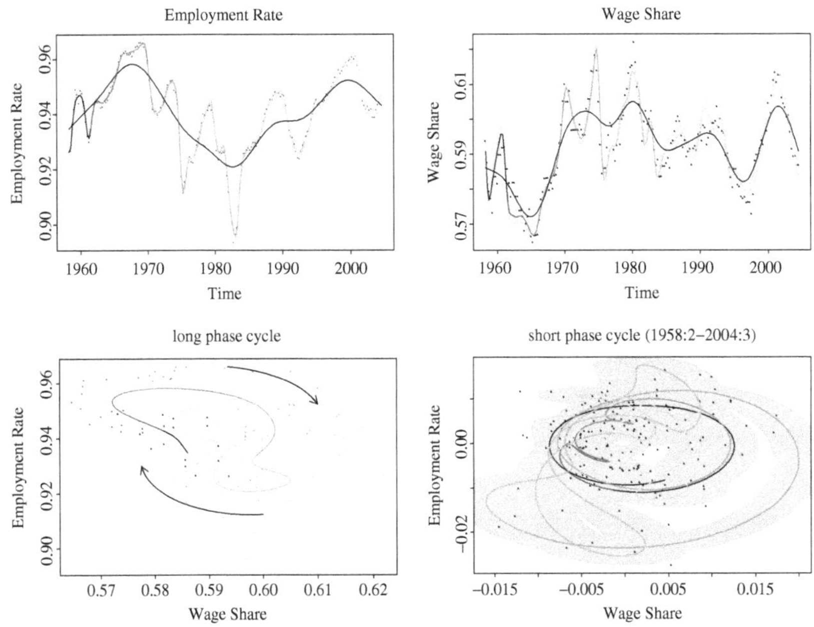

Figure 7.3 Separating the US distributive dynamics into short and long cycles.

There is however a further reason why the goods market dynamics should be negatively correlated with the labor share, namely the interaction between aggregate demand and supply reactions toward real wage changes.

As previously stated, a large body of empirical work – such as Bowles and Boyer (1995), Gordon (1995), Stockhammer and Onaran (2004), Naastepad and Storm (2007), Stockhammer *et al.* (2009) and Hein and Vogel (2008) – has addressed the question whether an economy is wage- or profit-led.[10]

In our view, however, these and the large majority of the existent empirical studies on the wage-led/profit-led debate oversee a central point, namely the discrepancy between aggregate demand and the realized (and observable) components of aggregate output. Indeed, the great majority of these studies often use measures of realized consumption and realized investment in order to find out whether consumption responds stronger (positively) than investment (negatively), in which case they would call the observed situation wage-led. But normally planned domestic consumption and investment (and their reaction to wage increases) do differ from their actual, realized levels due to the interplay of aggregate demand and supply as well as through the simultaneous influence of other macroeconomic variables such as the real interest or the real exchange rate, on the one hand, as well as the expectations of future developments, on the other, which may obscure significantly a clear-cut classification of the economy between wage- or profit-led categories.

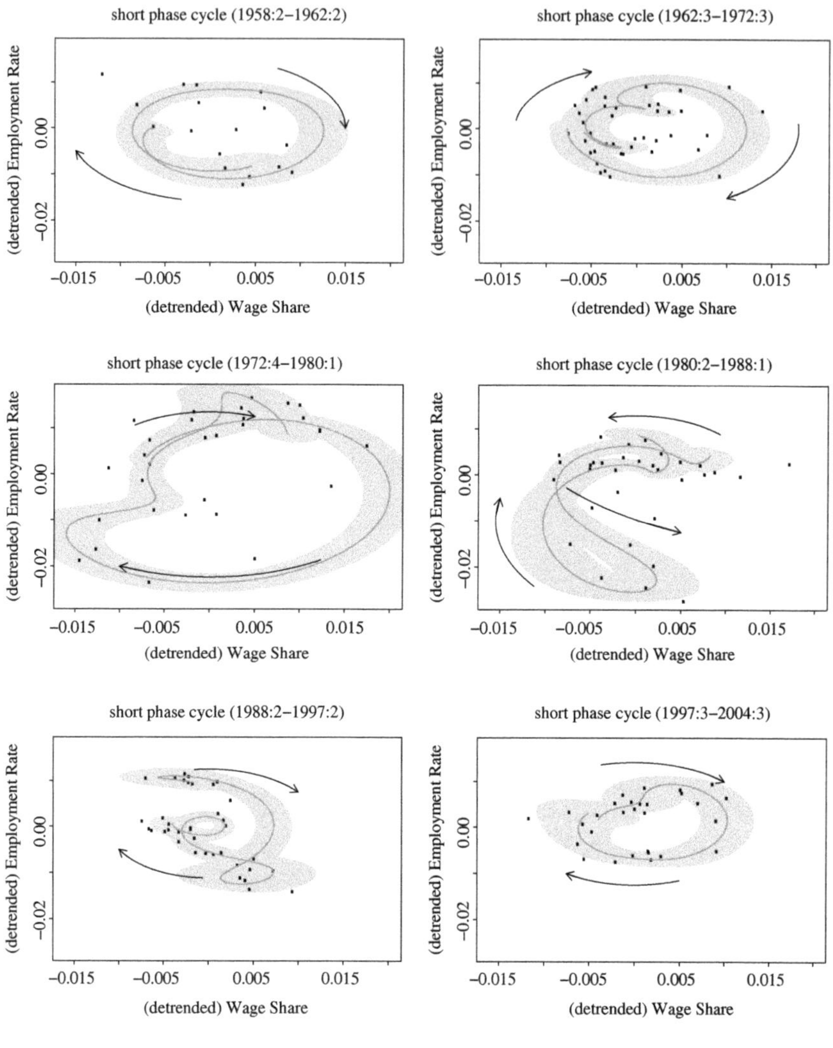

Figure 7.4 US distributive cycles of business cycle frequency.

The importance of a *joint* consideration of the concerned macroeconomic effects at work can be made clearer by the following simple example illustrated in Figure 7.5. Going back to Keynes's (1936) acceptance of the first classical postulate in his *General Theory*, we have on the one hand a supply curve (AS curve) that is positively sloped, since marginal costs increase with economic activity. On the other hand we have a demand curve (AD curve) that is negatively sloped due to its textbook IS–LM foundation.

If we assume, following Keynes, that real wages are negatively correlated with economic activity – due to the supply schedule of firms – and if we assume that

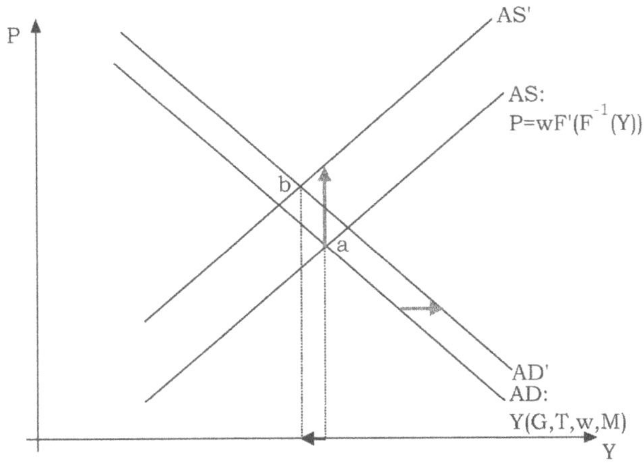

Figure 7.5 Wage-led demand implies profit-led activity in conventional Keynesian AD–AS analysis.

aggregate goods demand is wage-led as stressed for example by Stockhammer *et al.* (2009), the equality between goods demand and supply (the goods market equilibrium outcome in the AD–AS model) will always determine that only a negative correlation between economic activity (the output level) and the real wage can be observed, since only the intersection between demand and supply (which always moves along the supply curve) is actually observable. So even if aggregate goods demand was wage-led, the reaction of realized output to a real wage increase would suggest a profit-led economic activity, that is, lead to an observational profit-led outcome. As illustrated in Figure 7.5, nominal wage increases shift the demand curve to the right implying higher activity. But they also shift the AS curve to the left (or up). Since the shift of the AD curve has to be smaller in amount than the AS curve shift (as illustrated exemplarily in Figure 7.5) given the counteracting reactions of the different aggregate demand components to a real wage increase, a net reduction of the output level (with a de facto increase in the real wage) is observable as the final outcome.[11] A proper identification of the overall real wage (or the labor share) effect on output must thus take also into account the effect of output on the former variable.

In the next sections, however, we do not investigate further these empirical issues but analyze instead the interplay between the real wage and output using a simplified version of the Keynesian disequilibrium AD–AS model first introduced and investigated in Chen *et al.* (2006). As will be discussed below, this type of model questions the usual way of thinking in terms of an AD and an AS curve, whether static or dynamic, since it interprets its building blocks as providing equations for price and for quantity dynamics where in particular the latter represents an interaction of supply and demand and thus not an AD curve as is customarily believed. This further law of motion will, as a result of our formulation of a wage–price spiral in a

Keynesian framework, provide some sort of reasoning that seems to be in favor of the proponents of a wage-led theory of goods demand. We will get for the adjustment of the real wage from our formulation of the wage–price spiral that its growth rate depends positively on labor market activity (through money wage growth) and negatively on goods market activity (through price level growth). Depending on which of these effects is the stronger one, we get an overall positive dependence on the labor share if the labor market is dominant (a situation which we call labor market-led) and a negative dependence in the opposite case of a goods market-led wage–price spiral. This gives a positive link from economic activity to (the growth rate of) real wages, but one that comes not from goods demand, but from wage negotiations and the price setting behavior of firms. If a labor market-led wage–price spiral situation were coupled with a wage-led goods market dynamics, we would have two positive feedback effects between activity levels and real wages and thus would get explosiveness (maybe existing at the times when the Nixon administration exercised a stop to wages and prices). This situation may be understood as an environment where the money wage dominates the wage–price spiral (at least in an upward direction). This is the model of gradual wage, price and quantity adjustments that we will formulate and somewhat expand in the following. See Flaschel and Krolzig (2006) for a related approach or Barbosa-Filho and Taylor (2006) for a structuralist approach in this framework.

Our empirical investigation supports the theoretical intuition that real wage growth is actually labor market-led, but not due to positive link from goods demand, but instead due to the positive influence generated coming from wage negotiations and the price setting behavior of firms. This result, coupled with the empirical evidence suggesting that real activity growth is profit-led, will therefore imply stable cyclical adjustment processes in general. This may be understood as a weak form of the working of Keynes's (1936) first classical postulate in an environment where the money wage dominates the wage–price spiral (at least in an upward direction).

7.3 A dynamical (dis)equilibrium AD–AS model

In this section we consider a separate quantity from wage and price dynamics in the description of the model rather than AD vs. AS as was still the case in the previously mentioned work. In addition we formulate our dynamic price–quantity model in such a way that it can be reduced easily to a smaller dimensional dynamical system, the stability conditions of which can be investigated analytically to yield a variety of stability conclusions.

The goods and the labor markets

The model of this chapter is considered against the background of a fixed proportions technology, characterized by[12]

$$y^p = \ln(Y^p/K) = \text{const.}, \quad z = Y/L^d = \text{const.},$$

$$y = \ln(Y/Y^p), \quad e = L^w/L.$$

Potential output Y^p is here compared with actual output Y, which is demand determined in this model. Here y describes the output gap, defined as the log of the ratio of actual to potential output (which could also be considered as the rate of capacity utilization). To produce the output workers have to supply $L^d = Y/z$ hours of work. Their rate of utilization is therefore given by u^w. Finally, e represents the rate of employment on the labor market.

As is usually done in the macroeconomics literature (see e.g. Rudebusch and Svensson 1999), we model the dynamics in the goods markets by means of a law of motion of the type of a dynamic IS equation

$$\dot{y} = (\alpha_y - 1)y - \alpha_{yr}(i - \dot{p} - (i_0 - \pi_0)) + \alpha_{yv}(\omega - \omega_0), \tag{7.1}$$

with $\alpha_{yv} > 0$ or $\alpha_{yv} < 0$, depending on whether the overall reaction of the output dynamics with respect to real wage increases is positive or negative, that is, on whether aggregate demand is wage- or profit-led.

The reduced-form equation (7.1) has three important characteristics. (i) It reflects the dependence of output changes on aggregate income and thus on the rate of capacity utilization by assuming a negative, i.e. stable, (partial) dynamic multiplier relationship in this respect. (ii) It shows the joint dependence of consumption and investment on the real wage/wage share (which in the aggregate may in principle allow for positive or negative signs before the parameter β_{uv}, depending on whether consumption or investment is more responsive to real wage changes/wage share changes). (iii) It shows finally the negative influence of the real rate of interest on the evolution of economic activity. With respect to the link between the goods and the labor markets, for simplicity the validity of Okun's (1970) law is assumed, whereas

$$e/e_0 = (Y/Y^p)^{\alpha_{eu}} = \exp(\alpha_{ey}y) \iff e = \exp(\alpha_{ey}y)e_0, \tag{7.2}$$

with Y as the actual and Y^p as its potential level of output, and e as the employment rate.[13]

Wage–price dynamics

The core of our earlier theoretical framework, which allowed for nonclearing labor and goods markets and therefore for under- or over-utilized labor as well as capital, is the modeling of the wage–price dynamics, which are specified through two separate Phillips curves, each one led by its own measure of demand pressure (or capacity bottleneck), instead of a single one as done in baseline new Keynesian models as in Galí and Gertler (1999) and Galí *et al.* (2001).[14] The approach of estimating separate wage and price Phillips curves is not altogether new, however. Barro (1994) for example observes that Keynesian macroeconomics is (or should be) based on imperfectly flexible wages as well as prices and thus on the consideration of wage as well as price Phillips curves. Furthermore, Fair (2000) criticizes the low accuracy of reduced-form price equations, and in the same study estimates two separate wage and price equations for the USA, nevertheless using a single demand-pressure term, the NAIRU gap.

On the contrary, by modeling wage and price dynamics separately from each other, each one determined by their own measures of demand and cost pressures in the market for labor and for goods. By these means, we can analyze the dynamics of the real wages in the economy and identify oppositely acting effects as they might result from different labor and goods markets developments. Indeed, we believe that a Keynesian model of aggregate demand fluctuations should (independently of whether justification can be found for this in Keynes's (1936) *General Theory*) allow for under- (or over-) utilized labor *as well as* capital, and gradual wage as well as price adjustments in order to be general enough from the descriptive point of view.

Concerning the price Phillips curve, a similar procedure can be applied, based on desired markups of firms. Along these lines one in particular gets an economic motivation for the inclusion of (indeed the logarithm of) the real wage (or wage share) with negative sign in the wage Phillips curve and with positive sign in the price Phillips curve, without any need for log-linear approximations as in the new Keynesian approaches.

According to this modeling approach, the structural form of the wage–price dynamics can be expressed by

$$\begin{aligned}\dot{w} = {} & \beta_{we}(\exp(\alpha_{ey}y)e_0 - e_0) - \beta_{wv}(v - v_0) \\ & + \kappa_{wp}\dot{p} + (1-\kappa_{wp})\pi^c + \kappa_{wz}g_z, \qquad (7.3)\\ \dot{p} = {} & \beta_{py}\,y + \beta_{pv}(v - v_0) + \kappa_{pw}(\dot{w} - g_z) + (1-\kappa_{pw})\pi^c, \qquad (7.4)\end{aligned}$$

where w denotes the log nominal wage, p the log producer price level, v the log wage share and $g_z = \text{const.}$ the trend labor productivity growth. The respective demand-pressure terms in the wage and price Phillips curves $e - e_0$ and y in the market for labor and for goods, respectively,[15] are thus augmented by three additional terms: (1) the deviation of the log wage share v or real unit labor costs from its steady-state level (the error correction term discussed in Blanchard and Katz (1999, p. 71)); (2) a weighted average of corresponding expected cost-pressure terms, assumed to be model-consistent, with forward-looking, crossover wage and price inflation rates $\dot{w}$ and $\dot{p}$, respectively, and a backward-looking measure of the prevailing inertial inflation in the economy (the "inflationary climate," so to say) symbolized by $\pi^c = \text{const.}$;[16] and, finally, (3) trend labor productivity growth g_z (which is expected to influence wages in a positive and prices in a negative manner, due to the associated easing in production cost pressure).[17]

The microfoundations of our wage Phillips curve are of the same type as in Blanchard and Katz (1999) (see also Flaschel and Krolzig (2006)), which can be reformulated with the employment gap $e - \bar{e}$ and the output gap.

Our wage–price module is thus consistent with standard models of unemployment based on efficiency wages, matching and competitive wage determination, as well as markup pricing and can be considered as an interesting alternative to the – theoretically rarely discussed and empirically questionable – purely forward-looking new Keynesian form of staggered wage and price dynamics that we have discussed in Section 7.1.

Moreover, this wage–price mechanism can also be interpreted in terms of a post-Keynesian approach as formulated in Barbosa-Filho and Taylor (2006).[18]

The across-markets or *reduced-form* Phillips curves of the wage Phillips curve and the price Phillips curve are given by (with $\kappa = 1/(1-\kappa_w\kappa_p)$)[19]

$$\begin{aligned}\dot{w} &= \kappa[\beta_{we}(\exp(\alpha_{ey}y)e_0 - e_0) + \kappa_w\beta_{py}y + (\kappa_{wz} - \kappa_{wp}\kappa_{pw})g_z] + \bar{\pi}^c,\\ \dot{p} &= \kappa[\beta_{py}\,y + \kappa_p\beta_{we}(\exp(\alpha_{ey}y)e_0 - e_0) + \kappa_{pw}(\kappa_{wz} - 1)g_z] + \bar{\pi}^c,\end{aligned}$$

with inflation pass-through terms behind the κ_{wp} and κ_{pw} parameters. These reduced-form Phillips curves represent a considerable generalization of the conventional view of a single-market price Phillips curve with only one measure of demand pressure, namely the one in the labor market. They are easily derived when account is taken of the fact that the above equations can be rewritten as a system of two linear equations in the variables $\dot{w} - \pi^c$ and $\dot{p} - \pi^c$ and solved through the usual inversion of the 2×2 system matrix that is thereby obtained.

It should be pointed out that, as the wage–price mechanisms are formulated, the development of the inflation climate does not matter for the evolution of the domestic log wage share $v = w - p - z$, measured in terms of producer prices, the law of motion of which is given by (e given by equation (7.2))

$$\begin{aligned}\dot{v} = \kappa[&(1-\kappa_{pw})(\beta_{we}(\exp(\alpha_{ey}y)e_0 - e_0) - \beta_{wv}(v - v_0))\\ &- (1-\kappa_{wp})(\beta_{py}\,y + \beta_{pv}(v - v_0)) + (\kappa_{wz} - 1)(1-\kappa_{wz})g_z].\end{aligned} \tag{7.5}$$

As equation (7.5) clearly shows, due to the specification of the wage and price inflation dynamics, the labor share depends on both situations, in the goods and labor markets, on the state of income distribution in the economy as well as on the relative weights of crossover inflation expectations in the wage and price inflation adjustment equations. Since the focus of this chapter lies on the dynamics of the real wage and not of the wage share, we assume that the level of average labor productivity is $Z = 1$ (so that $v = w - p - \ln(Z) \Longleftrightarrow v = \omega$) and $g_z = 0$, and reformulate equation (7.5) as representing the dynamics of the log real wage (with $v_0 = \omega_0$), namely

$$\begin{aligned}\dot{\omega} = \kappa[&(1-\kappa_{pw})(\beta_{we}(\exp(\alpha_{ey}y)e_0 - e_0) - \beta_{wv}(\omega - \omega_0))\\ &- (1-\kappa_{wp})(\beta_{py}y + \beta_{pv}(\omega - \omega_0))].\end{aligned} \tag{7.6}$$

As can be clearly observed, equation (7.6) delivers a rationale for the (at least theoretically) ambiguous reaction of the real wages to increases in aggregate income, which is based on the crossover inflation weights κ_{wp} and κ_{pw} and the respective "slope" of the wage and price Phillips curves, taking note of their corresponding excess demand-pressure terms.[20]

The structural wage and price inflation adjustment equations (7.3) and (7.4) also imply the following reduced-form price Phillips curve

$$\dot{p} = \kappa[\beta_{we}(\exp(\alpha_{ey}y)e_0 - e_0) - \beta_{wv}(\omega - \omega_0) + \kappa_{pw}(\beta_{py}y + \beta_{pv}(\omega - \omega_0))] + \pi^c, \tag{7.7}$$

which is to be inserted into the IS equation given by (7.1).

Monetary policy

Concerning monetary policy, we model the nominal interest rate as being determined by a simple Taylor rule without interest rate smoothing (for comparison see Svensson 1999). Hereby we assume the target rate of the monetary authorities as being determined by

$$i = i_0 + \phi_\pi(\dot{p} - \pi_0) + \phi_y y. \tag{7.8}$$

The target rate of the central bank i is thus made dependent on the steady-state nominal rate of interest i_0, and is as usual dependent on the inflation gap and the capacity utilization gap (as a measure of the output gap).[21] For the time being we assume that there is no interest rate smoothing with respect to the interest target of the central bank, which therefore immediately sets its target rate at each moment in time. This allows the interest rate policy rule to be inserted directly into the law of motion characterizing the market for goods and thus saves one law of motion in the investigation of the economy.

Our simplified (disequilibrium) dynamical model thus reads

$$\begin{aligned}
\dot{y} &= (\alpha_y - 1)y - \alpha_{yr}(\phi_\pi - 1)(\dot{p} - \pi_0) + \alpha_{yv}(\omega - \omega_0), \\
\dot{\omega} &= \kappa[(1 - \kappa_{pw})(\beta_{we}(\exp(\alpha_{ey}y)e_0 - e_0) - \beta_{wv}(\omega - \omega_0)) \\
&\quad - (1 - \kappa_{wp})(\beta_{py}y + \beta_{pv}(\omega - \omega_0))],
\end{aligned}$$

after insertion of equation (7.8) into equation (7.1) (with ω instead of v), and $\dot{p}$ given by equation (7.7). We note that the steady state of the dynamics, due to its specific formulation, can be supplied exogenously as $e_0 = 1,\ v_0,\ \pi_0^c = \dot{p}_0 = \dot{w}_0 = 0$ and $y_0 = 0$, since the model has been constructed around a specific steady-state position.

In the next section we discuss (on the basis of the local stability analysis of the model thoroughly presented in the appendix to this chapter) the theoretical viability (in the sense of a dynamically stable economic system) of the wage- and profit-led hypothesis concerning the dynamics of the goods markets (taking into account their interaction with the wage–price dynamics).

7.4 Wage- and profit-led goods market dynamics and macroeconomic stability

In order to focus first on the intrinsic interaction of y and ω without the stabilizing influence of monetary policy and the Blanchard and Katz (1999) error correction terms in both wage and price adjustment equations, we begin by setting $\alpha_{yr} = 0$ and $\beta_{wv} = \beta_{pv} = 0$. The simplified system I is then given by

$$\dot{y} = (\alpha_y - 1)y + \alpha_{yv}(\omega - \omega_0),$$
$$\dot{\omega} = \dot{w} - \dot{p} = \kappa[(1 - \kappa_{pw})\beta_{we}(\exp(\alpha_{ey}y)e_0 - e_0) - (1 - \kappa_{wp})\beta_{py}y],$$

with $\dot{p}$ given by

$$\dot{p} = \kappa[\beta_{py}y + \kappa_{pw}\beta_{we}(\exp(\alpha_{ey}y)e_0 - e_0)] + \bar{\pi}^c. \tag{7.9}$$

The corresponding Jacobian of this simplified 2D system is given by

$$J^{\mathrm{I}} = \begin{pmatrix} \partial\dot{y}/\partial y & \partial\dot{y}/\omega \\ \partial\dot{\omega}/\partial y & \partial\dot{\omega}/\omega \end{pmatrix} = \begin{pmatrix} J_{11}^{\mathrm{I}} & J_{12}^{\mathrm{I}} \\ J_{21}^{\mathrm{I}} & J_{22}^{\mathrm{I}} \end{pmatrix}$$
$$= \begin{pmatrix} \alpha_y - 1 & \alpha_{yv} \\ \kappa[(1 - \kappa_{pw})\beta_{we}\alpha_{eu} - (1 - \kappa_{wp})\beta_{py}] & 0 \end{pmatrix} = \begin{pmatrix} - & ? \\ ? & 0 \end{pmatrix}.$$

According to Proposition 7.1 on the local stability of the model presented in the appendix of this chapter, if the goods markets dynamics are wage-led ($\alpha_{yv} > 0$, so that $\partial\dot{y}/\partial\omega > 0$), the real wage must react negatively with respect to output increases ($\partial\dot{\omega}/\partial y < 0$), i.e. the real wage dynamics must react anti-cyclically if the system's steady state is to be asymptotically stable and thus viable from an economic perspective. On the contrary, if the goods market dynamics are profit-led ($\alpha_{yv} < 0$, so that $\partial\dot{y}/\partial\omega < 0$), then the real wages must react positively to output increases ($\partial\dot{\omega}/\partial y > 0$).

The economic intuition behind the conditions of Proposition 7.1 is the following. If goods markets are wage-led, then an increase in the real wage leads to an economic expansion. If the adjustment of the real wage is positively dependent on the output gap, then the initial increase in the real wage would be the kick-off of an expansionary spiral boosted by the positive feedback between output and real wages. Such a situation cannot, however, be considered as economically viable (or desirable), at least in the long run. In the absence of other stabilizing channels, if the output dynamics are wage-led, then the real wage dynamics must be goods market-led (as we have labeled the situation where prices react more strongly than nominal wages to changes in the level of economic activity), i.e. $\partial\dot{\omega}/\partial y < 0$, if the economic system which is analyzed is supposed to be locally stable.

By setting $\alpha_{yr} > 0$ we can reincorporate the real interest rate channel into the dynamics of the new system II, which then reads

$$\dot{y} = (\alpha_y - 1)y - \alpha_{yr}(\phi_\pi - 1)(\dot{p} - \pi_0) + \alpha_{yv}(\omega - \omega_0),$$
$$\dot{\omega} = \kappa[(1 - \kappa_{pw})\beta_{we}(\exp(\alpha_{ey}y)e_0 - e_0) - (1 - \kappa_{wp})\beta_{pu}y],$$

with $\dot{p}$ given by equation (7.9).

Under the assumption of a sufficiently pronounced monetary policy represented by $\phi_\pi > 1$, which is able to overcome the destabilizing real interest rate channel, the incorporation of the real interest channel does not change the stability properties of the steady state. In this reduced system, a sufficiently aggressive monetary policy only increases the speed of convergence of a locally stable system toward its steady state, but cannot enforce the stability for an unstable system. The clear-cut correspondence of *wage-led/goods market-led* and *profit-led/labor market-led* cases stated in Proposition 7.1 for system I holds thus also for system II.

Now let β_{wv} and β_{pv} be greater than zero but assume again $\alpha_{yr} = 0$. In this case, the extended dynamical system III reads

$$\dot{y} = (\alpha_y - 1)y + \alpha_{yv}(\omega - \omega_0),$$
$$\dot{\omega} = \kappa[(1 - \kappa_{pw})(\beta_{we}(\exp(\alpha_{ey}y)e_0 - e_0) - \beta_{wv}(\omega - \omega_0)) - (1 - \kappa_{wp})(\beta_{py}y + \beta_{pv}(\omega - \omega_0))],$$

with $\dot{p}$ given by equation (7.7) and the corresponding Jacobian J^{III} being

$$J^{\text{III}} = \begin{pmatrix} \partial\dot{y}/\partial y & \partial\dot{y}/\omega \\ \partial\dot{\omega}/\partial y & \partial\dot{\omega}/\omega \end{pmatrix} = \begin{pmatrix} J^{\text{III}}_{11} & J^{\text{III}}_{12} \\ J^{\text{III}}_{21} & J^{\text{III}}_{22} \end{pmatrix} = \begin{pmatrix} \alpha_y - 1 & \alpha_{yv} \\ J^{\text{III}}_{21} & J^{\text{III}}_{22} \end{pmatrix},$$

with

$$J^{\text{III}}_{21} = \kappa[(1 - \kappa_{pw})\beta_{we}\alpha_{ey} - (1 - \kappa_{wp})\beta_{py}]$$

and

$$J^{\text{III}}_{22} = -\kappa[(1 - \kappa_{pw})\beta_{wv} + (1 - \kappa_{wp})\beta_{pv}].$$

As Proposition 7.3 makes clear, the introduction of a stabilizing self-referential feedback channel in the real wage dynamics changes to a certain extent the clear-cut correspondence of the *wage-led/goods market-led* and *profit-led/labor market-led* cases just discussed and treated by Propositions 7.1 and 7.2 in the appendix of this chapter. Indeed, as Proposition 7.3 shows, for $\beta_{wv}, \beta_{pw} > 0$, if the goods market is wage-led, the real wage dynamics do not necessarily have to be goods market-led; the partial derivative $\partial\dot{\omega}/\partial y$ can be either negative or positive, as long as it is of a sufficiently small dimension that does not threaten the stability of the system, i.e.

$$\frac{\partial\dot{\omega}}{\partial y} < \frac{(\partial\dot{y}/\partial y)(\partial\dot{\omega}/\partial y)}{\partial\dot{y}/\partial\omega}.$$

The economic intuition behind Proposition 7.3 is the following. If the economy is wage-led and the real wage dynamics depend negatively on their own level, then the reaction of the real wage with respect to output increases can be positive ($\partial\dot{\omega}/\partial y > 0$) and still not be system-destabilizing, as long as such a reaction is sufficiently small. If this is the case, then the system's steady state is locally stable without the need of additional stabilizing mechanisms such as monetary policy.

If the economy is *profit-led*, however, the possibility of such an ambiguity no longer exists since the upper-bound value for $\partial\dot{\omega}/\partial y$ is already negative, as shown in Proposition 7.3.

Finally, let us analyze the case of β_{wv}, β_{pv} *and* α_{yr} greater than zero. In this most general case the dynamical system IV is given by

$$\begin{aligned}\dot{y} &= (\alpha_y - 1)y - \alpha_{yr}(\phi_\pi - 1)(\dot{p} - \pi_0) + \alpha_{yv}(\omega - \omega_0),\\ \dot{\omega} &= \kappa[(1-\kappa_{pw})(\beta_{we}(\exp(\alpha_{ey}y)e_0 - e_0) - \beta_{wv}(\omega - \omega_0))\\ &\quad - (1-\kappa_{wp})(\beta_{py}y + \beta_{pv}(\omega - \omega_0))],\end{aligned}$$

with $\dot{p}$ given by equation (7.7), and the corresponding Jacobian being given by

$$J^{\mathrm{IV}} = \begin{pmatrix}\partial\dot{y}/\partial y & \partial\dot{y}/\omega\\ \partial\dot{\omega}/\partial y & \partial\dot{\omega}/\omega\end{pmatrix} = \begin{pmatrix}J_{11}^{\mathrm{IV}} & J_{12}^{\mathrm{IV}}\\ J_{21}^{\mathrm{IV}} & J_{22}^{\mathrm{IV}}\end{pmatrix},$$

with

$$\begin{aligned}J_{11}^{\mathrm{IV}} &= (\alpha_y - 1) - \alpha_{ur}(\phi_\pi - 1)\kappa(\beta_{py} + \kappa_{pw}\beta_{we}\alpha_{ey}),\\ J_{12}^{\mathrm{IV}} &= \alpha_{yv} - \alpha_{yr}(\phi_\pi - 1)\kappa(\beta_{pv} - \kappa_{pw}\beta_{wv}),\\ J_{21}^{\mathrm{IV}} &= \kappa[(1-\kappa_{pw})\beta_{we}\alpha_{ey} - (1-\kappa_{wp})\beta_{py}],\\ J_{22}^{\mathrm{IV}} &= -\kappa[(1-\kappa_{pw})\beta_{wv} + (1-\kappa_{wp})\beta_{pv}].\end{aligned}$$

According to Proposition 7.4, if the overall effect of real wage increases on the goods markets dynamics ($\partial\dot{y}/\partial\omega = J_{12}^{\mathrm{IV}}$) is positive – despite the positive effect of the real interest rate channel (which is however made negative by a sufficiently aggressive monetary policy ($\phi_\pi > 1$) – the real wage reaction with respect to output must be bounded from above – featuring a anti-cyclical ($\partial\dot{\omega}/\partial y < 0$) or a boundedly pro-cyclical ($J_{21}^{\mathrm{IV}\,\max} > \partial\dot{\omega}/\partial y > 0$) pattern – if the steady state of the system is to be locally asymptotically stable. Expressed differently, if the goods market is *wage-led* ($\partial\dot{y}/\partial\omega > 0$), then the corresponding effect of y on ω must not be too large for the economic system to be stable. In the same sense, if $\partial\dot{y}/\partial\omega < 0$, the reaction of the real wage dynamics toward output increases must be bounded from below – featuring a pro-cyclical ($\partial\dot{\omega}/\partial y > 0$) or a boundedly anti-cyclical pattern ($J_{21}^{\text{IV}\min} < \partial\dot{\omega}/\partial y < 0$).

Again, the economic intuition behind Proposition 7.4 is to be found in the nature of the interaction between real wage and output dynamics. If the goods markets are *wage-led* ($\partial\dot{y}/\partial\omega > 0$), then the reaction of the real wage dynamics to output increases must be either sufficiently small if positive or *labor market-led*, or simply negative (and therefore *goods market-led*) in order to allow the stabilizing effects $\partial\dot{y}/\partial y$ and $\partial\dot{\omega}/\partial\omega$ to ensure the stability of the whole system. In the same sense, if the goods markets are *profit-led* ($\partial\dot{y}/\partial\omega < 0$), then the real wage dynamics must be either *labor market-led* ($\partial\dot{\omega}/\partial y > 0$) or, if *goods market-led* ($\partial\dot{\omega}/\partial y < 0$), of a sufficiently small dimension in absolute terms.

The role of monetary policy

It should be noted that a central assumption in all the analyzed cases has been the existence of a sufficiently low degree of persistence of the output gap ($\alpha_y < 1$) and a sufficiently aggressive monetary policy rule in terms of the Taylor principle ($\phi_\pi > 1$). These two assumptions have assured that the trace of the Jacobian matrix J is unambiguously negative in all cases. In order to highlight the importance of these two assumptions, assume now that $\alpha_y = 1$ and $\phi_\pi < 1$ (with $\alpha_{yr} > 0$). In this case, for $\alpha_{yv} > 0$, the sign structure of J^{IV} is given by

$$J^{\text{IV}} = \begin{pmatrix} \partial\dot{y}/\partial y & \partial\dot{y}/\omega \\ \partial\dot{\omega}/\partial y & \partial\dot{\omega}/\omega \end{pmatrix} = \begin{pmatrix} J_{11}^{\text{IV}} & J_{12}^{\text{IV}} \\ J_{21}^{\text{IV}} & J_{22}^{\text{IV}} \end{pmatrix} = \begin{pmatrix} + & + \\ ? & - \end{pmatrix}.$$

since $J_{11}^{\text{IV}} = -\alpha_{ur}(\phi_\pi - 1)\kappa(\beta_{py} + \kappa_{pw}\beta_{we}\alpha_{ey}) > 0$ due to a monetary policy which is not sufficiently aggressive ($\phi_\pi < 1$) to tame the destabilizing real interest channel.

In this case, the only viable solution (from a dynamic perspective) is that $\partial\dot{\omega}/\partial y = J_{21}^{\text{IV}} < 0$ holds, with the additional necessary assumptions

$$J_{11}^{\text{IV}} < J_{22}^{\text{IV}} \quad \text{and} \quad J_{21}^{\text{IV}} < J_{21}^{\text{IV}\max'} = J_{11}^{\text{IV}} \cdot J_{22}^{\text{IV}} / J_{12}^{\text{IV}} < 0,$$

since $J_{11}^{\text{IV}}, J_{12}^{\text{IV}} > 0$ and $J_{22}^{\text{IV}} < 0$. The unstable dynamics in the goods markets (represented by $J_{11}^{\text{IV}}, J_{12}^{\text{IV}} > 0$) has thus been tamed by sufficiently stabilizing intrinsic real wage dynamics ($J_{22}^{\text{IV}} < 0$) and sufficiently strong anti-cyclical reactions of the log real wage with respect to output increases (represented by J_{21}^{IV}) if the economic system is to be stable.

For the opposite case $\alpha_{yv} < 0$ (assuming for the simplicity of the argument that $|\alpha_{yv}| > \alpha_{yr}(\phi_\pi - 1)\kappa(\beta_{pv} - \kappa_{pw}\beta_{wv})$), the sign structure of J^{IV} is given by

$$J^{\mathrm{IV}} = \begin{pmatrix} \partial\dot{y}/\partial y & \partial\dot{y}/\omega \\ \partial\dot{\omega}/\partial y & \partial\dot{\omega}/\omega \end{pmatrix} = \begin{pmatrix} J_{11}^{\mathrm{IV}} & J_{12}^{\mathrm{IV}} \\ J_{21}^{\mathrm{IV}} & J_{22}^{\mathrm{IV}} \end{pmatrix} = \begin{pmatrix} + & - \\ ? & - \end{pmatrix}.$$

In this case, the only viable solution (again from a dynamic perspective) is that $\partial\dot{\omega}/\partial y = J_{21}^{\mathrm{IV}} > 0$, with the additional necessary assumptions

$$J_{11}^{\mathrm{IV}} < J_{22}^{\mathrm{IV}} \quad \text{and} \quad J_{21}^{\mathrm{IV}} > J_{21}^{\mathrm{IV}\,\min'} = J_{11}^{\mathrm{IV}} \cdot J_{22}^{\mathrm{IV}} / J_{12}^{\mathrm{IV}} > 0.$$

For the profit-led case under an insufficiently aggressive monetary policy, strong pro-cyclical reactions of the log real wage with respect to output increases (represented by J_{21}^{IV}) and again sufficiently stabilizing intrinsic real wage dynamics ($J_{22}^{\mathrm{IV}} < 0$) are thus needed to assure the dynamic stability of the economic system.

As the analysis of this section shows, a sufficiently aggressive monetary policy ($\phi_\pi > 1$) not only increases the speed of convergence toward the locally stable steady state, but furthermore – through its stabilizing effect on the goods markets dynamics through J_{11}^{IV} and J_{22}^{IV} – even enables dynamics of the real wage which might be unfeasible otherwise, as the comparison between the proof of Proposition 7.4 and the above discussion of the role of monetary policy makes clear.

7.5 Conclusions

In this chapter we have studied the interaction between the dynamics of the real wage and goods markets activity under the perspective of the wage-led/profit-led debate, a central issue in the heterodox economics literature. Using a dynamic systems approach and taking into account the intrinsic ambiguity of the real wage channel already acknowledged by Rose (1967), as well as key stylized facts on the distributive and the business cycles in the US economy, we investigated the viability of wage- and profit-led regimes under different real wage adjustment scenarios and monetary policy rules.

The results of this chapter can be summarized as follows. If the dynamics of the goods markets are wage-led and monetary policy is not sufficiently aggressive or not present at all in the model, then the dynamics of the real wage must react negatively to aggregate income increases (and therefore must be goods market-led) if the steady state of the system is supposed to be locally stable. Analogously, if the goods market dynamics are profit-led and monetary policy is not sufficiently aggressive, then the real wage dynamics must be labor market-led, i.e. they should react positively to output increases. This characterization, however, is no longer that clear-cut under a sufficiently aggressive monetary policy rule. Indeed, the stabilizing effect of monetary policy on aggregate investment allows (for a bounded range of parameters) a combination of wage-led and labor market-led dynamics within a stable dynamical system.

As discussed in this chapter, the dynamic systems approach pursued here, which properly takes into account the main feedback mechanisms between the level of economic activity and real wages, allowed us to question the plausibility of *wage-led* compared to *profit-led* regimes in a modern economy, taking into account that the real wage dynamics seem to be primarily labor market-led (are by and large of a pro-cyclical nature). It is our view that the proper study of the macroeconomy (and the categorization into different "regimes") cannot really be performed simply through partial considerations, but has to be conducted by an integrated modeling of the economy as a closed dynamical system (microfounded or not), where the dynamic interactions of the relevant macroeconomic variables are properly modeled and investigated.

Appendix: local stability analysis of the model

The (disequilibrium) dynamical model of this chapter reads

$$
\begin{aligned}
\dot{y} &= (\alpha_y - 1)y - \alpha_{yr}(\phi_\pi - 1)(\dot{p} - \pi_0) + \alpha_{yv}(\omega - \omega_0),\\
\dot{\omega} &= \kappa[(1 - \kappa_{pw})(\beta_{we}(\exp(\alpha_{ey}y)e_0 - e_0) - \beta_{wv}(\omega - \omega_0))\\
&\qquad - (1 - \kappa_{wp})(\beta_{py}y + \beta_{pv}(\omega - \omega_0))],
\end{aligned}
$$

after the insertion of equation (7.8) into equation (7.1) (with ω instead of v), and $\dot{p}$ given by equation (7.7).

The Jacobian matrix of this 2D system evaluated at the model's steady state is

$$
J = \begin{pmatrix} \partial\dot{y}/\partial y & \partial\dot{y}/\omega \\ \partial\dot{\omega}/\partial y & \partial\dot{\omega}/\omega \end{pmatrix} = \begin{pmatrix} J_{11} & J_{12} \\ J_{21} & J_{22} \end{pmatrix},
$$

with

$$
\begin{aligned}
J_{11} &= (\alpha_y - 1) - \alpha_{ur}(\phi_\pi - 1)\kappa(\beta_{py} + \kappa_{pw}\beta_{we}\alpha_{ey}),\\
J_{12} &= \alpha_{yv} - \alpha_{yr}(\phi_\pi - 1)\kappa(\beta_{pv} - \kappa_{pw}\beta_{wv}),\\
J_{21} &= \kappa[(1 - \kappa_{pw})\beta_{we}\alpha_{ey} - (1 - \kappa_{wp})\beta_{py}],\\
J_{22} &= -\kappa[(1 - \kappa_{pw})\beta_{wv} + (1 - \kappa_{wp})\beta_{pv}].
\end{aligned}
$$

PROPOSITION 7.1 *Let $\alpha_y < 1$, $\alpha_{yr} = 0$, $\beta_{wv} = \beta_{pv} = 0$, and $\alpha_{uv} > 0$. Then the steady state of the simplified system I with the Jacobian matrix*

$$
J^{\mathrm{I}} = \begin{pmatrix} \alpha_y - 1 & \alpha_{yv} \\ \kappa[(1 - \kappa_{pw})\beta_{we}\alpha_{eu} - (1 - \kappa_{wp})\beta_{py}] & 0 \end{pmatrix}
$$

is locally asymptotically stable if and only if

$$
(1 - \kappa_{pw})\beta_{we}\alpha_{ey} < (1 - \kappa_{pw})\beta_{py}.
$$

Proof: It is easy to check that, for $\alpha_y < 1$, trace J^{I} is unambiguously negative. For the steady state to be locally asymptotically stable,

$$\det(J^{\mathrm{I}}) = -\alpha_{yv}[\kappa((1-\kappa_{pw})\beta_{we}\alpha_{eu} - (1-\kappa_{wp})\beta_{py})] > 0.$$

Since $\alpha_{yv} > 0$ by assumption, only for $(1-\kappa_{pw})\beta_{we}\alpha_{eu} < (1-\kappa_{pw})\beta_{py}$ (which implies $\partial\dot{\omega}/\partial y < 0$) can the second Routh–Hurwitz local stability condition be fulfilled. □

PROPOSITION 7.2 *Now let $\alpha_{yr} > 0$ but keep $\beta_{wv} = \beta_{pv} = 0$, and assume $\alpha_y < 1$ and $\phi_\pi > 1$. The reincorporation of the real interest rate channel by setting $\alpha_{yr} > 0$ (under the assumption of a sufficiently aggressive monetary policy represented by $\phi_\pi > 1$) into the dynamics of the system does not relativize Proposition 7.1.*

Proof: It is easy to check that, while the trace of the new system II is given by

$$\mathrm{trace}(J^{\mathrm{II}}) = \alpha_y - 1 - \alpha_{yr}(\phi_\pi - 1)\kappa(\beta_{py} + \kappa_{pw}\beta_{we}\alpha_{ey}) < 0,$$

the determinant of J^{II} remains unchanged with respect to $\det(J^{\mathrm{I}})$, being namely

$$\det(J^{\mathrm{II}}) = \alpha_{uv}[\kappa((1-\kappa_{pw})\beta_{we}\alpha_{eu} - (1-\kappa_{wp})\beta_{pu})],$$

since $J^{\mathrm{II}}_{22} = 0$. □

PROPOSITION 7.3 *Let $\alpha_y < 1$ and $\alpha_{yr} = 0$, but β_{wv}, β_{pv} and $\alpha_{uv} > 0$. Then the steady state of the new system III with the Jacobian matrix J^{III} is locally asymptotically stable if and only if*

$$(1-\alpha_y)\kappa[(1-\kappa_{pw})\beta_{wv} + (1-\kappa_{wp})\beta_{pv}]/\alpha_{yv}$$
$$> \kappa[(1-\kappa_{pw})\beta_{we}\alpha_{eu} - (1-\kappa_{wp})\beta_{py}].$$

Proof: Under Proposition 7.3, the trace of J^{III} is given by

$$\mathrm{trace}(J^{\mathrm{III}}) = \alpha_y - 1 - \kappa[(1-\kappa_{pw})\beta_{wv} + (1-\kappa_{wp})\beta_{pv}] < 0,$$

and is thus unambiguously negative, while the determinant of J^{III} is

$$\det(J^{\mathrm{III}}) = (1-\alpha_y)\kappa[(1-\kappa_{pw})\beta_{wv} + (1-\kappa_{wp})\beta_{pv}]$$
$$- \alpha_{yv}\kappa[(1-\kappa_{pw})\beta_{we}\alpha_{eu} - (1-\kappa_{wp})\beta_{py}].$$

Since $\alpha_{yv} > 0$ by assumption, it is obvious that $\det(J^{III}) > 0$ (the second Routh–Hurwitz local stability condition) can be fulfilled only if

$$(1-\alpha_y)\kappa[(1-\kappa_{pw})\beta_{wv} + (1-\kappa_{wp})\beta_{pv}]/\alpha_{yv}$$
$$> \kappa[(1-\kappa_{pw})\beta_{we}\alpha_{eu} - (1-\kappa_{wp})\beta_{py}],$$

that is, if

$$\frac{\partial \dot{\omega}}{\partial y} < \frac{(\partial \dot{y}/\partial y)(\partial \dot{\omega}/\partial y)}{\partial \dot{y}/\partial \omega}.$$

□

PROPOSITION 7.4 *Let $\alpha_y < 1$, $\phi_\pi > 1$ and β_{wv}, β_{pv}, α_{uv} and $\alpha_{yr} > 0$. Then the steady state of the extended system IV (which is the original system) with the Jacobian matrix J^{IV} is locally asymptotically stable, if for $\alpha_{yv} > \alpha_{yr}(\phi_\pi - 1)\kappa(\beta_{pv} - \kappa_{pw}\beta_{wv})$, $J_{21}^{\mathrm{IV}} < J_{21}^{\mathrm{IV\,max}} = J_{11}^{\mathrm{IV}} \cdot J_{22}^{\mathrm{IV}} / J_{12}^{\mathrm{IV}}$, and if for $\alpha_{yv} < \alpha_{yr}(\phi_\pi - 1)\kappa(\beta_{pv} - \kappa_{pw}\beta_{wv})$, $J_{21}^{\mathrm{IV}} > J_{21}^{\mathrm{IV\,min}} = J_{11}^{\mathrm{IV}} \cdot J_{22}^{\mathrm{IV}} / J_{12}^{\mathrm{IV}}$.*

Proof: It can be easily confirmed that in this case, the trace of J^{IV} is unambiguously negative. Concerning the determinant of J^{IV}

$$\det(J^{\mathrm{IV}}) = J_{11}^{\mathrm{IV}} \cdot J_{22}^{\mathrm{IV}} - J_{12}^{\mathrm{IV}} \cdot J_{21}^{\mathrm{IV}},$$

the sign of J_{12}^{IV} (and therefore the sign of $\det(J^{\mathrm{IV}})$) is not unambiguously determined only by the assumption $\alpha_{yv} > 0$, since in contrast to the previously analyzed cases, for $\alpha_{yr} > 0$, the sign of J_{21}^{IV} rather depends on whether $\alpha_{yv} - \alpha_{yr}(\phi_\pi - 1)\kappa(\beta_{pv} - \kappa_{pw}\beta_{wv})$ is greater or less than zero and, for $\alpha_{yv} > 0$ and $\phi_\pi > 1$, whether

$$\alpha_{yv} > \alpha_{yr}(\phi_\pi - 1)\kappa(\beta_{pv} - \kappa_{pw}\beta_{wv}) \quad \text{or} \quad \alpha_{yv} < \alpha_{yr}(\phi_\pi - 1)\kappa(\beta_{pv} - \kappa_{pw}\beta_{wv}).$$

For $\alpha_{yv} > \alpha_{yr}(\phi_\pi - 1)\kappa(\beta_{pv} - \kappa_{pw}\beta_{wv})$, J_{12}^{IV} is unambiguously greater than zero. In this case $\det(J^{\mathrm{IV}}) > 0$ (the second Routh–Hurwitz local stability condition) can be fulfilled if and only if

$$J_{21}^{\mathrm{IV}} < J_{21}^{\mathrm{IV\,max}} = J_{11}^{\mathrm{IV}} \cdot J_{22}^{\mathrm{IV}} / J_{12}^{\mathrm{IV}},$$

whereas $J_{21}^{\mathrm{IV}} = \partial \dot{\omega}/\partial y$ can be greater or less than zero, that is, whereas the dynamics of the log real wage react positively or negatively with respect to output increases.

For $\alpha_{yv} < \alpha_{yr}(\phi_\pi - 1)\kappa(\beta_{pv} - \kappa_{pw}\beta_{wv})$, $J_{12}^{\mathrm{IV}} < 0$. In this case the second Routh–Hurwitz local stability condition $\det(J^{\mathrm{IV}}) > 0$ can be fulfilled if and only if

$$J_{21}^{\mathrm{IV}} > J_{21}^{\mathrm{IV\,min}} = J_{11}^{\mathrm{IV}} \cdot J_{22}^{\mathrm{IV}} / J_{12}^{\mathrm{IV}},$$

whereas $J_{21}^{\mathrm{IV}} = \partial \dot{\omega}/\partial y$ can be greater or less than zero, that is, whereas the dynamics of the log real wage react positively or negatively with respect to output increases. □

8 DAD–DAS

Estimated convergence and the emergence of "complex dynamics"

8.1 Introduction

In this chapter[1] we present the analysis of an empirically oriented baseline model of disequilibrium aggregate demand–disequilibrium aggregate supply (DAD–DAS) type.[2] Its origins as far as the considered wage–price spiral is concerned date back to the chapter of Chiarella and Flaschel (1996b). This wage–price mechanism has recently been extended and studied analytically and numerically in Chiarella *et al.* (2005) in great detail. The results we obtain in the present chapter from this wage–price mechanism, augmented by a (partly) conventional Keynesian goods market dynamics, Okun's law and a conventional type of Taylor interest rate policy rule, stand in striking contrast – despite formal similarities – to the ones obtained from the comparable new Keynesian macrodynamics when staggered wage and price setting are assumed in this latter approach.

We use estimated parameter sets for studying the stability features of our model numerically as well as analytically. The strong convergence properties that we obtain in this way however only apply to the, by and large, linear version of our DAD–DAS system. They will completely disappear (in the downward direction) when this model type is enhanced by downward wage inflexibility, since the estimated DAD–DAS model is profit-led (where real wages increases are contractionary due to a dominance of investment over consumption). In a profit-led economy with downwardly rigid wages and (maybe only sluggishly) falling prices, it turns out that in a depressed situation real wages must increase, a fact which makes the ongoing depression ever deeper, until the economy either collapses or undergoes a significant change in behavior.

We finally consider also the case in which the economy is wage-led, where therefore increasing wage flexibility is bad for economic stability, since booms will tend to produce real wage increases which further stimulate the economy under such a regime. The same accelerator mechanism is of course then working in a downward direction, but can obviously (from a partial perspective) be stopped if there are floors to money wage deflation (or even inflation, as was shown to be the case by Hoogenveen and Kuipers (2000) for six European countries). In a wage-led regime a kink in the money wage Phillips curve therefore can limit the purely explosive behavior that exists in the unrestricted case and can indeed be shown to lead – even in a fairly advanced 5D system – to bounded and in fact economically viable dynamics. These dynamics moreover will be of a complex type if the unrestricted dynamics becomes strongly explosive. Our model is thus able to generate, quite naturally and without the imposition of economically unrealistic parameter values, the types of complex economic behavior that have been written about by J. Barkley-Rosser in a number of publications, in particular (Rosser 1999, 2000).

We thus in sum find interesting dynamical features in an advanced Keynesian aggregate supply/aggregate demand model with sluggish price, wage and output adjustments that allow for convergence results (in particular with an estimated version of the model) and thus for considerations that relate to the Frisch paradigm in business cycle theory. However, not totally unrelated to the estimated sizes of parameter values, we can also find situations where endogenously generated irregular business fluctuations are observed, which in our view confirm (though with time-invariant parameters still), the cycle theory advanced in Keynes's (1936) *General Theory*, which we would characterize as an anti-Frisch or, better, a Keynesian paradigm.

The chapter develops as follows. In Section 8.2 we introduce the basic relationships of our disequilibrium aggregate supply–disequilibrium aggregate demand model and obtain its reduced-form dynamics. In Section 8.3 we give an estimated version of the model, obtained in earlier work. We then simulate the model to gauge its response to positive real wage shocks. We also carry out an eigenvalue analysis around the steady state of the model in order to determine which parameters are most likely to be destabilizing. Section 8.4 discusses the stability properties of the model and proves a number of propositions about the stabilizing/destabilizing tendencies of various parameters. In Section 8.5 we introduce the midrange downward wage rigidity and discuss its role in stabilizing the model when it is subject to explosive fluctuations. Section 8.6 gives further simulations of the model with parameters chosen close to those of the estimated model, but now allowing a situation in which wage flexibility with respect to demand pressure is destabilizing. By analyzing phase plane projections and bifurcation diagrams we show how the dynamics can easily become complex. Section 8.7 draws some conclusions.

8.2 Baseline DAD–DAS macrodynamics

In this section we introduce a model of the DAD–DAS variety as an empirically motivated reformulation of a baseline model of the Keynesian AD–DAS variety as already investigated in Asada *et al.* (2006). This model type can be characterized as a matured redesign of the standard model of the old neoclassical synthesis and can be usefully contrasted with the corresponding model type of the now fashionable new (Keynesian) neoclassical synthesis.

In our baseline model – with its dynamic formulation of goods adjustment market behavior – we avoid the logical inconsistencies of the old neoclassical synthesis, described in detail in Asada *et al.* (2006), basically by formulating a wage–price spiral mechanism consisting of a money wage Phillips curve (WPC) and a price Phillips curve (PPC) that at first sight look very similar (from the formal perspective) to the wage–price dynamics of the new Keynesian model, when both staggered prices and wages are considered in the latter approach.

We observe qualitatively the same variables and the same parameter signs on the right-hand sides of these two Phillips curves (as far as the dependence of wage and price inflation on output and wage gaps are concerned), but use as in our earlier work on Keynesian macrodynamics – see Chiarella and Flaschel (1996b) for a first formulation – hybrid inflationary expectations formation for the accelerator terms that we employ. In our formulation of wage and price inflationary expectations formation, we have myopic perfect foresight, not as in the case of the new Keynesian wage–price dynamics on the own one-period-ahead rate of inflation (a self-reference mechanism), but rather with respect to other rate of inflation (a hetero-reference mechanism), as is appropriate when one speaks of cost-pressure items in the tradition of mainstream Phillips curve formulations. Owing to this crossover structure in the myopic perfect foresight component of Phillips curve accelerator terms, we are able furthermore to assume a neoclassical dating of these expectations, meaning thereby that time indices of inflation rates are the same on both sides of these two Phillips curves, whereas the new Keynesian Phillips curves use the current rate and the one-period-ahead wage inflation (or price) inflation rate on the left- and right-hand sides of their staggered wage (respectively price) adjustment rules. Finally, in contrast to the new Keynesian Phillips curves, we always include backward-looking expectations, but interpret such (adaptively updated) expectations as an inflation climate expression that agents form in addition to their correct myopic expectations, in order also to take into account the inflationary regime into which current inflation is embedded.

We thus make use of the following representation of a Keynesian wage–price spiral (still using the new Keynesian measures for the output and the wage gap, however).

The structural form of the Keynesian wage–price spiral (in discrete time)

$$d\ln w_{t+1} \overset{\text{WPC}}{=} \kappa_w E_t(d\ln p_{t+1}) + (1-\kappa_w)\pi_t^m + \beta_{wy}\ln Y_t - \beta_{w\omega}\ln\omega_t,$$

$$d\ln p_{t+1} \overset{\text{PPC}}{=} \kappa_p E_t(d\ln w_{t+1}) + (1-\kappa_p)\pi_t^m + \beta_{py}\ln Y_t + \beta_{p\omega}\ln\omega_t,$$

where d denotes the backward difference operator, all parameters are positive ($0 < \kappa_w, \kappa_p < 1$) and π^m denotes our inflationary climate expression,[3] here updated by a standard adaptive expectations process in order to simplify the analysis of the model. We thus have the same formal structure in these wage–price dynamics, but expectations are now based on weighted averages of corresponding cost-pressure terms, combining myopic perfect foresight with sluggishly adjusted inflationary regime expectations. The difference between the new Keynesian and our approach moreover lies in different microfoundations of the wage and price Phillips curves, based on what has been shown in Blanchard and Katz (1999), besides the significantly different way of treating forward- and backward-looking expectations.

Transferred into a deterministic continuous-time framework, the new Keynesian wage–price dynamics reads (using π^w, π^p to denote their wage and price inflation rates and setting $\ln Y = y, \theta = \ln w$)

$$\dot{\pi}^w = -\beta_{wy} y + \beta_{w\omega}\theta,$$
$$\dot{\pi}^p = -\beta_{py} y - \beta_{p\omega}\theta,$$

while our approach – now specifically in terms of the employment rate e on the labor market and the capacity utilization rate u on the market for goods – gives rise to ($\hat{x} = \dot{x}/x$ denotes the growth rate of a variable x) the following.

The structural form of the Keynesian wage–price spiral (in continuous time)

$$\widehat{w} \stackrel{\text{WPC}}{=} \beta_{we}(e-1) - \beta_{w\omega}\ln\omega + \kappa_w\hat{p} + (1-\kappa_w)\pi^m, \quad \kappa_w \in (0,1), \tag{8.1}$$

$$\hat{p} \stackrel{\text{PPC}}{=} \beta_{pu}(u-1) + \beta_{p\omega}\ln\omega + \kappa_p\widehat{w} + (1-\kappa_p)\pi^m, \quad \kappa_p \in (0,1). \tag{8.2}$$

There are several important differences between our approach and that of the new Keynesians to wage–price dynamics. First, we use on the left-hand sides inflation rates $\widehat{w}$, $\hat{p}$ for wage and price inflation in place of their time rate of change. Second, we use two measures for the output gap, one relating to the labor market (the deviation of the rate of employment from the NAIRU rate of employment $\bar{e} = 1$) and one relating to the goods market (the deviation of the rate of capacity utilization of firms from their intended normal rate of capacity utilization $\bar{u} - 1$). Finally, in both the wage Phillips curve and the price Phillips curve we use weighted averages for the cost-pressure measures of both workers and firms, based on myopic perfect foresight and our concept of an inflation climate π^m. Owing to these differences in wage and price inflation formation, we do not get the sign reversal in front of the output and wage gaps that is typical for the new Keynesian approach to wage and price dynamics.

The wage Phillips curve has been microfounded in Blanchard and Katz (1999) from the perspective of current theories of the labor market. Note that the log that appears in the formal representation of our wage Phillips curve is not due to a log-linear approximation of the originally given structural equation, but instead results (see Blanchard and Katz 1999) from a growth rate reformulation of a bargained real wage curve, initially represented in level form. For the price Phillips curve a formally similar procedure is adopted, based on an approach to flexible markup pricing. The two Phillips curves can be considered as a linear system of equations in the variables $\widehat{w} - \pi^m$ and $\hat{p} - \pi^m$ that can be easily solved, giving rise thereby to the law of motion (8.6) for the real wage ω and the reduced-form price Phillips curve (8.8). Together with the law of motion for the inflationary climate expression (8.7) we therefore obtain in sum three laws of motion that describe the disequilibrium adjustment of aggregate supply of our model (the DAS component) as is shown below.

The disequilibrium AD part of the model (the DAD component) is here still of a simple type, consisting of a dynamic multiplier equation (8.3) in terms of the rate of capacity utilization u, whose rate of growth is assumed to depend negatively on its level u (as in the simple textbook multiplier story), as usual on the (here actual) real rate of interest $r - \hat{p}$ and, with an ambiguous sign, on the real wage, which measures the impact of income distribution on the determination of aggregate demand and resulting output adjustments. We call a regime where $-\alpha_{u\omega}$ applies a *profit-led regime* and the opposite case a *wage-led regime*, characterizing in this way the situations where investment dominates consumption with respect to real wage changes and vice versa.

Adding to the law of motion for the rate of capacity utilization, we assume that the rate of employment e obeys some sort of Okun's law, following the rate of capacity utilization with a time delay as shown in equation (8.4). We finally have a standard form of a Taylor interest rate policy rule (8.5), including however interest rate smoothing. Note that parameter values are indexed in a way similar to the notation used in input–output tables and that all equations have been expressed in linearized form around their steady-state values, which are here supplied from the outside and thus treated as exogenously given.

Taken together the considered *dynamic DAD–DAS macromodel*, with real wage dynamics now in place of the nominal wage Phillips curve and price Phillips curve, thus consists of the following five laws of motion:

$$\hat{u} = -\alpha_{uu}(u-1) - \alpha_{ur}((r-\hat{p}) - (r_0 - \bar{\pi})) \pm \alpha_{u\omega} \ln \omega, \tag{8.3}$$

$$\hat{e} = \beta_{eu}(u-1) + \beta_{e\hat{u}}\hat{u}, \tag{8.4}$$

$$\dot{r} = -\gamma_{rr}(r - r_0) + \gamma_{rp}(\hat{p} - \bar{\pi}) + \gamma_{ru}(u-1), \tag{8.5}$$

$$\begin{aligned}\widehat{\omega} = \kappa[&(1-\kappa_p)(\beta_{we}(e-1) - \beta_{w\omega}\ln\omega) \\ &- (1-\kappa_w)(\beta_{pu}(u-1) + \beta_{p\omega}\ln\omega)],\end{aligned} \tag{8.6}$$

$$\dot{\pi}^m = \beta_{\pi^m}(\hat{p} - \pi^m), \tag{8.7}$$

representing the IS dynamics, Okun's law, the Taylor rule, the dynamics of income distribution or of the real wage, and the updating of the inflationary climate expression. Since steady-state values are parameters of the model we assume for reasons of numerical simplicity that they are given by 1 in the case of utilization rates and real wages and – from an annualized perspective – by 0.1 and 0.02 as far as the steady-state rate of interest and the inflation target of the central bank are concerned.

We need to use in addition the following reduced-form expression for the price inflation Phillips curve (obtained by solving simultaneously equations (8.1) and (8.2))[4]

$$\hat{p} = \kappa[\beta_{pu}(u-1) + \beta_{p\omega}\ln\omega + \kappa_p(\beta_{we}(e-1) - \beta_{w\omega}\ln\omega)] + \pi^m, \tag{8.8}$$

which has to be inserted into the above laws of motion in various places in order to obtain an autonomous system of differential equations in the state variables, capacity utilization u, the rate of employment e, the nominal rate of interest r, the real wage rate ω, and the inflationary climate expression π^m. We have written the laws of motion in an order that gives first the dynamic equations also present in the baseline new Keynesian model of inflation dynamics, and then the extension by our dynamics of income distribution and the inflationary climate in which the economy is operating. This modification and extension of the baseline AD–DAS model of Asada *et al.* (2006) goes beyond this earlier approach to the extent that it now also allows for positive effects of real wage changes on aggregate demand (in wage-led regimes), which not were present in the AD component of our original modification of the conventional AD–AS dynamics (which was always profit-led, due to the lack of an effect of income distribution on households' consumption).

We will find from the theoretical and empirical perspective that the laws of motion of the DAD–DAS model imply damped oscillations if the inflation climate is adjusting sufficiently sluggishly and if price inflation rates respond sluggishly to the excess demand on the market for goods. The DAD–DAS dynamics becomes explosive if inflationary climate expectations or price inflation itself are adjusting too fast. Its unboundedness must then be tamed by assuming behavioral nonlinearities at least far off the steady state that then limit the explosive nature of the dynamics such that they become bounded and thus economically viable. Strategies for finding meaningful trajectories for the new Keynesian and our matured Keynesian macrodynamics therefore differ radically from each other, and go to the root of the difference between the underlying paradigms of Frisch and Keynes, characterized by strong shock absorbers on the one hand (enforced by the so-called jump variable technique of the rational expectations school) and endogenously created business fluctuations (locally explosive dynamics – under certain side conditions on adjustment speeds – tamed by behavioral nonlinearities far off the steady state) on the other.

8.3 Simulating an estimated version of the model

The model (8.3)–(8.7) has been estimated for the US economy (1965:1–2002:4) on the structural level in Chen *et al.* (2006) with the following result for estimated parameter values, obtained from a system estimate where the inflationary climate was measured by a 12-quarter moving average with linearly declining weights denoted by π_t^{12}:

$$\begin{aligned}
d\ln u_{t+1} &= -0.09u_t - 0.17(r_t - d\ln p_{t+1}) - 0.74\ln\omega_t + 0.08,\\
d\ln e_{t+1} &= 0.21 d\ln u_{t+1} \quad (\text{or in integrated form} e_t = u_t^{0.21}),\\
r_{t+1} &= 0.90r_t + 0.41 d\ln p_{t+1} + 0.05u_t - 0.04,\\
d\ln w_{t+1} &= 0.12e_t - 0.09\ln\omega_t + 0.57 d\ln p_{t+1} + 0.43\pi_t^{12} - 0.11,\\
d\ln p_{t+1} &= 0.03u_t + 0.06\ln\omega_t + 0.32 d\ln w_{t+1} + 0.68\pi_t^{12} - 0.03.
\end{aligned}$$

We now have one law of motion less than before, since the adaptive expectations mechanism for the inflationary climate has been replaced here by the moving-average expression, which – when translated back into such a mechanism – gives rise to an adjustment speed of approximately $\beta_{\pi^m} = 0.15$ in the law of motion (8.7) for the climate π^m. Taken together we obtain the following numerical specification of the reduced-form 4D dynamics of Chen *et al.* (2006), where the measured form of Okun's law $e_t = u_t^{\beta_{e\hat{u}}} = u_t^{0.21}$ has been linearized around the steady state and where the above two linear structural equations for $d\ln w_{t+1} - \pi_t^{12}$ and $d\ln p_{t+1} - \pi_t^{12}$ have been solved and subtracted from each other in order to obtain the law of motion for real wages,

$$d\ln w_{t+1} - \pi_t^{12} - (d\ln p_{t+1} - \pi_t^{12}) = d\ln w_{t+1} - d\ln p_{t+1} = d\ln \omega_{t+1},$$

solely as function of the capacity utilization rates of firms and of workers and the current level of the real wage. We thus have

$$d\ln u_{t+1} = -0.09u_t - 0.17(r_t - d\ln p_{t+1}) - 0.74\ln\omega_t + 0.08, \tag{8.9}$$

$$r_{t+1} = 0.90r_t + 0.41d\ln p_{t+1} + 0.05u_t - 0.04, \tag{8.10}$$

$$d\ln\omega_{t+1} = 0.05u_t - 0.11\ln\omega_t + 0.02, \tag{8.11}$$

$$d\pi_t^m = 0.15(d\ln p_{t+1} - \pi_t^m). \tag{8.12}$$

As before we have to insert into (8.9)–(8.12) the following reduced-form expression for the price Phillips curve in order to get an autonomous system of difference equations in the state variables, capacity utilization u_t, the nominal rate of interest r_t, the real wage rate ω_t, and the inflationary climate expression π_t^m:

$$d\ln p_{t+1} = \kappa[\beta_{pu}(u_t - 1) + \beta_{p\omega}\ln\omega_t + \kappa_p(\beta_{we}(e_t - 1) - \beta_{w\omega}\ln\omega_t)] + \pi_t^m,$$

which here becomes

$$d\ln p_{t+1} = 0.05u_t + 0.03\ln\omega_t + \pi_t^m - 0.01 \tag{8.13}$$

when use is made again of Okun's law linearized around its steady-state value 1.

As noted, we have made use of Okun's law in integrated form also in the law of motion for real wages (see equation (8.6)), which when inserted into it gives the following parameter in front of the rate of capacity utilization u_t (by which e_t has been replaced in the demand-pressure term of the wage Phillips curve):

$$\alpha = \kappa[(1-\kappa_p)\beta_{we}\beta_{e\hat{u}} - (1-\kappa_w)\beta_{pu}].$$

This parameter α (which here equals 0.05) is the critical condition for the working of the so-called Rose or real wage effect, since – when α is positive – it states that real wage growth is positively correlated with economic activity and thus (due to the estimated form of the goods market dynamics, that is, the law of motion for the rate of capacity utilization) negatively responding to its level with a time delay, if this law of motion for u is taken into account in addition. Owing to these two laws of motion and the size of their estimated coefficients, the role of income distribution in the fluctuations generated by the model will surely be an important one, a fact that is rarely established in other macrodynamic analyses of the business cycle. The estimated system (8.9)–(8.13) clearly shows that there is a stabilizing crossover feedback channel between real wage changes and rates of capacity utilization changes that is further stabilized by the Blanchard and Katz error correction terms in the law of motion for real wages. Note however that the dynamics of income distribution are here embedded in a framework with estimated parameter sizes that are held constant over the whole observation period, that is, income distribution here works in a Keynesian environment with rigid (hence not systematically in time varying) propensities to consume and invest, in contrast to what has been suggested by (Keynes 1936, ch. 22) in his analysis of goods market dynamics. We therefore conclude that certain business cycle generators (accelerators) are still absent from the considered dynamics in their present form which means that the implied phase length for the cycle will exceed considerably those actually observed for the US economy, as is indeed shown in Figure 8.1.[5]

We thus get from the reduced-form representation (8.9)–(8.13) of our estimated DAD–DAS dynamics that the growth rates of u and ω depend negatively (respectively positively) in a crossover fashion on each other, establishing a stabilizing feedback chain between capacity utilization and real wage dynamics, or a normal Rose effect, which in contrast to Rose's (1967) model thus contributes to the stability of the system from a partial perspective. We also see here that the negative effect of real wages on the rate of change of capacity utilization (the profit-led

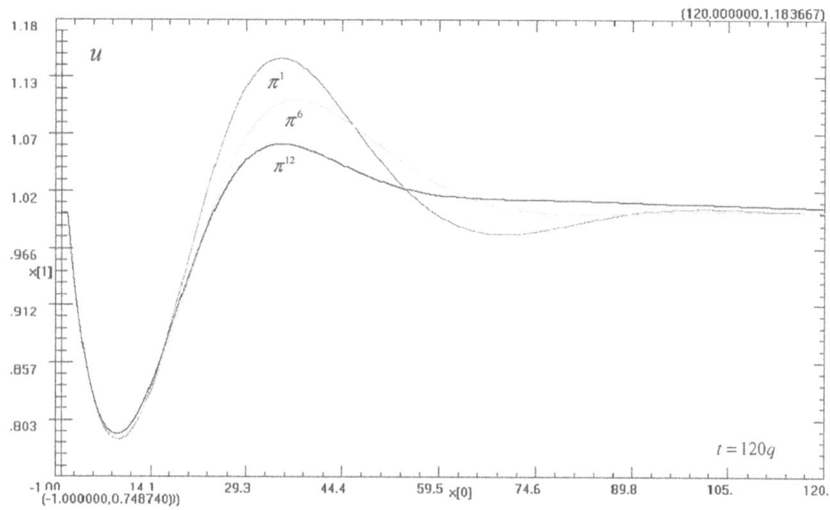

Figure 8.1 Responses to positive real wage shocks for the three sets of estimated parameter values (based on inflationary climate terms π^m with linearly declining weights with $m = 12, 6, 1$ quarter length).

mechanism) is a strong one, while the positive effect of capacity utilization on the rate of change of real wages (the market flexibility effect) is fairly weak, due to the observed fact that economic activity influences real wages both positively – through the employment rate channel – and negatively – through the direct effect of the rate of capacity utilization on the price level – and due to the fact that the (at first sight) apparently dominant effect of e on $\widehat{\omega}$ is significantly reduced by the weak link between the rate of employment (a stock ratio) and the rate of capacity utilization (a flow ratio) established through our estimate of Okun's law.

Besides the Rose effect we have the usual rate of interest channel in the law of motion for the rate of capacity utilization, whereby central bank policy can influence the economy in a stabilizing fashion, in fact a substitute for the conventional Keynes effect, but whereby also the destabilizing *Mundell effect* comes into play. This latter effect establishes a positive link between the rate of capacity utilization and its rate of change, since the real rate of interest depends negatively on the inflation rate and thereby also negatively on the rate of capacity utilization. However, since we have estimated that the parameter β_{pu} is likely to be very small (implying that there is no strong dependence of price inflation on demand pressure in the market for goods), the destabilizing Mundell effect will be relatively weak, despite a significant negative dependence of the growth rate of economic activity on the real rate of interest.

We have furthermore from the partial perspective a stable dynamic multiplier and a stabilizing influence of real wages on their rate of change, established by the Blanchard and Katz (1999) error correction terms in the wage and price Phillips curves. There is finally a positive link between changes in the inflation climate and the rate of capacity utilization, since the rate of price inflation and thus the inflationary climate depend positively on the rate of capacity utilization and since – again via the real rate of interest channel – the rate of change of the capacity utilization of firms depends positively on the inflation climate surrounding the current evolution of the economy (see the reduced-form (8.13) for the price Phillips curve as well as equations (8.12) and (8.9)). This supplements the findings that increasing reaction of wage inflation to demand pressure should contribute to stability, while the opposite is true for increasing reaction of price inflation to its measure of demand pressure. Of course, all these statements are only partial in nature and may be falsified as intuitive guidelines for the systems' (in)stability once the eigenvalues of the Jacobian of the full dynamical system are calculated numerically, since all these feedback chains only appear in part of the minors that are to be considered in the Routh–Hurwitz conditions for local asymptotic stability.

It has been established in Chen *et al.* (2006), and see also the next section, that the estimated sign structure always implies local asymptotic stability of the steady state if the reaction of price inflation to demand pressure is sufficiently small, if the inflationary climate is updated sufficiently slowly and if interest rate smoothing is sufficiently weak, with the interest rate reacting to inflation and capacity gaps. Taking everything together, we therefore should expect convergence back to the steady state when the considered dynamics are simulated numerically and shocked out of their steady-state position. This is indeed the case as is shown in Figure 8.1 where we also show that this situation is not much changed if our 12-quarter moving-average representation of the inflation climate is modified toward a six-quarter moving average (again with linearly declining weights) and the model re-estimated. Similar observations also hold even in the case where only one quarter is considered, that is, when the inflation climate is just represented by the inflation rate of the previous period as this is usually the case in theoretical analysis of the new Keynesian approach augmented toward the treatment of hybrid expectations (to which the concept of an inflation regime or climate is however then no longer associated). We thus get as a first numerical result that the economy seems to be very robust in the absorption of supply-side, demand-side and policy shocks. In Figure 8.1 we exemplify this result through the application of a positive real wage shock (caused by an increase in money wages or a decline in the general price level). The response is significant decline in the rate of capacity utilization for approximately three years and then a slow and overshooting recovery over the next seven years until the economy starts to converge back to its steady-state position with more or less mild fluctuations. This result holds unambiguously for the climate expressions of the discussed type, that is for π_t^{12}, π_t^6 and π_t^1. However the overshooting mechanism can be seen to become the stronger the faster the inflationary climate adjusts to the short-run fluctuations of the actual exchange rate.

It is a bit perplexing to know from the theoretical analysis of the model that it loses its stability by way of a Hopf bifurcation if the speed of adjustment of the inflationary climate becomes sufficiently fast and to find empirically that convergence of the dynamics back to its steady-state position is guaranteed even if only a one-quarter lag applies for the representation of the inflation climate (which is then literally speaking no longer interpretable as a climate expression). We believe that this is basically due to the fact that we did not allow in our estimation for nonlinear behavioral relationships, a task that still remains to be solved. The applied econometric methodology (see Chen *et al.* 2006 for details) and the by and large linear structure of the model thus prevent – in view of the bounded fluctuations contained in the employed dataset – the establishment of eigenvalues outside the unit circle (or with positive real part in the continuous-time version of the model). The only weak evidence for an increased tendency toward instability is the increase in volatility that is shown in Figure 8.1 when the time horizon in the formation of the inflation climate expression becomes smaller and smaller.

In the eigenvalue diagrams shown in Figure 8.2 we in addition have to take note of the fact that the loss of stability by way of a Hopf bifurcation (generally leading to the death of an unstable limit cycle around a stable corridor of the dynamics or the birth of a stable limit cycle after the loss of stability of the steady state) becomes more and more delayed if we use the estimated parameters for the cases π^{12}, π^6, π^1 in this order as shown on the left-hand side of Figure 8.2. Faster and faster adjustment of the inflationary climate expression in our continuous-time version of the dynamics thus does not lead to a decrease in the Hopf bifurcation point, but rather to its increase. We note here that, due to the estimated form of Okun's law, we have that one eigenvalue of the 5D dynamics must always be zero

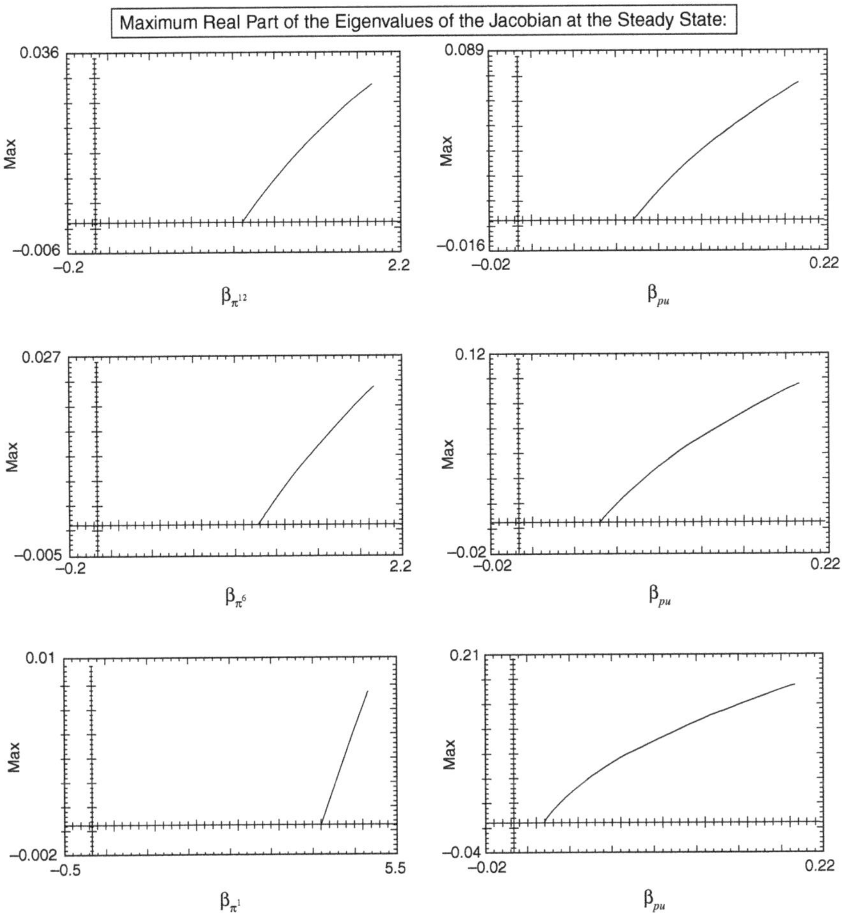

Figure 8.2 Eigenvalue diagrams for varying parameter sizes.

so that only the local instability range is clearly shown in the eigenvalue diagrams in Figure 8.2. The increased tendency toward instability if we run through the sequence $\pi_t^{12}, \pi_t^6, \pi_t^1$ can however be mirrored by our estimated models to a certain degree when we consider the same situation of a loss of stability by way of the parameter β_{pu} in place of the parameter $\beta_{\pi m}$ as is shown on the right-hand side of Figure 8.2. Here it can be seen that the interval for this parameter where stability prevails becomes smaller and smaller so that in the case of π^1 we even get loss of stability within the confidence interval for the parameter β_{pu}. We therefore find – even in the case where behavioral nonlinearities are ignored in theory and in estimation – that the vulnerability of the dynamics toward the establishment of explosive adjustment processes becomes larger the faster the inflation climate is adjusting in view of the actual course of price inflation.

We have found in addition in Chen *et al.* (2006) that all partial feedback chains (including the working of the Blanchard and Katz error correction terms) translate themselves into corresponding "normal" eigenvalue reaction patterns for the full 5D dynamics (with Okun's law added in its estimated derivative form), with the exception of the speed parameter β_{we}, where the eigenvalue analysis has shown that increasing wage flexibility may indeed become destabilizing if it becomes sufficiently large. This provides one example of the situation where partial economic insight can be misleading due to the fact that the corresponding feedback chain is only a small component of the many minors of the Jacobian of the dynamics at the steady state that have to be investigated in the application of the Routh–Hurwitz conditions to the full 4D dynamics (where Okun's law is applied in level form).

Increasing price flexibility has been found to be destabilizing, since the growth rate $\hat{e}$ of economic activity can thereby be made to depend positively on its level (via the real rate of interest channel, see equation (8.3)), leading to an unstable augmented dynamic multiplier process in the trace of the Jacobian J of the system under such circumstances. Furthermore, such increasing price flexibility will give rise to a negative dependence of the growth rate of the real wage on economic activity (whose rate of change in turn depends negatively on the real wage) and thus lead to further sign changes in the Jacobian J. Increasing price flexibility is therefore bad for the stability of the considered dynamics from at least two perspectives. Nevertheless as the model is estimated there seems to be no problem for the working of the economy, since economic shocks may have long-lasting consequences (due to our estimation of constant parameters) when sufficiently large, but are always absorbed by the economy through nearly monotonic adjustments, once the effect of the shock has become reversed.

This impression may however be misleading if one further aspect of the functioning of actual market economies is taken into account (to which attention has not yet been paid in our estimation procedures). Hoogenveen and Kuipers (2000) have established for six European countries that money wages are not only completely rigid downwards, but have in fact a floor for their rate of growth, which is bounded from below by a positive value. They basically therefore establish a kink in the wage Phillips curve at positive rates of wage inflation. Chen and Flaschel (2006) do not find such a strong result in the case of the US economy, but find also at least some evidence that money wages can be considered as being downwardly rigid. We thus now reconsider the above dynamical system for the new situation where wages can rise as specified by it, but cannot fall, that is, we exclude wage deflation now from consideration. In such a case we can establish the results shown in Figure 8.3 where the estimated model and its shock absorber properties are repeated for the case π^{12} (with an inflation target of the central bank of again 2%).

Adding complete downward money wage rigidity to the convergent dynamics exemplified in Figure 8.2 (and a monetary policy that is tighter in its inflation target, $\bar{\pi} = 0.003$) now however implies a radical change in the system's behavior. Since money wages cannot fall and since price can still fall in the depression

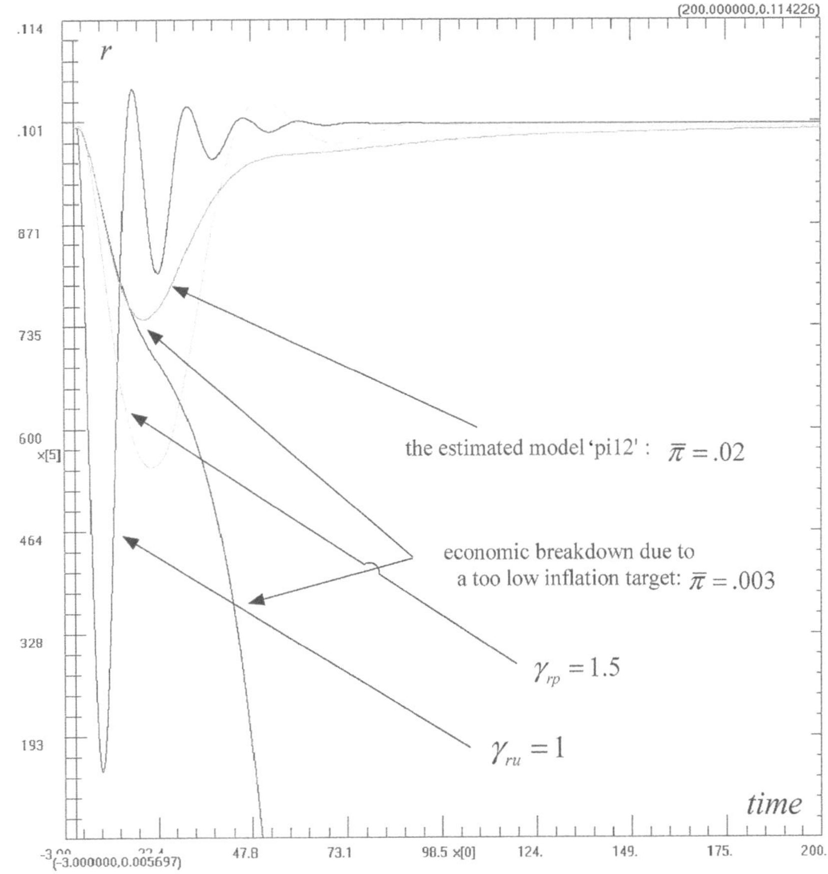

Figure 8.3 Downward money wage rigidity and too restrictive inflation targets.

generated by the assumed positive real wage shock – though price flexibility was measured as very sluggish – we get in such a situation that the real wage must increase. This downward adjustment mechanism continues to work and it makes the depression deeper and deeper until the economy breaks down, exemplified in Figure 8.3 by means of the evolution of the nominal rate of interest. There exists therefore a great danger for systems with profit-led goods market dynamics, since downward price flexibility coupled with downwardly rigid wages then necessarily lead the economy into a deflationary spiral when deflation begins to start through shocks or other events. We also show in this figure how a more active interest rate policy with respect to the inflation as well as the output gap can avoid such a breakdown if it is chosen sufficiently strong. For our purposes however, here we only need that a global floor to the evolution of the money wage (or its inflation rate) can be disastrous in a situation that initially appeared to be a very stable one, without such a nonlinearity. The question therefore is by which mechanisms such a monotonic tendency toward more and more severe depressions can be stopped or even reversed. This question is further pursued after the following section, which is devoted to a stability analysis of the dynamics with the estimated parameter signs and the theoretical occurrence of instability if a floor to money wage inflation is added to the model.

8.4 Analyzing the estimated version of the model

Based on our estimated equations (8.9)–(8.12), the theoretical model (8.3)–(8.7) can now be simplified to the following qualitative format (setting $b = \beta_{e\hat{u}}$ for notational simplicity so that $e = u^b$):

$$\hat{u} = -\alpha_{uu}(u-1) - \alpha_{ur}(r - \hat{p} - (r_0 - \bar{\pi})) - \alpha_{u\omega}\ln\omega, \tag{8.14}$$

$$\dot{r} = -\gamma_{rr}(r - r_0) + \gamma_{rp}(\hat{p} - \bar{\pi}) + \gamma_{ru}(u-1), \tag{8.15}$$

$$\begin{aligned}\widehat{\omega} = \kappa[&(1-\kappa_p)(\beta_{we}(u^b - 1) - \beta_{w\omega}\ln\omega) \\ &- (1-\kappa_w)(\beta_{pu}(u-1) + \beta_{p\omega}\ln\omega)],\end{aligned} \tag{8.16}$$

$$\dot{\pi}^m = \beta_{\pi^m}(\hat{p} - \pi^m), \tag{8.17}$$

$$\hat{p} = \kappa[\beta_{pu}(u-1) + \beta_{p\omega}\ln\omega + \kappa_p(\beta_{we}(u^b - 1) - \beta_{w\omega}\ln\omega)] + \pi^m, \tag{8.18}$$

where the $\hat{p}$ equation has to be inserted into equations (8.14), (8.15) and (8.17) in order to arrive at an autonomous system of differential equations. Doing this, linearizing around the steady state and rearranging items then gives rise to

$$\begin{aligned}
\hat{u} &= -[\alpha_{uu} - \kappa(\beta_{pu} + \kappa_p\beta_{we}b)]u - \alpha_{ur}r \\
&\quad - [\alpha_{u\omega} - \alpha_{ur}\kappa(\beta_{p\omega} - \kappa_p\beta_{w\omega})]\omega + \alpha_{ur}\pi^m + \text{const.} \\
&= -a_1u - a_2r - a_3\omega + a_4\pi^m \pm a_0, \\
\dot{r} &= [\gamma_{rp}\kappa(\beta_{pu} + \kappa_p\beta_{we}b) + \gamma_{ru}]u - \gamma_{rr}r \\
&\quad + \gamma_{rp}\kappa(\beta_{p\omega} - \kappa_p\beta_{w\omega})\omega + \gamma_{rp}\pi^m + \text{const.} \\
&= +b_1u - b_2r \pm b_3\omega + b_4\pi^m \pm b_0, \\
\widehat{\omega} &= \kappa\{[(1-\kappa_p)\beta_{we}b - (1-\kappa_w)\beta_{pu}]u \\
&\quad - [(1-\kappa_p)\beta_{w\omega} + (1-\kappa_w)\beta_{p\omega}]\omega\} + \text{const.} \\
&= +c_1u - c_3\omega \pm c_0, \\
\dot{\pi}^m &= \beta_{\pi^m}\kappa[(\beta_{pu} + \kappa_p\beta_{we}b)u + \kappa(\beta_{p\omega} - \kappa_p\beta_{w\omega})\omega] + \text{const.} \\
&= +d_1u \pm d_3\omega \pm d_0.
\end{aligned}$$

Note that all coefficients are positive, and where we write $\pm$ in front of a coefficient this is to indicate ambiguity of sign. Making qualitative use of our estimated parameter values we have assumed, on the one hand, in the law of motion for the rate of capacity utilization u that the $\hat{p}_u$, $\hat{p}_\omega$ components are dominated by the direct influences of u, ω on the growth rate of capacity utilization. In the law of motion for real wages we assume, on the other hand, in correspondence to our estimates, that the growth rate of real wages depends positively on the rate of capacity utilization (that is, $\beta_{\omega e}$ is the dominant term in this respect), though this positive dependence may be a weak one, since our estimate of Okun's law implies only a fairly weak impact effect of the capacity utilization rate on the rate of employment. By and large we thereby obtain an unambiguous sign structure for the partial derivatives of our dynamical system and thus its Jacobian J at the steady state, as is shown below (where the $\pm$ items are solely due the two opposing real wage or Blanchard and Katz error correction terms in the reduced-form price Phillips curve):

$$J = \begin{pmatrix} - & - & - & + \\ + & - & \pm & + \\ + & 0 & - & 0 \\ + & 0 & \pm & 0 \end{pmatrix}.$$

PROPOSITION 8.1 *Assume that the sign structure of the matrix J applies and that its entry J_{23} is sufficiently small. Then, the steady state of the dynamics (8.14)–(8.17), with (8.18) inserted into them, is locally asymptotically stable, if the inflationary climate expression π^m is updated in a sufficiently sluggish way, and if $\gamma_{rr} < \gamma_{rp}$ holds true.*

Proof: Let us first consider the case where $\beta_{\pi^m} = 0$ holds true. We consider the submatrix $J(3,3)$ for the remaining laws of motion, with J_{23} set equal to zero, which is then given by

$$J(3,3) = \begin{pmatrix} - & - & - \\ + & - & 0 \\ + & 0 & - \end{pmatrix}.$$

The characteristic polynomial of this matrix is given by

$$p(\lambda) = \lambda^3 + k_1\lambda^2 + k_2\lambda + k_3, \quad k_1 = -\text{trace}\, J(3,3), \quad k_3 = -\det J(3,3),$$

and it is easily shown to have only positive coefficients. Furthermore, the condition $k_1k_2 - k_3 > 0$ is also fulfilled, since $\det J(3,3)$ is completely dominated by the expressions that make up k_1k_2. We thus have that the Routh–Hurwitz conditions for local asymptotic stability apply to the given situation, implying that the real parts of the eigenvalues of this polynomial must all be negative.

Consider now the case $\beta_{\pi m} > 0$. According to our assumptions we then get for $\det J$ the sign structure

$$\det J = \det\begin{pmatrix} - & - & - & + \\ - & - & 0 & + \\ + & 0 & - & 0 \\ + & 0 & 0 & 0 \end{pmatrix} = \det\begin{pmatrix} 0 & - & 0 & + \\ 0 & - & 0 & + \\ 0 & 0 & - & 0 \\ + & 0 & 0 & 0 \end{pmatrix},$$

which implies a positive determinant due to our assumption on the relative sizes of the parameters γ_{rr} and γ_{rp}.

Making the parameter $\beta_{\pi m}$ slightly positive moves the eigenvalues with three negative real parts and one zero eigenvalue in such a way that they are now all in the negative half of the complex plane (since eigenvalues depend continuously on the parameters of the model and since the determinant is the product of all four eigenvalues). This implies the assertion of Proposition 8.1. □

PROPOSITION 8.2 *Assume that the sign structure of the matrix J applies and that its entry J_{23} is sufficiently small.*

1 *Increasing the adjustment speeds β_{pu} and β_{wu} to a sufficient degree gives rise to a Hopf bifurcation – via dynamic multiplier instability – where the system generally loses its asymptotic stability accompanied by the death of an unstable limit cycle or the birth of a stable limit cycle.*
2 *Assume $\alpha_{ur} = 0$, in which case assertion 1 does not apply. Then, increasing the adjustment speed β_{pu} to a sufficient degree again gives rise to a Hopf bifurcation toward the above type of instability, now via an adverse real wage adjustment (an adverse Rose effect).*
3 *Increasing the adjustment speed $\beta_{\pi m}$ to a sufficient degree also gives rise to the above type of Hopf bifurcation, now via an adverse real interest rate adjustment (the so-called Mundell effect).*

Proof:

1 In this case the entry J_{11}, characterizing the overall effect of utilization changes on the growth rate of capacity utilization, becomes positive and can be made as large as needed in order to arrive at a positive trace of the matrix J. The Hopf bifurcation then occurs when $k_1k_2 - k_3$ becomes zero, which must be the case before trace $J = 0$ is established because $(k_1k_2 - k_3)$ decreases with trace J and k_3 is positive.
2 In this case J_{11} remains negative, while $J_{12}J_{21}$ is zero. The only entry in the coefficient k_2 that then depends on the parameter β_{pu} is then given by $J_{13}J_{31}$, where J_{31} must become positive for increasing β_{pu}, while J_{13} remains negative, thereby establishing a positive feedback channel between capacity utilization

and real wages that makes k_2 negative if β_{pu} becomes sufficiently large. The Hopf bifurcation then occurs when $k_1k_2 - k_3$ becomes zero, which must be the case before $k_2 = 0$ is established.

3 This is obvious, since the parameter β_{π^m} only appears in the product $J_{14}J_{41}$ which establishes a positive link between the evolution of the inflation climate π^m and capacity utilization u, the destabilizing Mundell effect of conventional macrodynamic model-building. □

PROPOSITION 8.3 *Assume that the sign structure of the matrix J applies. Assume furthermore that monetary policy is impotent by setting* $\alpha_{ur} = 0$. *Assume finally that the negative Blanchard and Katz error correction mechanism in the real wage dynamics is sufficiently weak (that is, the term* $(1 - \kappa_w)\beta_{p\omega}$ *is chosen sufficiently small). Then, the steady state of the considered dynamical system is unstable in the downward direction, if there is a global floor to money wage inflation at its steady-state value, that is, any initial and contractionary u or* ω *shock then leads to an accelerating contraction of the economy.*

Proof: In the considered situation, the interacting dynamics are reduced to a 2D dynamical system in the rates u and ω. This system exhibits a negative determinant of its Jacobian at the steady state $u_0 = 1$, $\omega_0 = 1$ and two 1D stable manifolds that cannot be reached by contractions in u or expansions in ω. This implies that such shocks always lead to trajectories with a declining rate of capacity utilization along them. □

If monetary policy is only weakly influencing the private sector and if the Blanchard and Katz real wage error correction mechanism in the price Phillips curve is weak, we then have a situation in which the reaction of price levels to their corresponding demand-pressure item and the missing reaction of wages in this regard allow for an adverse adjustment, so that an increase in real wages will lead the economy into deeper and deeper depressions. The question then is whether interest rate effects in goods demand and interest rate steering by the central bank can help to avoid such an outcome, since of course the destabilizing Mundell effect will then also be present in the feedback interactions of our economy, or whether monetary policy needs a systematic overhaul in a situation where there is an adverse real wage effect at work. Our analytical findings in the estimated situation thus are that the economy may work like a shock absorber for certain ranges of its parameter values, but that this property may get lost in a variety of ways which then demand the introduction of further behavioral nonlinearities that can keep the resulting dynamics bounded despite the existence of centrifugal forces around its steady-state position.

In such situations our approach demands further behavioral nonlinearities in the case of explosive downward (or upward) business fluctuations, but not for the imposition of a new Keynesian mathematical boundedness condition that – if determinate – keeps the dynamics always in their steady-state position, a result that is not at all in line with Keynes's (1936) own analysis of the trade cycle mechanism – see his chapter 22 and the uses he there makes of his three central parameters, the marginal propensity to consume, the marginal efficiency of investment and the state of liquidity preference. However, concerning our own approach, we find that the results on various degrees of downward money wage rigidities do not unambiguously support Keynes' view that workers' resistance against money wage reductions is always good for economic stability.

8.5 Midrange downward money wage rigidity

In this section we show by means of an example that the problematic downward rigidity of money wages may to some extent be needed in order to stabilize the economy when it is subject to explosive fluctuations caused by an increase in the speed with which the inflationary climate expression is adjusted. This rigidity should not however be global in nature, but give way again to downward wage flexibility if the rate of employment becomes sufficiently low. This particular, not implausible, mix of different wage inflation regimes is a bit surprising with respect to its stability implications, but is at least not completely unmotivated, due to the fact that wage flexibility tends to be stabilizing and price flexibility destabilizing from the partial perspective of the real wage channel discussed above.

In order to formalize the envisaged three regimes of wage inflation needed for our subsequent simulations, we make use of the three alternatives shown in Figure 8.4 in our reformulation of the wage Phillips curve, from which the dynamics of real wages and price inflation in their reduced-form presentation must then be derived. Underlying these three situations is the assumption that wages behave as in the original model considered in Sections 8.2 and 8.3 when their rate of change is above a certain floor f and when the rate of employment is above a certain critical level $\underline{e}$ below which workers again accept faster decreases in their money wages than the level f. Wage inflation is in the latter case assumed to be driven by

$$\widehat{w} = \beta_{we}(e-1) + \kappa_w \hat{p} + (1-\kappa_w)\pi^m,$$

in place of the working of the Phillips curve in normal or overheated situations

$$\widehat{w} = \beta_{we}(e-1) - \beta_{w\omega}\ln\omega + \kappa_w \hat{p} + (1-\kappa_w)\pi^m.$$

In between we have – as stated – a regime where wage inflation (or deflation) is just given by a rate f.

These three scenarios translate themselves into reduced-form real wage and price level dynamics as follows, where we now denote by $\widehat{w}_{\text{red}}$ the reduced-form money wage Phillips curve of the original model:

$$\widehat{w}_{\text{red}} = \kappa[\beta_{we}(e-1) - \beta_{w\omega}\ln\omega + \kappa_w(\beta_{pu}(u-1) + \beta_{p\omega}\ln\omega)] + \pi^m.$$

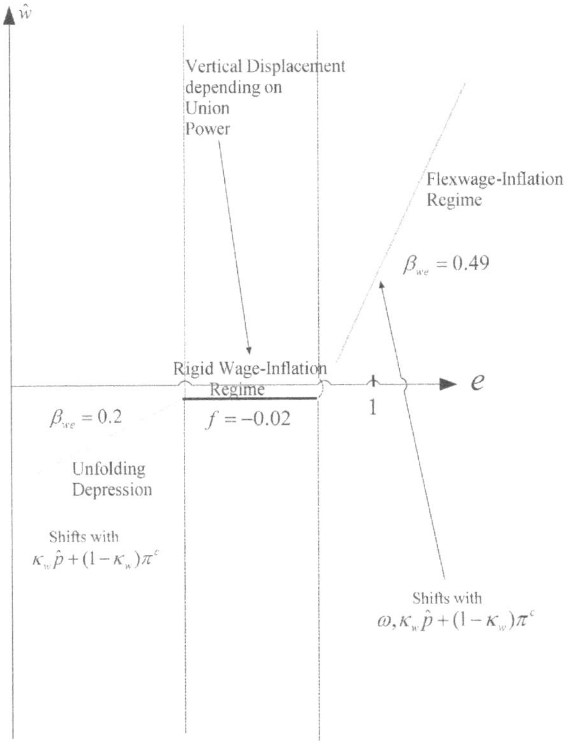

Figure 8.4 Three possible regimes for wage inflation.

If $\widehat{w}_{\text{red}} < f$ and $e \geq \underline{e}$, then

$$\widehat{\omega} = (1-\kappa_p)(f-\pi^m) - \beta_{pu}(u-1) + \beta_{p\omega}\ln\omega, \tag{8.19}$$

$$\hat{p} = \pi^m + \kappa_p(f-\pi^m) + \beta_{pu}(u-1) + \beta_{p\omega}\ln\omega, \tag{8.20}$$

if $\widehat{w}_{\text{red}} \geq f$ and $e \geq \underline{e}$, then the original dynamics (8.6) and (8.8) apply, while in all other situations we have to apply the equations

$$\widehat{\omega} = \kappa[(1-\kappa_p)\beta_{we}(e-1) - (1-\kappa_w)(\beta_{pu}(u-1) + \beta_{p\omega}\ln\omega)], \tag{8.21}$$

$$\hat{p} = \kappa[\beta_{pu}(u-1) + \beta_{p\omega}\ln\omega + \kappa_p\beta_{we}(e-1)] + \pi^m. \tag{8.22}$$

The money wage behavior underlying these modified dynamics is summarized in Figure 8.4. This situation represents an appropriate modification of Filardo's (1998) empirical analysis of such a type of Phillips curve, where however the price inflation gap (with respect to expected inflation) is used on the vertical axis. There is thus some evidence for such a three-regime Phillips curve, though in a somewhat different context.

When one applies this nonlinear wage Phillips curve to the estimated model, here with a tight inflation target of the central bank of $\bar{\pi} = 0.0077$, one gets the hierarchy of events shown in Figure 8.5. In situation 1 ($f = -\infty$), where there is no nonlinearity in the wage Phillips curve, we still have the convergent result of Figure 8.2 (a positive real wage shock of 4% is here applied), though indeed the inflation target is now somewhat below the floor to wage inflation. In situation 2 ($f = 0.01$, $\underline{e} = -\infty$), we have that the floor $f = 0.01$ applies globally and get again economic breakdown due to the adverse working of the Rose real wage effect. In situation 3 ($f = 0.01$, $\underline{e} = 0.99$) where wage flexibility becomes re-established again with the same parameter value β_{we}, below employment rates $e = 0.99$, we get an intermediate situation in which the rate of employment stays below 0.99, the rate of capacity utilization converges approximately to the value 0.95, and where there is ongoing deflation with the rate -0.01. The real wage however stays 2% above its original steady-state value and the nominal rate of interest remains positive, but is close to zero. The long run of the model therefore departs significantly from the steady-state values of the unrestricted dynamics with its linear wage Phillips curve. We therefore get from this example that the three-regime wage Phillips curve is better than the one with a global floor to money wage inflation, but the completely unrestricted model with its linear wage Phillips curve still provides the best outcome after a contractionary real wage shock has hit the economy in these three scenarios.

The example just discussed applies to the situation where the adjustment of the inflationary climate is still sufficiently sluggish to guarantee the stability properties shown in Figure 8.1. The obtained results thus characterize an economy that exhibits strong convergence back to the original steady state if not restricted by behavioral nonlinearities of the type discussed. Let us next investigate a situation where the economy is destabilized by a change in the speed of adjustment of the inflationary climate that is surrounding it. We now assume in place of the value 0.15 the value 1.52 for the parameter β_{π^m} and leave all other parameters as they were estimated in the case π^{12}. The result, in terms of capacity utilization, is shown in Figure 8.6 by the cyclical time series with symmetrically and rapidly increasing amplitudes of the cycle.

Figure 8.6 therefore shows in the completely unrestricted case a time series for the rate of capacity utilization that will sooner or later lead to economic collapse if there is no change in the behavior of the economy. Adding now a global floor of $f = -0.005$ to the dynamics in their wage Phillips curve component does not improve this situation, but leads again to monotonic economic breakdown instead. However if we allow for a third regime as described in Figure 8.4 on its left-hand side, we find that the evolution of the state variables of the model remains bounded to an economically meaningful domain. In addition, these dynamics are now of a mathematically complex type (but only somewhat irregular from the economic point of view) as is shown in Chen *et al.* (2006) by investigating the stable trajectory shown in Figure 8.6 in more detail.

With the assumed change in the adjustment speed of the inflationary climate expression the economy is therefore no longer viable in the long run (but cyclically

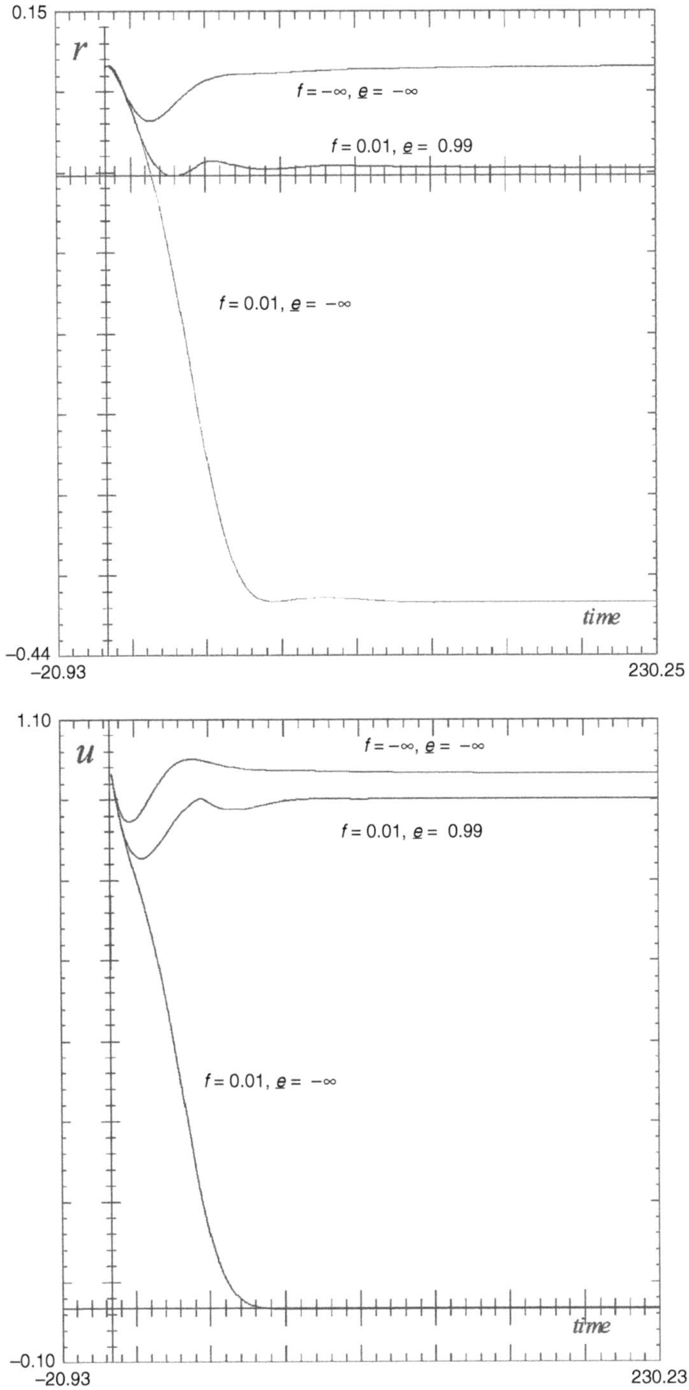

Figure 8.5 Convergent unrestricted dynamics and the role of piecewise nonlinear wage Phillips curves ($\bar{\pi} = 0.0077$) for the interest rate (top panel) and capacity utilization (bottom panel).

explosive) and it becomes even less viable if a global floor $f = -0.005$ is introduced into the estimated wage Phillips curve as shown in Figure 8.5. Yet assuming a wage Phillips curve as discussed in connection with Figure 8.4 overcomes not only this latter monotonic downturn, but also the explosive fluctuations of the unrestricted case. Some downward flexibility of money wages in a certain midrange interval, giving way however to downward flexibility of money wages again at 4% rate of unemployment, here provides viability to the evolution of the trajectories of the dynamics as indicated in Figure 8.6, here over a 50-year horizon.

8.6 Wage-led regimes, rising adjustment speeds and the emergence of complex dynamics

In this section we provide some further simulation of the general model with admissible, but no longer estimated, parameter values in order also to consider

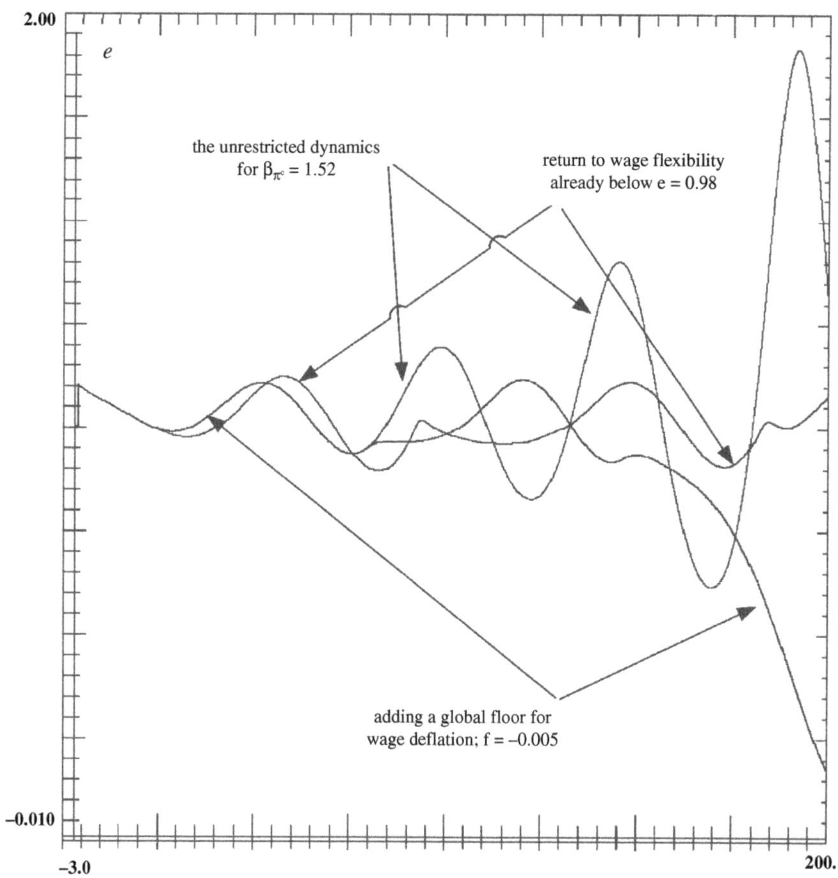

Figure 8.6 The role of regime changes in wage inflation dynamics.

in particular a situation where the Rose effect works in the opposite way, that is, where aggregate demand and the adjustment of the rate of capacity utilization depend positively on the real wage and where therefore wage flexibility with respect to demand pressure on the labor market should be destabilizing. In such a situation a global floor to wage inflation or deflation should therefore save the economy from economic breakdown, since downwardly rigid money wages combined with downwardly (somewhat) flexible prices leads to real wage increases which in the present situation stimulates economic activity and thus should lead the economy out of the depression. Yet, owing to the fact that the unrestricted economy is here in a strong way an explosive one, we find after each recovery that explosive forces come about, each time in a somewhat modified manner, until the economy falls back again into a depression with downward money wage rigidity avoiding its further destabilization until a new recovery sets in.

The base parameter set underlying the simulations is shown in Table 8.1. Speeds of price and wage adjustment are somewhat higher now, while the adjustment speed of the inflationary climate is only one-third of the value used in the preceding section. We have a positive real wage effect in the goods market dynamics (a wage-led regime now) and have now also included a negative real wage effect in the law of motion of the rate of employment, which furthermore now depends on the level of the rate of capacity utilization in addition to the growth rate of capacity utilization we have used so far as the sole determinant of the rate of employment changes. The rate of employment is thus no longer strictly positively correlated with the rate of capacity utilization as was the case in our estimate of the model, which makes the critical α condition considered in Section 8.3 more difficult to obtain, though of course wage flexibility must now be destabilizing. Finally, monetary policy is now more active with respect to the state of the business cycle and we have a floor to wage deflation that is practically zero. The result of this combination of parameter values is, as is shown below, that the nonlinear wage Phillips curve of Figure 8.2, now with a global floor ($\underline{e} = 0$) – in fact the only important nonlinearity in our 5D dynamical system – is capable of keeping a highly explosive unrestricted dynamics within economically meaningful bounds. This result is achieved in a way that makes the resulting attractors complex from the mathematical perspective, though not too irregular from the economic perspective.

We illustrate the complex dynamics that is generated by this specific parameter set at first by showing in Figure 8.7 projections of its now 5D format (since the rate

Table 8.1 Base parameter set used for simulation of the model with a positive real wage effect

$\beta_{pu} = 1$	$\beta_{p\omega} = 0.4$	$\kappa_p = 0.3$	$\beta_{we} = 0.8$	$\beta_{w\omega} = 0.4$
$\kappa_w = 0.7$	$\beta_{\pi^m} = 0.5$	$\alpha_{uu} = 0.22$	$\alpha_{u\omega} = -0.1$	$\alpha_{ur} = 0.25$
$\beta_{eu} = 0.15$	$\beta_{e\hat{u}} = 0.5$	$\beta_{e\omega} = 0.5$	$\gamma_{rr} = 0.1$	$\gamma_{rp} = 0.5$
$\gamma_{ru} = 1$	$f = -0.0001$	$\underline{e} = 0$	$\omega_{\text{shock}} = 1.01$	

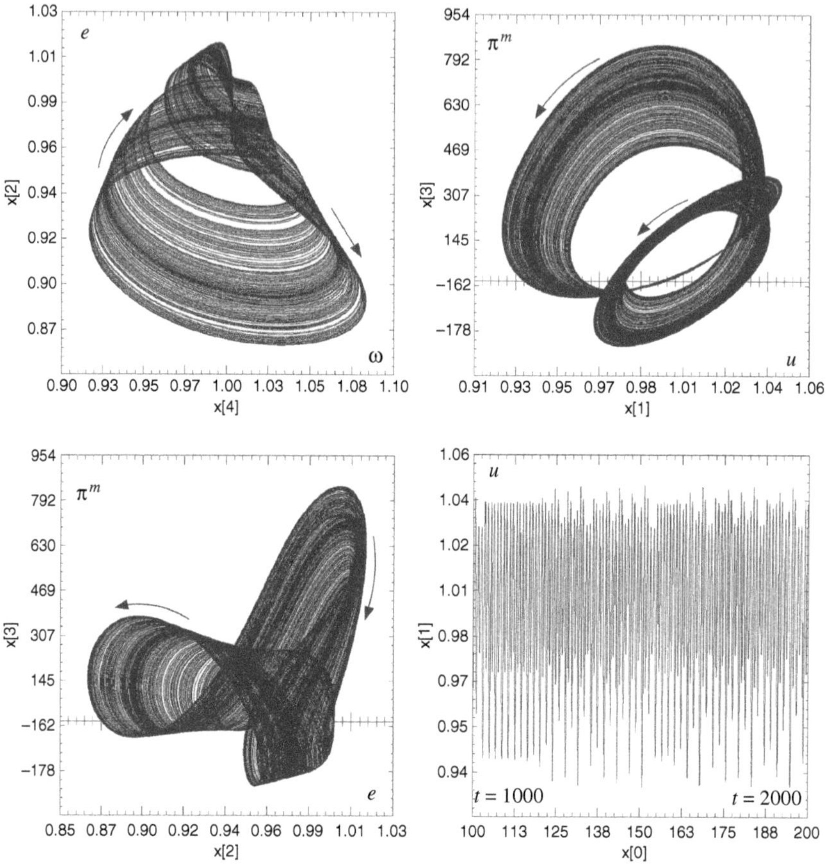

Figure 8.7 Projections and a time-series representation of the attractor of the dynamics.

of employment is now moving independently from the rate of capacity utilization to some extent) into 2D subplanes of the full 5D phase space.

We see top left in Figure 8.7 the partial phase plot of the real wage against the rate of employment with a by and large clockwise orientation and phase length corresponding to what is known from the Goodwin (1967) 2D growth cycle model and its empirical analog. In periods of high employment however the clockwise movement of these two state variables gives way to some local and fast fluctuations which represent the explosive part of the dynamics. Below this figure we see the projection of the attractor into the rate of employment/inflation climate subspace where we would expect, due to what is known from unemployment–inflation phase plots (and their clockwise orientation), a counterclockwise orientation which is not clearly visible there. This orientation is however typical for the projections of the attractor top right, there for a capacity utilization rate and inflation climate subspace projection. We see there too, that – when recovery sets in – the dynamics are squeezed through a small corridor (or eye of a needle) followed by a small stagflation cycle, which is then followed by a large cycle until the economy is squeezed back into the small corridor for its next upswing phase. The time series bottom right adds to this the information that the sequence of business fluctuations generated by the present parameter set is irregular and regular at one and the same time – irregular from the mathematical point of view in its amplitudes, and regular from the economic point of view due to the repetitive behavior in the succession of small and large cyclical patterns.

In Figure 8.8 we present some bifurcation diagrams (around the set of parameter values given in Table 8.1) which show the plots of local maxima and minima (in the vertical direction) plotted against one typical parameter on the horizontal axis. The figures show broad bands where these minima and maxima are (fairly) dense and at the end of the shown parameter ranges or in between limit cycle behavior which to some extent exhibits situations of period-doubling routes to complex dynamics.

Top left we have plotted the rate of capacity utilization against the parameter $\alpha_{u\omega}$ which determines the strength of the impact of real wages on goods market evolution. Top right the capacity utilization rate is plotted against the policy parameter γ_{ru} which determines the strength of the reaction of the central bank to the activity level of the economy (a parameter that is normally not so much at the center of interest as the one in front of the inflation gap). We can see there that positive values of $-\alpha_{u\omega}$ (profit-led regimes) and low γ_{ru} create viability problems for the considered economy. Note that we measure the positive effect of real wages on the growth rate of capacity utilization by negative numbers, since the negative effect was measured by a positive number in our estimates. Owing to the working of the global floor on money wage deflation we have a fairly stable corridor within which the rate of capacity utilization is fluctuating for a large domain of $\alpha_{u\omega}$ values, which is not true in a similar way for variations in the policy parameter γ_{ru}. In the latter case the complex dynamics can even be made to disappear as an outcome if the parameter γ_{ru} is increased a little bit beyond 1, the value we used to generate Figure 8.7 and its complex dynamics. There are also windows in the case of the parameter $\alpha_{u\omega}$ which however disappear if the parameter is set to even larger values.

In Figure 8.8 we see bottom left (for $\beta_{pu} = 0.8$ in place of $\beta_{pu} = 1$) the local maxima and minima of real wages plotted against the speed of adjustment of money wages with respect to demand pressure in the market for labor. We again have a fairly stable corridor (enclosed by the interval (0.9, 1.1)) within which the real wage is moving when the parameter is increased from close to zero up to 8. We have complex dynamics at the point that corresponds to the above parameter set with increases in maximum amplitudes thereafter, but with a sudden return to limit cycle behavior at approximately $\beta_{we} = 2.6$. Fluctuations thereafter even become less pronounced until there is again a period-doubling sequence back to complex dynamics. There is therefore no global property for the considered wage adjustment speed to be stabilizing in the sense of eigenvalue analysis as one might

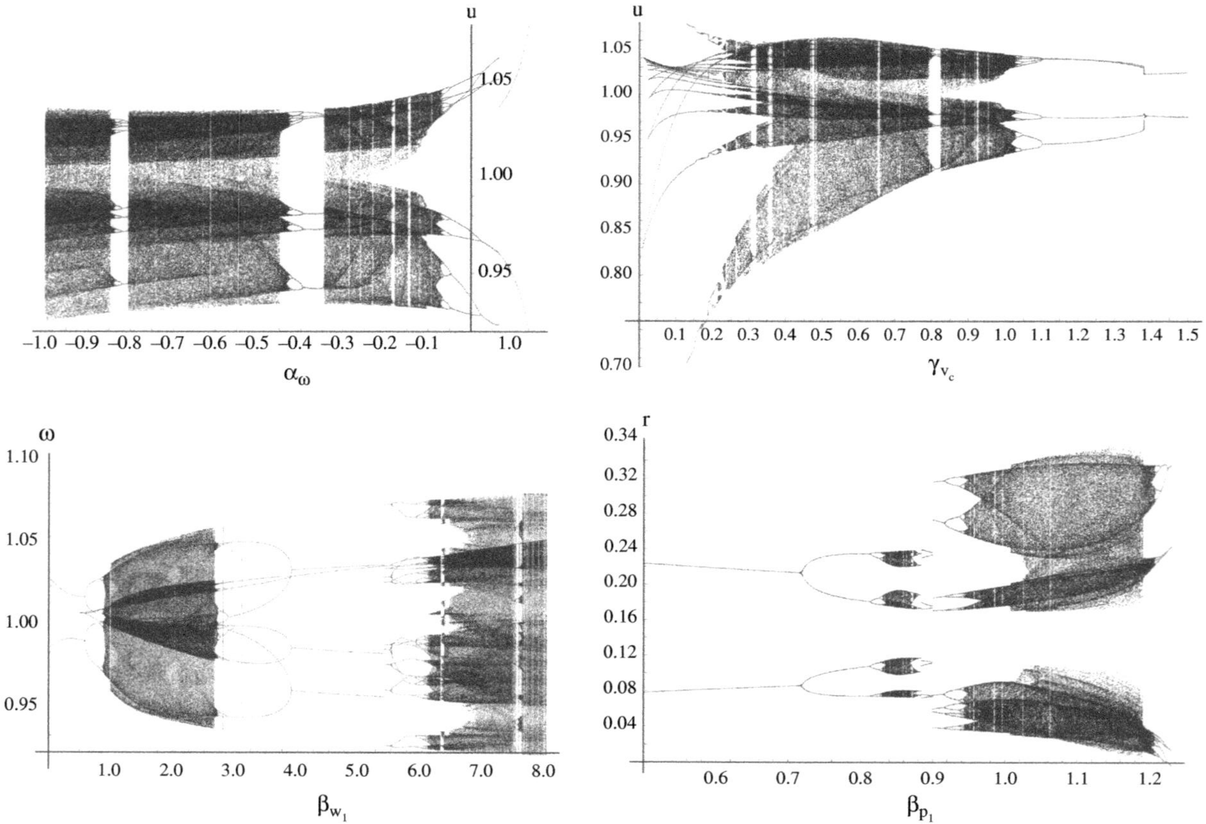

Figure 8.8 Bifurcation diagrams for selected adjustment speeds and behavioral coefficients of the dynamics.

expect from the partial reasoning concerning the real wage channel in a wage-led regime. Bottom right in Figure 8.8 finally we show the fluctuations in the nominal rate of interest (their local maxima and minima) plotted against the speed of adjustment of price inflation with respect to demand pressure in the market for goods. The system bifurcates systematically into complex dynamics as this speed of adjustment is increased, yet it still remains viable over a range from 0.95 to 1.2 approximately.

In sum we therefore get that increasing wage and price flexibility does not appear to be good for economic stability, even if tamed by a rigid floor to money wage declines, while the role of income distribution in the determination of goods market dynamics appears to be similar over wide ranges of the parameter $\alpha_{u\omega}$, though interrupted by phases of less complex dynamics (limit cycle behavior) and with tendencies toward instability if the economy switches from a wage-led regime to a profit-led one (where the impact of real wages on the growth rate of capacity utilization becomes a negative one). Finally, monetary policy that gives more and more weight to the state of the business cycle (as measured by u) becomes more and more stabilizing in the considered situation. It is obvious from these numerical simulations that the assumed kink in the wage Phillips curve is of great importance for the behavior of the considered economy, since it makes an unstable wage-led regime a viable one.

8.7 Conclusions

We conclude from what has been shown that higher-dimensional models can generate – even for parameter ranges that correspond to empirically observed parameter sizes – interesting patterns of business fluctuations, and this in continuous time, where too strong convergence properties do not give rise to over-adjustment and instability as in discrete-time systems. Complex dynamics was in our model not the outcome of such destabilizing overshooting and/or implausible and artificial nonlinearities as is often the case in the literature on chaotic dynamics. It was instead the plausible by-product of the combination of by and large conventional (though not very often considered) higher-dimensional Keynesian DAD–DAS analysis with an important factual institutional nonlinearity, here stylized in the form of a kinked money wage Phillips curve (with one or two kinks). In the present chapter, this latter outcome was primarily shown for a situation where the goods market was wage-led, while Chen *et al.* (2006) investigate the same issue for the profit-led case, again in the case of a double-kinked wage Phillips curve as estimated in Filardo (1998).

9 International linkages in a Keynesian two-country model

Economists have long been concerned with understanding the causes of the seemingly regular fluctuations in aggregate economic quantities. The extensive research on this topic has both an empirical and a theoretical dimension. The empirical research has focused on various statistical features and stylized facts of observed business cycles, refining considerably the early measures of Burns and Mitchell (1946). The focus of theoretical developments has been to seek a better understanding of the underlying economic mechanisms driving the business cycle. One may loosely categorize these developments into two broad camps. One approach has a distinctly microeconomic focus with a utility maximizing representative agent inter-temporally optimizing in reaction to external shocks. It would be fair to state that the way in which the stochastic processes for the external shocks are modeled plays an important role in the dynamic behavior of these models. Real business cycle theory is of course the prominent, currently very much in vogue, example of this type of modeling, and Cooley (1995) probably still provides the best overview. The other approach focuses on the macroeconomic aggregates themselves and models their interaction as dynamic adjustment processes in a disequilibrium or nonmarket-clearing framework. According to this view, business fluctuations come about when economic conditions are such that the destabilizing feedback chains dominate. For an exposition of this approach, one may consult Dore (1993) and Chiarella and Flaschel (2000a).

As far as international business cycles are concerned, interest among economists has been equally intense, especially in recent decades with the liberalization of exchange rate regimes, the resulting increase in international capital flows and the increasing globalization of world trade. In addition to the issues concerning closed economies, empirical research has also focused on the co-movement of macroeconomic aggregates across countries – see, for example, Gregory *et al.* (1997) and Baxter and Stockman (1989). The two broad approaches referred to above have been extended by theoretical modeling to the two-(or multi-) country situation. A good example of the real business cycle approach can be found in Canova and Marrinan (1998), while Asada *et al.* (2003a) discuss the disequilibrium approach.

In this chapter,[1] we contribute to the disequilibrium literature with a model that focuses on the co-movement of prices and the terms of trade, developed by extending to a two-country world the integrated disequilibrium macromodeling of Chiarella and Flaschel (2000a). This framework allows analysis of international business cycles and of basic economic feedback chains; specifically, the interactions of stabilizing and destabilizing dynamic economic processes.

9.1 Introduction

During the last decade and especially after the prominent contribution by Obstfeld and Rogoff (1995), there was an important paradigm change concerning the theoretical modeling approach of open economies. After the long-lasting predominance of Mundell–Fleming–Dornbusch type models in the academic as well as in the more policy-oriented literature, the so-called "new open-economy macroeconomics" approach has become the workhorse framework in the mainstream academic literature for the analysis of open-economy issues in recent years.

As in their closed-economy dynamic stochastic general equilibrium (DSGE) counterparts, such as the ones discussed by Erceg *et al.* (2000) and Smets and Wouters (2003), a central feature in this type of model is the assumption of rational expectations. However, even though theoretically appealing, the notion of fully rational agents is still quite controversial in the academic literature, and especially in the literature on nominal exchange rate dynamics. As pointed out, for example, by De Grauwe and Grimaldi (2005b), efficient markets rational expectations models are unable to match empirical data on foreign exchange (FX) rate fluctuations as well as the occurrence of speculative bubbles, herding behavior and runs. "Nonrational" models, that is, models which feature heterogeneous beliefs by the economic agents or different types of agents with different attitudes or trading schemes, seem much more successful in this task. Such models, on the other hand, often constrain themselves on the analysis of the FX markets and do not analyze the effects of such nonrational behavior by the FX market participants for the dynamic stability at the macroeconomic level.

In this chapter we attempt to fill in this gap in this alternative literature by setting up a two-country semistructural macroeconomic model with a baseline formulation of the nominal exchange rate dynamics, which however could be easily reformulated and expanded by means of a chartist/fundamentalist module, as done for example in Proaño (2008). As we formulate the present model, it reacts to disequilibrium situations in both goods and labor markets in a sluggish manner primarily due to the only gradual adjustment of nominal wages and prices to such situations. This is the first logical step for the understanding of real effects of monetary and fiscal policy in economies which are highly interrelated with each other through a variety of markets and channels, when one allows for the nonclearing of markets at every point in time and for gradual adjustments to such market disequilibrium situations.

To do so we reformulate the theoretical disequilibrium model of AD–AS growth investigated in Chen *et al.* (2006) and Proaño *et al.* (2007), for the case of two large open economies, first each in isolation and then in their interaction as two subsystems within a large closed dynamical system. The proposed model structure is similar in spirit to the two-country KMG model considered in Chiarella *et al.* (2006b), but is appropriately simplified in order to have a framework more suitable for empirical estimation and also for the study of the role of contemporary interest rate policy rules.

The remainder of the chapter is organized as follows. In Section 9.1 we describe the theoretical two-country semistructural framework for the case of an open economy. Section 9.2 integrates two open economies and discusses in more detail the linking channels between both economies, as well as the dynamics of the nominal exchange rate (the financial link) and the steady-state conditions. In Section 9.3 we estimate the model and discuss the resulting dynamic adjustments of the variables of the calibrated framework. In Section 9.4 we investigate by means of eigenvalue analysis the consequences of wage and price flexibility as well as of monetary policy for the stability of the dynamical system. Section 9.5 draws some concluding remarks.

9.2 The baseline open-economy framework

In this section we describe the macroeconomic module of our theoretical framework by extending the closed-economy, semistructural macroeconomic model discussed in Chen *et al.* (2006) and Proaño *et al.* (2007) through the incorporation of trade, price and financial links between two similar economies with imperfectly flexible nominal wages and prices. Hereby we assume that both economies have the same macroeconomic structure and are additionally conducted with the same type of monetary policy. Therefore we discuss in this section only the structure of the domestic economy, denoting with the superscript f foreign economy variables and assuming equivalent formulations for the foreign economy (with the effect of the log real exchange rate $\eta = s + \ln(p^f) - \ln(p)$ adequately adjusted).

The goods and labor markets

Concerning the real part of the economy, we follow a semistructural approach assuming that the dynamics of output and employment can be summarized by the following laws of motion:

$$\begin{aligned} \hat{u} = & -\alpha_{uu}(u - u_0) - \alpha_{uv}(v - v_0) - \alpha_{ur}(i - \hat{p} - (i_0 - \pi_0)) \\ & + \alpha_{u\eta}\eta + \alpha_{uu^f}\hat{u}^f, \qquad (9.1) \\ \hat{e} = & \, \alpha_{e\hat{u}}\hat{u} - \alpha_{ev}(v - v_0). \qquad (9.2) \end{aligned}$$

The first law of motion is of the type of a dynamic backward-looking open-economy IS equation, here represented by the growth rate of the capacity utilization rate of firms. Concerning the closed-economy dimension, it has three important domestic characteristics: (i) it reflects the dependence of output changes on aggregate income and thus on the rate of capacity utilization by assuming a negative, i.e. stable dynamic multiplier, relationship in this respect; (ii) it shows the joint dependence of consumption and investment on the domestic income distribution, which in the aggregate in principle allows for positive or negative signs before the parameter α_{uv}, depending on whether consumption, investment or the next exports are more responsive to relative real wage and wage share changes;[2] and (iii) it incorporates the negative influence of the real rate of interest on the evolution of economic activity. Additionally, in contrast to the closed-economy model discussed and investigated in Proaño *et al.* (2007), we incorporate: (iv) the positive effect of foreign goods demand (represented by the *growth rate* of capacity utilization in the foreign economy; and (v) the positive influence of the deviation of the log real exchange rate $\eta = s + \ln(p^f) - \ln(p)$ (s being the log nominal exchange rate, the law of motion of which will be defined below) from its PPP consistent steady-state level $\eta_0 = 0$.

In the second law of motion, for the growth rate of the rate of employment, we assume that the employment policy of firms follows – in the form of a generalized Okun's law – the growth rate of capacity utilization (with a weight $\alpha_{e\hat{u}}$).[3] Moreover, we additionally assume that an increasing wage share has a negative influence on the employment policy of firms. Employment is thus in particular assumed to adjust to the level of current activity, since this dependence can be shown to be equivalent to the use of a term $(u/u_0)^{\alpha_{e\hat{u}}}$ when integrated, i.e. the form of Okun's law in which this law was originally specified by Okun (1970) himself.

The wage–price dynamics

As for example Barro (1994) observes, perhaps the most important feature that theoretical Keynesian models should comprise is the existence of imperfectly flexible wages as well as prices. This is a common characteristic between our approach and advanced new Keynesian models such as Erceg *et al.* (2000) and Woodford (2003). However, even though the resulting structural wage and price Phillips curves equations of our approach resemble to a significant extent those included in those theoretical models, their microfoundations are completely different. Indeed, instead of assuming monopolistic power in the price and wage setting of forward-looking, purely rational firms and households under a Calvo (1983) pricing scheme,[4] our wage and price inflation adjustment equations are based on the more descriptive structural approach proposed by Chiarella and Flaschel (2000a) and Chiarella *et al.* (2005), which, being a Keynesian framework of aggregate demand fluctuations which allows for under- (or over-) utilized labor *as well as* capital, is based on gradual adjustments to disequilibrium situations of all real variables of the economy.

By allowing for disequilibria in both goods and labor markets, we can discuss the dynamics of wages and prices separately from each other in their structural forms, assuming that both react to their own measure of demand pressure, namely $e - e_0$ and $u - u_0$, in the market for labor and for goods, respectively.[5] Here we denote by e the rate of employment on the labor market and by e_0 the NAIRU equivalent level of this rate, and similarly by u the rate of capacity utilization of the capital stock and u_0 the normal rate of capacity utilization of firms.

As in Chiarella and Flaschel (2000a) and Chiarella *et al.* (2005), we model the expectations in both wage and price Phillips curve in a hybrid way, with crossover myopic perfect foresight (model-consistent) expectations with respect to short-run wage and domestic price inflation, on the one hand, and an adaptive updating inflation climate expression (symbolized by π_c) concerning the evolution of the CPI inflation ($\hat{p}_c$), on the other. Note that, through this specification, our model features, while not rational, nevertheless model consistent expectations concerning the evolution of the wage and price inflation and also incorporate a similar degree of inertia obtained in new Keynesian models only through also *ad hoc* "rules of thumb" or price indexation assumptions – see e.g. Galí and Gertler (1999) and Galí *et al.* (2001).

More specifically, we assume concerning the wage Phillips curve that the short-run price level considered by workers in their wage negotiations is set by the producer, so that producer price inflation gives the rate of inflation that is perfectly foreseen by workers as their short-run cost-push term. Additionally, in order to incorporate the role of import price inflation for the dynamics of the economy, we assume that the measure that is taken by workers to judge the medium-run evolution of prices in their respective economies is the consumer price index (CPI), defined as

$$p_c = p^{\gamma}(Sp^f)^{1-\gamma},$$

the geometric average of domestic and import prices – with p^f being foreign price level and S the nominal exchange rate.

Consequently, the CPI inflation $\hat{p}_c$ includes both domestic inflation (with a specific weight γ) and imported goods price inflation (with weight $1-\gamma$), so that

$$\hat{p}_c = \gamma\hat{p} + (1-\gamma)(\dot{s} + \hat{p}^f), \tag{9.3}$$

with $s = \ln(S)$. Because of the uncertainty linked with nominal exchange rate movements, we assume for both workers and firms' decision-taking processes that CPI inflation is updated in an adaptive manner according to[6]

$$\dot{\pi}_c = \beta_{\pi_c}(\hat{p}_c - \pi_c) = \beta_{\pi_c}\gamma(\hat{p} - \pi_c) + \beta_{\pi_c}(1-\gamma)(\hat{p}^f + \dot{s} - \pi_c). \tag{9.4}$$

We thereby arrive at the following two Phillips curves for wage and price inflation, which in this core version of Keynesian AD–AS dynamics are – from a qualitative perspective – formulated in a fairly symmetric way.

The structural form of the wage–price dynamics is

$$\widehat{w} = \beta_{we}(e - e_0) - \beta_{wv}\ln(v/v_0) + \kappa_{wp}\hat{p} + (1-\kappa_{wp})\pi_c + \kappa_{wz}\hat{z}, \tag{9.5}$$

$$\hat{p} = \beta_{pu}(u - u_0) + \beta_{pv}\ln(v/v_0) + \kappa_{pw}(\widehat{w} - \hat{z}) + (1-\kappa_{pw})\pi_c, \tag{9.6}$$

where $\hat{z}$ denotes the growth rate of labor productivity (which we assume here just to be equal to $g_z = \hat{z} = \text{const.}$ (g_z denoting the trend labor productivity growth).

Note that as the wage–price mechanisms are formulated, the development of the CPI inflation does not matter for the evolution of the domestic wage share $v = (w/p)/z$, measured in terms of producer prices, the law of motion of which is given by (with $\kappa = 1/(1-\kappa_{wp}\kappa_{pw})$)

$$\hat{v} = \kappa[(1-\kappa_{pw})f_w(e,v) - (1-\kappa_{wp})f_p(u,v) + (\kappa_{wz}-1)(1-\kappa_{pw})g_z], \tag{9.7}$$

with

$$f_w(e,v) = \beta_{we}(e-e_0) - \beta_{wv}\ln(v/v_0)$$

and

$$f_p(y,v) = \beta_{pu}(u-u_0) + \beta_{uv}\ln(v/v_0),$$

which follows easily from the following obviously equivalent representation of the above two Phillips curves:

$$\begin{aligned}
\widehat{w} - \pi_c &= \beta_{we}(e-e_0) - \beta_{wv}\ln(v/v_0) + \kappa_{wp}(\hat{p} - \pi_c),\\
\hat{p} - \pi_c &= \beta_{pu}(u-u_0) + \beta_{pv}\ln(v/v_0)) + \kappa_{pw}(\widehat{w} - \pi_c),
\end{aligned}$$

by solving for the variables $\widehat{w} - \pi_c$ and $\hat{p} - \pi_c$. It also implies the following two across-markets or *reduced-form* Phillips curves:

$$\begin{aligned}
\widehat{w} &= \kappa[\beta_{we}(e-e_0) - \beta_{wv}\ln(v/v_0) + \kappa_{wp}(\beta_{pu}(u-u_0) + \beta_{pv}\ln(v/v_0))\\
&\quad + (\kappa_{wz} - \kappa_{wp}\kappa_{pw})g_z] + \pi_c,\\
\hat{p} &= \kappa[\beta_{pu}(u-u_0) + \beta_{pv}\ln(v/v_0) + \kappa_{pw}(\beta_{we}(e-e_0) - \beta_{wv}\ln(v/v_0))\\
&\quad + \kappa_{pw}(\kappa_{wz} - 1)g_z] + \pi_c,
\end{aligned}$$

which represent a considerable generalization of the conventional view of a single-market price Phillips curve with only one measure of demand pressure, the one in the labor market, as used in the majority of new Keynesian models.

Equation (9.7) shows the ambiguity of the stabilizing role of the real wage channel, already discussed by Rose (1967), which arises – despite the incorporation of specific measures of demand and cost pressure on both the labor and the goods markets – if the dynamics of the employment rate and the workforce utilization are linked to the fluctuations of the firms' capacity utilization rate via Okun's law. Indeed, as sketched in Figure 9.1, a real wage increase can act, taken by itself, in a stabilizing or destabilizing manner, depending among other things on whether the

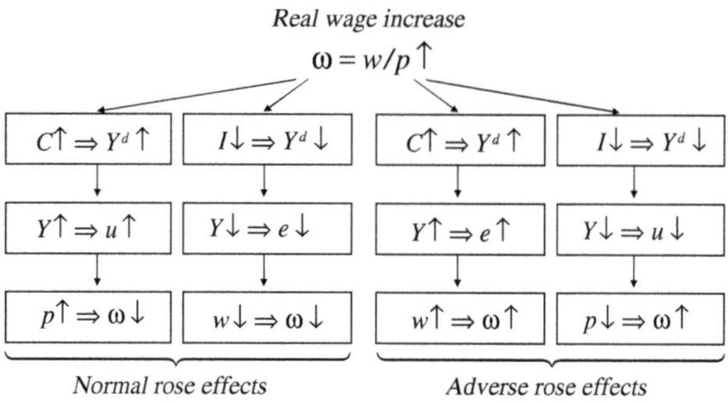

Figure 9.1 Normal (convergent) and adverse (divergent) Rose effects: the real wage channel of Keynesian open-economy macrodynamics.

dynamics of the capacity utilization rate depends positively or negatively on the real wage (i.e. on whether consumption reacts more strongly to real wage changes than investment and, in an open economy, net exports, or vice versa) *and* whether price flexibility is greater than nominal wage flexibility with respect to their own demand-pressure measures.

Monetary policy

As standard in modern macroeconomic models, we assume that money supply accommodates to the interest rate policy pursued by the central bank and thus does not feed back into the core laws of motion of the model. As interest rate policy we assume the following classical type of Taylor rule:

$$i_{\mathrm{T}} = (i_0 - \pi_0) + \hat{p} + \phi_{ip}(\hat{p} - \pi_0) + \phi_{iu}(u - u_0). \tag{9.8}$$

The target rate of the central bank i_{T} is thus assumed to depend on the steady-state real rate of interest – augmented by actual inflation back to a nominal rate – on the inflation gap and on the capacity utilization gap (as a measure of the output gap). We assume furthermore that the monetary authorities, when pursuing this target rate, do not react automatically but rather adjust to it in a smooth manner according to

$$\dot{i} = \alpha_{ii}(i_{\mathrm{T}} - i), \tag{9.9}$$

with α_{ii} determining the adjustment speed of the nominal interest rate.[7] Inserting i_{T} in the above and rearranging terms we obtain from this expression the following dynamic law of motion for the nominal interest rate:

$$\dot{i} = -\gamma_{ii}(i - i_0) + \gamma_{ip}(\hat{p} - \pi_0) + \gamma_{iu}(u - u_0), \tag{9.10}$$

where we have $\gamma_{ii} = \alpha_{ii}$, $\gamma_{ip} = \alpha_{ii}(1+\phi_{ip})$, i.e. $\phi_{ip} = \gamma_{ip}/\alpha_{ii} - 1$, and $\gamma_{iu} = \alpha_{ii}\phi_{iu}$. Note that the actual (perfectly foreseen) rate of inflation $\hat{p}$ is used to measure the inflation gap with respect to the inflation target π_0 of the central bank. Note also that we could have included (but have not done this here yet) a new kind of gap in the above Taylor rule, the wage share gap, since we have in our model a dependence of aggregate demand on income distribution and the real wage. The state of income distribution matters for the dynamics of our model and thus might also play a role in the decisions of the central bank.[8]

The nominal exchange rate dynamics

A common procedure in the open-economy DSGE type of models is to assume that the dynamics of the nominal exchange rate are driven by the validity of the purchasing power parity (PPP) postulate (see e.g. Obstfeld and Rogoff 1995). Through a log-linearization around the general equilibrium "rational expectations" steady state of the system, the – correctly – expected depreciation rate of the nominal exchange rate between two economies is simply determined by

$$E_t[s_{t+1} - s_t] = \pi_t - \pi_t^f,$$

with s_t denoting the log of the nominal exchange rate and π_t and π_t^f the domestic and foreign price inflation rates, respectively. Under the assumption that the price inflation rate is determined by the difference between money and consumption growth differentials, the actual nominal exchange rate can be expressed (applying the no-bubbles condition) as (see Walsh 2003, p. 277)

$$s_t = \frac{1}{1+\delta}\sum_{i=0}^{\infty}\left(\frac{1}{1+\delta}\right)^i [(m_{t+i} - m_{t+i}^*) - (c_{t+i} - c_{t+i}^*)],$$

with δ as the intertemporal discount rate, m and m^* as the money supplies, and c and c^* as the consumption levels in the domestic and foreign economies. Thus, in the new Keynesian framework, the actual nominal exchange rate between two countries depends on the current and future paths of the nominal money supply and consumption differentials between both economies.

Though straightforward in a theoretical rational expectations general equilibrium framework, this solution implies nevertheless the existence of (solely) purely rationally handling agents in the financial markets, an assumption that has been proven to be unable to explain major stylized facts of the nominal exchange rate dynamics. As shown for example in Ehrmann and Fratzscher (2005), the volatility of fundamentals (modeled in that study through an index of interest rate and output growth differentials and current account deficits) is by far not as large as the dynamics of the corresponding nominal exchange rates.

Owing to the empirical failure of rational expectations models, a large literature based on the assumption of heterogeneous expectations or beliefs among the traders in the foreign exchange market has arisen in the last decade. The inclusion of such heterogeneity, and therefore of a somewhat "nonrational" behavior by the economic agents, has proven quite valuable in providing insights and explanations concerning some of the "puzzles" which arise when "rationality" is assumed.[9]

In the most basic heterogeneous expectations framework (see e.g. Frankel and Froot 1990), two basic types of traders with different belief patterns (or expectations) concerning the future behavior of the nominal exchange rate are modeled, the fundamentalists and the chartists. The fundamentalists typically believe that the nominal exchange rate is driven by macroeconomic fundamentals such as interest rate differentials, different developments of production and employment and/or the validity of the PPP postulate and consequently trade conforming to this belief. In contrast, the chartists are assumed to follow the market tendencies, acting thus in principle in a destabilizing manner. The dynamics and stability of the resulting nominal exchange rate, therefore, depend on the relative strength and proportion of these two groups in the foreign exchange market.

In more advanced theoretical frameworks about heterogeneous beliefs, a wide variety of extensions concerning the endogenous determination of the trader groups composition can be found: in Kirman (1993), for example, the determination of the two groups is determined by a purely stochastic factor; in Lux (1995b) the "contagion" effect, that is, the change in the trading strategy, depends on the overall "mood" of the market and on the observed realized returns. De Grauwe and Grimaldi (2005a), in a similar manner, assume the *group change* probability as a function of the relative probability of the forecasting rules of the two groups and the *risk* associated with their use.[10]

In our theoretical framework though we will leave these possible model extensions for future research and assume for simplicity a delayed adjustment of the nominal exchange rate based on the uncovered interest rate parity (UIP) postulate, namely

$$\dot{s} = \beta_s(i^f - i + \hat{s}^e), \tag{9.11}$$

with

$$\hat{s}^e = \beta_{s\eta}(-\eta)$$

denoting the expected nominal depreciation rate (specified here through the expectational equation (9.11)). This law of motion together with the price inflation adjustment equations for the domestic and the foreign economies deliver

$$\begin{aligned}\dot{\eta} &= \dot{s} + \hat{p}^f - \hat{p} \\ &= \beta_s(i^f - i + \hat{s}^e) + \hat{p}^f - \hat{p}.\end{aligned} \tag{9.12}$$

Taken together, the model of this section consists of the following six laws of motion (with the derived reduced-form expressions as far as the wage–price spiral is concerned and with reduced-form expressions by assumption concerning the goods and the labor market dynamics).[11]

The one-country submodule

$$\hat{u} \overset{\text{dynamic IS}}{=} -\alpha_{uu}(u-u_0) - \alpha_{ur}(i - \hat{p} - (i_0 - \pi_0))$$
$$- \alpha_{uv}(v - v_0) + \alpha_{u\eta}\eta + \alpha_{uu^f}\hat{u}^f, \tag{9.13}$$

$$\hat{e} \overset{\text{Okun's law}}{=} \alpha_{e\hat{u}}\hat{u} - \alpha_{ev}(v - v_0), \tag{9.14}$$

$$\hat{v} \overset{\text{wage share}}{=} \kappa[(1-\kappa_{pw})(\beta_{we}(e-e_0) - \beta_{wv}\ln(v/v_0))$$
$$-(1-\kappa_{wp})(\beta_{pu}(u-u_0) + \beta_{pv}\ln(v/v_0)) + \rho g_z] \tag{9.15}$$

with

$$\rho = (\kappa_{wz} - 1)(1 - \kappa_{pw}),$$

$$\dot{\pi}_c \overset{\text{CPI climate}}{=} \beta_{\pi_c}(\hat{p}_c - \pi_c), \quad \hat{p}_c = \gamma\hat{p} + (1-\gamma)(\hat{s} + \hat{p}^f), \tag{9.16}$$

$$\dot{i} \overset{\text{Taylor rule}}{=} -\gamma_{ii}(i - i_0) + \gamma_{ip}(\hat{p} - \pi_0) + \gamma_{iu}(u - u_0), \tag{9.17}$$

$$\dot{\eta} \overset{\text{real exchange}}{=} \beta_s(i^f - i - \beta_{s\eta}\eta) + \hat{p}^f - \hat{p}. \tag{9.18}$$

The above equations represent, in comparison to the baseline model of new Keynesian macroeconomics, the IS goods market dynamics, here augmented by Okun's law as link between the goods and the labor market, and of course the Taylor rule. There is now also a law of motion for the wage share $\hat{v}$ that makes use of the same explaining variables as in the new Keynesian model with both staggered prices and wages (but with inflation rates $\hat{p}, \widehat{w}$ in place of their time rates of change and with no accompanying sign reversal concerning the influence of output and wage gaps), and finally the law of motion that describes the updating of the inflationary climate expression. We have to make use in addition of the reduced-form expression for the price inflation rate or the price Phillips curve, our law of motion for the price level p in place of the new Keynesian law of motion for the price inflation rate π^p:

$$\hat{p} = \kappa[\beta_{pu}(u-u_0) + \beta_{pv}\ln(v/v_0) + \kappa_{pw}(\beta_{we}(e-e_0) - \beta_{wv}\ln(v/v_0))] + \pi_c, \tag{9.19}$$

which has to be inserted into the above laws of motion in various places in order to get an autonomous nonlinear system of differential equations in the state variables, capacity utilization u, the rate of employment e, the nominal rate of interest i, the wage share v, and the inflationary climate expression π_c. We stress that one can consider equation (9.19) as a sixth law of motion of the considered dynamics which however – when added – leads a system determinant which is zero and which therefore allows for zero-root hysteresis for certain variables of the model (in fact in the price level if the target rate of inflation of the monetary authorities is zero and if interest rate smoothing is present in the Taylor rule). We have written the laws of motion in an order that gives first the dynamic equations also present in the baseline new Keynesian model of inflation dynamics, and then our formulation of the dynamics of income distribution and of the inflationary climate in which the economy is operating.

In sum, therefore, our dynamic AD–AS growth model exhibits a variety of features that are much more in line with a Keynesian understanding of the characteristics of the trade cycle than is the case for the conventional modeling of AD–AS growth dynamics or its radical reformulation by the new Keynesians (where – if nondeterminacy can be avoided by the choice of an appropriate Taylor rule – only the steady-state position is a meaningful solution in the related setup we considered in the preceding section).

Local stability analysis: the small open-economy case

We start our analysis of the stability properties of the system with the small open-economy case, assuming that the foreign economy is and remains at its steady-state level ($u^f = u_0^f$, $e^f = e_0^f$, $v^f = v_0^f$). We note that the steady state of the 5D subdynamics, due to its specific formulation, can be supplied exogenously. As this submodule is formulated it exhibits five gaps, to be closed in the steady state, and has five laws of motion, which when set equal to zero, exactly imply this result (assuming that the foreign economy stays at its steady-state level).

Since we assume the same structure for both economies, the local stability of one subsystem would imply the same for the other subsystem, assuming that similar parameter dimensions.

As discussed in Chen *et al.* (2006), the steady state of the dynamics of the closed-economy version of this model is asymptotically stable under certain sluggishness conditions that are reasonable from a Keynesian perspective, loses its asymptotic stability cyclically (by way of so-called Hopf bifurcations) if the system becomes too flexible, and becomes sooner or later globally unstable if (generally speaking) adjustment speeds become too high. If the model is subject to explosive forces, it requires extrinsic nonlinearities in economic behavior – like downward money wage rigidity – to manifest themselves at least far off the steady state in order to bound the dynamics to an economically meaningful domain in the considered 5D state space.

In order to investigate the role of heterogeneous expectations in the foreign exchange market as well as more traditional international transmission channels for the stability of the whole macroeconomic system in an analytical manner, we reduce the dimensions of our theoretical framework through the following simplifying assumptions.

- The monetary authorities do not pursue an interest rate smoothing strategy, so that $i = i_{\mathrm{T}}$ always holds. This is the case when $\alpha_{ii} \to \infty$.

- $\beta_{\pi^c} = 0$. In this case the inflationary climate is constant (hereby we assume that $\pi_c = 0$).
- We can replace e through $\alpha_{eu}u$ in the wage and price inflation adjustment equations without loss of generality.

Under the simplifying assumptions, the initial 5D dynamical system can be reduced to the following 3D subsystem:

$$\hat{u} = -\alpha_{uu}(u-u_0) - \alpha_{ur}(\phi_{ip}(\hat{p}-\pi_0) + \phi_{iu}(u-u_0)) \\ - \alpha_{uv}(v-v_0) + \alpha_{u\eta}\eta, \tag{9.20}$$

$$\hat{v} = \kappa[(1-\kappa_{pw})(\beta_{we}(\alpha_{eu}u - e_0) - \beta_{wv}\ln(v/v_0)) \\ - (1-\kappa_{wp})(\beta_{pu}(u-u_0) + \beta_{pv}\ln(v/v_0)) + \rho g_z], \tag{9.21}$$

$$\dot{\eta} = \beta_s[i_0^f - (i_0 + (1+\phi_{ip})(\hat{p}-\pi_0) + \phi_{iu}(u-u_0)) - \beta_{s\eta}\eta] - \hat{p}, \tag{9.22}$$

with

$$\hat{p} = \kappa[\beta_{pu}(u-u_0) + \beta_{pv}\ln(v/v_0) + \kappa_{pw}(\beta_{we}(\alpha_{eu}u - u_0) - \beta_{wv}\ln(v/v_0))] \tag{9.23}$$

to be inserted in several places.

The corresponding Jacobian of this reduced 3D subsystem

$$J_{3D} = \begin{bmatrix} J_{11} & J_{12} & J_{13} \\ J_{21} & J_{22} & J_{23} \\ J_{31} & J_{32} & J_{33} \end{bmatrix},$$

with

$$J_{11} = \frac{\partial \hat{u}}{\partial u} = -\alpha_{uu} - \alpha_{ur}\left(\phi_{ip}\kappa\left(\beta_{pu} + \kappa_{pw}\beta_{we}\alpha_{eu}\right) + \phi_{iu}\right) < 0, \tag{9.24}$$

$$J_{12} = \frac{\partial \hat{u}}{\partial v} = -\alpha_{uv} - \alpha_{ur}\phi_{ip}\kappa\left(\frac{\beta_{pv} - \kappa_{pw}\beta_{wv}}{v_0}\right) < 0, \tag{9.25}$$

$$J_{13} = \frac{\partial \hat{u}}{\partial \eta} = \alpha_{u\eta} > 0, \tag{9.26}$$

$$J_{21} = \frac{\partial \hat{v}}{\partial u} = \kappa((1-\kappa_{pw})\beta_{we}\alpha_{eu} - (1-\kappa_{wp})\beta_{pu}), \tag{9.27}$$

$$J_{22} = \frac{\partial \hat{v}}{\partial v} = -\kappa\left(\frac{(1-\kappa_{pw})\beta_{wv} + (1-\kappa_{wp})\beta_{pv}}{v_0}\right) < 0, \tag{9.28}$$

$$J_{23} = \frac{\partial \hat{v}}{\partial \eta} = 0, \tag{9.29}$$

$$J_{31} = \frac{\partial \dot{\eta}}{\partial u} = -\beta_s((1+\phi_{ip})\kappa(\beta_{pu} + \kappa_{pw}\beta_{we}\alpha_{eu}) + \phi_{iu})$$
$$- \kappa(\beta_{pu} + \kappa_{pw}\beta_{we}\alpha_{eu}) < 0, \tag{9.30}$$

$$J_{32} = \frac{\partial \dot{\eta}}{\partial v} = -\beta_s(1+\phi_{ip})\kappa\left(\frac{\beta_{pv} - \beta_{wv}\kappa_{pw}}{v_0}\right) - \kappa\left(\frac{\beta_{pv} - \beta_{wv}\kappa_{pw}}{v_0}\right), \tag{9.31}$$

$$J_{33} = \frac{\partial \dot{\eta}}{\partial \eta} = -\beta_s\beta_{s\eta} < 0, \tag{9.32}$$

has the following sign structure

$$J_{3D} = \begin{bmatrix} - & - & + \\ ? & - & 0 \\ - & ? & - \end{bmatrix}.$$

According to the Routh–Hurwitz stability conditions for a 3D dynamical system, asymptotic local stability of a steady state is fulfilled when

$$a_i > 0, \quad i = 1, 2, 3, \quad \text{and} \quad a_1 a_2 - a_3 > 0,$$

where $a_1 = -\text{trace}(J)$ and $a_2 = \sum_{k=1}^{3} J_k$ with

$$J_1 = \begin{vmatrix} J_{22} & J_{23} \\ J_{32} & J_{33} \end{vmatrix}, \quad J_2 = \begin{vmatrix} J_{11} & J_{13} \\ J_{31} & J_{33} \end{vmatrix}, \quad J_3 = \begin{vmatrix} J_{11} & J_{12} \\ J_{21} & J_{22} \end{vmatrix},$$

and $a_3 = -\det(J)$.

Our reduced 3D dynamical system is stable around its interior steady state, if the following proposition is fulfilled.

Proposition 9.1 *Assume that (i) $\beta_{we}\alpha_{eu} > \beta_{pu}$, that is, that wage inflation reacts more strongly to changes in capacity utilization than price inflation, and additionally that (ii) κ_{pw} is of a sufficiently small dimension so that $(1 - \kappa_{pw})\beta_{wv} + (1 - \kappa_{wp})\beta_{pv} > 0$ and $\partial\hat{u}/\partial v < 0$ is fulfilled.*

Then, the Routh–Hurwitz conditions are fulfilled and the unique steady state of the reduced 3D dynamical system is locally asymptotic stable.

Proof: As can be easily observed, according to the formulation of the dynamics of the nominal exchange rate, these are unambiguously asymptotically stable, since $\partial\dot{\eta}/\partial\eta < 0$. Under Proposition 9.1 $\partial\hat{v}/\partial v < 0$, and the trace of J is then unambiguously negative (and $a_1 > 0$ holds), since

$$\text{trace}(J) = J_{11} + J_{22} + J_{33} < 0. \tag{9.33}$$

Condition (i) additionally ensures the partial derivative of $\dot{\eta}$ with respect to v to be negative, that is $\partial\dot{\eta}/\partial v < 0$. Condition (ii) assures that $\partial\hat{v}/\partial u > 0$.

If conditions (i) and (ii) hold, the sign structure of the Jacobian matrix is given by

$$J_{3D} = \begin{bmatrix} - & - & + \\ + & - & 0 \\ - & - & - \end{bmatrix}.$$

Under such a sign structure, J_1, J_2 and J_3, the second-order minors of J, are given by

$$\begin{aligned} J_1 &= J_{22} \cdot J_{33} - J_{32} \cdot J_{23} \\ &= \beta_s \beta_{s\eta} \kappa \left(\frac{\beta_{wv}(1 - \kappa_{pw}) + \beta_{pv}(1 - \kappa_{wp})}{v_0} \right) > 0, \end{aligned} \tag{9.34}$$

$$\begin{aligned} J_2 &= J_{11} \cdot J_{33} - J_{31} \cdot J_{13} \\ &= \beta_s \beta_{s\eta} [\alpha_{uu} + \alpha_{uv}(\phi_{ip}\kappa(\beta_{pu} + \kappa_{pw}\beta_{we}\alpha_{eu}) + \phi_{iu})] \\ &\quad + \alpha_{u\eta}[\beta_s((1 + \phi_{ip})\kappa(\beta_{pu} + \kappa_{pw}\beta_{we}\alpha_{eu}) + \phi_{iu}) \\ &\quad + \kappa(\beta_{pu} + \kappa_{pw}\beta_{we}\alpha_{eu})] > 0, \end{aligned} \tag{9.35}$$

$$\begin{aligned} J_3 &= J_{11} \cdot J_{22} - J_{21} \cdot J_{12} \\ &= [\alpha_{uv} + \alpha_{ur}(\phi_{ip}\kappa(\beta_{pv} - \beta_{wv}\kappa_{pw}) + \phi_{iu})] \\ &\quad \cdot \kappa \left(\frac{(1 - \kappa_{pw})\beta_{wv} - (1 - \kappa_{wp})\beta_{pv}}{v_0} \right) \\ &\quad + \kappa[(1 - \kappa_{pw})\alpha_{eu}\beta_{we} - (1 - \kappa_{wp})\beta_{pu}] \\ &\quad \times \left[\alpha_{uv} + \alpha_{ur}\phi_{ip}\kappa \left(\frac{\beta_{pv} - \kappa_{pw}\beta_{wv}}{v_0} \right) \right] > 0. \end{aligned} \tag{9.36}$$

It can be easily confirmed that $a_2 = \sum_{k=1}^{3} J_k > 0$ and $a_3 = -\det(J) > 0$, as well as the critical condition $a_1 a_2 - a_3 > 0$ for local asymptotic stability of the steady state of the system hold under the assumed parameter constellation.

Concerning the determinant of J, from the sign structure of the 3D Jacobian it can be easily seen that it is negative, so that $a_3 = -\det(J) > 0$. □

With regard to the local asymptotic stability properties of the 6D subsystem, we can infer without an analytical proof that it will lose stability if (a) the conditions (i) and (ii) in Proposition 9.1 are no longer fulfilled, (b) the adjustment speed of the inflationary climate β_{π^c} approaches infinity or (c) the nominal interest rate does not adjust sufficiently fast to the target rate pursued by the monetary authorities, that is, when the interest rate smoothing parameter α_{ii} is insufficiently low.

9.3 The two-country framework: estimation and evaluation

After having set up the basic structure of an open economy of Keynesian nature, in this section we integrate two economies (and therefore two small open-economy dynamic models if considered separately) with similar characteristics (as the Eurozone and USA) into a consistent whole.

Considering both economies as a single macroeconomic framework, the resulting 11D dynamical system comprises 11 dynamic variables with the gaps

$$u-u_0, \quad e-e_0, \quad v-v_0, \quad i-i_0, \quad \hat{p}-\pi_0, \quad \eta-\eta_0,$$

plus the five ones for the foreign economy that correspond to the first (domestic) five of the list shown above.

For the unique determination of the steady-state position we set $\hat{u}, \hat{e}, \hat{v}, \dot{i}$ equal to zero (and of course have the same situation for the foreign economy). This holds only when all gaps are zero simultaneously, which additionally delivers (for $\eta = \eta_0 = 0$) $\dot{s} = 0$.

Assuming a constant steady-state nominal exchange rate s, we moreover get from the reduced-form price Phillips curves

$$\begin{aligned}
\hat{p}_0 &= \pi_{co} = \gamma\pi_{co} + (1-\gamma)\pi_{co}^f,\\
\hat{p}_0^f &= \pi_{co}^f = \gamma^f\pi_{co}^f + (1-\gamma^f)\pi_{co}\\
&\iff \pi_c = \pi_c^f.
\end{aligned}$$

By inserting again equation (9.3) and its foreign economy counterpart, we obtain

$$\gamma\hat{p}_0 + (1-\gamma)\hat{p}_0^f = \gamma^f\hat{p}_0 + (1-\gamma^f)\hat{p}_0^f,$$

which only holds true for $\hat{p} = \hat{p}^f$. At the steady state, thus, both countries share the same inflationary climate and equilibrium inflation rate, independently of the actual composition of the CPI index in both economies. Under this condition, the nominal exchange rate equation (9.11) delivers indeed a constant nominal exchange rate at the steady state, and therefore also a constant real exchange rate, since $\eta = \eta_0$.

The two-country model

$$\begin{aligned}
\hat{u} &= -\alpha_{uu}(u-u_0) - \alpha_{ur}(i-\hat{p}-(i_0-\pi_0)) - \alpha_{uv}(v-v_0)\\
&\quad + \alpha_{u\eta}\eta + \alpha_{uu^f}\hat{u}^f,\\
\hat{e} &= \alpha_{e\hat{u}}\hat{u} - \alpha_{ev}(v-v_0),\\
\hat{v} &= \kappa[(1-\kappa_{pw})f_w(e,v) - (1-\kappa_{wp})f_p(u,v) + \rho g_z],\\
\dot{\pi}_c &= \beta_{\pi_c}(\hat{p}_c - \pi_c), \quad \hat{p}_c = \gamma\hat{p} + (1-\gamma)(\dot{s} + \hat{p}^f),\\
\dot{i} &= -\gamma_{ii}(i-i_0) + \gamma_{ip}(\hat{p}-\pi_0) + \gamma_{iu}(u-u_0),\\
\dot{\eta} &= \beta_s^f(i^f - i - \eta) + \hat{p}^f - \hat{p},
\end{aligned}$$

$$\begin{aligned}
\hat{u}^f &= -\alpha_{uu}(u^f - u_0) - \alpha_{ur}(i^f - \hat{p}^f - (i_0 - \pi_0)) - \alpha_{uv}(v^f - v_0) \\
&\quad - \alpha_{u\eta}\eta + \alpha_{uu^f}\hat{u}, \\
\hat{e}^f &= \alpha_{e\hat{u}}\hat{u}^f - \alpha_{ev}(v^f - v_0), \\
\hat{v}^f &= \kappa[(1-\kappa_{pw})f_w(e^f, v^f) - (1-\kappa_{wp})f_p(u^f, v^f) + \rho g_z^f], \\
\dot{\pi}_c^f &= \beta_{\pi_c}(\hat{p}_c^f - \pi_c^f), \quad \hat{p}_c^f = \gamma\hat{p}^f + (1-\gamma)(-\dot{s} + \hat{p}), \\
\dot{i}^f &= -\gamma_{ii}(i^f - i_0) + \gamma_{ip}(\hat{p}^f - \pi_0) + \gamma_{iu}(u^f - u_0).
\end{aligned}$$

The structure of the 11D dynamical system is summarized in Figure 9.2. This figure shows at its top the interaction of the foreign exchange market with the two economies and toward the bottom the interaction of both economies through their goods markets.

As this diagrammatic exposition of quantity and price trade channels linking the two economies shows, the macroeconomic interaction between them seems apparently intrinsically stable, and the sole obvious source of instability or even chaos is laid on the foreign exchange markets. Indeed, in the absence of predominant unstable nominal exchange rate dynamics, the dynamics of the two-country framework seem to be of a self-regulating nature through the interaction of quantity and price trade linkages. This, however, is not necessarily the case. So, for example, on the one hand, an exogenous increase in the foreign demand ($u^f \uparrow$) leads to an increase of price and (through the related increase in foreign employment) wage inflation abroad, which in turn leads to a loss of competitiveness ($\eta \uparrow$) and to a cooling down of the economy. On the other hand, though, an increase in u^f leads (through the "locomotive" effect) to an increase in the domestic level of economic activity, to an increase in domestic wage and price inflation and subsequently to a fall of η, which, in turn, is likely to boost furthermore the economic activity abroad. The net effect of these two opposite effects and therefore the stability of

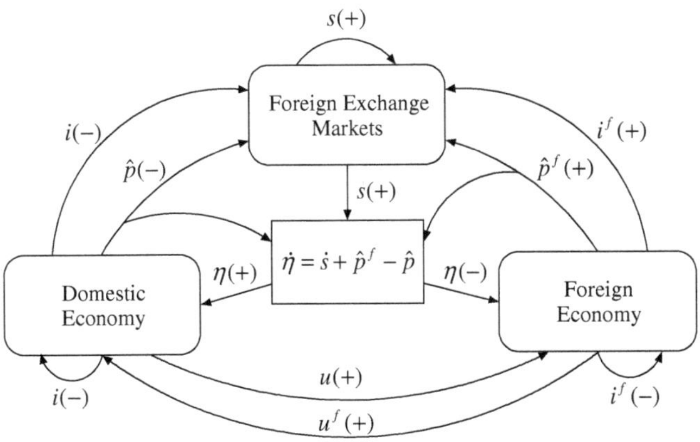

Figure 9.2 The real and financial links of the two-country model.

the system thus depends to an important extent on the degree of wage and price flexibility in both economies. However, since a thorough analytical calculation of the Routh–Hurwitz local stability conditions for a 11D system would be an extremely complicated and, more importantly, nontransparent task, we will investigate the stability of the system in a numerical manner focusing on the role of the wage and price flexibility for the stability of the system by means of an eigenvalue analysis in Section 9.4.

Stylized facts of monetary policy

Since the seminal contribution by Sims (1980), vector autoregressive (VAR) models have become a standard tool for the study of the transmission of monetary policy in industrialized economics.

In the majority of existing studies the VAR analysis is performed under the implicit assumption that the studied economies have "closed" or "small open-economy" characteristics due to the possible collinearity and identification problems which can arise if a large number of variables is incorporated in the VAR model. From the econometric perspective, this means that foreign variables, if included in the estimated VAR model, are assumed to be exogenously determined. Indeed, most of the prominent studies on monetary policy transmission, such as Bernanke and Blinder (1992), Bernanke and Mihov (1998) and Christiano *et al.* (1999) for the US economy, Kim (1999) for the G7 countries and Peersman and Smets (2003) for the Euro area, are based on a "small open-economy" assumption.

Under such a specification the main stylized facts concerning the monetary policy transmission mechanism can be summarized as follows.

- An unexpected increase in the US nominal interest rate (a contractionary monetary policy shock) leads to a slowdown of economy activity, which reaches its peak after five quarters, approximately.
- The response of employment resembles the output reaction, though in a somewhat delayed manner.
- Price inflation initially increases (the price puzzle discussed, for example, by Sims (1992)), but, after some quarters, an unambiguously negative effect can be observed.
- The domestic currency appreciates due to, among other things, the interest rate parity.

Concerning the international transmission of monetary policy, Kim (2001) discusses two main findings from his VAR estimations. First, that monetary policy in the non-US G6 countries follows US monetary policy shocks (a result which corroborates the findings of Eichenbaum and Evans (1995) concerning the dynamic behavior of spread between foreign and US interest rates after such types of shocks). Second, that US monetary expansions have a positive spillover effect on the remaining G7 countries primarily due to the resulting reduction in world interest. This result is also found by Bluedorn and Bowdler (2006) and Eickmeier (2007), the latter concerning the effect of US monetary shocks on Germany.

The empirical evidence on the reaction of nominal exchange rates to monetary policy shocks is, on the contrary, not as undisputed. While Eichenbaum and Evans (1995, p. 976), for example, find that "the maximal effect of a contractionary monetary policy shock on US exchange rates is not contemporaneous; instead the dollar continues to appreciate for a substantial period of time [a finding which] is inconsistent with simple rational expectations overshooting models of the sort considered by Dornbusch (1976)," Kim and Roubini (2000), Kalyvitis and Michaelides (2001) and Bluedorn and Bowdler (2006) find little evidence for such behavior for the G7 nominal exchange rates after the inclusion of alternative measures of monetary policy shocks as well as of relative output and prices in their specifications.

Next the strength of international transmission channels between the USA and the Euro area, two large economies which are likely to indeed influence each other by a variety of macroeconomic channels, are investigated by means of econometric methods.

Data sources and descriptive statistics

In order to analyze the interaction of two economies which indeed are of sufficiently large dimension to significantly influence each other, we take as examples the economies of the USA and the Euro area. The empirical data of the corresponding time series stem from the Federal Reserve Bank of St. Louis dataset (see http:/www.stls.frb.org/fred) and the OECD database for the USA and the Euro area, respectively. The variables are listed in Table 9.1. The data are quarterly, seasonally adjusted and concern the period from 1980:1 to 2004:4.

The logarithms of wages and prices are denoted $\ln(w_t)$ and $\ln(p_t)$, respectively. Their first differences (backwardly dated), i.e. the current rate of wage and price inflation, are denoted $\widehat{w}_t$ and $\hat{p}_t$ as in the theoretical framework. The inflationary climate π^c of the theoretical part of this chapter is approximated here in a very simple way by a linearly declining moving average of price inflation rates with linearly decreasing weights over the past 12 quarters, denoted π_t^{12}.

Figure 9.3 shows the time series of both the US and the Euro area described in Table 9.1. As can be observed in Figure 9.3, the USA and the Euro area have featured in the last two decades a remarkable similarity in their respective wage and price inflation developments, as well – to a somewhat lesser extent – as in the dynamics of the capacity utilization and the output gap, respectively (see Table 9.2).

This, however, does not hold for the dynamics of the employment rate and the wage share of both economies. As can be observed in Figure 9.3, while the US unemployment rate has fluctuated, roughly speaking, around a constant level over the last two decades, the European employment (unemployment) rate described a persistent downwards (upwards) trend over the same time period. This particular European development has been explained by Layard *et al.* (1991) and Ljungqvist and Sargent (1998) by an overproportional increase in the number of long-term

Table 9.1 US and Euro area dataset

Variable		*Description of the original series*
e	USA	Employment rate
	Euro area	Employment rate (HP cyclical component, $\lambda = 640\,000$)
u	USA	Capacity utilization: manufacturing, percent of capacity
	Euro area	Output gap
w	USA	Non-farm business sector: compensation per hour, 1992 = 100
	Euro area	Business sector: wage rate per hour
p	USA	Gross domestic product: implicit price deflator, 1996 = 100
	Euro area	Gross domestic product: implicit price deflator, 2000 = 100
z	USA	Non-farm business sector: output per hour of all persons, 1992 = 100
	Euro area	Labor productivity of the business economy
v	USA	Non-farm business sector: real compensation per output unit, 1992 = 100
	Euro area	Business sector: real compensation per output unit (HP cyclical component, $\lambda = 640\,000$)
i	USA	Federal funds rate
	Euro area	Short-term interest rate
s		EUR/USD nominal exchange rate

unemployed (i.e. workers with an unemployment duration over 12 months) with respect to short-term unemployed (workers with an unemployment duration of less than 12 months) and the phenomenon of hysteresis especially in the first group. Because long-term unemployed become less relevant in the determination of nominal wages (since primarily the short-term unemployed are taken into account), the potential downward pressure on wages resulting from the unemployment of the former diminishes, with the result of a higher level of the NAIRU (see Blanchard and Wolfers 2000). When the long-term unemployment is high, the aggregate unemployment rate of an economy thus, "becomes a poor indicator of effective labor supply, and the macroeconomic adjustment mechanisms – such as downward pressure on wages and inflation when unemployment is high – will then not operate effectively" (OECD 2002, p. 189).

Since time-series data for long-term unemployment in the Euro area are not available for the analyzed sample period, we used the adjusted cyclical component of the unemployment rate as a proxy for the short-term unemployment. This series was calculated as the difference between the actual unemployment rate and the Hodrick–Prescott (HP) trend series obtained on the basis of a smoothing factor $\lambda = 640\,000$ (interpretable as a proxy for the actual development of long-term unemployment in the Euro area), normalized to zero in 1970:1, where unemployment (and also long-term unemployment) was extremely low on the European continent.[12] In our econometric estimation, thus, we implicitly assume the existence of a variable NAIRU in the Euro area, despite the fact that we did not explicitly model it in the theoretical framework of the previous section.

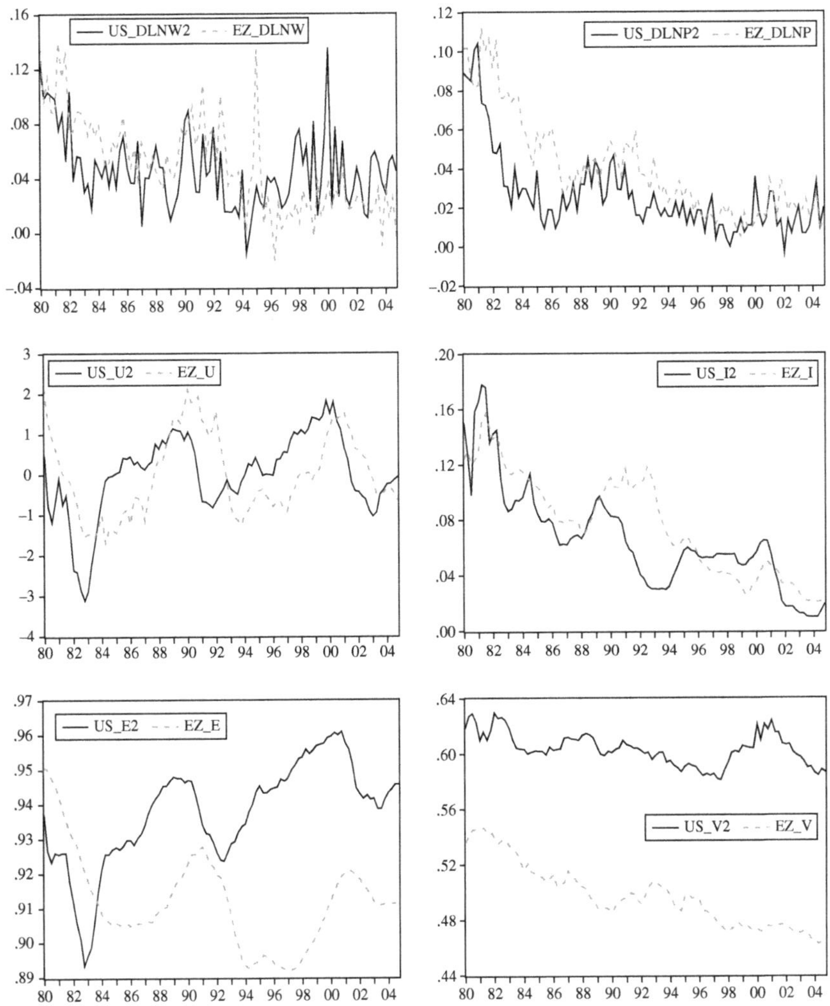

Figure 9.3 US and Euro area aggregate time series.

In order to check the stationarity of the analyzed time series, Phillips–Perron unit root tests were computed in order to account, besides residual autocorrelation as done by the standard ADF tests, also for possible residual heteroskedasticity. The Phillips–Perron test specifications and results are shown in Table 9.3. The applied unit root tests reject the hypothesis of a unit root for all series with the exception of the Euro area nominal interest rate i. However, we interpret these results as only providing a hint that the nominal interest exhibit a strong autocorrelation due to the known low power of the unit root tests.

Table 9.2 US and Euro area dataset: descriptive statistics

	u	e	$d\,ln(w)$	$d\,ln(p)$	v	i	nxr
Euro area							
Mean	0.893	0.977	0.049	0.040	0.599	0.077	
Median	0.891	0.975	0.045	0.034	0.599	0.079	
Max.	0.929	0.997	0.140	0.112	0.617	0.157	
Min.	0.864	0.958	−0.020	0.005	0.578	0.020	
Std. dev.	0.017	0.012	0.034	0.026	0.009	0.037	
J.B. prob.	0.058	0.013	0.085	0.000	0.453	0.060	
Sum	89.32	97.71	4.995	4.049	59.98	7.714	
Sum sq. dev.	0.029	0.014	0.117	0.068	0.009	0.135	
Obs.	100	100	100	100	100	100	
USA							
Mean	0.987	0.948	0.046	0.026	0.604	0.066	0.899
Median	0.988	0.947	0.042	0.019	0.604	0.058	0.860
Max.	1.027	0.964	0.135	0.104	0.629	0.178	1.370
Min.	0.920	0.911	−0.015	−0.003	0.581	0.010	0.620
Std. dev.	0.022	0.012	0.027	0.021	0.012	0.037	0.157
J.B. prob.	0.000	0.000	0.003	0.000	0.487	0.000	0.004
Sum	98.78	94.84	4.605	2.639	60.37	6.615	89.92
Sum sq. dev.	0.047	0.014	0.073	0.044	0.013	0.139	2.424
Obs.	100	100	100	100	100	100	100

Table 9.3 Phillips–Perron unit root test results: sample 1980:1 to 2004:4

Country	*Variable*	*Lag length*	*Determ.*	*Adj. test stat.*	*Prob.**
USA	$\widehat{w}$	–	const.	−6.7769	0.0000
	$\hat{p}$	–	const.	−2.7647	0.0671
	$\hat{u}$	–	–	−7.0655	0.0000
	$\hat{e}$	–	–	−4.8206	0.0000
	i	–	–	−1.8553	0.0608
Euro area	$\widehat{w}$	–	const.	−3.4982	0.0100
	$\hat{p}$	–	none	−2.3617	0.0183
	$\hat{u}$	–	const.	−8.0891	0.0000
	$\hat{e}$	–	–	−3.1516	0.0019
	i	–	–	−1.4810	0.1290

*One-sided p-values (Davidson and MacKinnon 2004).

Structural estimation results

We discuss now the system estimations of both countries carried out based on the parameter restrictions stemming from the theoretical model discussed in Section 9.2.

As discussed in the previous section, the law of motion for the real wage rate, given by equation (9.7), represents a reduced-form expression of the two structural equations for $\widehat{w}_t$ and $\hat{p}_t$. Noting again that the inflation climate variable is defined in the estimated model as a linearly declining function of the past 12 price inflation rates, the dynamics of the system (9.13)–(9.16) can be reformulated as

$$\begin{aligned}
\widehat{w}_t^j &= \beta_{we}(e_{t-1}^j - e_0^j) - \beta_{wv}\ln(v_{t-1}^j/v_0^j) + \kappa_{wp}\hat{p}_t^j + \kappa_{w\pi}{}_{12}\pi_t^{12,j} \\
&\quad + \kappa_{wz}\hat{z}_t^j + \epsilon_{wt}, \\
\hat{p}_t^j &= \beta_{pu}(u_{t-1}^j - u_0^j) + \beta_{pv}\ln(v_{t-1}^j/v_0^j) + \kappa_{pw}(\widehat{w}_t^j - \hat{z}_t^j) \\
&\quad + \kappa_{p\pi}{}_{12}\pi_t^{12,j} + \epsilon_{pt}, \\
\ln u_t^j &= \ln u_{t-1}^j - \gamma_{uu}(u_{t-1}^j - u_0^j) - \alpha_{ur}(i_{t-1}^j - \hat{p}_t^j) \\
&\quad \pm \alpha_{uv}(v_t^j - v_0^j)\alpha_{u\eta}\eta_{t-4} + \epsilon_{ut}, \\
\hat{e}_t^j &= \alpha_{eu-1}\hat{u}_{t-1}^j + \alpha_{eu-2}\hat{u}_{t-2}^j + \alpha_{eu-3}\hat{u}_{t-3}^j + \epsilon_{et}, \\
i_t^j &= \phi_i i_{t-1}^j + (1-\phi_i)\phi_\pi \hat{p}_t^j + (1-\phi_i)\phi_y u_{t-1}^j + \epsilon_{it}, \quad \text{with } j = us, ez, \\
s_t &= i_{t-1}^{us} - i_{t-1}^{ez} + \alpha_{ss}s_{t-1} - \lambda\beta_s^f\eta_t + (1-\lambda)\beta_s^c\hat{s}_{t-1},
\end{aligned}$$

with $\gamma_{uu} = 1 - \alpha_{uu}$ and sample means denoted by a subscript o.

In order to investigate the differences between a single-country system estimation and a two-country system estimation for the values of the parameters of the model for the USA and Euro area, we estimated the structural equations of both countries separately and jointly by means of three-stage least-squares (3SLS), in order to account for a possible regressor endogeneity and heteroskedasticity. As can be observed in Table 9.4, we find wide support for the theoretical formulation discussed in the previous section. In the first place we find similar and statistically significant coefficients for $\ln(v/v_0)$, the Blanchard–Katz error correction terms, in both the wage and price adjustment equations of both the USA and the Euro area.

In the second place, our crossover formulation of the inflationary expectations cannot be rejected statistically in the wage and price inflation equations of both economies. As Table 9.4 shows, the inclusion of the market specific demand-pressure terms (the capacity utilization in the price and the employment rate in the wage Phillips curve equations) is also corroborated by our estimations, as well as the fact that wage flexibility is higher than price flexibility (concerning their respective demand-pressure measures) in both the USA and the Euro area, a result in line with the findings of Chen and Flaschel (2006), Proaño *et al.* (2007) and Flaschel *et al.* (2008b).

Concerning the estimated open-economy IS equation, the 3SLS estimations summarized in Table 9.4 show, as expected, the negative influence of the expected real interest rate on the dynamics of capacity utilization in both economies. The same holds true for the effect of $v - v_0$ in both the USA and Euro area, the deviation of the labor share from its steady-state level, showing that a relatively high labor share (or real average unit labor costs) has a negative impact on the domestic rate

Table 9.4 3SLS parameter estimates: one-country specification

Estimation sample: 1980:1 to 2004:4							
$\widehat{w}_t$	β_{we}	β_{wv}	κ_{wp}	$\kappa_{w\pi}12$	κ_{wz}	$\bar{R}^2$	*DW*
Euro area	0.481	−0.424	0.878	0.254	0.238	0.705	1.608
	[2.669]	[−3.643]	[3.584]	[1.091]	[2.843]		
USA	0.684	−0.352	0.685	0.634	0.376	0.317	1.828
	[3.425]	[−2.744]	[2.618]	[2.462]	[5.239]		
$\hat{p}_t$	β_{pu}	β_{pv}	κ_{pw}	$\kappa_{p\pi}12$		$\bar{R}^2$	*DW*
Euro area	0.274	0.136	0.083	0.864		0.898	1.518
	[4.644]	[2.471]	[2.081]	[23.240]			
USA	0.250	0.097	0.085	0.833		0.774	1.354
	[4.604]	[1.769]	[2.311]	[18.084]			
$\ln u_t$	γ_{uu}	α_{ur}	α_{uv}	$\alpha_{u\eta}$	α_{uuf}	$\bar{R}^2$	*DW*
Euro area	−0.136	−0.059	−0.203	0.012	0.070	0.927	1.839
	[−3.896]	[−2.905]	[−3.292]	[2.183]	[0.988]		
USA	−0.069	−0.044	−0.048	−0.001	0.185	0.904	1.495
	[−2.454]	[−1.804]	[−1.557]	[−1.458]	[1.845]		
$\hat{e}$	α_{eu1}	α_{eu2}	α_{eu3}			$\bar{R}^2$	*DW*
Euro area	0.139	0.129	0.071			0.616	1.121
	[7.284]	[6.791]	[3.881]				
USA	0.138	0.092	0.045			0.357	1.377
	[4.763]	[3.097]	[1.541]				
i	ϕ_i	ϕ_{ip}	ϕ_{iu}			$\bar{R}^2$	*DW*
Euro area	0.926	1.519	1.468			0.981	1.364
	[43.669]	[10.705]	[2.524]				
USA	0.820	2.217	0.611			0.927	1.887
	[29.764]	[15.661]	[2.578]				
s	α_{ss}	β_s	$\beta_{s\eta}$			$\bar{R}^2$	*DW*
Euro area	0.903	0.340	0.145			0.917	1.409
	[17.192]	[1.737]	[0.578]				
USA	0.908	0.309	0.048			0.917	1.413
	[17.322]	[1.578]	[0.678]				

of capacity utilization, something that holds for a profit-led economy. The coefficient α_{uuf}, which represents the effect of foreign goods demand on the dynamics of the domestic capacity utilization rate, are both positive and significant (with the US coefficient of an unexpectedly high value) for both economies.

The parameter estimates in the dynamic Okun's law and Taylor rule equations of both economies are positive, statistically significant and of reasonable dimension, with nevertheless a much higher reaction coefficient to inflation than output in the USA than in the Euro area for the analyzed sample period. Concerning the law of motion of the log nominal exchange rate, both the log real exchange rate as well as the interest rate differential influence the level of the log nominal exchange rate, the former in a negative and the latter in a positive manner.

Besides the one-country 3SLS estimations just discussed, we estimated both countries as a single system by means of 3SLS.[13] Compared with the single-country 3SLS estimations just described, Table 9.5 delivers quite similar values concerning all estimated parameters, corroborating the robustness of our results. There are nevertheless two remarkable differences. While in the 3SLS estimations we obtained a quite high coefficient for α_{uu^f} in the US equation (representing the role of the growth rate of capacity utilization in the Euro area for the dynamics of the same variable in the USA), in Table 9.5 we obtained a parameter estimate of more reasonable dimension (though still too high if compared with the coefficient in the Euro area $\ln u$ equation, if one takes into account that the USA is probably more important for the Euro area than otherwise).[14] The second remarkable difference between the one-country and the two-country 3SLS estimations concerns the influence of the log real exchange rate on the log nominal exchange rate. While in the estimations summarized in Table 9.4 its coefficient was highly significant and in line with our theoretical formulation, in the second estimation described in Table 9.5 that coefficient seems to be statistically insignificant.

Dynamic adjustments

In order to evaluate the empirical plausibility of our theoretical framework, we simulate an approximate discrete-time version of the semistructural model discussed in Section 9.2 based on the estimated 3SLS structural model parameters discussed in the last section.[15] Additionally, we calibrate the parameters concerning the theoretical CPI inflationary climate for both countries with the following values

$$\beta_{\pi_c} = 0.25, \quad \kappa_{\pi_c} = 0.5, \quad \gamma = 0.85.$$

Both countries have thus the same degree of inflation climate inertia (represented by β_{π_c}, the adjustment coefficient of the CPI inflationary climate), whereafter each new (quarterly) CPI inflation rate observation updates with only a 0.25 weight the inflationary climate. Both countries have also the same degree of credibility in the monetary policy target (κ_{π_c}) as well as the same composition of domestic and foreign goods in the CPI index.[16]

A US monetary policy shock

In Figure 9.4 we show the dynamic adjustments to a 1% (100 basis points) monetary policy shock in the US economy of the two countries using the structural parameters estimates of both the USA and the Euro area depicted in Table 9.5. As

Table 9.5 3SLS parameter estimates: two-country specification

Estimation sample: 1980:1 to 2004:4							
$\widehat{w}_t$	β_{we}	β_{wv}	κ_{wp}	$\kappa_{w\pi 12}$	κ_{wz}	$\bar{R}^2$	*DW*
Euro area	0.462	−0.412	0.888	0.244	0.234	0.705	1.615
	[2.594]	[−3.589]	[3.672]	[1.059]	[2.836]		
USA	0.661	−0.386	0.484	0.582	0.352	0.341	1.830
	[4.158]	[−2.933]	[1.797]	[3.107]	[5.112]		
$\hat{p}_t$	β_{pu}	β_{pv}	κ_{pw}	$\kappa_{p\pi 12}$		$\bar{R}^2$	*DW*
Euro area	0.252	0.115	0.076	0.870		0.898	1.522
	[4.334]	[2.135]	[1.965]	[23.907]			
USA	0.130	0.138	0.107	0.579		0.789	1.391
	[2.757]	[2.450]	[3.168]	[19.324]			
$\ln u_t$	γ_{uu}	α_{ur}	α_{uv}	$\alpha_{u\eta}$	α_{uu^f}	$\bar{R}^2$	*DW*
Euro area	−0.109	−0.064	−0.161	0.012	0.101	0.927	1.746
	[−3.412]	[−3.264]	[−2.693]	[2.408]	[1.540]		
USA	−0.094	−0.040	−0.118	−0.008	0.161	0.906	1.529
	[−3.485]	[−1.937]	[−2.193]	[−1.330]	[1.634]		
$\hat{e}$	α_{eu1}	α_{eu2}	α_{eu3}			$\bar{R}^2$	*DW*
Euro area	0.137	0.129	0.076			0.616	1.132
	[7.237]	[6.886]	[4.199]				
USA	0.153	0.101	0.045			0.371	1.444
	[5.334]	[3.418]	[1.559]				
i	ϕ_i	ϕ_{ip}	ϕ_{iu}			$\bar{R}^2$	*DW*
Euro area	0.925	1.534	1.769			0.981	1.358
	[48.649]	[11.237]	[3.048]				
USA	0.823	2.157	0.375			0.928	1.890
	[31.627]	[15.271]	[1.756]				
s	α_{ss}	β_s	$\beta_{s\eta}$			$\bar{R}^2$	*DW*
	0.909	0.383	0.111			0.917	1.412
	[17.628]	[1.995]	[0.534]				

Figure 9.4 shows, the numerical simulations of the calibrated theoretical discrete-time model resemble to a large extent the stylized facts of monetary policy briefly discussed in the previous section.

As expected, a positive monetary policy shock in the USA leads to a depreciation of the EUR/USD nominal exchange rate primarily via the uncovered interest rate parity (UIP) condition in the law of motion of the log nominal exchange rate. This nominal appreciation of the US dollar, together with the effect of the interest

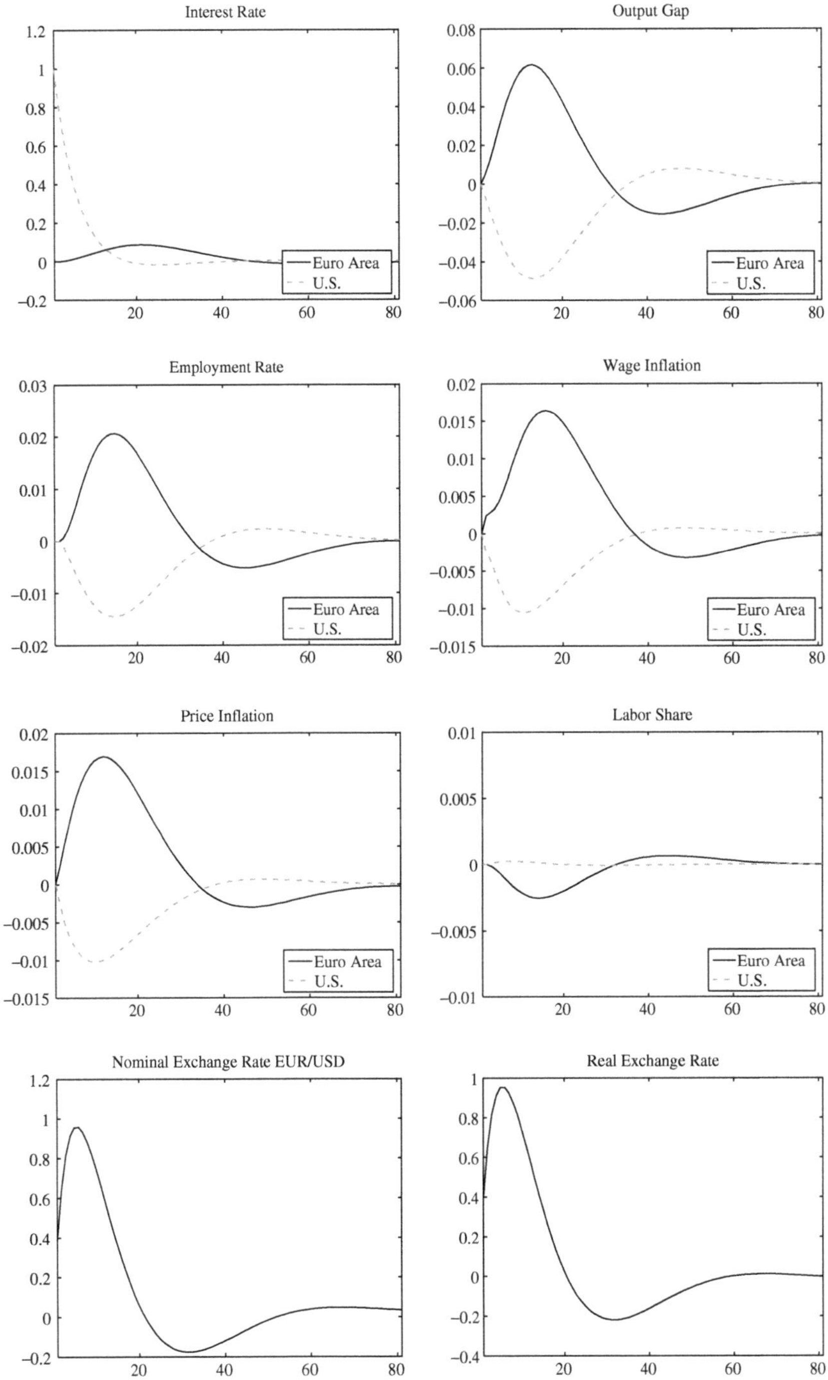

Figure 9.4 Simulated responses to a 1% US monetary policy shock.

rate increase, leads to a slowdown of the US economy, observable in the decrease in capacity utilization. Following the downturn of this variable, employment also falls, as well as wage and price inflation start falling after some quarters below baseline. The Euro area is affected from the contractionary US monetary policy shock through three macroeconomic channels, the nominal depreciation of the euro, the drop in foreign aggregate demand and the gain of relative competitiveness resulting from an increase in η. As Figure 9.4 shows, the activation of these three channels leads to an increase in economic activity in the Euro area.

A Euro area monetary policy shock

As a second simulation experiment, we compute the dynamic adjustments of both the USA and the Euro area after a monetary policy shock by the European Central Bank (ECB) with our calibrated model.

The dynamics depicted in Figure 9.5 resemble to a large extent the dynamic adjustments to a US monetary shock previously discussed. However, we can identify one main important difference. Indeed, while the Euro area was largely affected by the contractionary monetary policy shock in the USA, the opposite does not hold by far for the US economy, due to the relatively lower foreign goods demand coefficient $\alpha_{u u f}$ coefficient as well as due to the absence of a significant influence of the real exchange rate and the relative competitiveness channel.[17]

It should be stressed that the overshooting nominal (and real) exchange rate dynamics observable in Figures 9.4 and 9.5 arise due to its specific formulation in our model. However, even though this overshooting behavior is concordant with the findings by Eichenbaum and Evans (1995), this result should not be over-interpreted given the contrary empirical evidence by the alternative studies previously discussed.

9.4 Eigenvalue-based stability analysis

As previously mentioned, if the stability of a macrodynamic system is not simply imposed through the rational expectations assumption, the relative strength of the different macroeconomic channels interacting in an economy become central for the local and global stability properties of the system analyzed.

The main purpose of this section is to highlight this issue within the semistructural two-country macro-framework discussed and estimated in the previous sections. For this an eigenvalue stability analysis is used taking as the benchmark parameters the estimated values presented in the previous section. After calibrating the 11D continuous-time system, the eigenvalues of the system are calculated *ceteris paribus* for different parameters of the models (mostly in the 0–1 interval) using the SND software.[18]

In Figures 9.6–9.9 the maximal eigenvalues of the system for varying parameter values in the closed-economy (the one-country submodule under $\alpha_{u u f}, \alpha_\eta = 0$ and $\xi = 1$, calculated with the US parameter estimates of Proaño *et al.* (2007), shown in Table 9.6) and in the open-economy cases are sketched.

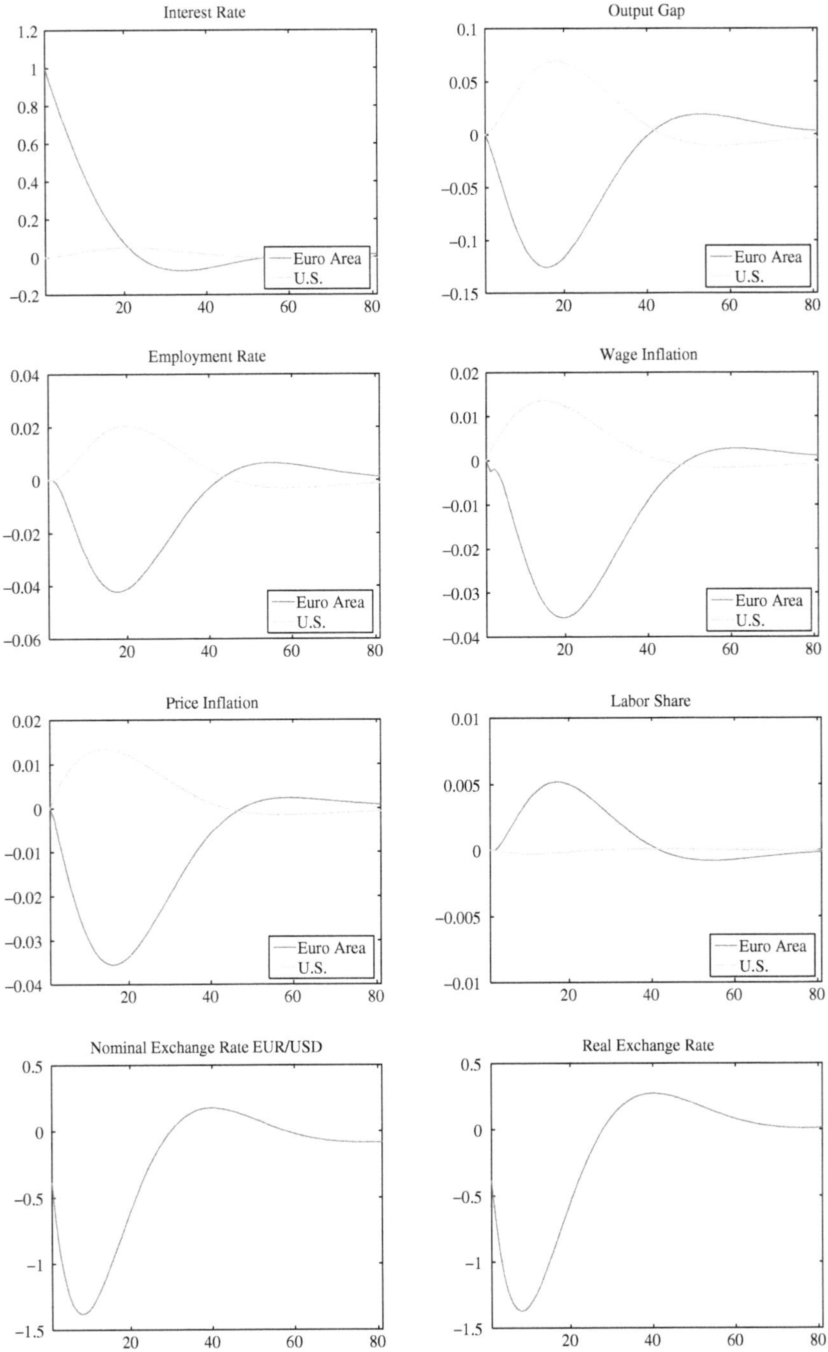

Figure 9.5 Simulated impulse responses to a one-standard-deviation Euro area monetary policy shock.

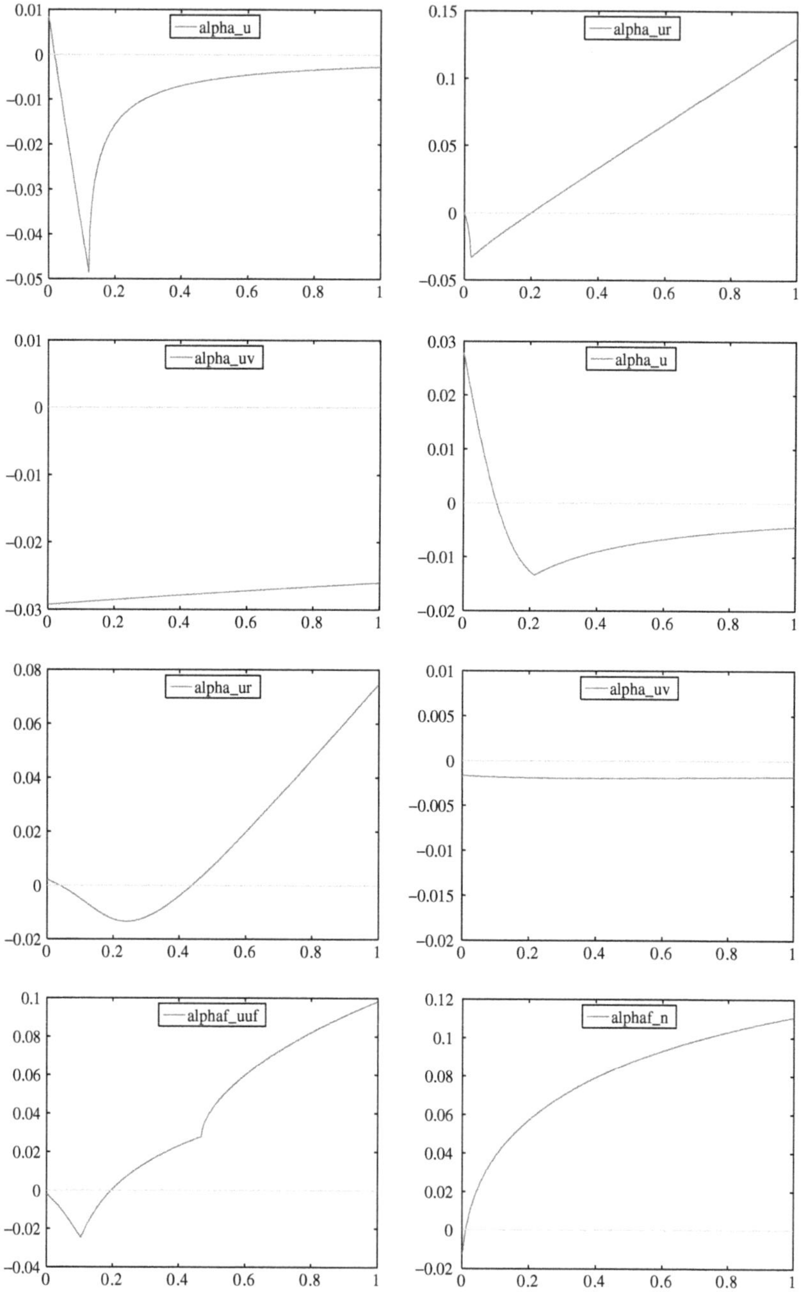

Figure 9.6 Eigenvalue-based stability analysis: the real economy.

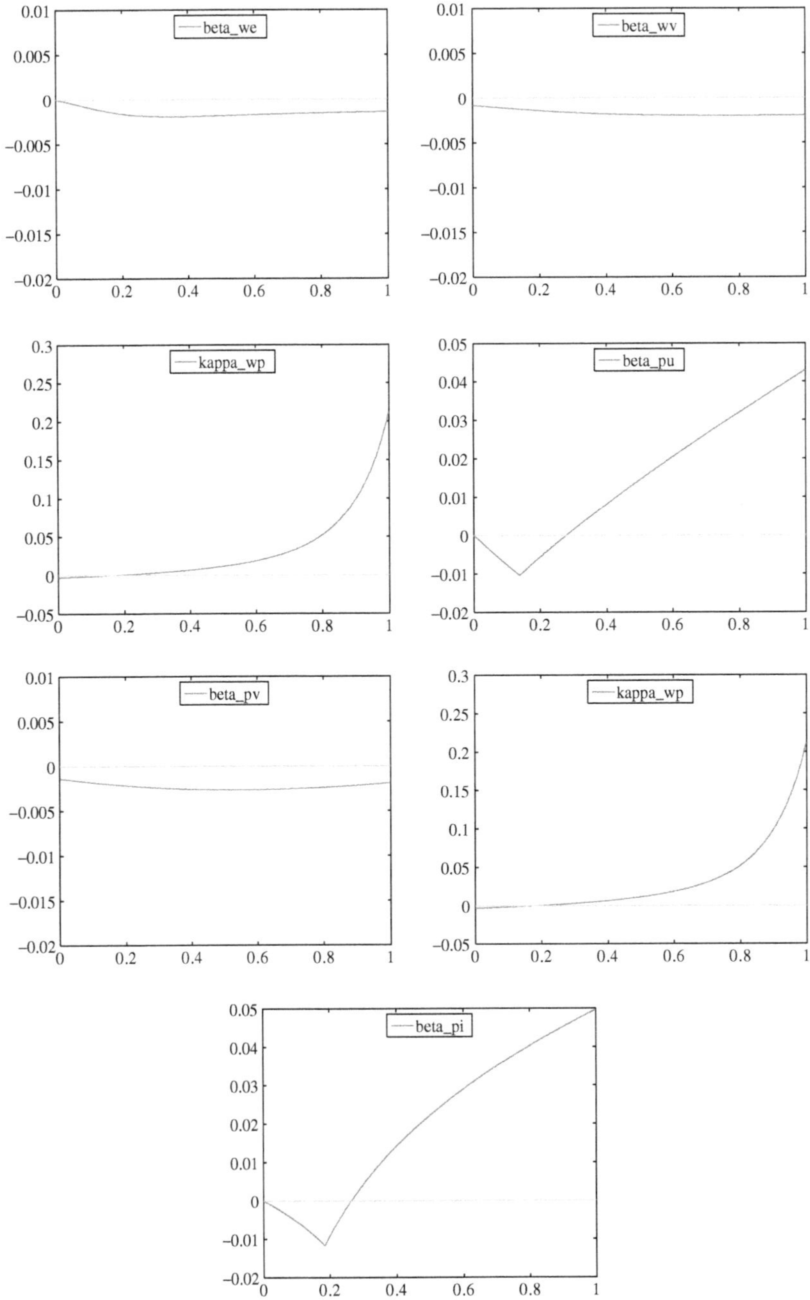

Figure 9.7 Eigenvalue-based stability analysis Ib: wage–price dynamics (the open-economy case).

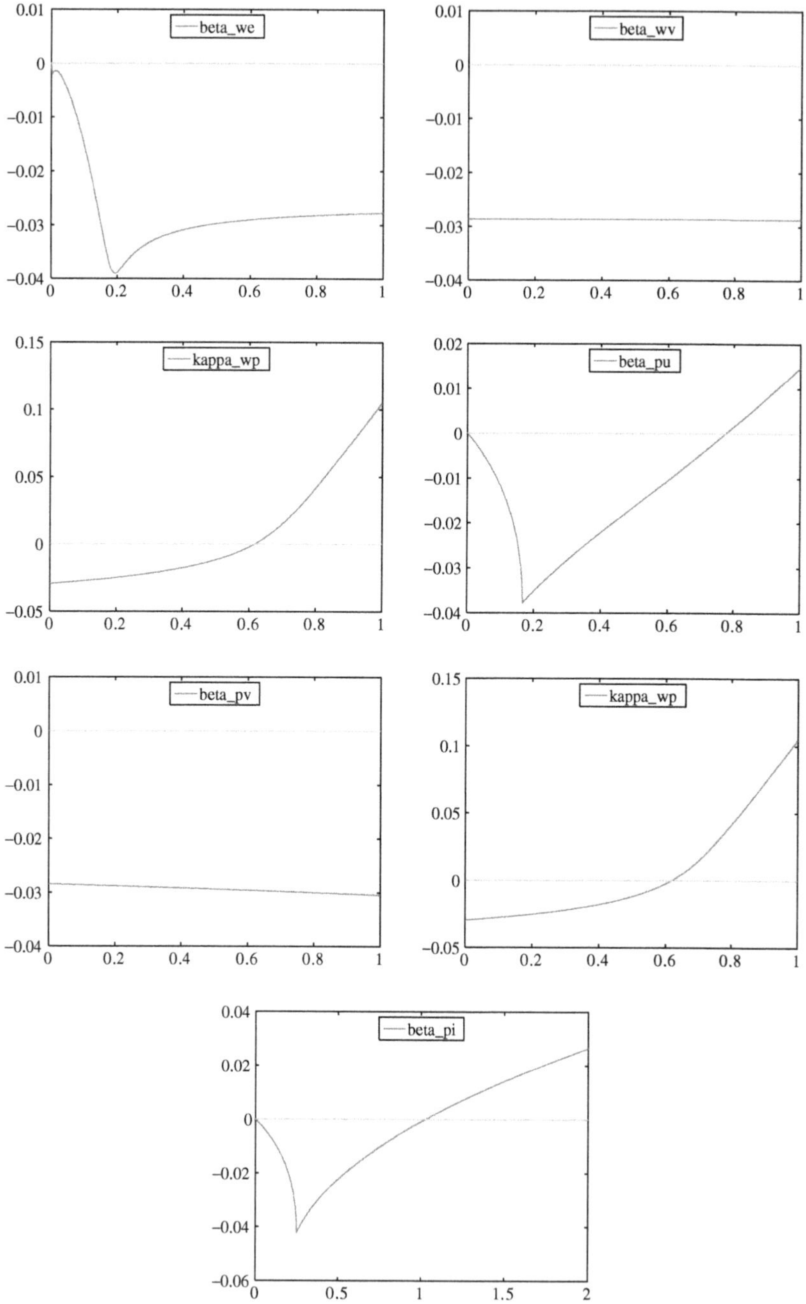

Figure 9.8 Eigenvalue-based stability analysis: wage–price dynamics (the closed-economy case, using the parameter values estimated in Proaño *et al.* (2011)).

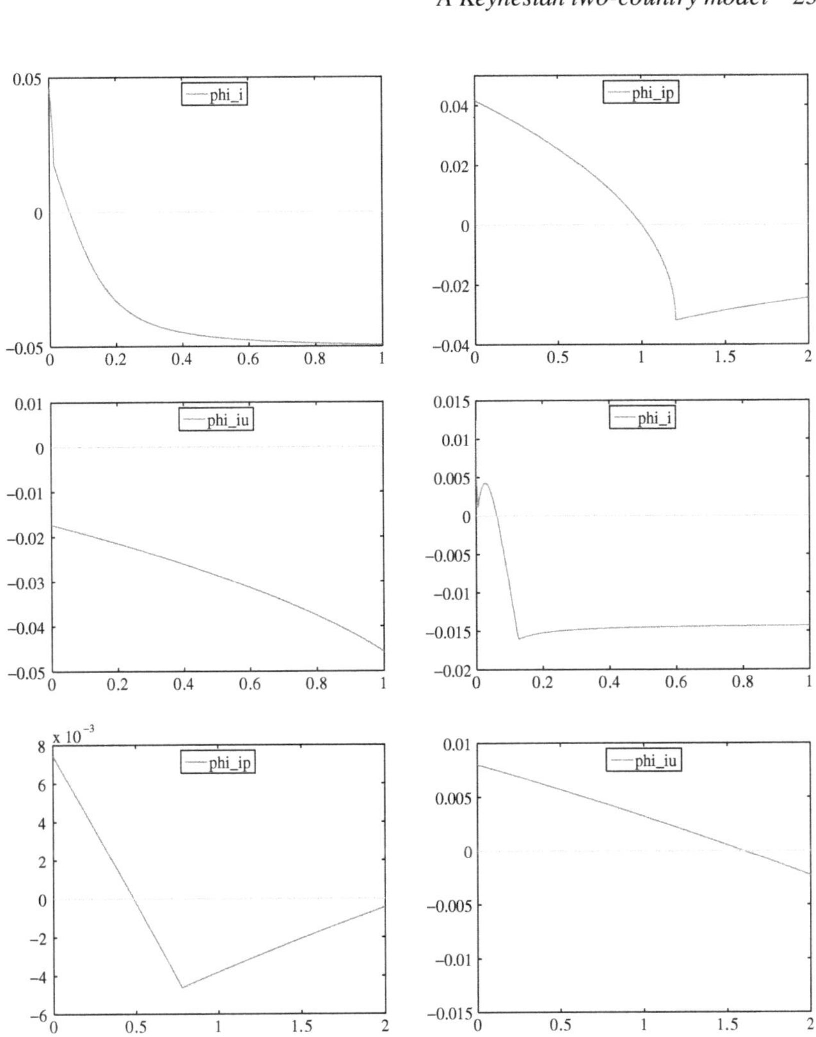

Figure 9.9 Eigenvalue-based stability analysis: monetary policy.

The comparison between the eigenvalue diagrams of the closed-economy and open-economy cases depicted in Figures 9.6–9.8 reveals by and large the same qualitative implications of a variation of the analyzed coefficients for the stability of the system (and the two- and one-country case). So, while the stability properties of the respective systems seem to be invariant for different parameters of α_{uv} (the reaction strength of capacity utilization to an increase in the wage share), β_{we} (the wage inflation reactiveness parameter with respect to labor marker disequilibrium situations), as well as β_{wv} and β_{pv} (the Blanchard–Katz error correction terms in both the wage and price inflation adjustment equations), the same does not hold for the remaining real economy parameters. Indeed, high coefficients

Table 9.6 Closed-economy model – calibration parameters (Proaño *et al.* 2007)

Goods markets	γ_{uu} 0.077	α_{ur} 0.042	α_{yv} −0.173	
Labor markets	α_{eu1} 0.201	α_{eu2} 0.113	α_{eu3} 0.039	α_{ev} 0.100
Wage Phillips curve	β_{we} 0.679	β_{we} 0.208	κ_{wp} 0.420	$1-\kappa_{wp}$ 0.580
Price Phillips curve	β_{we} 0.294	β_{we} 0.113	κ_{wp} 0.044	$1-\kappa_{wp}$ 0.956
Monetary policy rule	α_{ii} 0.830	ϕ_{ip} 2.17	ϕ_{iu} 0.423	

of α_{ur}, the real interest rate reactiveness of the capacity utilization, both κ_{wp} and κ_{pw}, the crossover inflation terms in the wage and price Phillips curve equations, a high price flexibility with respect to goods market disequilibrium situations (represented by the parameter β_{pu}) as well as a high adjustment of the inflationary climate π_c, determined by β_{π_c}, seem to induce instability in the system.

Concerning the open-economy dimension of the model, Figure 9.6 shows that both a high reactiveness of capacity utilization toward the real exchange rate *and* the dynamics of the foreign economy (determined by α_η and α_{uu^f}, respectively), are likely to induce instability of the system due to an eventual oversynchronization of both economies which might feature reinforcing properties.

Figure 9.9 shows the eigenvalue diagrams resulting from variations in the monetary policy parameters. As expected, while an increase in α_{ii} (that is, a lower degree of interest rate smoothing in the nominal interest rate law of motion, or, in other words, the faster adjustment speed of the actual nominal interest rate with respect to i_T) induces stability in both the closed- and the open-economy systems, the steady-state stability properties seem to be invariant to changes in ϕ_{iu} (the reaction coefficient of the monetary policy instrument with respect to the output gap).

This, however, does not hold for ϕ_{ip}, the reaction coefficient with respect to the inflation gap. Indeed, consistently with the academic literature on monetary policy, we find for the closed-economy case that the steady state of the economic system is stable only if $\phi_{ip} > 1$, that is, only if monetary policy reacts in a sufficiently active manner with respect to inflationary developments, as discussed for example in Walsh (2003) and Woodford (2003). In the open-economy case, however, the eigenvalue diagram of ϕ_{ip} shows that the threshold value for stability lies much lower than in the closed-economy case, relativizing up to a certain extent the validity of the prominent Taylor principle, at least for large economies such as the USA and the Euro area. This result, though somewhat surprising at first sight, is actually quite reasonable. In contrast to the closed-economy case, in an open economy the monetary policy transmission mechanism is, additionally to traditional transmission channels such as the credit and the balance sheet channels, enriched by other transmission channels such as the nominal exchange rate and the competitiveness channels. So, for example, an interest rate increase leads not only to higher borrowing costs and therefore to a lower consumption and investment demand, but also, in an open economy, to a nominal (and real) appreciation of the domestic currency, which in turn leads to a decrease in the net exports. In an open economy, thus, monetary policy can rely on the activation of more transmission channels and therefore does not need to be as aggressive as in the closed-economy case.

9.5 Conclusions

In this chapter we studied a basic theoretical two-country framework based on the disequilibrium approach by Chiarella and Flaschel (2000a) and Chiarella *et al.* (2005), where two large open economies interacted with each other and indeed influenced each other through trade, price and financial channels.

Despite the straightforwardness of the theoretical formulation of this semistructural two-country model, we were able to perform an insightful analysis of the macroeconomic interaction of two large economies at both the theoretical and empirical levels. At the theoretical level, we were able to identify the stability conditions of the continuous-time dynamical system, highlighting primarily the role of wage flexibility for macroeconomic stability. At the empirical level, the econometric estimations of the Euro area and the US economy (two large open economies which are in fact highly interrelated through a variety of macroeconomic channels) showed, on the one hand, the empirical plausibility of our theoretical framework, corroborating the results of the closed-economy model discussed in Part I of this book. On the other hand, they showed the remarkable similarities between the Euro area and the US economy not only in the wage and price inflation equations, but also in the dynamics of the goods and labor markets. Furthermore, using the parameter estimates of the Euro area and the US economy, we were able to generate dynamic impulse–response functions quite concordant with the VAR evidence discussed in the academic literature.

An important issue worth highlighting is the eigenvalue analysis performed in the previous section. Given the actual predominance of rational expectations models where the model stability is given by assumption and by the associated model solution method, the present analysis shows an alternative – and also valid – perspective on the analysis of model stability. This alternative approach allowed us to identify and to highlight, among other things, the role of wage and price stability, as well as the importance of an active monetary policy, for the stability of the system. Additionally, we could investigate, in a graphical and insightful manner, the differences in the stability conditions between closed and open economies. Concerning this last point, a remarkable result of the eigenvalue analysis was the different threshold values of ϕ_{ip}, the inflation gap coefficient in the Taylor rule, in the closed- and open-economy cases. As previously discussed, our analysis showed that the coefficient value dividing a "passive" from an "active" monetary policy is, in our theoretical formulation and given our parameterization, lower in the open-than in the closed-economy case. Though still preliminary, this result stresses the necessity to incorporate open-economy factors in macroeconomic models when studying the effectiveness and adequacy of different monetary policy rules.

Part IV

The structural Keynes–Metzler–Goodwin model

10 Integrating macromodels of employment, price and inventory dynamics

10.1 Introduction

In this chapter[1] we continue in a self-contained way the analysis of the dynamic properties of a general model of Keynesian monetary growth begun in Chiarella and Flaschel (1995a). This model exhibits a conventional IS–LM block based on goods market disequilibrium in place of the conventional multiplier equilibrium. Quantities in the goods market adjust through a Metzlerian inventory mechanism that refers to sales expectations and planned vs. actual inventory changes. Corresponding to this sluggish adjustment of quantities there are also sluggish price and wage adjustments, the former in the light of expected sales of firms and their thereby implied level of capacity utilization, and the latter in the basically conventional way of an expectations augmented wage Phillips curve, here with demand-pull and cost-push components. These real and nominal adjustment processes are supplemented by a money market equilibrium equation as theory of the nominal rate of interest.

Aggregate demand is based on differential saving habits of households, an investment function which depends on profit rate differentials and the degree of capacity utilization of firms, and on government's demand for goods. Labor force growth is driven exogenously, capital stock growth is determined by planned investment and the money growth rate is set exogenously by the monetary authority. Inflation is determined in a demand-pull and cost-push fashion and it operates in a climate of expected inflation – both backward- and forward-looking – that adds to its momentum.

These are the essential building blocks of the model, which is made a complete model by specifying the budget equations of households, firms and the government and some further details. The structural equations of the model differ in some details from those used in Chiarella and Flaschel (1995a), making the model from a mathematical point of view less intertwined by simplifying its Metzlerian inventory process to some extent. Modified in this way the model provides an intermediate step between the Kaldorian and the Metzlerian model introduced in Chiarella and Flaschel (1995b).

By introducing appropriate state variables in intensive form the model can be reduced to a nonlinear differential equation system of dimension six with however only five state variables that are really interdependent. We here stress that the functional forms of the various equations of the model have been chosen – as in Chiarella and Flaschel (1995a) – as linear as it is possible. The nonlinearities that characterize this dynamical system are thus of a minimal nature or "intrinsic" to it as they are due to the facts that

- certain laws of motions must be formulated in terms of rates of growth and not just time derivatives, and
- certain state variables must be multiplied with each other in particular in expressions deriving from the rate of employment and the rate of profit.

There are thus only some nonavoidable nonlinearities involved in the formulation of this model of monetary growth which nevertheless allow for the existence of limit cycles and more complex attractors and which to some extent render this model a viable one even in the presence of locally explosive dynamics around the steady state. In our view it is very important to start from such intrinsic nonlinearities to demonstrate thereby not only that complex macrodynamic behavior is due to strong nonlinearities in the employed behavioral equations, but also that it can arise in a much more fundamental way simply through the type of interaction of the state variables of complete macroeconomic models.

Our model of monetary growth integrates three important partial (2D) views on the working of the macroeconomy: a Rose (1967) type of real growth dynamics, a Tobin (1975) type of inflation dynamics and a Metzler (1941) type of inventory dynamics, the latter, as stated, in a less complete way than in Chiarella and Flaschel (1995a). In view of this we start our investigation of the general 6D dynamics by considering first these component 2D dynamics in isolation. One may hope that the results obtained for these prototypic subdynamics will to some extent also be characteristic for the integrated system, as there is otherwise not much sense in the prevailing consideration of such partial macrodynamic views.

A study of the integrated dynamics from an analytical and a numerical point of view, however, then reveals that the qualitative features of the subdynamics are not preserved through their integration. Instability in the 2D cases is turned into stability in 6D. Flexibilities that are bad for economic stability on the 2D level are good for it on the 6D level and vice versa. Finally, complex behavior can occur in the 6D case that is not possible on the 2D level. We conclude that the use of partial models that separate growth from inflation and from inventory adjustments may be very misleading with respect to the implications they have for stability, types of fluctuations and economic policy when compared with the results that their interaction generates.

Assuming in the considered model type high speeds of adjustment for prices or quantities will however generally destroy the viability of this only intrinsically nonlinear model. It then becomes obvious that important nonlinearities – which are due to changing economic behavior far off the steady state of the model – are still lacking. After providing a list of the most basic quantity or value constraints that may come into being in larger business fluctuations we choose one (and only one) particular type of behavioral nonlinearity in order to attempt to restrict the explosive nature of the dynamics for higher adjustment speeds. This nonlinearity concerns a basic fact of the postwar period, namely that there has been no deflation in the general level of wages even in periods of large unemployment. The wage inflation Phillips curve of the model – which generally operates in an inflationary environment – is thus modified such that no *decrease* in the wage level is allowed for. This simple change in the model's dynamics – the exclusion of nominal wage deflation – has dramatic consequences for its viability as well as its complexity, as will be shown by means of phase plots and bifurcation diagrams.

Integrated Keynesian models of monetary growth have been rarely studied in the literature, partly due to the involved mathematical complexities. Some of these complexities are investigated in the present chapter, showing that this model type exhibits very interesting dynamics even on its most fundamental level of formulation. However, there remains much to be done in order to really understand the cyclical growth patterns to which these models give rise.

10.2 A complete Keynesian model of monetary growth

In this section we briefly introduce the building blocks of our Keynesian model of monetary growth. This model integrates certain aspects of Rose's (1967) employment cycle and its wage–price dynamics, an inflationary dynamics akin to the Tobin (1975) inflationary process and its extensions, and a sales expectations and inventory dynamics of the Metzler (1941) type. The model therefore combines in the context of monetary growth prominent examples of the purely real, the purely monetary and the inventory dynamics. One topic of the chapter is that views on the working of the economy that can be drawn from the isolated perspectives of each of these three model types are not at all supported by the dynamical results that come about when these separate dynamic mechanisms become interdependent. Another topic will be the intrinsic nonlinearities that this model type exhibits – and their consequences – and how they can be enhanced to allow for economic viability when economically meaningless trajectories occur.

The following model structure represents a somewhat simplified version of the model type considered in Chiarella and Flaschel (1995a). Here, more stress is laid on mathematical simplification in place of full economic interaction. In contrast to the six interdependent state variables of the Chiarella and Flaschel (1995a) model the sixth state variable of the present model will not feed back here into the first five laws of motion of the model. Nevertheless, with respect to economic content the model is very close to that of Chiarella and Flaschel (1995a) and will therefore be introduced here only briefly (leaving out all equations that are necessary for economic completeness but that do not contribute to the final dynamic form of the model). The reader is referred to Chiarella and Flaschel (1995a) for such and other details.

The equations of this model of IS–LM growth with a wage–price sector and an inventory adjustment mechanism are as follows:

1. *Definitions:*

$$\omega = w/p, \quad \rho^e = (Y^e - \delta K - \omega L^d)/K. \tag{10.1}$$

This set of equations introduces variables that are of use in the following structural equations of the model, namely the definition of real wages ω and of the expected rate of profit ρ^e on capital K.

Household behavior is described next by the following set of equations:

2. *Households (workers and asset-holders):*

$$M^d = h_1 pY^e + h_2 pK(r_0 - r), \tag{10.2}$$

$$C = \omega L^d + (1 - s_c)[\rho^e K + rB/p - T], \tag{10.3}$$

$$\widehat{L} = n = \text{const.} \tag{10.4}$$

Money demand M^d is specified as a simple linear function of the nominal value of expected sales (as a proxy for expected transactions) pY^e and the rate of interest r (r_0 the steady-state rate) in the usual way. The form of this function has been chosen in this way to allow for a simple linear formula for the rate of interest in terms of the state variables of the model, i.e. it is determined to some extent by the mathematical reason that the model's structural form should be as linear as it is possible. Nonlinear money demand functions with real wealth in place of the capital stock are in fact more appropriate and thus should replace this simple function later on.

Consumption C is based on classical saving habits with savings out of wages set equal to zero for simplicity. For the time being we assume that real taxes T are paid out of (expected) profit and interest income solely and in a lump sum fashion. Workers supply labor L inelastically at each moment in time with a rate of growth $\widehat{L}$ given by n, the so-called natural rate of growth.

3. *Firms (production units and investors):*

$$Y^p = y^p K, \quad y^p = \text{const.}, \quad U = Y^e/Y^p = y^e/y^p \quad (y^e = Y^e/K), \tag{10.5}$$

$$L^d = Y^e/x, \quad x = \text{const.}, \quad V = L^d/L = Y^e/(xL), \tag{10.6}$$

$$I = i_1(\rho^e - (r - \pi))K + i_2(U - 1)K + nK, \tag{10.7}$$

$$\widehat{K} = I/K. \tag{10.8}$$

Firms expect to sell commodities in amount Y^e and produce them in the technologically simplest way possible, by way of a fixed proportions technology characterized by the normal output capital ratio $y^p = Y^p/K$ and a fixed ratio x between expected sales Y^e and labor L^d needed to produce this output. This simple concept of technology allows for a straightforward definition of the rate of utilization U, V of capital as well as labor.

Note here that firms may produce more or less than expected sales, depending on their inventory policy. In order to suppress some economic feedback effects for reasons of mathematical simplicity we have assumed that the economic actions of firms are based on a measure of capacity utilization U as defined above and that they pay their workforce on the basis of the employment generated by expected sales, while planned changes in inventories are accompanied by over- or under-time work of the employed (that does not show up in the wage bill). This is one important difference to the model considered in Chiarella and Flaschel (1995a). Investment per unit of capital I/K is driven by two forces: the rate of return differential between the expected rate of profit ρ^e and the real rate of interest $r-\pi$, and the deviation of actual capacity utilization U from the normal or nonaccelerating inflation rate of capacity utilization, 1. There is also an unexplained trend term in the investment equation which is set equal to the natural rate of growth for reasons of simplicity. The last equation, finally, states that (fixed business) investment plans of firms are always realized in this Keynesian (demand-oriented) context – by way of corresponding inventory changes.

We now turn to a brief description of the government sector:

4. *Government (fiscal and monetary authority):*

$$T = t^n K + rB/p \quad (t^n = (T - rB/p)/K = \text{const.}), \tag{10.9}$$

$$G = gK, \quad g = \text{const.}, \tag{10.10}$$

$$\hat{M} = \mu = \text{const.} \tag{10.11}$$

The government sector is here described in as simple a way as is possible. (Lump sum) real taxes net of interest are assumed to be collected in a way such that their ratio t^n to the capital stock remains constant. Similarly, government expenditures per unit of capital g are assumed as constant – in order to ease the calculation of intensive forms and steady states of the model. Money supply growth μ is also assumed as constant.

We have equilibrium in the asset markets of the economy, described by:

5. *Equilibrium condition (money market):*

$$M = M^d = h_1 pY^e + h_2 pK(r_0 - r). \tag{10.12}$$

Goods market adjustment is however less than perfect and represented by the following set of equations:

6. *Disequilibrium situation (goods market adjustments):*

$$Y^d = C + I + \delta K + G, \tag{10.13}$$

$$N^d = \beta_{nd} Y^e, \quad \mathcal{I} = nN^d + \beta_n (N^d - N), \tag{10.14}$$

$$Y = Y^e + \mathcal{I}, \tag{10.15}$$

$$\dot{Y}^e = nY^e + \beta_{y^e}(Y^d - Y^e), \tag{10.16}$$

$$\dot{N} = Y - Y^d. \tag{10.17}$$

The first equation defines aggregate demand Y^d which is never constrained in the present model. Desired inventories N^d are assumed to be a constant proportion of expected sales Y^e and intended inventory investment $\mathcal{I}$ is determined on this basis via the adjustment speed β_n multiplied by the current gap in inventories $N^d - N$, augmented by a growth term that integrates in the simplest way the fact that this inventory adjustment rule is operating in a growing economy. Output of firms Y is the sum of expected sales and planned inventory adjustments and sales expectations Y^e are here formed in a purely adaptive way, again augmented by a growth term. Finally, actual inventory changes $\dot{N}$ are given by the discrepancy between output Y and actual sales Y^d.

We now turn to the last module of our model which is the wage–price sector:

7. *Wage–price sector (adjustment equations):*

$$\widehat{w} = \beta_w(V-1) + \kappa_w \hat{p} + (1-\kappa_w)\pi, \tag{10.18}$$

$$\hat{p} = \beta_p(U-1) + \kappa_p \widehat{w} + (1-\kappa_p)\pi, \tag{10.19}$$

$$\dot{\pi} = \beta_{\pi_1}(\hat{p}-\pi) + \beta_{\pi_2}(\mu - n - \pi). \tag{10.20}$$

This "supply-side" description is based on fairly symmetric treatment on the causes of wage and price inflation. Wage inflation $\widehat{w}$ is driven, on the one hand, by a demand-pull component, given by the deviation of the actual rate of employment V from the NAIRU-based one, 1, and, on the other, by a cost-push term measured by a weighted average of the actual rate of price inflation $\hat{p}$ and a medium-run expected rate of inflation π. Similarly, price inflation $\hat{p}$ is driven by the demand-pull term $U-1$ and the weighted average of the actual rate of wage inflation $\widehat{w}$ and the medium-run expected rate of inflation π. This latter expected rate of inflation is in turn determined by a composition of backward-looking (adaptive) and forward-looking (regressive) expectations.

This model integrates the interaction between real wages and capital accumulation, between inflation and the expected rate of inflation, and between expected sales and actual inventory levels, the latter in a less complete way than in Chiarella and Flaschel (1995a). An integrated model of this type exhibits six (here only five) interacting state variables and is thus of a dynamic dimension that is rarely considered in the economic literature. Nevertheless, assuming finite adjustment speeds in the labor and the goods markets – in the latter for prices and quantities – makes this number of state variables unavoidable.

10.3 The implied 6D dynamics

The above general model of Keynesian monetary growth can be reduced to the following six-dimensional (6D) dynamical system in the variables $\omega = w/p, l = L/K, m = M/(pK), \pi, y^e = Y^e/K$ and $\nu = N/K$:

$$\widehat{\omega} = \kappa[(1-\kappa_p)\beta_w(V-1) + (\kappa_w - 1)\beta_p(U-1)], \tag{10.21}$$

$$\hat{l} = -i_1(\rho^e - r + \pi) - i_2(U-1), \tag{10.22}$$

$$\widehat{m} = \mu - \pi - n - \kappa[\beta_p(U-1) + \kappa_p\beta_w(V-1)] + \hat{l}, \tag{10.23}$$

$$\dot{\pi} = \beta_{\pi_1}\kappa[\beta_p(U-1) + \kappa_p\beta_w(V-1)] + \beta_{\pi_2}(\mu - n - \pi), \tag{10.24}$$

$$\dot{y}^e = \beta_{y^e}(y^d - y^e) + \hat{l}y^e, \tag{10.25}$$

$$\dot{\nu} = y - y^d + (\hat{l} - n)\nu. \tag{10.26}$$

For output per capital $y = Y/K$ and aggregate demand per capital $y^d = Y^d/K$ we have the following expressions:

$$y = (1 + n\beta_{n^d})y^e + \beta_n(\beta_{n^d}y^e - \nu), \tag{10.27}$$

$$\begin{aligned} y^d &= \omega y^e/x + (1 - s_c)(\rho^e - t^n) + i_1(\rho^e - r + \pi) + i_2(U-1) + n + \delta + g \\ &= y^e + (i_1 - s_c)\rho^e - i_1(r - \pi) + i_2(U-1) + \text{const.} \end{aligned} \tag{10.28}$$

Furthermore, we have made use of the abbreviations

$$V = l^d/l = y^e/(lx), \quad U = y^e/y^p, \quad \rho^e = y^e(1 - \omega/x) - \delta,$$
$$r = r_0 + (h_1y^e - m)/h_2.$$

This presentation of the model shows that the variable ν does not appear on the right-hand side of the first five laws of motion. It is thus of secondary importance in the following.

There is a *unique steady-state solution* or point of rest of the dynamics (10.21)–(10.26) fulfilling $\omega_0, l_0, m_0 \neq 0$ which is given by

$$y_0^e = y_0^d = y^p, \quad l_0 = y_0^e/x, \quad y_0 = (1 + n\beta_{n^d})y_0^e,$$
$$m_0 = h_1y_0^e, \quad \pi_0 = \mu - n, \quad \rho_0^e = t^n + (g - t^n + n)/s_c,$$
$$r_0 = \rho_0^e + \mu - n, \quad \omega_0 = (y_0^e - \delta - \rho_0^e)/l_0, \quad \nu_0 = \beta_{n^d}y_0^e.$$

We assume that the parameters of the model are chosen such that the steady-state values for ω, l, m, ρ^e, r are all positive. Before we start to investigate the dynamic properties of this 6D dynamical system, let us consider in the next section first what we can learn about its dynamical behavior from its three 2D prototype constituents, the Rose-type employment cycle model, the Tobin-type interaction between inflation and inflationary expectations, and the Metzlerian adjustment mechanism of sales expectations and inventories, by considering these 2D dynamics in isolation from each other.

10.4 Three prototype "subdynamics"

The real wage dynamics

Prototype models of Keynesian real growth dynamics generally assume goods market equilibrium at each point in time coupled with no inventory holdings of firms $y = y^e = y^d$, $\nu = \nu^d = 0$. They furthermore neglect interest rate phenomena and inflationary expectations. The rate of price and wage inflation, and thus the real wage dynamics, are driven by disequilibrium in the rate of utilization of the capital stock[2] and the labor force as they both result from the state of effective demand on the goods market.

The above assumptions can be described with respect to our general 6D model of monetary growth as follows: $\beta_{y^e} = \beta_n = \infty, \beta_{n^d} = 0, y = y^e = y^d, \nu = \nu^d = 0$ (goods market equilibrium with no inventories); $h_2 = \beta_{\pi_2} = \infty, r = r_0, \pi = \pi_0 = \mu - n$ (liquidity trap at the steady state and long-run steady-state inflationary expectations). This indicates that the isolated real dynamics is not obtained from the general case in a mathematically simple fashion. Under these assumptions the real part of the 6D model can be reduced to the interaction of the two state variables ω and l which then form an autonomous system of differential equations of dimension two:

$$\widehat{\omega} = \kappa[(1-\kappa_p)\beta_w(V-1) + (\kappa_w - 1)\beta_p(U-1)], \tag{10.29}$$

$$\hat{l} = -i_1(\rho - r_0 + \pi_0) - i_2(U-1) = n + g - t^n - s_c(\rho - t^n), \tag{10.30}$$

with

$$U = y/y^p, \quad V = (y/x)/l, \quad \rho = y(1-\omega/x) - \delta.$$

The value of $y = Y/K$ has now to be calculated from the goods market equilibrium condition

$$\begin{aligned} y = {} & \omega y/x + (1-s_c)(y(1-\omega/x) - \delta - t^n) \\ & + i_1(y(1-\omega/x) - \delta - r_0 + \pi_0) + i_2(y/y^p - 1) + n + \delta + g. \end{aligned}$$

In the *steady state* of the above dynamics, we have

$$\rho_0 = t^n + (n + g - t^n)/s_c$$

(via $\hat{l} = 0$) and $i_1(\cdot) = 0$ via $r_0 = \rho_0 + \pi_0$. Employing again $\hat{l} = 0$ then gives $y_0 = y^p$ and thus $l_0 = y_0/x$ due to $\widehat{\omega} = 0$. The steady-state value of ω finally is given by definition of ρ as $\omega_0 = (y_0 - \delta - \rho_0)/l_0$. These steady-state values coincide with the steady-state values of ω, l of the 6D dynamics.

The above goods market equilibrium condition gives for the equilibrium output per capital

$$y(\omega) = \frac{(i_1 - s_c)(1-\omega_0/x)y^p + i_2}{(i_1 - s_c)(1-\omega/x)y^p + i_2}\, y^p. \tag{10.31}$$

This nonlinear function represents a condensed form of the following feedback chain of the general model

$$\omega \rightarrow y^d \rightarrow y^e \rightarrow y,$$

since the last three magnitudes are identified in the present subdynamics. The function $y(\omega)$ is discussed with respect to its range of definition and its properties in Chiarella and Flaschel (1995b, ch. 4), giving rise there to three different situations. One of these cases is excluded here from consideration by way of the assumption $Z = (i_1 - s_c)(1 - \omega_0/x)y^p + i_2 > 0$. This restricts the set of admissible parameters i_1, i_2, s_c such that $\rho'(\omega) < 0$ holds true, whenever the profit rate function

$$\rho(\omega) = \frac{Zy^p}{(i_1 - s_c)y^p + i_2/(1 - \omega/x)} - \delta$$

is well defined. The dependence of the rate of profit ρ on the real wage rate ω is therefore the conventional one in our remaining cases. Nevertheless, the sign of $y'(\omega)$ will be ambiguous at and around the steady state, since it then follows that

$$\operatorname{sign} y'(\omega) = \operatorname{sign}(i_1 - s_c).$$

The real dynamics (10.29) and (10.30) therefore allows – even under the assumption $Z > 0$ just made – for two very different situations of the dependence of output y, capacity utilization U and rate of employment V on the real wage ω.

PROPOSITION 10.1 *The Hopf bifurcation locus of the dynamics (10.29) and (10.30) in the* (β_p, β_w) *parameter space is given by the straight line*

$$\beta_w^H = \frac{1 - \kappa_w}{1 - \kappa_p}\beta_p.$$

The steady state of this real 2D dynamics is locally asymptotically stable above this line (for $\beta_w > \beta_w^H$*) and unstable below it if* $i_1 < s_c$ *holds. The opposite is true in the alternative situation* $i_1 > s_c$.

Proof: The proof is similar to that in Chiarella and Flaschel (1995a). □

In sum, we can state that we learn from this 2D model type that increased wage flexibility ($\beta_w \uparrow$) is destabilizing in the case where goods market equilibrium y responds positively (based on $i_1 > s_c$) to changes in income distribution (changes in the real wage), since real wage increases then increase employment and thus the upward pressure on nominal and on real wages. By contrast, increased price flexibility ($\beta_p \uparrow$) will be stabilizing in this case. The opposite is true in the "orthodox" case where equilibrium output responds negatively to an increase in the real wage.

The nominal dynamics

Prototype models of monetary dynamics generally also assume goods market equilibrium at each point in time coupled with no inventory holdings of firms $y = y^e = y^d$, and they neglect real wage phenomena and their interaction with capital accumulation. These latter assumptions can be represented in the 6D dynamics by assuming $\beta_w = 0, \kappa_w = 1$, i.e. $\widehat{w} = \hat{p}(\widehat{\omega} = 0)$ and in addition $\omega(0) = \omega_0, l = l_0$ $(n = 0)$. We thus in particular exclude the Rose real growth cycle of the preceding subsection from consideration here. It is again obvious that this 2D economic prototype model is obtained as a mathematical limit of the general model that is not easy to handle from a mathematical point of view.

The monetary part of the general model can then be reduced to the following two state variables m, π which now form an autonomous system of differential equations of dimension two

$$\widehat{m} = \mu - \pi - \kappa\beta_p(U - 1), \tag{10.32}$$

$$\dot{\pi} = \beta_{\pi_1}\kappa\beta_p(U - 1) + \beta_{\pi_2}(\mu - \pi), \tag{10.33}$$

where $U = y/y^p - 1$ and where the equilibrium output y is now given by

$$y = \omega_0 y/x + (1 - s_c)(\rho - t^n) + i_1(\rho - r + \pi) + i_2(y/y^p - 1) + \delta + g, \tag{10.34}$$

with

$$\rho = y(1 - \omega_0/x) - \delta, \quad r = r_0 + (h_1 y - m)/h_2.$$

Solving $\widehat{m} = 0, \dot{\pi} = 0$ for the unknown steady-state values $\mu - \pi_0$, $U_0 - 1$ gives $\pi_0 = \mu$, $U_0 = 1$, i.e. $y_0 = y^p$. Owing to the choice of the stationary level of real wages ω_0, equation (10.34) then implies $r_0 = \rho_0 + \pi_0 = y^p(1 - \omega_0/x) - \delta + \pi_0$ and thus $m_0 = h_1 y^p$ for our second dynamic variable. The *steady-state* values of this dynamics are therefore once again identical to the corresponding ones of the 6D dynamics (but $n = 0$ now).

Making use of these steady-state values of m, π, equation (10.34) can be transformed to the form

$$y(m, \pi) = y^p\left(1 + \frac{(i_1/h_2)(m - m_0) + i_1(\pi - \pi_0)}{h_1 i_1 y^p/h_2 - Z}\right), \tag{10.35}$$

where Z is given as in the preceding subsection. Viewed from the perspective of the preceding subsection (where $h_2 = \infty$ was assumed), the related case $h_2 < \infty$ (but large) gives a negative denominator in (10.35) and therefore gives rise to a function $y(m, \pi)$ with $y_m < 0$, $y_\pi < 0$. With respect to conventional macrostatics these two partial derivatives represent an abnormal Keynes and a negative Mundell effect (of m and π) on effective demand, since an increase in real balances (via a decrease in the price level p) is then contractionary and an increase in π does not stimulate investment *and* effective demand, but will reduce the latter. We thus can expect that this case will give rise to unconventional results with respect to the joint working on the Keynes and the Mundell effect. Both effects will be positive ($y_m, y_\pi > 0$) or normal if and only if h_2 is decreased sufficiently, such that

$$h_2 < h_2^0 = h_1 i_1 y^p / Z, \quad Z = (i_1 - s_c)(1 - \omega_0/x)y^p + i_2 > 0$$

holds true.

PROPOSITION 10.2

1 *The dynamics (10.32) and (10.33) give rise to saddle-path behavior around its steady state* (det < 0) *if* $h_2 > h_2^0$ *holds and it exhibits a positive determinant of its Jacobian in the opposite case.*
2 *The Hopf locus in* (β_p, β_{π_1}) *space of the latter case is given by*

$$\beta_{\pi_1}^H = \frac{\beta_{\pi_2} Q}{\beta_p \kappa i_1} + \frac{h_1 y^p}{h_2}, \quad Q = \frac{h_1 i_1 y^p}{h_2} - Z > 0.$$

This locus is therefore a simple decreasing function of the parameter β_p.
3 *The dynamics (10.32) and (10.33) are (for* $Q > 0$*) locally asymptotically stable below this locus and unstable above it.*

Proof: The proof is similar to that in Chiarella and Flaschel (1995a). □

In sum, we can state that we learn from this prototype subdynamics that local instability prevails throughout in the case of an abnormal Keynes and Mundell effect (of p and π on equilibrium output y). In the opposite case, a simultaneous increase in price flexibility ($\beta_p \uparrow$) as well as in the speed of adjustment of inflationary expectations ($\beta_\pi \uparrow$) – if sufficiently pronounced – is bad for economic stability.

The quantity dynamics

As in the preceding subsection this prototype dynamics ignores accumulation and real wage dynamics and it – in line with the real dynamics – abstracts furthermore from interest rate and inflationary phenomena. We therefore assume stationarity in ω, l, π and r at their steady-state values (and also $n = 0$). Instead, we now allow for goods market disequilibrium, changing sales expectations and the Metzlerian output and inventory adjustment process based on such sales expectations. This shows again that the here considered 2D prototype dynamics is also not a simple special case from the mathematical point of view of the general 6D model, though the variable y^e is independent of the variable ν in both cases.

The above assumptions give rise to the following 2D dynamics in sales expectations and inventories per unit of the capital stock:

$$\dot{y}^e = \beta_{y^e}(y^d - y^e), \tag{10.36}$$

$$\dot{\nu} = y - y^d, \tag{10.37}$$

with $y - y^e = \beta_n(\beta_{n^d} y^e - \nu)$, $\rho^e = y^e - \delta - \omega_0 y^e/x$ and

$$\begin{aligned} y^d - y^e &= (i_1 - s_c)\rho^e + i_2(y^e/y^p - 1) - t^n(1 - s_c) - i_1(r_0 - \pi_0) + g \\ &= [(i_1 - s_c)(1 - \omega_0/x) + i_2/y^p]y^e + \text{ const.} = (Z/y^p)y^e + \text{ const.} \end{aligned}$$

At the *steady state* of this dynamics we have $y_0^d = y_0^e$ and $y_0 = y_0^d$. Therefore $\nu_0 = \beta_{n^d} y_0^e$. Moreover, $\omega = \omega_0, r = r_0, \pi = \pi_0$ imply via goods market equilibrium $y_0 = y^p$, i.e. the steady-state values of (10.36) and (10.37) are again the ones obtained from the steady-state solution for the 6D dynamics (but $n = 0$ now).

Proposition 10.3

1 *The dynamics (10.36) is autonomous and purely explosive for all adjustment speeds of sales expectations* $\beta_{y^e} > 0$.
2 *The dynamics (10.37) is in itself stable but must follow a saddle-path dynamics due to its dependence on the unstable sales expectations dynamics*

Proof: This is obvious. □

Owing to our assumption $Z > 0$ we thus get an explosive goods market dynamics whenever sales expectations depart from the level of aggregate demand y^d. The Metzlerian approach thus gives rise to a somewhat unusual result in the present setup. This problematic dynamics in the inventory component of the general model is here simply due the fact that the multiplier is unstable under the assumed side condition $Z > 0$. From a Kaldorian trade cycle perspective this seems to demand the introduction of, for example, a nonlinear investment function in order to tame this instability of the above linear inventory mechanism. We shall see in the following that nothing of this sort may be necessary. Local asymptotic stability can be retained simply by integrating the three 2D prototype dynamics into a consistent whole. Depending on parameter choices there will however exist local or global instabilities in the general 6D dynamics. At this stage then, the introduction of outward stabilizers may become necessary and should be considered. Yet, at the present stage, we have still to investigate how much can be gained for the analysis of viable models of cycles and growth simply by proceeding to an integrated analysis of the views of this section on the working of the real, the monetary and the inventory dynamics.

10.5 Dynamic properties of the integrated Rose–Tobin–Metzler dynamics

Let us now return to the investigation of the general 6D system and a comparison of its results with the three 2D subsystems considered in the preceding section.

PROPOSITION 10.4 *Consider the Jacobian (the linear part) of the dynamics (10.21)–(10.26) at the steady state. The determinant of this 6×6 matrix, $\det J$, is always positive. It follows that the system can only lose or gain asymptotic stability by way of a so-called Hopf bifurcation (if its eigenvalues cross the imaginary axis with positive speed).*

Proof: For the proof, see Chiarella and Flaschel (1995b). □

PROPOSITION 10.5 *For the entries in the trace of J the following hold.*

1 $J_{11} = 0$, *i.e. the Rose effect no longer shows up in the trace of J.*
2 $J_{22} = 0$ *as in the corresponding 2D case of real growth.*
3 $J_{33} < 0$, *due to the Keynes effect $r(p), r'(p) > 0$ in the $\hat{l}$ term of the third dynamic law. Note here that the state variable y^e prevents an immediate impact of the Keynes effect (and its consequences on aggregate demand) on factor utilization rates U, V and thus on the rate inflation and the corresponding state variable m.*
4 $J_{44} < 0$, *due to the forward-looking component in the fourth dynamic law. The above remark on the Keynes effect here applies to the Mundell effect $Y^d_\pi > 0$, i.e. there is no longer a destabilizing influence of the parameter β_{π_1} present in the trace of the Jacobian (as there was in the 2D case).*
5 $J_{55} = \beta_{y^e}(-Q/y^p) + y^e_0(Q/y^p - s_c(1 - \omega_0/x))$, *where Q has been defined in Proposition 10.2. It follows that the system must be locally unstable for values of β_{y^e} sufficiently large if $Q < 0$, since this adjustment parameter is – besides the always stabilizing parameter β_{π_2} – the only one among the adjustment speed parameters that shows up in the trace of J.*
6 $J_{66} = y_\nu < 0$ *and $J_{i6} = 0$ for $i = 1, \ldots, 5$. It follows from Proposition 10.4 that the determinant of the Jacobian of the (independent) 5D subdynamics (10.21)–(10.25) is negative at the steady state.*

Proof: It is straightforward to prove these. □

We thus have that the destabilizing (or stabilizing) role of the parameters $\beta_w, \beta_p, \beta_{\pi_1}$ can no longer be obtained by just considering the trace of the matrix J. The determinant being positive and the trace of J being basically negative (if β_{y^e} is chosen appropriately), it therefore depends on the other principal minors (of dimension two to four) whether the steady state of the considered dynamics is locally asymptotically stable or not.

There are, for example, 15 principal minors of J of dimension two, three of which are given by the three determinants considered in the preceding section. The calculation of the corresponding (and even more of the other) Routh–Hurwitz conditions for local asymptotic stability is thus a formidable task. It is nevertheless tempting to conjecture that these Routh–Hurwitz stability conditions might be fulfilled for either generally sluggish or generally fast adjustment speeds. The following numerical investigations of the model however show that nothing of this sort will hold true in general.

In the presentation of the general Keynesian monetary growth model in Section 10.2 we have made use of linear relationships as much as this was possible. Technology, behavioral relationships and adjustment equations were all chosen in a linear fashion. Though nonlinear in extensive form, money demand was chosen such that it gave rise to a linear equation for the rate of interest when transformed to intensive form. Yet, certain relationships such as the wage dynamics must refer to rates of growth in order to make sense economically. Furthermore and quite naturally there are certain products of variables involved such as total wages ωL^d or the rate of employment L^d/L. Such occurrences make the model a nonlinear one in a natural or intrinsic way. It is one of our aims in the present chapter to investigate the model's dynamic properties in this naturally nonlinear form in order to see to what extent the generated dynamics represents an (economically or at least mathematically) viable one despite the negative findings obtained in the preceding section for its three prototype subsystems. Of course, it is not to be expected that the dynamics is viable for all of its meaningful parameter constellations. Further nonlinearities – in particular from the supply side – will become operative in a variety of situations. Nevertheless it is often not necessary to use nonlinearities in wage adjustment, in technology, in investment, and so on, in a first step in order to get a bounded behavior. Where the 2D cases suggest the use of such additional nonlinearities, the corresponding 6D situation may nevertheless be asymptotically stable or – if not – give rise to limit cycle behavior over certain ranges of the parameters due to the natural nonlinearities that are present.

In the intensive form and with respect to the state variables used in equations (10.21)–(10.26) there are three types of nonlinearities induced by the structural form of the model.

- Three of the state variables give rise to a growth rate law of motion (ω, l, m).
- Owing to their formulation in per-capital terms, two of the state variables (y^e, ν) give rise to products of the form $\hat{l}y^e, \hat{l}\nu$.
- There are natural products or quotients of some of the state variables in the form $V = y^e/l$ for the rate of employment V and $\rho^e = y^e - \delta - \omega y^e/x$ for the rate of profit ρ^e.

Note here that the replacement of the state variable l by the state variable $k = 1/l$ transforms all nonlinearities into product form. Note furthermore that the terms $\hat{l}z = -\hat{k}z$ with $z = m, y^e, \nu$ lead to trilinear expressions in their respective laws of motion.

In this representation of the dynamics we have – besides growth rates and the products just mentioned – nonlinearities present only in the $\beta_w(\cdot)$ term, in ρ^e and due to that term also in the aggregate demand term y^d. Up to growth rate

Table 10.1 Parameter model for simulation of 6D dynamics

$\beta_p = 1$	$\beta_w = 0.16$	$\beta_{\pi_1} = 0.1$	$\beta_{\pi_2} = 1$	$\beta_n = 0.75$	$\beta_{y^e} = 1$	$\beta_{n^d} = 0.2$
$\kappa_w = \kappa_p = 0.5$	$n = \mu = 0.05$	$i_1 = 0.5$	$i_2 = 0.5$	$s_c = 0.8$		
$h_1 = 0.1$	$h_2 = 0.2$					
$t^n = 0.3$	$g = 0.32$	$\delta = 0.1$				
$y^p = 1$	$x = 2$	$[r_0 = \rho_0 = 0.3875]$				

formulations we have thus basically only two types of nonlinearities involved in the laws of motion of the system and they both relate to the Rose subdynamics of the model. Though these terms reappear in various places it may therefore be stated that the present dynamics is comparable to the Rössler system (one bilinear term) and the Lorenz system (two bilinear terms).

Let us now turn to a numerical investigation of the 6D dynamics. We shall employ the basic parameter set displayed in Table 10.1 in the numerical illustrations given below (and shall later on only state the changes taking place with respect to it).

Corresponding to the three subdynamics considered in the preceding section we here look at the stabilizing or destabilizing role of the pairs of adjustment speeds β_w, β_p, and β_{π_1}, β_p, and β_{y^e}, β_n (denoted by bp, etc., in the following figures). The shaded areas in Figures 10.1 and 10.2 show the parameter domain where the 6D dynamics is locally asymptotically stable. The boundary of these domains is the Hopf bifurcation locus where the system loses its local asymptotic stability either by way of a so-called supercritical Hopf bifurcation (where a stable limit cycle is born after the boundary has been crossed) or by way of a subcritical Hopf bifurcation (where an unstable limit cycle is shrinking to "zero" when the boundary is approached). Along the bifurcation line there also exist degenerate Hopf bifurcations separating super – from subcritical bifurcations (where there are no limit cycles existing to the left and to the right of this boundary).[3] We have found in many numerical investigations of the model that the bifurcations in the following diagrams are generally of a supercritical nature. The only important exception is the bifurcation line on the right-hand side of the (β_{y^e}, β_n) parameter space where the system again loses stability (at $\beta_{y^e} = 4.82$) for high adjustment speeds of the parameter β_{y^e}.

Proposition 10.6 *The following holds with respect to the above choice of parameter values. The steady state of the dynamics (10.21)–(10.26) is locally asymptotically stable for a high adjustment speed of prices, a low adjustment speed of wages, a low adjustment speed of inflationary expectations and all inventory adjustment speeds. The adjustment speed of sales expectations, by contrast, must be in the interval* $(0.98, 4.82)$*, i.e. it should be neither too high nor too low.*

The corresponding situation of the three 2D subdynamics is shown in the small rectangles in Figure 10.1. We can see that the combination of an explosive real cycle with (unstable) saddle-point situations in the monetary and the inventory

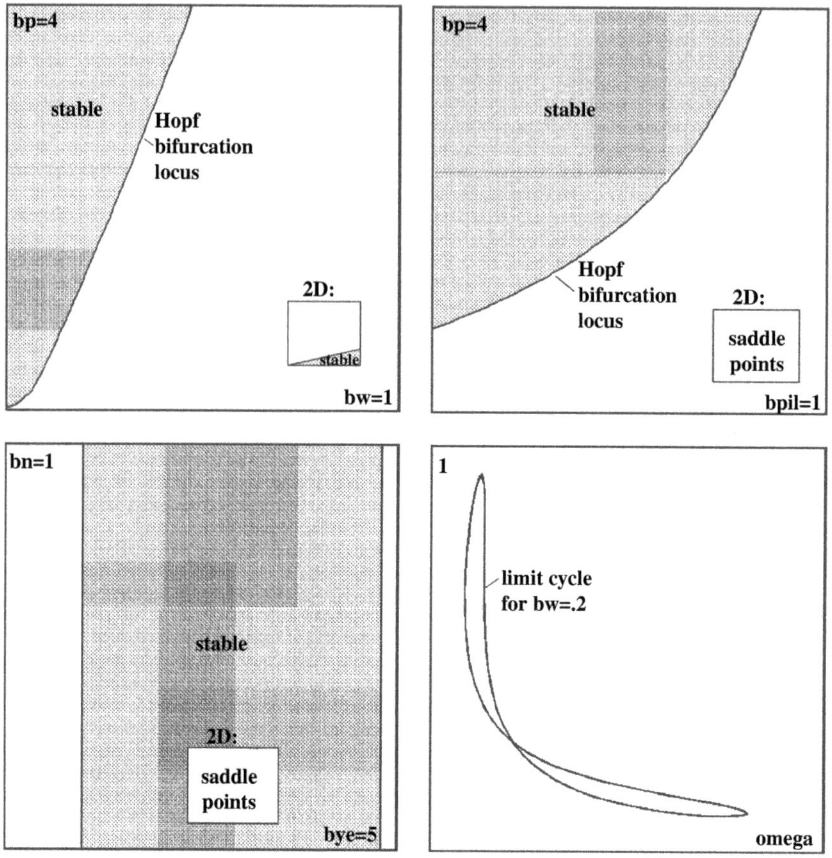

Figure 10.1 6D bifurcation loci and a limit cycle for $h_2 = 0.2$ ($Q < 0$).

subsystem gives rise to asymptotic stability in the integrated 6D system. Note here that there are no perverse Keynes effects $Y_p^d > 0$ or Mundell effects $Y_\pi^d < 0$ with respect to the aggregate demand function of the 6D system – in contrast to the corresponding 2D situation. Furthermore we have the next result.

Proposition 10.7 *The following holds with respect to the above choice of parameter values. The stabilizing properties of price and wage adjustment in the 6D system are just the opposite of those suggested by the disintegrated real cycle model.*

The partial model thus gives the wrong information concerning an important policy issue, the adequate degree of wage flexibility for economic stability. Sluggish wages are now good for economic stability, while flexible wages are not. With respect to the parameter β_w the bifurcation point where local stability gets lost is approximately given by $\beta_w^H = 0.16$. The final picture in Figure 10.1 shows the projection onto the (ω, l) plane of the stable limit cycle that is generated beyond this point at $\beta_w = 0.2$. This limit cycle increases considerably in amplitude when this parameter is increased toward $\beta_w = 0.3$. Thereafter the dynamics becomes purely explosive.

In Figure 10.1 we have considered an example of the situation where the monetary 2D dynamics is of saddle-point type ($Q < 0$). In the opposite case $Q > 0$ the 2D situation also exhibits a Hopf bifurcation line (see Proposition 10.2) which is shown in the small square in the following figure (the situation for the other 2D dynamics has remained unchanged). Ignoring very small adjustment speed in the price level, the 6D dynamics has not changed very much qualitatively by the assumption of a parameter value for h_2 that gives rise to $Q > 0$. Yet, the domain of stability is quantitatively seen to be significantly increased with respect to $\beta_{y^e}, \beta_{\pi_1}$ by the possibility of stability for the monetary subdynamics. Note that price flexibility (starting from an unstable steady state) can bring back stability to the 6D dynamics, but not to the 2D dynamics of the monetary subsystem.

In Figure 10.2 we also show some effects of parameter changes on the position of the Hopf bifurcation line. In the first of its panels we can see that an increase of the parameter β_{π_1} from 0.1 to 0.4 may increase the stable domain for wage flexibility. The same holds true in the second and third panels where a decrease of β_w from 0.16 to 0.1 and a decrease of β_{π_1} from 0.4 to 0.1 is considered, respectively. The main point shown by these panels is however that 2D explosive situations are again combined in the integrated dynamics such that local asymptotic stability can be obtained for its steady state.

We have pointed above to the "naturally" nonlinear structure of our dynamical system. The question arises whether this basically "bilinear" system allows for a period-doubling sequence toward complex dynamics as for example the Rössler system with its single bilinear term – see, for example, Strogatz (1994, p. 377) for a graphical presentation of this system. Figure 10.3 provides such an example for the dynamical system of this chapter and the basic parameter set given above (but $h_2 = 0.08, \beta_{\pi_1} = 0.4$).

Figure 10.4 shows the kind of attractor that may be generated by such a sequence of period-doubling bifurcations of the limit cycle obtained by varying the bifurcation parameter β_w. Note that all these figures represent projections of the dynamics that is taking place in 6D phase space.

These numerical simulations also show that the cycle generated in this way becomes larger and larger and by no means stays in an economically meaningful subset of the phase space. Increasing the parameter further than shown above will also destroy mathematical boundedness. From an economic point of view it is thus clear that additional forces must come into being when certain ceilings or floors are approached with respect to quantity or value magnitudes. This is the topic of the following section.

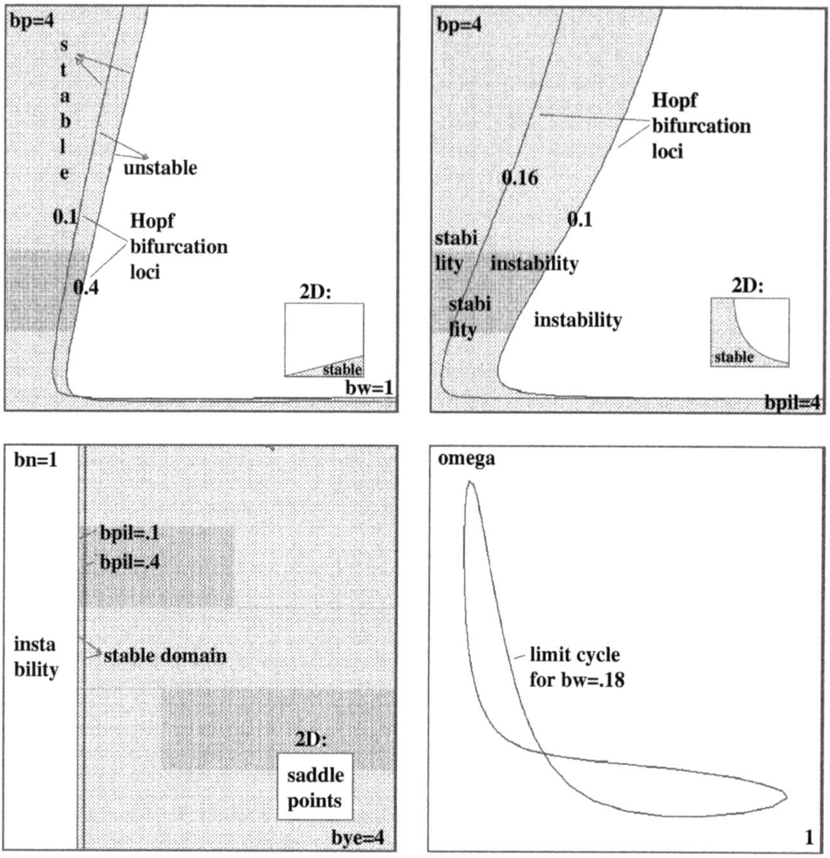

Figure 10.2 6D bifurcation loci and a limit cycle for $h_2 = 0.08$.

10.6 The case of no nominal wage deflation

When the fluctuations generated by the naturally nonlinear model of this chapter become very large – as in the situation shown in Figure 10.4 – or even unbounded, they may or will leave the domain of economically admissible values. Then – or even much before such a point is reached – other economic forces come into being which at least attempt to avoid such occurrences.

A complete list of absolute ceilings and floors for economic fluctuations in our Keynesian monetary growth model could be the following:

- $V \leq V_{\max}$ for the rate of employment,
- $U \leq U_{\max}$ for the rate of capacity utilization,
- $\nu \geq 0$ for inventory holdings,
- $I \geq -\delta K$ for net investment (gross investment $I + \delta K \geq 0$),

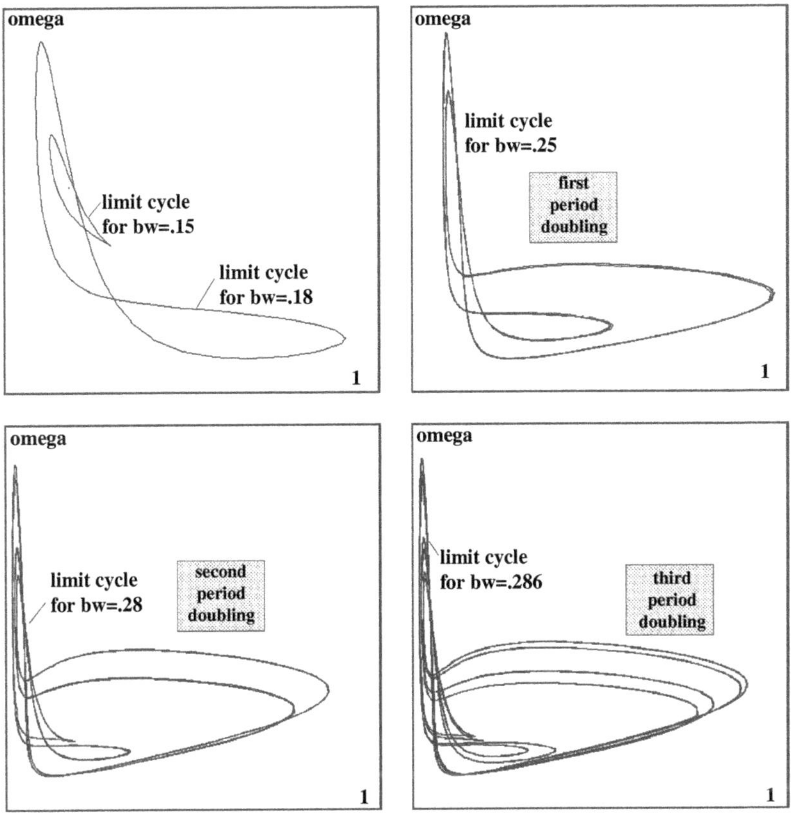

Figure 10.3 Period-doubling route to complex dynamics ($h_2 = 0.08$, $\beta_{\pi_1} = 0.4$).

- $r \geq 0$ for the nominal rate of interest,
- $\omega < x$ for real wages ω and labor productivity x.

The first two items state that there are two constraints for the output of firms at each point in time t, one ($Y^K_{\max} = U_{\max} y^p K$) determined by the size of the capital stock which is in existence in t and which describes the maximum usage to which the physical means of production can be put ($y^p K$ the normal usage), and one ($Y^L_{\max} = V_{\max} x L$) which describes the maximum of labor effort available from a given labor force L (xL the normal usage). The output that is actually produced at each moment of time is thus given by

$$Y = \min\{Y^e + \mathcal{I}, Y^K_{\max}, Y^L_{\max}\}.$$

This equation should be used in place of equation (10.15) when such limits are approached. It can however be expected that the behavior of the economy changes significantly before such limits are reached.

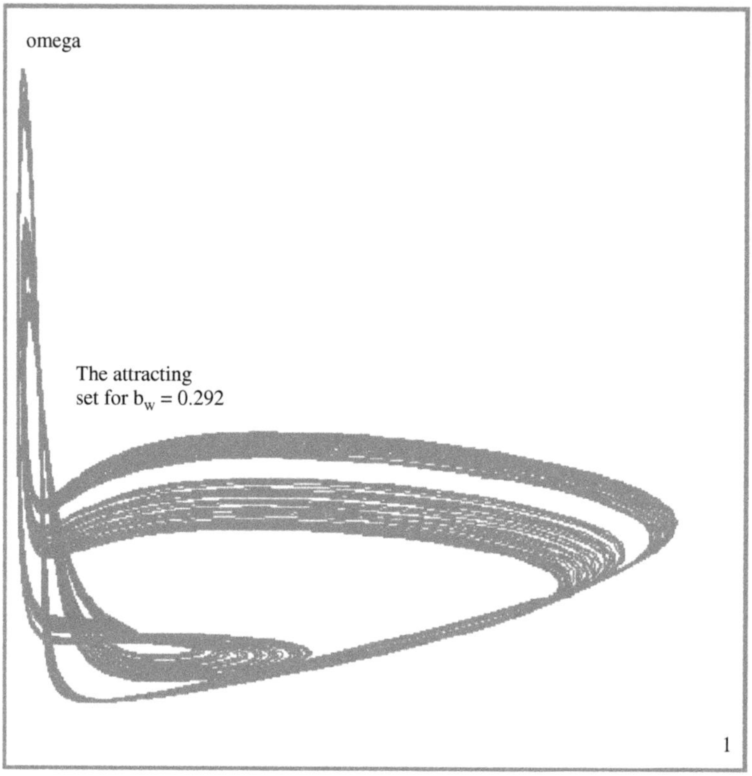

Figure 10.4 At the edge of mathematical boundedness ($h_2 = 0.08$, $\beta_{\pi_1} = 0.4$).

The third of the above items states that inventories cannot become negative. It is not so binding as it appears at first sight, since unfilled orders can be – and are in fact – treated as negative inventories in the present model (they are subsequently served on a first-come first-served basis until inventories become positive again). The fourth item is also not as binding as it looks at first sight, since the depreciation rate may become endogenous in times of crisis where gross investment approaches zero. These items are all quantity constraints, while the last two items represent price or value constraints. Negative nominal rates of interest r will not come about due to the behavior of asset markets if this floor is approached. Finally, the mechanism that keeps real wages ω below labor productivity x is not so obvious and has been controversial throughout the history of economic theory.

Of course, prices p, w as well as the capital stock K have to stay positive also, but this is assured by the formulation of their dynamics in terms of rates of growth. The above listed barriers – when approached – demand the integration of various types of nonlinearities (or additional reaction patterns such as overtime work, changes in the participation rate and immigration in the case of the full employment barrier) that may often prevent the described bound from actually being reached (and thus the Keynesian effective demand regime is left).

Astonishingly, however, all of the above additions to our demand constrained Keynesian model of monetary growth can be bypassed in many circumstances when one simple fact of modern economies is taken into account and added to the model, i.e. the nonexistence of an economy-wide wage deflation $\widehat{w} < 0$. In an inflationary economy workers may demand very small nominal wage increases in the face of high unemployment, i.e. they may not attempt to resist real wage decreases when they occur in this way. By contrast, the resistance to nominal wage decreases may be formidable due to the institutional structure of the economy. Such and further related arguments have been put forth in a pronounced way by Keynes (1936) in particular and they here provide the basis for the following simple modification of the money wage Phillips curve (10.18):

$$\widehat{w} = \min\{\beta_w(V-1) + \kappa_w \hat{p} + (1-\kappa_w)\pi, 0\}.$$

This modified wage equation which excludes the occurrence of a nominal wage deflation has dramatic consequences for the stability and the pattern of fluctuations that are generated by the thereby revised model. This will be demonstrated here by a series of simulations of this new model which create economically meaningful trajectories for all relevant variables despite pronounced increases in the formerly rapidly destabilizing adjustment parameter β_w.

Let us briefly describe how the model of Sections 10.2 and 10.3 is modified by our reformulation of the money wage Phillips curve. The wage and price adjustment equations of these sections can be represented in the form

$$\widehat{w} - \pi = \beta_w(V-1) + \kappa_w(\hat{p} - \pi),$$
$$\hat{p} - \pi = \beta_p(U-1) + \kappa_p(\widehat{w} - \pi),$$

which gives rise to the following expressions for $\widehat{w} - \pi$ and $\hat{p} - \pi$:

$$\widehat{w} - \pi = \kappa[\beta_w(V-1) + \kappa_w\beta_p(U-1)], \tag{10.38}$$
$$\hat{p} - \pi = \kappa[\kappa_p\beta_w(V-1) + \beta_p(U-1)]. \tag{10.39}$$

The simultaneous determination of wage and price deflation is thereby solved and shows that both inflation rates depend on the state of excess demand in both the market for labor and for goods and on expected medium-run inflation. Subtracting the second from the first equation then gives the law of motion of the real wage we have employed in Section 10.3. Yet, when the rule of downwardly rigid nominal wages applies, i.e. in the case where

$$\kappa[\beta_w(V-1) + \kappa_w\beta_p(U-1)] + \pi < 0$$

holds true, we have

$$\widehat{w} = 0, \quad \hat{p} = \beta_p(U-1) + (1-\kappa_p)\pi,$$

and thus get for the real wage dynamics in this case

$$\widehat{\omega} = -\beta_p(U-1) - (1-\kappa_p)\pi. \tag{10.40}$$

This is the modification to be made to equation (10.21) whenever the above inequality holds true. Furthermore, both equations (10.23) and (10.24) make use of the expression

$$\hat{p} - \pi = \kappa[\kappa_p\beta_w(V-1) + \beta_p(U-1)],$$

which in the case of the above inequality must be replaced by

$$\hat{p} - \pi = \beta_p(U-1) - \kappa_p\pi. \tag{10.41}$$

This completes the set of changes induced by the assumption of downwardly rigid nominal wages.

Let us now look at the consequences of this simple modification of the model. A first example is provided by Figure 10.5. This figure is based on the data of Figure 10.4 ($\mu = n$, i.e. no steady-state inflation in particular and also $h_2 = 0.08, \beta_{\pi_1} = 0.4$) and differs from the model of that figure only by the above extension of the Phillips curve. In this case the revision of the model has two basic consequences.

- The steady state of the model is now (for $\mu = n$) no longer uniquely determined in the interior of the phase space as far as the rate of employment V_0 (and l_0) are concerned. The rate V_0 may now be lower than 1 in the steady state, since the then implied wage deflation is prevented by the above change in the wage adjustment mechanism of the model (all other steady values are the same as before).
- The set of steady states of the revised model is now globally asymptotically stable in a very strong way (see Figure 10.5 for an example). Owing to the changed behavior of workers the economy is rapidly trapped in an underemployment equilibrium that may be much higher than the NAIRU rate of unemployment of the former steady-state situation.

We thus have that downward wage rigidity prevents the fluctuations shown in Figure 10.4 in a radical way, but is accompanied by a more depressed labor market in the steady state than before. These results are in our view due to the fact that there is a floor or ratchet built into the model right at the edge of the steady state.

This observation suggests that there will be more fluctuations if there is steady-state inflation, i.e. if $\mu > n$ is assumed, since the behavior of the economy is

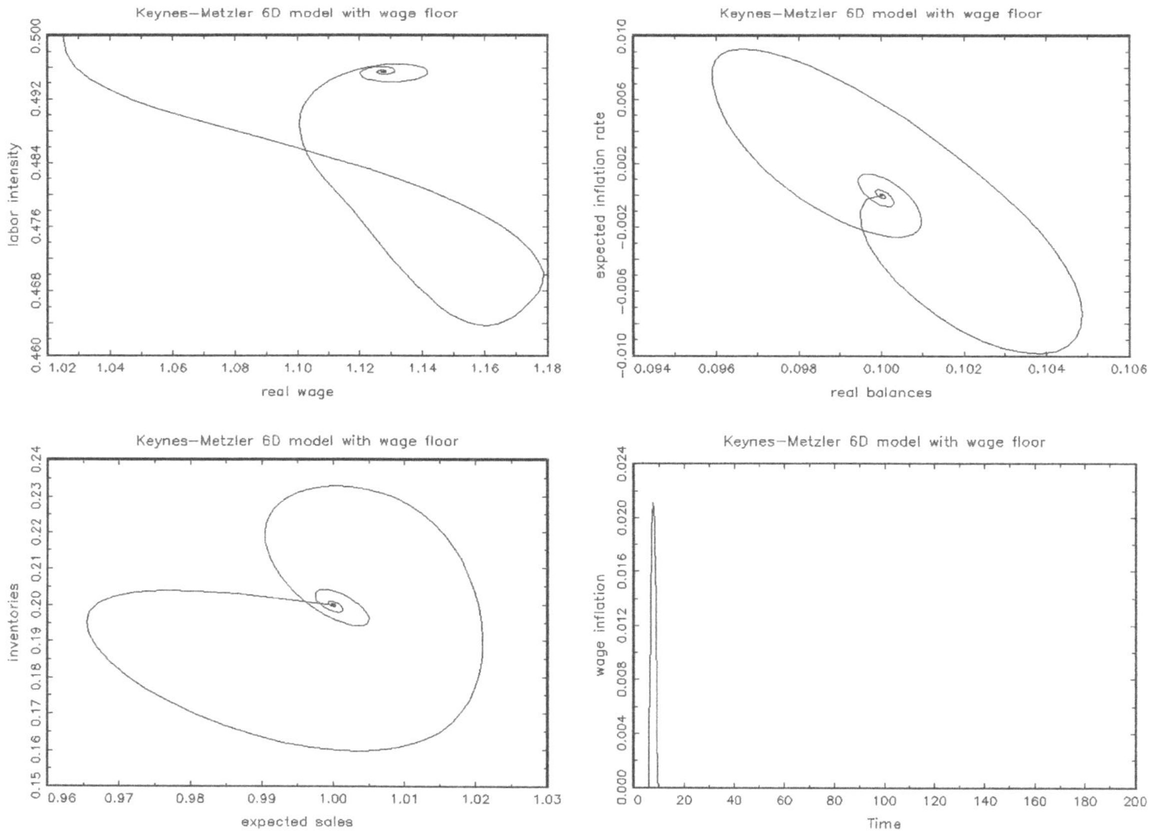

Figure 10.5 No steady-state inflation ($\mu = n = 0.05$, $\beta_w = 0.292$ as in Figure 10.4).

then only modified further away from the steady state which in this case is again uniquely determined as in the preceding model. Locally it is thus of the form of the preceding section. The interesting question then is whether the dynamics is again radically modified by the ratchet situation that the level of nominal wages may rise, but cannot fall. Figures 10.6–10.12 illustrate this for a wage adjustment speed β_w that varies from 2 to 26, i.e. over a range where the previous model would collapse immediately.

This series of figures shows that the period-doubling route to complex dynamics shown in Figures 10.3 and 10.4 can also be demonstrated to exist in this model variant, but now for extremely high adjustment speeds β_w of nominal wages w and amplitudes of fluctuations that stay within economically meaningful bounds. Note that wage inflation can get as high as 130% and that inventories may become slightly negative in the last figure where the case $\beta_w = 26$ is considered (Figure 10.12).

Figures 10.6–10.12 each show three projections of the 6D dynamics onto the (ω, l), the (m, π) and the (y^e, ν) subspaces as well as the development of wage inflation as a time series. This series of figures demonstrates several things:

- the model is now extremely viable, but – as expected – no longer asymptotically stable;
- the model exhibits large but economically meaningful persistent fluctuations;
- the model undergoes a period-doubling sequence as the parameter β_w is increased further and further;
- the model shows only weak changes in amplitude while the parameter β_w is increased significantly;
- the economic length of the cycle stays approximately 20 years, while the mathematical period of course doubles along the period-doubling route.

The dynamics therefore eventually becomes complex as the parameter β_w is increased further and further. The dynamics of the naturally nonlinear model is thus radically changed from a global – though not from a local[4] – perspective.

10.7 Conclusions

In Keynes (1936, pp. 14 and 269) it is stated:

> Thus it is fortunate that workers, though unconsciously, are instinctively more reasonable economists than the classical school, inasmuch as they resist reductions of money wages, which are seldom or never of an all-round character . . .
>
> The chief result of this policy (of flexible wages, C.C./P.F.) would be to cause a great instability of prices, so violent perhaps as to make business calculations futile . . . .

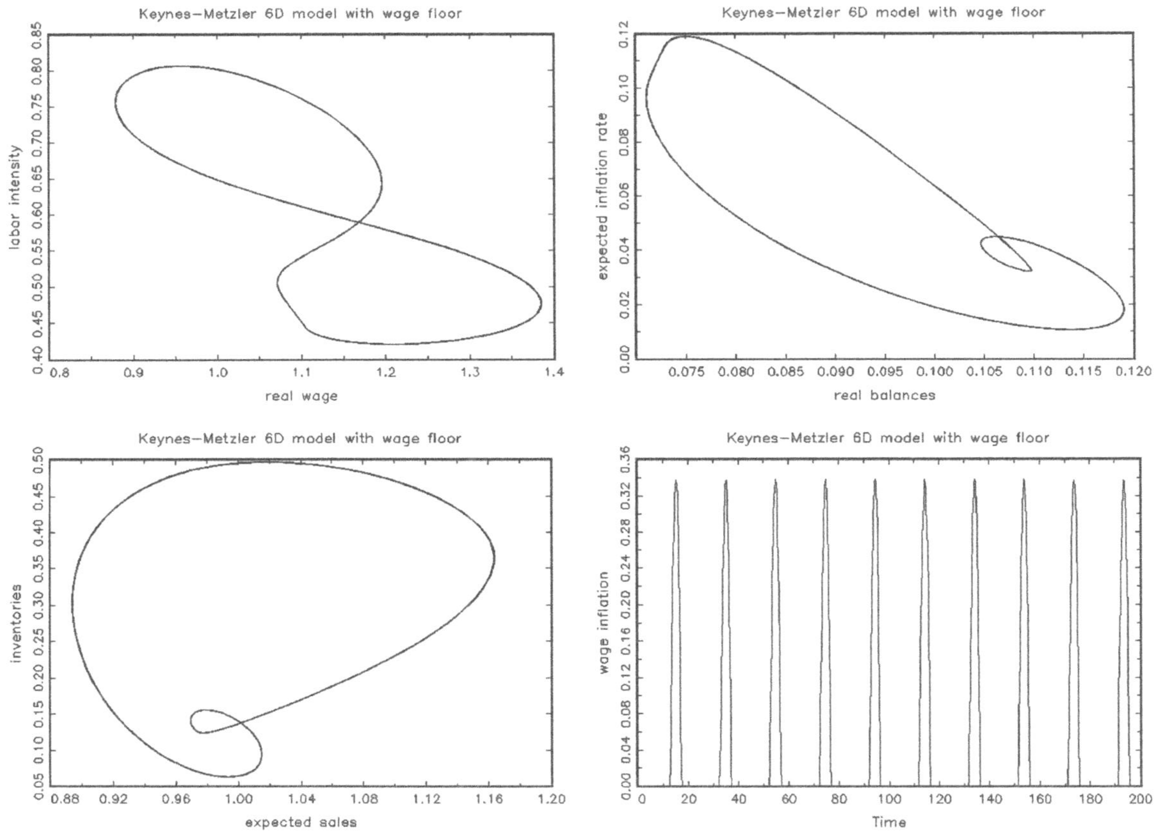

Figure 10.6 Steady-state inflation ($\mu = 0.1 > n = 0.05$) and period-1 limit cycles ($\beta_w = 2$).

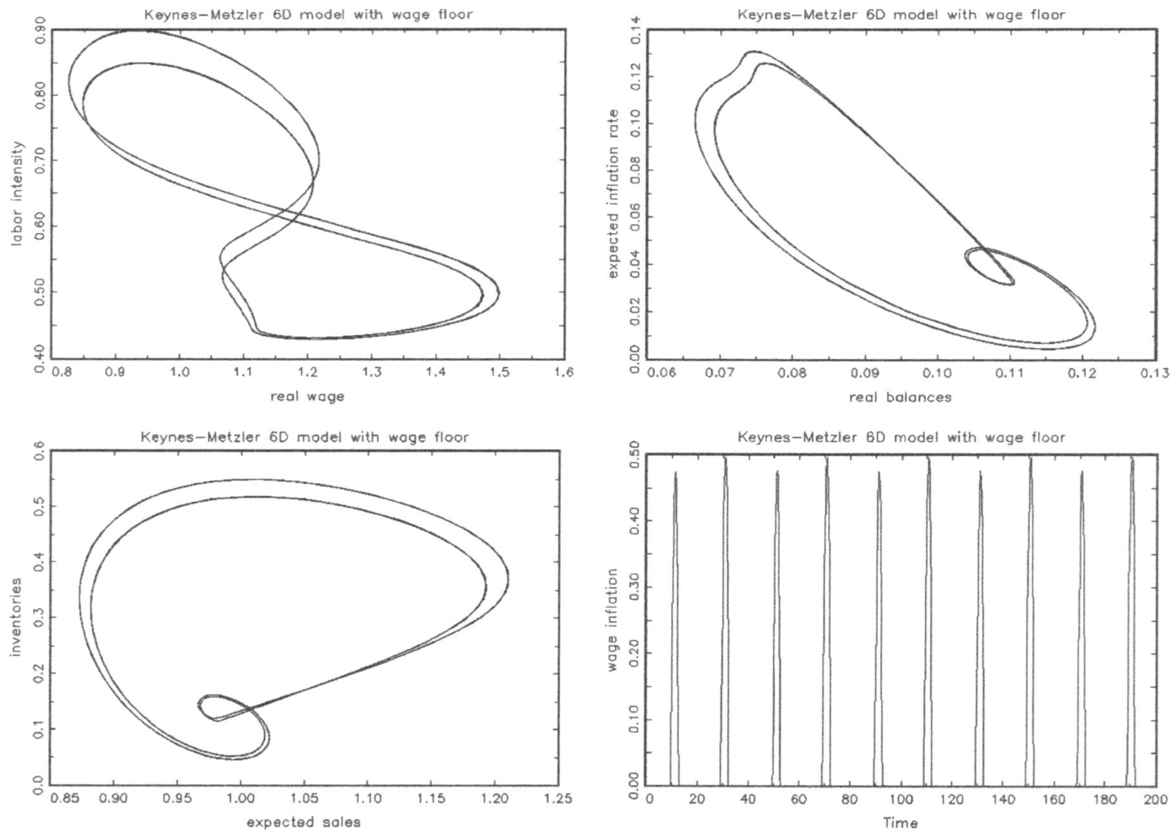

Figure 10.7 Steady-state inflation and period-2 limit cycles ($\beta_w = 5$).

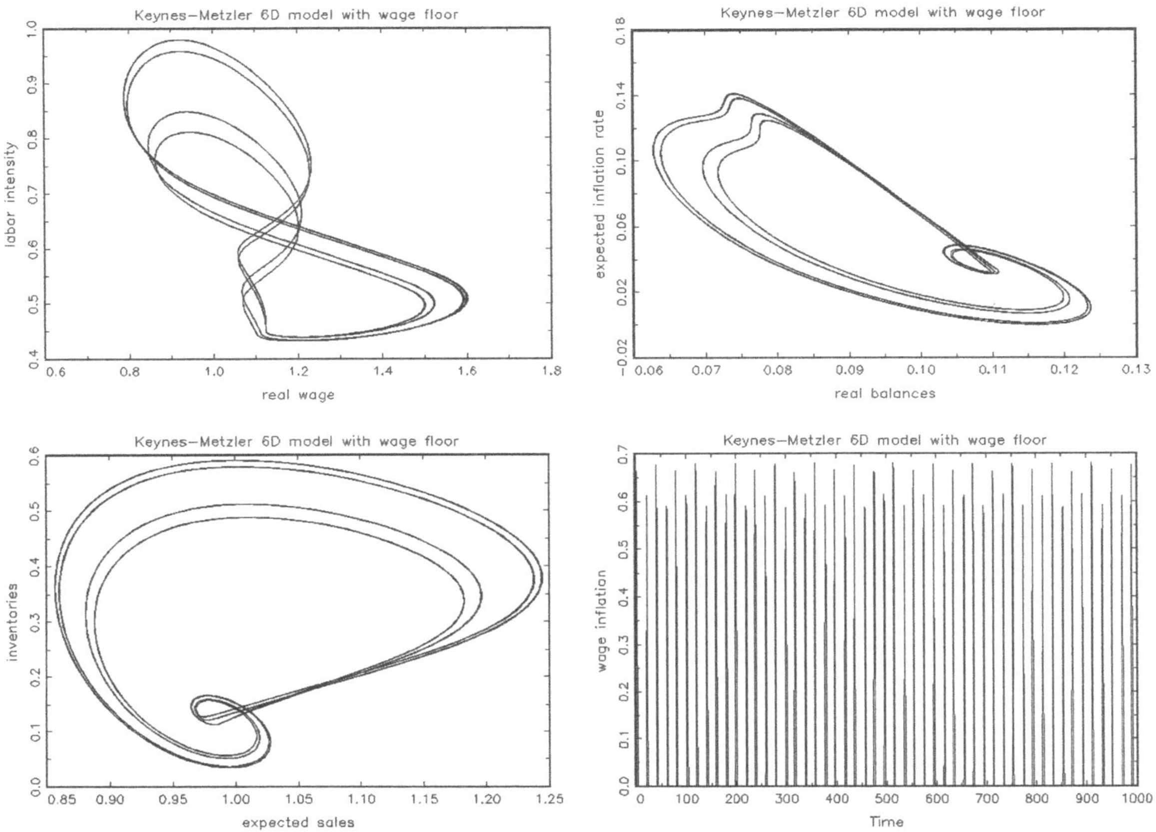

Figure 10.8 Steady-state inflation and period-4 limit cycles ($\beta_w = 10$).

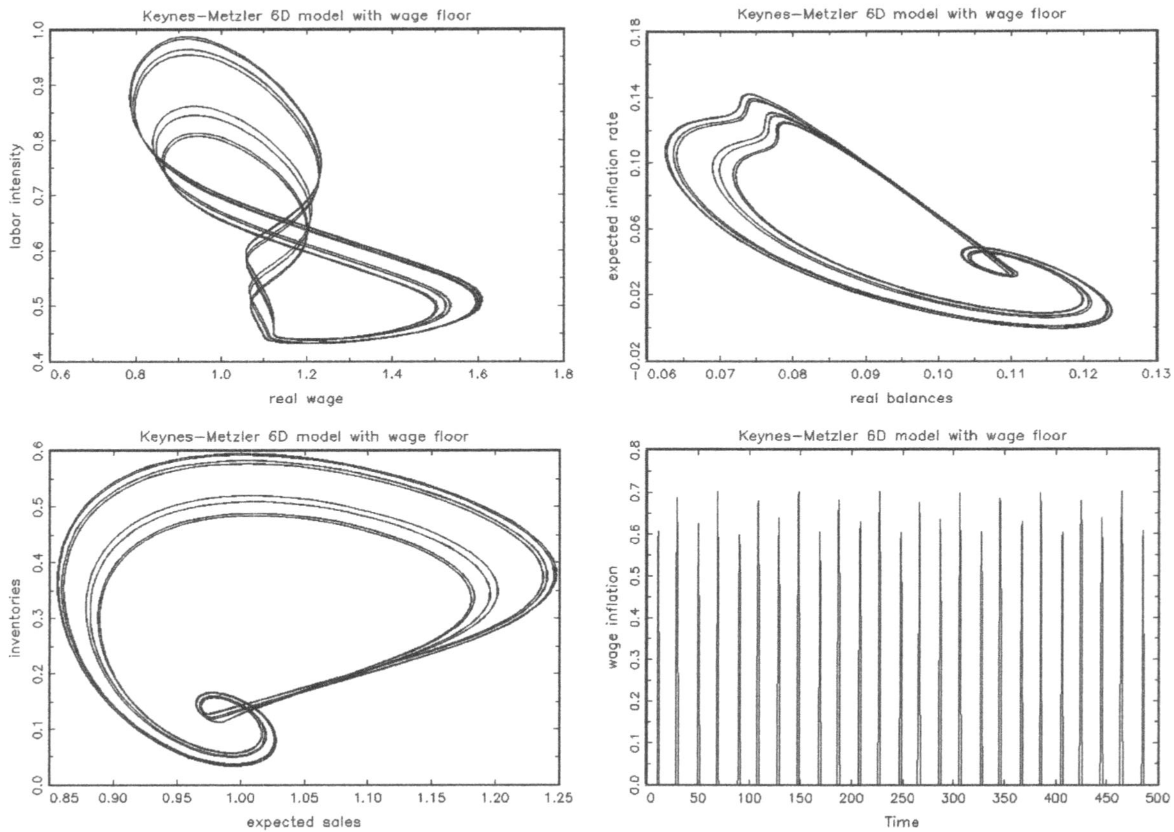

Figure 10.9 Steady-state inflation and period-8 limit cycles ($\beta_w = 10.7$).

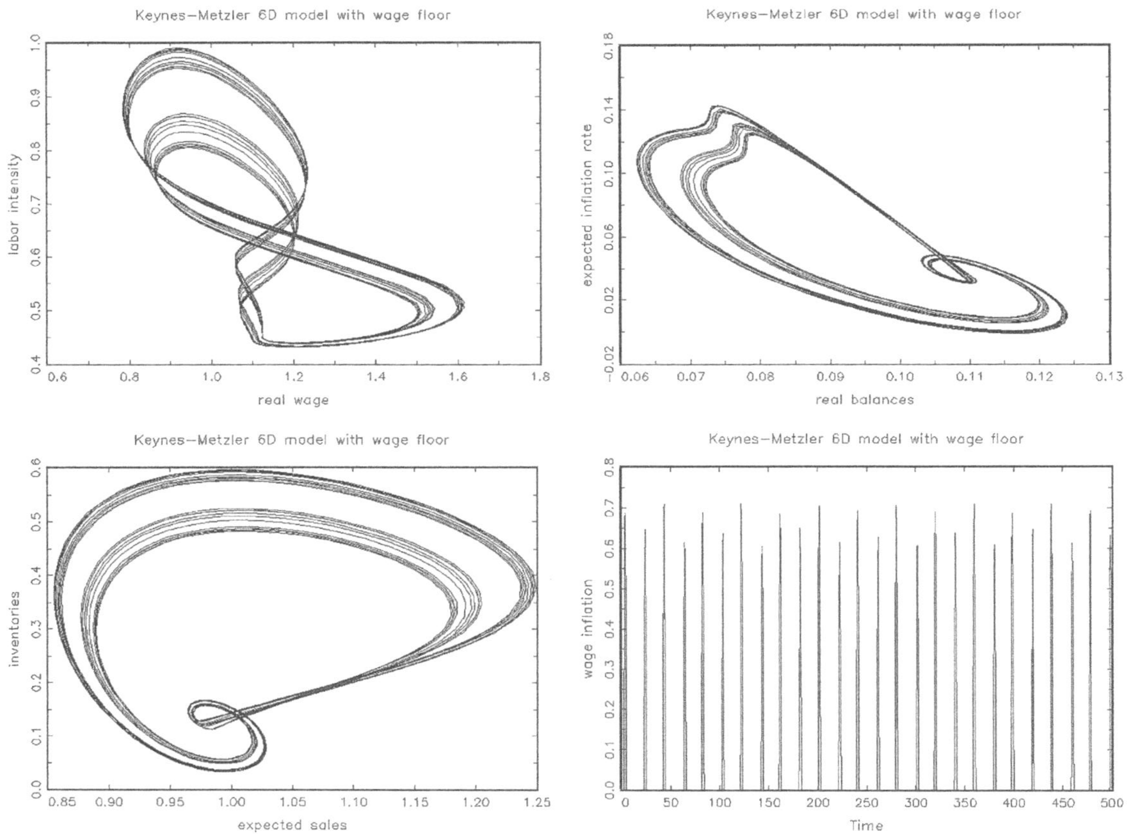

Figure 10.10 Steady-state inflation and period-16 limit cycles ($\beta_w = 11$).

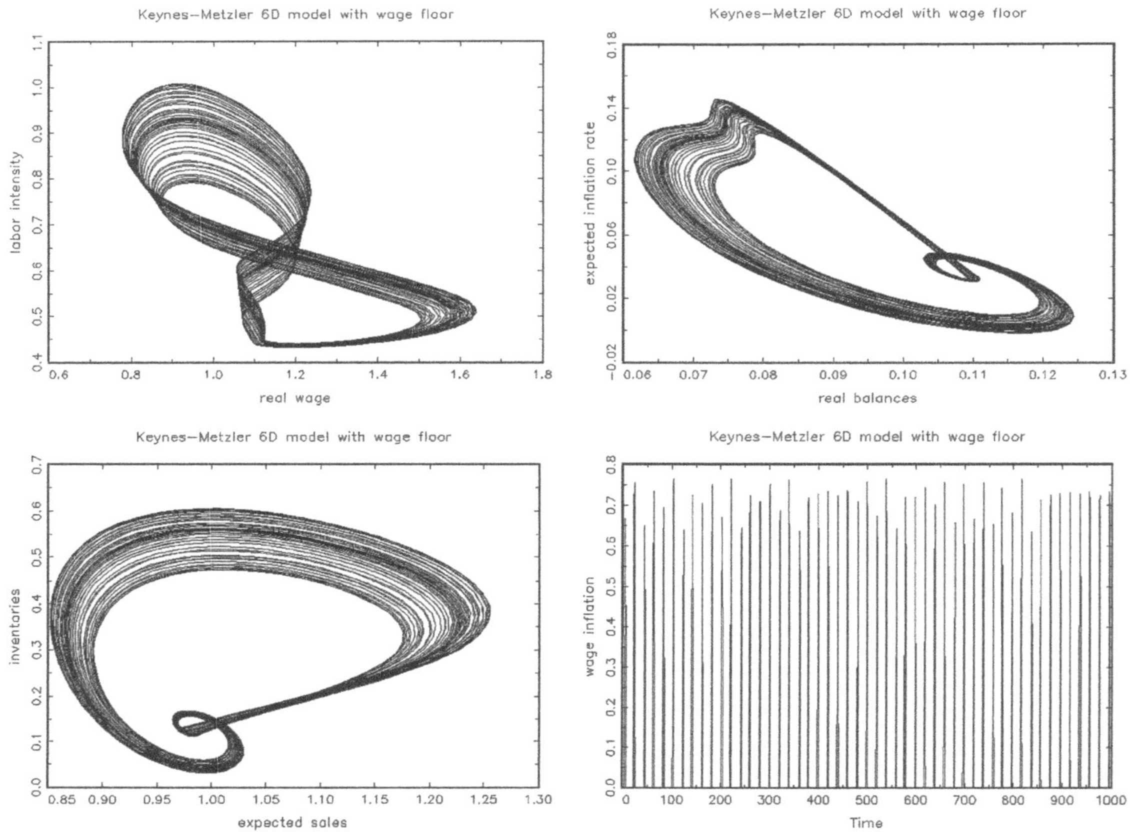

Figure 10.11 Steady-state inflation of high period ($\beta_w = 13$).

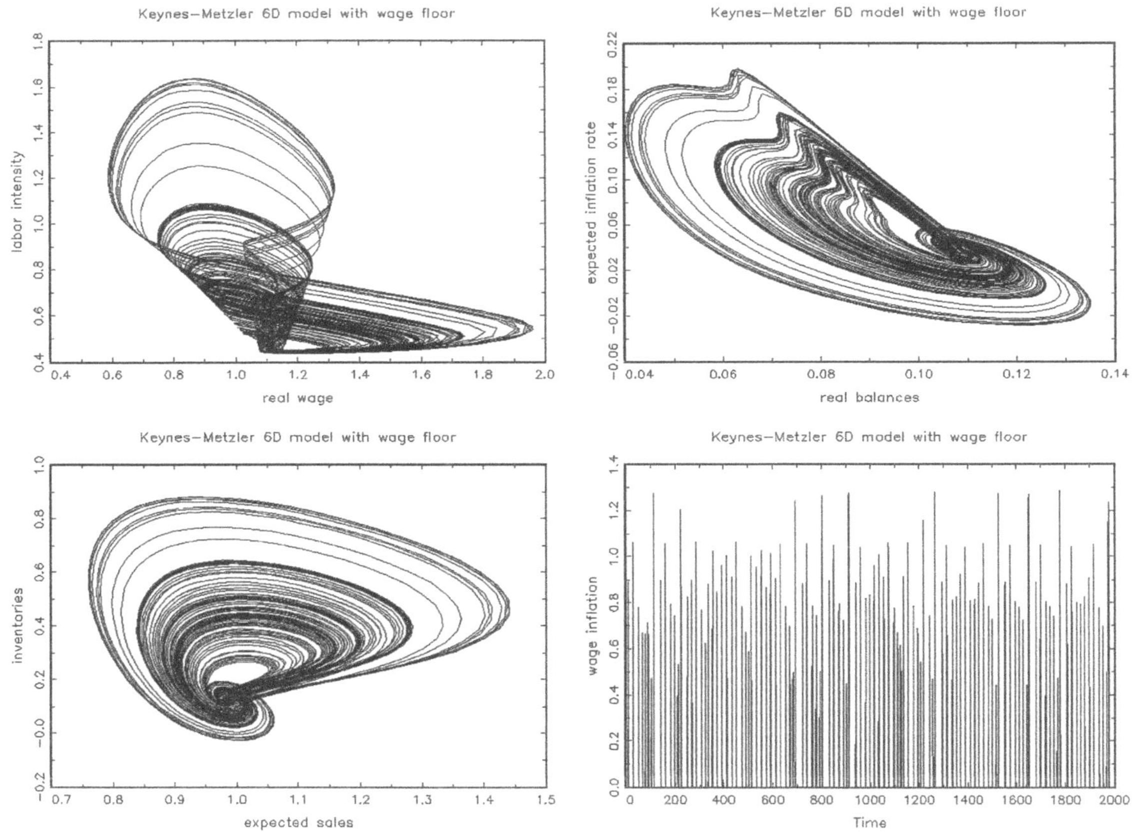

Figure 10.12 Steady-state inflation and complex dynamics ($\beta_w = 26$).

The present Keynesian model of monetary growth has demonstrated the validity of this view by means of numerical simulations of a system with laws of motion having considerable completeness and complexity. Of course, other sources for stability may also exist, but must be left for future research.

11 Calibration of an unobservable inflation climate

11.1 Introduction

The new Keynesian Phillips curve is currently the dominating concept to represent nominal rigidity in macroeconomic theory and the analysis of monetary policy. While its treatment of expected inflation as rational expectations is elegant and theoretically appealing, there is, however, growing awareness that the model is hard to square with the facts. Generally, econometric support is not only lacking for the canonical sticky-price model but also for the hybrid versions that combine forward-looking and backward-looking expectations. A study that has recently worked this out is Rudd and Whelan (2005). At the end the authors arrive at the definite conclusion that the new Keynesian Phillips curve "cannot serve as an adequate approximation to the empirical inflation process" (Rudd and Whelan 2005, p. 18).

Even if this upshot is accepted, the appropriate steps to be taken are less obvious. An interesting example of how to proceed in this situation is the paper by Fuhrer (1997). Though with more elementary methods, he similarly states that "expectations of future prices are empirically unimportant in explaining price and inflation behavior" (Fuhrer 1997, p. 349). Noting that the data cannot reject the hypothesis with any confidence that expectations are rather purely backward-looking (ibid, p. 344), he then goes on to examine the dynamic implications of a backward-looking, accelerationist Phillips curve with those of a mixed forward-looking and backward-looking specification. In a disinflation experiment he finds that the former "implies implausibly long and vigorous responses to events many years ago" (ibid, p. 347), whereas the time path of the model with some forward-looking price behavior conforms considerably better to the conventional wisdom that monetary policy does not have pronounced long-run effects. Thus, for policy simulations, a combination of forward-looking and backward-looking elements may yield more reasonable long-run behavior than the accelerationist Phillips curve, without sacrificing too much on empirical performance (Fuhrer 1997, p. 349).

While this may appear to be a revaluation of the new Keynesian approach, the last two sentences with which Fuhrer (1997, p. 349) concludes his observations put it again in a state of suspense: "Still, this is a relatively weak basis for incorporating forward-looking behavior in price specifications. Other alterations to the model may do just as well in stabilizing model dynamics." In fact, our chapter can be seen as taking up this final remark and its implicit invitation, or challenge. We will propose such an alternative model of the inflation dynamics that distinguishes itself by the following three features.

(1) It is conceptually more ambitious than an accelerationist Phillips curve, though technically speaking it is still backward-looking.
(2) By combining estimation and calibration methods in a new way, we are able to obtain satisfactory "estimates" of its numerical coefficients.
(3) The implied impulse–response properties avoid the high inflation persistence just mentioned.

The discussion of our inflation module is organized as follows. The next section is a brief overview of the basic conceptual ideas and of our approach to assign numerical values to the structural parameters. Section 11.3 introduces the formal modeling equations. The numerical values for its parameters are obtained in Section 11.4, which is the methodological core of the chapter. The way in which estimation and calibration procedures are here combined allows us to construct bootstrap samples of shocks to the model, so that an entire frequency distribution of appropriate numerical parameters can be computed. Section 11.5 is a sensitivity analysis that investigates how the optimal solutions of our fitting problem change, and the optimal fit itself deteriorates, if some of the model's parameter are exogenously varied. Dynamic implications of the inflation module are studied in Section 11.6; in particular, its impulse–response functions are compared with those from an a theoretical vector autoregression that serves as a frame of reference. Section 11.7 concludes.

11.2 Overview of modeling approach and methodology

The Phillips curve that we put forward is formally similar to the baseline case of the new Keynesian Phillips curve and has likewise been derived within the by now standard framework of Calvo's (1983) time-contingent price setting. The assumption of homogeneous and rational expectations has, however, been dropped. In effect, expected inflation in the Phillips curve for the next period is replaced with the notion of a general inflation climate, which is the aggregate of the firms' heterogeneous beliefs about inflation. Specifically, these individual judgements summarize in a single number the rate of inflation that the firm expects to prevail on average over the whole future, where the "average" is based on a discounting procedure with Calvo's probability that, in a given period, the firm would not receive a signal to reset its price.[1]

These microfoundations are one pillar on which the concept of the inflation climate rests; the other is the specification of its law of motion. Shifting the discussion to the macroeconomic level, it is here assumed that the climate variable responds not only to current inflation, which would be an ordinary adaptive expectations mechanism, but also to the level of economic activity and its recent changes. Furthermore, the central bank's target rate of inflation may be taken into account, according to the credibility of monetary policy. Considering these few variables will already yield a sufficiently rich and flexible theory of the output–inflation nexus.

We think of these adjustments of the inflation climate as being brought about by firms that are not rational in the abstract sense of the theory, but adaptive in the common sense that they react in reasonable ways to the arrival of new information in an uncertain environment. For this reason the adjustment module will be called the *adaptive inflation climate* (AIC).[2] The modeling of the Phillips curve together with AIC is intended to follow the famous KISS ("keep it sophisticatedly simple") principle of Zellner (1992, 2002). The expectations of the heterogeneous firms are certainly less elaborate than rational expectations, but also less naive than adaptive expectations. Hence, we would rather like to characterize the firms' expectation formation as *sophisticatedly simple*.

Besides the usual slope coefficient in the Phillips curve, the AIC module comprises four reaction coefficients, which have to be numerically specified. They cannot be directly estimated from the data since the inflation climate is an unobservable variable. While it might be proxied by a survey measure of expected inflation, we prefer another approach which as far as we are aware of is a new method of parameter "estimation."

The method is based on the idea of simulating the model (with an empirical output series) and searching for a combination of the parameters such that the model-generated time path of the inflation rate comes close to actual inflation. Essentially, this can still be regarded as a calibration procedure.[3] The problem, however, is that these simulations should explicitly take into account the effects that are exogenous to the model's output–inflation nexus; otherwise the parameter values would have to produce not only the model's inflation dynamics but also its exogenous perturbations, so that the values might be possibly distorted.

We thus face the question of how to identify the "exogenous" forces. Our solution is alternatively to describe the output–inflation nexus in a straightforward a theoretical way such as has proved useful in many applications. That is, we estimate the nexus by a VAR, which can be interpreted to represent the interrelated feedbacks of output, inflation and now the inflation climate in a reduced form. What remains unexplained in the VAR's inflation equation is thus exogenous to the determination of inflation within an output–inflation context. Accordingly, the residuals of the VAR's inflation component serve to specify the forces that are considered to be exogenous to our modeling framework.

Against this background, we simulate the model by adding, in the Phillips curve, in each period the estimated residual from the VAR as this period's exogenous perturbation. The inflation series generated in this way can then be fitted to actual inflation.

The values of the parameters that minimize the distance between the artificial and the actual time series is what we are basically looking for. In addition, it is possible to examine the robustness of these coefficients. To this end a convenient bootstrap device can be utilized, which means that in period t no longer this period's estimated residual is added in the Phillips curve, but a randomly drawn perturbation from the entire set of the estimated residuals. The optimal coefficients will generally differ from one such sample run to another, and by replicating them sufficiently often we can obtain a frequency distribution for each coefficient of the model. The distribution allows us to compute a mean value of the coefficient and gauge a confidence interval around it. Interestingly, if we leave the underlying model simulations aside, these bootstrap operations with their repeated fitting to actual inflation are again more akin to an "estimation" procedure.

After deciding on a set of parameter values on the basis of these Monte Carlo experiments, it still has to be checked whether the model's dynamic implications can be accepted. Two tests are employed for this evaluation. First, we consider the time path of the inflation climate, which was disregarded so far, and compare it with the evolution of its empirical proxy of a survey measure of expected inflation. It will not be required that the climate trajectory generated by our coefficients are as good a prediction of the survey measure as a prediction from a regression estimation. What we nevertheless demand from the climate is that its time path shares the most important qualitative features of the survey measure, or that the deviations can be satisfactorily explained when they appear too pronounced.

The second test is of a similar type as the disinflation experiment to which Fuhrer (1997) subjected the accelerationist Phillips curve, which it failed to pass (see the introduction). Our test criterion is provided by the impulse–response functions from the above-mentioned VAR. Starting the deterministic AIC dynamics with the same shocks, the resulting trajectories should show a similar speed of convergence back to the equilibrium values as the VAR time paths. It may be anticipated that both tests will not be much of a problem to our AIC theory of price inflation.

The remainder of the chapter has now to provide the details that are underlying this general description of the model's achievements.

11.3 Formulation of the AIC module

In the Calvo (1983) framework of monopolistic competition and time-contingent price setting, each firm must precommit to a price until it receives a signal that it can change the price, which in a given period it is allowed to do with a probability $1-\theta$. If there were no price rigidities, then in period t firm f would set its price, in logs, as $(p_t^f)^\star = p_t + \eta\, y_t^f$, where p_t is (the log of) the aggregate price level, η the elasticity of its upward-sloping supply curve (supposed to be uniform for simplicity), and y_t^f the firm's output gap, i.e. the percentage deviation of its current output from potential output. In an inflationary environment, however, and being aware that it may not be able to change its price for multiple periods, the firm will charge a higher price to guard against these "losses." The (log of the) firm's reset price z_t^f will thus be given by

$$z_t^f = (1-\theta)\sum_{k=0}^{\infty}\theta^k E_t^f\,(p_{t+k}^f)^\star = (1-\theta)\sum_{k=0}^{\infty}\theta^k E_t^f\,(p_{t+k}+\eta y_{t+k}^f). \qquad (11.1)$$

It is easily recognized that z_t^f is the average frictionless price until the next price adjustment. Attaching the superscript f also to the expectation operator makes explicit that the individual firms may differ in their beliefs about the future price level.

In contrast, the new Keynesian theory assumes that all firms are homogeneous and entertain rational expectations. With π_t being the rate of inflation in period t, it is well known that this results in the baseline case of the new Keynesian Phillips curve,

$$\pi_t = E_t\pi_{t+1} + \frac{(1-\theta)^2\eta}{\theta} y_t. \tag{11.2}$$

Whereas the new Keynesian firms, either directly or by suitably manipulating the formal structural equations describing the economy, can predict an entire time profile of future price levels p_{t+k} and the demand directed to themselves, a firm that is not blessed with rational expectations must cope with the future in a more elementary manner. Our central idea for such a firm f is that, in period t, it captures future inflation inherent in the price series p_{t+k} by a single, firm-specific number π_t^f (which, of course, will change over time).

In detail, consider the expected price level for $t+k$ and, invoking the rates of inflation until that time, write it as

$$E_t^f\, p_{t+k} = p_t + \sum_{j=1}^{k} E_t^f\, \pi_{t+j}.$$

When the firm seeks to grasp future inflation by its summarizing rate π_t^f, we have

$$E_t^f\, p_{t+k} = p_t + \sum_{j=1}^{k}[\pi_t^f + E_t^f\,\pi_{t+j} - \pi_t^f] = p_t + k\pi_t^f + \sum_{j=1}^{k}(E_t^f\,\pi_{t+j} - \pi_t^f).$$

Denoting the accumulated residuals for period $t+k$ by $e_{t+k}^f = e_{t+k}^f(\pi_t^f)$, the expected price level is split up into

$$E_t^f\, p_{t+k} = p_t + k\pi_t^f + e_{t+k}^f(\pi_t^f),$$

where

$$e_{t+k}^f(\pi_t^f) = \sum_{j=1}^{k}(E_t^f\,\pi_{t+j} - \pi_t^f). \tag{11.3}$$

What the number π_t^f should accomplish is that these residuals average out on the whole. Realistically, however, the firm sees itself in an uncertain inflationary environment. It has no reliable basis to build up a probability distribution of future inflation rates, on which it could really expect the residuals to cancel out by a suitable choice of π_t^f. On the other hand, the firm has to settle down on a definite reset price in the end. So it proceeds *as if* π_t^f were able to satisfy this condition. The firm is aware that this will not be perfectly the case, but for lack of a better (and not more costly) procedure it is willing to accept the possible errors. Accordingly, in using (11.3) to determine its reset price z_t^f, the firm sets the total sum of the probability-discounted errors equal to zero,

$$\sum_{k=1}^{\infty} \theta^k e_{t+k}^f(\pi_t^f) = 0. \tag{11.4}$$

This rule completes the firm's treatment of future prices in (11.1). Expectations about its output gap need not take any secular growth rate into account. Since we want to stay close to the conventional Phillips curves where output expectations have no explicit role to play, it is then convenient to approximate the infinite output sum in (11.1) by "extrapolating" the most recent output gap and its change,

$$\sum_{k=0}^{\infty} \theta^k E_t^f y_{t+k}^f = \xi_1 y_{t-1}^f + \xi_2 \Delta y_{t-1}^f \tag{11.5}$$

(here $\xi_1 > 0$ and $\xi_2 \geq 0$ are only homogeneous across firms to simplify the notation below).[4]

Describing the distribution of firms by a density function $s = s(f)$, it is shown in Franke (2005, secs. 2.2 and 2.3) that equations (11.3)–(11.5) together with the updating equation for the aggregate price level give rise to the following equation for the economy's rate of inflation:

$$\pi_t = \int_0^1 \pi_t^f \, ds(f) + \frac{(1-\theta)^2 \eta}{\theta} [(1+\xi_1) y_{t-1} + \xi_2 \Delta y_{t-1}]. \tag{11.6}$$

Again, in order to preserve a close affinity with the usual Phillips curve specifications we disregard the changes in the economy-wide output gap and put $\xi_2 = 0$. The remaining composed term $(1-\theta)^2 \eta (1+\xi_1)/\theta$ may be summarized by the latter β_y. Lastly, for the aggregation of the firm-specific rates of inflation π_t^f we introduce the symbol

$$\pi_t^c = \int_0^1 \pi_t^f \, ds(f), \tag{11.7}$$

and call this variable the general *inflation climate* in the economy (therefore the superscript c). In sum, we arrive at the Phillips curve formulation

$$\pi_t = \pi_t^c + \beta_y y_{t-1}. \tag{11.8}$$

The analogy of (11.8) to the new Keynesian Phillips curve (11.2) is obvious. Apart from the minor issue of the dating of the output term, the model-consistent mathematical expectations of next period's inflation, $E_t\pi_{t+1}$, is here replaced with a variable that reflects the firms' heterogeneous beliefs about average (suitably discounted) inflation in the whole future. So far, however, the inflation climate π_t^c mainly emphasizes the heterogeneity of firms and that they must form expectations in less than perfect ways. To breathe life into this notion, it has next to be laid out how firms come to set up their rates π_t^f.

For our purpose it is appropriate to discuss this kind of expectation directly at the macrolevel, that is, we have to put forward a dynamic process that governs the adjustments of π_t^c. In Franke (2005, sec. 3), the formulation of such a process is motivated by the patterns one can identify in survey measure data on expected rates of inflation. Here we immediately turn to the description of the process. To begin with, the inflation climate π_t^c is predetermined in a given period t and modified by the firms at the beginning of the next period as the period-t variables are observed. The updating procedure is based on the concept of a general benchmark rate of inflation, toward which the current value of π_t^c is adjusted in a gradual manner. This benchmark is a combination of four single components which, of course, are themselves varying over time.

Regarding the beginning of period $t+1$ when π_t^c has to be updated, the four benchmark components are: (i) the current rate of inflation, π_t; (ii) the (constant) target rate of inflation, $\pi^\star$, which is set by the central bank and publicly known; (iii) an output-adjusted rate of inflation, $\pi_t + \zeta_y y_t$ for some $\zeta_y > 0$, which expresses the idea that the firms see a tendency for higher inflation if economic activity is presently above normal; and (iv) a growth-adjusted rate of inflation, $\pi_t + \zeta_g \Delta y_t$ for some $\zeta_g > 0$ ($\Delta y_t = y_t - y_{t-1}$), which expresses the idea that the firms see a tendency for higher inflation if the economy is presently growing faster than potential output.

Given adjustment speeds δ_a and weights ω_a summing up to zero ($a = \pi, s, y, g$), these components induce the following changes of the inflation climate:

$$\pi_{t+1}^c = \pi_t^c + \sum_{a=\pi,s,y,g} \omega_a \delta_a \Delta\pi^{c,a},$$

where

$$\Delta\pi^{c,\pi} := \pi_t - \pi_t^c, \quad \Delta\pi^{c,y} := \pi_t + \zeta_y y_t - \pi_t^c,$$
$$\Delta\pi^{c,s} := \pi^\star - \pi_t^c, \quad \Delta\pi^{c,g} := \pi_t + \zeta_g \Delta y_t - \pi_t^c.$$

Clearly, as it should be, with $\pi^c = \pi^\star$ the equation allows the Phillips curve to support a steady state $\pi = \pi^\star$, $y = 0$ of the economy.

This structural representation of the dynamics of the inflation climate contains ten behavioral coefficients. While they are useful in order to distinguish the four single benchmark concepts from each other, they are not all needed in the further analysis. We reduce them to the four parameters:

$$\alpha_c := \omega_\pi \delta_\pi + \omega_y \delta_y + \omega_g \delta_g + \omega_s \delta_s, \quad \alpha_y := \omega_y \delta_y \zeta_y / (\omega_\pi \delta_\pi + \omega_y \delta_y + \omega_g \delta_g),$$
$$\gamma := \omega_s \delta_s / a_c, \qquad \alpha_g := \omega_g \delta_g \zeta_g / (\omega_\pi \delta_\pi + \omega_y \delta_y + \omega_g \delta_g),$$

and write the above equation equivalently as

$$\pi^c_{t+1} = \pi^c_t + \alpha_c[\gamma\pi^\star + (1-\gamma)(\pi_t + \alpha_y y_t + a_g \Delta y_t) - \pi^c_t]. \tag{11.9}$$

Equation (11.9) summarizes how the single firm's views about future inflation cause the general inflation climate to change in an adaptive way; where, as usual in the learning literature on heterogeneous agents, the expression "adaptive" is used in a broader sense than just an "adaptive expectations" rule. The equation can thus be said to describe the concept of an *adaptive inflation climate*. In short, the combination of the updating rule (11.9) and the Phillips curve (11.8) will be referred to as the *AIC module*.

The parameter α_c is plainly the general speed of adjustment in the updating of the inflation climate. The economic significance of the coefficient γ and its relationship to the literature is less evident. To reveal it, consider an elementary specification of expectations in the Phillips curve which can reflect the faith that firms have in the conduct of monetary policy. Following Freedman (1996, p. 235ff.), such a Phillips curve may read

$$\pi_t = \mu\pi^\star + (1-\mu)A(L)\pi_{t-1} + \underline{y}_{t-1}, \tag{11.10}$$

where $A(L)$ is a polynomial lag function indicating that expected inflation is tied to the past rates of inflation, whose coefficients add up to unity. The weight μ expresses the degree to which inflation expectations are anchored on the target rate of inflation. In this sense the coefficient can be interpreted as measuring the credibility of the central bank.[5] On the other hand, $1-\mu$ as the sum of the coefficients on the lagged rates of inflation is commonly viewed as a measure of inflation persistence.

The AIC module can be compared to (11.10) by dating (11.9) one period backward and substituting it in (11.8). In this way $\pi^\star$, π_{t-1} and π^c_{t-1} show up on the right-hand side of the Phillips curve. The latter can be substituted by (11.9) dated two periods backward, which in turn introduces π_{t-2} and π^c_{t-2}. Repeating this procedure infinitely often and using $\sum_{k=0}^{\infty}(1-\alpha_c)^k = 1/\alpha_c$, we finally get

$$\pi_t = \gamma\pi^\star + (1-\gamma)\sum_{k=0}^{\infty}\alpha_c(1-\alpha_c)^k \pi_{t-k-1} + \beta_y y_{t-1}$$
$$+ \alpha_c(1-\gamma)\sum_{k=0}^{\infty}(1-\alpha_c)^k(\alpha_y y_{t-k-1} + \alpha_g \Delta y_{t-k-1}). \tag{11.11}$$

Since the terms $\alpha_c(1-\alpha_c)^k$ sum up to unity, we can summarize

$$\begin{array}{rl} \gamma & \text{credibility of the central bank,} \\ 1-\gamma & \text{inflation persistence in the Phillips curve.} \end{array} \qquad (11.12)$$

In addition to highlighting the role of the parameter γ, (11.11) shows the main difference of the AIC module from the familiar Phillips curves. Even if they include a target rate of inflation when rewritten as a backward-looking Phillips curve, our approach not only includes the (discounted) past rates of inflation, as implied by a textbook adaptive expectations mechanism, but also the entire history of output evolution.

11.4 Fitting model-generated inflation to actual inflation

Identification of exogenous forces

The AIC module has been put forward to be incorporated in larger macroeconomic models, which now requires a numerical specification of its parameters, i.e. of the slope β_y in the Phillips curve and the four AIC coefficients α_c, γ, α_y and α_g. A straightforward strategy in this respect is to proxy the inflation climate by one of the survey measures of expected inflation and estimate (11.9) by elementary regression methods. Using the consumer price index (CPI) and the Survey of Professional Forecasters (SPF) for its quarterly rate of change four quarters ahead, this was done in Franke (2005). However, while these results looked quite satisfactory at first sight, problems arose when SPF entered regressions of the Phillips curve. For this reason we here propose an alternative approach to obtaining the numerical parameters.[6]

Since the inflation climate is an unobservable variable, information about the AIC coefficients without using a proxy can only be gained by studying their implications for the rate of inflation, which is observable. We can thus combine (11.8) and (11.9), simulate them with empirical values for the output gap, and compare the resulting inflation series with actual inflation. It is then an immediate idea to look for a set of parameters such that this model-generated inflation comes as close as possible to actual inflation, where the distance between the two series can be measured by the root mean square deviation (RMSD). In this sense model-generated inflation can be said to be fitted to actual inflation.

Note that grounding the parameter search on simulations of a theoretical model is more akin to calibration, whereas minimizing an objective function such as the RMSD might already be classified as estimation. However, the procedure just outlined calls for a second thought, leading to the consequence that estimation will have an additional role to play.

The starting point of the following discussion is the elementary calibrationist wisdom that every model is false. The AIC module, as any Phillips curve, is not the exact truth but merely an approximate, theoretically motivated description of macroeconomic price setting. It focuses on the output–inflation nexus and leaves the possible influence from other sources aside. They are just exogenous forces, which are present in the real world but not yet in the formulation of the Phillips curve in (11.8). This implies that the RMSD minimizing set of coefficients derived as sketched above not only produces (in an approximate manner) the inflation dynamics as far as they are originating with the output–inflation nexus, but also accounts for the exogenous forces to which actual inflation has responded. The parameter values may therefore possibly be distorted; they may partly capture reactions to something outside the output–inflation nexus for which they were not designed.

We learn from these arguments that the model simulations should explicitly include a variable $\varepsilon_{\pi,t}$ in the Phillips curve that represents the exogenous forces. We also now make our adjustment period explicit, which will be one quarter. Denoting the actual values of the output gap by y_t^{emp} and taking over the updating equation (11.9), the model's series of the inflation rate is recursively generated by the three equations,

$$\pi_t^c = (1-\alpha_c)\pi_{t-1}^c + \alpha_c[\gamma\pi^\star + (1-\gamma)(\pi_{t-1} + \alpha_y y_{t-1} + \alpha_g \Delta y_{t-1})], \tag{11.13}$$

$$\pi_t = \pi_t^c + \beta_y y_{t-1} + \varepsilon_{\pi,t}, \tag{11.14}$$

$$y_t = y_t^{\text{emp}}, \quad t = 1961{:}1\text{–}2003{:}1. \tag{11.15}$$

The output gap is based on production of the nonfinancial corporations and conveniently given by the percentage deviations from the Hodrick–Prescott (HP) trend.[7] The sample period 1961:1–2003:1 is chosen such that its beginning and end are marked by pronounced trough values. On the whole, the 42 years cover five major cycles that may well be conceived as business cycles. The HP trend itself is computed over a longer period (1958:1–2004:3) to avoid the end-of-period effects.

While at the theoretical level the terms $\varepsilon_{\pi,t}$ in (11.14) are unexplained random shocks to the inflation dynamics, for a calibration of the model's numerical parameters we have to be more specific about them. As the AIC module is a theoretical approximation to the output–inflation nexus as a whole, our problem for the calibration is to extract from the data what, within our sample period, we regard as exogenous to the latter. The "true" output–inflation nexus is, of course, unknown. However, it can be captured in a manner that is widely, in very different applications, acknowledged as satisfactory if we are content with an a theoretical (linear) description, the appropriate tool for which is a vector auto regression (VAR). That is, since the AIC module is only concerned with the one direction from output to prices (and the repercussions of lagged prices on themselves), it suffices to consider the inflation component of such a VAR. Accordingly, using the actual data on the output gap (y_t^{emp}) and inflation (π_t^{emp}) we estimate the regression

$$\pi_t^{\text{emp}} = \sum_{k=1}^{4} a_{\pi k}\pi_{t-k}^{\text{emp}} + \sum_{k=1}^{4} a_{yk} y_{t-k}^{\text{emp}} + u_{\pi,t} \tag{11.16}$$

(by ordinary least squares (OLS) over the same sample period 1961:1–2003:1; four lags prove to be a suitable lag length).[8] The two sums $\sum_k a_{\pi k}\pi_{t-k}$ and $\sum_k a_{yk}y_{t-k}$ represent the output–inflation nexus in reduced form, whose details are of no interest here. Important for us are rather the estimated residuals from the regression, designated $\hat{u}_{\pi,t}$: they are the exogenous forces that we sought to identify. Therefore, equations (11.13)–(11.15) are complemented by assuming that

$$\varepsilon_{\pi,t} = \hat{u}_{\pi,t}. \tag{11.17}$$

We note that generally the Phillips curve (11.14) is a stochastic equation. Under (11.17), however, and with given coefficients α_c, γ, etc., we are considering a sample run where the shocks to the inflation rate are already determined by another device, namely, by the outcome of a regression estimation.

Figure 11.1 summarizes the relationship between regression (11.16) and the model simulations (11.13)–(11.15) and (11.17). The upper part sketches the outcome of the a theoretical regression approach, whose role is to furnish us with estimates $\hat{u}_{\pi,t}$ for the exogenous influences on the output–inflation nexus. The lower part makes clear that these residuals are plugged into the Phillips curve to specify the exogenous shocks to the theoretical model. In combination with the AIC adjustment equation and the impact of actual output, suitable coefficients α_c, α_y, etc., should make it possible that these feedback mechanisms generate an inflation series that approximates actual inflation.

Even if this procedure yields meaningful structural coefficients in the AIC module and produces a satisfactory fit of the model-generated inflation series, and even if in (11.16) four lags are a suitable choice in terms of the Schwarz or Akaike information criterion, it might be asked for the robustness of this result if the estimated residuals with which the model simulations are provided were obtained by another lag length in the regression. To check this problem, (11.16) was re-estimated with (a) six lags and (b) eight lags of inflation as well the output gap. Comparing the residuals here obtained with the $\hat{u}_{\pi,t}$ from (11.16), close correlations are found: they are as high as 0.980 and 0.966 for case (a) and (b), respectively. As this also shows that the deterministic parts of these versions are very similar, not too much should depend on the four lags that we have chosen – in particular, if we turn to the more general bootstrap procedures discussed in Sections 4.3 and 4.4.

A first result

We are thus ready to simulate system (11.13)–(11.15) under assumption (11.17) and search for numerical values of the parameters that minimize the RMSD of the model outcome π_t from actual inflation π_t^{emp}. To this end, the downhill simplex method (Press *et al.* 1986, p. 289ff.) is employed; it does not require the computation of any derivatives and proves quite efficient. While this is an unconstrained optimization procedure, the nonnegativity constraints on the coefficients can be conveniently treated by adding a high penalty for their violation in the objective function (see Judd 1998, p. 123ff.).

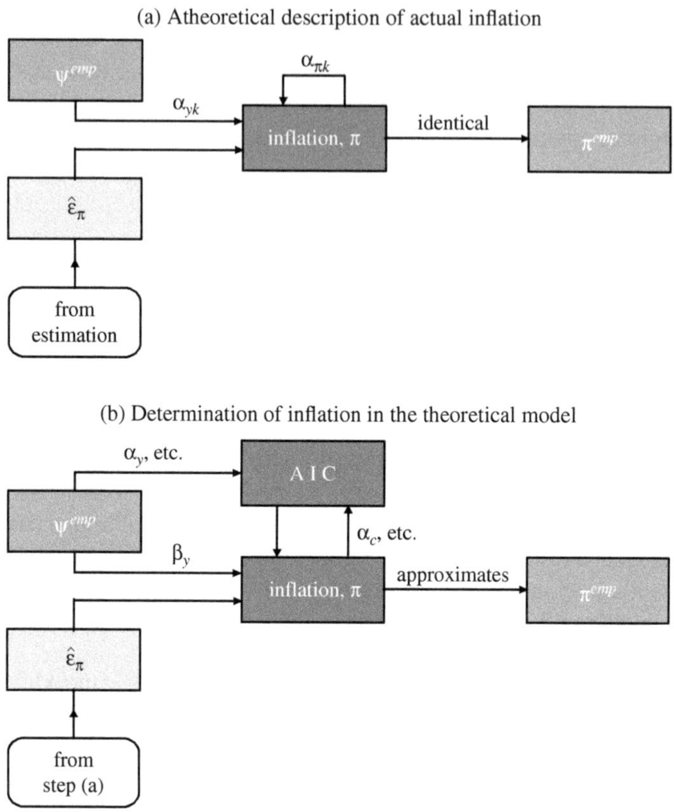

Figure 11.1 Relationship between actual and model-generated inflation.

As will be seen below, it is useful to control for the slope of the parameter β_y in the Phillips curve. We base our first simulations on $\beta_y = 0.14$, which is the estimate of Rudebusch and Svensson (1999, p. 208) for their (quarterly) accelerationist Phillips curve (with four lags of inflation).[9] The model's inflation rate π_{t-1} for t = 1961:1 is naturally initialized with its empirical value. At an exploratory stage of our investigations, the starting value of the inflation climate was still included as an additional "parameter" to minimize the RMSD. It was then fixed close to the value that has been found to solve the present optimization, namely, at $\pi^c_{t-1} = 1.00\%$ for t = 1961:1.

Regarding the AIC coefficients proper the nonnegativity constraint takes effect for α_g; in the present as well as in almost all other fitting experiments we get $\alpha_g = 0$. Unless it becomes slightly positive in some marginal cases, the coefficient will therefore not be further mentioned in the following. Then, the first row in Table 11.1 reports the three coefficients α_c, γ and α_y that prove salient. All three of them are of a reasonable order of magnitude. The adjustment speed α_c and

Table 11.1 RMSD minimizing coefficients under $\beta_y = 0.14$.

	α_c	γ	a_y	$RMSD$
A. $\varepsilon_{\pi,t} = \hat{u}_{\pi,t}$ (estimated residuals)				
Coefficients	0.409	0.412	0.287	0.272
B. $\pi_t \equiv$ estimated residuals				
"Fit"	—	—	—	0.968
C. Shocks $\varepsilon_{\pi,t}$ drawn from $\hat{u}_{\pi,t}$, (11.18)				
Coefficients	0.410	0.453	0.292	0.301
Standard dev.	0.021	0.014	0.024	0.016
Lower 2.5%	0.372	0.423	0.242	0.271
Upper 2.5%	0.453	0.478	0.339	0.333
D. Shocks $\varepsilon_{\pi,t}$ drawn from $N(0, s_u^2)$				
Coefficients	0.410	0.453	0.292	0.301
Standard dev.	0.021	0.014	0.024	0.014
Lower 2.5%	0.372	0.423	0.243	0.274
Upper 2.5%	0.455	0.477	0.339	0.330

Note: The coefficients in parts C and D are the mean values across 5000 bootstrap samples (in each of which the optimal coefficient α_g is zero).

credibility γ are both distinctly less than one, and also the responsiveness α_y to output does not appear overly strong.

To assess the goodness of fit it has to be taken into account that quarterly inflation is a rather jagged time series. Average deviations as they are given by $RMSD = 0.272\%$ can thus be judged to be very small. This is clearly confirmed by Figure 11.2, which contrast the model's predictions with the actual data. There are in fact only a few short intervals where the two series can be told apart.

The fit demonstrated in Figure 11.2 may even appear to be too good. That is, it could be suspected that the exact tracking of the many spikes in the inflation series is primarily accomplished by the estimated residuals that have been added in the Phillips curve equation, which says that the merits of the AIC modeling itself would be rather limited. To check these doubts we discard the model equations for a moment and suppose that inflation is solely given by the estimated residuals, i.e. $\pi_t = \hat{u}_{\pi,t}$ for all t. Measuring the deviations of this series from actual inflation, RMSD = 0.968 results; see row B in Table 11.1. Hence the improvement in the fit by the structural model and suitable numerical parameters, as it is documented in row A of Table 11.1, is sizeable.[11] We consider this finding to be a sound justification for the inflation module.

Numerical coefficients from a bootstrap procedure

It has been made clear enough that our procedure to obtain numerical values for the model's structural parameters is a combination of estimation and calibration. Because of the iterated model simulations in the search for the RMSD minimizing

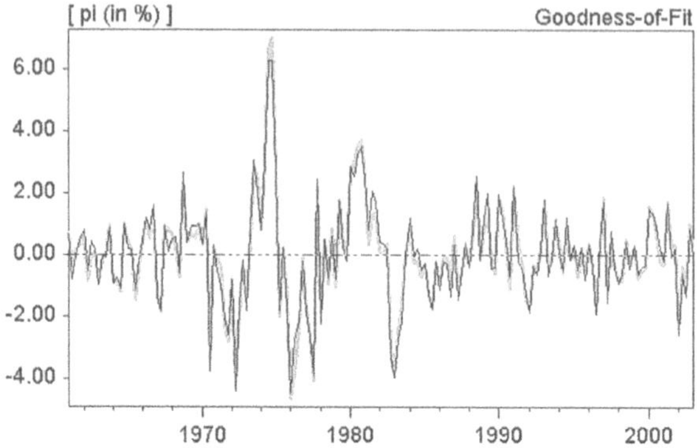

Figure 11.2 Actual (detrended) inflation (grey line) and model-generated inflation (solid line).[10]

coefficients it is, however, appropriate to emphasize the calibration element. For lack of a better expression, the optimal coefficients may nevertheless be called the "estimates" for the model.[12]

Such as estimates in econometric applications are susceptible to randomness and there exist methods to assess the reliability of the coefficients obtained from a specific sample, it is now time to ask how much we can trust our estimate, i.e. in the coefficients given in row A of Table 11.1. To shape this discussion, we proceed as if (11.16) were an accurate reduced-form representation of the dynamic process generating inflation. Although the AIC module is meant to be a succinct theoretical description of the output–inflation nexus or, what in this context amounts to the same, of the deterministic part of (11.16), the concrete coefficients minimizing RMSD will to some degree still depend on the specific random forces that were at work in the sample period. If we imagine that the same deterministic output–inflation nexus (over another period or in a different country, say) had been affected by different exogenous forces, the estimates of α_c, γ, α_y, α_g would have somewhat departed from the present result.

In order to interpret our estimates in this perspective, we generate artificial data. We want to know, at least approximately, how the estimates are distributed if assumption (11.17) is dropped and, instead of the estimated residuals $\hat{u}_{\pi,t}$ from (11.16), the Phillips curve is subjected to alternative sequences of shocks $\varepsilon_{\pi,t}$. To this end we have to make an assumption about the probability distribution of these shocks, which will certainly be based on the properties of the estimated residuals. It is helpful that the latter show no sign of serial correlation or heteroskedasticity, so the shocks can be safely assumed to be independent and identically distributed.

An immediate hypothesis, then, is to draw the shocks from a normal distribution whose standard deviation is given by the standard error of the regression. However, the residuals in (11.16) are not very likely to be normally distributed; depending on the test statistic the estimated residuals exhibit p-values of 0.033 and 0.023.

When admitting nonnormal shocks we can make use of the fact that the empirical distribution function of the error terms in (11.16) is a consistent estimator of the unknown error distribution. This allows us to draw the error terms from the empirical distribution of the residuals (Davidson and MacKinnon 2004, p. 161): at each t the shock $\varepsilon_{\pi,t}$ is assigned the value of one of the estimated residuals, with equal probability. It is understood that a residual that has been pulled out of the "hat" into which metaphorically speaking all residuals are thrown is subsequently replaced. With U indicating the uniform distribution and the time index t ranging from 1961:1, which is identified with $t = 1$, to 2003:1, which is identified with $t = T = 169$, this probability distribution of the shocks can be briefly denoted by

$$\varepsilon_{\pi,t} \sim U[\hat{u}_{\pi,1}, \hat{u}_{\pi,2}, \ldots, \hat{u}_{\pi,T}], \quad t = 1, \ldots, T.$$

However, one subtlety has still to be taken into account. While this distribution has variance $(1/T)\sum_t \hat{u}^2_{\pi,t}$, the unbiased estimate of the variance of the error terms in (11.16) with its eight regressors is $[1/(T-8)]\sum_t \hat{u}^2_{\pi,t}$. To correct for the downward bias the distribution of the $\varepsilon_{\pi,t}$ should therefore be rescaled (Davidson and MacKinnon 2004, p. 163). Accordingly, we assume that the shocks to the Phillips curve are distributed as

$$\varepsilon_{\pi,t} \sim \left[\frac{T}{T-8}\right]^{1/2} U[\hat{u}_{\pi,1}, \hat{u}_{\pi,2}, \ldots, \hat{u}_{\pi,T}], \quad t = 1, \ldots, T = 169. \tag{11.18}$$

The kind of resampling here described is called bootstrapping, though in econometrics these errors are usually directly plugged in a regression equation (Davidson and MacKinnon 2004, p. 159ff.). A set $\varepsilon_{\pi,t}$ for $t = 1, \ldots, T$ obtained from (11.18) is correspondingly called a bootstrap sample.

If system (11.13)–(11.15) is combined with a sequence of random shocks from (11.18), then also the inflation series to which the model is to be fitted has to be modified. It can no longer be actual inflation that serves this purpose, but from the pivotal role stated for the deterministic part of (11.16) it follows that the estimated residuals in this equation have to be replaced with the same shocks. That is, given a bootstrap sample $b = \{e_{\pi,t}\}_{t=1}^{T}$ and the estimated coefficients $\hat{a}_{\pi k}$ and $\hat{a}_{yk}$ from (11.16), the inflation series to be fitted has to be simulated as

$$\pi^\star_t = \sum_{k=1}^{4} \hat{a}_{\pi k}\pi^\star_{t-k} + \sum_{k=1}^{4} \hat{a}_{yk} y^{\text{emp}}_{t-k} + \varepsilon_{\pi,t}, \quad t = 1, \ldots, T, \tag{11.19}$$

where for $t = -3, \ldots, 0$ the inflation rates are initialized with their historical values. Of course, different bootstrap samples b give rise to different reference series $\pi^\star_t = \pi^\star_{t,b}$. Denoting likewise by $\pi_{t,b}$ the inflation series that is generated by the model (11.13)–(11.15) and (11.18) on the basis of a bootstrap sample b, then (still maintaining the Phillips curve slope $\beta_y = 0.14$) for each such sample b numerical values for α_c, γ, α_y and α_g have to be found that minimize RMSD$(\pi_{t,b}, \pi^\star_{t,b})$.

In this way we draw 5000 bootstrap samples, which proves to be more than sufficient, simulate the model and compute the corresponding RMSD minimizing coefficients. Row C in Table 11.1 reports the mean values of the optimal AIC coefficients (α_g always turns out to be zero) and the RMSD they bring about. Concerning the goodness of fit, it is on average somewhat worse than when the estimated residuals are underlying, though in a time-series diagram one would hardly be able to see any difference with the naked eye. It is also seen in the table that the average adjustment speed α_c and the average output responsiveness α_y are practically the same as in row A, whereas the credibility coefficient γ is considerably higher. In this respect, the order at which the $\hat{u}_{\pi,t}$ have arrived in time seems to give rise to a special case.

The entire distributions of the 5000 optimal coefficients and the corresponding minimal RMDSs, which are shown in Figure 11.3, are indicative of their relevant range. At first sight these magnitudes appear to be nearly normally distributed, as the thin lines of the density of the normal distribution suggest. The eye, however, tends to underestimate the discrepancies between the two distributions. Taking the large number of observations into account, the normality hypothesis is mainly rejected by the test statistics.[13] For this reason Table 11.1 reports not only the standard deviations but also the 2.5% and 97.5% quantiles. To avoid confusion, the expression "confidence interval" should perhaps be better avoided, so we say that the bootstrap experiments provide us, for each of the structural coefficients, with an interval of numerical values that can be regarded as feasible. According to this criterion, the credibility coefficient γ obtained from the estimated residuals in row A of the table, which falls outside this range, is not fully trustworthy. At the present stage of the discussion one may prefer to decide in favour of a higher value.[14]

Checking the results with normally distributed shocks

We proceed in this subsection with another bootstrap procedure, which readily allows us to examine the sensitivity of the optimal AIC coefficients to a change in the probability distribution of the inflation shocks $\varepsilon_{\pi,t}$. We maintain the variance of the estimated residuals from (11.16) for them and confine ourselves to the most obvious benchmark of an alternative distribution, which is the normal distribution. (Recall that the estimated residuals are unlikely to be normally distributed.) Accordingly, we substitute

$$\varepsilon_{\pi,t} \sim N(0, \sigma^2), \quad \sigma = \text{SER}(15) = 1.36, \tag{11.20}$$

for the empirical distribution in (11.18) (SER(11.16) = 1.36 is the rounded standard error of regression (11.16)). Everything else is the same as in the bootstrap experiment in the previous subsection. The results are documented in part D of Table 11.1. It is immediately seen that for all practical purposes they are virtually identically with part C of the table, where the empirical distribution of the estimated residuals was underlying for the shocks to the model's Phillips curve.

This finding gives additional support to the evaluation at the end of Section 4.4, that the particular lag specification in the a theoretical equation (11.16) to identify the shocks $\varepsilon_{\pi,t}$ is not a very serious issue. Given that, as mentioned there, the deterministic part of (11.16) is only marginally affected by different lag lengths like six or eight quarters, another choice of the lags would have led to very similar results, at least in the stochastic framework where apparently the (nonnormal) empirical distribution could well be replaced by an ordinary normal distribution function with the same variance. From a slightly different point of view, the robustness of the numerical features of our inflation module is also confirmed by the sensitivity analysis in Section 11.5.

11.5 A sensitivity analysis

Variations of the slope coefficient in the Phillips curve

The discussion so far has been concerned with finding suitable numerical values for the AIC parameters, while the slope of the Phillips curve was exogenously given, $\beta_y = 0.14$. This supposition is now dropped and we examine how the

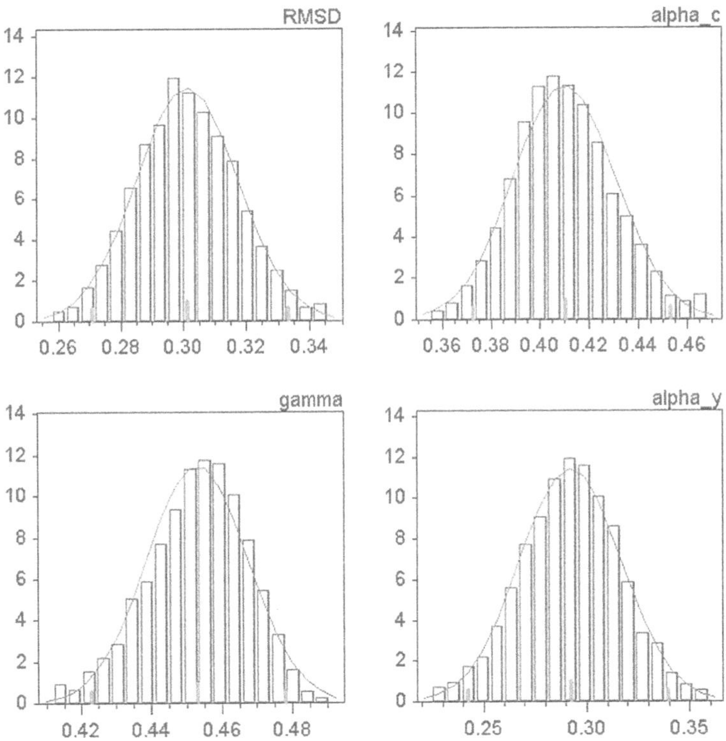

Figure 11.3 Frequency distributions of the AIC coefficients from the bootstrap experiments.[15]

previous results are affected by this greater flexibility. However, rather than add β_y to the set of coefficients that minimize the RMSD of model (11.13)–(11.15), it proves more useful to continue to treat β_y as a given coefficient. Its value is thus systematically varied over a relevant range, and for each such value again the optimal AIC coefficients α_c, γ, α_y and α_g are computed.

To this end, we begin directly with the bootstrap procedure that selects the inflation shocks from the estimated residuals, i.e. the $\varepsilon_{\pi,t}$ are distributed according to (11.18) and on the whole 5000 random sequences of these shocks are drawn for each β_y to simulate inflation. The results for a few chosen values of β_y between 0 and 0.20 are collected in Table 11.2. They contain already all the information we need.

The second column of Table 11.2 shows that the fit of the model can be improved by reducing the value of the slope β_y. The table ends at $\beta_y = 0$, but negative values would on average lead to a further reduction in RMSD. Nevertheless, the feasibility intervals (the range between the lower and upper 2.5% quantiles of the bootstrap samples) have a similar extension as in Table 11.1 and so still overlap, although the average RMSD is systematically declining with β_y. More importantly, if a model-generated inflation series is contrasted with its reference series $\pi_t^\star$ from (11.19), one would not be able to recognize these improvements on an RMSD like that in Figure 11.2, which already showed a nearly perfect fit. We therefore conclude that, with respect to fitting, any one of the first five rows in Table 11.2 would be practically as good as any other.

The virtually equally close fits reported in the table can be better understood by comparing the a theoretical regression equation (11.16) with the model's expression (11.11) for the rate of inflation, where lagged inflation and output are substituted for the inflation climate π_t^c in the structural Phillips curve (11.8). As documented in the last row of Table 11.2, in the estimation of (11.16) the four coefficients a_{yk} on y_{t-k}^{emp} $(k = 1, \ldots, 4)$ sum up to 0.298. On the other hand, the optimal AIC coefficients α_c, γ, α_y vary in such a way with the changes in β_y that the sum of the first four coefficients on the lagged output gaps in (11.11),

Table 11.2 RMSD minimizing coefficients under variations of β_y

β_y	*RMSD*	α_c	γ	α_y	$\sum_{k=1}^{4} \tilde{a}_{yk}$
0.20	0.341	0.402	0.439	0.170	0.283
0.14	0.301	**0.410**	**0.453**	**0.292**	0.280
0.10	0.279	0.420	0.462	0.373	0.278
0.05	0.257	0.436	0.473	0.474	0.275
0.00	0.240	0.454	0.482	0.576	0.272
(11.16)	—	—	(0.511)	—	0.298

Note: Entries 2–5 of each of the upper rows are the averages of 5000 bootstrap samples employing (11.18) for the shocks $\varepsilon_{\pi,t}$ (again, the optimal α_g is always zero). With respect to (11.16) in the last row, $\tilde{a}_{yk}$ indicates the estimated output coefficients of this regression; for the remainder of the table, they stand for the first four output coefficients in (11.11), $\sum_k \tilde{a}_{yk} = \beta_y + \alpha_c(1-\gamma)a_y \sum_{k=0}^{3}(1-\alpha_c)^k$. The number 0.511 in the last row equals one minus the sum of the estimated $a_{\pi k}$ in (11.16).

which equals $\beta_y + \alpha_c(1-\gamma)a_y \sum_{k=0}^{3}(1-\alpha_c)^k$, remains almost invariant; and with values between 0.272 and 0.280 or 0.283 is fairly close to the sum of the four estimated output coefficients in (11.16).

It may also be noted that the inflation persistence $\sum_{k=1}^{4} \hat{a}_{\pi k}$ in (11.16), which was estimated as 0.489, is not very different from the inflation persistence implied by (11.11). Table 11.2 mentions this in terms of its complement, the credibility coefficient γ, which by (11.12) is 1 – persistence. In fact, decreasing β_y below zero would further increase the optimal γ toward $1 - 0.489 = 0.511$.

Since regarding fitting we are essentially free to choose any of the numerical parameter sets in Table 11.2, additional criteria can be invoked for a suitable choice. For example, as indicated in Section 4.2, we may wish to relate our inflation module and its dynamic properties, when it is integrated in a broader modeling framework, to the accelerationist Phillips curves from the literature, whose estimates of the slope have a typical order of magnitude of 0.14; whereas in the context of another discussion, somewhat higher or lower values of β_y may be preferred.

Even the case $\beta_y = 0$ bears some attention. This value is, of course, meaningless if we think of the theoretical background sketched in Section 11.3 where, as made explicit in (11.6), β_y is given by the composed term $\beta_y = (1-\theta)^2\eta(1+\xi_1)/\theta$ and η, ξ_1 and θ are positive structural parameters (and $\theta < 1$). However, an alternative (and perhaps simpler) story might be told to introduce the special case of (11.14), $\pi_t = \pi_t^c + \varepsilon_{\pi,t}$. Using (11.13) and this relationship for $t-1$, the equation for the rate of inflation can be reformulated as a generalized accelerationist Phillips curve,

$$\begin{aligned} \pi_t &= \pi_{t-1} - \alpha_c\gamma(\pi_{t-1} - \pi^\star) + \alpha_c(1-\gamma)a_y y_{t-1} + \varepsilon_{\pi,t} - (1-\alpha_c)\varepsilon_{\pi,t-1} \\ &= \pi_{t-1} - 0.22(\pi_{t-1} - \pi^\star) + 0.14 y_{t-1} + \varepsilon_{\pi,t} - 0.55\varepsilon_{\pi,t-1}. \end{aligned} \quad (11.21)$$

As it is written, the equation also emphasizes the mean-reverting nature of this generalization, whose strength is measured by the parameter γ. Apart perhaps from the moving average of the perturbations ε_π, the equation as such does not look unattractive.[16] It is furthermore quite remarkable that the coefficient on the output gap again turns out to be 0.14, which could underline the workability of this particular specification.

Variations of the AIC coefficients

Since from the fitting criterion no strong preference for a particular value of the slope β_y in the Phillips curve can be derived, in the remainder of this chapter we fix it again at the original $\beta_y = 0.14$. As an average across our set of 5000 bootstrap samples of inflation shocks $\varepsilon_{\pi,t}$ drawn from the empirical distribution (11.18), the optimal numerical values for the triple α_c, γ, α_y are then given by the bold-face figures in Table 11.2 (besides $\alpha_g = 0$). To put them in perspective, we now ask for the sensitivity of the average RMSD if the AIC coefficients moderately depart from these values.

Given the dispersion of the minimal RMSD values within the bootstrap samples, which was reported in Table 11.1, a fit that increases its RMSD from the (on average) minimal 0.301 to 0.330, say, would not be deemed too severe a deterioration. We can also once again refer to the time-series plots of the model-generated π_t vs. $\pi_t^\star$ as in Figure 11.2, where still no great changes would be visible. Hence we want to get an idea of the range over which the AIC coefficients deteriorate the fit of π_t to $\pi_t^\star$ by, on average, no more than 10%. These combinations could be judged as being not essentially worse than the optimal coefficients.

The problem is easier to treat if only two parameters are simultaneously considered. We set the output coefficient α_y at its optimal value $\alpha_y = 0.292$ (and of course α_g at zero) and let α_c and γ vary almost symmetrically around their optimal values 0.410 and 0.453, respectively. Precisely, a grid with $0.250 \le \alpha_c \le 0.550$ and $0.350 \le \gamma \le 0.550$ in width and a resolution 101×101 is considered. For each pair (α_c, γ) on the grid the same 500 bootstrap samples of shocks $\varepsilon_{\pi,t}$ from (11.18) are drawn, the model trajectories of the inflation rate π_t and the corresponding reference series $\pi_t^\star$ from (11.19) are simulated, and lastly their RMSD$(\pi_t, \pi_t^\star)$ are computed.[17]

The 1%, 5% and 10% contour lines in the (α_c, γ) plane resulting from this experiment are shown in Figure 11.4. Regarding their shape it is interesting to note that, though the lines appear to be fairly elliptic, they are not symmetrical around the optimal pair of (α_c, γ) from Table 11.1, which is marked by the cross in the middle. The contours have a somewhat wider extension to the south-west than to the north-east, a phenomenon that illustrates the (mildly) nonlinear features of the fitting problem.

The regions enclosed by the contour lines are in fact relatively large. We are accordingly not very heavily dependent on the exact optimal values of the coefficients. In other words, our theoretical approximation to the true inflation process can be considered to be numerically quite robust to the specification of the a theoretical VAR-like reference model of (11.16), to which the model's parameters are to be fitted.

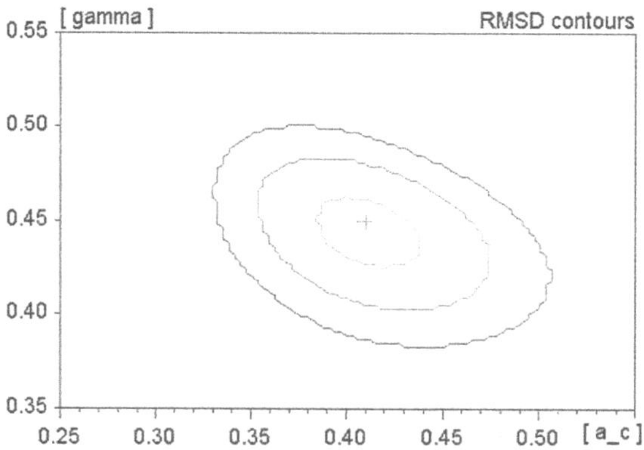

Figure 11.4 RMSD contour lines in the (α_c, γ) plane (at 1%, 5% and 10%).[18]

Just to find the contour lines of the RMSD function, certainly more intelligent and time-saving devices are conceivable than its straightforward evaluation on all points of a grid. A side effect of this procedure, however, is that it allows us to check the properties of this function in finer detail. In particular, we have established that at the cross in Figure 11.4, which indicates the local minimum tracked down by the search algorithm, the RMSD attains its minimal value also over the grid. Beyond the security measures that had already been taken when testing the algorithm, we are thus confirmed that this point is indeed the global solution to the RMSD minimization problem.

Moreover, we find that everywhere on the grid the RMSD function is decreasing in α_c at lower values of the coefficient and increasing at higher values. Likewise, it is decreasing in γ at lower and increasing at higher values of this parameter. This monotonicity property is a more than sufficient condition for a minimum to be globally unique. We can also reasonably expect that this convenient feature or at least its implication is preserved in the experiments that we are going to conduct next, so that these solutions of the search algorithm need no longer be so carefully controlled for their global validity.

Optimal fits with respect to given speeds of adjustment α_c

If for some reason outside the present discussion a higher adjustment speed was preferred over the optimal value $\alpha_c = 0.410$, Figure 11.4 gives an impression of how far we could go to the right if the credibility coefficient γ were to be held constant and we were willing to accept a perhaps 10% loss in the fit. It is also seen that at the same price a higher α_c could be bought if simultaneously γ were to be suitably decreased, and conversely, though in lower magnitudes, if lower values of α_c were to be favored.

To investigate these relationships in greater numerical precision, we change the role of α_c and treat it in this subsection as an exogenous parameter, too. We let it vary over the range from 0.20 to 0.60. Endogenous, in the sense that they are the control variables to bring about the optimal fit, are here only γ, α_y and α_g. For each value of α_c in the given range, the RMSD minimizing values of this triple have to be computed. Figure 11.5 illustrates how they and the fit itself change with the variations of α_c.

The shaded area is again based on 5000 bootstrap samples or error sequences $\varepsilon_{\pi,t}$ drawn from the empirical distribution (11.18); they are the same for each α_c considered. For a given value of α_c, the area contains the interval of optimal values of RMSD, γ, α_y from the inner 95% quantile of their bootstrap frequency distribution (where each such value is optimal with respect to one of the bootstrap sample sequences $\varepsilon_{\pi,t}$). In Section 4.3 these values were characterized as feasible, so analogously to a confidence band, the entire shaded area formed by these intervals may for short be called a feasibility band.

The intervals given by dotted vertical lines where the adjustment speed is fixed at $\alpha_c = 0.410$ are practically identical with the feasibility intervals documented in Table 11.1, part C (although there α_c is not exogenous but also determined as part

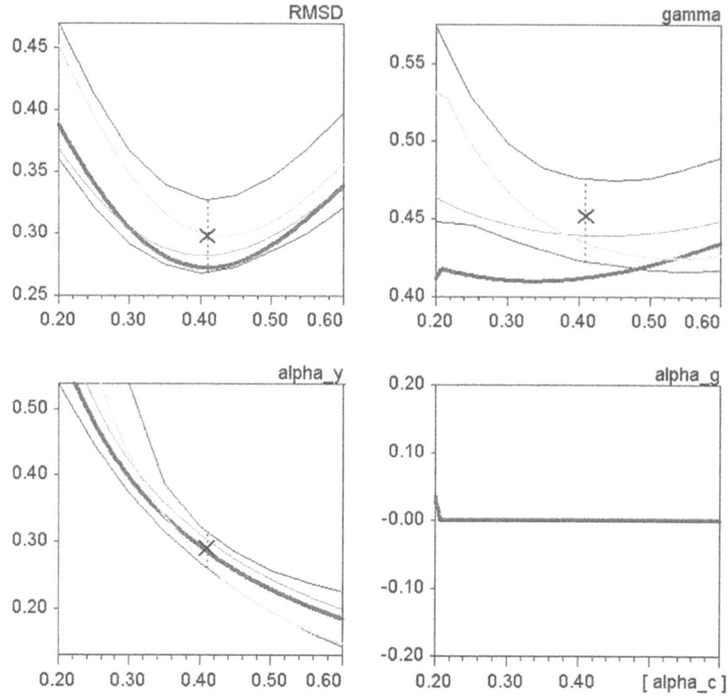

Figure 11.5 RMSD minimization under variations of α_c.[19]

of the optimal solution). The diagonal crosses on the dotted lines are the values in the first row of part C.

The bold line in Figure 11.5 represents the optimal values when, as in Section 4.2, the shocks in the simulations of the inflation rate are given by the estimated residuals, $\varepsilon_{\pi,t} = \hat{u}_{\pi,t}$ from equation (11.17). We already know from Table 11.1 that in this case the RMSD minimizing γ is outside the feasibility interval when α_c is endogenous to the optimization problem, and this equally holds true for the exogenously frozen $\alpha_c = 0.410$. For sufficiently high values of α_c, however, the optimal γ "returns" into the feasibility band. Regarding RMSD and α_y, their optimal values under $\varepsilon_{\pi,t} = \hat{u}_{\pi,t}$ happen to be within the feasibility band over the whole range of α_c.

The two thinner lines in Figure 11.5 represent the optimal values from two selected $\varepsilon_{\pi,t}$ bootstrap samples (the same sequence for each α_c). For RMSD, α_y and now also γ, both of them are fully contained in the feasibility band. On the other hand, it is seen that they do not maintain the ordering of the coefficients; over some range of α_c, one sample yields a higher optimal γ or α_y than the other, and over another range of α_c it yields a lower value. Furthermore, while for both bootstrap samples the optimal α_y decreases as α_c rises, this monotonicity may fail to apply for the optimal value of γ. Contrary to what might have been expected from the contour lines in Figure 11.4, there are bootstrap samples of the shocks that induce the optimal γ to rise rather than to fall in response to an increase in α_c, and γ also rises if α_c is sufficiently diminished; though with other samples monotonicity prevails, as shown by the second thin line in the upper right panel. These phenomena elucidate that systematic, or "nice," relationships between the parameters may only exist for the mean values across a larger number of bootstrap samples.

The inverse relationship between α_c and the optimal values of α_y underlines the significance of the output channel in the adjustments of the inflation climate. Clearly, if the adjustment speed α_c decreases, which *ceteris paribus* would deteriorate the fit, there should be one or several other parameters that can at least partially compensate for this effect. As it turns out, this task is not so much fulfilled by a stronger influence of inflation, via a change in γ (cf. equation (11.13)), but by a stronger role for the output gap, via a rise in α_y.

A last observation is on the coefficient α_g on output changes in AIC. As shown in the bottom right panel of Figure 11.5, it continues to be always zero in the optimal parameter set, except when the adjustment speed becomes as small as $\alpha_c = 0.20$. Near this value the optimal α_g begins to turn positive, which in the panel is exemplified for the case $\varepsilon_{\pi,t} = \hat{u}_{\pi,t}$. The kink in the bold line in the upper right panel shows a slight shift in the roles that α_g and γ play for fitting. It is here also seen that a similar kink may, but need not yet, occur for the single bootstrap samples.

Zero values of α_g are therefore not a universal requirement for a good fit. Noticing this, we learn that the coefficient should not be preliminarily discarded from the modeling equations, because it might gain some relevance again in other, perhaps more elaborate, applications of the AIC concept. For example when additional driving forces are included in the Phillips curve, or when a price Phillips curve is combined with a wage Phillips curve.

11.6 Additional criteria for the numerical coefficients

The implied motions of the inflation climate

Our study has so far been concerned with minimizing the distance between model-generated and actual inflation (or an artificial substitute for actual inflation), whereas the inflation climate has been completely neglected. Although we can be quite content with these fitting results, it should now be asked if also the implied time paths of the inflation climate π_t^c make economic sense. We consider this to be a necessary condition for the validity of our approach, though the judgement itself will be of a more qualitative, or informal, nature.

It has been pointed out above that, while the concept of the adaptive inflation climate has no direct empirical counterpart, its trajectories should exhibit similar patterns as the survey measures of expected inflation. As one such measure to which the model's π_t^c may be compared, let us take the Survey of Professional Forecasters (SPF). More precisely, we choose the mean forecasts of the (annualized) quarterly rate of change of CPI inflation four quarters ahead, from 1981:3 (the quarter when this survey was initiated) until 2001:3. The series is displayed as the bold line in Figure 11.6.

Over the last eight years of the sample period, the SPF series is compared to the inflation rates it has to forecast.[21] This illustrates the much greater smoothness of SPF, which the AIC concept is set out to reproduce (other survey data exhibit a similar smoothness). We add that the inflation rates are even more volatile in the time before; the series is only cut to avoid clutter.

Without invoking any Phillips curve, our adjustment equation (11.13) for the inflation climate can be directly tested by using SPF_t as a proxy for π_t^c and running a regression. Regarding target inflation, the general downward tendency in Figure 11.6 suggests replacing the constant number of the model with a variable (Hodrick–Prescott) trend rate of inflation, π_t^{trend}. Thus the corresponding regression reads

$$\begin{aligned}\text{SPF}_t = (1-\alpha_c)\text{SPF}_{t-1} + \alpha_c[\gamma\pi_t^{\text{trend}} \\ + (1-\gamma)(\pi_{t-1}^{\text{emp}} + \alpha_y y_{t-1}^{\text{emp}} + \alpha_g \Delta y_{t-1}^{\text{emp}})] + \eta_t.\end{aligned} \tag{11.22}$$

Estimating (11.22) by nonlinear least squares over 1982:1–2001:2 (excluding the high inflation rates from $t-1 = 1981{:}3$), the coefficients given in the first row of Table 11.3 are obtained. The standard error of the regression (SER) and the R^2 testify to the good fit to SPF_t, which is made possible by the high degree of smoothness in that series. In the table, α_y is written as zero since it was distinctly insignificant, so to speak. The other three coefficients are significant. While all these coefficients are economically meaningful and so the estimation could be taken as further support for the general concept of AIC, the values themselves are fairly different from the orders of magnitudes encountered in Section 11.4.

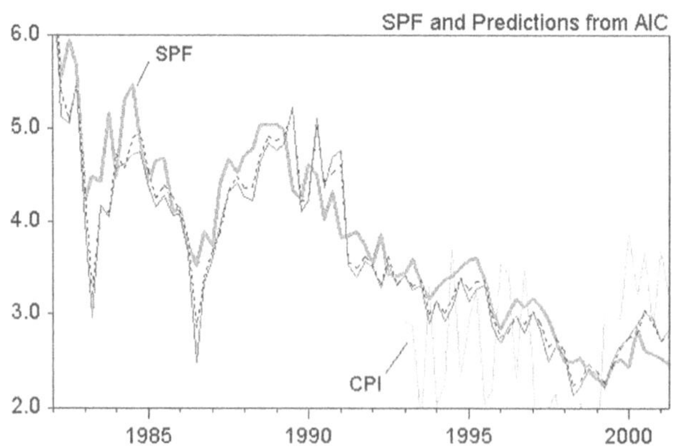

Figure 11.6 Alternative AIC predictions of SPF.[20]

Table 11.3 AIC predictions of SPF from (11.22)

α_c	γ	α_y	α_g	*SER*	R^2
Estimation					
0.211	0.700	0.000	2.917	0.300	0.908
0.410	0.453	0.292	0.000	0.434	0.808
0.300	0.470	0.470	0.000	0.372	0.859

Especially α_g attains a large positive value, whereas before it has (nearly) always vanished.[22]

Nevertheless, let us ask by how much the fit to SPF is aggravated if the calibrated coefficients from Table 11.1 are plugged into equation (11.22). The standard error and the R^2 they give rise to are reported in the second row of Table 11.3. Clearly, the deterioration is substantial and plainly unsatisfactory by the usual econometric standards. However, plotting the predictions from (11.22) (where $\eta_t \equiv 0$) as the thin solid line (over the entire sample period) in Figure 11.6, it is seen where the bad fit comes from. Mainly responsible for it are the two sharp troughs in $t = 1983{:}2$ and $t = 1986{:}3$, which are caused by the inflation rates $\pi_{t-1}^{emp} = 0.27\%$ and $\pi_{t-1}^{emp} = -1.95\%$, respectively. These shocks are completely ignored by the Professional Forecasters (though from the complete SPF data source it can be read that these low rates were already essentially perceived by them). By contrast, our AIC updating module cannot decide to neglect these as outliers, as subsequently they proved to be; their influence is only weakened by the partial adjustments with their speed $\alpha_c = 0.410$.

In the logic of the model, appreciable downward reactions in the two critical quarters cannot only be accepted – we may not even want the model to remain without perceptible response to the observed sudden fall in inflation. In this way the problem becomes a matter of the intensity of the reaction, where it might be felt that the agents in the model should be somewhat more cautious. This idea can be allowed for by choosing a slower adjustment speed of $\alpha_c = 0.30$, say. Maintaining $\alpha_g = 0$, suitable values for γ and α_y can be found by looking at the feasibility bands of Figure 11.5; from their interior we pick $\gamma = 0.47$ and $\alpha_y = 0.47$. The last row in Table 11.3 shows that this alternative indeed improves the fit to SPF_t, even considerably so.

On the other hand, drawing the predictions from these coefficients as the dotted line in Figure 11.6 and comparing them to the previous predictions from $\alpha_c =$ 0.410, etc. (the solid line), the differences between the two time series appear relatively minor to the eye. Which of the two one prefers might be just a matter of taste.

Given the limited framework we are working in, it can be concluded that both predictions are meaningful and can be considered to be satisfactory. That is, the implied motions of the inflation climate variable π_t^c are quite acceptable. From this side there are no serious objections to the AIC inflation module and the numerical results of Section 11.4.

Impulse–response functions

In the investigation of the dynamic implications of the numerical coefficients, we now return to our frame of reference for the output–inflation nexus. This was the a theoretical equation (11.19) for the rate of inflation, which we conceived as one component of an elementary VAR in inflation and the output gap. Having established that the inflation generated by the AIC module comes close to the series produced by this reference equation, it will be expected that the model also exhibits similar dynamic properties in general.

A basic property of a dynamic system is its speed of convergence in the absence of shocks and its reaction patterns to exogenous perturbations. These features are conveniently studied by means of impulse–response functions. Accordingly, we estimate the a theoretical output equation corresponding to the inflation equation (11.19), compute the resulting impulse–response functions of the estimated two-variable VAR in π_t and y_t, and lay the confidence bands of ± 2 standard deviations around them. Then we impose the same initial shocks on our otherwise deterministic modeling equations and compute the thus initialized trajectories. The model and the above calibration pass the convergence speed test if the variables return sufficiently fast to their equilibrium values. The more demanding reaction pattern test is passed if the trajectories also remain within the VAR confidence bands.

In the present context the expression "model" has to include an output equation. Since we have not put forward any theory for these adjustments in this chapter, we resort to the output component of the VAR. Thus, to be exact, the following system is simulated, where $\hat{b}_{\pi k}$ and $\hat{b}_{yk}$ are the estimated VAR coefficients of the output equation

$$\pi_t = \pi_t^c + \beta_y y_{t-1}, \tag{11.23}$$

$$y_t = \sum_{k=1}^{4} \hat{b}_{\pi k}\pi_{t-k} + \sum_{k=1}^{4} \hat{b}_{yk} y_{t-k}, \tag{11.24}$$

$$\pi_t^c = (1-\alpha_c)\pi_{t-1}^c + \alpha_c[\gamma\pi^\star + (1-\gamma)(\pi_{t-1} + \alpha_y y_{t-1} + \alpha_g \Delta y_{t-1})], \tag{11.25}$$

$$\pi_0 = \varepsilon_{\pi,0}, \quad y_0 = \varepsilon_{y,0}. \tag{11.26}$$

Of course, at $t = -1, \ldots, -4$, output, inflation and the inflation climate are still at their equilibrium values $y = 0$ and $\pi = \pi^c = \pi^\star$.

The outcome of this exercise is illustrated in Figure 11.7. The thin solid line are the VARs' estimated impulse–response functions (π_t as deviations from $\pi^\star$), their confidence bands are given by the shaded areas, and the bold lines display the response of system (11.23)–(11.26) to the initial shocks. Regarding the order of the innovations, it is assumed in the VAR estimation that an output innovation in $t = 0$ has no direct impact on the rate of inflation. In the two panels to the left, output is shocked by an almost 1% increase and inflation begins to react only from the next quarter on; $\varepsilon_{y,0} = 0.94$ and $\varepsilon_{\pi,0} = 0$. On the other hand, the initial shock to π in the two panels to the right induces a simultaneous moderate fall in output; $\varepsilon_{\pi,0} = 1.33$ and $\varepsilon_{y,0} = -0.15$.

Of course, the essential information is the response of the rate of inflation to the two shocks. If this variable moves similarly to the VAR response, then by construction the output paths will remain close to each other, too. What we see in the upper two panels for the rate of inflation is that convergence in system (11.23)–(11.26) is as fast as in the VAR (perhaps even a bit faster); this is in contrast to the familiar backward-looking, accelerationist Phillips curves that would in fact imply a much slower convergence. Regarding the pattern of the adjustments, the VAR exhibits a mild overshooting, which is mimicked by our model, though to a weaker extent. As far as the response to the shock in π is concerned, over a transition phase of four or six quarters one should not expect the two inflation series to move too perfectly in line. It has here to be taken into account that in the VAR the inflation rate is influenced by four lags of itself and one of the coefficients is weakly negative (which, by the way, explains the minor kink after four quarters). Thus, convergence in (11.23)–(11.26) is first slower and then faster. Nevertheless, on the whole the dynamics of the model's rate of inflation in the upper two panels can be reckoned to be fairly satisfactory.

In addition to the simulations just discussed, we have also examined the adjustment paths brought about by other parameter sets. Our overall finding is a great

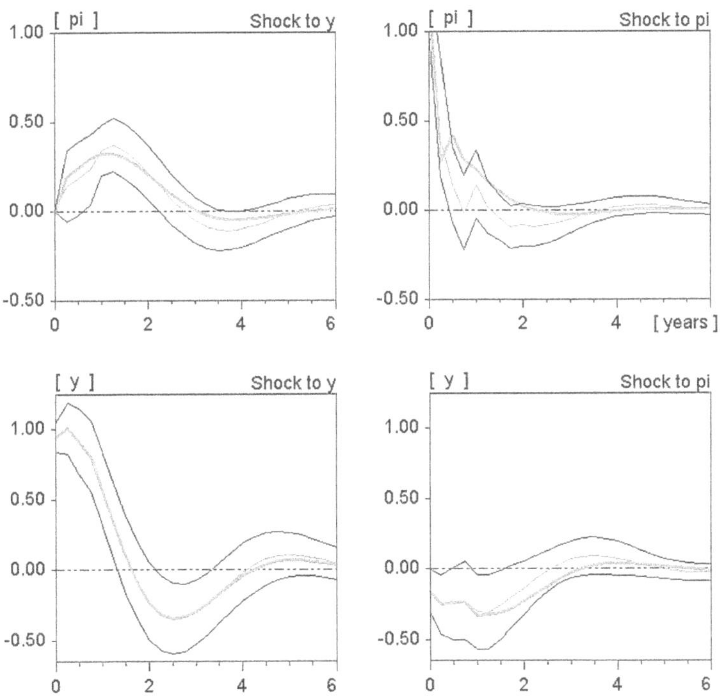

Figure 11.7 Estimated and model-generated impulse–response functions.[23]

robustness. The features shown in Figure 11.7 are preserved over a wide (indeed very wide) range of the parameters; in particular, if the coefficients are chosen from within the feasibility bands of Figure 11.5 when α_c is varied. Likewise, variations of the Phillips curve slope β_y have no notable effects if α_c, γ and α_y adjust to these changes according to Table 11.2. It can therefore be concluded that our model's impulse–response functions exhibit all the features that at the present stage it seems reasonable to require.

11.7 Conclusions

The baseline case of the new Keynesian Phillips curve as well as its hybrid variants with forward-looking expectations have come under severe econometric criticism, the crucial argument being that this approach cannot explain the role played by lagged dependent variables in inflation regressions. It is thus time to consider alternative, backward-looking versions, which, however, should not fall back on simple adaptive expectations as in the traditional interpretation. Abjuring rational expectations and taking heterogeneous expectations of firms seriously, the present chapter deals with a reinterpretation of the expectational variable in the Phillips curve as a general inflation climate, which was proposed in Franke (2005). Rather than refer to inflation in the next period, this concept seeks to summarize in a single number the expectations about suitably discounted inflation over the entire future.

Updating of the climate in response to new information proceeds in a gradual manner. The adjustments are not only oriented toward current inflation but also take the level and change of the output gap into account as well as the central bank's target rate of inflation. These are in our view the basic ingredients of any reasonable expectation formation process about inflation. Our aim has been to model such a process in a sophisticatedly simple way. The four-parameter specification at which we arrived was then called the adaptive inflation climate (AIC).

Numerical values of the parameters were obtained from combining the inflation climate adjustments with the Phillips curve and simulating this model, where the output gap was still treated as an exogenous variable (the actual deviations of GDP from a Hodrick–Prescott trend). In fitting this model to actual inflation, the other exogenous forces were identified by an a theoretical VAR-like estimation. The sequence of shocks to the Phillips curve thus obtained was also used to construct additional bootstrap samples of shocks. This allowed us to compute not only a set of numerical parameters that minimizes the distance between model-generated and actual inflation, but an entire frequency distribution of these parameters. Since the parameter search is based on simulations of a theoretical model, it is essentially a calibration procedure, which, however, is supported by the estimation of an a theoretical reference system.

This approach, the theoretical model and our method of combining calibration and estimation elements, proved workable in that the reference series could be closely approximated, and that the corresponding parameter values were all in an economically meaningful range. A sensitivity analysis showed that the good fitting properties are robust to wide variations of the parameters; in particular if they are also suitably coordinated. Nevertheless, if we are to settle down on just one particular set of numerical coefficients, we can offer the benchmark combination in bold type in Table 11.2.

We furthermore checked the dynamic implications of the numerical results. Comparing it to the time series of a survey measure of expected inflation, we ensured that the time path of the model's inflation climate variable, which so far remained in the background, is sufficiently reasonable. In addition, it was confirmed that the impulse–response functions of the model are quite similar to their counterparts from VAR estimation, especially as regards the speed of convergence.

The natural field of application for our inflation module are small models to study monetary policy. While the use of the new Keynesian Phillips curve in these models has an understandable theoretical appeal, its implications may not be innocuous. The fact that here current inflation summarizes the entire sequence of expected future output gaps for the economy is a strong prediction that may well have a bearing on the kind of optimal policy. To quote Rudd and Whelan (2005, p. 20): "given that this prediction is soundly rejected by the data, the use of these models for policy analysis strikes us as questionable at best." Even if one does not fully share this harsh assessment, substituting our alternative model with the numerically specified adaptive inflation climate for the new Keynesian Phillips curve should be worth investigating.

12 A macroeconometric framework for the analysis of monetary policy

12.1 Introduction

Recently, in macroeconomics the quantitative study of monetary policy rules has been undertaken in a variety of frameworks. Such frameworks are, for example, the large-scale macroeconometric models (Fair 1984 and the contributions collected in Taylor 1999), the VAR (Bernanke and Blinder 1992; Sims 2000) and the optimization-based approach (Rotemberg and Woodford 1999; Christiano and Gust 1999). Usually two alternative monetary policy rules have been considered, namely the monetary authority targeting (1) monetary aggregates or (2) the interest rate. The former implies an indirect and the latter a direct inflation targeting. The latter rule originates in Taylor (1993) and has also been called the Taylor rule.[1] As has been shown historically, most central banks of OECD countries switched during the 1980s from the policy of controlling monetary aggregates to targeting inflation rates through controlling short-term interest rates.[2] The second type of monetary policy rule, the Taylor rule, has recently been given much attention and has been evaluated extensively in the context of macroeconometric frameworks (see Taylor 1999).

This chapter[3] employs a small-scale Keynesian integrated macromodel to evaluate the above monetary rules of central banks. Our approach is novel in the sense that we employ a consistently formulated and complete Keynesian macroeconometric framework to study monetary policy issues. The Keynesian model presented and estimated here exhibits along the lines of Flaschel *et al.* (1997) asset market clearing, disequilibrium in product and labor market, sluggish price and quantity adjustments, two Phillips curves for the wage and price dynamics and expectations formulation which represents a combination of adaptive and forward-looking behavior. Moreover, as in Chiarella and Flaschel (2000a), the current chapter also includes real growth, inflationary dynamics and inventory adjustment. As to the historical tradition, on the demand side it is Keynesian, it makes use of Kaldor's distribution theory, uses the asset market structure as in Sargent's (1987) Keynesian model, employs Malinvaud's (1980) investment theory, and a Metzler-type inventory adjustment process, and uses an expectations mechanism that is forward- and backward-looking.[4]

The model's dynamic features for the two policy regimes are explored for certain parameter constellations. The general dynamic behavior of our system can be analytically studied locally but the global behavior has to be inferred from numerical simulations. For the model with money supply rule it is indicated that for a certain range of parameter constellations interesting dynamics, for example, persistent cycles, may arise. On the other hand, the Taylor rule appears to add further stabilizing forces to this type of model, since it counteracts the destabilizing Mundell effect of inflationary expectations and thus brings more stability into the macromodel.

In order to match the model with the US macroeconomic time-series data, we estimate key parameters through single equation or subsystem estimations using US quarterly data from 1960:1 to 1995:1. In the estimation of the parameters for the wage–price dynamics and for the inventory dynamics as well as investment and consumption functions expectations variables appear which are not observables. We can, however, transform the equations to be estimated and estimate the adjustment speeds involved in the expectations dynamics. Those estimations are undertaken with two-stage least squares (2SLS). We want to remark that this kind of estimation strategy can also be found in recent literature on macro-estimations for large systems with many parameters. Note that, since we are interested here in developing a model that replicates the empirical effects of policy actions we explore less to what extent our model improves the forecast of particular time-series data but rather whether our model can match some time-series properties of the data. Our econometric method resembles the method that has been used in the calibration literature – see, for example, the work by Rotemberg and Woodford (1999).

In the last step then, for our parameter estimates, we explore the stability properties of our two policy rules and study the question whether the impulse–response functions of our model variants match those of the data. Since both policy rules are defined here as feedback rules we find that they generate less instability than compared with studies that employ only exogenous policy shocks, for example, autoregressive processes for the monetary policy.[5] This means that discretionary monetary policy that is following some feedback rule will be stabilizing. This is a property that many Keynesian models have predicted. Moreover, our model is able to replicate well-known stylized facts obtained, for example, from VAR studies of macroeconomic variables.

The remainder of the chapter is organized as follows. Section 12.2 gives a broad overview on the various feedback structures of the model. Section 12.3 introduces the small-scale integrated monetary macromodel. Section 12.4 studies the steady state and the dynamics of the model, in intensive form. In Section 12.5 we describe our econometric estimation strategy and report results from our estimations. Section 12.6 evaluates our results and Section 12.7 concludes the chapter.

12.2 Adjustment mechanisms and feedback dynamics

As mentioned above, the ideas of disequilibrium models come from a long tradition of Keynes, Kaldor, Metzler, Malinvaud, Tobin and Sargent. Their contributions consist in describing the interaction of markets for goods, labor money and financial assets and they study the possible stabilizing or destabilizing feedback mechanisms at work in market economies. Before we describe the details of each market, the macroeconometric model and its dynamics, we want to give a rough description of the structure of the model and dynamic feedback mechanisms involved.

We consider a closed three-sector economy (households, firms and government), where there exist five distinct markets, for labor, goods, money, bonds and equity (which are perfect substitutes of bonds). In order to summarize our model briefly, we use Table 12.1. In the table real magnitudes are represented and the index d refers to demand and the symbol with no index represents supply. The symbols in the following table denote the following: $L =$ labor, $C =$ consumption, $I =$ investment, $Y =$ income, $M =$ money, $G =$ government expenditure, $\delta K =$ depreciation, $B =$ bonds and $E =$ equity. The table shows the interaction of the sectors and the markets, where the rows represent the sectors and the columns the markets.

This is the basic structure of the closed-economy model considered in this chapter. Concerning the modeling of disequilibria we want to note that firms have desired capacity and desired inventories. Temporary deviation from those benchmarks are caused by unexpected changes in aggregate goods demand. We presume that a distinguishing feature of Keynesian models, in particular in contrast to equilibrium macromodels, is that under- or over-utilized capital as well as under- or over-utilized labor force are important. Except in Malinvaud (1980) this has often been neglected even in the Keynesian tradition. Moreover, our small-scale model is complete in the sense that we consider all the major markets and define the financing conditions and budget restrictions of households, firms and the government. The model gives rise to seven interdependent laws of motion or – via a suitable assumption on wealth effects and tax collection – to a 6D integrated dynamic system.

There are, however, basic macroeconomic feedback mechanisms at work in the dynamics of our model that we need to make more explicit. For the description of those feedback mechanisms we need to refer to both real and nominal magnitudes.[6] Figure 12.1 shows the macroeconomic feedback mechanisms that have been discussed in macroeconomics since the 1930s and which are also inherent in our model. They are composed of the interaction of the Keynes effect, the Mundell effect, the Metzlerian accelerator effect and the so-called Rose effect. Since our model, however, does not model the details of the financial market and

Table 12.1 The structure of a closed three-sector economy

	Labor market	*Goods market*	*Money market*	*Bonds market*	*Equities market*
Households	L	C	M^d	B^d	E^d
Firms	L^d	$Y,\ I+\delta K$	—	—	E
Government	—	G	M	B	—

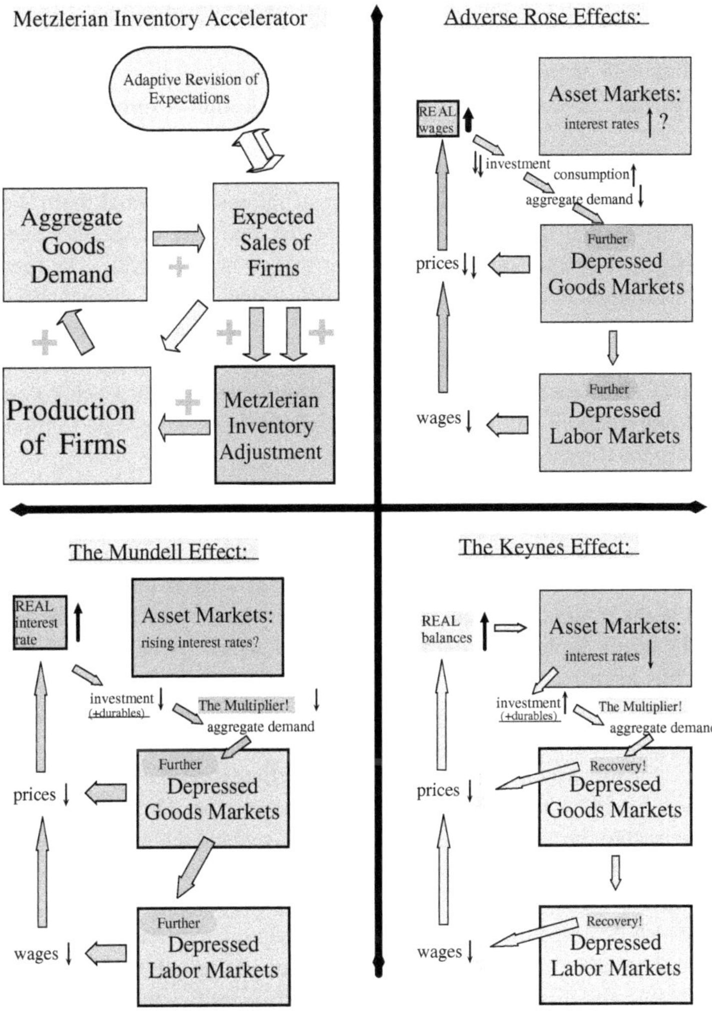

Figure 12.1 The feedback chains of the model.

its interaction with the real side, we neglect here the Fisher debt effects, the Pigou wealth effects, and various types of accelerator mechanisms in the financial–real interaction.

The Keynes effect, Figure 12.1 bottom right, is well known and it basically means that falling wages and prices increase real liquidity which *ceteris paribus* decreases the nominal rate of interest, which in turn increases aggregate demand and the output of firms and employment. This counteracts a further fall in wages and prices and thus helps to stabilize the economy. The same conclusions of course hold for rising wages and prices. This, however, is the sole definitely stabilizing mechanism in the model, since the Metzlerian inventory accelerator mechanism, shown in Figure 12.1 top left, is only stabilizing when inventory adjustments are sluggish and – on this basis – the sales expectations mechanism sufficiently fast (coupled with a propensity to spend that is smaller than one), which in fact then provides but a rigorous form of the well-known dynamic multiplier story.

The partial Mundell effect, bottom left in Figure 12.1, is a real rate of interest effect on the economy (with the nominal rate of interest kept fixed then). Falling wages and prices and thus deflation increase the real rate of interest and thus reduce aggregate demand (investment and consumption in general). The resulting decline in the output and the employment of firms gives further momentum to the ongoing deflation and thus implies a deflationary spiral if no other mechanism – such as the Keynes effect – stops this deflationary tendency. Of course, this destabilizing effect also works in inflationary environments with increasing demand, output and employment and thus increasing inflation where expected inflation is changing into the direction of actual inflation.

Finally, though known for a long time, the Rose (1967) real wage effect is rarely discussed in the literature. It encompasses several possibilities, one of which is shown in Figure 12.1 top right. Assume again that wages and prices are falling, but that prices are falling faster than wages. The real wage is therefore rising and is assumed in the figure to depress investment more than it increases consumption demand. The initial depressed situation on the markets for goods is therefore deepening and thus leads to further declines in prices and wages. This again gives rise to a deflationary spiral if the considered process repeats itself. In the case when consumption demand is increasing more than investment demand is decreasing we get the opposite conclusion and thus improvements on the market for goods and for labor that move the economy out of the depression. This is a normal Rose effect in contrast to the adverse one considered beforehand. Of course when wages are falling faster than prices we get the opposite of what has just been said, and thus a normal Rose effect followed by an adverse one.

It should also be noted that all behavioral and technical relationships in the following model have been chosen to be linear as much as possible. It is not difficult to introduce into the model some well-known nonlinearities that have been used in the literature on real, monetary and inventory dynamics of Keynesian type. We use only unavoidable nonlinearities in the model. Such nonlinearities naturally arise from the growth rate formulation of certain laws of motion, certain unavoidable ratios and the multiplicative interaction of variables. Already on the basis of these most basic types of nonlinearities it can be shown that interesting dynamic properties will arise – without any "bending of curves" often employed to tame the assumed explosive dynamical behavior of the partial submodels. We thus purposely kept the dynamic equations simple in order to preserve the original effects of the macroeconomic feedback mechanisms.

In order to evaluate the strength of the stabilizing or destabilizing effects arising from our aforementioned macroeconomic feedback mechanisms and to evaluate the overall stability of those feedback mechanisms under certain policy actions, we need to model in detail the interaction of the sectors and markets and estimate the parameters involved.

12.3 A monetary macrodynamic model

We formulate a monetary macromodel in discrete time which makes the time structure of the model transparent.[7] We provide a structural form of the model that is theoretically coherent in its use of budget constraints, dating of activities and expectations and that can be investigated from the empirical point of view. The model is presented in terms of modules. Our Keynesian disequilibrium model uses in particular the following variables characterizing income distribution and asset allocation.

1. *Definitions (real remunerations, real wealth and rates of growth):*

$$\omega_t = w_t/p_t, \quad u_t = \omega_t/x_t, \quad \rho_t^e = (Y_t^e - \delta K_{t-1} - \omega_t L_t^d)/K_{t-1}, \tag{12.1}$$

$$W_t = (M_{t-1} + B_{t-1} + p_{et} E_{t-1})/p_t, \quad p_b = 1, \tag{12.2}$$

$$\rho_t^n = (Y_t^{dn} - \delta K_{t-1} - \omega_t L_t^n)/K_{t-1}, \tag{12.3}$$

$$Y_t^{dn} = \bar{U} Y^p/(1 + n\beta_{nd}), \quad Y_t^n = \bar{U} Y^p, \quad L_t^n = Y_t^n/x_t, \tag{12.4}$$

$$\hat{z}_t = \Delta z_t/z_{t-1} = (z_t - z_{t-1})/z_{t-1}, \quad \text{growth rate of variable } z_t. \tag{12.5}$$

The set of definitions in equation (12.1) represent real wages ω_t and the wage share u_t, the expected real rate of return on capital, ρ_t^e, based on sales expectations Y_t^e at $t-1$ for the present point in time t. Equation (12.2) represents current stock of real wealth W_t. Note that stocks that exist at time t are indexed by $t-1$, while their actual reallocation and revaluation happen in t and are thus indexed by t. Current real wealth held by households in t is here composed of money M_{t-1}, fixed price bonds $B_{t-1}(p_b = 1)$ and equities E_{t-1} as in Sargent (1987)[8] and is determined on the basis of the current market prices for equities, p_{et}, and output, p_t. In equation (12.4) current output is produced with the capital stock given at $t-1$ and with labor that is paid in t. Note furthermore that the definition of growth rates $\hat{z}_t$, and of first differences, is indexed forward in order to ease the presentation of the intensive form of the model later on. Note finally that we have added here in equation (12.3) the definition of the normal rate of return on capital, which is based on full capacity operation and which thus only varies with the real wage rate, in order to allow for an investment function that separates profitability effects from changes in actual activity levels.

Describing income distribution and savings along the line of Kaldor (1966) we propose the behavior of households, represented by workers and asset-holders, to be determined by the following set of equations. All behavioral equations are chosen as linear as possible. Only intrinsic "natural" nonlinearities are allowed for at present. Later, extrinsic nonlinearities may be added in a systematic way.

2. *Households (workers and asset-holders):*

$$C_t = (1 - s_w)(\omega_t L_t^d + r_t B_{t-1}^w / p_t - T_t^w) \\ + (1 - s_c)(\rho_t^e K_{t-1} + r_t B_{t-1}^c / p_t - T_t^c), \quad (12.6)$$

$$S_{pt} = s_w(\omega_t L_t^d + r_t B_{t-1}^w / p_t - T_t^w) \\ + s_c(\rho_t^e K_{t-1} + r_t B_{t-1}^c / p_t - T_t^c), \quad (12.7)$$

$$W_t + S_{pt} = (M_t^d + B_t^d + p_{et} E_t^d)/p_t, \quad (12.8)$$

$$\widehat{L}_{t+1} = n_l = \text{const.} \quad (12.9)$$

Aggregate consumption of households, C_t, see equation (12.6), is based on differentiated saving ratios, s_w, s_c, of workers and pure asset-holders. Workers save in the form of bonds and thus have real interest income of amount $r_t B_{t-1}^w / p_t$ in addition to their real wage income $\omega_t L_t^d$. We assume for both types of households that their real taxes, T_t^w, T_t^c, are paid out of their income in a lump sum fashion (see module 4). Equation (12.7) provides the definition of real private savings, S_{pt}, of both workers and pure asset-holders, which is, in equation (12.8), allocated to the actual changes in the stock of money, of bonds and of equities. Equation (12.8) thus states how real wealth and real savings act as budget restriction for aggregate stock demand for real money balances, real bond and real equity holdings of both workers and asset-owners at time t (Walras's law of stocks and flows). The supply of labor, L_t, is inelastic at each moment in time with a rate of growth, $\widehat{L}_{t+1}$, given by n_l, the natural rate of growth.

The production sector and the behavior of firms are described by the following set of equations.

3. *Firms (production, investment and inventory):*

$$Y_t^p = y^p K_{t-1}, \quad y^p = \text{const.}, \quad U_t = Y_t / Y_t^p, \quad (12.10)$$

$$L_t^d = Y_t / x_t, \quad \hat{x}_t = n_x = \text{const.}, \quad V_t = L_t^d / L_t = Y_t / (x_t L_t), \quad (12.11)$$

$$I_t / K_{t-1} = i_1(\rho_t^m - \xi - (r_t^m - \pi_t^m)) + i_2(U_t - \bar{U}) + n, \quad n = n_l + n_x, \quad (12.12)$$

$$S_{ft} = Y_{ft} = Y_t - Y_t^e = \mathcal{I}_t, \quad (12.13)$$

$$Y_t^e \neq Y_t^d = C_t + I_t + \delta K_{t-1} + G_t, \quad (12.14)$$

$$\frac{p_{et} \Delta E_t}{p_t} = I_t + Y_t^e - Y_t^d = I_t + \Delta N_t - \mathcal{I}_t,$$

$$\Delta E_t = E_t - E_{t-1}, \quad \Delta N_t = N_t - N_{t-1}, \quad (12.15)$$

$$\widehat{K}_t = \Delta K_t / K_{t-1} = I_t / K_{t-1}, \quad \Delta K_t = K_t - K_{t-1}. \quad (12.16)$$

According to equations (12.10) and (12.11), firms produce output, Y_t, in the technologically simplest way, via a fixed proportions technology characterized by the given potential output/capital ratio $y^p = Y_t^p / K_{t-1}$ and the ratio x_t between actual output Y_t and employed labor L_t^d which grows in time with the given rate n_x. This simple concept of a fixed proportions technology exhibiting Harrod neutral technical progress allows for a straightforward definition of the rate of utilization of capital, U_t, and labor, V_t. Note that current investment I_t will not have a capacity effect in the current point in time t, i.e. capacity output is restricted by the capital stock K_{t-1}, and that labor is paid ex post, at t, from the proceeds obtained from current sales, Y_t^d.

In equation (12.12) investment per unit of capital, I_t/K_{t-1}, is driven by two forces, the excess of the normal rate of return on capital, ρ_t^m, over the real rate of interest, $r_t^m - \pi_t^m$, and the deviation of actual capacity utilization U_t from the normal or nonaccelerating inflation rate of capacity utilization $\bar{U}$. Note that all these rates are understood as medium-run averages to be explained below. Note also that we have added a constant risk premium to the real rate of interest in comparison to the real rate of return on capital. There is also an unexplained trend term in the investment equation which is set equal to the natural rate of growth, plus the rate of technical progress, for reasons of simplicity – see also Sargent (1987, ch. 5) in this regard.[9]

Savings of firms, equation (12.13), is equal to the excess of output over expected sales (caused by planned inventory changes). We assume in this model that expected sales are the basis of firms' dividend payments (after deduction of capital depreciation, δK_{t-1}, and real wage payments, $\omega_t L_t^d$.) Equation (12.14) shows the excess of expected demand over actual demand. In the present version of the model any such excess demand has to be financed by firms by issuing new equity (or gives rise to windfall profits if this excess is negative). It follows, as expressed in equation (12.15), that the total amount of new equity issued by firms must equal the intended fixed capital investment and unexpected inventory changes, $Y_t^e - Y_t^d = N_t - N_{t-1} - \mathcal{I}_t$; compare our formulation of the inventory adjustment mechanism in module 6. Finally, equation (12.16) states that (fixed business) investment plans of firms are always realized in this Keynesian (demand-oriented) context, by way of corresponding inventory changes.

We now turn to a brief description of fiscal and monetary policy rules where the former are here still chosen in a way that is as simple as possible in the context of a growing economy, since we want to concentrate on the behavior of the private sector of the economy and on monetary policy rules in the following. Tax rates in equation (12.17) and government expenditure are described by simple rules to be used in the intensive form of the model. Government saving is defined in equation (12.19) and the government budget restriction is given by equation (12.22), which however is of no importance for the dynamics of the model due to our neglect of interest income and wealth effects.

4. *Government (fiscal and monetary authorities):*

$$t^w = \frac{T_t^w - r_t B_{t-1}^w / p_t}{K_{t-1}} = \text{const.}, \qquad t^c = \frac{T_t^c - r_t B_{t-1}^c / p_t}{K_{t-1}} = \text{const.}, \qquad (12.17)$$

$$G_t = gK_{t-1}, \quad g = \text{const.} \quad (T_t = T_t^w + T_t^c), \tag{12.18}$$

$$S_{gt} = T_t - r_t B_{t-1}/p_t - G_t = (t^w + t^c - g)K_{t-1}, \tag{12.19}$$

$$\hat{M}_t = \Delta M_t / M_{t-1} = \mu_t, \quad \Delta M_t = M_t - M_{t-1}, \tag{12.20}$$

$$\mu_{t+1} = \mu_t + \beta_{m_1}(\bar{\mu} - \mu_t) + \beta_{m_2}(\bar{\pi} - \hat{p}_{t+1}) + \beta_{m_3}(\bar{U} - U_t), \quad \beta_{m_i} > 0, \tag{12.21}$$

$$\Delta B_t = p_t G_t + r_t B_{t-1} - p_t T_t - \Delta M_t, \quad \Delta B_t = B_t - B_{t-1}. \tag{12.22}$$

The money supply rule has been extended in comparison to earlier presentations of the macromodel in order to be directly comparable to the interest rate policy rule to be described below.[10]

As regards the monetary policy we will explore alternative rules. Module 4 above assumes that the monetary authority, for controlling inflation, targets the supply of money, as represented in equation (12.21). We formulate the money supply rule as a feedback rule. The future growth rate of the money supply, $\mu_{t+1} = \hat{M}_{t+1}$, is assumed to be steered toward a constant target term $\bar{\mu}$, but subject to temporary deviations when currently developing inflation differs from the target level which in turn is subject to further deviations by a term that characterizes the current state of the business cycle. Too high inflation as compared to the target level thus, for example, induces the central bank to moderate its adjustment toward the growth target $\bar{\mu}$ and this the more so the higher the activity in the business cycle. Note that one has to assume as consistency condition for the money supply rule that $\bar{\pi} = \bar{\mu} - n$ holds.

As a modern alternative to this money supply-oriented policy we also investigate the Taylor rule according to which the monetary authority aims at setting the nominal rate of interest in response to deviations of the interest rate from its steady-state value, the deviations of the actual rate of inflation, $\hat{p}_t$, from a target rate of inflation, $\bar{\pi}$, and the deviations of the actual rate of capacity utilization from the target rate of capacity utilization – see equation (12.23) below. We also assume, as in Clarida *et al.* (1998), some interest rate smoothing in the application of the Taylor rule. This alternative rule, often called the central bank's reaction function, thus reads

$$r_{t+1} = r_t - \beta_{r_1}(r_t - r_0) + \beta_{r_2}(\hat{p}_{t+1} - \bar{\pi}) + \beta_{r_3}(U_t - \bar{U}), \quad \beta_{r_i} > 0. \tag{12.23}$$

Note that the rate of inflation employed here is a forward rate of inflation[11] where we, in contrast to our use of expected medium-run averages, disregard errors in expectations formation – see our presentation of the wage–price sector in module 7 of the model. There (forward-looking) myopic perfect foresight interacts with (backward-looking) medium-run expectations of inflation in the mutual interdependence of the wage and price setting process. Note finally that the above Taylor rule assumes that money demand is always realized at the nominal rate of interest set by the monetary authority. In view of the fiscal rules for government and either of the monetary rules for the central bank, the issue of new bonds by the government (net of open market operations by the central bank) is then determined residually via equation (12.22). This states that the resulting money and bond financing must exactly cover the deficit in government expenditure financing. This holds also for the Taylor rule.[12]

We now describe the asset market equilibrium conditions of the model.

5. *Equilibrium conditions (asset markets):*

$$W_t + S_{pt} = (M_t^d + B_t^d + p_{et} E_t^d)/p_t, \tag{12.24}$$

$$M_t = M_t^d = h_1 p_t Y_t + h_2 p_t K_{t-1}(r_0 - r_{t+1}), \tag{12.25}$$

$$\begin{aligned} r_{t+1} &= \frac{p_{t+1} Y_{t+1}^e - \delta p_{t+1} K_t - w_{t+1} L_{t+1}^d}{p_{et} E_t} + \frac{(p_{e,t+1} - p_{et}) E_t}{p_{et} E_t} \\ &= \frac{\rho_{t+1}^e p_{t+1} K_t}{p_{et} E_t} + \hat{p}_{e,t+1}, \end{aligned} \tag{12.26}$$

$$B_t = B_{t-1} + \Delta B_t = B_t^d, \quad E_t = E_{t-1} + \Delta, E_t = E_t^d. \tag{12.27}$$

The source of the stock demands for financial assets is again shown in (12.24) as the aggregate real value of the existing stock at current market prices plus real savings of workers and the asset-owning households. Money demand is specified as a simple linear function of nominal output, $p_t Y_t$, and interest r_{t+1} to be paid on the currently traded bonds in the next period (r_0 is the steady-state rate of interest), but with K_t in place of W_{t+1} as measure of real wealth. This equation determines the rate of interest for the period $[t, t+1]$ on the basis of predetermined values for the other variables of the money demand equation.[13] Note also that money market equilibrium (12.25) does not feed back into the rest of the model in the case of the Taylor monetary policy rule, in which case money supply is always adjusted in order to meet money demand at the nominal rate of interest r_{t+1} set by the central bank. The form (12.25) of the money demand function is chosen in the above way in order to allow for a simple formula for the nominal rate of interest in the intensive form of the model.[14]

Asset markets are assumed to clear at all times. Equation (12.25) describes this assumption for the money market, providing the equation for the current market rate of interest to be used for the payments of interest in the next point in time in the case of the money supply rule (12.21). Bonds and equities are assumed to be perfect substitutes, see equation (12.26), their markets being cleared as the money market is cleared. This equation assumes myopic perfect foresight and equates on this basis the interest rate with the expected rate of return on equities, i.e. the sum of the dividend rate of return and of the actual capital gains per share in the period $[t, t+1]$. Yet, there is no feed back into the rest of the dynamics.

The disequilibrium in the goods market is described by the following set of equations.

6. *Disequilibrium in the goods market (adjustment mechanism):*

$$S_t = S_{pt} + S_{gt} + S_{ft} = p_{et} \Delta E_t / p_t + \mathcal{I}_t = I_t + \Delta N_t, \tag{12.28}$$

$$
\begin{aligned}
Y_t^d &= C_t + G_t + I_t + \delta K_{t-1}, \\
&= (1-s_c)Y_t^e + (s_c - s_w)\omega_t L_t^d + \gamma K_{t-1} \\
&\quad + [i_1(\rho_t^m - \xi - (r_t^m - \pi_t^m)) + i_2(U_t - \bar{U}) + n + \delta]K_{t-1}, \\
&\quad \gamma = -(1-s_w)t^w - (1-s_c)(\delta + t^c) + g, \qquad (12.29)
\end{aligned}
$$

$$N_t^d = \beta_{nd} Y_t^e, \qquad (12.30)$$

$$\mathcal{I}_t = n N_t^d + \beta_n (N_t^d - N_{t-1}), \qquad (12.31)$$

$$Y_t = Y_t^e + \mathcal{I}_t, \qquad (12.32)$$

$$Y_{t+1}^e = Y_t^e + n Y_t^e + \beta_{y^e}(Y_t^d - Y_t^e), \qquad (12.33)$$

$$N_t = N_{t-1} + Y_t - Y_t^d. \qquad (12.34)$$

It is easy to check, by means of the presented budget equations and savings relationships, that the consistency of new money and new bonds flow supply and demand implies the consistency of the flow supply and demand for equity. Equation (12.28) of this disequilibrium block of the model describes on this basis simple identities that can be related with the ex post identity of total savings S_t and total investment I_t^a for a closed economy. It is here added for accounting purposes solely. Equation (12.29) defines aggregate demand, Y_t^d, which is assumed to be never constrained in the present model.

In equation (12.31) desired inventories N_t^d are assumed to be a constant fraction of expected sales, Y_t^e, and intended inventory investment, $\mathcal{I}_t$, is determined on this basis via the adjustment speed β_n multiplied by the current gap between intended and actual inventories $(N_t^d - N_t)$. The latter is augmented by a growth term that integrates in the simplest way the fact that this inventory adjustment rule is operating in a growing economy. Output of firms, Y_t, in equation (12.32) is the sum of expected sales and planned inventory adjustments. Sales expectations are formed in a purely adaptive way, see equation (12.33). Finally, in equation (12.34), actual inventory changes are given by the discrepancy between actual output, Y_t, and actual sales, Y_t^d.

We now turn to the last and most important module of our model, which is the wage–price module. It decomposes the standard across-markets Phillips curve mechanism into two dynamic equations augmented by a law of motion for inflationary expectations formation concerning the medium run.

7. *Wage–price module (adjustment equations):*

$$\widehat{w}_{t+1} = \beta_w(V_t - \bar{V}) + \kappa_w(\hat{p}_{t+1} + n_x) + (1-\kappa_w)(\pi_t + n_x), \qquad (12.35)$$

$$\hat{p}_{t+1} = \beta_p(U_t - \bar{U}) + \kappa_p(\widehat{w}_{t+1} - n_x) + (1-\kappa_p)\pi_t, \qquad (12.36)$$

$$\pi_{t+1} = \pi_t + \beta_\pi(\hat{p}_{t+1} - \pi_t). \qquad (12.37)$$

Our above representation of the wage–price module of the model is based on fairly symmetric assumptions on the causes of wage and price inflation. Wage inflation for $[t, t+1]$, according to equation (12.35), is driven, on the one hand, by a demand-pressure component, given by the deviation of the actual rate of employment, V_t, from the NAIRU rate, $\bar{V}$. On the other hand, it is driven by a cost-push term, measured by a weighted average of the short-run future rate of price inflation, $\hat{p}_{t+1}$ (representing myopic perfect foresight) and an expected rate of inflation, π_t, which we interpret as concerning the medium run, both augmented by the growth rate of labor productivity. Similarly, in equation (12.36), price inflation is driven by the demand-pressure term, $(U_t - \bar{U})$, where $\bar{U}$ is the NAIRU rate of capacity utilization, and a cost-pressure term, represented by the weighted average of the short-run future rate of wage inflation $\widehat{w}_{t+1}$, again allowing for myopic perfect foresight in the short run, to be diminished by the growth rate of labor productivity, and again the rate of inflation π_t expected to hold over the medium run.[15] The rate of inflation π_t, expected to hold over the medium run, is in turn determined by assuming that it follows a weighted average of past inflation rates, leading to an inflationary expectations mechanism as in (12.37).

We stress that we have assumed myopic perfect foresight as far as asset markets and short-run expectations in the wage–price mechanism are concerned. This is unproblematic for the Keynesian structure of the model as long as wage and price adjustment does not solely depend on these short-run measures of cost pressure, but is also paying attention to adaptively formed medium-run or average inflation rate. This is sufficient to introduce inertia into the accelerator terms of the wage–price dynamics regarding upward or downward adjustments of wages and prices. The short-run accelerator coefficients in the wage and price Phillips curves are thus both smaller than one, which reduces the power of the myopic perfect foresight assumption to a rather secondary issue (though rational expectations are in fact assumed in order to put not too much weight on possible short-run errors in inflationary expectations). Yet, as far as sales expectations are concerned, we still rely in this model on a simple adaptive expectations mechanism.

Short-run expectations of price and wage inflation (as said for reasons of simplicity without any error term) thus do not translate themselves one to one and immediately into wage claims or price level changes, but they are here further increased (diminished) if past inflation rates have been higher (lower) and/or if future inflation over the medium run is expected to be higher (lower) compared to what is currently the case. These aspects of our wage–price sector introduce inertia in a new way without violation of the condition that the labor market and the goods market must be balanced at the steady state. Assuming errors in the judgements on currently occurring wage and price inflation would make the model more realistic, but would not alter its dynamics significantly, since the important thing in this module is represented by the fact that the coefficients in front of current price and wage cost pressures are in general less than unity[16] (as was found in empirically oriented studies of the short-run accelerator term in the conventional price Phillips curve). We thus neglect errors in wage–price changes that are currently occurring and thus include into our model a perfectness that is generally considered a problem for conducting Keynesian type aggregate demand analysis, but which indeed is only an assumption of very secondary importance in the demand-driven model of this chapter.

Overall, although there are still some simplified specifications present in our model, for example concerning fiscal policy and the financial markets, we have provided a model that is ready for use. Those incomplete specifications do not prevent us from successfully calibrating the model.

Lastly we want to remark that we have assumed in the investment function (12.12) as expression for the expected rate of inflation the medium-run rate determined in the wage–price module of the model. Therefore we have to use a medium-run time horizon in this investment behavior with respect to nominal interest and real profitability as well, which here for reasons of simplicity are determined as follows:[17]

$$\rho_t^m = \sum_{i=0}^{11} \delta_i^\rho \rho_{t-i}^n, \quad \sum_{i=0}^{11} \delta_i^\rho = 1,$$

$$r_t^m = \sum_{i=0}^{11} \delta_i^r r_{t-i}, \quad \sum_{i=0}^{11} \delta_i^r = 1,$$

$$\pi_t^m = \pi_t \quad \text{(as before).}$$

Here it is also appropriate to relabel the former variable π_t by π_t^m, to clearly show where we use concepts that refer to a medium-run horizon. Note that such an extension introduces further lags into the model that reflect the adjustment of expectations with respect to a medium-run horizon, but we do not expect that they will alter the dynamics of the model significantly.

12.4 The dynamics of the private sector under alternative monetary policy rules

Next, we first study in the context of our Keynesian dynamics a special case of the money supply rule (12.21) of the monetary authority. After that we explore the dynamics of the macromodel in the case where the monetary authority follows the Taylor rule.

In the derivation of the intensive form of the wage–price dynamics, module 7, we solve the two wage–price equations (12.35) and (12.36) for the two unknowns $\widehat{w}_{t+1} - \pi_t - n_x$ and $\hat{p}_{t+1} - \pi_t$, which gives rise to the following explicit expressions for these two variables[18]

$$\widehat{w}_{t+1} - \pi_t - n_x = [\beta_w(V_t - \bar{V}) + \kappa_w\beta_p(U_t - \bar{U})]/[1 - \kappa_w\kappa_p], \tag{12.38}$$

$$\hat{p}_{t+1} - \pi_t = [\kappa_p\beta_w(V_t - \bar{V}) + \beta_p(U_t - \bar{U})]/[1 - \kappa_w\kappa_p]. \tag{12.39}$$

These equations in turn imply for the dynamics of the share of wages $u_t = \omega_t/x_t$ the law of motion

$$\begin{aligned}\hat{u}_{t+1} &= \widehat{w}_{t+1} - \hat{p}_{t+1} - n_x \\ &= [(1 - \kappa_p)\beta_w(V_t - \bar{V}) - (1 - \kappa_w)\beta_p(U_t - \bar{U})]/[1 - \kappa_w\kappa_p].\end{aligned} \tag{12.40}$$

This statement, however, is only true when one neglects second-order terms, for example in the formula that relates the nominal rates of wage and price inflation with the growth rate of the real wage. Such second-order terms are repeatedly neglected in all following calculations of the intensive form of the model. The above law (12.40) provides the first dynamical equation of this intensive form. Note also that the formula for $\hat{p}_{t+1} - \pi_t$ is inserted into the following laws of motion of the intensive form of the model in various places.

Neglecting second-order terms we get from the model of the preceding section the following autonomous 6D dynamic system in the variables, share of wages $u_t = \omega_t / x_t$, labor intensity in efficiency units[19] $l_t = x_t L_t / K_{t-1}$, real balances per unit of capital $m_t = M_t / (p_t K_{t-1})$, inflationary expectations π_t^m, sales expectations per unit of capital $y_t^e = Y_t^e / K_{t-1}$ and inventories per unit of capital $\nu_t = N_{t-1} / K_{t-1}$, which describe the laws of motion of the private sector of our economy:[20]

$$\hat{u}_{t+1} = \kappa[(1-\kappa_p)\beta_w(V_t - \bar{V}) + (\kappa_w - 1)\beta_p(U_t - \bar{U})], \tag{12.41}$$

$$\hat{l}_{t+1} = -i(\cdot) = i_1(\rho_t^m - \xi - (r_t^m - \pi_t^m)) + i_2(U_t - \bar{U}), \tag{12.42}$$

$$\hat{m}_{t+1} = \mu_{t+1} - \pi_t - n - \kappa[\beta_p(U_t - \bar{U}) + \kappa_p \beta_w (V_t - \bar{V})] - i(\cdot), \tag{12.43}$$

$$\pi_{t+1}^m = \pi_t^m + \beta_\pi[\kappa(\beta_p(U_t - \bar{U}) + \kappa_p \beta_w (V_t - \bar{V}))], \tag{12.44}$$

$$y_{t+1}^e = y_t^e + \beta_{y^e}(y_t^d - y_t^e) - i(\cdot) y_t^e, \tag{12.45}$$

$$\nu_{t+1} = \nu_t + y_t - y_t^d - (i(\cdot) + n)\nu_t. \tag{12.46}$$

For output per capital $y_t = Y_t / K_{t-1}$ and aggregate demand per capital $y_t^d = Y_t^d / K_{t-1}$ we have the following expressions:

$$y_t = (1 + n\beta_{n^d}) y_t^e + \beta_n(\beta_{n^d} y_t^e - \nu_t), \tag{12.47}$$

$$\begin{aligned} y_t^d &= (1 - s_w)(u_t y_t - t^w) + (1 - s_c)(\rho_t^e - t^c) + i(\cdot) + n + \delta + g \\ &= (1 - s_c) y_t^e + (s_c - s_w) u_t y_t + i(\cdot) + n + \delta + \gamma, \end{aligned} \tag{12.48}$$

with $\gamma = -(1 - s_w)t^w - (1 - s_c)(\delta + t^c) + g$, assumed to be positive. We make use in addition of the expressions and abbreviations (in the case of a money supply rule)

$$V_t = l_t^d / l_t, \quad U_t = y_t / y^p, \quad l_t^d = x_t L_t^d / K_{t-1} = y_t,$$

$$\rho_t^e = y_t^e - \delta - u_t y_t, \quad r_{t+1} = r_0 + (h_1 y_t - m_t)/h_2,$$

$$\rho_t^n = y_t^{dn} - \delta - u_t y_t^n, \quad y_t^{dn} = \bar{U} y^p / (1 + n\beta_{n^d}), \quad y_t^n = \bar{U} y^p,$$

$$i(\cdot) = i_1(\rho_t^m - \xi - (r_t^m - \pi_t^m)) + i_2(U_t - \bar{U}),$$

$$\mu_{t+1} = \hat{M}_{t+1} = \mu_t + \beta_{m_1}(\bar{\mu} - \mu_t) + \beta_{m_2}(\bar{\pi} - \hat{p}_{t+1}) + \beta_{m_3}(\bar{U} - U_t),$$

$$\rho_t^m = \sum_{i=0}^{11} \delta_i^\rho \rho_{t-i}^n, \quad \sum_{i=0}^{11} \delta_i^\rho = 1, \quad r_t^m = \sum_{i=0}^{11} \delta_i^r r_{t-i}, \quad \sum_{i=0}^{11} \delta_i^r = 1.$$

We next show that the above dynamics have a uniquely determined steady state which is locally asymptotically stable under reasonable assumptions on the parameters of the dynamics and which loses its stability by way of a Hopf bifurcation if certain adjustment speeds become large enough. We assume the standard condition $s_w < s_c$ to hold in the following proposition.

Proposition 12.1 *There is a unique steady-state solution or point of rest of the dynamics (12.40) and (12.41), fulfilling $u_0, l_0, m_0 \neq 0$, which is given by the following expressions:*

$$y_0 = \bar{U} y^p, \quad l_0^d = y_0, \quad l_0 = l_0^d / \bar{V}, \quad y_0^e = y_0^d = \frac{y_0}{1 + n\beta_{n^d}}, \tag{12.49}$$

$$u_0 = \frac{s_c y_0^e - (\gamma + \delta + n)}{(s_c - s_w) y_0}, \quad \rho_0^e = y_0^e - \delta - u_0 y_0, \tag{12.50}$$

$$m_0 = h_1 y_0, \quad \pi_0 = \bar{\pi} = \bar{\mu} - n, \quad r_0 = \rho_0^e + \pi_0 - \xi, \quad \nu_0 = \beta_{n^d} y_0^e. \tag{12.51}$$

We assume that the parameters of the model are such that the steady-state values for u, ρ^e, r are all positive.[21]

Proof: The proof basically rests on the fact that equations (12.41) and (12.43), set equal to zero, imply, combined with equations (12.42) and (12.44), two independent linear equations in the unknowns $V_t - \bar{V}$ and $U_t - \bar{U}$ which therefore are both zero in the steady state. The remaining steady-state conditions are then easily obtained from these two equilibrium situations by setting the remaining right-hand sides of (12.41)–(12.46) equal to zero. □

Proposition 12.2 *(For the continuous-time limit case with $\delta_0^\rho = 1, \delta_0^r = 1.$[22]) Assume that the parameters $\beta_w, \beta_p, \beta_{\pi^m}, \beta_n, h_2$ are all sufficiently small and the parameter β_{y^e} sufficiently large (and $\mu_t = \bar{\mu}$ for reasons of simplicity). Then, the steady state of the dynamics (12.41)–(12.46) is locally asymptotically stable.*

Sluggish wage–price adjustments (including expectations), low interest rate sensitivity of money demand and a small inventory accelerator coupled with a fast multiplier process thus make the system convergent and thus provide a proper starting point for the investigation of its dynamics. A detailed statement and proof of this proposition is provided in Köper (2003) where it is also shown that loss of such stability always comes about by way of Hopf bifurcations and thus in particular in a cyclical fashion. Around the parameter value where the Hopf bifurcation occurs the system loses its local stability in general either by the birth of an attracting limit cycle after the bifurcation point has been passed (the supercritical case) or the death of a repelling limit cycle when the bifurcation point is approached from below (the subcritical case). The occurrence of supercritical Hopf bifurcation, and thus of persistent and attracting limit cycles, is demonstrated numerically for a simpler version of the dynamics in Chiarella and Flaschel (2000a). These results also hold in the case of the Taylor interest rate policy rule, but are more difficult to obtain in the case of an active money supply rule, since this adds another differential equation to the model and makes the dynamical system a seven-dimensional (7D) one.

We now come to a discussion of the feedback mechanisms that are at work in the dynamics (12.41)–(12.46). They are, as discussed in Section 12.2, composed of the interaction of the Keynes effect, the Mundell effect, the Metzlerian accelerator effect and the so-called Rose effect. In order to evaluate those effects on aggregate demand we need estimates of the aggregate goods demand function from a reduced-form representation of consumption and investment demand. The functions, to be estimated in the next section, are

$$\begin{aligned} c+g &= (1-s_c)y_t^e + (s_c - s_w)u_t y_t + \gamma = a_1 y_t^e - a_2 u_t y_t + a_3, \\ i+\delta &= -(i_1 y_0)u_t^m - i_1(r_t^m - \pi_t^m) + i_2 U_t + i_1(y_0^e - \delta - \xi) - i_2\bar{U} + n + \delta, \\ &= -b_1 u_t^m - b_2(r_t^m - \pi_t^m) + b_3 U_t + b_4. \end{aligned}$$

Estimating the parameters a_i and b_j of the above two equations will provide us with just enough equations from which the parameters of the aggregate demand function can be calculated and inference on the above stability problems can be made.

Through the subsequent estimation we will get the partial derivatives of y^d, our aggregate demand function, with respect to sales expectations, the current wage share, the nominal rate of interest and the expected rate of inflation (both medium-run values) and finally the level of inventories per unit of capital. We hereby make use of the relationship

$$y_t = (1 + n\beta_{n^d})y_t^e + \beta_n(\beta_{n^d} y_t^e - \nu_t)$$

between output and sales expectations and inventories. The coefficients of the aggregate demand function are related as follows:[23]

$$\begin{aligned} y_{y^e}^d &= (1-s_c) + (s_c - s_w)u_0(1 + n\beta_{n^d} + \beta_n\beta_{n^d}) \\ &\quad + (i_2/y^p)(1 + n\beta_{n^d} + \beta_n\beta_{n^d}) \approx 0.98, \\ y_u^d &= (s_c - s_w)y_0 \approx 0.53, \quad y_{r^m}^d = -i_1 \approx -0.16, \quad y_{\pi^m}^d = i_1 \approx 0.16. \end{aligned}$$

We thus can guess that the Metzlerian type of quantity adjustment process will be stable, since aggregate demand increases by less than one, following an increase in sales expectations, and leads in turn to an increase in sales expectations that is less than the initial increase. Of course, such a statement is still only an intuitive and partial one and must be based on an investigation of the Jacobian of the dynamics at the steady state in order to be proved. Wage share adjustment by contrast is not stabilizing from such a partial perspective if wages respond more strongly to changes in economic activity than prices, since aggregate demand, and thus sales expectations and output, respond positively to an increase in real wages and the wage share, which due to the dominance of wage flexibility gives rise to further increases in real wages and the wage share. Next, increases in the nominal interest rate, with inflationary expectations being given, decrease aggregate demand, and thus sales expectations and economic activity, which reduces the pressure on the price level and thus on the nominal rate of interest, which thus is a stylizing feedback chain, the Keynes effect in fact. By contrast, increases in inflationary expectations, with the nominal rate of interest now being given, increase aggregate demand, sales expectations and economic activity, and thus give rise to further increases in inflation and expected inflation, an unstable feedback mechanism we discussed under the name of the Mundell effect.

The question arises as to which one of these two effects, both of which work through the real rate of interest channel, will be the dominant one in the presently considered situation. To give a tentative answer to this question we temporarily disregard the use of the medium-run moving average in the investment function and assume as real rate expression in the investment function the short-run version $r_t - \hat{p}_{t+1}$. This gives rise to the formula

$$r_t - \hat{p}_{t+1} = r_0 - \left(\frac{1}{h_2}\right) m_t + \pi_t^m + \left(\frac{h_1 y^p}{h_2} - \kappa[\beta_p + \kappa_p \beta_w]\right) U_t + \text{const.},$$

if we disregard the difference between V_t and U_t as measures of economic activity, as is often done. The stabilizing Keynes effect is thus the dominant one if h_2 is chosen sufficiently small (β_p and β_w given), since an increase in economic activity and the price level will then increase the real rate of interest unambiguously and thus lead to counteracting changes in economic activity. By contrast, sufficiently high adjustment speeds for prices (and wages, h_2 now being given) will imply that increases in economic activity (as measured by U_t) will decrease the real rate of interest and thus lead to further increases in economic activity. In this case the destabilizing Mundell effect is the dominant one, in particular if there are expectations that respond quickly to changes in the inflation rate.

Finally we have an (immediate) negative effect of inventory accumulation on aggregate demand, sales expectations and output, given by

$$y_\nu^d = -(i_2/y^p + (s_c - s_w)u_0)\beta_n,$$

which can be viewed as potentially destabilizing since a decrease in aggregate demand piles up inventories, which decreases goods demand even further. Note here in addition that this process becomes the stronger the higher the speed of adjustment of inventories becomes. Such an increase furthermore can destabilize the output adjustment process considered above in addition since the partial derivative $y_{y^e}^d$ becomes larger than one if the parameter β_n is made sufficiently large.

Yet, for the parameter values of the next section the quantity adjustments are all stabilizing, while the real wage and real interest rate adjustments are destabilizing. In sum this gives rise to local instability for the steady state of our model of monetary growth, here still with a constant rate of growth of the money supply, since the price adjustment processes dominate the quantity adjustment processes. The question thus becomes what changes have to be made to the model in order to make its steady state attracting or – if this is not possible – in order to bound the dynamics to economically meaningful domains when it departs too much from the steady state. Note that decreases in wage flexibility are unambiguously stabilizing since they make the adverse Rose effect less pronounced (or disappear) and since they reduce the destabilizing power of the Mundell effect. By contrast, decreased price flexibility reduces the destabilizing potential of the Mundell effect, but makes the adverse Rose effect a stronger one. While decreasing β_w, h_2 and β_n is thus always good for stability in the considered situation, the same does not hold true for decreases (or increases) in price flexibility β_p.

Quantity adjustment thus appears to be stable, distributional adjustments unstable, and the Mundell effect seems to dominate the Keynes effect at the interest rate sensitivity measured in the next section (where we obtain $h_2 = 2.14$). The longer the time horizon in the excess profitability measure in investment, the stronger this short-run destabilizing mechanism becomes. The question, therefore, arises how active monetary policy – our generalized money supply rule or the Taylor interest rate rule – can bring stability to an economy that appears to be slightly explosive (slightly above the Hopf bifurcation point) in their cyclical dynamics. We only claim here that anti-inflationary policy rules, of both types, can indeed stabilize the dynamics of the private sector and make them convergent. This has been shown by numerical simulations of the theoretical model in Flaschel *et al.* (1998) and will here be considered only from the empirical perspective on the basis of the empirical estimates in the following section.

12.5 Estimation of the model parameters

Next, we turn to the estimation of the structural parameters of the model. These parameters are used to simulate the model and to undertake an impulse–response study.

We first remark that it is technically impossible, and also not necessary, to estimate all the parameters according to the reduced intensive form as expressed in (12.41)–(12.48). The system includes many expected variables which are not observable. Although the equations are all expressed in linear form, the parameters often appear in multiplicative form and hence are nonlinearly related. What facilitates our estimation is the fact that we treat the entire system as being recursive or block recursive. This allows, whenever possible, the parameters to be estimated by a single equation (either in reduced form or in structural form). Only for those parameters that appear in a simultaneous system, such as in the price–wage dynamics, do we use the standard method, for example 2SLS, to estimate the parameters. We shall remark that such an estimation strategy can also be found in

Christiano and Eichenbaum (1992) who use such a strategy for a large system with many structural parameters.

We can divide all the estimated structural parameters into seven subsets. Table 12.2 provides the estimates and the standard errors.

Before we elaborate on how we have estimated these parameters we first remark that in equation (12.36) we have set β_p to zero in our estimation of the price–wage dynamics. The estimated β_p is close to zero and not significant according to the estimation procedure described below.[24] Given this result, we can expect that the standard demand–supply forces in determining prices and wages do not appear to be empirically significant, at least according to US time-series data. The estimations appear to support the markup theory of pricing.

Table 12.2 The estimates of structural parameters (standard errors are given in parentheses)

Set 1	Sales expectation	$\beta_{y^e} = 1.2610$ (0.1067) $\beta_n = 0.0414$(0.0105) $\beta_{n^d} = 0.4691$ (0.0203)
Set 2	Price–wage dynamics	$\beta_w = 0.0958$ (0.0285) $\beta_p = 0$ (0.0000) $\beta_x = 0.4702$ (0.0520) $\beta_\pi = 0.6537$ (0.1753) $\kappa_p = 0.3430$ (0.0843) $\kappa_w = 0.9081$ (0.1387)
Set 3	Consumption function	$\gamma = 0.0829$(0.0145) $s_c = 0.6230$ (0.0654) $s_w = 0.0510$ (0.0258)
Set 4	Investment function	$i_1 = 0.1363$ (0.0509) $\xi = 0.1500$ (0.0069) $i_2 = 0.0340$ (0.0076)
Set 5	Money demand function	$h_1 = 0.1769$ (0.0028) $h_2 = 2.1400$ (0.1771)
Set 6	Reaction functions of monetary authority	$\beta_{r_1} = 0.0463$ (0.0315) $\beta_{r_2} = 0.0781$ (0.0327) $\beta_{r_3} = 0.0184$ (0.0056) $\beta_{m_1} = 0.5524$ (0.0814) $\beta_{m_2} = 0.0499$ (0.0938) $\beta_{m_3} = 0.0481$ (0.0168)
Set 7	Other parameters	$r_0 = 0.0221$(0.0089) $y_p = 0.5091$ (0.0167) $\pi = 0.0074$ (0.0119) $\mu = 0.0154$ (0.0095) $U = 0.8231$ (0.0468) $V = 0.9403$ (0.0164) $\delta = 0.0468$ (0.0034) $n_l = 0.0049$ (0.0029) $n_x = 0.0032$ (0.0081) $n = 0.0081$ (0.0079)

Next we explain how we have obtained those estimates as expressed in Table 12.2. We start from below. The parameters in set (12.7) are those parameters that can be either expressed in terms of an average, or are defined in a single structural equation with a single parameter. This allows us to apply moments estimation by matching the first moments of the model and the related data. The parameters in set (12.6) are estimated by applying OLS directly to (12.21) and (12.23).

To estimate the parameters in set (12.5), we use equation (12.25) divided by $p_t K_{t-1}$. Then we obtain from this

$$r_{t+1} - r_0 = a_1 y_t + a_2 m_t, \tag{12.52}$$

where r_0 is given in set (12.6). The OLS regression on (12.52), gives us the estimated parameters a_1 and a_2. By setting $a_1 = h_1/h_2$ and $a_2 = -1/h_2$, we then obtain the estimated h_1 and h_2. Since the structural parameters h_1 and h_2 appear multiplicatively in a_1 and a_2, we are not able to obtain the standard deviations directly from the OLS regression. We therefore treat these estimates of h_1 and h_2 as being nonlinear least-squares (NLS) estimates and use the method as discussed in Judge *et al.* (1998, pp. 508–510) to derive their standard deviations. We use the Gauss procedure GRADP to calculate the derivative matrix that is necessary to derive the variance–covariance matrix of the estimated parameters. We shall remark that the same principle is also applied to other similar cases whenever parameters appear in multiplicative form or NLS is applied.

The remaining parameters are more complicated to estimate. For their estimations we need, either directly or indirectly, the expectation variables that are not observables. Let us first discuss how we estimate the parameters related to sales expectation, i.e. set (12.1). We estimate this parameter set based on the consideration that actual and predicted y_t can be matched as close as possible via equation (12.47). This gives

$$y_t = b_1 y_t^e + b_2 \upsilon_t. \tag{12.53}$$

Here we should regard the time series y_t^e as being a function of β_{y^e} via the adaptive rule (12.45),[25] given the initial condition y_0^e, which we set here to be y_0. We therefore can construct an objective function $f(\beta_{y^e})$

$$f(\beta_{y^e}) = e_y(\beta_{y^e})' e_y(\beta_{y^e}), \tag{12.54}$$

where $e_y(\beta_{y^e})$ is the error vector of OLS regression on (12.53) at the given β_{y^e} and hence the series y_t^e. Minimizing $f(\beta_{y^e})$ by applying an optimization algorithm, we obtain the estimate of β_{y^e}. Given the estimate of β_{y^e} and hence the series y_t^e the OLS is applied to (12.53). This gives us the estimates of b_1 and b_2. By setting $b_1 = 1 + (n + \beta_n)\beta_{n^d}$ and $b_2 = -\beta_n \beta_{n^d}$ with n given in set (12.7), one then obtains the estimates of β_n and β_{n^d}. Apparently, all these estimates can be regarded as an NLS, and therefore the standard deviation can be derived in a similar way as discussed in Judge *et al.* (1998, pp. 508–510).

Next, we discuss how we estimate parameter set (12.2). Given the time series π_t, the structural parameters β_p, β_w, β_x, κ_p and κ_w can be estimated by the method of 2SLS. The first stage is the OLS regression of the following reduced form (derived from (12.38) and (12.39))

$$\widehat{w}_{t+1} - \pi_t = w_1(V_t - \overline{V}) + w_2(U_t - \bar{U}) + w_3 n_{x,t+1}, \tag{12.55}$$

$$\hat{p}_{t+1} - \pi_t = p_1(V_t - \overline{V}) + p_2(U_t - \bar{U}). \tag{12.56}$$

This will yield instrument variables for $\widehat{w}_{t+1}$ and $\hat{p}_{t+1}$ on the right-hand sides of the following structural equations to which our second stage of OLS regression will be applied

$$\widehat{w}_{t+1} - \pi_t = \beta_w(V_t - \overline{V}) + \kappa_w(\hat{p}_{t+1} - \pi_t) + \beta_x n_{x,t+1}, \tag{12.57}$$

$$\hat{p}_{t+1} - \pi_t = \beta_p(U_t - \bar{U}) + \kappa_p(\widehat{w}_{t+1} - \pi_t - \beta_x n_{x,t+1}). \tag{12.58}$$

However, these estimations are based on the assumption of given time series π_t, whose dynamics is governed by the adaptive rule (12.37). Therefore we shall first, as in the case of y_t^e, estimate β_π to obtain π_t. The difference is now that we have to match both $\widehat{w}_{t+1}$ and $\hat{p}_{t+1}$ and thus a set of weighting coefficients is needed. Since both $\widehat{w}_{t+1}$ and $\hat{p}_{t+1}$ are measured in terms of growth rates, it is reasonable to assume an equal weight in matching $\widehat{w}_{t+1}$ and $\hat{p}_{t+1}$. This consideration allows us to construct the objective function

$$f(\beta_\pi) = \begin{bmatrix} e_w(\beta_\pi)' & e_p(\beta_\pi)' \end{bmatrix} \begin{bmatrix} e_w(\beta_\pi) \\ e_p(\beta_\pi) \end{bmatrix}, \tag{12.59}$$

where e_w and e_p are the error vectors of $\widehat{w}_{t+1}$ and $\hat{p}_{t+1}$ with respect to the 2SLS estimation for (12.55)–(12.56) and (12.57)–(12.58) respectively. An optimization algorithm is then applied to minimize $f(\beta_\pi)$ to obtain the NLS estimate of β_π.

Once β_{y^e} and β_π are estimated we can construct the time series y_t^e and π_t. This not only allows us to estimate the parameters in the equations for sales expectations and the price–wage dynamics but also is necessary to estimate the parameters in the consumption and investment functions. To estimate the consumption function we use an OLS regression for

$$c_t + g_t = c_0 + c_1 y_t^e + c_2 u_t y_t. \tag{12.60}$$

The structural parameters are obtained by setting $c_0 = \gamma$, $c_1 = 1 - s_c$ and $c_2 = s_c - s_w$. The OLS regression equation for the investment function takes the form

$$i_t - (n + \delta) = i_1(\rho_t^m - \xi - (r_t^m - \pi_t^m)) + i_2(U_t - \bar{U}). \tag{12.61}$$

For the above, n, δ and $\bar{U}$ are given in set 7 in Table 12.2; ξ is estimated by the method of moments, i.e. setting the mean of $\rho_t^m - \xi - (r_t^m - \pi_t^m)$ to 0.

Given the parameter estimates of our model, reported in Table 12.2, we can evaluate the performance of our macroeconometric models for the above stated monetary policy rules.

12.6 Evaluating the macroeconometric model and the monetary policy rules

In evaluating our Keynesian macroeconometric framework and the two policy rules we employ our estimated parameters. First, we want to report on how our estimated equations can track the empirical time-series data. Employing our estimated parameters, we report in Figures 12.2 and 12.3 the actual and predicted macroeconomic time series generated from some key behavioral functions. [26] One can observe that most macroeconomic variables are well predicted.

The fit, however, is less successful for investment. It is even less successful for the interest rate derived from the money demand function. This will create a difficulty for the exercise to simulate the impact of the money supply rule, which will be discussed below. However, we shall remark that the parameters that we estimate here for the money demand function are statistically significant. This indicates that the explanatory variables, y_t and m_t, do have some power to explain the interest rate r_{t+1}. Yet, admittedly there may be a better explanation for it (which may take, for example, a nonlinear form). The same argument may also be applied to the investment function.

Yet, whereas the fit for the interest rate derived from the money demand function does not replicate the variation in the interest rate but solely the trend of the interest rate, the estimated investment function at least partially captures the variation in investment. Given that empirical estimates notoriously fail to properly capture money demand and investment functions we still may view our estimates for those two functions as a relative success given our limited aim to study the effects of monetary policy rules in a low-dimensional macroeconometric model.

Next, we undertake some system simulations. The aim of those simulations is, first, to find out whether the actually estimated parameters will allow us to arrive at similar conclusions as predicted in Section 12.4, however only for certain ranges of parameters and partial effects. Here now the interaction of all feedback effects can be explored and monetary policy effects with generalized feedbacks can be studied. Second, we are aiming at comparing our results on monetary policy rules and actions with results obtained from VAR studies.

If we simulate our macroeconometric model with the estimated parameters as reported in Table 12.2 for both policy rules, assuming that either the actual interest rate is determined by the money supply rule or the Taylor rule, we obtain Figures 12.4 and 12.5.

For both policy feedback rules the macroeconomic variables exhibit a slight instability although the instability occurs less for the Taylor rule – compare Figures 12.3 and 12.4. This was also predicted in Section 12.4. When we, however, (strongly) increase the reactions of the money supply rule and the interest rate reaction to the output gap and inflation gap, both rules lead to convergence results (although cyclically fluctuating).

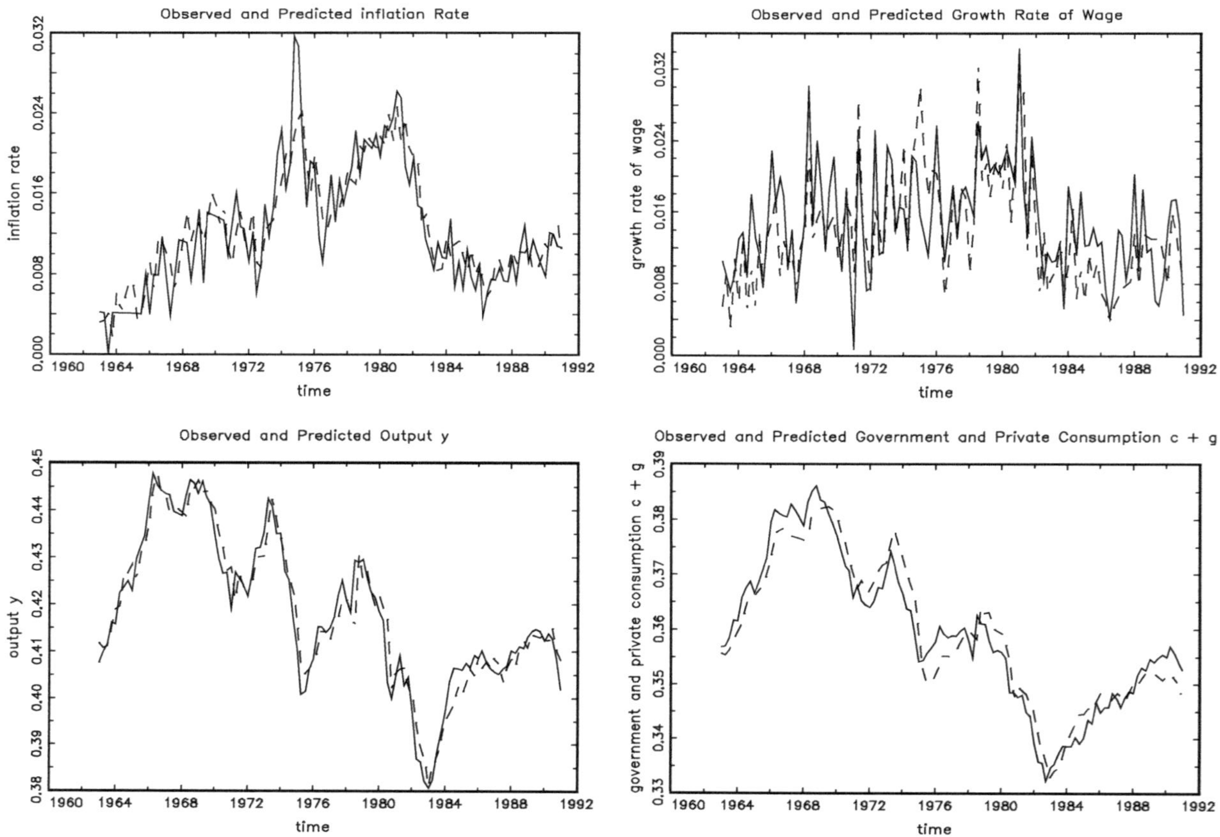

Figure 12.2 Four observed and predicted variables.

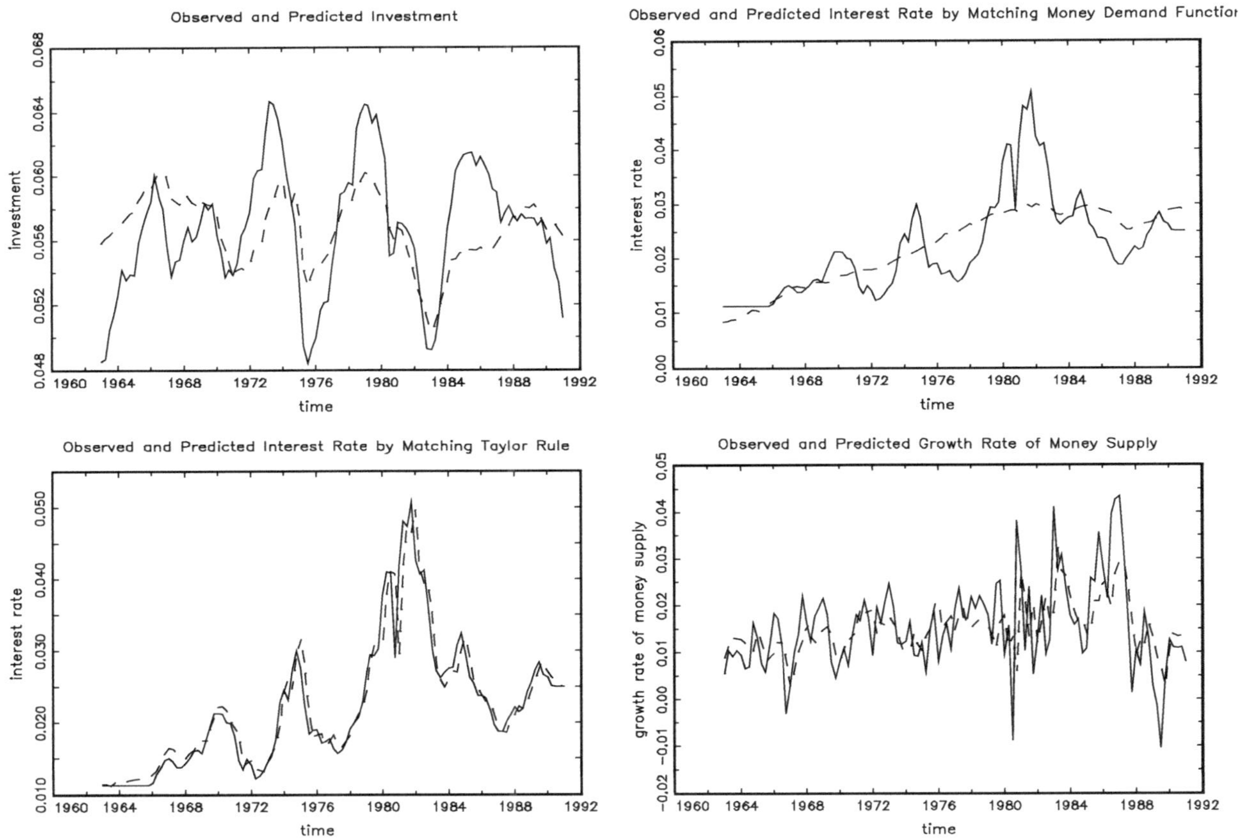

Figure 12.3 Another four observed and predicted variables.

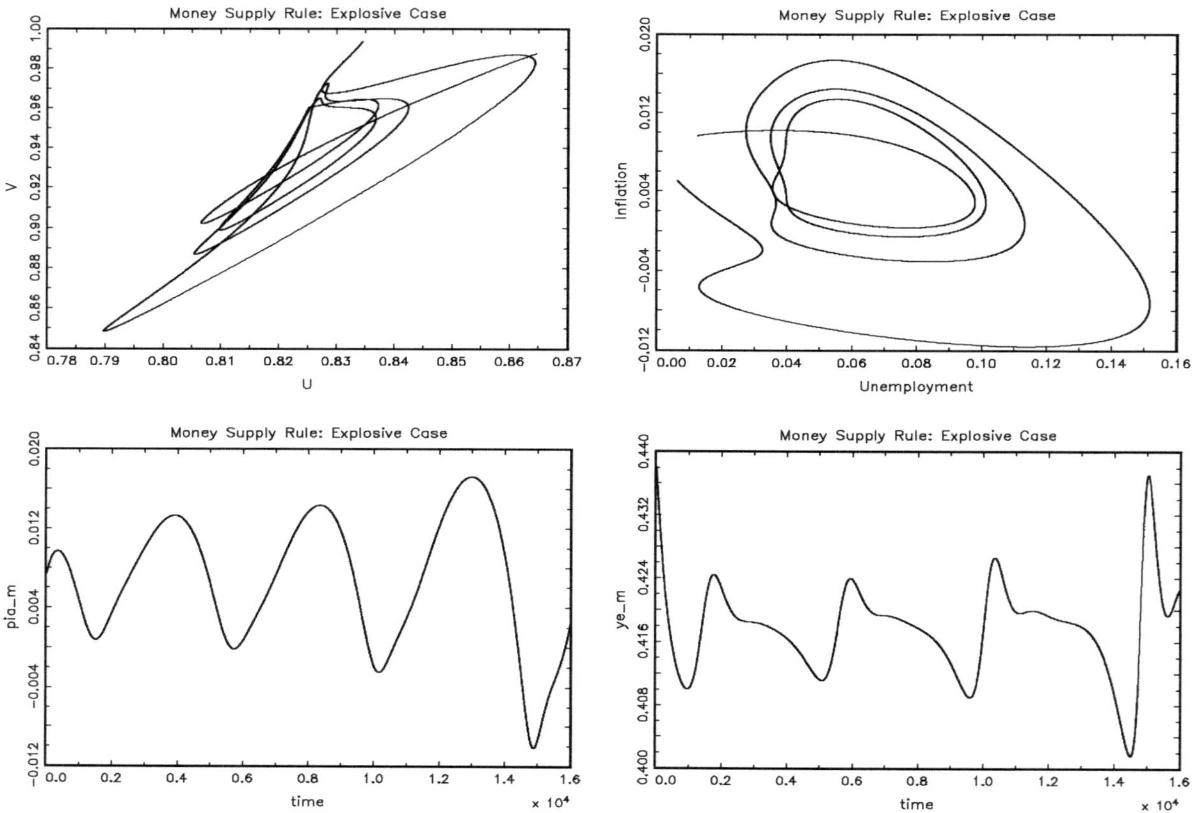

Figure 12.4 Simulation of the model with money supply rule (unstable case).

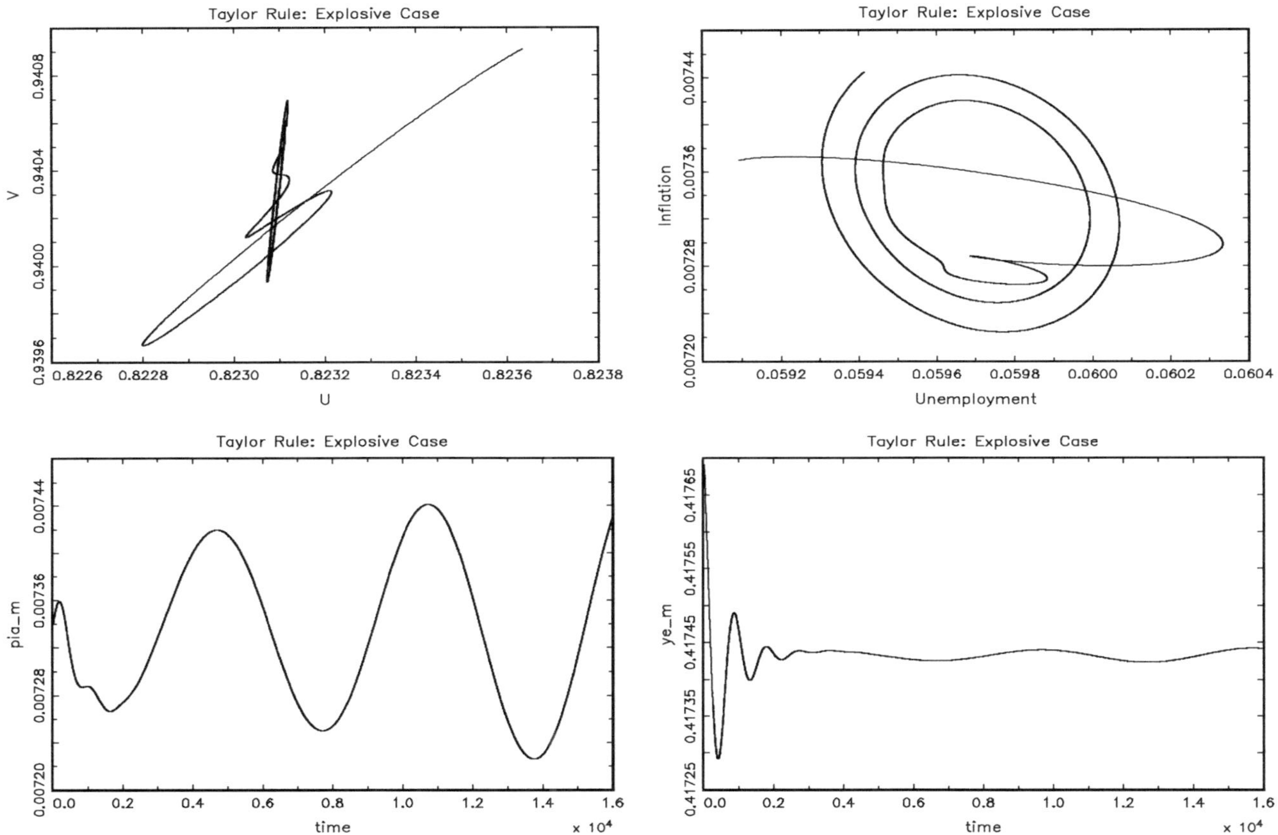

Figure 12.5 Simulation of the model with Taylor rule (unstable case).

The convergence results are depicted for the money supply rule in Figure 12.6 and for the Taylor rule in Figure 12.7.

Note that since the actions based on the two policy rules are endogenized it is in fact reasonable to expect a removal of instability – or increase in stability. This result, which has already been conjectured in Section 12.4, would imply that discretionary monetary policy that responds to the state of macrovariables will be stabilizing. In fact, the possible instability generated by monetary policy rules have been the topic of recent studies on monetary policy – see the various contributions in Taylor (1999). Christiano and Gust (1999), for example, show, although in an optimizing framework, that if the Taylor rule puts strong emphasis on the output gap, indeterminacy and instability of macroeconomic variables may be generated. Instability also occurs under their version of the money supply rule. Their result suggest that central banks should not pursue too much of a discretionary policy. Yet, in their formulation of the money supply rule they use an AR(2) process (autoregressive model of order two) to stylize a money supply process. Thus, there is no feedback of the money supply to other economic variables such as, for example, in our case to the inflation and output gaps. We also have, for reason of comparison, employed such an AR(2) process for the money supply and indeed obtained too completely unstable paths of our macrovariables. This complete instability can only be overcome by feedback rules as we have formulated them for our money supply and Taylor interest rate policy rules.

Finally we want to study whether our model exhibits typical impulse–response functions well known from many recent macroeconomic studies – see for example Christiano *et al.* (1994) and Christiano and Gust (1999). In those studies macrovariables respond to liquidity shocks as follows. In the short run with liquidity increasing the interest rate falls, capacity utilization and output rise, employment rises and, due to sluggish price responses, prices only rise with a delay. Very similar responses can be seen in the context of our model variants for both money supply shocks, Figure 12.8, and direct interest rate shocks (through the Taylor rule), Figure 12.9.

Note that we have shown the trajectories in deviation form from the steady state. For the money supply rule, Figure 12.8, we have assumed that first there is a non-steady-state increase in the growth of money supply. This gives rise to an interest rate fall, rise of employment, utilization of capacity, investment, consumption and, with a delay, a rise in the inflation rate. Finally in the long run all variables, although cyclically, move back to their steady-state levels.

Similar results can be observed in Figure 12.9 for the Taylor rule except that there we displace the interest rate through a shock from its steady-state value. The interest rate is decreased but it moves back in the direction of its steady-state value. The other variables also respond as one would expect from VAR studies of macroeconomic variables. With the fall of the interest rate there is a rise in capacity utilization, output, employment, investment and consumption and, again with a delay, a rise in the inflation rate. The latter can be observed from the fact that the inflation rate peaks later than the utilization of capacity, output and employment. Overall, our model is roughly able to replicate well-known stylized facts obtained

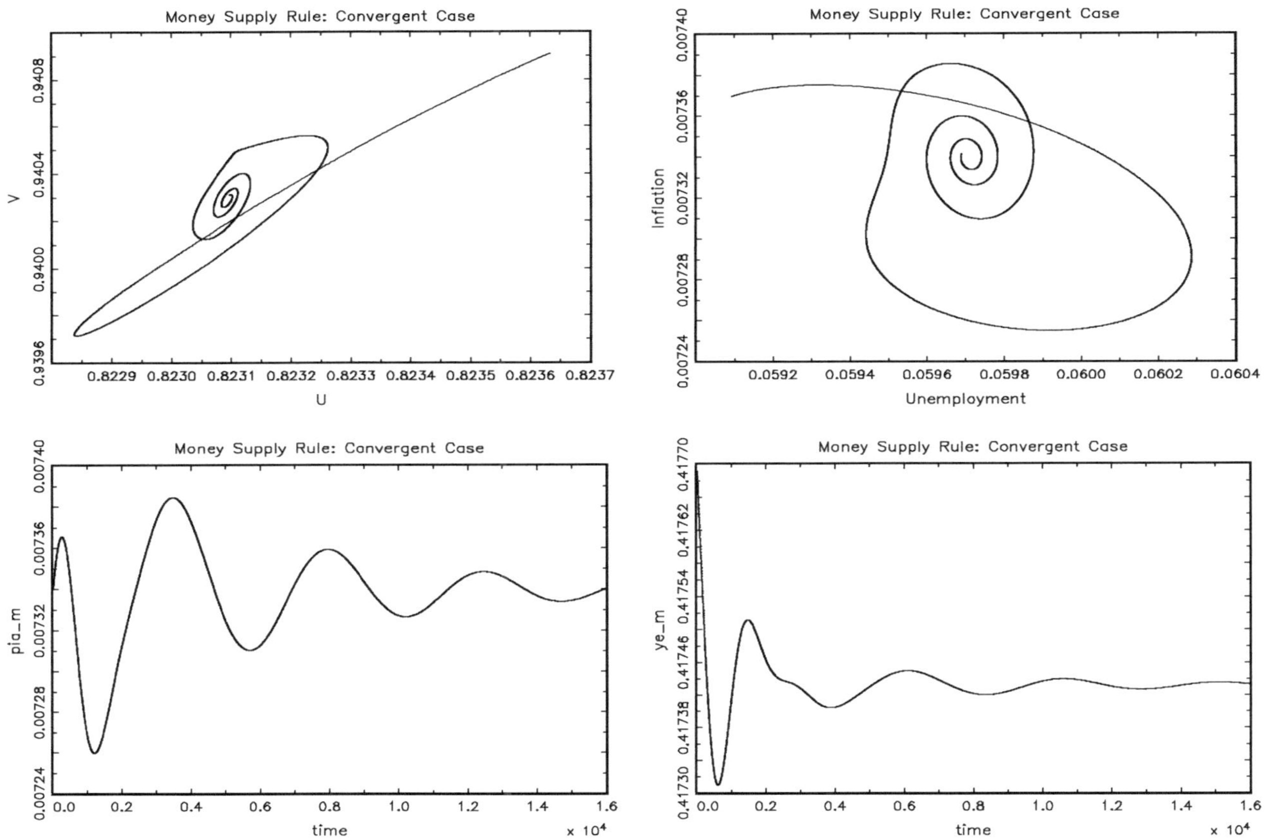

Figure 12.6 Simulation of the model with money supply rule (stable case).

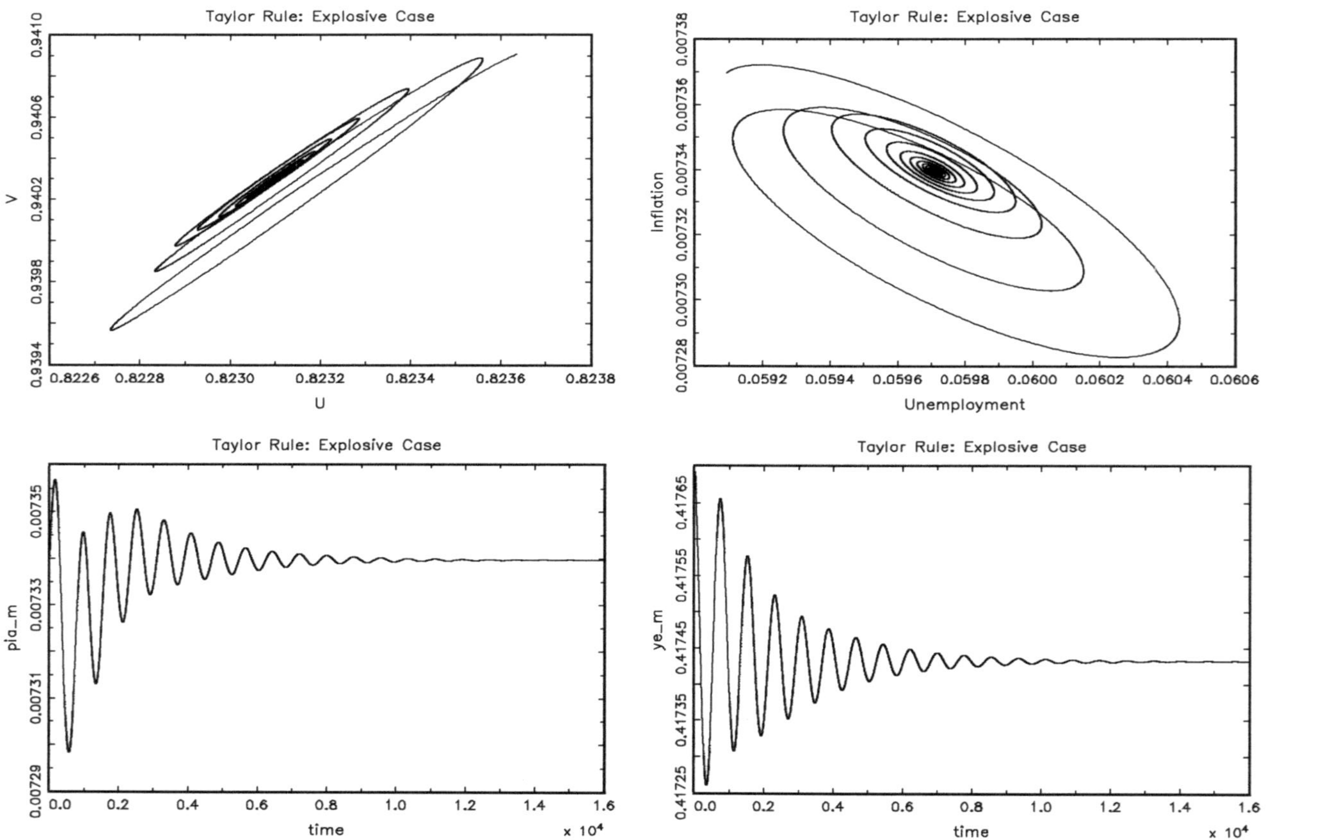

Figure 12.7 Simulation of the model with Taylor rule (stable case).

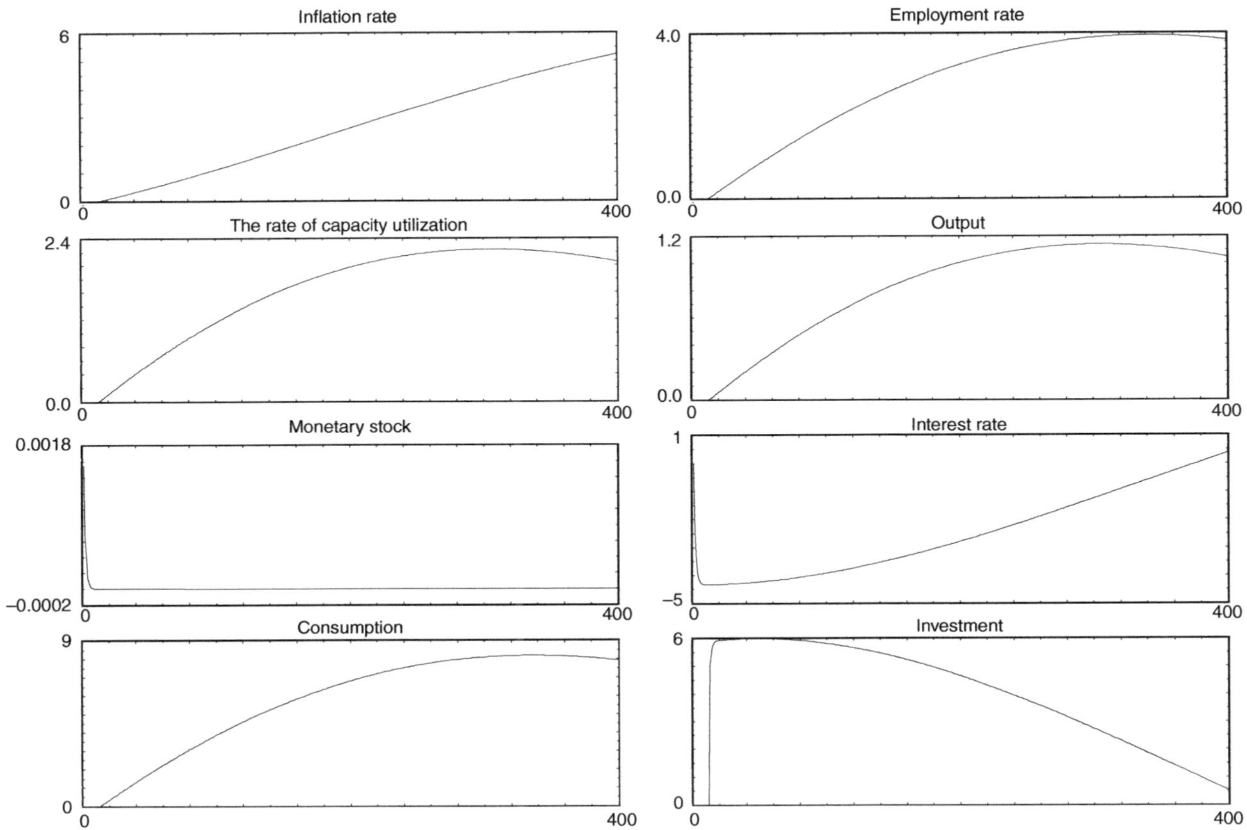

Figure 12.8 Impulse responses for money supply rule.

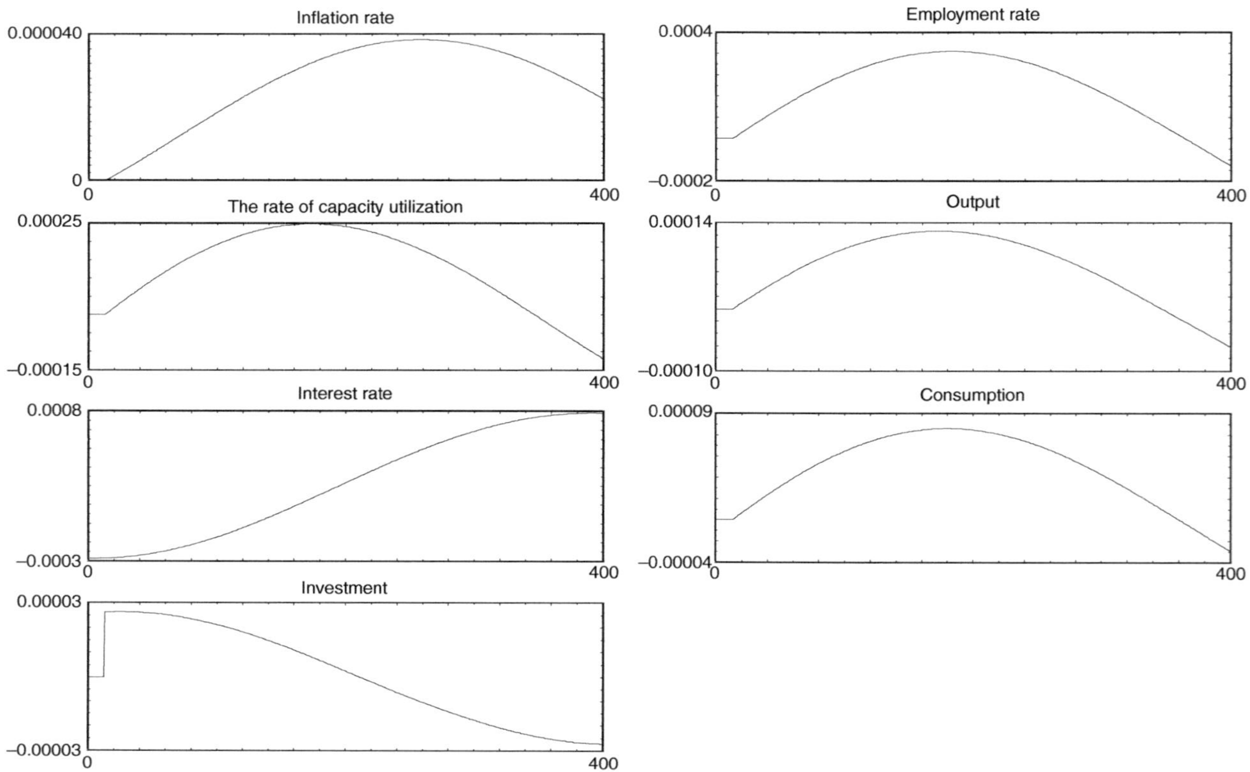

Figure 12.9 Impulse responses for Taylor rule.

from VAR studies of macroeconomic variables. Since our model is rather large, is nonlinear and involves more macroeconomic feedback mechanisms than a VAR study, our results on the impulse–response functions are encouraging.

12.7 Conclusions

In the chapter we have chosen a Keynesian-based macroeconometric framework for studying macrodynamics and monetary policy. In our framework disequilibrium is allowed in the product and labor markets whereas the financial markets are always cleared. There are sluggish price and quantity adjustments and expectations formation represents a combination of adaptive and forward-looking behavior. We consider two monetary policy rules. These policy rules are the money supply rule (12.1) and the interest rate targeting by the monetary authority (12.2). We demonstrate the implication of those policy rules for a monetary macromodel of Keynesian type, and study how the private sector behaves under those alternative policy rules. We estimate the parameters of the model employing US macroeconomic time-series data from 1960:1 to 1995:1.

Based on the estimation of the parameters, obtained partly from subsystems and partly from single equations, we study, using simulations, the dynamic properties for economies which employ either the money supply or the Taylor rule. As we could show with respect to volatility of the macroeconomic variables the model with the Taylor rule seems to perform better in the sense that it gives rise to a faster convergence of macroeconomic variables. We also show that discretionary monetary policy that responds to the state of macroeconomic variables appears to be stabilizing – at least if the policy is pursued with sufficient strength. This is contrary to what one obtains from purely exogenous policy shocks. Moreover, the impulse–response functions for our two model variants show roughly the same features as shown by empirical impulse–response functions based on VAR studies. Our results thus show that our disequilibrium model can compete with currently widely used equilibrium macromodels.

Of course, more empirical work needs to be done in order to confirm or evaluate the findings of this chapter. Yet, AD–AS disequilibrium models that include a treatment of income distribution, the role for aggregate demand and economic growth have not yet been discussed in the theoretical and applied literature to a sufficient degree and thus deserve more attention than they have received so far.

Part V

Extensions

13 The dynamics of "natural" rates of growth and employment

13.1 Introduction

In this chapter[1] we use the integrated 5D Kaldor–Tobin model of monetary growth (KT model) introduced in Chiarella and Flaschel (2000a, ch. 7) in order to investigate on this basis the role played by a variety of labor market and employment adjustment processes. We introduce these additional processes in order to give more weight to labor market considerations in an otherwise traditional Keynesian setup of a growing monetary economy. Increasing the weight of labor market adjustments in Keynesian disequilibrium analysis in our view represents an important step forward in the medium- as well as the long-run analysis of the underemployment situations faced in particular by Europe.

The model, presented in extensive form in the appendix to this chapter, is complete with respect to agents (households, firms and government) and markets (goods, labor and financial assets) all of whose interactions are consistent with respect to budget constraints. In this framework we assume a sluggish adjustment of wages, prices as well as output, the latter however (somewhat simplified) in the tradition of Kaldor (1940) and Tobin (1975).[2] The model is described in its economic building blocks in Chiarella and Flaschel (2000a, ch. 7) and is here motivated immediately on the level of its typical intensive form state variables and their laws of motion. From the KT model with its simple formulation of the labor market it inherits as state variables the share of wages u, labor intensity l, real balances m, inflationary expectations π and the rate of output per unit of capital y which is the minimum set of state variables to be employed in the presence of sluggish adjustments of wages, prices, expectations and quantities (output and growth).[3]

We add to these state variables in the present chapter a sluggish adjustment of the employment of firms V (in view of the over- or undertime work within the firm), adjustment processes for the so-called NAIRU rate of employment $\bar{V}$ and the so-called "natural" rate of growth n and corresponding to this also an adjustment process for the trend growth rate of investment per capital γ. These additions allow an analysis of endogenous growth (without technical change, however), of endogenous long-run employment, and of insider–outsider effects in the process of wage formation.

The structure of the model is "naturally" nonlinear, i.e. no nonlinear economic behavioral relationships are imposed. This allows us to investigate the role of its intrinsic nonlinearities first. The dynamics of the model are capable of generating limit cycles (via Hopf bifurcations), hysteresis effects with respect to "natural" growth as well as "natural" unemployment and also (period-doubling sequences toward) more complex dynamic behavior, if a very basic nonlinearity (or kink) in the employed money wage Phillips curve is taken into account.

One consequence of our choice of the endogeneity of these rates is that there is now hysteresis[4] in the dynamics, i.e. these rates are no longer uniquely determined and there is now also path dependence in the long-run behavior of the trajectories of the dynamics. Also, in order to allow for an adjustment of the NAIRU rate of employment we have to distinguish now, on the one hand, between the rate of employment that refers to the labor market and, on the other, the one within firms (the rate of employment of the employed labor force). This introduces further delays in the adjustment of the rate of employment on the labor market (by distinguishing inside from outside effects) and it makes the description of employment relationships also more realistic.

In sum, we reduce in this chapter the reliance on exogenously given so-called natural rates of employment and growth and also take account of further important feedback loops within firms and in the labor market. The chapter thereby achieves the integration of Keynesian sluggish wage/price as well as quantity adjustments with endogenous trend growth as well as with an endogenous determination of the long-run rate of employment of the labor force into the Keynesian monetary growth framework we have introduced in Chiarella and Flaschel (2000a, chs. 4 and 7). In this way we generate a dynamic structure that has interesting qualitative as well as quantitative dynamic features concerning economic fluctuations and their impact on long-run growth and employment. Future work in this area could extend such Keynesian models of monetary growth to small or interacting open economies of the Dornbusch (1976) type and could also improve on the structure of the financial markets which in the present framework is taken from Sargent (1987, chs. 1–5) as the simplest approach to a complete modeling of the financial decisions of households, firms and the government.

13.2 The KT model with endogenous "natural" growth and employment

In this section we introduce the extended KT monetary growth model of Chiarella and Flaschel (2000a, ch. 8) immediately in intensive form[5] as a nine-dimensional (9D) autonomous dynamical system in the following state variables: wage share u, labor intensity l, real balances per capital m, medium-run inflationary expectations π, output per capital y, rate of employment V, "natural" or NAIRU rate of employment $\bar{V}$, trend capital stock growth γ, and "natural" growth n. We shall explain the economic contents of the laws of motion of these state variables immediately on this intensive form level in order to save space.[6] The dynamics implied by the model will be investigated in the remainder of this chapter from an analytical as well as a numerical point of view.

Our in general 9D Keynesian monetary growth dynamics reads as follows with respect to the above list of its state variables:

$$\hat{u} = \kappa[(1-\kappa_p)(\beta_{w_1}(V-\bar{V}) + \beta_{w_2}(V^w - 1)) + (\kappa_w - 1)\beta_p(U-\bar{U})], \tag{13.1}$$

$$\hat{l} = n - (\gamma + i_1(\rho - r + \pi) + i_2(U - \bar{U})), \tag{13.2}$$

$$\widehat{m} = \mu_0 - \pi - n + \hat{l} - (\hat{p} - \pi), \tag{13.3}$$

$$\dot{\pi} = \beta_{\pi_1}(\hat{p} - \pi) + \beta_{\pi_2}(\mu_0 - n - \pi), \tag{13.4}$$

$$\dot{y} = +\beta_y(y^d - y) - (i_1(\rho - r + \pi) + i_2(U - \bar{U}))y, \tag{13.5}$$

$$\widehat{V} = \gamma + \beta_v(V^w - 1) - n, \tag{13.6}$$

$$\dot{\bar{V}} = \beta_{\bar{v}}(V - \bar{V}), \tag{13.7}$$

$$\dot{\gamma} = \beta_\gamma(I/K - \gamma), \tag{13.8}$$

$$\dot{n} = \beta_n(n(V,\gamma) - n), \quad n(V,\gamma) = n_v(V - \underline{V}) + n_\gamma(\gamma - \underline{\gamma}) + \underline{n}. \tag{13.9}$$

Here we employ as abbreviations:[7]

$$\hat{p} - \pi = \kappa[\beta_p(U - \bar{U}) + \kappa_p(\beta_{w_1}(V - \bar{V}) + \beta_{w_2}(V^w - 1))],$$

$$\rho = y(1-u) - \delta, \quad \text{rate of profit,}$$

$$r = r_0 + (h_1 y - m)/h_2, \quad \text{nominal rate of interest,}$$

$$V^w = L^d/L^w = y/(xVl), \quad \text{employment rate of employed workforce,}$$

$$U = y/y^p, \quad \text{rate of capacity utilization,}$$

$$c = C/K = uy + (1 - s_c)(\rho - t^n), \quad \text{consumption per capital,}$$

$$i = I/K = i_1(\rho - r + \pi) + i_2(U - \bar{U}) + \gamma, \quad \text{net investment per capital,}$$

$$g = G/K = t^n + \mu_0 m, \quad \text{government expenditure per capital,}$$

$$y^d = c + i + \delta + g, \quad \text{aggregate demand per capital.}$$

For simplicity we have based the above dynamical system on a fixed proportions technology characterized by constant output/employment and (potential) output'capital ratios x, y^p.[8] The real wage ω and the share of wages u are thus in fixed proportion to each other $u = \omega/x$. Equation (13.1) – the first important block of our model – describes on this basis the rate of change of real wages as being driven by the outside rate of employment V in its deviation from the "natural" or NAIRU rate of employment $\bar{V}$, by the inside (of firms) given rate of employment V^w of the employed workers compared to their normal level of employment, here given by 1, and by the rate of capacity utilization within firms, U, in its deviation from the normal rate of capacity utilization $\bar{U}$. The coefficients β represent speeds of adjustment and the $\kappa \in (0, 1)$ weights that determine the extent to which the cost-push terms in the money wage and price-level inflation rates are determined by short-run expressions for price and wage inflation, respectively, or by medium-run expectations on these rates of inflation. We therefore assume here two Phillips curves of the usual inflation augmented type, one for wages and one for prices, each depending on the corresponding level of factor utilization and inflationary expectations concerning prices and wages, respectively. Since prices concern the denominator in the real wage dynamics, the dependence of $\widehat{\omega}$ on the rate of capacity utilization must be negative, while the inside and outside rates of utilization of the labor force act positively on the real wage dynamics.

The use of two Phillips curves of the type

$$\widehat{w} = \beta_{w_1}(V - \bar{V}) + \beta_{w_2}(V^w - 1) + \kappa_w \hat{p} + (1 - \kappa_w)\pi,$$
$$\hat{p} = \beta_p(U - \bar{U}) + \kappa_p \widehat{w} + (1 - \kappa_p)\pi,$$

for money wage and price level inflation in place of only one (for price inflation) can be conceived as a considerable generalization of many other formulations of wage/price inflation, for example of models which basically only employ demand-pull forces with respect to the labor market and cost-push ones on the market for goods. Note here also that money wage dynamics depends on the employment rate V outside as well as the employment rate V^w inside the firms and thus pays attention to outsider as well as insider effects.

These wage and price inflation curves can be reduced to two linear equations in the unknowns $\widehat{w} - \pi$ and $\hat{p} - \pi$ which are easily solved and give rise to the following expressions for these two unknowns:

$$\widehat{w} - \pi = \kappa[\beta_{w_1}(V - \bar{V}) + \beta_{w_2}(V^w - 1) + \kappa_w \beta_p(U - \bar{U})], \tag{13.10}$$
$$\hat{p} - \pi = \kappa[\kappa_p(\beta_{w_1}(V - \bar{V}) + \beta_{w_2}(V^w - 1)) + \beta_p(U - \bar{U})]. \tag{13.11}$$

These equations in turn immediately imply for the dynamics $\widehat{\omega} = \widehat{w} - \hat{p}$ of the real wage $\omega = w/p$ the equation (13.1).

Equation (13.2) describes the evolution of labor intensity $l = L/K$ as determined by endogenous labor force growth and investment per capital $\widehat{K} = I/K$, the latter depending on trend growth in investment γ, on the real rate of return differential $\rho - r + \pi$ and on the state of excess demand as reflected through the term $U - \bar{U}$.

Equation (13.3) on the dynamics of real balances per capital $m = M/(pK)$ is purely definitional and it needs the above expression for $\hat{p} - \pi$ in order to make explicit the law of motion to which it gives rise. This observation also holds true for the dynamics of the expectations of medium-run inflation, equation (13.4), which combines adaptive (backward-looking) and regressive (forward-looking) behavior, the latter with respect to the currently prevailing steady-state rate of inflation $\mu_0 - n$ for simplicity.

Equation (13.5) describes the adjustment of the output/capital ratio $y = Y/K$ as the consequence of the output adjustment equation $\dot{Y} = \gamma Y + \beta_y(Y^d - Y)$, which is the dynamic multiplier of the Kaldor (1940) trade cycle and the Tobin (1975) inflation dynamics model reformulated for a growing economy (Y^d aggregate demand). Equations (13.2)–(13.5) thus in sum represent an integration of the Kaldor (1940) trade cycle/Tobin (1975) inflationary dynamics model into the context of a growing economy and thus provide the KT portion of our model of monetary growth.

We now turn to a description to the final block of our model, i.e. to employment decisions, "natural" rates dynamics and the dynamics of the trend term in capital stock growth. Equation (13.6) assumes a type of adjustment for the employment decision of firms of the form

$$\dot{L}^w = \gamma L^w + \beta_v(L^d - L^w),$$

where L^w denotes the workforce employed by the firms and L^d the employment of this workforce according to the level of aggregate demand, so that $L^d = Y/x$, with $V^w = L^d/L^w$ the employment of the employed and with $V = L^w/L$ the employment rate on the labor market. Note that this adjustment equation is similar in spirit to the dynamic multiplier equation assumed to hold for the output adjustments of firms. Firms thus respond sluggishly also in adjusting their labor force to actual employment of this labor force; for example, "USA" would represent a case of a relatively high adjustment speed, while "Japan" may be considered to be at the other end of the spectrum. The next equation (13.7) represents a simple feedback loop from the actual rate of employment V on the NAIRU rate of employment $\bar{V}$ motivated by the simple fact that employment above this "natural" rate improves the skills of the labor force and thereby increases the flexibility of the labor market, while employment below the natural rate deteriorates labor market conditions and thus reduces the steady-state rate of employment $\bar{V}$. Similarly, in equation (13.8), capital stock growth I/K above the trend γ tends to raise this trend term (and vice versa). Finally, such a feedback loop is also applied to the trend in labor force growth n which depends on the state of employment V and the trend growth of the economy γ, but working with some delay and relative to some benchmarks $\underline{V}$, $\underline{\gamma}$ with respect to these indicators of the well-being of the economy. This dynamic law is based on the view that there is always a reserve of people available who can join the workforce when needed and who are repelled into the "subsistence sector" in the opposite situation. This closes the block of the labor market adjustment processes of our monetary growth model.

We add to the above description of the dynamics of our model that the rate of profit ρ is defined as shown above and depends on output per capital y and the share of wages u in the usual way. Furthermore, money market equilibrium solved for the nominal rate of interest r – by assumption – implies a simple linear relationship between this rate and y, m as is customary in elementary textbook discussions. Policy rules are such that $g = t^n + \mu_0 m$ holds for government expenditures per unit of capital, where t^n, capital taxes net of interest per unit of capital, are assumed to be a given magnitude[9] and where μ_0 denotes the exogenously given rate of growth of the money supply. Finally, we have the definitional relationships $V^w = L^d/L^w = y/(xVl)$ and $U = Y/Y^p = y/y^p$ for the two rates of utilization we employ in our model (on the level of firms), and for aggregate demand per unit of capital we have

$$y^d = uy + (1 - s_c)(\rho - t^n) + i_1(\rho - r + \pi) + i_2(U - \bar{U}) + n + \delta + g,$$

due to assumptions on savings and investment behavior (s_c is the rate of savings out of capital income).[10]

We stress that we have chosen all behavioral equations as linearly as possible in order to concentrate on the "natural" or intrinsic nonlinearities of the dynamics and their implications. This in particular holds for the function $n(V, \gamma)$ which implies that there is a unique solution γ_0 to the equation

$$n(\bar{V}, \gamma_0) = \gamma_0: \quad \gamma_0 = \frac{n_v(\bar{V} - \underline{V}) + \underline{n} - n_\gamma \underline{\gamma}}{1 - n_\gamma}, \quad n_\gamma < 1,$$

for each level of the NAIRU rate of employment $\bar{V} \in (0, 1)$. In view of the linear structure of the assumed technological and behavioral equations, the above presentation of our model shows that its nonlinearities are, on the one hand, due to the necessity of using growth laws in various cases and, on the other, to multiplicative expressions for some of the state variables of the form uy, $y/(xVl)$ and $\hat{l}y$. Though intrinsically nonlinear of the kind of the Rössler and the Lorenz dynamical system, our 9D system may, however, still be characterized as being of a simple type, in particular since these nonlinearities do not too often appear in its nine equations.

For any choice of the NAIRU-based rate of employment $\bar{V}$ it is easily shown that there is a unique interior steady-state solution for the remaining state variables of the above dynamical system if one adds to it the equation $n_0 = \gamma_0$ (with γ_0 as determined above), i.e.[11]

$$y_0^d = y_0 = \bar{U} y^p, \quad l_0^d = y_0/x, \tag{13.12}$$

$$m_0 = h_1 y_0, \tag{13.13}$$

$$\pi_0 = \mu_0 - n_0, \tag{13.14}$$

$$\omega_0 = [y_0 - \delta - t^n - (n_0 + \mu_0 m_0)/s_c]/l_0^d, \tag{13.15}$$

$$\rho_0 = y_0 - \delta - \omega_0 l_0^d, \tag{13.16}$$

$$r_0 = \rho_0 + \mu_0 - n_0, \tag{13.17}$$

$$V_0 = \bar{V}, \quad l_0 = l_0^d/\bar{V}. \tag{13.18}$$

The set of economically meaningful steady states of the considered 9D dynamics is thus given by a ray in $\Re^9$. The model is assumed to have sufficiently large buffers $1 - \bar{V}$ and $1 - \bar{U}$ at its steady state so that the Keynesian demand regime we have assumed above to prevail at each point in time (in each short run of the model) can indeed be maintained along the trajectories of the dynamics.

13.3 Stability analysis of the 6D core subdynamics

In this section we shall consider some stability properties of the subdynamics of the model (13.1)–(13.9) that is given by its first six laws of motion, the natural rates of growth and employment being given magnitudes ($n = \gamma$) here. We thus investigate the special cases:

- $\beta_\gamma = 0, \; \gamma(0) = n = \text{const.},$
- $\beta_n = 0, \; n(0) = n = \text{const.},$
- $\beta_{\bar{V}} = 0, \; \bar{V}(0) = \bar{V} = \text{const.} \in (0, 1).$

The remaining six laws of motion contain the KT portion (13.2)–(13.5) of the model (the dynamics of K, Y and p, π) and they enrich this structure by a real wage dynamics of the Rose (1990) type and a more or less sluggish adjustment process of the outside rate of employment in view of current inside over- or underemployment.

In order to obtain stability results for this 6D dynamical system we start from an appropriately chosen 3D subdynamics where the Routh–Hurwitz stability conditions can be considered explicitly and where specific economic reasons allow one to expect asymptotic stability of the steady state of the model.[12]

Proposition 13.1 *Assume* $\beta_{w_1} = \beta_{w_2} = \beta_p = \beta_\pi = \beta_v = 0$ *and that* ω, π, V *are given by their steady-state values. Then, the steady state of the 3D dynamical system (13.2), (13.3) and (13.5) is locally asymptotically stable if the parameter* h_2 *is chosen sufficiently small and the parameter* β_y *sufficiently large.*

Proof: This is a lengthy, but straightforward, application of the Routh–Hurwitz theorem; see Chiarella and Flaschel (2000a, Lemma 7.1) for a proof in a related situation. □

The above proposition states that the isolated l, m, y dynamics is locally asymptotically stable when the Keynes effect (i.e. the link $m \to r$, see the preceding section) is sufficiently strong and the dynamic multiplier (which is then stable) works with sufficient strength. Since inflationary expectations are still constant here, the assertion of Proposition 13.1 is therefore not too surprising when considered from the perspective of the Kaldor (1940) trade cycle and the Tobin (1975) inflationary dynamics.

Proposition 13.2 *Assume* $\beta_{w_1} = \beta_{w_2} = \beta_p = \beta_v = 0$ *and that* ω, V *are given by their steady-state values. Then, the steady state of the 4D dynamical system (13.2)–(13.5) is locally asymptotically stable if the parameters* h_2 *and* β_π *are chosen sufficiently small and the parameter* β_y *sufficiently large.*

Proof: By exploiting linear dependences in the Jacobian of the considered 4D dynamics at the steady state one can show that the determinant of this Jacobian is always positive for $\beta_\pi > 0$. The eigenvalue 0 corresponding to $\beta_\pi = 0$ must therefore become negative if the situation considered in Proposition 13.1 is modified toward a small positive value of β_π. □

This proposition says that the Tobin (1975) type of monetary instability cannot yet come about for inflationary expectations the adaptive component of which is still sufficiently sluggish.

PROPOSITION 13.3 *Assume that $\beta_v = 0$ and that V is given by its steady-state value. Then, the steady state of the 5D dynamical system (13.1)–(13.5) is locally asymptotically stable if the parameters h_2, β_π, β_{w_1}, β_{w_2} and β_p are chosen sufficiently small and the parameter β_y sufficiently large.*

Proof: The proof is of the same type as that for Proposition 13.2. □

This proposition simply states that the stability assertion of Proposition 13.2 also holds for wage/price dynamics and thus for real wage dynamics that are sufficiently sluggish.

PROPOSITION 13.4 *Assume that the parameters h_2, β_{w_1}, β_{w_2}, β_p, β_π and β_v are chosen sufficiently small and the parameter β_y sufficiently large. Then, the steady state of the 6D dynamical system (13.1)–(13.6) is locally asymptotically stable.*

Proof: This is of the same type as the one for Proposition 13.2. □

This proposition states that a "Japanese" type of economy where inside over- or underemployment is only sluggishly transferred to changes in the workforce employed by firms remains stable under the conditions considered in Proposition 13.3.

In closing this section we simply state that the above stability scenarios will change toward local instability via so-called Hopf bifurcations. There local asymptotic stability gets lost via the birth of a stable limit cycle or the death of an unstable limit cycle if the parameters h_2 or β_π or β_v or either β_{w_i} or β_p become sufficiently large. The basic reason for this occurrence is that the determinant of the Jacobian of the 6D system at the steady state is always positive. The 6D dynamics therefore in particular loses stability in a cyclical fashion and thus generates a theory of endogenous business fluctuations in these (as well as most other) situations.[13]

13.4 Hysteresis effects in "natural" employment and/or growth

To quote Franz (1990, p. 2):

> In general terms hysteresis is a property of dynamics systems. Hysteretic systems are path-dependent systems. The long-run solution of such a system does

> not only depend on the long-run values of the exogenous variables (as usually) but also on the initial conditions of each state variable. These systems have a long-lasting memory and are therefore "historical" systems. Loosely speaking, where you get to is determined by how you get there.

We will briefly consider in this section hysteretic effects in our full 9D dynamics (and appropriate subsystems) based on the occurrence of one or more zero roots in the characteristic equation of the Jacobian (at the steady state) of our continuous-time dynamics. In the next section the consequences of such an occurrence are combined with an assumption that prevents money wage deflation and are there investigated from the numerical point of view with respect to interesting medium- and long-run dynamical behavior to which the model and its subdynamics give rise.

PROPOSITION 13.5 *Consider the 7D dynamical system where $\beta_n = \beta_\gamma = 0$ holds with given initial rates $n = \gamma$. Then the following hold.*

1 *For any choice of the NAIRU-based rate of employment $\bar{V}$ there is a unique steady-state solution for the remaining state variables as described in Section 13.2. The set of economically meaningful steady states of the considered 7D dynamics is thus given by a ray in $\Re^7$.*
2 *Corresponding to the situation just described we have* det $J = 0$ *for the Jacobian J of the considered dynamical system at the steady state and thus one eigenvalue of the dynamical system equal to zero.*
3 *Apart from path dependence with respect to the values of $\bar{V}$ and l the conditions for local asymptotic stability with respect to the above ray are the same as for the previously considered 6D dynamical system if the parameter $\beta_{\bar{v}}$ is chosen sufficiently small.*

Proof:

1 This is straightforward; see equations (13.12)–(13.18).
2 The laws of motion for the state variables V, $\bar{V}$ allow removal of the expressions for the wage Phillips curve from the first four laws of motion as far as the calculation of determinants is concerned. It is then easy to see that both the m equation as well as the π equation can be further simplified and both can then be shown to depend on the state variable π solely. This makes these two equations proportional to each other and thus implies that the determinant of the Jacobian of the dynamics must be zero at the steady state.
3 This is a straightforward exercise in eigenvalue analysis on the basis of the preceding section. □

Neither the isolated addition of the dynamical law (13.8) nor of the law (13.9) to our 6D dynamics considered in the preceding section can give rise to hysteretic effects in the resulting 7D dynamical systems as was the case for the endogenous determination of the NAIRU-based rate of employment $\bar{V}$. The following proposition will, however, show that combined adjustment processes for n and γ are capable of producing hysteresis now with respect to the growth rate of the economy.

PROPOSITION 13.6 *Assume* $\beta_{\bar{V}} = 0$ *and* $\bar{V} \in (0, 1)$. *Assume furthermore* $n(V, \gamma) = \gamma$. *We consider the 8D dynamical system brought about by adding the dynamical laws (13.8) and (13.9) to our 6D dynamics. Then the following hold.*

1. *For any choice of the trend growth rate γ in the investment function there is a unique steady-state solution for the remaining state variables of the type described in Section 13.2 (if one adds to them the equation $n_0 = \gamma$). The set of economically meaningful steady states of the considered 8D dynamical system is thus given by a ray in $\Re^8$.*
2. *Corresponding to the situation just described we have* $\det J = 0$ *for the Jacobian J of the considered dynamical system at the steady state and thus one eigenvalue is always zero.*
3. *Apart from path dependence the conditions for local asymptotic stability with respect to the above described ray are the same as for the considered 6D subdynamics if the parameters β_γ and β_n are chosen sufficiently small.*

Proof:

1. This is straightforward; see equations (13.12)–(13.18).
2. It is sufficient to note here that the equation governing the law of motion of l can be expressed in the present case as a simple linear combination of the two laws for n and γ.
3. This is a straightforward exercise in eigenvalue analysis on the basis of the preceding section. □

Finally, we come to an investigation of the full dynamical structure of the KT model with endogenous long-run growth and long-run labor force participation. We here proceed in two steps: (1) the integration of the 7D/8D cases (with $n(V, \gamma) = \gamma$) we have considered above, and (2) the investigation of the model with a general function $n(V, \gamma) \neq \gamma$ as far as the dynamics of the natural rate of growth n is concerned.

PROPOSITION 13.7 *Consider the full 9D dynamical system (13.1)–(13.9) on the basis of $n(V, \gamma) = \gamma$. Then we have the following.*

1. *For any choice of the NAIRU-based rate $\bar{V}$ and the trend growth rate γ in the investment function there is a unique steady-state solution for the remaining state variables of the type described in Section 13.2 (if one adds to them the equation $n_0 = \gamma$). The set of economically meaningful steady states of the considered 9D dynamical system is thus given by a surface in $\Re^9$.*

2 *Corresponding to the situation just described* rank$(J) = 7$ *for the Jacobian J of the considered dynamics at the steady state and thus two eigenvalues are always zero.*

Proof:

1 This is straightforward; see equations (13.12)–(13.18).
2 It is sufficient to note again that the equation governing the law of motion of l can be expressed in the present case as a simple linear combination of the two laws for n and γ and that in addition the further linear dependence we considered in Proposition 13.5 can be shown to hold true. □

This twofold hysteretic situation can again be reduced to a (single) hysteretic evolution in the NAIRU (and l) by way of Proposition 13.8.

PROPOSITION 13.8 *Consider the full 9D dynamical system (13.1)–(13.9) on the basis of a function* $n(V, \gamma)$ *that differs from the special choice* $n(V, \gamma) = \gamma$. *Assume furthermore that the equation* $n(\bar{V}, \gamma_0) = \gamma_0$ *has a unique positive solution* γ_0 *for each* $\bar{V} \in (0, 1)$. *Then we have the following.*

1 *For any choice of the NAIRU-based rate* $\bar{V}$ *there is a unique steady-state solution for the remaining state variables of the type described in Proposition 13.6 (if one adds to them the equation* $n_0 = \gamma_0$, *with* γ_0 *as determined above). The set of economically meaningful steady states of the considered 9D dynamical system is thus given by a ray in* $\Re^9$.
2 *Corresponding to the situation just described* rank$(J) = 8$ *for the Jacobian J of the considered dynamical system at the steady state and thus one eigenvalue is always zero. This again gives rise to hysteresis effects or a path-dependent convergence to long-run steady-state positions just as in Proposition 13.5.*

With this proposition we terminate the theoretical discussion of the general 9D dynamical system with endogenous growth and endogenous NAIRUs. It is obvious that we have formulated with these propositions only very basic results for our 9D extension of the KT dynamics. This must suffice here as an outlook on Keynesian monetary growth theory which attempts to endogenize important "natural" rates of economic theory.

13.5 Some numerical simulations

Simulating the "naturally" nonlinear dynamics of Section 13.2 allows one to illustrate the results on asymptotic stability of Section 13.3 (also in the large), to search for the Hopf bifurcations we have pointed to at the end of that section (often leading to cyclical explosiveness when the respective parameters are further increased) and to exemplify the hysteretic situations discussed in Section 13.4. These numerical illustrations are however of a fairly straightforward type and are thus not presented here due to space limitations. Instead, we will now add one further important labor market nonlinearity to the model (13.1)–(13.9) which at one and the same time makes the model's dynamics look much more interesting and also more relevant from an empirical point of view. This nonlinearity concerns the money wage Phillips curve which we now modify in the following way:

$$\widehat{w} = \max\{\beta_{w_1}(V - \bar{V}) + \beta_{w_2}(V^w - 1) + \kappa_w \hat{p} + (1 - \kappa_w)\pi, 0\}.$$

This modification assumes in line with many empirical observations that there may be wage inflation, but that there is hardly any deflation in the general level of money wages. We insert this basic empirical fact into our money wage Phillips curve in the simplest way possible, namely by keeping its linear shape in the case of wage inflation and by assuming it as identically "zero" otherwise. We refer to this type of Phillips curve as the kinked Phillips curve in the following.[14]

On the basis of this modification, we now provide some numerical illustrations of the dynamical systems we have considered in the preceding sections. We stress again that the full dynamical system is characterized by a variety of adjustment lags of employment and of endogenous growth which taken together may be briefly summarized as follows:

$$V \to V^w, \quad \gamma \to \widehat{K}, \quad n \to \gamma \quad [\text{or } n(V, \gamma)], \quad \bar{V} \to V.$$

These various routes of adjustment will be switched off or on in the following simulation studies and will thereby provide us, though still in a way that has to be expanded, with a quantitative impression of the working of these various feedback mechanisms in isolation as well as in their interaction.

Let us start with the 6D core dynamical system of in fact no endogenous growth and no endogenous NAIRU rate of employment, but only delayed output and employment adjustments besides somewhat sluggish wage and price adjustments and inflationary expectations. We make use here of the parameter set of Table 13.1, where a number of adjustment coefficients are to be chosen as zero in order to reflect this 6D case properly.[15]

Note that money supply is here assumed to grow faster than the real economy, so that there is steady-state inflation. The kink in the Phillips curve thus becomes operative only somewhat below the steady state. Figure 13.1 nevertheless shows

Table 13.1 The basic parameter set for the following simulations

$s_c = 0.8$	$\delta = 0.1$	$y^p = 1$	$x = 2$	
$\underline{n} = \underline{\gamma} = 0.05$	$n_0 = \gamma_0 = 0.05$	$\underline{V} = 1$		
$h_1 = 0.1$	$h_2 = 0.05$	$i_1 = 0.25$	$i_2 = 0.5$	
$\beta_{w_1} = 2.5$	$\beta_{w_2} = 2.5$	$\beta_p = 1$	$\kappa_w = 0.5$	$\kappa_p = 0.5$
$\beta_{\pi_1} = 0.6$	$\beta_{\pi_2} = 1$	$\beta_n = \beta_\gamma = \beta_{\bar{v}} = 0$	$\beta_y = 2$	$\beta_v = 2$
$n_v = 0$	$n_\gamma = 1$	$\mu_0 = 0.08$	$\mu_2 = 0.08$	$t^n = 0.08$

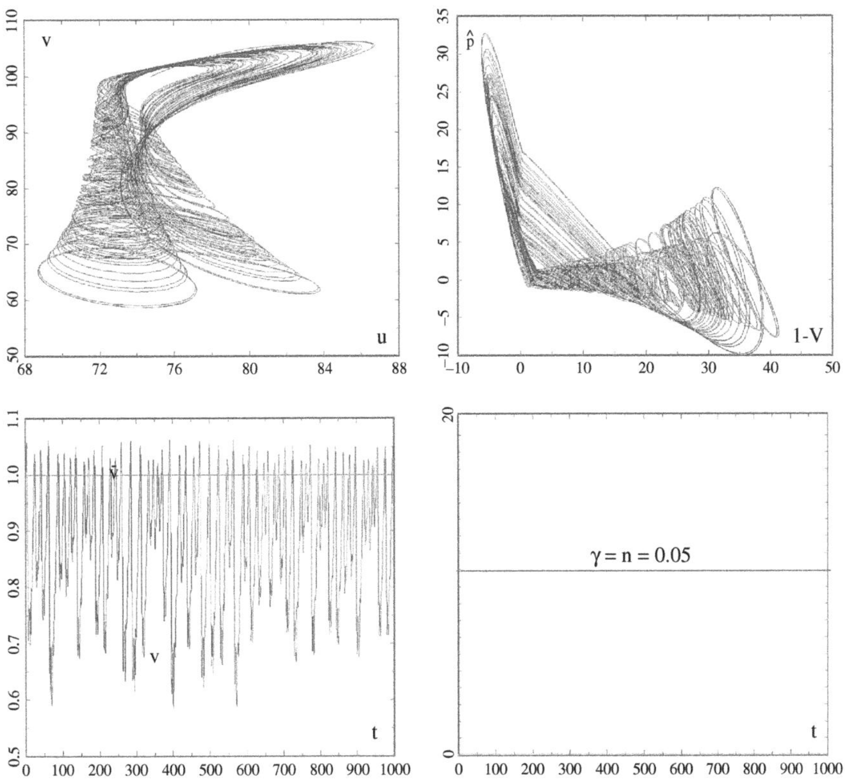

Figure 13.1 Phase plots and time-series representations over a time horizon of 1,000 years (6D case).[16]

the effects of the kink in the Phillips curve in a dramatic way, since the model without this kink would not be mathematically viable even over a much shorter time horizon, due to the high adjustment speed of money wages in particular. The kinked Phillips curve (which excludes wage deflation from the dynamics) therefore restricts the dynamics significantly and it leads to the irregular fluctuations shown (by way of a sequence of period doublings of limit cycles, not shown). We note here that the shown downward fluctuations, in particular in the rate of employment, are significantly larger than the upward fluctuations, due to the kink in the Phillips curve which makes depressions much deeper and last much longer as compared to the booms. Note also that there is price level deflation in the model since we did not assume a kink in the price Phillips curve as well.

The occurrence of large fluctuations can be reduced if the extent of steady-state inflation is decreased by moving μ_0 closer to n, so that the kink in the Phillips curve becomes more important. In the limit $\mu_0 = n$, it is operative right at the steady state which implies a continuum of steady-state rates of employment

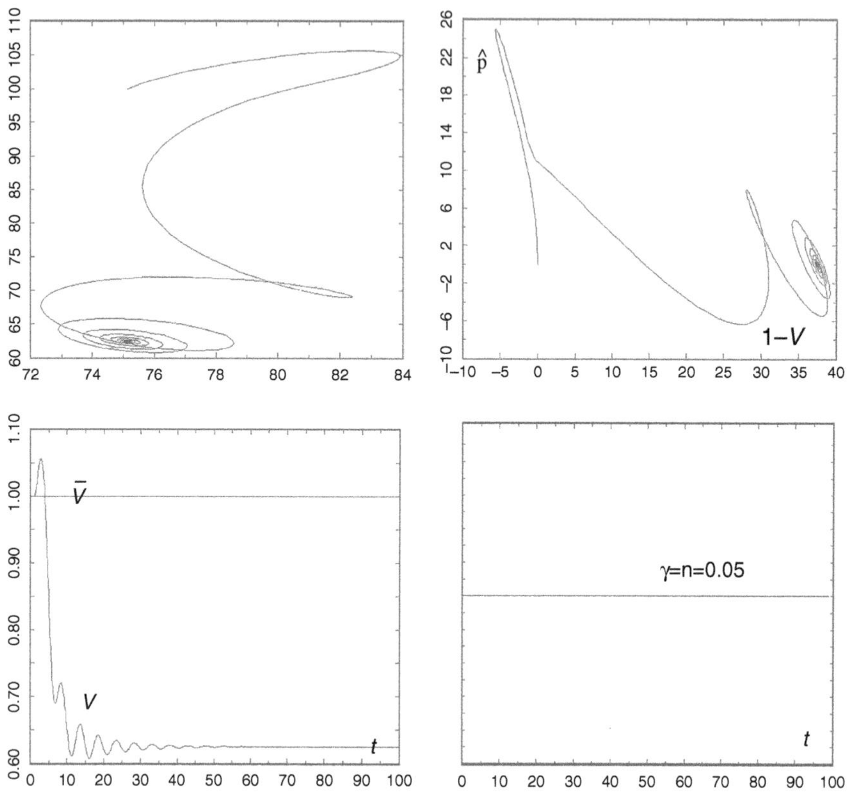

Figure 13.2 Downwardly rigid money wages at the inflationless steady state.

V_0 below $\bar{V}$ to which the economy can now tend because money wages do not fall in these depressed situations. This occurrence of long-run "unnatural" unemployment is generally accompanied by very stable adjustment processes toward such a situation as Figure 13.2 exemplifies. The economy therefore gets stuck in a depressed state and this in a way that no longer allows for the irregular and persistent fluctuations we observed in Figure 13.1.

Growth rates of money supply between 0.08 and 0.05 therefore generate economically viable situations with less and less irregular fluctuations of decreasing amplitude as the parameter μ_0 is decreased and with longer and longer situations of depression. However, different from the case $\mu_0 = n$, the economy will always recover from such depressed situations as shown in Figure 13.1.

The simulations we have thus far shown indicate that there is an important choice for monetary policy to be made between a situation where the economy is very stable, but also (very) depressed, as in Figure 13.2, and one, as in Figure 13.1, where the economy in fact recovers from each depression, but this at the cost of large and persistent fluctuations around the original steady state (of "full" employment). There is thus an important role for inflation in the steady state (based on $\mu_0 > n_0$), since it avoids the permanent implementation of an institutional constraint in the wage–price module at this steady state which would alter the behavior of the economy in the radical fashion shown in Figure 13.2.

Let us now, however, return to inflationary steady-state situations and come to the inclusion of endogenous growth into the situations of fluctuations and exogenous trend growth just considered. Figure 13.3 shows the resulting 8D dynamics over a time horizon of 500 years after the steady state has been shocked at time $t = 1$ by a 10% increase in the money supply. We stress here once again that assuming high adjustment speeds for wages, prices and expectations is responsible for the large amplitudes we observe in the cycles shown. From an empirical point of view one may therefore be inclined to reduce the corresponding parameters in size

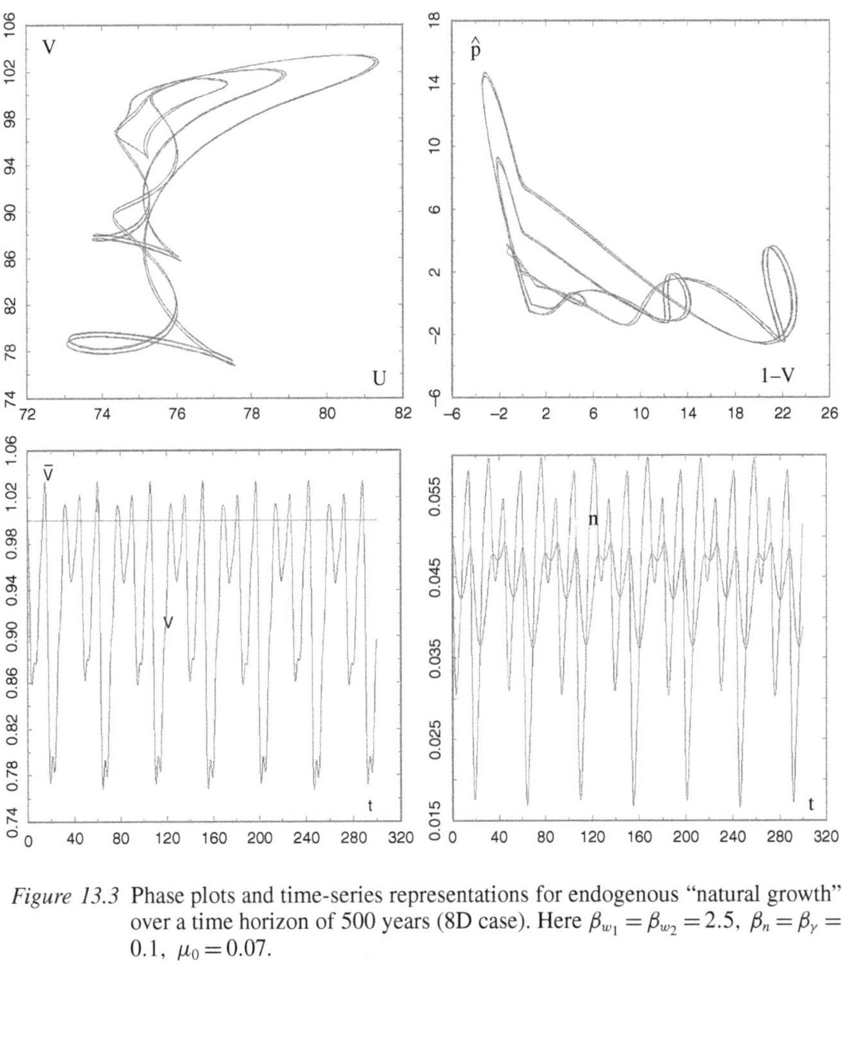

Figure 13.3 Phase plots and time-series representations for endogenous "natural growth" over a time horizon of 500 years (8D case). Here $\beta_{w_1} = \beta_{w_2} = 2.5,\ \beta_n = \beta_y = 0.1,\ \mu_0 = 0.07$.

or to reduce again the level of steady-state inflation in order to get an economically viable dynamics with only "moderate" fluctuations in particular in the state variables V, n. However, the fact that in theory there are often situations where these adjustment parameters are set equal even to infinity makes it worth while to consider what in fact comes about in situations of flexible price and trend growth adjustments.

Figure 13.3 shows (at the bottom right) that the natural rate of growth and trend growth in investment are now moving in time – the first following the movement of the latter rate γ in an adaptive fashion and with levels that are definitely below the initial steady-state value of $n = 0.05$. Observe also that the NAIRU-based rate $\bar{V}$ is still constant in this simulation of endogenous growth. Note finally that the amplitude of the fluctuations shown is still large, due to the high speeds of adjustment assumed in the wage–price module of the model.

The general impression again is that the cycle has no tendency to become of a simple limit cycle type or the like as time evolves so that one might conjecture that

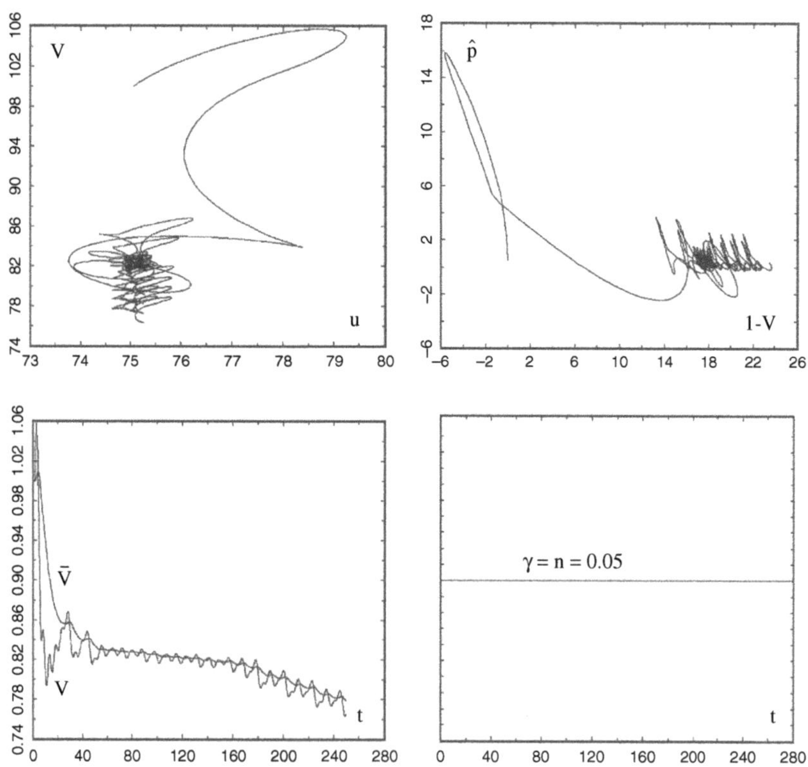

Figure 13.4 Phase plots and time-series representations of an endogenous determination of the NAIRU-based rate $\bar{V}$ (7D case).

the attractor of the dynamics shown could be complex in nature. This impression is, however, not confirmed when the model is iterated further, since it suddenly settles down at a fairly simple limit cycle (at $t = 800$ as further simulations, not displayed, have shown). This limit cycle is subject to hysteresis with respect to initial conditions as well as speeds of adjustment that do not enter the calculation of the steady-state positions.

Let us now turn to an endogenous determination of the NAIRU-based rate $\bar{V}$ and consider this situation first for growth rates γ, n that are given exogenously. We thus assume as (modified) parameter values $\beta_{\bar{v}} = 0.1$ and $\beta_\gamma = \beta_n = 0$ and the adjustment speeds of wages β_{w_1} and β_{w_2} are now set equal to 1.5. In this case we get, despite an inflationary steady-state situation, that the economy becomes more and more depressed, since the predominant existence of low employment rates deskill unemployed workers thereby reducing the rate $\bar{V}$ which in turn allows for lower and lower actual rates of employment V. As Figure 13.4 suggests there is no real end to this process above the level of zero employment. We thus get the result that each following depression is more severe than the preceding one with

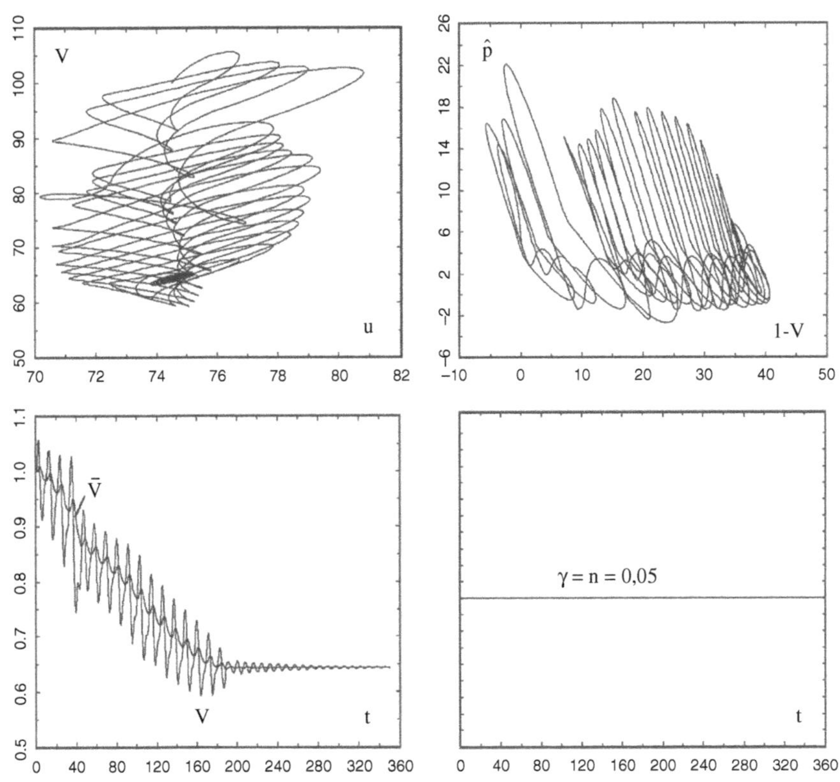

Figure 13.5 Phase plots and time-series representations of an endogenous determination of the NAIRU-based rate of employment $\bar{V}$ (7D case).

no sign that this process will come to a standstill. This combines hysteresis due to the kinked Phillips curve with hysteretic effects caused by the law that governs the evolution of the "natural" rate of employment.

Decreasing the adjustment speed of wages, however, can alter this situation and remove the downward trend in the model at some later point in time. This is shown in Figure 13.5, where the adjustment speeds β_{w_i} of money wages have both again been reduced to the value 1. Here, the model converges to a very low level of the actual as well as the NAIRU-based rate of employment, $V,\ \bar{V}=0.63$ approximately.

The economic dynamics considered in Figure 13.5 can change significantly with the size of the monetary shock that is exercised at time $t=1$. Expansive shocks above the current multiplicative one (1.1) confirm the situation shown in Figure 13.5, while shocks below this value (and in particular contractive ones) give rise to the same type of monotonic behavior, but accompanied by persistent fluctuations in place of the asymptotic adjustment shown in the Figure 13.5. This example shows that there can be little path dependence with respect to averages, but instead path dependence with respect to the type of fluctuations that occur. This is not surprising if one takes into account that point attractors need not be the only attractors in the present dynamical system.

Finally, we consider the situation where all three rates $\bar{V},\ \gamma,\ n$ are determined endogenously. Here, too, we get a long period of cyclical downturns now with respect to employment and growth which, however, as before come to a halt after approximately 350 years, see Figure 13.6, with a damped cyclical movement around the steady state that is then established. The figures drastically exemplify how downturns that are longer than upturns, due to the asymmetry in the money wage Phillips curve, can drag the rates of employment and the rates of growth down to levels that must be considered as highly problematic if not catastrophic. Such situations of self-enforcing depressions to some extent may have characterized the period of growth slowdown that followed the 1960s and early 1970s. They are here established through the interaction of the kinked Phillips curve with hysteretic effects in "natural" and trend growth as well as "natural" employment.

Let us contrast this result with a situation where the economy fluctuates in such a mild way around its inflationary steady state that the kink in the money wage Phillips curve does not become operative, here based on a sluggish wage adjustment of the type $\beta_{w_1}=\beta_{w_2}=0.3$. As Figure 13.7 shows there are then no longer self-enforcing downturns, but there is here in fact a slight increase in the steady-state rate of employment, due to the path dependence of the "natural" rates of growth and employment. Such a situation may be (loosely) compared with the development in the 1960s and 1970s where in fact the growth rate of money wages did not approach the value zero where the kink in the Phillips curve would have become operative. Note that the comparison of Figures 13.6 and 13.7 suggests that there are significant effects of speeds of adjustments (on which the steady-state solutions do not depend) on the long-run behavior of the economy.

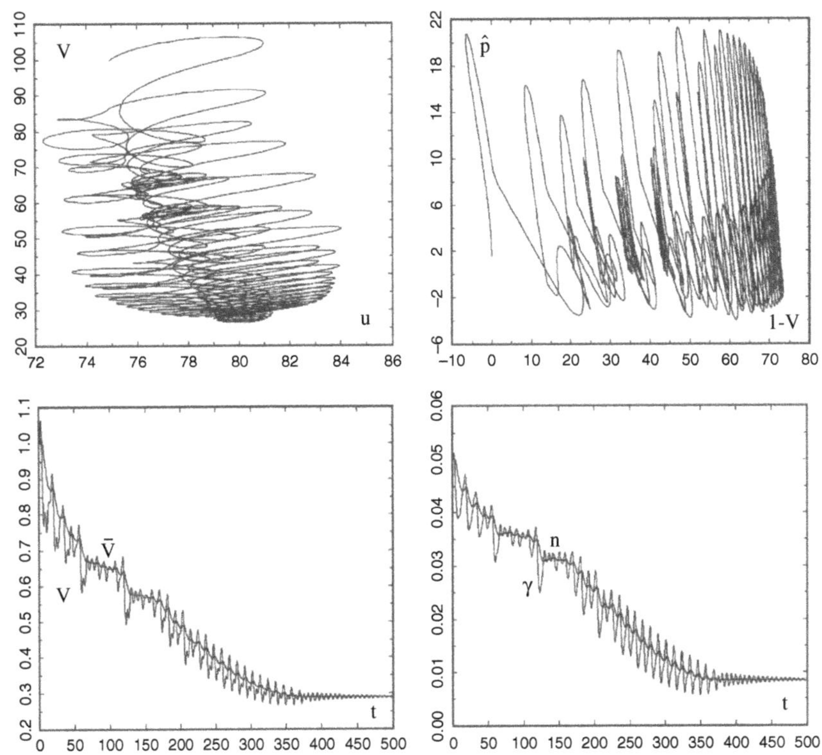

Figure 13.6 Phase plots and time-series representations with an endogenous determination of $\bar{V}$, γ, n (9D case). Here $\beta_{w_1} = \beta_{w_2} = 2$, $\beta_v = 5$, $\beta_n = \beta_{\bar{v}} = 0.1$, $\beta_\gamma = 0.05$, $\mu_0 = 0.066$.

This ends our numerical investigation of the general 9D dynamics and its various subcases. We have seen that a variety of interesting dynamics may occur with amplitudes that may still be considered too high, but which can be significantly reduced if lower adjustment speeds in the wage–price module and in the level of inflation that prevails in the steady state are allowed for. We have furthermore provided examples of a weak dependence of long-run behavior on initial conditions and a much stronger dependence of the long run on speeds of adjustment (that do not enter the calculation of the steady states).

We close this section and the chapter with the conclusion that wage–price flexibility can be bad for economic stability, and that downwardly rigid money wages are very important for the economic viability of the dynamics. This is in particular true in an inflationary environment where the occurrence of ever-lasting depressions is avoided through price inflation leading to damped fluctuations around a prosperous steady state when supported by sluggish adjustments in the wage–price module of the model.

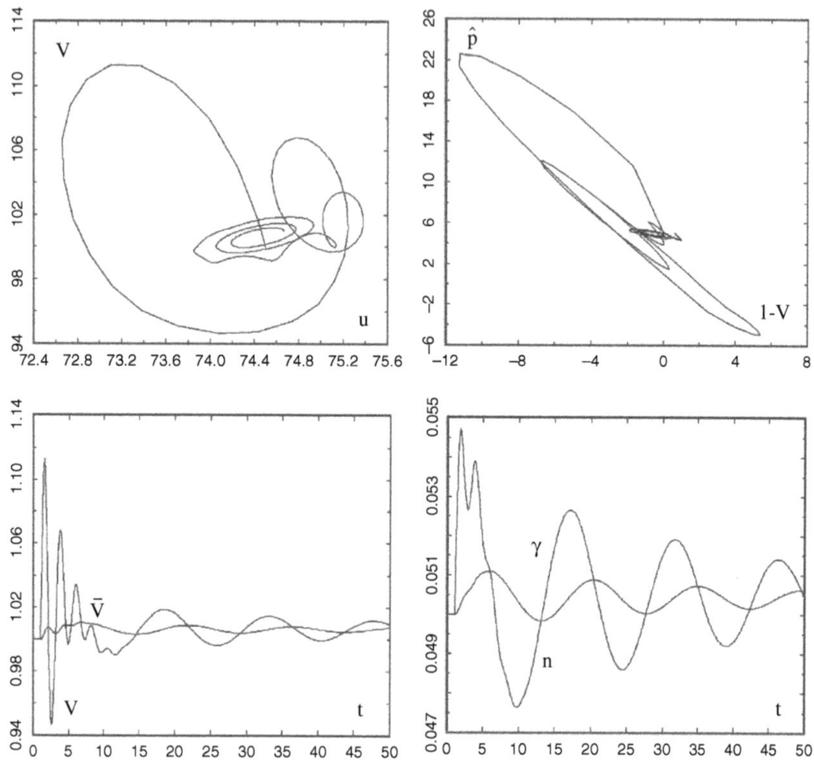

Figure 13.7 Phase plots and time-series representations for small fluctuations in the level of economic activity.

Appendix: the model in extensive form

The KT model of the chapter which is presented in this appendix in extensive form is based on the formal structure of markets and agents used in Sargent (1987, chs. 1–5), but extended to a treatment of sluggish price/wage as well as output adjustments and disequilibrium on the labor market as well as within firms.

1. *Definitions (remunerations and wealth):*

$$\omega = w/p, \quad \rho = (Y - \delta K - \omega L^d)/K,$$

$$W = (M + B + p_e E)/p, \quad p_b = 1.$$

2. *Households (workers and asset-holders):*

$$W = (M^d + B^d + p_e E^d)/p, \quad M^d = h_1 pY + h_2 pK(1-\tau)(\bar{r} - r),$$

$$C = \omega L^d + (1 - s_c)[\rho K + rB/p - T], \quad s_w = 0,$$

$$S_p = \omega L^d + Y_c^D - C = Y - \delta K + rB/p - T - C$$
$$= s_c[\rho K + rB/p - T] = s_c Y_c^D$$
$$= (\dot{M}^d + \dot{B}^d + p_e \dot{E}^d)/p,$$
$$\widehat{L} = n, \quad \dot{n} = \beta_n(n(V,\gamma) - n), \quad n_i(V,\gamma) > 0, \quad i = 1,2.$$

3. *Firms (production units and investors):*

$$Y^p = y^p K, \quad y^p = \text{const.}, \quad U = Y/Y^p = y/y^p \quad (y = Y/K),$$
$$L^d = Y/x, \quad x = \text{const.}, \quad V = L^w/L, \quad V^w = L^d/L^w,$$
$$\dot{L}^w = \gamma L^w + \beta_v(L^w - L^d),$$
$$I = i_1(\rho - (r - \pi))K + i_2(U - \bar{U})K + \gamma K,$$
$$p_e \dot{E}/p = I + (S - I) = I + Y - \delta K - C - G = Y - Y^d,$$
$$\widehat{K} = I/K \neq S/K,$$
$$\dot{\gamma} = \beta_\gamma(\widehat{K} - \gamma).$$

4. *Government (fiscal and monetary authority):*

$$t^n = (T - rB/p)/K = \text{const.},$$
$$G = T - rB/p + \mu_2 M/p,$$
$$S_g = T - rB/p - G \quad [= -(\dot{M} + \dot{B})/p, \text{ see below}],$$
$$\hat{M} = \mu_0,$$
$$\dot{B} = pG + rB - pT - \dot{M}.$$

5. *Equilibrium conditions (asset markets):*

$$M = M^d = h_1 pY + h_2 pK(1 - \tau)(\bar{r} - r) \quad [B = B^d, \ E = E^d],$$
$$p_e E = (1 - \tau)\rho p K/((1 - \tau)r - \pi),$$
$$\dot{M} = \dot{M}^d, \quad \dot{B} = \dot{B}^d \quad [\dot{E} = \dot{E}^d].$$

6. *Disequilibrium situation (goods market adjustment):*

$$S = p_e \dot{E}^d = S_p + S_g = Y - \delta K - C - G = p_e \dot{E} \neq I,$$
$$Y^d = C + I + \delta K + G,$$
$$\widehat{Y} = \gamma + \beta_y(Y^d/Y - 1) = \gamma + \beta_y((I - S)/Y),$$
$$\dot{N} = \delta_2 K + S - I, \quad S = S_p + S_g = Y - \delta K - C - G.$$

7. *The dynamics of the labor market NAIRU:*

$$\dot{\bar{V}} = \beta_{\bar{v}}(V - \bar{V}).$$

8. *Wage–price sector (adjustment equations):*

$$\widehat{w} = \beta_{w_1}(V - \bar{V}) + \beta_{w_2}(V^w - 1) + \kappa_w \hat{p} + (1 - \kappa_w)\pi,$$

$$\hat{p} = \beta_p(U - \bar{U}) + \kappa_p \widehat{w} + (1 - \kappa_p)\pi,$$

$$\dot{\pi} = \beta_{\pi_1}(\hat{p} - \pi) + \beta_{\pi_2}(\mu_0 - n - \pi).$$

14 High-order disequilibrium growth dynamics

14.1 Introduction

In this chapter[1] we motivate and analyze a disequilibrium monetary growth model of a small open economy. The model consists of the dynamic interaction of a real sector and a nominal one. The dynamics of the real sector are determined by employment and labor intensity dynamics and an inventory dynamics. In the nominal part of the model price and inflationary expectations dynamics interact with dynamics of the foreign exchange rate and expectations of exchange rate depreciation. The resulting model is expressed as an 8D dynamical system which incorporates sluggish price and quantity adjustments, allows for fluctuations in both capital and labor utilization and allows for international trade in goods as well as financial assets.

Our aim is to understand the main stabilizing and destabilizing economic forces driving the dynamics of the model and to analyze their potential to generate complex dynamic behavior.

In Section 14.2 we lay out and motivate the eight differential equations governing the dynamics of our model. In Section 14.3 we discuss the five main economic feedback chains, the Rose effect, the Mundell effect, the Metzler effect, the Dornbusch effect and the Keynes effect, and show that their conflicting stabilizing and destabilizing influences drive the dynamic behavior of the model. We show that eigenvalue analysis indicates that local stability is lost via Hopf bifurcations in a way that is dependent in particular on the speeds of adjustment of prices and expectations. In this section we also discuss the intrinsic (or "natural") nonlinear features of the model. Simulations reveal however that the aforementioned intrinsic nonlinearities are generally not sufficient to bound the dynamics when the equilibrium is locally unstable. Therefore in Section 14.4 we introduce (and motivate) an extrinsic nonlinearity into the function modeling net capital flows by taking account of the fact that these are bounded by international wealth. This extrinsic nonlinearity in conjunction with rapid speeds of adjustment of exchange rates and of expectations of exchange rate depreciation give rise (close to the limiting case of myopic perfect foresight) to a relaxation oscillation between the exchange rate and its expected rate of depreciation. Simulations reveal that movements away from the locally unstable equilibrium remain bounded on some sort of complex attractor. However high-frequency movements in the foreign exchange sector here lead to unrealistic high-frequency movements in the real sector of the model.

In Section 14.5 the frequency of the movements in the real sector is made more realistic by introducing a ninth differential equation which allows for sluggish adjustment of the trade balance based on a sluggish adjustment of the terms of trade that govern imports and exports. Simulations here reveal motion to high-order limit cycles, but now with fluctuations in the real sector which exhibit more realistic frequencies.

In Section 14.6 we introduce a further nonlinearity, this time both into the real and the nominal part of the economy, namely that nominal wage deflation (and thus part of real wage determination) is subject to some kind of floor. This nonlinearity also gives rise to high-order limit cycles and also complex attractors, in particular when coupled with the other modifications of the model discussed above. Period-doubling routes to such complex attractors are considered in Section 14.7. Section 14.8 draws some conclusions and makes suggestions for further research.

14.2 Disequilibrium growth in small open economies

We consider a disequilibrium model of monetary growth of an open economy with sluggish adjustment of all prices and of output (coupled with imbalances in the utilization rates of both labor and capital) and where real and financial markets interact, here primarily by way of international capital mobility and the trade balance. The state variables of the model are $\omega = w/p$, the real wage, $l = L/K$, the labor/capital ratio, p, the price level, π, the expected rate of inflation, $y^e = Y^e/K$, sales expectations per unit of capital, $\nu = N/K$, inventories per unit of capital, e, the nominal exchange rate, and ϵ, the expected rate of change of the exchange rate. These state variables are fundamental for any disequilibrium approach to monetary growth with sluggish price as well as quantity adjustments on the market for labor, for goods and also to some extent on the market for foreign exchange. We show in Asada *et al.* (2003a) that the evolution of these state variables is governed by the dynamical system (14.1)–(14.8) below.

These equations are based on growth laws in four cases ($\hat{x}$ the growth rate of a variable x) and on simple time derivatives in the four remaining laws of motion. They have to be inserted into each other in three cases. One has to make use of the static relationships shown below in addition in order to obtain an explicit representation of this system as an autonomous eight-dimensional (8D) system of differential equations:

$$\widehat{\omega} = \kappa[(1-\kappa_p)\beta_w(V-\bar{V}) + (\kappa_w - 1)\beta_p(U-\bar{U})], \tag{14.1}$$

$$\hat{l} = -i_1(\rho^e - r + \pi) - i_2(U-\bar{U}), \tag{14.2}$$

$$\dot{y}^e = \beta_{y^e}(y^d - y^e) + \hat{l}y^e, \tag{14.3}$$

$$\dot{v} = y - y^d - (n - \hat{l})v. \tag{14.4}$$

The above real dynamics are investigated in Chiarella and Flaschel (2000a) on various levels of generality. They basically consist of a Rose (1967) employment cycle approach where economic growth or labor intensity l is interacting with real wage formation, ω, and a Metzler (1941) inventory cycle mechanism where expected sales per capital, y^e, and actual inventories per capital, v, drive the adjustment of production and inventories made by firms.

$$\hat{p} = \pi + \kappa(\beta_p(U - \bar{U}) + \kappa_p\beta_w(V - \bar{V})), \tag{14.5}$$

$$\dot{\pi} = \beta_\pi(\alpha_\pi(\hat{p} - \pi) + (1 - \alpha_\pi)(-\pi)), \tag{14.6}$$

$$\widehat{e} = \beta_e(\beta(r_0^* + \epsilon - r) - nx), \tag{14.7}$$

$$\dot{\epsilon} = \beta_\epsilon[\alpha_\epsilon(\hat{e} - \epsilon) + (1 - \alpha_\epsilon)(-\epsilon)]. \tag{14.8}$$

The above nominal dynamics consist of two similar mechanisms which both are known to be destabilizing, the Tobin (1975) inflationary spiral based on the so-called Mundell effect and the Dornbusch (1976) exchange rate dynamics based on some sort of external Mundell effect. In both cases an increase in expectations stimulates the actual rate of change of the considered variable and thus further increases the change in expectations, leading to cumulative instability if the involved adjustment parameters are sufficiently large. Here, the internal or Tobin case concerns the price level p and inflationary expectations π, and the external or Dornbusch situation concerns the expected rate of change, ϵ, of the exchange rate e.

Taken together these dynamics basically extend the presentation of Keynesian dynamics given in Sargent (1987, ch. V) toward sluggish price adjustment and fluctuating utilization rates of the capital stock, sluggish output and inventory adjustment of firms and a foreign sector of Dornbusch type which in our view represents the minimum extension for an open-economy model that can truly be considered as Keynesian. Note here that markets and sectors are the same as in the Sargent model (with the exception of the external ones). The Sargent approach to Keynesian dynamics is investigated in its details in Flaschel *et al.* (1997) and extended into the direction of the above dynamics in Chiarella and Flaschel (2000a) and Asada *et al.* (2003a).

We have for output per unit of capital $y = Y/K$, for aggregate demand per unit of capital $y^d = Y^d/K$ and for the trade balance per unit of capital nx the expressions

$$y = y^e + n\beta_{n^d}y^e + \beta_n(\beta_{n^d}y^e - v), \tag{14.9}$$

$$\begin{aligned} y^d = {} & (1 - \tau_w)\omega y/x + \gamma_c(\eta)(1 - s_c)(\rho^e - t^n) + c_1^*(\eta) \\ & + i_1(\rho^e - r + \pi) + i_2(U - \bar{U}) + n + \delta + g, \end{aligned} \tag{14.10}$$

$$nx = c_1^*(\eta) - (1 - \gamma_c(\eta))(1 - s_c)(\rho^e - t^n). \tag{14.11}$$

We have employed the following as abbreviations in the presentation of the above dynamics:

$$V = y/(xl), \quad U = y/y^p, \quad \text{rate of employment and of capacity utilization,}$$

$$\rho^e = y^e - \delta - \omega y/x, \quad \text{expected rate of profit,}$$

$$r = r_0 + (h_1 y - m_0 l/p)/h_2, \quad \text{nominal rate of interest,}$$

$$\eta = p/ep_0^*, \quad \text{terms of trade,}$$

$$\kappa = (1 - \kappa_w \kappa_p)^{-1}, \quad m_0 = (M/L)(0), \quad \text{some constants.}$$

The 8D autonomous nonlinear system of differential equations (14.1)–(14.8) will be investigated in this chapter from the theoretical as well as from the numerical point of view. For the sake of brevity we here motivate the intensive form dynamics directly and refer the reader to Asada *et al.* (2003a) for discussions of the extensive or structural form of the model.

For simplicity we have based the above dynamical system on a fixed proportions technology[2] characterized by constant output/employment and (potential) output/capital ratios x, y^p, i.e. given expressions for labor as well as capital productivity. The real wage ω and the share of wages u are thus in fixed proportion to each other $u = \omega/x$ and potential output Y^p grows in line with the capital stock K. Equation (14.1) describes the law of motion for real wages, which are driven by the rate of employment V in its deviation from the NAIRE rate of employment $\bar{V}$, and by the rate of capacity utilization within firms, U, in its deviation from their normal rate of capacity utilization, $\bar{U}$. The coefficients β represent speeds of adjustment and the $\kappa \in (0, 1)$ are weights that determine the extent to which the cost-push terms in the money wage and price-level Phillips curves are determined by short-run expressions for price and wage inflation, $\hat{p}$, $\widehat{w}$ or by medium-run expectations of average inflation π. We therefore assume here two Phillips curves of the usual inflation augmented type, one for wages and one for prices, each depending on the corresponding level of factor utilization and on inflationary expectations concerning prices and wages, respectively. Since prices concern the denominator in the real wage dynamics, the dependence of $\widehat{\omega}$ on the rate of capacity utilization must be negative, while the rate of utilization of the labor force acts positively on the real wage dynamics.

This usage of two Phillips curves of the type

$$\widehat{w} = \beta_w(V - \bar{V}) + \kappa_w \hat{p} + (1 - \kappa_w)\pi, \tag{14.12}$$

$$\hat{p} = \beta_p(U - \bar{U}) + \kappa_p \widehat{w} + (1 - \kappa_p)\pi \tag{14.13}$$

for money wage and price inflation $\widehat{w}$, $\hat{p}$ in place of only one (for price inflation) represents a considerable generalization of many other formulations of wage/price inflation, for example of models which basically only employ cost-push forces in the market for goods. It is assumed that workers only consume the domestic product. We thus only need the domestic price level change in the money wage Phillips curve, which makes the feedback structure easier to handle. Domestic price and wage inflation, however, depend on foreign consumption habits, since these are part of the aggregate demand function (to be discussed below) which directs expected sales and thus the output and employment decision of firms.

These wage and price inflation curves can be transformed to two linear equations in the unknowns $\widehat{w} - \pi$ and $\hat{p} - \pi$ which are easily solved, giving rise to

$$\widehat{w} - \pi = \kappa[\beta_w(V - \bar{V}) + \kappa_w \beta_p(U - \bar{U})], \tag{14.14}$$

$$\hat{p} - \pi = \kappa[\kappa_p(\beta_w(V - \bar{V}) + \beta_p(U - \bar{U})]. \tag{14.15}$$

These equations in turn immediately imply equation (14.1) for the dynamics $\widehat{\omega} = \widehat{w} - \hat{p}$ of the real wage $\omega = w/p$ and equation (14.5) for the dynamics of the price level p.

Equation (14.2) describes the evolution of labor intensity $l = L/K$ as determined by exogenous labor force growth with rate n and investment per unit of capital $\hat{K} = I/K$, the latter depending on trend growth[3] in investment n, on the expected real rate of return differential $\rho^e - (r - \pi)$ and on the state of excess demand in the market for goods as reflected by the term $U - \bar{U}$, the excess utilization rate of the capital stock. Taken together, equations (14.1) and (14.2) describe growth and income distribution dynamics in a way that is related to the medium-run dynamics considered in Solow and Stiglitz (1968) and Malinvaud (1980). Its real roots are however in Rose's (1967) analysis of the employment cycle and the extensions provided in this respect in Rose (1990).

Equation (14.3) describes the change in sales expectations as being governed by trend growth and by the observed expectational error (between aggregate demand Y^d and expected sales Y^e), here already in a form that is reduced to per unit of capital expressions y^d, y^e. Similarly, equation (14.4) states that actual inventories N change according to the discrepancy between actual output Y and actual demand Y^d (which in our Keynesian context is never rationed), again reduced to per unit of capital terms and thus to lower case in place of the above upper-case letters. This subdynamics represent an extension of Metzlerian ideas (see also Franke and Lux 1993) to a growing economy as in Franke (1996).

This ends the description of the real part of the model. We now turn to the evolution of its nominal variables as represented by the price level p and the nominal exchange rate e and expectations about the rates of change of these two magnitudes.

Equation (14.5), the dynamics of the price level, has already been considered above (as an intermediate step in the determination of the law of motion for real wages), while the dynamics of the expectations of medium-run inflation, equation (14.6), combines adaptive (backward-looking) and regressive (forward-looking) behavior, the latter for simplicity with respect to the steady-state rate of inflation, which is here zero,[4] since we assume that money grows at the same rate as output in the steady state.[5] The subdynamics (14.5) and (14.6) are the internal nominal dynamics of our model and represent a general form of Tobin (1975) type dynamics.

We now turn to a description of the final block, i.e. to the open-economy part of the model which is as in Dornbusch (1976). Equation (14.7) makes use of the expressions ncx ($=\beta(r_0^* + \epsilon - r)$) and nx which describe net capital export and net exports per unit of capital, respectively. Net capital exports in turn depend, as shown, on the interest rate differential on foreign and domestic bonds, where the former expression also contains the expected currency depreciation in the usual way.[6] Since ncx is finite, we have imperfect capital mobility. Furthermore, the term $ncx - nx$ represents the imbalance caused by capital and goods trade on the market for foreign exchange. Equation (14.7) assumes on this basis that the rate of change of the exchange rate depends positively, and for the moment also linearly, on this imbalance, i.e. besides imperfect capital mobility, we have also a finite adjustment speed of the exchange rate in place of the interest rate parity condition usually used in models of the Dornbusch (1976) type. Equation (14.8) then adds that exchange rate expectations are formed qualitatively in the same way as inflationary expectations, with an adaptive, backward-looking component and a regressive, forward-looking component which for reasons of simplicity, and on the basis of the PPP theorem, refers to the steady-state rate of change of the exchange rate, which is zero in the present context.[7]

Equations (14.1)–(14.6) are formally the same as for the closed economy (see Chiarella and Flaschel 2000a). They interact with the foreign sector, (14.7) and (14.8), by way of aggregate demand and the domestic rate of interest, the former depending on the exchange rate through international trade and the latter being influenced by the output and price decisions of firms through a conventional LM curve approach.

Let us finally briefly comment on the static relationships of our dynamical model. Equation (14.9) is based on the Metzlerian inventory adjustment process according to which, in its simplest format, desired inventories per capital $\beta_{n^d} y^e$ are proportional to expected sales per capital y^e. The discrepancy to actual inventories per capital ν then determines desired inventory changes (with adjustment speed β_n and augmented by the term $n\beta_{n^d} y^e$ that accounts for growth). This sum $n\beta_{n^d} y^e + \beta_n(\beta_{n^d} y^e - \nu)$ thus represents the portion of production (per capital) that is intended for inventories, to which we have to add expected sales per capital y^e in order to arrive at the actual output y (per unit of capital) that firms will produce.

Equation (14.10) represents the aggregate demand term y^d (per unit of capital) that firms will face and on the basis of which they will revise their sales expectations. It is composed of the real wage sum (after taxes) per unit of capital $(1 - \tau_w)\omega y/x$ (which in this model is totally spent on domestic goods) and of $\gamma_c(\eta)(1 - s_c)(\rho^e - t^n)$, i.e. that part of profits per unit of capital $\rho^e - t^n$ (after lump sum taxes t^n) that is spent on domestic goods, $(1 - s_c)(\rho^e - t^n)$, based on a proportionality factor $\gamma_c(\eta) \in [0, 1]$ that depends on the terms of trade η. The expression for aggregate demand furthermore contains $c_1^*(\eta)$, i.e. the foreign demand for the domestic good (per unit of capital), which is also dependent on the terms of trade η and contains gross investment (per unit of capital) $i_1(\rho^e - r + \pi) + i_2(U - \bar{U}) + n + \delta$, and finally government expenditure (per unit of capital) g which just as t^n is considered as a given magnitude (as we do not consider policy rules and policy experiments here). Aggregate demand therefore depends on income distribution, on the savings rate s_c out of profit income, on the terms of trade η and on the determinants of the investment decision as they were described above.

Equation (14.11) describes net exports nx per unit of capital, which are given by exports $c_1^*(\eta)$ minus imports $(1-\gamma_c(\eta))(1-s_c)(\rho^e - t^n)$, which is the complementary expression to the above demand out of profits that went into the domestic good (wage owners only consume the domestic good by assumption). Assuming the same situation in the rest of the world provides us with an understanding of the term $c_1^*(\eta)$ which however would then include an expression for the relative sizes of the capital stocks and would thus depend on the profit rate expected abroad. These additional ratios make the dynamics more involved and are held constant in the present analysis.[8] Taken together we here therefore suppress certain feedback mechanisms by taking certain ratios (g, t^n and the ones just mentioned) as fixed.

We add to the above description of the dynamics of our model that employment L^d/K per unit of capital is given by $y/x = (Y/K)/(Y/L^d)$ and that on this basis the expected rate of profit ρ^e is to be defined as shown above (δ is the rate of depreciation). Furthermore, money market (LM) equilibrium solved for the nominal rate of interest r – by assumption – implies a simple linear relationship between this rate and output y and real balances (per capital) $m_0 l/p$ as is customary on the textbook level. We stress in this regard that we want to keep the model as linear as possible, since we want to concentrate on its intrinsic nonlinearities[9] at first (which are later augmented by two basic extrinsic nonlinearities, but not yet by nonlinearities in the behavioral relationships). Note also that, since labor and money are assumed to grow at the same pace, the ratio M/L must be constant in time and has to be used as a scale factor that determines the steady-state values of the nominal magnitudes.

This ends the description of our Keynesian monetary growth model of the open economy, which exhibits sluggish adjustments of prices, wages and quantities (and corresponding to this the occurrence of over- or under-utilized labor and capital in the course of the cycles that it generates). The interested reader is referred to Chiarella and Flaschel (2000a) and Asada *et al.* (2003a) for more details on this model type.

14.3 Partial feedback chains and stability issues

Feedback chains

As the model is formulated we can distinguish five important feedback chains which we will describe below in isolation from each other, but which of course interact in the full 8D dynamics so that one or other can become dominant when parameters are chosen appropriately.

1. The Rose effect (economic activity–real wage interaction)

In order to explain this effect we assume for the time being IS–LM equilibrium and thus know from our above presentation of aggregate goods demand that output and in the same way the rate of employment and the rate of capacity utilization will depend positively or negatively on real wages, due to their opposite effects on the consumption of workers and on investment (and consumption out of profits). According to the law of motion for real wages (14.1) we thus get a positive or negative feedback effect of real wages on their rate of change, depending on the relative adjustment speed of nominal wages and prices. Either price or wage flexibility will therefore be destabilizing, depending on investment and saving propensities, i_1, s_c, with respect to the expected rate of profit. The destabilizing Rose effect (of whatever type) will be weak if both wage and price adjustment speeds β_w, β_p are low.

2. The Metzler effect (expected sales/inventory changes mechanism)

As equation (14.9) shows, output y depends positively on expected sales y^e and this the stronger the higher the speed of adjustment β_n of planned inventories. The time rate of change of expected sales in equation (14.3) therefore depends positively on the level of expected sales when the parameter β_n is chosen sufficiently large. Flexible adjustment of inventories coupled with a high speed of adjustment of sales expectations thus work against economic stability. There will, of course, exist other situations where an increase in the latter speed of adjustment may increase the stability of the dynamics.

3. The Mundell effect (internal nominal dynamics)

We assume IS–LM equilibrium again in order to explain this often neglected effect with respect to the sixth dynamic law of our model. Since net investment depends (as is usually assumed) positively on the expected rate of inflation π we have that aggregate demand and thus output and the rates of capacity utilization depend positively on this expected inflation rate. This implies a positive dependence of $\hat{p} - \pi$ on π and thus a positive feedback from the expected rate of inflation on its time rate of change if β_p, β_w are chosen sufficiently large (see equation (14.6)). Faster adjustment speeds of inflationary expectations will therefore destabilize the economy in this situation (for all positive α_π).

4. The Dornbusch effect (external nominal dynamics)

Increasing the parameters β_e, β for exchange rate flexibility and capital mobility will increase the positive influence of the expected exchange rate changes ϵ on the actual rate of change of the exchange range without bound. For positive α_ϵ we get in this way a positive feedback of exchange rate expectations on their time rate of change which becomes the more destabilizing the faster these expectations are adjusted. This effect is similar to the Mundell effect we considered previously.

So far we have only considered feedback chains that may give rise to instability for certain parameter constellations. The next and last of these feedback chains is definitely not of this sort and represents the original concession that Keynes (1936) made to full employment theorists.

5. The Keynes effect (nominal price/interest co-movements and economic activity)

We again assume IS–LM equilibrium in order to explain this well-known effect in simple terms with respect to the fifth dynamic law of our model. According to LM equilibrium the nominal rate of interest r depends positively on the price level p. Aggregate demand and thus output and the rates of capacity utilization therefore depend negatively on the price level, implying a negative dependence of the inflation rate on the level of prices through this channel. A high sensitivity of the nominal rate of interest with respect to the price level (a low parameter h_2, the opposite of the liquidity trap) thus should exercise a strong stabilizing influence on the dynamics of the price level (14.5) and on the economy as a whole, which is further strengthened if price and wage flexibility increases.

This brief discussion of the basic 2D feedback mechanism in our full 8D dynamics on balance suggests that increases in the speeds of adjustment of the dynamics will generally be bad for economic stability or viability. Exceptions to this rule are given by either wage or price flexibility and by the sales expectations mechanism, e.g. if inventories are adjusted sufficiently slowly. Of course, we do not have IS equilibrium in the full 8D dynamics as was assumed above. This however simply means that the effects discussed above work with some lag or more indirectly, due to the delayed interaction of aggregate demand, expected sales and output decisions. Mathematically speaking the above destabilizing effects will thus not appear in the trace of the Jacobian of the system at the steady state, but will be hidden somewhere in the principal minors that underlie the calculation of the Routh–Hurwitz conditions for local asymptotic stability.

Assumptions

In order to have all behavioral functions as linear as possible we assume for the foreign sector the behavioral relationships:

$$\gamma_c(\eta) = \gamma_c^0 + \gamma(\eta_0 - \eta),$$
$$c_1^*(\eta) = c_0 + c_1(\eta_0 - \eta),$$
$$c_0 = (1 - \gamma_c(\eta_0))(1 - s_c)(\rho_0^e - t^n).$$

The first assumption of course cannot be true in the large, since $\gamma_c(\eta) \in [0,\ 1]$ must hold true. The second and third assumptions guarantee that there is a balanced trade account, and thus a balanced capital account, in the steady state with η_0 as steady-state terms of trade, and $r_0 = r_0^*$.

Proposition 14.1 *There is a* unique steady-state solution *or point of rest of the dynamics (14.1)–(14.8) fulfilling* $\omega_0,\ l_0,\ p_0,\ e_0 \neq 0$ *which is given by*[10]

$$y_0 = \bar{U} y^p, \quad l_0 = (y_0/x)/\bar{V}, \quad y_0^e = y_0^d = y_0/(1+n\beta_{n^d}), \quad \nu_0 = \beta_{n^d} y_0^e,$$

$$\omega_0 = \frac{s_c(y_0^e - \delta - t^n) + t^n - g - n}{(s_c - \tau_w) y_0/x}, \quad \rho_0^e = y_0^e - \delta - \frac{\omega_0 y_0}{x},$$

$$p_0 = m_0 l_0/(h_1 y_0), \quad \pi_0 = 0, \quad r_0 = \rho_0^e,$$

$$e_0 = p_0 \quad \textit{if } \eta_0 = 1, \quad p_0^* = 1, \quad \epsilon_0 = 0.$$

For a proof of Proposition 14.1 the reader is referred to Asada *et al.* (2003a). We assume that the parameters of the model are chosen such that the steady-state values for $\omega,\ l,\ m,\ \rho,\ r,\ \eta$ are all positive. With respect to the above steady-state solution the following then holds.

Proposition 14.2 *The following statements hold with respect to the 8D dynamical system (14.1)–(14.8).*[11]

1. *Assume that the corresponding steady state of the subdynamics for the closed economy is locally asymptotically stable for* $\eta,\ \epsilon$ *frozen at their steady-state values* $\eta_0,\ \epsilon_0$.[12] *Then, the steady state of the full 8D dynamics is locally asymptotically stable for all adjustment speeds* $\beta_e,\ \beta_\epsilon$ *that are chosen sufficiently small.*
2. *The determinant of the Jacobian of the dynamics (14.1)–(14.8) at the steady state is always positive.*
3. *On the other hand, if* β_e *(or* β*) and* β_ϵ *are chosen sufficiently large then the steady-state equilibrium is locally repelling. The system therefore generally undergoes Hopf bifurcations at intermediate values of these adjustment parameters for the foreign sector.*

The stability and Hopf bifurcation results we obtained in the case of a closed economy in Chiarella and Flaschel (2000a) therefore generalize to the open-economy situation and can thus be extended to include the above considered parameter changes. We thus know of situations where the Routh–Hurwitz conditions for local asymptotic stability hold and further where they are violated, by increasing the adjustment speed of certain expectation mechanisms and of certain prices. The Hopf bifurcation theorem implies the existence of limit cycles for our dynamical system, either unstable ones that shrink to zero as the bifurcation point is approached, or stable ones that are born when the bifurcation point is passed.

In the following numerical sections of the chapter we shall by and large apply as basic set of parameters the ones displayed in Table 14.1, modified in specific ways in order to get interesting dynamics.

The set of parameter values shown in Table 14.1 provides a case somewhat below the situation of a Hopf bifurcation as considered in Proposition 14.2 and

Table 14.1 Parameter set for the basic simulation of the high-order disequilibrium growth dynamics model

$s_c = 0.8$	$\delta = 0.1$	$n = 0.05$	$h_1 = 0.1$	$h_2 = 0.4$	$(m_o = 0.05,\ m_o$ shock:1.1)		
$y^p = 1$	$x = 2$	$\beta_w = 0.35$	$\beta_p = 1$	$\kappa_w = 0.5$	$\kappa_p = 0.5$	$\beta_\pi = 1$	$\alpha_\pi = 0.5$
$i_1 = 0.3$	$i_2 = 0.25$	$\beta_{n^d} = 0.1$	$\beta_{y^e} = 9$	$\beta_n = 10$	$t^n = 0.3$	$g = 0.33$	
$\beta_e = 0.5$	$\beta = 1$	$\beta_\epsilon = 1$	$\alpha_\epsilon = 0.5$	$c_1 = 0.15$	$\gamma_c^o = 0.5$	$\gamma = 1$	

thus gives rise to convergent cyclical dynamics back to the steady state (which due to space limitations are not shown here). Increasing adjustment speeds for prices, quantities or expectations will generally make the dynamics globally explosive, which means that extrinsic nonlinearities have to be added to them in order to obtain economic boundedness. Additional nonlinearities are then generally needed when local asymptotic stability is lost through a faster adjustment of prices, quantities and expectations. Such nonlinearities will be investigated in isolation and in combination in the following Sections 14.4–14.7.

14.4 Relaxation oscillations in the market for foreign exchange

Assuming as point of departure for the following numerical investigations of the model a much higher adjustment speed for the exchange rate $\beta_e = 2.5$ and a strong adjustment of the corresponding expectational dynamics $\beta_\epsilon = 5$, $\alpha_\epsilon = 0.8$ implies nearly immediate collapse of (extremely strong divergence from) the steady state for the considered dynamics. To make these dynamics nevertheless a bounded one we therefore in addition integrate into the model the fact that net capital flows are bounded by international wealth and thus must remain limited.

Specifically we are here assuming for the reaction of net capital exports (per unit of capital) with respect to interest rate differentials

$$\beta(r_0^* + \epsilon - r) = \beta_1 \tanh[\beta(r_0^* + \epsilon - r)/\beta_1], \quad \beta_1 = 0.05.$$

This function of the interest rate differential has the same slope as the earlier linear function $\beta(r_0^* + \epsilon - r)$ at the steady state, but its values remain less than 0.1 in absolute amount (for $\beta_1 = 0.05$), however large interest rate differentials may become.

Before turning to a numerical illustration of the resulting dynamics (see Figure 14.2), we briefly discuss by means of Figure 14.1 from a 2D perspective why and how so-called relaxation oscillation must occur in such a situation.[13] We know from equation (14.7) that the exchange rate e is driven by excess demand in the market for foreign currency

$$\hat{e} = \beta_e\{\beta_1 \tanh[\beta(r_0^* + \epsilon - r)/\beta_1] - nx(\eta, \rho^e)\},$$

with speed β_e. These dynamics are depicted as a function of ϵ in Figure 14.1 with the additional term $nx(\eta, \rho^e)$, $\eta = p/e$, acting as shift term with respect to the curve shown.

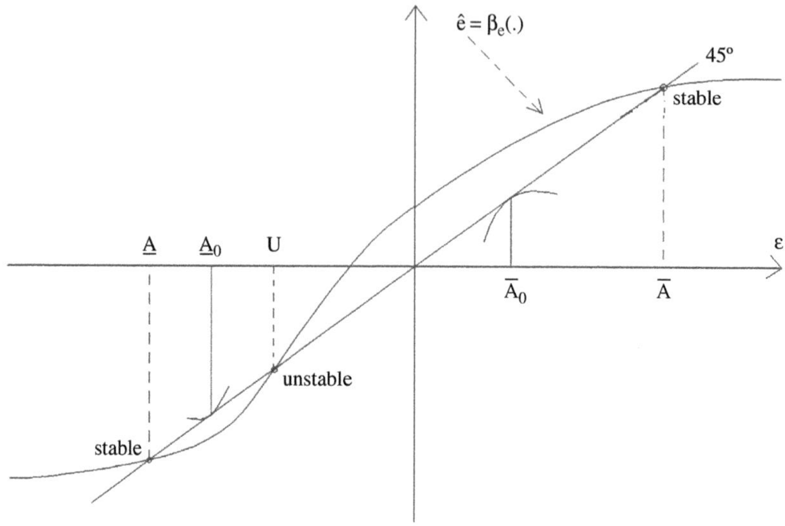

Figure 14.1 Exchange rate dynamics and myopic perfect foresight equilibria.

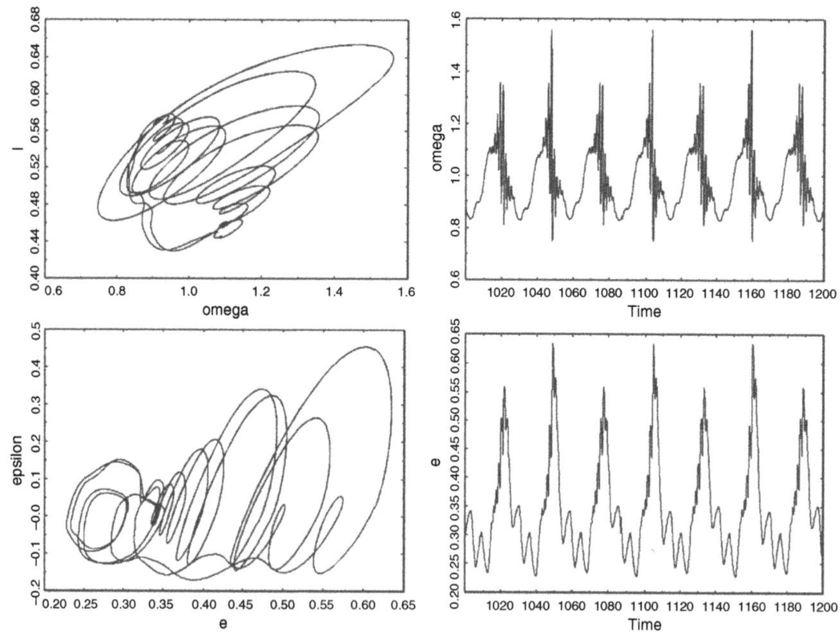

Figure 14.2 The contours of the attractor of the 8D dynamics with near to perfect foresight relaxation oscillations.

There are three perfect foresight equilibria in the depicted situation, points $\underline{\mathrm{A}}$, U and $\overline{\mathrm{A}}$. Furthermore, and for example, an adaptive revision of expectations

$$\dot{\epsilon} = \beta_\epsilon(\hat{e} - \epsilon)$$

will produce in Figure 14.1 convergence to either the perfect foresight equilibrium $\underline{\mathrm{A}}$ or $\overline{\mathrm{A}}$, depending on initial conditions, while the one in the middle, U, is unstable under adaptive expectations.

We start from a situation where $nx(\eta, \cdot) > 0$ holds, i.e. where there is a trade surplus initially (at point $\overline{\mathrm{A}}$). Again, fast adaptive expectations ($\beta_\epsilon \uparrow$) ensure that the economy is at or close to this point $\overline{\mathrm{A}}$. However, at this point $\overline{\mathrm{A}}$, we have $\hat{e} = \epsilon > 0$ and thus a rising nominal exchange rate and falling terms of trade $\eta = p/e$ (the opposite conclusion holds at $\underline{\mathrm{A}}$). The trade surplus $nx(\eta, \cdot)$ at $\overline{\mathrm{A}}$ is therefore increasing in size, which shifts the $\beta_e(\cdot)$ curve downwards and point $\overline{\mathrm{A}}$ to the left toward a lower level of $\hat{e} = \epsilon$. The ongoing depreciation of the home country's currency is thereby slowed down and it moves the economy into the direction of the steady state $\hat{e} = 0$.

This process continues until point $\overline{\mathrm{A}}_0$ is reached where the upper perfect foresight equilibrium disappears. From then on the lower perfect foresight equilibrium is the only stable equilibrium which is rapidly (or instantaneously) approached by way of our mechanism of (infinitely) fast adaptive expectations (for example). When this point is approached we get however $\hat{e} = \epsilon < 0$ and thus now rising terms of trade η. The $\beta_e(\cdot)$ curve therefore then starts to shift upwards, and the point $\underline{\mathrm{A}}$ starts moving to the right. There results an ongoing appreciation of the home country's currency which slowly reduces the now existing trade balance deficit until again a critical point $\underline{\mathrm{A}}_0$ of the considered dynamics is reached, where the lower stable equilibrium on which this process rested disappears. The process then returns (immediately) to a situation of the type $\overline{\mathrm{A}}$ and the above described situation starts to repeat itself.

This is the open-economy analog to the well-known Kaldor (1940) trade cycle mechanism with its fast variable Y, the output of firms, and its slow variable K, the capital stock of firms. In the present model, the fast variable is the expected rate of depreciation or appreciation ϵ and the (relatively) slow variable is the rate of exchange e which is working in the Kaldorian way through the trade imbalance $nx(\eta, \cdot)$, $\eta = p/e$.

The above is of course only an intuitive analysis of the dynamics generated by equations (14.7) and (14.8) in the presence of a nonlinearity of the $\beta(\cdot)$ type. A complete analysis demands a planar representation of the above dynamics of the variables ϵ, e, so far based on one law of motion and a slowly shifting parametric term $nx(\eta, \cdot)$. There are indeed many representations of this limit cycle mechanism and its limiting case (a limit limit cycle) which, however, are not reviewed here again.

From the 8D point of view there are further factors that influence this Kaldorian relaxation oscillation, namely the price level p, the nominal rate of interest r and its determinants and the expected rate of profit ρ^e. The relaxation oscillation just described thus interacts in a specific way with the remaining six state variables of the dynamics. This situation is described in detail in Asada *et al.* (2003a). Figure 14.2 shows the contours of the attractor of the 8D dynamics with near to perfect foresight relaxation oscillations.[14]

Owing to the high speed of adjustments in the market for foreign exchange[15] we have a high frequency of the wave-forms shown also for the real sector of the economy (which appears to be unrealistic). The important thing here however is that the assumed nonlinearity has established the viability of the dynamics in a pronounced way. Nonlinearities in international capital flows may therefore represent an important stabilizing force even in situations where adjustments are very fast (and in particular even if perfect foresight is assumed to prevail).

In Figure 14.3 we show a bifurcation diagram corresponding to the situation considered in Figure 14.2. This diagram shows the local maxima and minima of the time series for the real wage ω for parameter values β_ϵ between 0 and 5.6 after a transient period of 1000 years up to year 1250. We can see from this figure (which may still include some transient behavior) that the shape of the attractor is varying considerably over the range of the bifurcation parameter with relatively limited fluctuations of the real wage for β_ϵ between 0.6 and 2 – and with boundedness of the dynamics for all values of β_ϵ that are considered.

There may be problems in interpreting this type of bifurcation diagram and the false type of bifurcation they may suggest are discussed in Parker and Chua (1989, p. 218ff.). This discussion nevertheless shows that this type of bifurcation diagram can be of use if it is interpreted with care. We will return to such diagrammatic

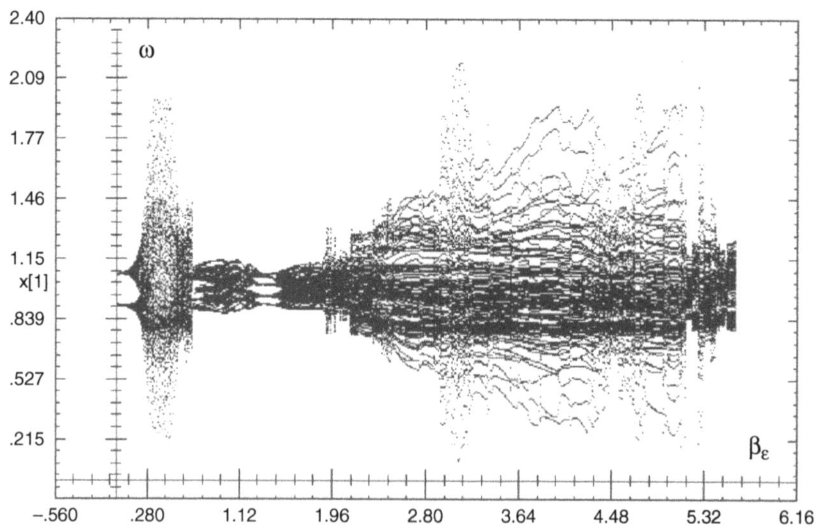

Figure 14.3 A bifurcation diagram along the attracting sets of the dynamics.

representations in Section 14.7 when period-doubling routes to complex dynamics are investigated for a 9D extension of the model.

14.5 Adding sluggish trade balance adjustments

In order to remove the high-frequency cycles at least from the real part of the model we now assume that the terms of trade that apply to exports and imports only sluggishly adjust to the terms of trade fluctuations, $p/(ep^*)$, as they are caused by the net capital flows in the market for internationally traded bonds. Specifically we assume here for the relationship between these two (real) rates of exchange η_{trade} and η the following delayed response of the former rate to the movement of the latter:

$$\dot{\eta}_{\text{trade}} = \beta_t(\eta - \eta_{\text{trade}}), \qquad \beta_t > 0,$$

where $1/\beta_t$ gives the time delay with which the trade rate is responding to the capital market-determined rate[16] η. Assuming for example for the delay $1/\beta_t$ the value 2.5 we obtain for the situation considered in the preceding section the simulations shown in Figure 14.4.[17]

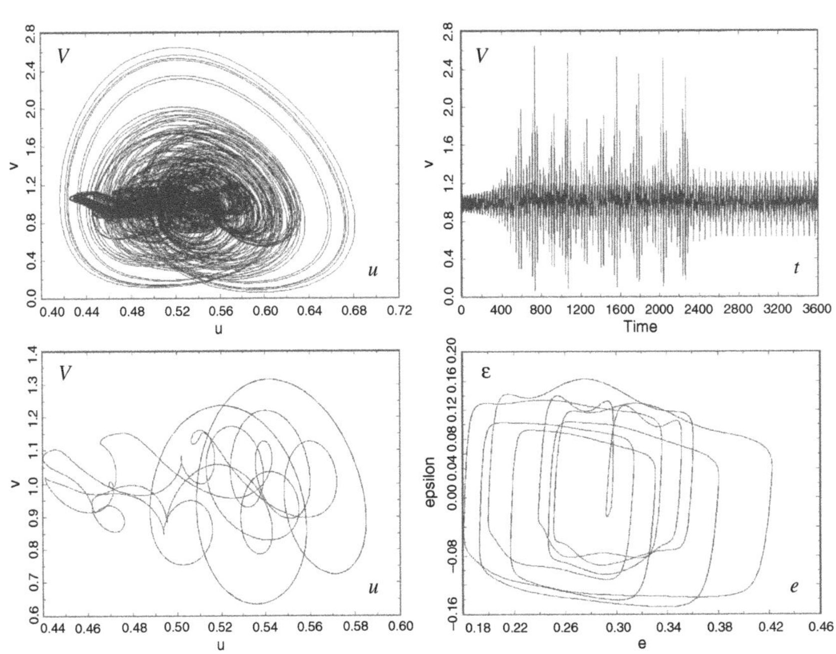

Figure 14.4 The 8D dynamics with perfect foresight relaxation oscillations and sluggishly adjusting international trade, transient and limit behavior.

We see that the 2D relaxation oscillation in the foreign exchange market has become somewhat more pronounced now as its interaction with the real sector is less tight here (and as the speed of adjustment of exchange rate expectations has been increased). The limit behavior of the dynamics thus appears to be of the type of a high-order limit cycle in both real and nominal magnitudes.

14.6 Kinked Phillips curves

We now turn to our second type of extrinsic nonlinearity[18] which is much easier to introduce, in particular in the following stylized form. We assume that wage inflation is determined as described in Section 14.2, but that wage deflation is subject to a floor $f < 0$, saying that wages will adjust downwards at most with speed f. This gives rise to the following modification of the money wage Phillips curve of the model (14.1)–(14.8):

$$\widehat{w} = \max\{f, \beta_w(V - \bar{V}) + \kappa_w \hat{p} + (1 - \kappa_w)\pi\},$$

which implies for price inflation the expression

$$\hat{p} = \beta_p(U - \bar{U}) + \kappa_p f + (1 - \kappa_p)\pi,$$

when the floor f is reached, and for the dynamics of real wages in this case

$$\widehat{\omega} = -\beta_p(U - \bar{U}) + (1 - \kappa_p)(f - \pi).$$

Adding this modification to the model (14.1)–(14.8) also changes its dynamics and its degree of viability dramatically. This is also true without the occurrence of relaxation oscillations, as Figures 14.5 and 14.6 demonstrate.[19]

Figure 14.5 shows on this basis a situation where there is a (mild) floor to nominal wage deflation, $f = -0.03$, and considers this over a time horizon of 100 years. Top left in Figure 14.5 we see the phase plot for the share of wages $u = \omega/x$ as against the rate of employment $V = y/(xl)$ (the variables of the Goodwin (1967)–Rose (1967) employment cycle). This plot shows a cycle that is basically of Goodwin–Rose growth cycle type though with added freely fluctuating and explosive movements in the phase of high employment and thereafter with fluctuations with decreasing amplitude when the kink in the Phillips curve becomes partly operative. The economy thereby slowly gets stuck (for a while) in a depressed situation and is thereafter showing slow monotonic recovery of the rate of employment accompanied by significant decreases in the share of wages[20] back to high levels of employment (where the explosive fluctuations again set in).[21] States of high employment are thus accompanied by superimposed shorter cycles, while nothing of this type occurs in states of depression during which the "kink" is fully operative (see again Figure 14.5, top left). The plot top right shows – besides the share of wages u – the time series of the rates of employment V and of capacity utilization U which during the depression are negatively correlated and thus contradict the usual understanding of Okun's law (see Okun 1970).

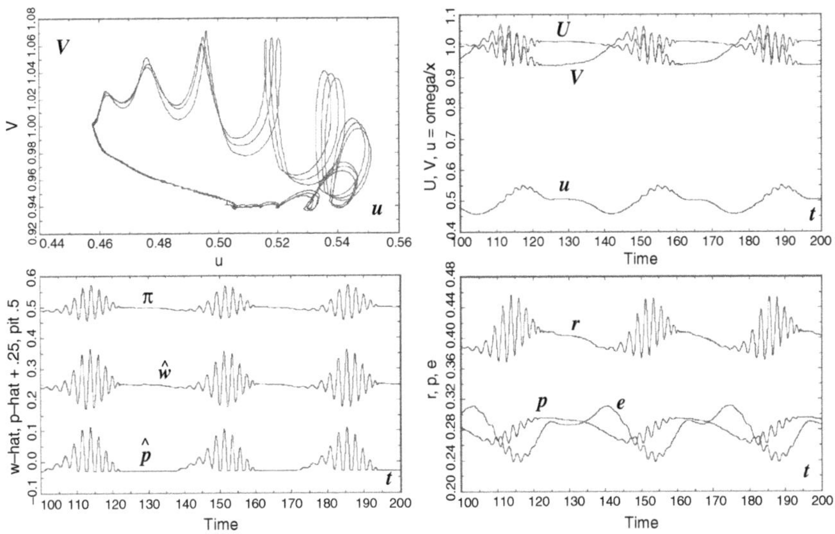

Figure 14.5 The 8D dynamics with a kinked Phillips curve for $t \in [100, 200]$ $(f = -0.03)$.[22]

During phases of high employment both rates start to fluctuate in line with each other, which is in line with Okun (1970). It is thus obvious that the cycle has a very typical asymmetric structure where Okun's law holds for part of the time, but not at other times.

Bottom left in Figure 14.5 we see the rates of growth of wages, prices and the expected rate of inflation which – in order to distinguish them from another in one and the same figure – have been augmented by constant terms and thus lifted along the vertical axis (by 0.25, 0.5 respectively). The period where the kink in the Phillips curve is operative is clearly visible. Finally, we see bottom right that there is a strict co-movement between the nominal rate of interest and the price level (at least in phases of depression), which has been called the Gibson paradox in the literature. While relaxation oscillations in the market for foreign exchange give rise to high-frequency fluctuations of the economy (which need to be damped in their impact on the real part of the economy), a kink in the money wage Phillips curve gives rise to long cycles in employment and income distribution (superimposed by shorter cycles during the phase of high employment).

A remarkable observation in the latter case (see Figure 14.6) is that the recovery back to full and overemployment need not occur under all circumstances, in particular when the kink in the Phillips curve is sufficiently close to zero and when relaxation oscillations are present. In such a situation the actual employment rate may stay completely below the NAIRU rate of employment (here equal to one) in the course of the cycle due to the fact that each upswing is too weak to reach or go beyond the steady-state value of employment. We thus can have "unnaturally" low

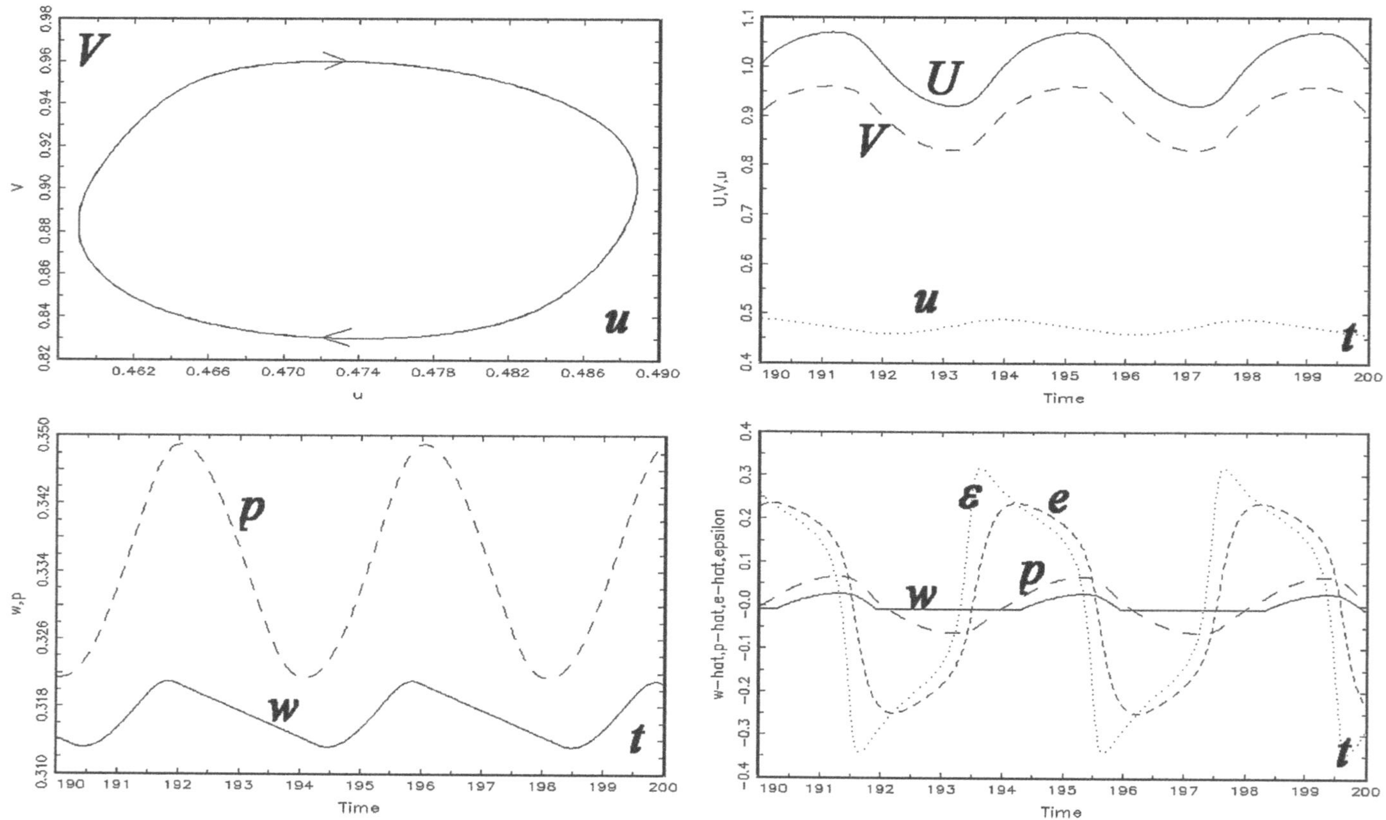

Figure 14.6 A persistent depressed employment cycle ($f = -0.01$).

employment rates all over the cycle, and thus also on average, caused by the existence of persistent cycles which prevent the economy from climbing back to (or going beyond) their uniquely determined steady-state situation. Note that capacity utilizations of capital and labor move in line with each other in Figure 14.6, while there is again a quarter phase displacement of the wage share reflecting the overshooting mechanism of the Goodwin (1967) model. As Figure 14.6 bottom right shows we have again relaxation oscillations in the foreign exchange market which here account for the relatively high-frequency movement that is observed and which in fact help to keep the real cycle below the NAIRE rate of employment $\bar{V} = 1$.[23]

14.7 Period-doubling routes to chaos

In this section we finally display some simulations based on the simultaneous operation of the considered extrinsic nonlinearities and also on a sluggish adjustment of the trade balance. The parameter set used is displayed in Table 14.2 and is basically the same as the one for Figure 14.5 of the preceding section, up to wage and inflationary expectations adjustment speeds and again a stricter floor to nominal wage decreases $f = -0.01$, which now however does not prevent endogenous recovery to situations above "full" employment.

With respect to this parameter set we find that, as wage flexibility β_w is increased, there is a period-doubling sequence toward complex dynamics which in fact repeats itself to some degree as the wage adjustment speed becomes more and more pronounced. We thus see by way of these numerical examples that the integrated dynamics of small open economies with their intrinsic and only two extrinsic nonlinearities of a fairly natural type allows for period-doubling routes to chaos if, in the presence of a kinked Phillips curve, the wage adjustment speed β_w becomes sufficiently strong.

The 3D and 2D projections of the full 8D dynamics shown in Figures 14.7 and 14.8 in particular clearly show a sequence of period doublings that leads to more than quasi-periodic behavior at the parameter values $\beta_w = 1.55$, 2.4 and 3.03, and thus to chaos, as for example discussed in Parker and Chua (1989, ch. 1). It is also astonishing to see that further increases in wage adjustment speed give rise to a return to simple periodic behavior, wherefrom a new sequence of period doublings is started and where the already observed pattern seems to repeat itself.

Table 14.2 Parameter set for the basic simulation of the high-order disequilibrium growth dynamics model: period-doubling routes to chaos

$s_c = 0.8$	$\delta = 0.1$	$n = 0.05$	$h_1 = 0.1$	$h_2 = 0.1$	($m_o = 0.05$, m_o shock:1.1)				
$y^p = 1$	$x = 2$	$\beta_w = 1.3$	$\beta_p = 1$	$\kappa_w = 0.5$	$\kappa_p = 0.5$	$\beta_\pi = 1$	$\alpha_\pi = 1$		
$i_1 = 0.3$	$i_2 = 0.25$	$\beta_{n^d} = 0.1$	$\beta_{y^e} = 5$	$\beta_n = 10$	$t^n = 0.3$	$g = 0.33$			
$\beta_e = 2$	$\beta = 1$	$\beta_\epsilon = 1$	$\alpha_\epsilon = 0.5$	$c_1 = 0.15$	$\gamma_c^o = 0.5$	$\gamma = 1$		$\beta_1 = 0.05$	$\beta_t = 0.5$

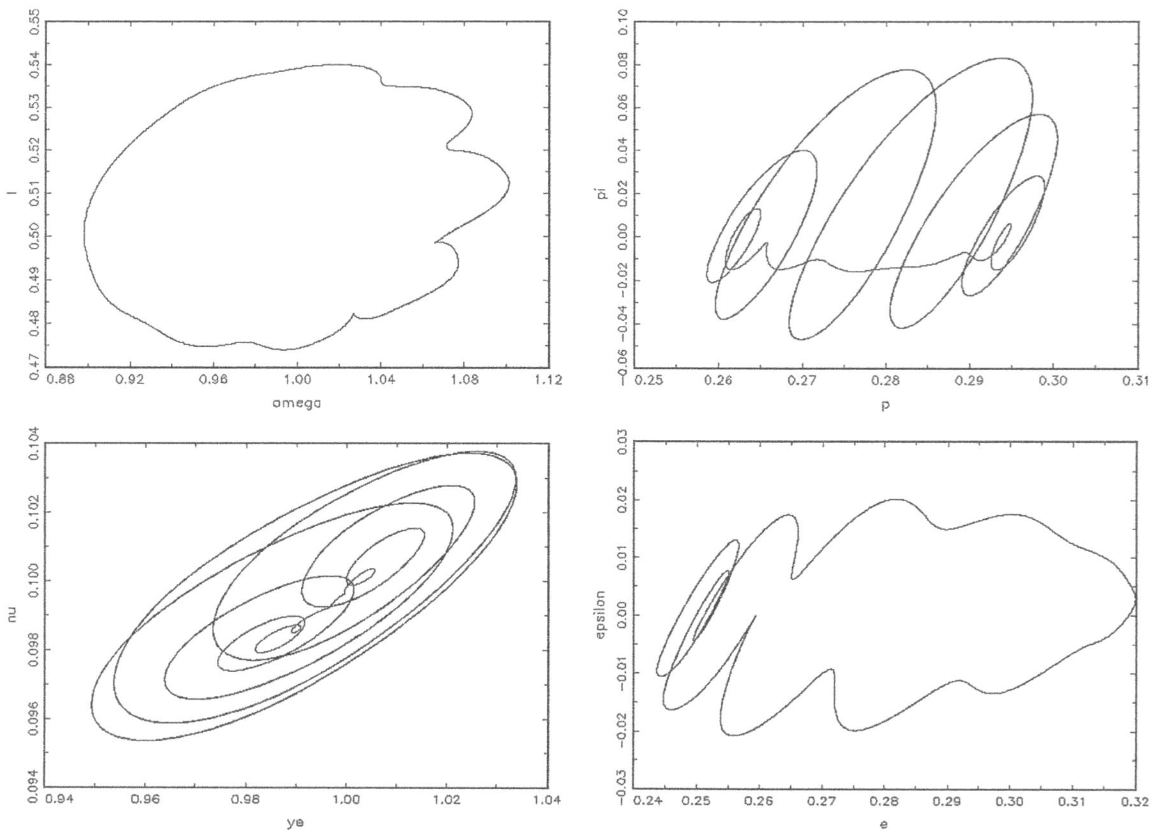

Figure 14.7 A 3D projection of a period-doubling route toward “complex dynamics.”

With Figure 14.9 we provide further evidence on the mentioned series of period doublings, again by way of a bifurcation diagram as suggested and discussed in Parker and Chua (1989) – see also the critical comments on such bifurcation diagrams in their chapter 8. Figure 14.9 provides a very compact impression of what is going on when the adjustment speed of nominal wage is increased from 0.5 to 3.5 as far as the local maxima and minima of the time series of the evolution of real wages are concerned.

14.8 Conclusions

We have set up and analyzed an 8D disequilibrium monetary growth model of a small open economy. We have discussed how the model's cycle generating behavior arises from the balance between stabilizing and destabilizing influences of its basic economic feedback structures, namely the Rose effect, the Metzler

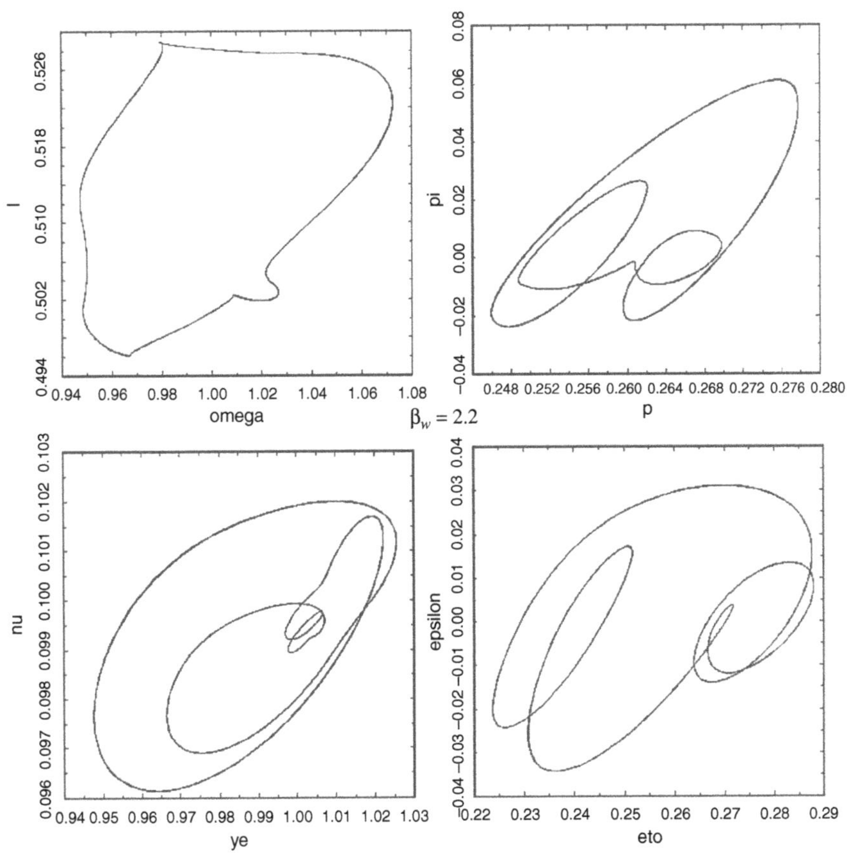

Figure 14.8 Subsequent period-doubling sequences toward complex dynamics (the four 2D projections, as in Figure 14.2).

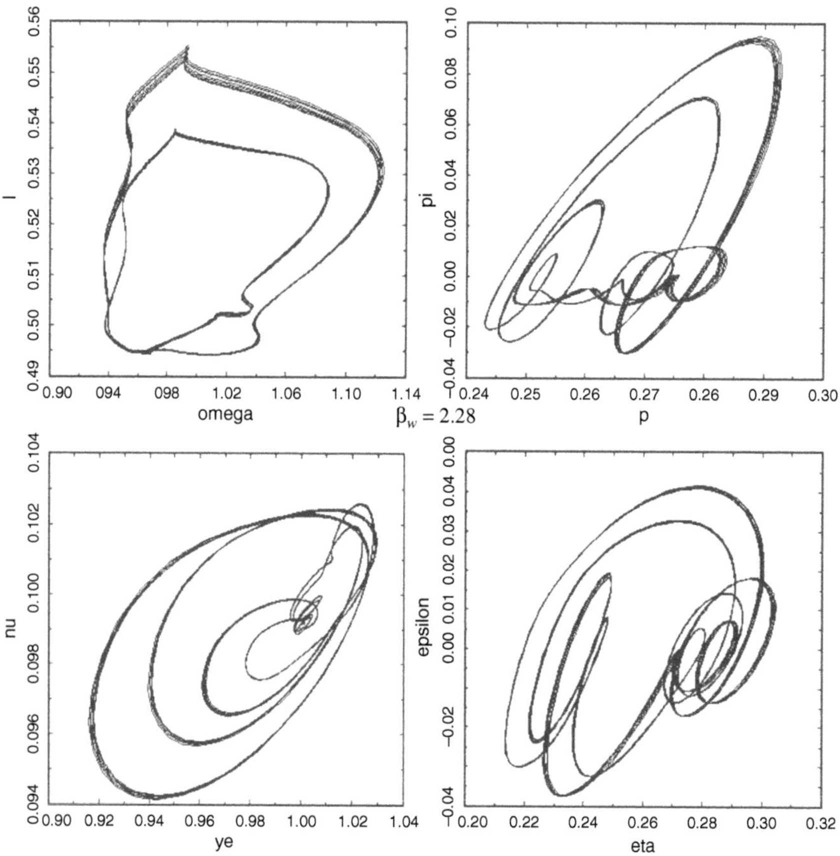

Figure 14.8 Continued.

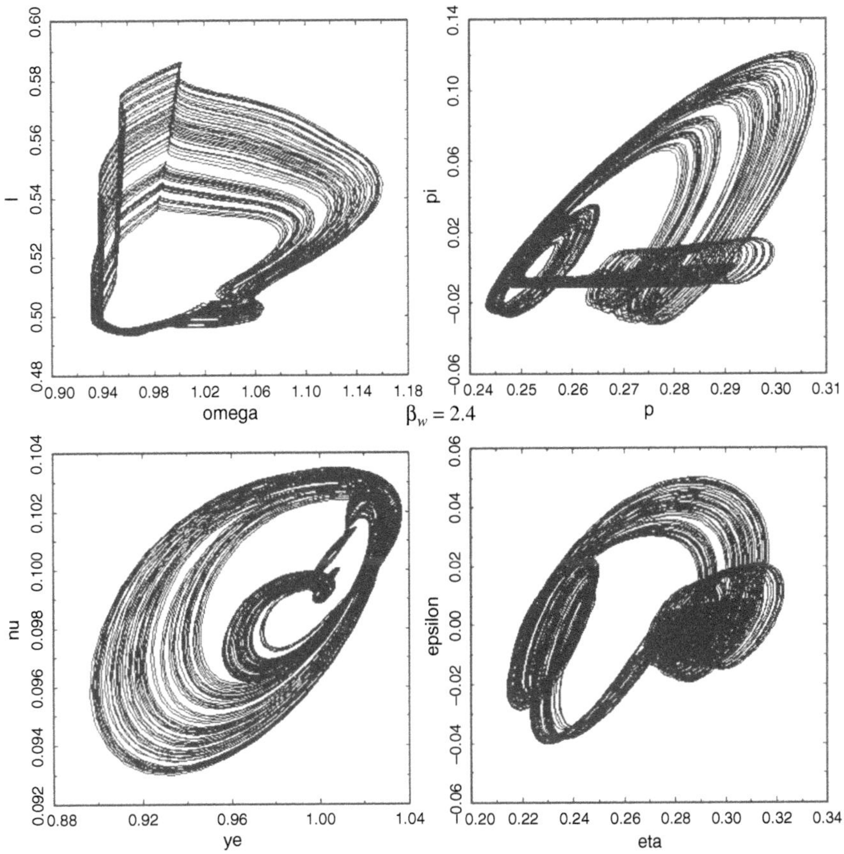

Figure 14.8 Continued.

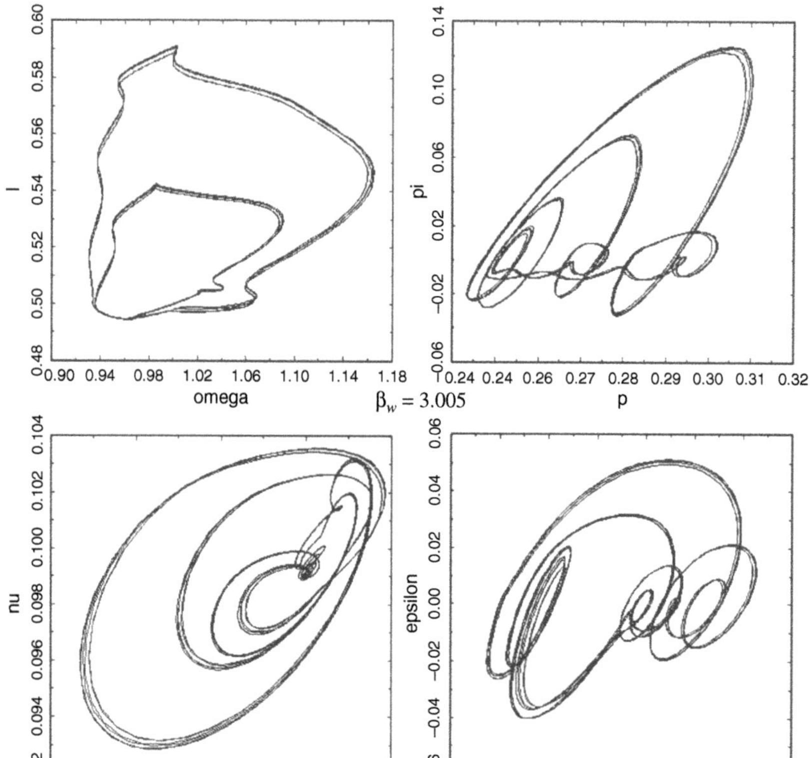

Figure 14.8 Continued.

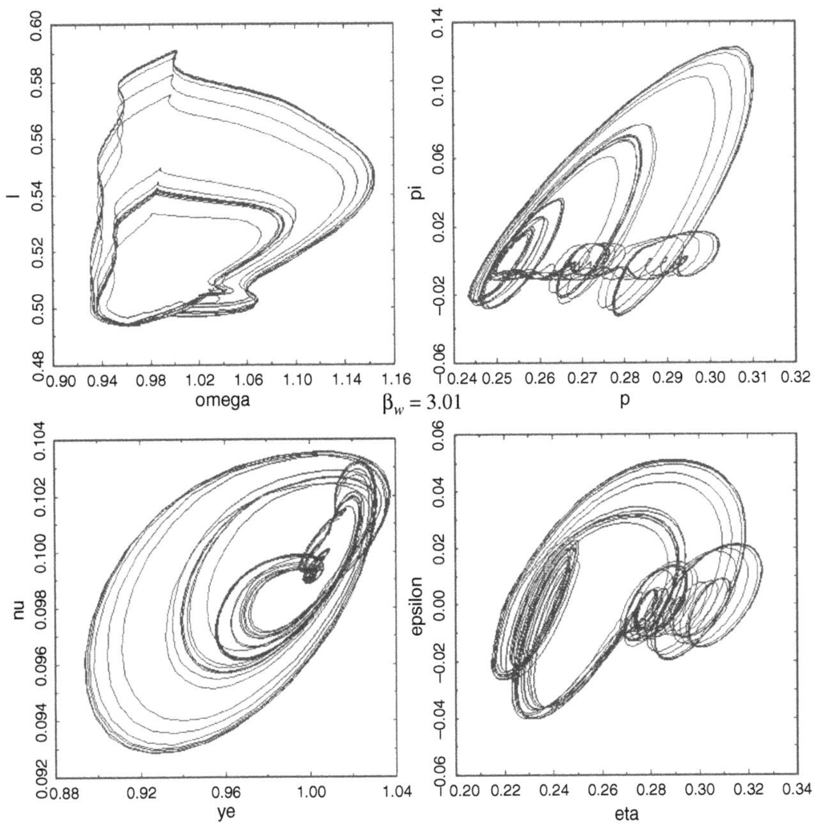

Figure 14.8 Continued.

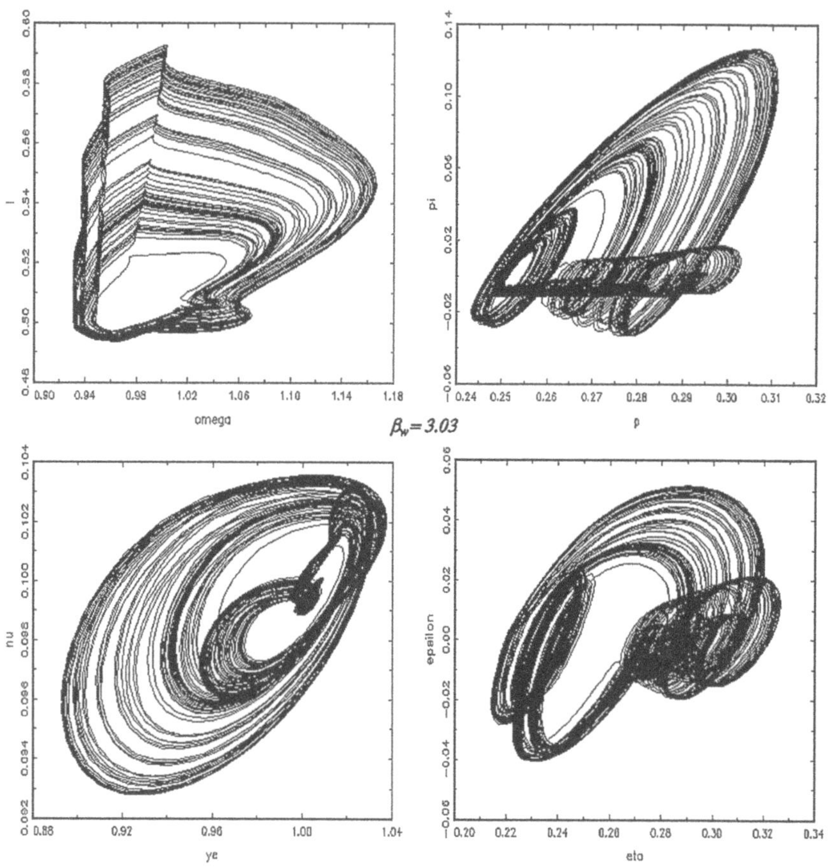

Figure 14.8 Continued.

effect, the Mundell effect, the Dornbusch effect and the Keynes effect. We have seen via numerical simulations that the model's intrinsic nonlinearities are generally not able to bound the dynamic motion when the equilibrium is locally unstable. We have therefore introduced two extrinsic nonlinearities, one in the

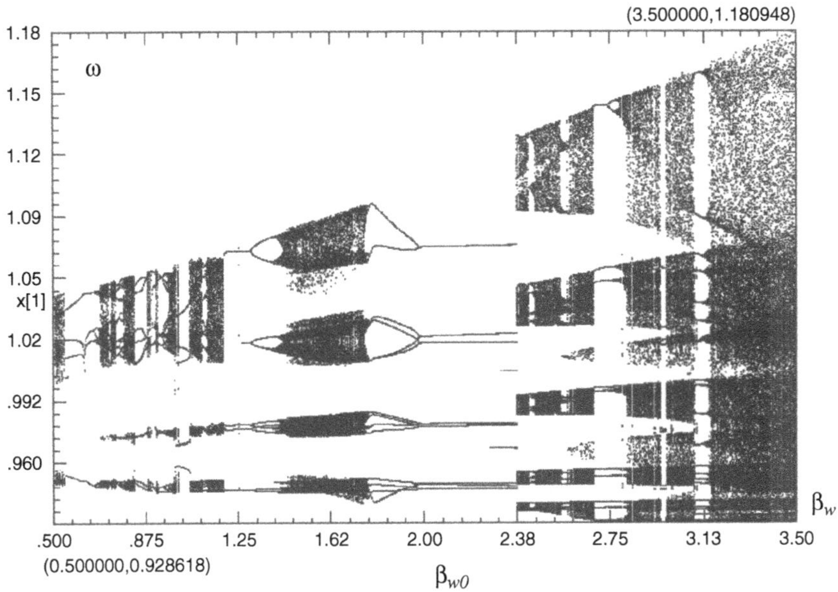

Figure 14.9 A bifurcation diagram corresponding to Figures 14.7 and 14.8.

flow of internationally traded interest-bearing assets, the other in the form of a floor on nominal wage depreciation in the presence of high unemployment rates.

We have used numerical simulations and bifurcation diagrams to study the impact of these nonlinearities on the resulting dynamics. With the nonlinearities operating separately or together the motion now remains bounded for a wide range of parameter values. Bifurcation diagrams reveal regions of high-order limit cycles as well as regions of apparently chaotic motion. We have also introduced sluggish adjustment of the trade balance to exchange rate changes, which increases the dimension of the system by one but leads to more realistic frequencies of cycles in the real part of the model for medium-sized wage and price adjustment speeds.

Further developments of the model studied here would include the introduction of the government budget constraint and of policy rules that may add further stability to the system and allowing in a more explicit way for heterogeneous agents (chartists and fundamentalists) in the foreign exchange market. A much larger list is provided in Asada *et al.* (2003a).

15 AD–AS disequilibrium dynamics and endogenous growth

15.1 Introduction

Models of AD–AS growth, such as the one in Sargent (1987, ch. 5), allow only for one type of disequilibrium, in the labor market, which is interpreted as being due to the assumed sluggish wage adjustment based on a conventional augmented money wage Phillips curve. The goods market is in equilibrium in a twofold way. Firms are on their supply or AS curve, operating at the desired level of capacity utilization. There is Keynesian goods and money market (or AD) equilibrium, since the price level, which is completely flexible, adjusts such that the Keynesian regime or quantity constraint becomes compatible with the profit-maximizing choice of output of firms, but not compatible with labor market equilibrium. There has been an extensive discussion in the recent literature whether this is a sensible scenario for describing a Keynesian rationing of firms on the market for goods – see Chiarella *et al.* (2000b, sec. 7.10) for a brief survey.

We do not enter into this discussion here, but simply avoid the situation described above by positing that a Keynesian theory of fluctuations and growth should allow for both the stock of labor and the stock of capital to be under- or over-utilized. In line with Keynes (1936, p. 4) we therefore should provide an explanation of the actual employment of all available resources, not only just labor. The traditional way to start the modeling of such a situation is to assume a sluggish adjustment of the price level as well – of a form that is still to be determined – and to study on this basis the evolution of IS–LM equilibria and the price level in time. One could follow thereby the example of the macroeconometric model in Powell and Murphy (1997) by assuming that prices sluggishly adjust toward competitive conditions as encapsulated in the AS curve.

Further reflection, however, shows that this is still too much equilibrium to start with, since firms always adjust toward IS–LM equilibrium with infinite speed. Assuming instead, and in line with price adjustment, also a somewhat sluggish quantity adjustment indeed makes the Keynesian structure of the considered dynamics even more obvious and, as shown in Chiarella and Flaschel (2000a), also easier to analyze, though the number of dynamic variables is increased by two. In the place of ambiguous equilibrium descriptions we have a clear sequence of causal events, which thus allows AD–AS equilibrium growth to be understood from the perspective of disequilibrium growth, to be presented below.

The following AS–AS model of disequilibrium growth in this chapter[1] is thus based on sluggish wage, price and quantity adjustment processes (including expectations) giving rise in particular to under- or over-utilized labor as well as capital in the dynamics it implies. We obtain a (minimally) complete and consistent structural form of a Keynesian monetary growth model with goods as well as labor market disequilibrium, based on consistently formulated budget equations for households (workers and asset-holders), firms and the government. We include Harrod neutral technical change of an exogenous rate n_l, supplementing natural growth n in the usual way, in order to approach the subject of the chapter, the role of endogenously generated technical change in such models of AD–AS disequilibrium growth.

15.2 AD–AS disequilibrium growth: exogenous technical change

The static and dynamic equations of this general continuous-time model of disequilibrium growth are the following ones.[2]

First, households' behavior (workers and asset-holders) is described by the following equations.[3]

1. *Households (workers and asset-holders):*

$$C = (1-\tau_w)\omega L^d + (1-s_c)[\rho^e K + rB/p - T_c], \tag{15.1}$$

$$S_p = s_c[\rho^e K + rB/p - T_c] = (\dot{M}^d + \dot{B}^d + p_e\dot{E}^d)/p, \tag{15.2}$$

$$\widehat{L} = n = \text{const.}, \quad \text{growth rate of labor supply,} \tag{15.3}$$

$$\omega = w/p, \quad \text{real wage,} \quad u = \omega/x = wL^d/(pY), \quad \text{wage share,} \tag{15.4}$$

$$\rho^e = (Y^e - \delta K - \omega L^d)/K, \quad \text{expected real rate of profit.} \tag{15.5}$$

Aggregate consumption C is based on classical saving habits, s_w, s_c, with the savings rate out of wages, s_w, set equal to zero for simplicity. We assume that wages are taxed with a uniform rate τ_w and that property income is subject to lump sum taxation T_c, again for reasons of simplicity. Allowing savings out of wages and other taxation schemes does not make much difference – see (Chiarella and Flaschel 2000a, 1999) in this regard. We denote by L^d actual employment, by K the capital stock, and by L labor supply, which grows at the natural rate n. Bonds B are of the fixed price variety, with a money market-determined nominal rate of interest r and with price set equal to 1. Real private savings S_p, here out of disposable interest income of asset-holders solely, are allocated to desired changes in the stock of money, bonds and equities (E) held, the financial assets that exist in the considered economy.

The production and investment behavior of firms is described next by the following set of equations.[4]

2. *Firms (production units and investors):*

$$Y^p = y^p K, \quad y^p = \text{const.}, \quad U = Y/Y^p, \tag{15.6}$$

$$L^d = Y/x, \quad x = x_0 \exp(n_l t), \quad \hat{x} = n_l = \text{const.}, \quad V = L^d/L, \tag{15.7}$$

$$I = i_1(\rho^e - (r - \pi))K + i_2(U - \bar{U})K + (n + n_l)K, \tag{15.8}$$

$$S_f = Y_f = Y - Y^e = \mathcal{I}, \tag{15.9}$$

$$p_e \dot{E}/p = I + (\dot{N} - \mathcal{I}), \tag{15.10}$$

$$\widehat{K} = I/K. \tag{15.11}$$

According to equations (15.6) and (15.7), firms produce commodities in amount Y in the technologically simplest way possible, via a fixed proportions technology characterized by the potential output/capital ratio $y^p = Y^p/K$ and the ratio x between actual output Y and employment L^d needed to produce this output, where labor productivity x is assumed to rise with a constant rate of amount n_l. This simple concept of technology allows for a straightforward definition of the rate of utilization U, V of capital as well as labor.[5]

In equation (15.8) investment per unit of capital I/K is driven by three forces: by the rate of return differential between the expected rate of profit ρ^e and the real rate of interest $(r - \pi)$; by the deviation of actual capacity utilization U from the normal or nonaccelerating inflation rate of capacity utilization $\bar{U}$; and by an unexplained trend term $n + n_l$ which is determined such that capital widening in the steady state, where the first two terms are zero, is just sufficient to allow for "full employment." Savings S_f ($=$ income Y_f) of firms, equation (15.9), is equal to the excess of output Y over expected sales Y^e (and equal to planned inventory changes), since we assume in this model that expected sales are the basis of firms' dividend payments (after deduction of capital depreciation δK and real wage payments ωL^d).

The next equation shows the financial deficit of firms, due to the planned investment I and to unintended inventory changes $\dot{N} - \mathcal{I}$ (where N denotes the stock of inventories) which has to be financed by firms by issuing new equities. We assume here, as in Sargent (1987), that firms issue no bonds and retain no expected earnings. It follows, as expressed in equation (15.10), that the total amount of new equities $\dot{E}$ issued by firms, valued at current share price p_e, must equal in value the sum of intended fixed capital investment and unexpected inventory changes – compare our later formulation of the inventory adjustment mechanism. Finally, equation (15.11) states that (business fixed) investment plans of firms are always realized in this Keynesian (demand-oriented) context, by way of corresponding inventory changes.

We now turn to a brief description of the government sector which in the present chapter is not of central interest and is thus formulated in the simplest possible way in view of later steady-state calculations.[6]

3. *Government (fiscal and monetary authority):*

$$T_w = (1-\tau_w)\omega L^d, \quad \text{wage taxation,} \tag{15.12}$$

$$T_c \quad \text{s.t.} \quad (T_c - rB/p)/K = t_c^n = \text{const.}, \quad \text{property income taxation,} \tag{15.13}$$

$$G = T_w + gK, \quad g = \text{const.}, \quad \text{government expenditure,} \tag{15.14}$$

$$S_g = T - rB/p - G, \quad T = T_w + T_c, \quad \text{budget surplus (or deficit),} \tag{15.15}$$

$$\hat{M} = \mu = \text{const.}, \quad \text{growth rate of money supply } M, \tag{15.16}$$

$$\dot{B} = pG + rB - pT - \dot{M}, \quad \text{accommodating debt financing.} \tag{15.17}$$

Government is here characterized by assuming as in Sargent (1987, ch. 5) that real (property income) taxes net of interest are constant and that the money supply grows at a constant rate μ. The consequences of these assumptions for government savings and debt financing are shown in equations (15.15) and (15.17) in an obvious way. Much less restrictive fiscal and monetary policy rules are discussed in Chiarella *et al.* (1999).

The disequilibrium situation in the goods market is an important component driving the dynamics of the economy. This situation, as far as quantity adjustment processes are concerned, is described by the following equations.

4. *Disequilibrium situation (goods market adjustments):*

$$S = S_p + S_g + S_f = p_e\dot{E}^d/p + \mathcal{I} = I + \dot{N} = p_e\dot{E}/p + \mathcal{I}, \tag{15.18}$$

$$Y^d = C + I + \delta K + G, \tag{15.19}$$

$$N^d = \beta_{n^d} Y^e, \quad \mathcal{I} = (n+n_l)N^d + \beta_n(N^d - N), \tag{15.20}$$

$$Y = Y^e + \mathcal{I}, \tag{15.21}$$

$$\dot{Y}^e = (n+n_l)Y^e + \beta_{y^e}(Y^d - Y^e), \tag{15.22}$$

$$\dot{N} = Y - Y^d = S - I. \tag{15.23}$$

Equation (15.18) of this disequilibrium block of the model describes various identities that can be related with the ex post identity of savings and investment for a closed economy. It is here added solely for accounting purposes. Equation (15.19) then defines aggregate demand Y^d which is never constrained in the present model.

In equation (15.20) desired inventories N^d are assumed to be a constant proportion of expected sales Y^e and intended inventory investment $\mathcal{I}$ is then determined on this basis via the adjustment speed β_n multiplied by the current gap between intended and actual inventories $(N^d - N)$ and augmented by a growth term that integrates in the simplest way the fact that this inventory adjustment rule is operating in a growing economy. Output of firms Y in equation (15.21) is the sum of expected sales Y^e and planned inventory adjustments $\mathcal{I}$. Sales expectations are here formed in a purely adaptive way, again augmented by a growth term to take account of long-run natural growth; see equation (15.22). Finally, in equation (15.23), actual inventory changes $\dot{N}$ are given by the discrepancy between output Y and actual sales Y^d equal to the difference between total savings S and fixed business investment I.

We now turn to the wage–price module or the supply side of the model as it is often characterized in the literature.[7]

5. *Wage–price adjustment equations and inflationary expectations):*

$$\widehat{w} = \beta_w(V - \bar{V}) + \kappa_w(\hat{p} + n_l) + (1 - \kappa_w)(\pi + n_l), \tag{15.24}$$

$$\hat{p} = \beta_p(U - \bar{U}) + \kappa_p(\widehat{w} - n_l) + (1 - \kappa_p)\pi, \tag{15.25}$$

$$\dot{\pi} = \beta_\pi(\alpha\hat{p} + (1 - \alpha)(\mu - (n + n_l)) - \pi). \tag{15.26}$$

This "supply-side" description is based on fairly symmetric assumptions on the causes of wage and price inflation. Money wage inflation $\widehat{w}$ according to equation (15.24) is driven, on the one hand, by a demand-pull component, given by the deviation of the actual rate of employment V from the NAIRU rate $\bar{V}$, and, on the other, by a cost-push term measured by a weighted average of the actual rate of price inflation $\hat{p}$, augmented by the rate of productivity growth n_l,[8] and a medium-run expected rate of inflation π, again augmented in the just described way. Similarly, in equation (15.25), price inflation is driven by the demand-pressure term $(U - \bar{U})$, where $\bar{U}$ denotes the nonaccelerating inflation rate of capacity utilization, and the weighted average of the actual rate of wage inflation $\widehat{w}$ and a medium-run expected rate of inflation π, the former diminished by productivity growth, since this reduces the cost pressure that firms are experiencing. The latter rate of inflation, expected as the average over the medium run, is in turn determined by a composition of backward-looking (adaptive) and forward-looking (regressive) expectations. It is easy to show, under suitable assumptions, that this amounts to an inflationary expectations mechanism as in (15.26) where expectations are governed in an adaptive way by a weighted average of the actual and the steady-state rate of inflation. It is also easy to extend this mechanism to more refined backward-looking procedures as well as to more refined price forecasting rules (so-called p^* concepts and the like).[9]

Finally, we have the following set of equilibrium conditions with respect to the financial assets considered in this model.

6. *Equilibrium conditions (asset markets):*

$$M = M^d = h_1 pY + h_2 pK(r_0 - r) \quad [B = B^d,\ E = E^d], \tag{15.27}$$

$$r = (\rho^e pK + \dot{p}_e E)/p_e E, \tag{15.28}$$

$$\dot{M} = \dot{M}^d, \quad \dot{B} = \dot{B}^d \quad [\dot{E} = \dot{E}^d]. \tag{15.29}$$

Asset markets are assumed to clear at all times, due to interest rate flexibility and the perfect substitute assumption as far as bonds and equities are concerned. The nominal interest rate r adjusts to clear the money market, equation (15.27), while the remainder of financial wealth is allocated to bonds and equities in a way that need not be considered explicitly in the following since asset-holders are indifferent between these assets, because, as stated, bonds and equities are assumed to be perfect substitutes; see equation (15.28). Finally, in equation (15.29), it is assumed that wealth-owners accept the inflows of money and bonds issued by the state for the current period, reallocating them only in the next period by adjusting their portfolios then anew. It is easy to check by means of the considered saving relationships that the assumed consistency of money and bonds flow supply and flow demand implies the consistency of the flow supply and demand for equities.

Block 6 of the model provides us with a simple formula for the rate of interest on the intensive form level and is in all other respects irrelevant for the dynamical analyses that follow, since equities and bonds will not feed back into the dynamics of the private sector due to our choice of property income taxation and investment function, where the price of shares is not needed explicitly. Of course, the restrictive assumptions underlying this situation must be relaxed later on; see Köper and Flaschel (1999) in this regard.

Money demand, as well as all other behavioral and technological relationships, have been specified as simple linear functions. We use such linear relationships throughout since we want to formulate the dynamics on the basis of their intrinsic or unavoidable nonlinearities first. Behavioral nonlinearities may be important later on in order to get global boundedness in the case of instability, but they should then be introduced in a systematic fashion as a reflected response to the destabilizing feedback structures that may be obtained from the model in its present form.

It is obvious from this description of the model that it is, on the one hand, already a very general description of macroeconomic dynamics. On the other, it is still dependent on very special assumptions, in particular with respect to financial markets and the government sector. This can be justified at the present stage of analysis by observing that many of its simplifying assumptions are indeed typical for macrodynamic models which attempt to provide a complete description of a closed economy – see in particular the model of Keynesian dynamics of Sargent (1987, part I). We have considerably extended such a conventional model of a three-sector/five-market approach to economic dynamics in module 2 (the sector of firms), module 4 (the disequilibrium adjustment process of the quantities produced) and module 5 (the wage–price sector and the determination of inflationary expectations) above. Other extensions of this framework (a more plausible treatment of wealth W and less primitive policy rules) must here remain for future research. This is in line with the project begun in Chiarella and Flaschel (2000a), namely to develop a class of models of Keynesian variety (beginning with the supply-side-oriented Keynes–Wicksell model considered in Chiarella and Flaschel (1996b)) where each successor model removes at least one problematic feature of the directly preceding model type. The present model type is much further up in this hierarchy of Keynesian models. It provides a purely demand-determined description of the macroeconomy with a particular emphasis on the behavior of firms and sluggish price as well as quantity adjustments. The stage meanwhile reached in the modeling of disequilibrium growth is surveyed in detail in Chiarella *et al.* (2000b). At present it is however still the distorting lack of investigations of integrated models of this type – and not their specific form – which the research agenda of this chapter seeks to address, here by incorporating the important issue of endogenous technological change in addition (see Section 15.4)

15.3 The dynamics of the private sector

It is easy to reduce the extensive-form dynamics of the preceding section to intensive form or state variable expressions (see Chiarella and Flaschel 2000a for the details), giving rise to an integrated 6D dynamical system in the wage share $u=\omega/x$, the full employment labor intensity in efficiency units $l^e = L\exp(n_l t)/K$, real balances per unit of capital $m = m/(pK)$, inflationary expectations π, sales expectations per unit of capital $y^e = Y^e/K$ and actual inventories per unit of capital $\nu = N/K$. There are further laws of motion (for bonds and equities per unit of capital) which however do not feed back into the core dynamics and are therefore here ignored for reasons of simplicity (see Chiarella and Flaschel 2000a for their description). We denote in the following by β_{π_1} and β_{π_2} the expressions $\beta_\pi\alpha$ and $\beta_\pi(1-\alpha)$, respectively:

$$\hat{u} = \kappa[(1-\kappa_p)\beta_w(V-\bar{V}) + (\kappa_w - 1)\beta_p(U-\bar{U})], \tag{15.30}$$

$$\hat{l}^e = -i_1(\rho^e - r + \pi) - i_2(U-\bar{U}), \tag{15.31}$$

$$\begin{aligned}\widehat{m} = \mu - (n+n_l) - \pi - [\kappa(\beta_p(U-\bar{U}) + \kappa_p\beta_w(V-\bar{V}))],\\ - (i_1(\rho^e - r + \pi) + i_2(U-\bar{U})),\end{aligned} \tag{15.32}$$

$$\dot{\pi} = \beta_{\pi_1}\kappa[\beta_p(U-\bar{U}) + \kappa_p\beta_w(V-\bar{V})] + \beta_{\pi_2}(\mu - (n+n_l) - \pi), \tag{15.33}$$

$$\dot{y}^e = \beta_{y^e}(y^d - y^e) - (i_1(\rho^e - r + \pi) + i_2(U-\bar{U}))y^e, \tag{15.34}$$

$$\dot{\nu} = y - y^d - (i_1(\rho^e - r + \pi) + i_2(U-\bar{U}) + n + n_l)\nu. \tag{15.35}$$

These laws of motion are to be supplemented by the following algebraic equations, for output per unit of capital $y = Y/K$, aggregate demand per unit of capital $y^d = Y^d/K$ and the nominal rate of interest r that clears the money market, in order to make them an autonomous system of six differential equations in the six state variables enumerated above:

$$\begin{aligned}y &= (1 + n\beta_{n^d})y^e + \beta_n(\beta_{n^d}y^e - \nu),\\ y^d &= uy + (1-s_c)(\rho^e - t_c^n) + i_1(\rho^e - r + \pi) + i_2(U-\bar{U})\\ &\quad + n + n_l + \delta + g,\\ r &= r_0 + (h_1 y - m)/h_2.\end{aligned}$$

Note that these algebraic equations and the laws of motion are furthermore based on the following defining expressions for rates of capacity utilization, labor demand per unit of capital, and the expected rate of profit:

$$V = l^{de}/l^e, \quad U = y/y^p, \quad l^{de} = L^d \exp(n_l t)/K = y/x_0,$$
$$\rho^e = y^e - \delta - uy.$$

Note finally that the above dynamical equations make use of the following solution of the wage–price block:

$$\widehat{w} - \pi - n_l = \kappa[\beta_w(V - \bar{V}) + \kappa_w \beta_p(U - \bar{U})], \quad \kappa = (1 - \kappa_w \kappa_p)^{-1},$$
$$\hat{p} - \pi = \kappa[\beta_p(U - \bar{U}) + \kappa_p \beta_w(V - \bar{V})], \quad \kappa = (1 - \kappa_w \kappa_p)^{-1},$$

in various places. Subtracting the second from the first equation furthermore implies

$$\hat{u} = \widehat{w} - \hat{p} - n_l = \kappa[(1 - \kappa_p)\beta_w(V - \bar{V}) + (\kappa_w - 1)\beta_p(U - \bar{U})],$$

which gives the first of the differential equations shown.

In these reduced-form equations, the interdependent wage and price Phillips curves defined in the preceding section have been separated from each other and now based on demand-pressure expressions augmented by inflationary expectations in a seemingly conventional way, yet here based on demand pressure in the labor *and* the goods market, which now appear (with differing weights) in both of these equations for wage and price inflation.

PROPOSITION 15.1 *There is a* unique interior steady-state solution *or point of rest of the dynamics (15.30)–(15.35) fulfilling* $u_0, l_0^e, m_0 \neq 0$ *which is given by the following expressions:*

$$y_0 = \bar{U} y^p, \quad \bar{V} l_0^e = l_0^{de} = y_0/x_0, \quad y_0^e = y_0^d = y_0/(1 + (n + n_l)\beta_{n^d}),$$
$$m_0 = h_1 y_0, \quad \pi_0 = \mu - (n + n_l), \quad r_0 = \rho_0^e + \pi_0, \quad \nu_0 = \beta_{n^d} y_0^e,$$
$$\rho_0^e = \frac{g - t_c^n + n + n_l}{s_c} + t_c^n, \qquad u_0 = \frac{y_0^e - \delta - \rho_0^e}{y_0}.$$

Proof: For the proof, see Chiarella and Flaschel (2000a). □

PROPOSITION 15.2 *Consider the Jacobian J of the dynamics (15.30)–(15.35) at the steady state. The determinant of this* 6 × 6 *matrix,* det *J, is always positive. It follows that the system can only lose or gain asymptotic stability by way of a Hopf bifurcation (if its eigenvalues cross the imaginary axis with positive speed).*

Proof: The assertion is proved by exploiting appropriately linear dependences between the rows of the Jacobian of the full dynamics at the steady state. See Chiarella and Flaschel (2000a, Proposition 6.4) for details. □

PROPOSITION 15.3 *This steady state is locally asymptotically stable for all adjustment speeds β_w, β_p, β_π, β_n chosen sufficiently low, and also h_2 sufficiently low, and for sales expectations β_{y^e} that are revised sufficiently fast.*

Proof: Freezing u, π, ν at their steady-state values (and setting β_n, β_p, β_π equal to zero) allows one to apply to the remaining 3D dynamics (in l^e, m, y^e) the Routh–Hurwitz theorem if h_2 is chosen sufficiently small and β_{y^e} sufficiently large, implying that the three eigenvalues of these reduced dynamics (at the steady state) must all have negative real parts in such a case. Next, one can show that the determinant of the Jacobian of the 4D dynamics (now including π) at the steady state, where β_{π_1}, β_{π_2} (or β_π) are now chosen positive (in fact for all $\beta_{\pi_2} > 0$), must be positive which means that a small β_{π_1} will preserve the negativity of the real parts of the considered eigenvalues and add a further negative one, due to the continuity of eigenvalues with respect to the parameters of the dynamics. The same procedure applies to β_n which when made positive implies a negative determinant and thus gives rise to a negative real eigenvalue together with unchanged signs in the real parts of the other ones if the change in β_n is again sufficiently small. Finally, due to Proposition 15.2, the determinant of the Jacobian of the full dynamics is always positive at the steady state and thus allows for another application of this procedure when the adjustment speeds of wages and prices are chosen sufficiently small. See also Chiarella and Flaschel (2000a, ch. 6) for further considerations of this type.[10] □

PROPOSITION 15.4 *The system will lose its local asymptotic stability – as described in Proposition 15.3 – if either β_w or β_p is chosen sufficiently large, if β_{π_1} is made large enough, or if β_n, β_{y^e} are chosen sufficiently large.*

Proof: Assuming for example β_{π_1} sufficiently large will give rise to a negative principal minor of order two that dominates the sum of the other principal minors of order two, which implies that one of the necessary conditions for local asymptotic stability of the Routh–Hurwitz criterion will no longer hold in such a situation. □

We thus have that either wage or price flexibility must be destabilizing, that fast inflationary expectations are destabilizing as well as the Metzlerian inventory adjustment process when based on a sufficiently fast accelerator mechanism. Further, this proposition (when combined with the preceding ones) claims that such fast adjustments of prices, expectations or inventories will lead at certain critical parameter values to a cyclical loss of stability, either by the death of an unstable limit cycle as the Hopf bifurcation value is approached or by the birth of a stable limit cycle when this bifurcation value is passed (since degenerate Hopf bifurcations will generally not occur in these intrinsically nonlinear dynamics).

15.4 Endogenous technical change

There exist various possibilities in the literature to model endogenous technical change; see Barro and Sala-i Martin (1995) or Aghion and Howitt (1998) in this regard. We here follow Schneider and Ziesemer (1994, p. 17) and use as representation of such technical change an approach based on Uzawa (1965) and Romer (1986), synthesized by Lucas (1988), called the URL approach in the following. Other representations of endogenous change will not significantly alter the conclusions of this section which therefore serves the purpose of illustrating the implications of an integration of the production of technological change into the AD–AS disequilibrium growth model of this chapter.

The URL approach to endogenous technical change can be described by means of the following two equations, characterizing the productive activities of firms:

$$\dot{A} = \eta(L_2^d/L^d)A, \quad \eta' > 0, \quad \text{research unit,} \tag{15.36}$$

$$Y = K^\beta (AL_1^d)^{1-\beta} A^\xi, \quad \xi > 0, \quad \text{production unit.} \tag{15.37}$$

The activities of the employed workforce $L^d = L_1^d + L_2^d$ are here split between the production of output (15.37), described by a Cobb–Douglas production function based on the measure of labor productivity A and augmented by the Romer externality A^ξ, and the production of labor productivity growth, described by equation (15.36). The production function (15.37) is easily reformulated as

$$Y = K^\beta (A^{(1-\beta+\xi)/(1-\beta)} L_1^d)^{1-\beta} = K^\beta (xL_1^d)^{1-\beta},$$

and shows in this way that it is of the usual type (Harrod neutral technical change), yet with a growth rate $\hat{x}$ of aggregate labor productivity x that exceeds the growth rate $\hat{A}$ produced by the firms due to the Romer externality $\hat{x} = (1 + \xi/(1-\beta))\hat{A}$. This approach to the production of technological change is considered in detail in Barro and Sala-i Martin (1995, ch. 4).

In view of our approach of using linear relationships as much as possible in the initial formulation of our disequilibrium growth dynamics we reduce the above technological presentation to the case of fixed proportions in production and a linear production function for technical progress, which in place of (15.36) and (15.37) gives rise to

$$\hat{A} = \eta L_2^d/L^d, \quad \eta > 0, \tag{15.38}$$

$$Y = \min\{y^p K, AL_1^d A^\xi\} = \min\{y^p K, A^{1+\xi} L_1^d\} = \min\{y^p K, xL_1^d\}, \tag{15.39}$$

in the notation used for our approach to disequilibrium growth in Sections 15.2 and 15.3. The variable x of this earlier approach is now based on the relationship

$$x = A^{1+\xi}, \quad \text{i.e.} \quad n_l = \hat{x} = (1+\xi)\hat{A} = (1+\xi)\eta h,$$

where $h = L_2^d/L^d$ denotes the proportion of employed workers that is devoted to the production of technological change. Depending on the variations of the scalar

h there is thus now varying labor productivity growth n_l in the model in place of the former assumption of a given rate of growth n_l of labor productivity x.

For illustrative purposes we assume as law of motion for the labor allocation ratio h the simple but plausible rule

$$\dot{h} = \beta_h(V - \bar{V}), \quad V = L^d/L. \tag{15.40}$$

Firms therefore increase their efforts to increase labor productivity growth if the labor market gets tighter, and vice versa, since this signals how much buffer is available should, for example, the trend growth in labor demand exceed the growth rate of labor supply. This statement in fact implies that certain growth rates should also matter in the above law of motion for h, an extension of the model that will be considered in future extensions of this chapter. We thus now have fluctuating employment in the aggregate and fluctuating allocation of the employed labor force between production proper and the production of technological change, producing fluctuations in labor productivity which in turn add to the fluctuations of the rate of employments V_1 in production as they are generated by the 6D dynamics.

We have now to distinguish between the overall rate of employment, $V = L^d/L$, and the one based on the production sector solely, $V_1 = L_1^d/L$, by way of the following revised algebraic relationships:

$$\begin{aligned} l^{de} &= l_1^{de}/(1-h), \quad l_1^{de} = xL_1^d/K = y, \\ V &= l^{de}/l^e = (l_1^{de} + l_2^{de})/l^e = V_1 + V_2 = V_1 + hV = V_1/(1-h), \\ \text{i.e.} \quad V_1 &= y/l^e, \quad V = y/((1-h)l^e), \quad \rho^e = y^e - \delta - ul^{de}. \end{aligned}$$

We note that labor measured in efficiency units, for example labor supply, is now represented by xL in place of $\exp(n_l t)L$, which however only means that all the former expressions are augmented by the given factor x_0. This does not change the form of the dynamics to a noteworthy degree, but is easier to read in the present situation. We observe that the formal structure of the model of the preceding sections is obtained, when $\beta_h = 0,\ h(0) > 0$ is assumed.

The first impression is that the dynamics have become more complex by the addition of endogenous technical change, since further intrinsic nonlinearities are introduced through the addition of a simple law of motion for the variable h, the ratio by which firms divide their workforce into productive and researching units. On the other hand, the wage–price block gives rise to the same formal expressions as in the case of given technical change, due to the treatment of productivity increases in the formation of wage and price inflation. A second view however reveals that the state variable h, though it enters the initially considered dynamical system in various places, does so only via V, $n_l = \hat{x}$ and ρ^e. Furthermore, the rate of employment V is the only variable of the initial dynamical system that affects the new dynamical law for h.

The interior steady-state solution for the above dynamics is no longer uniquely determined, since the variable h cannot be uniquely determined from setting the laws of motion to rest, due to the fact that an appropriate combination of the first six laws of motion generate the new law of motion (for h). The set of possible interior steady-state solutions is thus now given by the following equations:

$$y_0 = \bar{U} y^p, \quad l_{10}^{de} = y_0, \quad \bar{V} l_0^e = l_0^{de} = l_{10}^{de}/(1-h_0), \tag{15.41}$$

$$y_0^e = y_0^d = y_0/[1 + (n + (1+\xi)\eta h_0)\beta_{n^d}], \tag{15.42}$$

$$m_0 = h_1 y_0, \quad \pi_0 = \mu - (n + (1+\xi)\eta h_0), \tag{15.43}$$

$$r_0 = \rho_0^e + \pi_0, \quad \nu_0 = \beta_{n^d} y_0^e, \tag{15.44}$$

$$\rho_0^e = \frac{g - t_c^n + n + (1+\xi)\eta h_0}{s_c} + t_c^n, \quad \omega_0 = \frac{y_0^e - \delta - \rho_0^e}{l_0^d}, \tag{15.45}$$

where h_0 can be any economically admissible number.

Proposition 15.5 *There is a curve of* interior steady-state solutions *or points of rest of the dynamics which is given by the expressions (15.41)–(15.45) parameterized by an arbitrary choice of* $h \in (0, 1)$.

Proposition 15.6 *These steady states are locally attracting for all adjustment speeds* β_h *sufficiently low in all cases where the 6D subdynamics are locally asymptotically stable.*

This assertion follows directly from the fact that the dynamics with a given rate of labor productivity growth is qualitatively of the same type as the one where the variable h is of a given magnitude. Sufficiently sluggish wage, price and inflationary expectations adjustments coupled with fast sales expectations and a weak inventory accelerator mechanism, now also combined with slow shifts of employment between the production and research units of firms, will therefore be favorable for local asymptotic stability. Note in this context that there is some kind of accelerator mechanism with regard to the research activities of firms which works as follows. In the case of a high employment rate V, on the one hand, firms want to increase the growth of labor productivity by enlarging the number of workers in the R&D sector. On the other hand, the number of employees concerned with the production of goods is already determined by aggregate demand, which results in a further increase of V, leading firms to chose again a higher value of h and so on. Thus, a destabilizing feedback mechanism emerges. Note furthermore that the above stability assertions are here coupled with the situation of shock-dependent convergence toward a continuum of steady states as the attractors of the dynamics. Should there be convergence to steady states it will be a path-dependent one, where history and shocks matter.

Proposition 15.7 *Consider the Jacobian J of the dynamics at the steady state. The determinant of this* 7×7 *matrix,* $\det J$, *is always zero, while the upper* 6×6 *principal minor is always positive (as in the 6D case of the preceding section).*

It follows that the system can only lose or gain asymptotic stability by way of a Hopf bifurcation (if its eigenvalues cross the imaginary axis with positive speed).

Note for the considered situation that one eigenvalue must always be equal to zero, while no further eigenvalue can become zero in addition. Loss of stability therefore always takes place by the occurrence of two purely imaginary eigenvalues when the bifurcation point is reached. As before we get close to this situation either by shrinking an unstable limit cycle before the bifurcation point is reached or by expanding stable ones after it has been passed.

PROPOSITION 15.8 *The system will lose its local asymptotic stability if β_h is made sufficiently large.*

This proposition is proved in the same way as related ones for the system with exogenous technical change, here by simply showing that the parameter β_h appears in the trace of the Jacobian J of the dynamics at the steady state only once and there with a positive coefficient (due to the law of motion $\dot{h} = \beta_h[y/((1-h)l^e) - \bar{V}]$ for the allocation of research workers h) which can be made arbitrarily large by means of the parameter β_h without change in the other elements in the trace of J.

The proofs for Propositions 15.5–15.8 are thus not difficult to provide, since they are basically of the same type as the ones for the propositions of the preceding section. We thus in sum arrive at the conclusion that the attractors of the dynamics with endogenous technical change should not be very different from the ones of the dynamics considered in Section 15.3, but are shock-dependent, including the stable limit cycles that may be generated by the asserted existence of Hopf bifurcations. This means that the rate of productivity change of the economy will depend on average or in the limit on the history of the evolution of this economy.

15.5 Conclusions

In this chapter we have investigated the dynamic properties of a Keynesian AD–AS disequilibrium model including not only sluggish wage adjustment but also sluggish prices as well as a Metzlerian inventory dynamics. Owing to these elements the analysis, which is carried out first with exogenous Harrod neutral technical change and then with endogenous technological progress of the Uzawa–Romer type, is much easier than it would be on the basis of a conventional IS–LM approach (see Flaschel *et al.* 1999). We have found that the dynamics are dominated by the AD–AS structure in both variants of technical progress. This means that stability is supported by sluggish adjustments of wages, prices and inflationary expectations, by fast sales expectations and an inventory accelerator that is not too strong. If technical change is produced by the research activities of firms, stability furthermore requires that the shifts of employment between the production of goods and the research sector are sufficiently slow. Thus, the inclusion of endogenous technical change adds realism to the model, but does not alter its behavior in a significant way.

Part VI

The road ahead

Financial markets

16 Stabilizing an unstable economy and the choice of policy measures

16.1 Introduction

> As we approach the last decade of the twentieth century, our economic world is in apparent disarray. After two secure decades of tranquil progress following World War II, in the late 1960s the order of the day became turbulence – both domestic and international. Bursts of accelerating inflation, higher chronic and higher cyclical unemployment, bankruptcies, crunching interest rates, and crises in energy, transportation, food supply, welfare, the cities, and banking were mixed with periods of troubled expansions. The economic and social policy synthesis that served us so well after World War II broke down in the mid-1960s. What is needed now is a new approach, a policy synthesis fundamentally different from the mix that results when today's accepted theory is applied to today's economic system.
>
> Minsky (1982)

As a result of the financial crisis which started in the relatively small US subprime housing sector, the world has experienced in recent years the largest downturn of economic activity since the Great Recession. Since the end of 2007 a hyperactive monetary and fiscal policy implemented in the great majority of countries has aimed at preventing a further financial meltdown, and now the world economy as a whole seems to be on the brink of a stable recovery. It is now time to evaluate our previous understanding of how our economic system works. Further macroeconomic work is thus needed.

As the history of macroeconomic dynamics and business cycles (which recently have been developed as boom–bust cycles) has taught us, fragilities and destabilizing feedbacks are known to be potential features of all markets – the product markets, the labor market and the financial markets. In this chapter[1] we will focus in particular on the financial market. We use a Tobin-like macroeconomic portfolio approach, coupled with the interaction of heterogeneous agents on the financial market, to characterize the potential for financial market instability. Though the study of the latter has been undertaken in many partial models, we focus here on the interconnectedness of all three markets. Furthermore, we study what potential labor market, fiscal and monetary policies can have in stabilizing intrinsically unstable macroeconomies (it was Minsky (1982) in particular who put forward many ideas to stabilize an unstable economy). Beside other stabilizing policies in particular we propose an anti-cyclical monetary policy that sells assets – more specifically, equities of the nonfinancial sector – in the boom and purchases them in recessions. Modern dynamic and stability analyses are brought to bear to demonstrate the stabilizing effects of those suggested policies.

The chapter builds on work by Chiarella and Flaschel (2000a), Köper (2003) and Chiarella *et al.* (2005) by using models of that research agenda as the starting point for the proper design of a macrodynamic framework – as well as for the evaluation of labor market, fiscal and monetary policies – which allows in general for large swings in financial and real economic activity. Such a framework revives the macroeconomic portfolio approach that was suggested by Tobin (1969), building on baseline models of the dynamic interaction of the labor market, the product market and financial markets with risky assets. Furthermore, we also build on recent work on the interaction of heterogeneous agents in the financial market.[2] We allow for heterogeneity in share and goods price expectations and study the financial, nominal and real cumulative feedback chains that may give rise to destabilizing dynamics at the macroeconomic level. The work connects to traditional Keynesian business cycle analysis as Tobin, Minsky and Akerlof have suggested and thus seems appropriate given that governments worldwide have resorted to Keynesian-type policies to combat the current global financial crisis.

The remainder of the chapter is organized as follows. Section 16.1 sketches the main modules of a portfolio approach to Keynesian business cycle theory. The model's steady-state properties, as well as the comparative statics of the asset markets, are also explored in Section 16.1. The potential for fragility and destabilizing feedbacks as well as the proper design of labor market, fiscal and monetary policies are studied in Section 16.2. Section 16.2 also proposes a new form of monetary policy that is not only concerned with interest rates, but in particular with anti-cyclical selling and buying of assets (as recently also proposed by Farmer 2010) which is, in spirit, close to Minsky's (1982) ideas. The stabilizing effects of this policy are also explored. Section 16.3 concludes.

16.2 Asset markets and Keynesian business cycles: a portfolio approach

In the tradition of Tobin (1969), we will depart from the mainstream macroeconomic theory and will provide the structural form of a growth model using a portfolio approach and building on the behavior of heterogeneous agents in the asset markets. In order to discuss details we split the model into appropriate modules that refer to the different sectors of the economy, namely households, firms and the government (fiscal and monetary authority). Beside presenting a detailed structure of the asset market, we also represent the wage–price interactions, and connect the financial market to the labor and product market dynamics.

Households

We disaggregate the sector of households into worker households and asset-holder households. We begin with the description of the behavior of workers.

Worker households:

$$\omega = w/p, \tag{16.1}$$

$$C_w = (1-\tau_w)\omega L^d, \tag{16.2}$$

$$S_w = 0, \tag{16.3}$$

$$\widehat{L} = n = \text{const.} \tag{16.4}$$

Equation (16.1) gives the definition of the real wage ω before taxation, where w denotes the nominal wage and p the actual price level. We follow the Keynesian framework by assuming that the labor demand of firms can always be satisfied out of the given labor supply.[3] Then, according to equation (16.2), real income of workers equals the product of real wages times labor demand, which net of taxes $\tau_w \omega L^d$ equals workers' consumption, since we do not allow for savings of the workers as postulated in equation (16.3).[4] No savings implies that the wealth of workers is zero at every point in time. This in particular means that the workers do not hold any assets and that they consume instantaneously their disposable income. As is standard in theories of economic growth, we finally assume in equation (16.4) a constant growth rate n of the labor force L based on the assumption that labor is supplied inelastically at each moment in time. The parameter n can be easily reinterpreted to be the growth rate of the working population plus the growth rate of labor augmenting technical progress.

The income, consumption and wealth of the asset-holders are described by the following set of equations.

Asset-holding households:

$$r_k^e = (Y^e - \delta K - \omega L^d)/K, \tag{16.5}$$

$$C_c = (1-s_c)[r_k^e K + iB/p - T_c], \quad 0 < s_c < 1, \tag{16.6}$$

$$S_p = s_c[r_k^e K + iB/p - T_c] \tag{16.7}$$

$$= (\dot{M} + \dot{B} + p_e \dot{E})/p, \tag{16.8}$$

$$W_c = (M + B + p_e E)/p, \quad W_c^n = pW_c. \tag{16.9}$$

The first equation (16.5) of this module of the model defines the expected rate of return on real capital r_k^e to be the ratio of the currently expected real cash flow and the real stock of business fixed capital K. The expected cash flow is given by the expected real revenues from sales Y^e diminished by real depreciation of capital δK and the real wage sum ωL^d. We assume that firms pay out all expected cash flow in the form of dividends to the asset-holders. These dividend payments are one source of income for asset-holders. The second source is given by real interest payments on short-term bonds (iB/p) where i is the nominal interest rate and B the stock of such bonds. Summing up these types of interest incomes and taking account of lump sum taxes T_c in the case of asset-holders (for reasons of simplicity) we obtain the disposable income of asset-holders given by the terms in the square brackets of equation (16.6), which together with a postulated fixed propensity to consume $(1 - s_c)$ out of this income gives us the real consumption of asset-holders.

Real savings of pure asset-owners is real disposable income minus their consumption as shown in equation (16.7). The asset-owners can allocate the real savings in the form of new money holdings $\dot{M}$, or buy other financial assets, namely short-term bonds $\dot{B}$ or equities $\dot{E}$ at the price p_e, the only financial instruments that we allow for in the present reformulation of the KMG growth model. Hence, the savings of asset-holders must be distributed to these assets as stated in equation (16.8). Real wealth of pure asset-holders is thus defined in equation (16.9) as the sum of the real cash balance, real short-term bond holdings and real equity holdings of asset-holders. Note that the short-term bonds are assumed to be fixed price bonds with a price of one, $p_b = 1$, and a flexible interest rate i.

Along the lines of Tobin's work of portfolio theory, we assume imperfect substitution between three financial assets M (money), B (bonds) and E (equities). The demand for these three financial assets is given by the following set of equations:

$$p_e E^d = f_e(r_e^e, i) W_c^n, \tag{16.10}$$

$$B^d = f_b(r_e^e, i) W_c^n, \tag{16.11}$$

$$M^d = f_m(r_e^e, i) W_c^n, \tag{16.12}$$

with

$$f_m(\cdot) + f_b(\cdot) + f_e(\cdot) \equiv 1$$

and

$$r_e^e = \frac{r_k^e pK}{p_e E} + \pi_e^e = \frac{r_k^e}{q} + \pi_e^e, \tag{16.13}$$

where the expected rate of return on equities r_e^e consists as usual of real dividends per unit of equity $r_k^e pK/p_e E = r_k^e/q$ (by making use of the definition of Tobin's average $q = p_e E/pK$) and the expected capital gains π_e^e, the latter being nothing other than the expected growth rate of equity prices.

The assumed gross substitution property of the analyzed financial assets can be expressed by

$$\frac{\partial f_e(\cdot)}{\partial r_e^e} > 0, \quad \frac{\partial f_e(\cdot)}{\partial i} < 0,$$

$$\frac{\partial f_b(\cdot)}{\partial r_e^e} < 0, \quad \frac{\partial f_b(\cdot)}{\partial i} > 0,$$

$$\frac{\partial f_m(\cdot)}{\partial r_e^e} < 0, \quad \frac{\partial f_m(\cdot)}{\partial i} < 0,$$

which means that the demand for all other assets increases whenever the rate of return of the considered asset decreases (for a formal definition see for example Mas-Colell *et al.* (1995)).[5]

While the case of strict inequalities is treated in detail in Köper (2003), in order to characterize in this chapter the limits of monetary policy in a more focused way, in the following we assume that[6]

$$\frac{\partial f_e(\cdot)}{\partial i} = 0 \quad \text{and} \quad \frac{\partial f_m(\cdot)}{\partial r_e^e} = 0,$$

while all other partial derivatives are strict inequalities. The consequence of the above assumption is that now equations (16.10)–(16.12) postulate a clearly defined portfolio decision-making by the asset-holders according to which the demand for equities is primarily determined by the expected rate of return on equities r_e^e, the demand for government bonds by r_e^e *as well as* by the nominal interest rate i, and the money demand solely by i. Accordingly, after determining in every moment of time the fraction of their financial wealth to be invested in equities and the fraction to be held in broad money holdings $M_2 = M + B$, asset-holders thus choose their demand for bonds and their transactions demand M^d as components of M_2. This hierarchy in the portfolio decision-making is supposed to reflect the situation where asset markets are focused almost exclusively on expected capital gains and where the asset-holders may only consider the possibility of significant increases in their money holdings as a second or third best alternative.

The consequence of the above assumptions concerning the partial derivatives of the equity and money demand functions is that the subdivision of M_2 into transactions money and savings deposits takes place primarily on the basis of interest rate changes, so that we thus have an endogenous adjustment of M and B, but not of M_2. Furthermore, due to the trading process in the background of this situation, in stock market equilibrium $E = \bar{E}$ again holds, but under a new share price p_e and thus also a new money demand M_2. At the end of this process thus the supply of equities is again held by asset-holders and the demand for M_2 is back at the given stock of it. So for example in times of stress (for the equity market) where people want to go into money hoarding, the equity price will fall significantly without the possibility for the asset-holders as a whole to change their actual stock of equities.

Under normal conditions, asset-holders thus consider their portfolio choice between M_2 and E with a strong focus on equities as the central component of their wealth, demanding more (less) equities than they currently hold if the expected rate of return r_e^e is higher (lower) than its steady-state value. This in turn determines the share price p_e. Equity demand (vs. hoarding) represents therefore the crucial part in the decisions made on the financial markets, while cash management between money $M = M_1$ and B is a relatively trivial matter.[7]

In order to complete the modeling of asset-holders' behavior, we need to describe the evolution of π_e. In the tradition of recent work on heterogeneous agents in asset markets (see e.g. De Grauwe and Grimaldi 2006), we assume here that there are two types of asset-holders who differ with respect to their expectation formation of equity prices.[8] There are behavioral traders, called *chartists*, who in principle employ the following adaptive expectations mechanism

$$\dot{\pi}_{ec} = \beta_{\pi_{ec}}(\hat{p}_e - \pi_{ec}), \tag{16.14}$$

where $\beta_{\pi_{ec}}$ is the adjustment speed toward the actual growth rate of equity prices. The other asset-holders, the *fundamentalists*, employ a forward-looking expectation formation mechanism

$$\dot{\pi}_{ef} = \beta_{\pi_{ef}}(\eta - \pi_{ef}), \tag{16.15}$$

where η is the fundamentalists' expected long-run growth rate of share prices. Assuming that the aggregate expected rate of share price increases π_e is a weighted average of the two expected growth rates, where the weights are determined according to the sizes of the groups, we obtain

$$\pi_e = \alpha_{\pi_{ec}}\pi_{ec} + (1 - \alpha_{\pi_{ec}})\pi_{ef}, \tag{16.16}$$

where $\alpha_{\pi_{ec}} \in (0, 1)$ is the ratio of chartists to all asset-holders.

Note that the addition of such expectations schemes has an ambiguous effect on the stock market stability properties, with the fairly tranquil fundamentalists' expectations and in contrast the chartists' expectations coming from the behavioral traders, which tend to be destabilizing if they adjust with sufficient strength. Indeed, as suggested, for example, by Brunnermeier (2008), instabilities, bubbles and crashes are overwhelmingly due to the fact that there are heterogeneous agents in the asset market, giving rise to heterogeneous information, heterogeneous beliefs and limits to arbitrage, as also discussed in Abreu and Brunnermeyer (2003).[9]

Firms

We consider the behavior of firms by means of two submodules. The first describes the production framework and their investment in business fixed capital and the second introduces the Metzlerian approach of inventory dynamics concerning expected sales, actual sales and the output of firms.

Firms: production and investment:

$$Y^p = y^p K, \tag{16.17}$$

$$u = Y/Y^p, \tag{16.18}$$

$$L^d = Y/x, \tag{16.19}$$

$$e = L^d/L = Y/(xL), \tag{16.20}$$

$$q = p_e E/(pK), \tag{16.21}$$

$$I = i_q(q-1)K + i_u(u-\bar{u})K + nK, \tag{16.22}$$

$$\widehat{K} = I/K, \tag{16.23}$$

$$p_e \dot{E} = pI + p(\dot{N} - \mathcal{I}). \tag{16.24}$$

Firms are assumed to pay out dividends according to expected profits (expected sales net of depreciation and minus the wage sum) – see the above module for the asset-owning households. The rate of expected profits r_k^e is expected real profits per unit of capital as stated in equation (16.5). Firms produce output utilizing a production technology that transforms demanded labor L^d combined with business fixed capital K into output. For convenience we assume that the production process takes place with a fixed proportion technology.[10] According to equation (16.17) potential output Y^p is given at each moment of time by a fixed coefficient y^p times the existing stock of physical capital. Accordingly, the utilization of productive capacities is given by u, the ratio of actual production Y and the potential output Y^p. The fixed proportions in production give rise to a constant output/labor coefficient x, by means of which we can deduce labor demand from goods market-determined output as in equation (16.19). The ratio L^d/L thus defines the rate of employment in the model.

The economic behavior of firms must include their investment decision with regard to business fixed capital, which is determined independently of the savings decision of households. We here model investment decisions per unit of capital as a function of the deviation of Tobin's q (see Tobin 1969) from its long-run value 1, and the deviation of actual capacity utilization from a normal rate of capital utilization. We employ here Tobin's average q which is defined in equation (16.21) as the ratio of the nominal value of equities and the reproduction costs for the existing stock of capital. Investment in business fixed capital is thus reinforced when q exceeds one, and is reduced when q is smaller than one. This influence is represented by the term $i_q(q-1)$ in equation (16.22). The term $i_u(u-\bar{u})$ models the component of investment which is due to the deviation of utilization rate of physical capital from its nonaccelerating inflation value $\bar{u}$. The last component nK (n being the exogenously given natural growth rate) takes account of the natural growth rate n which is necessary for steady-state analysis if natural growth is considered as exogenously given. Equation (16.24) is the budget constraint of the firms. Investment in business fixed capital and unintended changes in the inventory stock $p(\dot{N} - \mathcal{I})$ must be financed by issuing equities, since equities are the only financial instrument of firms in this chapter. Capital stock growth finally is given by net investment per unit of capital I/K in this demand-determined model of the short-run equilibrium position of the economy.

Next we discuss the inventory dynamics following Metzler (1941) and Franke (1996).

Firms output adjustment:

$$N^d = \alpha_{n^d} Y^e, \tag{16.25}$$

$$\mathcal{I} = nN^d + \beta_n (N^d - N), \tag{16.26}$$

$$Y = Y^e + \mathcal{I}, \tag{16.27}$$

$$Y^d = C + I + \delta K + G, \tag{16.28}$$

$$\dot{Y}^e = nY^e + \beta_{y^e}(Y^d - Y^e), \tag{16.29}$$

$$\dot{N} = Y - Y^d, \tag{16.30}$$

$$S_f = Y - Y^e = \mathcal{I}, \tag{16.31}$$

where $\alpha_{n^d}, \beta_n, \beta_{y^e} \geq 0$.

Equation (16.25) states that the desired stock of physical inventories, denoted by N^d, is assumed to be a fixed proportion of the expected sales. The planned investments in inventories $\mathcal{I}$ follow a sluggish adjustment process toward the desired stock N^d according to equation (16.26). Taking account of this additional demand for goods, equation (16.27) writes the production Y as equal to the expected sales of firms plus $\mathcal{I}$.

To explain the expectation formation for goods demand, we need the actual total demand for goods which in (16.28) is given by consumption (of private households and the government) and gross investment by firms. From the observation of current actual demand Y^d, which is assumed to be always satisfied, the dynamics of expected sales is given in equation (16.29), which models expectations as the outcome of an error correction process that incorporates also the natural growth rate n in order to take account of the fact that this process operates in a growing economy. The adjustment of sales expectations is driven by the prediction error $(Y^d - Y^e)$, with an adjustment speed that is given by β_{y^e}. Actual changes in the stock of inventories are described in equation (16.30) by the deviation of production from goods demanded.

The savings of the firms S_f is as usual defined by income minus consumption. Because firms are assumed not to consume anything, their income equals their savings and is given by the excess of production over expected sales, $Y - Y^e$. According to the production account in Table 16.1 the gross accounting profit of firms finally is $r_k^e pK + p\mathcal{I} = pC + pI + p\delta K + p\dot{N} + pG$. Substituting in the definition of r_k^e from equation (16.5), we compute that $pY^e + p\mathcal{I} = pY^d + p\dot{N}$ or equivalently $(Y - Y^e) = \mathcal{I}$ as stated in equation (16.31).

Fiscal and monetary authorities

The role of the government in this chapter is to provide the economy with public (nonproductive) services within the limits of its budget constraint:

$$T = \tau_w \omega L^d + T_c, \tag{16.32}$$

Table 16.1 The four activity accounts of the firms

Uses	*Resources*
Production account of firms:	
Depreciation $p\delta K$	Private consumption pC
Wages wL^d	Gross investment $pI + p\delta K$
Gross accounting profits $\Pi = r_k^e pK + p\mathcal{I}$	Inventory investment $p\dot{N}$
	Public consumption pG
Income account of firms:	
Dividends $r_k^e p_y K$	Gross accounting profits Π
Savings $p\mathcal{I}$	
Accumulation account of firms:	
Gross investment $pI + p\delta K$	Depreciation $p\delta K$
Inventory investment $p\dot{N}$	Savings $p\mathcal{I}$
	Financial deficit FD
Financial account of firms:	
Financial deficit FD	Equity financing $p_e\dot{E}$

$$T_c - iB/p = t_c K, \quad t_c = \text{const.}, \tag{16.33}$$

$$G = gK, \quad g = \text{const.}, \tag{16.34}$$

$$S_g = T - iB/p - G, \tag{16.35}$$

$$\hat{M} = \mu, \tag{16.36}$$

$$\dot{B} = pG + iB - pT - \dot{M}. \tag{16.37}$$

Public purchases (and interest payments) are financed through taxes, through newly printed money, or newly issued fixed-price bonds ($p_b = 1$). Note that the budget constraint gives rise to some repercussion effects between the public and the private sector.[11] We model the tax income consisting of taxes on wage income and lump sum taxes on capital income T_c. With regard to the real purchases of the government for the provision of government services we assume, again as in Sargent (1987), that these are a fixed proportion g of real capital, which taken together allows us to represent fiscal policy by means of simple parameters in the intensive form representation of the model and in the steady-state considerations to be discussed later on. The real savings of the government, which is a deficit if it has a negative sign, is defined in equation (16.35) by real taxes minus real interest payments minus real public services.

Concerning monetary policy, it should be clear that under a totally inelastic equity demand function with respect to the interest rate (as assumed above), a monetary policy only based on the management of the short-term rate of interest is ineffective in terms of macroeconomic stabilization, unless it is capable of impacting capital gains expectations on the stock market. This holds for money supply steering as well as for the now fashionable interest rate policy rules of Taylor type, since such policies would only affect the cash management process within the given stock of liquid assets, as previously assumed. This result is a limit case of what Keynes (1936) already observed in the *General Theory*, where he wrote:

> Where, however, (as in the United States, 1933–1934) open-market operations have been limited to the purchase of very short-dated securities, the effect may, of course, be mainly confined to the very short-term rate of interest and have but little reaction on the much more important long-term rates of interest.

For reasons of expositional simplicity we thus assume for now that money supply grows at a given rate $\mu = \text{const.}$ (we will relax this assumption below). Equation (16.36) thus shows that money is assumed to enter the economy via open market operations of the central bank, which buys short-term bonds from the asset-holders when issuing new money. Then the changes in the short-term bonds supplied by the government are given residually in equation (16.37), which is the budget constraint of the governmental sector.

Wage–price interactions

We now turn to a module of our model that can be the source of significant centrifugal forces within the complete model. These are the three laws of motion of the wage–price spiral. Picking up the approach of Rose (1967)[12] of two short-run Phillips curves, (i) the wage Phillips curve and (ii) the price Phillips curve, the relevant dynamic equations can be written as

$$\widehat{w} = \beta_w(e - \bar{e}) + \kappa_w \hat{p} + (1 - \kappa_w)\pi^c, \tag{16.38}$$

$$\hat{p} = \beta_p(u - \bar{u}) + \kappa_p \widehat{w} + (1 - \kappa_p)\pi^c, \tag{16.39}$$

$$\dot{\pi}^c = \beta_{\pi^c}(\alpha \hat{p} + (1 - \alpha)(\mu - n) - \pi^c), \tag{16.40}$$

where β_w, β_p, $\beta_{\pi^c} \geq 0$, $0 \leq \alpha \leq 1$ and $0 \leq \kappa_w$, $\kappa_p \leq 1$. This approach makes use of the assumption that relative changes in money wages are influenced by demand pressure in the market for labor and price inflation (cost-pressure) terms. Price inflation in turn depends on demand pressure in the market for goods and on money wage (cost-pressure) terms. Wage inflation therefore is described in equation (16.38) on the one hand by means of a demand-pull term $\beta_w(e - \bar{e})$, which states that relative changes in wages depends positively on the gap between actual employment e and its NAIRU value $\bar{e}$. On the other hand, the cost-push elements in wage inflation is the weighted average of short-run (perfectly anticipated) price inflation $\hat{p}$ and medium-run expected overall inflation π^c, where the weights are given by κ_w and $1 - \kappa_w$. The price Phillips curve is quite similar, and also displays a demand-pull and a cost-push component. The demand-pull term is given by the gap between capital utilization and its NAIRU value $(u - \bar{u})$, and the cost-push element is the κ_p and $1 - \kappa_p$ weighted average of short-run wage inflation $\widehat{w}$ and expected medium-run overall inflation π^c.

What is left to model is the expected medium-run inflation rate π^c. We postulate in equation (16.40) that changes in expected medium-run inflation are due to an adjustment process toward a weighted average of the current inflation rate and steady-state inflation. Thus we introduce here a simple kind of forward-looking expectations into the economy. This adjustment is driven by an adjustment velocity β_{π^c}.

Asset markets equilibrium

Based on the Tobin (1969) portfolio approach to the behavior of asset-holders (see also Franke and Semmler 1999), we postulate that the following equilibrium conditions for the asset markets

$$p_e E = p_e E^d = f_e(r_e^e) W_c^n, \quad r_e^e = r_k^e/q + \pi_e^e, \tag{16.41}$$

$$B = B^d = f_b(r_e^e, i) W_c^n, \tag{16.42}$$

$$M = M^d = f_m(i) W_c^n. \tag{16.43}$$

always hold and thus determine the nominal rate of interest i and the price of equities p_e as statically endogenous variables in the model, as the trade between the asset-holders induces a process that makes asset prices fall or rise in order to equilibrate demands and supplies.

In the short run (in continuous time) the structure of wealth of asset-holders W_c^n is, disregarding changes in the share price p_e, given to them and for the model. Since the functions $f_m(\cdot)$, $f_b(\cdot)$ and $f_e(\cdot)$, introduced in equations (16.10)–(16.12), satisfy the well-known conditions

$$f_m(\cdot) + f_b(\cdot) + f_e(\cdot) \equiv 1, \tag{16.44}$$

$$\frac{\partial f_m(\cdot)}{\partial z} + \frac{\partial f_b(\cdot)}{\partial z} + \frac{\partial f_e(\cdot)}{\partial z} \equiv 0, \quad \forall\, z \in \{i, r_e^e\}. \tag{16.45}$$

These conditions guarantee that the number of independent equations is equal to the number of statically endogenous variables (i, p_e) that the asset markets are assumed to determine at each moment in time. Note also that all asset supplies here are given magnitudes at each moment in time and recall from equation (16.13) that r_e^e is given by $r_k^e/q + \pi_e$ and thus varies at each point in time solely due to variations in the share price p_e.[13]

The model in intensive form

The model's intensive form (see the appendix to this chapter for the derivation of the following equations) is given by

$$\widehat{\omega} = \kappa[(1-\kappa_p)\beta_w(e-\bar{e}) + (\kappa_w - 1)\beta_p(u-\bar{u})], \tag{16.46}$$

$$\dot{\pi^c} = \alpha\beta_{\pi^c}\kappa[\beta_p(u-\bar{u}) + \kappa_p\beta_w(e-\bar{e})] + (1-\alpha)\beta_{\pi^c}(\mu - n - \pi^c), \quad (16.47)$$

$$\hat{l} = n - i(\cdot) = -i_q(q-1) - i_u(u-\bar{u}), \quad (16.48)$$

$$\dot{y}^e = \beta_{y^e}(y^d - y^e) + (n - i(\cdot))y^e, \quad (16.49)$$

$$\dot{\nu} = y - y^d - i(\cdot)\nu, \quad (16.50)$$

$$\dot{\pi}_e = \alpha_{\pi ec}\beta_{\pi ec}(\hat{p}_e - \pi_{ec}) + (1-\alpha_{\pi ec})\beta_{\pi_{ef}}(\eta - \pi_{ef}), \quad (16.51)$$

$$\dot{b} = g - t_c - \tau_w\omega l^d - \mu m - b\{\kappa[\beta_p(u-\bar{u}) + \kappa_p\beta_w(e-\bar{e})] + \pi^c + i(\cdot)\}, \quad (16.52)$$

$$\dot{m} = m\mu - m\{\kappa[\beta_p(u-\bar{u}) + \kappa_p\beta_w(e-\bar{e})] + \pi^c + i(\cdot)\}. \quad (16.53)$$

As shown above, the dynamics in extensive form can therefore be reduced to eight differential equations, where however the law of motion for share prices has not yet been determined, or to seven differential and one integral equation, which is easier to handle than the alternative representation, since there is then no law of motion for the development of future share prices to be calculated. Note with respect to these dynamics that economic policy (fiscal and monetary) is still represented in very simple terms here, since money supply is growing at a given rate and since government expenditures and taxes on capital income net of interest payments per unit of capital are given parameters. This makes the dynamics of the government budget constraint (see equation (16.52), the law of motion for bonds per unit of capital b) a very trivial one as in Sargent (1987), and thus leaves the problems associated with these dynamics a matter for future research. The advantage is that fiscal policy can be discussed in a very simple way here by means of just three parameters.

A comparison of the present dynamics with those of the previous models of the authors[14] reveals that there are now two variables from the financial sector that feed back to the real dynamics in this extended system, the bond to capital ratio b representing the evolution of government debt and Tobin's average q. The first (dynamic) variable however only influences the real dynamics since it is one of the factors that influences the statically endogenous variable q which in turn enters the investment function as a measure of the firms' performance. Government bonds do not influence the economy in other ways, since there are not yet wealth effects in consumption and since the interest income channel to consumption has been suppressed by the particular assumption about tax collection concerning capital income.

It should be pointed out that in the present theoretical framework the influence of the (real) interest rate in the investment function is now absent, and that Tobin's q provides instead the channel by which investment behavior is reacting to the results brought about by the financial markets. We do this mainly for expositional clarity as our focus primarily lies on the interaction between stock and real markets, and also because its inclusion would not significantly change the stability properties of the model as long as equity prices are primarily focused on capital gains expectations and thus not directly affected by changes in the nominal interest rate. The case of a direct impact of the nominal and real rate of interest in the investment function against the background of a Taylor-like monetary policy rule is treated in detail in Chiarella *et al.* (2005).

A feature of the present dynamics is that there are no laws of motion left implicit. The model contains now a completely formulated dynamics, but still one where the real-financial interaction is represented in very basic terms. Price inflation (via real balances and real bonds) and the expected rate of return on capital (via the rate of return on dividends) influence the behavior of asset markets via their laws of motion such as gross substitution of assets and expectation dynamics for asset prices, while the reaction of asset markets feeds back into the real part of the economy instantaneously through the change in Tobin's q that they (and the dynamics of expected capital gains) bring about.

Before we come to a consideration of the model's steady state and its stability properties, as well as among other things the potentially destabilizing role of chartist-type capital gains expectations, we discuss the full structure of our model by means of what is shown in Figure 16.1. This figure highlights the destabilizing role of the wage–price spiral, where now – due to the assumed investment behavior – we always have a positive impact of real wages on aggregate demand and thus the result that wage flexibility will be destabilizing (if not counteracted by its effects on expected profits and their effect on financial markets and Tobin's q). We have already indicated that financial markets adjust toward their equilibrium in a stable manner as long as we disregard the expectations dynamics on the financial market. Monetary policy, whether money supply oriented and thus of type $M(i, p)$ or of a Taylor type $i(M, \hat{p})$, should – via the gross substitution effects – also contribute to the stability of the financial markets, and fiscal policy impacts the goods and financial markets, either in the orthodox manner or in a Keynesian anti-cyclical kind of way. Note however that due to the very intertwined dynamical structure of the model it is not clear how fiscal policy in detail might contribute to the shaping of the business cycle. Finally, there remains the discussion of the self-reference within the asset markets (that is, the closed loop structure between capital gains expectations and actual capital gains) which must also be the most difficult part of the considered dynamical system, the details of which must be left to future research.

Steady-state considerations

In this section we show the existence of a steady state in the economy under consideration. We here stress that this can be done independently of the analysis given in the following section on the comparative statics of the asset market equilibrium system, since Tobin's q is given by 1 in the steady state via the real part of the model and since the portfolio equations can be uniquely solved in conjunction with the government budget constraint for the three variables i, m, b which they then determine.[15]

As the model is formulated we have the nine state variables m, b, y^e, ω, l, ν, π^c, π_{ef}, π_{ec} in the considered dynamical system. We have written these state

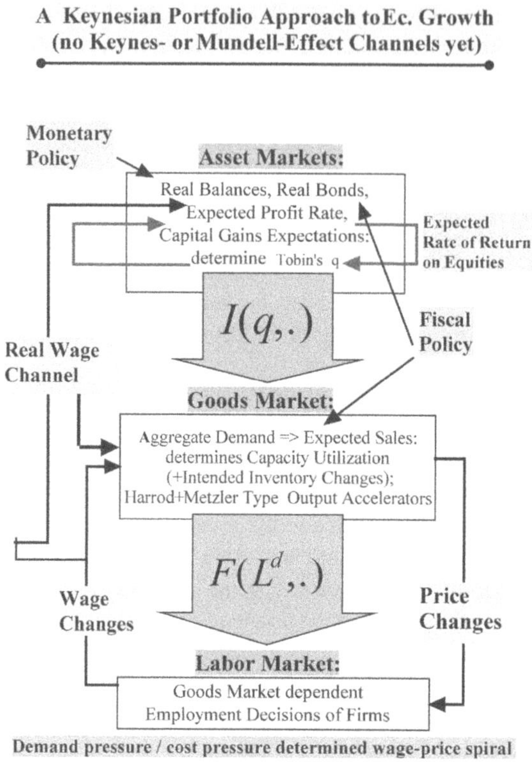

Figure 16.1 Keynes' causal downward nexus (from self-contained financial markets dynamics to economic activity), repercussive feedback chains (from economic activity to expected returns on equities), supply-side dynamics (the wage–price spiral) and policy rules in a Keynesian model with portfolio dynamics.

variables in the order they will used in the stability analysis in a following section. This order is generally not the same as in the steady-state analysis of the model where causalities of a different type (than in stability analysis) are involved.

LEMMA 16.1 *Assume that $s_c > \tau_w$ and $s_c r^{e0} > n + g - t_c$. Assume furthermore that the ratio*

$$\bar{\phi} = \frac{g - t_c - \tau_w \omega l^{do}}{g - t_c - \tau_w \omega l^{do} + \mu},$$

to be explicitly derived below, has a positive numerator, meaning that the government runs a primary deficit in the steady state. The dynamical system given by equations (16.46)–(16.53) possesses a unique interior steady-state solution

$(\omega^0, l^0, m^0 > 0)$ with equilibrium on the asset markets if the fundamentalist long-run reference of the increase in equity prices equals the steady-state inflation rate of goods prices

$$\eta = \hat{p}^0$$

and if

$$\lim_{i\to 0}(f_m(i, r^{e0} + \pi_e^0) + f_b(i, r^{e0} + \pi_e^0)) < \bar{\phi}$$

$$\text{and} \quad \lim_{i\to\infty}(f_m(i, r^{e0} + \pi_e^0) + f_b(i, r^{e0} + \pi_e^0)) > \bar{\phi}$$

hold true.[16]

Proof: If the economy rests in a steady state, then all intensive variables stay constant and all time derivatives of the system become zero. Thus by setting the left-hand sides of the system of equations (16.46)–(16.53) to zero, we can deduce the steady-state values of the variables.

From equation (16.48) we can derive that $i(\cdot)^0 = n$ holds, from equation (16.49) we get $y^{eo} = y^{do}$, and from equation (16.53) that

$$\mu = \kappa[\beta_p(u - \bar{u}) + \kappa_p\beta_w(e - \bar{e})] + \pi^c + i(\cdot).$$

Substituting the last relation into equation (16.40) and using $i(\cdot)^0 = n$ we obtain with $\alpha\beta_\pi \neq -(1-\alpha)\beta_\pi^c$ that $\mu - n - \pi^c = 0$ and $\kappa[\beta_p(u - \bar{u}) + \kappa_p\beta_w(e - \bar{e})] = 0$. Thus we have for $u - \bar{u}$ and $e - \bar{e}$ the two equations

$$u - \bar{u} = -\kappa_p\beta_w(e - \bar{e})/\beta_p,$$
$$u - \bar{u} = (1 - \kappa_p)\beta_w(e - \bar{e})/[(1 - \kappa_w)\beta_p].$$

By assumption we have $\beta_p, \beta_w > 0$ and $0 \le \kappa_p, \kappa_w \le 1$, so $e - \bar{e}$ must equal zero in order that the last two equations be fulfilled. When $e = \bar{e}$, then according to equation (16.46) we know that $u = \bar{u}$. Then equation (16.48) leads to $q^0 = 1$.

With these relations one can easily compute the unique steady-state values of the variables $y^e, l, \pi^c, \nu, \omega$ as

$$y^{eo} = \frac{y^0}{1 + n\alpha_{n^d}}, \quad \text{with } y^0 = \bar{u}y^p, \tag{16.54}$$

$$l^0 = y^0/(\bar{e}x), \tag{16.55}$$

$$\pi^{co} = \mu - n, \tag{16.56}$$

$$\nu^0 = \alpha_{n^d} y^{eo}, \tag{16.57}$$

$$\omega^0 = \frac{y^{eo} - n - \delta - g - (1 - s_c)(y^{eo} - \delta - t_c)}{(s_c - \tau_w)l^{do}}, \tag{16.58}$$

$$r^{e0} = y^{eo} - \delta - \omega^0 l^{do}. \tag{16.59}$$

All these values are determined on the goods and labor markets. The steady-state value of the real wage has in particular been derived from the goods market equilibrium condition that must hold in the steady state and it is positive under the assumptions made in Lemma 16.1.

We next take account of the asset markets, which determine the values of the short-term interest rate i (which now bears the burden of clearing the asset markets), but now in conjunction with the determination of the steady state for m and b, where $m+b$ is determined through the government budget constraint. This is the case because the steady-state rate of return on equities relies, on the one hand, solely on r^{e0} (since q has been determined through the condition $i(\cdot)=n$ and shown to equal one in steady state) and, on the other, on the expected inflation rate of share prices

$$r_e^{e0} = r^{e0} + \pi_e^0,$$

which equals the goods price inflation rate in the steady state as will be shown below.

The steady-state values of the two kinds of expectations about the inflation rate of equity prices (of chartists and fundamentalists) are

$$\pi_{ef}^0 = \eta, \quad \pi_{ec}^0 = \eta, \tag{16.60}$$

from which one can derive that $\pi_e^0 = \eta = \hat{p}^0 = \pi^{co} = \mu - n$ must hold. We have seen that, in the steady state, Tobin's q equals one and its time derivative equals zero, so that we can derive

$$\dot{q} = \frac{(\dot{p}_e E + p_e \dot{E})pK - p_e E(\dot{p}K + p\dot{K})}{p^2 K^2} = 0,$$

$$\Longrightarrow \quad \frac{\dot{p}_e E + p_e \dot{E}}{pK} = \hat{p} + n.$$

According to equation (16.24) we have $p_e \dot{E} = pI + p(\dot{N} - \mathcal{I})$; we thus get in the steady state that $p_e \dot{E} = pI$. Inserting this into the last implication shown we get $\hat{p}_e = \hat{p}$ and thus as an important finding that $\eta = \mu - n$ must hold in order to allow for a steady state.

Let us now determine the steady-state values of the stocks of real cash balances and the stock of bonds. These values have to be solved for in conjunction with the steady-state interest rate i^0 which is now solely responsible for clearing the asset markets, because the result that Tobin's $q=1$ has already been determined on the real markets.

The budget constraint of the government is given in intensive form by

$$\dot{b} + \dot{m} = g - t_c - \tau_w \omega l^d - (b+m)(\hat{p} + i(\cdot)). \tag{16.61}$$

One therefore obtains in the steady state that

$$b^0 + m^0 = (g - t_c - \tau_w \omega l^d)/\mu. \tag{16.62}$$

Furthermore, consider the asset demand functions given by equations (16.12) and (16.11), namely

$$m = f_m(\cdot)(m + b + q), \quad q = 1, \tag{16.63}$$

$$b = f_b(\cdot)(m + b + q), \quad q = 1. \tag{16.64}$$

The left-hand sides of the last two equations are the supplied amounts and the right-hand sides represent the demand for the assets $m,\ b$.

Using now equation (16.62) in the form

$$\mu(m^0 + b^0) = g - t_c - \tau_w \omega l^d, \tag{16.65}$$

the system of three linear independent equations (16.63)–(16.65) can be used to deduce the three unique steady-state values i^0, b^0 and m^0 which we will show below.

Beginning with the steady-state interest rate we sum equations (16.63) and (16.64) and multiply by μ, obtaining

$$\mu(m^0 + b^0) = (f_m^0 + f_b^0)\mu(m^0 + b^0 + 1),$$

where f_m^0 and f_b^0 respectively denote the values of $f_m(i^0, r^{e0} + \pi_e^0)$ and $f_b(i^0, r^{e0} + \pi_e^0)$. Substituting in the budget constraint in the form of equation (16.65) we get

$$f_m^0 + f_b^0 = \bar{\phi},$$

with

$$\bar{\phi} = \frac{g - t_c - \tau_w \omega^0 l^{do}}{g - t_c - \tau_w \omega^0 l^{do} + \mu}.$$

From property (16.45) and (16.14) we can conclude that

$$\frac{\partial(f_m + f_b)}{\partial i} > 0, \tag{16.66}$$

which implies that the cumulated demand for money and bonds is a strictly increasing function in the variable i.

If

$$\lim_{i \to 0}(f_m(i, r^{eo} + \pi_e^0) + f_b(i, r^{eo} + \pi_e^0)) < \bar{\phi}$$

and

$$\lim_{i \to \infty} (f_m(i, r^{eo} + \pi_e^0) + f_b(i, r^{eo} + \pi_e^0)) > \bar{\phi},$$

then by monotonicity and continuity there must be a value of i that equilibrates the asset markets in the above aggregated form. Then, steady-state supplies of m and b can be calculated by equations (16.63) and (16.64) in a unique way, based on the steady-state interest rates $i = i^0$ and $r_e^{e0} = r^{e0} + \pi_e$. This concludes the derivation of the uniquely determined steady-state values for our dynamical system (16.46)–(16.53) which in turn when inserted into this system indeed imply that the dynamics is at a point of rest in this situation. □

Note that inflation rates are uniform throughout in this model type (also for stock prices) and that government debt B is growing with the same rate as money supply μ in the steady state, while the real sector is growing with the natural rate n (which is also the growth rate of equity supply). We observe finally that the calculation of the steady-state value of the rate of change of the wage and the rate of return on capital can be simplified when it is assumed that government expenditures are given by $g + \tau_w \omega l^d$ in place of only g.

16.3 Dampening unstable business cycles

As we have shown in previous related work – see e.g. Chiarella and Flaschel (2000a) and Chiarella *et al.* (2000b) – the considered model type discussed above is capable of producing various dynamic outcomes and is thus a very open one with respect to possible business cycle implications. In particular, it features a variety of macroeconomic channels which may be of an intrinsically destabilizing nature, even though – through their interaction with other (stabilizing) mechanisms – they may not necessarily lead to fully fledged macroeconomic instability. There are for example two accelerator effects involved in the dynamics, the Metzlerian inventory accelerator mechanism and the Harrodian fixed business investment accelerator. We therefore expect that increasing the parameters β_n and i_u will also be destabilizing and also lead to Hopf bifurcations and other complex dynamic behavior. Either wage or price flexibility will, through their effects on the expected rate of return on capital, and from there on asset markets, be destabilizing and lead to Hopf bifurcations, limit cycles or (locally) purely explosive behavior eventually.[17]

Given the potentially destabilizing influence of these and other macroeconomic channels, the proper choice and design of active labor, fiscal and monetary policy is central for the achievement of a stable macroeconomic environment. In the following we discuss various policy options meant to assure such a macroeconomic stability.

Labor market and fiscal policies

Next we want to raise the question of what might stabilize our macroeconomic dynamics. Let us first suppose that all assumptions stated in Lemma 16.1 hold.

What is left to analyze then is the dynamical behavior of the system, when it is displaced from its steady-state position, but still remains in a neighborhood of the steady state. In the following we provide propositions, which in sum imply that there must be a locally stable steady state, if some sufficient conditions that are very plausible from a Keynesian perspective are met.

We begin with an appropriate subsystem of the full dynamics for which the Routh–Hurwitz conditions can be shown to hold. Setting $\beta_p = \beta_w = \beta_{\pi_{ef}} = \beta_{\pi_{ec}} = \beta_n = \beta_{\pi^c} = 0$, $\beta_{y^e} > 0$, and keeping π^c, π_e, ω, ν thereby at their steady-state values we get the following subdynamics of state variables m, b and y^e which are then independent of the rest of the system[18]

$$\begin{aligned} \dot{m} &= m(\mu - [\pi_0^c + i(\cdot)]), \\ \dot{b} &= g - t_c - \tau_w \omega(y/x) - \mu m - b(\pi_0^c + i(\cdot)), \\ \dot{y}^e &= \beta_{y^e}[c + i(\cdot) + \delta + g - y^e] + y^e(n - i(\cdot)). \end{aligned} \tag{16.67}$$

Proposition 16.1 *The steady state of the system of differential equations (16.67) is locally asymptotically stable if β_{y^e} is sufficiently large, the investment adjustment speed i_u concerning deviations of capital utilization from the normal capital utilization is sufficiently small and the partial derivatives of desired cash balances with respect to the interest rate $\partial f_m/\partial i$ and the rate of return on equities $\partial f_m/\partial r_e^e$ are sufficiently small. Moreover the equity market must be in a sufficiently tranquil state, i.e. the partial derivative $\partial f_e/\partial r_e^e$ must also be sufficiently small.*

Proof: See Köper (2003) for the proof of this, along with all the other following propositions in this section. □

The proposition asserts that local asymptotic stability at the steady state of the considered subdynamics holds when the demand for cash is not very much influenced by the rates of return on the financial asset markets,[19] the accelerating effect of capacity utilization on the investment behavior is sufficiently small, and the adjustment speed of expected sales toward actual demand is fast enough. Moreover, and this is an important condition, the stock markets must be sufficiently tranquil in the reaction to changes in the rate of return on equities, i.e. they are in particular not close to a liquidity trap.

In order to show how policy can enforce the validity of this situation we need some preliminary observations first. In the given structure of financial markets it is natural to assume that even $\partial f_m/\partial r_e^e = 0$ and $\partial f_e/\partial i = 0$ hold true, since fixed price bonds are equivalent to saving deposits and thus form together with money M just what is named M_2 in the literature. The internal structure of M_2 is however just a matter of proper cash management and should therefore imply that the rate of return r_e^e on equities does not matter for it. The latter only concerns the demand for equities vs. the demand for the aggregate M_2 which both solely then depend on the rate of return for equities, since the dependence on the rate of interest cancel when M_2 is formed.

Moreover, since the transaction costs for reallocations within M_2 can be assumed to be fairly small and the speed of adjustment of the dynamic multiplier (which is infinite if IS equilibrium is assumed) may be assumed to be large, we have only one critical parameter left in the above proposition which may be crucial for the stability of the considered subsystem of the dynamics, the investment parameter i_u, potentially representing an accelerator of Harrodian type. This suggests that fiscal policy should be used to counteract the working of this accelerator mechanism which leads from higher capacity utilization to higher investment to higher goods demand and thus again to higher capacity utilization.

The following proposition formulates how fiscal policy should be designed in order to create damped oscillations around the balanced growth path of the model (if they are yet present).

THEOREM 16.1 *Assume an independent fiscal authority solely responsible for the control of business fluctuations (acting independently from the business cycle neutral fiscal policy of the government) which implements the following two rules for its activity-oriented expenditures and their funding:*

$$g^u = -g_u(u - \bar{u}), \quad t^u = g_u(u - \bar{u}).$$

The budget of this authority is always balanced and we assume that the tributes t^u are paid by asset-holding households. The stability condition on i_u is now extended to the consideration of the parameter $i_u - g_u$. Then, an anti-cyclical policy g^u that is chosen in a sufficiently active way will enforce damped oscillations in the considered subdynamics if the savings rate s_c of asset-holders is sufficiently close to one (and if stock markets are sufficiently tranquil).

Therefore, an anti-cyclical policy that is chosen in a sufficiently active way will enforce damped oscillations in the considered subdynamics (1) if the savings rate of asset-holders is sufficiently close to one and (2) if stock markets are sufficiently tranquil. Note that neither the steady state nor the laws of motion are changed through this introduction of such a self-determined business cycle authority, if $s_c = 1$ holds true, which we assume to hold true in the following for reasons of simplicity.

Next we consider the same system but allow β_p to become positive, though only small in amount. This means that ω which had previously entered the m, b, y^e subsystem only through its steady-state value now becomes a dynamic variable, giving rise to the 4D dynamical system

$$\dot{m} = m\left(\mu - \left[\kappa\beta_p\left(\frac{y}{y^p} - \bar{u}\right) + \pi_0^c + i(\cdot)\right]\right),$$

$$\dot{b} = g - t_c - \tau_w\omega\frac{y}{x} - \mu m - b\left[\kappa\beta_p\left(\frac{y}{y^p} - \bar{u}\right) + \pi_0^c + i(\cdot)\right], \tag{16.68}$$

$$\dot{y}^e = \beta_{y^e}\left[c + i(\cdot) + \delta + g - y^e\right] + y^e(n - i(\cdot)),$$
$$\dot{\omega} = \omega\kappa(\kappa_w - 1)\beta_p\left(\frac{y}{y^p} - \bar{u}\right).$$

PROPOSITION 16.2 *The interior steady state of the dynamical system (16.68) is locally asymptotically stable if the conditions in Proposition 16.1 are met and β_p is sufficiently small.*

Note here that the implication of this new condition for the considered subdynamics is also obtained by the assumption $\kappa_w = 1$, i.e. workers and their representatives should always demand a full indexation of their nominal wages to the rate of price inflation. This implies the following result.

THEOREM 16.2 *Assume that the cost-push term in the money wage adjustment rule is given by the current rate of price inflation (which is perfectly foreseen). Then the considered 4D subdynamics implies damped oscillations around the given steady-state position of the economy.*

This type of a *scala mobile* thus implies stability instead of – as might be expected – instability, since it simplifies the real wage channel of the model considerably. It needs however the following theorem in addition in order to really tame the wage–price spiral of the model.

Enlarging the system (16.68) by letting β_w become positive we get the subsystem

$$\dot{m} = m\left(\mu - \left(\kappa\left[\beta_p\left(\frac{y}{y^p} - \bar{u}\right) + \kappa_p\beta_w\left(\frac{y}{xl} - \bar{e}\right)\right] + \pi_0^c + i(\cdot)\right)\right),$$
$$\dot{b} = g - t_c - \tau_w\omega\frac{y}{x} - \mu m$$
$$- b\left(\kappa\left[\beta_p\left(\frac{y}{y^p} - \bar{u}\right) + \kappa_p\beta_w\left(\frac{y}{xl} - \bar{e}\right)\right] + \pi_0^c + i(\cdot)\right),$$
$$\dot{y}^e = \beta_{y^e}[c + i(\cdot) + \delta + g - y^e] + y^e(n - i(\cdot)), \tag{16.69}$$
$$\dot{\omega} = \omega\kappa\left[(1 - \kappa_p)\beta_w\left(\frac{y}{xl} - \bar{e}\right) + (\kappa_w - 1)\beta_p\left(\frac{y}{y^p} - \bar{u}\right)\right],$$
$$\dot{l} = l\left[-i_q(q - 1) - i_u\left(\frac{y}{y^p} - \bar{u}\right)\right].$$

PROPOSITION 16.3 *The steady state of the dynamical system (16.69) is locally asymptotically stable if the conditions in Proposition 16.2 are met and β_w is sufficiently small.*

THEOREM 16.3 *We assume that the economy is a consensus-based one, where labor and capital have reached an agreement with respect to the scala mobile principle in the dynamics of money wages. Assume furthermore that capitalists and* *workers also agree against this background on the precept that additional money wage increases should be small in the boom $(u - \bar{u})$ and vice versa in the recession. This makes the steady state of the considered 5D subdynamics asymptotically stable.*

We now enlarge the system further by letting β_n become positive to obtain

$$\begin{aligned}
\dot{m} &= m\left(\mu - \left(\kappa\left[\beta_p\left(\frac{y}{y^p} - \bar{u}\right) + \kappa_p\beta_w\left(\frac{y}{xl} - \bar{e}\right)\right] + \pi_0^c + i(\cdot)\right)\right),\\
\dot{b} &= g - t_c - \tau_w\omega\frac{y}{x} - \mu m\\
&\quad - b\left(\kappa\left[\beta_p\left(\frac{y}{y^p} - \bar{u}\right) + \kappa_p\beta_w\left(\frac{y}{xl} - \bar{e}\right)\right] + \pi_0^c + i(\cdot)\right),\\
\dot{y}^e &= \beta_{y^e}[c + i(\cdot) + \delta + g - y^e] + y^e(n - i(\cdot)), \qquad (16.70)\\
\dot{\omega} &= \omega\kappa\left[(1-\kappa_p)\beta_w\left(\frac{y}{xl} - \bar{e} + (\kappa_w - 1)\beta_p\left(\frac{y}{y^p} - \bar{u}\right)\right)\right],\\
\dot{l} &= l\left[-i_q(q-1) - i_u\left(\frac{y}{y^p} - \bar{u}\right)\right],\\
\dot{\nu} &= y - (c + i(\cdot) + \delta + g) - \nu i(\cdot).
\end{aligned}$$

PROPOSITION 16.4 *The steady state of the dynamical system (16.70) is locally asymptotically stable if the conditions in Proposition 16.3 are met and β_n is sufficiently small.*

THEOREM 16.4 *The Metzlerian feedback between expected sales and output is given by*

$$y = (1 + \alpha_{n^d}(n + \beta_n))y^e - \beta_n\nu.$$

This static relationship implies that lean production α_{n^d} or cautious inventory adjustment β_n (or both) can tame the Metzlerian output accelerator.

We here do not introduce any exogenous regulating process for these Metzlerian sales inventory adjustments, but simply assume that this inventory accelerator process is of a secondary nature in the business fluctuations generated by the dynamics, in particular if the control of the Harrodian goods market accelerator is working properly.

We now let β_{π^c} become positive so that we then are back at the differential equation system

$$\begin{aligned}
\dot{m} &= m\mu - m(\kappa[\beta_p(u - \bar{u}) + \kappa_p\beta_w(e - \bar{e})] + \pi^c + i(\cdot)),\\
\dot{b} &= g - t_c - \tau_w\omega l^d - \mu m\\
&\quad - b(\kappa[\beta_p(u - \bar{u}) + \kappa_p\beta_w(e - \bar{e})] + \pi^c + i(\cdot)),\\
\dot{y}^e &= \beta_{y^e}(y^d - y^e) + y^e(n - i(\cdot)), \qquad (16.71)
\end{aligned}$$

$$\dot{\omega} = \omega\kappa[(1-\kappa_p)\beta_w(e-\bar{e}) + (\kappa_w - 1)\beta_p(u-\bar{u})],$$
$$\hat{l} = n - i(\cdot) = -i_q(q-1) - i_u(u-\bar{u}),$$
$$\dot{\nu} = y - y^d - i(\cdot)\nu,$$
$$\dot{\pi^c} = \alpha\beta_{\pi^c}\kappa[\beta_p(u-\bar{u}) + \kappa_p\beta_w(e-\bar{e})] + (1-\alpha)\beta_{\pi^c}(\mu - n - \pi^c).$$

PROPOSITION 16.5 *The steady state of the dynamic system (16.71) is locally asymptotically stable if the conditions in Proposition 16.4 are met and β_π^c is sufficiently small.*

THEOREM 16.5 *Assume that the business cycle is controlled in the way we have described so far and that this implies that the fundamentalist expectations of inflation become dominant in the adjustment rule for the inflationary climate*

$$\dot{\pi^c} = \beta_{\pi^c}(\alpha\hat{p} + (1-\alpha)(\mu - n) - \pi^c).$$

Choosing α sufficiently small guarantees the applicability of the preceding proposition.

The economy will thus exhibit damped fluctuations if the parameter α in the law of motion of the inflationary climate expression π^c is chosen sufficiently small, which is a reasonable possibility if the business cycle is damped and actual inflation, here only generated by the market for goods

$$\hat{p} \sim \beta_p(u-\bar{u})/(1-\kappa_p) + \pi^c,$$

is moderate. A stronger orientation of the change in the inflation climate on a return to the steady-state rate of inflation thus helps to stabilize the economy.

Note here that the consideration of expectation formation on financial markets is still ignored (assumed as static). It is however obvious that an enlargement of the dynamics by these expectations does not destroy the shown stability properties if only fundamentalists are active, since this enlarges the Jacobian by a negative entry in its diagonal solely. Continuity then implies that a portion of chartists that is relatively small as compared to fundamentalists will also admit to preserve the damped fluctuations we have shown to exist in the above sequence of propositions.

PROPOSITION 16.6 *The steady state of the dynamic system (16.71) is locally asymptotically stable if the parameter α_{π_e} is sufficiently small.*

In order to get this result enforced by policy action, independently of the size of the chartist population, we introduce the following type of Tobin tax on the capital gains of equities

$$\dot{\pi}_{ef} = \beta_{\pi_{ef}}(\eta - \pi_{ef}), \tag{16.72}$$
$$\dot{\pi}_{ec} = \beta_{\pi_{ec}}((1-\tau_e)\hat{p}_e - \pi_{ec}). \tag{16.73}$$

THEOREM 16.6 *The Tobin tax parameter τ_e implies that damped business fluctuations remain damped for all tax rates chosen sufficiently large (below 100%).*

The objective for implementation of such a Tobin tax (for all traders, irrespective of their expectations formation schemes, which are of course not observable) is to restrict to a certain extent the accelerating equity price expectations mechanism. The consequence of the implementation of such a tax is that the expectations of equity price gains – the relevant variable for the investment decisions of the chartists – are diminished by τ_e, being thus not $\hat{p}_e$ but $(1-\tau_e)\hat{p}_e$. Fundamentalists, in contrast, have a longer-term orientation and thus will quite likely care less for short-term variations in the equity prices and the gains resulting from them. As a result, the development of the equity prices may be more oriented toward fundamentals and less toward the expectations of pure equity price gains.[20]

Furthermore, it should be pointed out that the introduction of such a capital gain tax also implies the establishment of a public agency which accumulates or decumulates the reserve funds R resulting from the financial markets taxation according to the rule

$$\dot{R} = \tau_e \dot{p}_e E.$$

In order to keep again the laws of motion of the economy unchanged (to allow the application of the above stability propositions) we assume here that this public agency is independent of the other public institutions. The steady-state value ρ^0 of the reserve funds – expressed per value unit of capital pK – of this new agency is

$$\rho^0 = (R/pK)^0 = \tau_e(\mu - n)/\mu < 1.$$

This easily follows from the law of motion

$$\hat{\rho} = \hat{R} - \hat{p} - \widehat{K} = \frac{\dot{R}}{R}\frac{R}{pK} - \hat{p} - \widehat{K},$$

since $\hat{p} - \widehat{K} = \mu$ and $\hat{E} = n,\ q = 1,\ \hat{p}_e = \hat{p}$ hold in the steady state. It is assumed that the reserves of this institution are sufficiently large so that they will not become exhausted during the damped business fluctuations generated by the model.

The stability results of the propositions are intuitively very appealing in view of what we know about Keynesian feedback structures and from what has been discussed in the preceding sections, since it basically states that the wage spiral must be fairly damped, that the Keynesian dynamic multiplier be stable and not too much distorted by the emergence of Metzlerian inventory cycles, that the Harrodian knife-edge growth accelerator is weak, and that inflationary and capital gains expectations are fundamentalist in orientation and money demand subject to small transaction costs and fairly unresponsive to rate of return changes on financial assets (that is, money demand is not close to a liquidity trap). Such assumptions represent indeed fairly natural conditions from a Keynesian perspective.

On this basis we obtained in the above theorems the result that independently conducted anti-cyclical fiscal policy can limit the fluctuations on the goods market, that an appropriate consensus between capital and labor can tame the wage–price spiral and that a Tobin tax can tame the financial market accelerator. Metzlerian inventory dynamics and fluctuations in the inflationary climate that is surrounding the economy may then also be weak and thus not endanger asymptotic stability. But what about monetary policy?

Monetary policy

So far we have presumed that in the baseline model traditional monetary policy (as money supply and interest rate policy) is ineffective in the control of the economy between the short and the medium run. As monetary policy is set up it only affects the cash management process of asset-holders, but leaves $M_2 = M + B$ invariant.[21] Note however that such a monetary policy can be dangerous in the case of the liquidity trap, since this model allows for the equity-owners to attempt to a large degree to sell their equities against the fully liquid assets M and B. This would imply – as in the current financial crisis – that the public could end up sitting on the bad assets.

The alternative is to suggest that the central bank buys the bad assets and drives up asset prices again. This is a demanding policy option that must be investigated and discussed in more detail. Yet this policy seems to have been pursued in the current financial market meltdown and this variant of monetary policy has recently come to the forefront in the discussion. Details may be beyond the scope of the present chapter but we might make, as to this policy, some important observations. The fiscal authorities, the US Treasury, has extensively purchased equity, for example by taking over Fannie Mae and Freddie Mac, and taking over shares of automobile companies. The Federal Reserve has purchased, in order to clean up banks' balance sheets, a large amount of complex securities (mortgage-backed securities and collateralized debt obligations) to avoid a "fire sale" of bad assets and a downward spiral. It also undertook extensive lending to the private sector by accepting bad assets as collateral. This extensive purchase, or acceptance, of equity assets was a new policy variant coming to the forefront as the financial meltdown evolved in 2008 and 2009. This attempt to rescue the financial and banking sectors, through the purchase of securities, was widely viewed as a step to prevent a system-wide breakdown.[22] Next we want to build into our macromodel some elements of this new policy.

So far, in our baseline portfolio approach to Keynesian macrodynamics, we have first formulated a truly tranquil monetary policy as far as the long run is concerned, i.e. we assumed a constant growth rate of the money supply $\mu > n$. This policy was oriented toward the long run and implied in our model a positive inflation rate in the steady state. This rate should be chosen high enough to allow the avoidance of deflationary situations where the above-described compromise between capital and labor may break down – since labor may be very opposed to money wage reductions (as Keynes (1936) already noted as a behavioral rule, a fact ignored by those economists who disregard the psychology of workers).

As previously stated, in the type of portfolio model we have presented here, a monetary policy only oriented toward the short-term rate of interest is ineffective unless it impacts the long-term interest rates and capital gain expectations on the stock market. Since long-term bonds are not included in the present model[23] nor the debt issuing by firms (which only use equities as means of financing their investment),[24] we interpret the following proposal of Keynes for the stock market in order to discuss his implications (Keynes 1936, p. 205):

> If the monetary authority were prepared to deal both ways on specified terms in debts of all maturities, and even more so if it were prepared to deal in debts of varying degrees of risk, the relationship between the complex of rates of interest and the quantity of money would be direct.

We do this in addition to the above monetary policy that concerns the long run by assuming in extension of the "Friedmanian" rule $\dot{M} = \mu M, \ \mu = \text{const.}$, as integration of the long- as well as short- and medium-run orientation of monetary policy a "Keynesian" rule as follows:[25]

$$\hat{M} = \mu - \beta_{mq}(q - q^0), \quad \text{with}$$
$$\mu M = \dot{B}_c, \quad \dot{M} - \mu M = -\beta_{mq}(q - q^0)M = p_e \dot{E}_c. \tag{16.74}$$

This additional policy of the central bank takes the state of the stock market as measured by the gap between Tobin's q and its steady-state value $q^0 = 1$ as reference point in order to increase money supply above its long-run rate in the bust, by purchasing equities and by selling stock and decreasing therewith money supply below its long-run trend value in the boom. This is clearly a monetary policy that attempts to control the fluctuations in equity prices since it buys stocks when the stock market is weak and sells stocks in the opposite case. We stress that this policy is meant to be applied under normal conditions on financial markets and may not be so easily available in the cases where a liquidity trap is in operation.

In the treatment of the implications of the government (see also Sargent 1987, p. 16), we denoted by B the bonds held in the household sector and represented the ones currently purchased by the central bank ($\dot{B}_c$) by putting the corresponding supply of new money into the (aggregated) government budget constraint (assuming as usual that interest payments to the central bank are channeled back into the actual government sector). Moreover taxes net of interest were assumed as being a parameter (per unit of capital) in order to suppress the interest income effects in the consumption function of asset-holders. We now go one step further by continuing to use E for equities that are privately held and by assuming for the ones held by the central bank (E_c) that they have a reduced status only (exhibit no dividend payments and no voting rights). Dividend payments to the household sector thus remain as before. On this basis we assume that only $q = p_e E/pK$ enters the investment function of firms. This is clearly a restrictive assumption but it allows in the following Theorem 16.7 (indicating a route for future research) that only the law of motion for real balances per unit of capital is changed by the above addition of a Keynes-type open market policy rule.

Transferred to the intensive form level this rule, which we call a Tobin rule in the following, then gives rise to the following law of motion for real balances per unit of capital,

$$\hat{m} = \mu - \beta_{mq}(q - q^0) - (\hat{p} + \widehat{K}) \tag{16.75}$$

$$= \mu m - \beta_{mq}(q(m+b, r_k^e + \pi_e) - 1) \\ - \{\kappa[\beta_p(u - \bar{u}) + \kappa_p \beta_w(e - \bar{e})] + \pi^c + i(\cdot)\}m, \tag{16.76}$$

as the only change in the model of this chapter. In addition to holding government bonds it is assumed that the central bank holds equities in a sufficient amount in order to pursue its short-run-oriented stock market policy. This policy is sustainable in the long run, since the central bank buys stock when cheap and sells it when expensive.

We consider a proof for the statement that such a policy adds to the stability of the steady state of the dynamics by reconsidering only the first stage by our previous cascade of stable matrices approach (see e.g. Chiarella *et al.* 2006a).

THEOREM 16.7 *The initially considered, now augmented 3D subdynamics of the full 9D dynamics*

$$\dot{m} = m[\mu - \beta_{mq}(q - q^0) - (\pi_0^c + i(\cdot))],$$
$$\dot{b} = g - t_c - \tau_w \omega(y/x) - \mu m - b(\pi_0^c + i(\cdot)), \tag{16.77}$$
$$\dot{y}^e = \beta_{y^e}\left[c + i(\cdot) + \delta + g - y^e\right] + y^e(n - i(\cdot)),$$

can be additionally stabilized (by increasing the parameter range where damped oscillations are established and by making the originally given damped oscillations even less volatile) by an increasing parameter value β_{mq} of the new term $-\beta_{mq}(q - q^0)m$ in the law of motion for real balances, if anti-cyclical fiscal policy is sufficiently active to make the dynamic multiplier process a stable one (by neutralizing the Harrodian investment accelerator) and if the savings rate s_c of asset-holders is sufficiently close to one (which allows one to ignore effects from taxation on the consumption of asset-holders).

Proof: Under the conditions assumed to hold on the asset markets we can again solve for Tobin's q explicitly and get

$$q = \frac{f_e(r_e^e)}{1 - f_e(r_e^e)}(m+b) = q(r_e^e, m+b),$$

that is,

$$\frac{\partial q}{\partial r_e^e} = \frac{f_e'(r_e^e)}{(1 - f_e(r_e^e))^2}(m+b) > 0.$$

The Routh–Hurwitz polynomial of the Jacobian matrix is thereby augmented by the principal minors to be obtained from the additional matrix

$$\begin{aligned}
\dot{m} &= -\beta_{mq}(q - q^0)m, \\
\dot{b} &= g - t_c - \tau_w \omega(y/x) - \mu m - b(\pi^c + i(\cdot)), \\
\dot{y}^e &= \beta_{y^e}\left[c + i(\cdot) + \delta + g - y^e\right] + y^e(n - i(\cdot)),
\end{aligned}$$

which only differs from the original one in its first row. This row can be used to eliminate the $i_q(\cdot)$ term in the $i(\cdot)$ function when calculating the principal minors of this additional Jacobian matrix. From this simplification one then easily gets that the Routh–Hurwitz coefficients a_1, a_2 and a_3 of the characteristic polynomial of the augmented Jacobian exceed the originally given ones (note that according to Lemma 16.1 we have $q_m > q_b$), while the determinant of the Jacobian in the final Routh–Hurwitz condition $a_1a_2 - a_3$ is dominated by the additions to a_1 and a_2. □

The important means to stabilize the economy or to make it at least less volatile are therefore given here by Keynesian anti-cyclical demand management, consensus-based wage management, and Tobin-type management of the financial market accelerating processes and – in the full dynamical system hopefully – also by the above willingness of the central bank to trade not only in bonds, but also in equities (or in long-term bonds as in Köper (2003)). Owing to space limitations this latter statement must however be left here for future research, in particular if an impact of the equities that are held by the central bank on the real side of the economy is taken into consideration.

16.4 An applicable model of the real-financial disequilibria interaction: a next step

In Chapter 6 we have investigated the following semistructural model from the theoretical, empirical and numerical perspective, exhibiting four laws of motion: for capacity utilization u^c, the goods market dynamics; for the employment rate e, Okun's law; for the wage share v, describing the real wage channel; and for the inflationary climate expression π^c (supplemented by a reduced-form price Phillips curve). As the model was formulated we had no real anchor for its steady-state rate of interest and thus had to assume here that it is the monetary authority that enforces a certain steady-state value for the nominal rate of interest. Thus

$$\hat{u}^c = -\beta_{uu}(u^c - \bar{u}^c) - \beta_{ui}((i - \hat{p}) - (i_0 - \pi_0)) \pm \beta_{uv}(v - v_0), \tag{16.78}$$

$$\dot{e} = \beta_{eu}\frac{y^p}{zl_0}\left(\frac{u^c}{e} - \frac{\bar{u}^c}{e_0}\right), \quad y^p, z, l_0 \text{ given}, \tag{16.79}$$

$$\begin{aligned}\hat{v} &= \widehat{w} - \hat{p} \\ &= \kappa\left[(1-\kappa_p)\left(\beta_{we}(e-\bar{e}) + \beta_{wu}\frac{y^p}{zl_0}\left(\frac{u^c}{e} - \frac{\bar{u}^c}{e_0}\right) - \beta_{wv}\ln\left(\frac{v}{v_0}\right)\right)\right. \\ &\quad \left. - (1-\kappa_w)\left(\beta_{pu}\left(u^c - \bar{u}^c\right) + \beta_{pv}\ln\left(\frac{v}{v_0}\right)\right)\right],\end{aligned} \tag{16.80}$$

$$\dot{\pi}^c = \beta_{\pi^c}(\hat{p} - \pi^c), \tag{16.81}$$

with the supplementary equations

$$\begin{aligned} i &= i_0 - \pi_0 + \alpha_{ip}(\hat{p} - \bar{\pi}) + \alpha_{iu}(u^c - \bar{u}^c) + \alpha_{iv}(v - v_0), \\ \hat{p} &= \kappa[\beta_{pu}(u^c - \bar{u}^c) + \beta_{pv}\ln(v/v_0) \\ &\qquad + \kappa_p(\beta_{we}(e - \bar{e}) + \beta_{wu}(u^w - \bar{u}^w) - \beta_{wv}\ln(v/v_0))] + \pi^c, \end{aligned}$$

to be inserted into these laws of motion in order to get an autonomous system of differential equations. We could immediately insert the Taylor rule into the goods market dynamics and obtain the result that the negative feedbacks in this law of motion will be enhanced thereby, showing that the sign in front of the wage share in the law of motion for u^c can depend on much more than just the aggregate demand function of the economy.

In view of what happened on the financial markets during the financial crisis we have just gone through, it is of course too idealistic to represent their working only by the working of a short-term risk-free monetary policy rule as is the case above. This would suggest that monetary policy has full control over the financial markets by just setting the federal funds rate and allowing money supply to adjust accordingly.

In order to make a first step away from this situation at the end of this book (and in order to motivate the analysis of the third volume of our trilogy) we extend – in view of what we have investigated in this chapter – therefore the empirically motivated model of Chapter 6 by a single risky financial asset, represented through the stock market, as discussed in the preceding sections. However, we now use (somewhat) gradual stock adjustment processes not only on the market for goods and for labor, but also on the stock market, in order to circumvent the explicit treatment of stock demand, which is now translated into an implied low demand that then drives stock prices. This assumes that desired stocks are realized not instantaneously, but through more or less gradual stock adjustment principles.

We thus now use a dynamic approach in place of the Tobinian equilibrium determination of the share price of the preceding section, by assuming that stock imbalances in households' gross portfolio

$$\frac{p_e E^d - p_e E}{p_e E} = f_e(r_e^e), \quad r_e^e = \frac{r(u)}{p_e} + \pi_e^e, \quad f_e(r_{eo}^e) = 0, \quad f_e^{'} > 0,$$

lead to a fractional flow demand for assets of amount $\alpha_e(E^d - E)/E$, $\alpha_e \in (0, 1)$, which in turn leads to share price inflation or deflation of amount $\hat{p}_e = \beta_e \alpha_e (E^d - E)/E$, with β_e the adjustment speed of share prices, whereby equilibrium in the stock market is re-established. Relative excess demand $\alpha_e(E^d - E)/E$ – as shown – depends on the rate of return on equities r_e^e which is composed of the dividend rate of return $r(u)/p_e$ and expected capital gains π_e^e. Expected capital gains are based here on chartist behavior solely which is modeled on the theoretical level by simple forward and backward expectations formation mechanisms. One can of course use nested adaptive expectations (humped shaped explorations of the past) of even sophisticated econometric techniques as well for the backward-looking part, if the model is estimated, but theoretical stability analysis may be very demanding in such cases. Adding more sophisticated forward-looking fundamentalists' behavior on the other hand could be used to add stabilizing elements to the considered expectations formation, but again there is no real change implied by such modifications in the message of this section.

The laws of motion shown below therefore represent our modeling of the dynamics of financial markets, primarily driven by the interaction between actual capital gains and expected ones:

$$\dot{p}_e = \beta_e \alpha_e f_e \left(\frac{r(u)}{p_e} + \pi_e^e \right) p_e,$$

$$\dot{\pi}_e^e = \beta_{\pi_e^e,1}(\hat{p}_e - \pi_e^e) + \beta_{\pi_e^e,2}(\hat{p}_{eo} - \pi_e^e)$$

$$= \beta_{\pi_e^e,1} \left(\beta_e \alpha_e f_e \left(\frac{r(Y)}{p_e} + \pi_e^e \right) - \pi_e^e \right) + \beta_{\pi_e^e,2}(0 - \pi_e^e).$$

In the theoretical model with its stationary steady-state solution we assume for the long-run view of fundamentalists that they expect capital gains to converge to zero. This however is to be revised appropriately when the model is brought to the data.

The formation of capital gain expectations can be further motivated by the fact that the portion of chartists in the stock market is given by α and the portion of fundamentalists by $1 - \alpha$. Average capital gain expectations are defined on this basis by

$$\pi_e^e = \alpha\pi_{ec}^e + (1-\alpha)\pi_{ef}^e,$$

with respect to these two groups of economic agents, and they are subject to the above law of motion if we define $\beta_{\pi_e^e,1}$ by $\beta_{\pi_e^e}\alpha$ and $\beta_{\pi_e^e,2}$ by $\beta_{\pi_e^e}(1-\alpha)$ using a common adjustment speed of capital gain expectations with respect to this average expectation formulation.

The Jacobian of these dynamics is given (at the steady state) by

$$J_0 = \begin{pmatrix} \beta_e\alpha_e[-f_e'(\cdot)r(\cdot)/p_e^2]p_e & \beta_e\alpha_e f_e'(\cdot)p_e \\ \beta_{\pi_e^e,1}\beta_e\alpha_e[-f_e'(\cdot)r(\cdot)/p_e^2] & \beta_{\pi_e^e,1}[\beta_e\alpha_e f_e'(\cdot)-1-\beta_{\pi_e^e,2}] \end{pmatrix}$$

$$= \begin{pmatrix} - & + \\ - & \pm \end{pmatrix}.$$

Stability analysis is simple in this case since the determinant of the matrix J is always positive and the trace of J gives rise to the critical stability condition

$$\beta_{\pi_e^e,1}^H = \frac{\beta_e\alpha_e f_e'(\cdot)r(\cdot)/p_e}{\beta_e\alpha_e f_e'(\cdot)-1-\beta_{\pi_e^e,2}} > 0,$$

if the entry J_{22} is positive and thus representing a danger for asymptotic stability. This asymptotic stability gets lost at the Hopf bifurcation point $\beta_{\pi_e^e}^H$, where the system loses its stability in a cyclical fashion, in general through the disappearance of a stable corridor around the steady state or the birth of an attracting limit cycle (persistent fluctuations in share prices) if the system is a nonlinear one (where degenerate Hopf bifurcations are of measure zero in the considered parameter space).

The considered Hopf bifurcation represents in general however only a local phenomenon, around the considered bifurcation parameter. We expect therefore that the systems tends to become globally unstable when the adjustment speed of capital gain expectations $\beta_{\pi_e^e,1}$ becomes larger and larger.

In order to connect this financial dynamics with the real part of the economy, it suffices to interpret the share price p_e as representing the state of confidence of the economy and to add it to the dynamics of the goods market utilization rate by introducing into its law of motion the additional term

$$+\beta_{up_e}(p_e - p_{eo}).$$

We call this effect a Tobinian stock market effect and it gives rise to a financial accelerator process, since economic activity thereby depends positively on share prices and share prices – via dividends – depend positively on economic activity. Capital gain expectations may add further cumulative forces to this destabilizing feedback loop, but this is of course to be investigated in more detail than done here.

The steady state of this semistructural model type is given by an easy extension of the one derived in Chapter 5 (since it is unique and must therefore fulfill $p_e = p_{eo}, \pi_e^e = 0$). Its stability can be investigated by applying the methods of Chapter 5 and the present one, since the feedback structure is of the same type (though somewhat simplified) as the one of the Keynes–Metzler–Goodwin–Tobin (KMGT) model of this chapter. In case of local explosiveness, we have again to add behavioral nonlinearities such as kinked money wage Phillips curves. In the financial part of the model such issues are however only solved so far by applying certain policy measures such as Tobin taxes. The role of this sector in its interaction with the real part of the economy therefore has to be investigated further, in particular if further risky assets such as long-term bonds or credit supplied by commercial banks enter the scene.

This concludes our brief introduction of an applicable model of the dynamic stochastic general disequilibrium (DSGD) variety that can be considered as providing a polar case in comparison to the now fashionable dynamic stochastic general equilibrium (DSGE) models. The stochastic elements are of course not present in the above presentation of the model, but come into being when the model is estimated and should then give rise to the question of the relevance of the stochastic components in comparison to the deterministic feedback chains that this model contains and that were discussed in this book from a variety of angles. A detailed discussion of this final section remains however reserved for the third volume of our trilogy.

16.5 Outlook: toward a dynamic stochastic general disequilibrium model

Summing up, according to the theoretical approach pursued in this chapter, it is not so much the individual behavior of economic agents (firms, households, institutions), but rather the interconnectedness of agents and markets which can produce the stabilizing or destabilizing feedback effects within the dynamical system we have investigated in this chapter. The behavior of the agents was by and large a fairly simple one, while the dynamics they generated were subject to Harrodian and Metzlerian quantity accelerators, concerning the capacity utilization rate of firms and their inventory holdings, as well as the positive interaction between the state of confidence, measured by Tobin's q, and private investment and thus economic activity. Moreover, such centrifugal forces were also present in the financial part of the model, there concerning the interaction of capital gains and capital gains expectations, operating in an otherwise stable portfolio model which was characterized by gross substitutability. Finally, the real-financial market interaction between these two accelerating mechanisms was also strongly impacted by a wage–price spiral, also characterized by centrifugal dynamical forces under certain assumptions on its adjustment parameters.

In the context of our proposed model we then argued for the necessity of adequate labor, fiscal and monetary policies that may induce stability in an otherwise – when left to itself – unstable macroeconomic environment. More specifically, we have shown that anti-cyclical labor market and fiscal policies, in terms of wage management characterized by cooperation between capital and labor in a corporative system resulting in a tranquilized wage–price spiral and anti-cyclical demand management by a fiscal authority, may be powerful means to make the business cycle not only less volatile, but in fact damped and perhaps also monotonically converging to the balanced growth path of the economy.

Within the theoretical closed-economy framework discussed in this chapter, however, these fiscal and labor market policies are necessary but not sufficient conditions for a comprehensive macroeconomic stabilization economic policy setup. Indeed, as we have discussed here, if the financial markets are primarily driven by the expectation of future capital gains in the equity markets and only to a much lesser extent by short-term interest rate changes, a necessary condition for the dampening of business cycles at the macrolevel is a monetary policy focused on the stabilization of financial markets. On the basis of the results of the reduced 3D system analyzed in the previous section, this should be undertaken by the introduction of a Tobin tax on capital gains, together with the implementation of a Tobin rule – by means of buying and selling equities of the nonfinancial sector (and other risk-bearing securities) – in place of a Taylor rule which, as assumed here, may turn out to be incapable of stabilizing the real and financial markets.

In a final section we have reformulated and somewhat simplified the KMGT approach of this chapter from the applied perspective by simplifying the quantity dynamics to a certain degree and by adding financial accelerator dynamics. In order to get the model into a form that can be estimated we however suppressed the explicit representation of the stock demands of our Tobinian portfolio approach and have proxied the equity market adjustment process by way of a flow-oriented stock adjustment principle where adjusting flow demand, and on this basis adjusting equity prices, are driven by the expected rate of return (the dividend rate plus expected capital gains) in its deviation from the steady-state rate of return. This provides a model with disequilibrium in the financial markets which – when applied to the data – then gives rise to a model which can be considered as being of the DSGD variety. However in the present book we cannot pursue this topic in more depth and thus leave it for future research.

Appendix: derivation of the model in intensive form

In its intensive form, all stock and flow variables are expressed in per unit of capital terms in the laws of motion and also in the associated algebraic equations (which need to be inserted into the laws of motion in order to obtain an autonomous dynamical system). We thus divide nominal stock and flow variables by the nominal value of the capital stock pK and all real ones by K, the real capital stock.

This allows the determination of a (unique) economic steady-state solution as an interior point of rest of the resulting nine state variables.

We begin with the intensive form of some necessary definitions or identities, which we need to represent the dynamical system in a sufficiently comprehensible form. Thus we set

$$\begin{aligned}
Y/K &= y = (1+\alpha_{n^d}(n+\beta_n))y^e - \beta_n \nu,\\
Y^e/K &= y^e,\\
N/K &= \nu,\\
L^d/K &= l^d = y/x,\\
L/K &= l,\\
e &= l^d/l,\\
u &= y/y^p,\\
r_k^e &= y^e - \delta - \omega l^d,\\
C/K &= c = (1-\tau_w)\omega l^d + (1-s_c)(y^e - \delta - \omega l^d - t_c),\\
I/K &= i(\cdot) = i_q(q-1) + i_u(u-\bar{u}) + n,\\
Y^d/K &= y^d = c + i(\cdot) + \delta + g,\\
p_e E/(pK) &= q = q(m, b, r_k^e, \pi_e),\\
r_e^e &= r_k^e/q + \pi_e,\\
\pi_e &= \alpha_{\pi_e}\pi_{ec} + (1-\alpha_{\pi_e})\pi_{ef}.
\end{aligned}$$

The above equations describe output and employment per unit of capital, the rate of utilization of the existing stock of labor and capital, the expected rate of return on capital, consumption, investment and aggregate demand per unit of capital, Tobin's average q, and the expected rate of return on equities (including expected capital gains π_e).

Now we translate the laws of motion of the dynamically endogenous variables into capital intensive form. The law of motions for the nominal wages and price level stated in equations (16.38) and (16.39) interact instantaneously and thus depend on each other. Solving these two linear equations for $\widehat{w}$ and $\hat{p}$ gives[26]

$$\widehat{w} = \kappa(\beta_w(e-\bar{e}) + \kappa_w\beta_p(u-\bar{u})) + \pi^c, \tag{16.82}$$

$$\hat{p} = \kappa(\beta_p(u-\bar{u}) + \kappa_p\beta_w(e-\bar{e})) + \pi^c, \tag{16.83}$$

with $\kappa = (1-\kappa_w\kappa_p)^{-1}$. From these two inflation rates one can compute the growth law of real wages $\omega = w/p$ by means of the definitional relationship $\widehat{\omega} = \widehat{w} - \hat{p}$, from which equation (16.46) arises.

Next we obtain the set of equations that explains the dynamical laws of the expected rate of inflation, the labor capital ratio, the expected sales, and the stock of inventories in intensive form given by equations (16.47)–(16.50), respectively.

Equation (16.47) is almost the same as in the extensive-form model, but here the term $\hat{p} - \pi^c$ is substituted by use of equation (16.83). Equation (16.48), the law of motion of relative factor endowment, follows from equations (16.4) and (16.23) and is given by the (negative) of the investment function as far as its dependence on asset markets and the state of the business cycle are concerned. Equation (16.49) is obtained by taking the time derivative of y^e, so that

$$\dot{y}^e = \frac{d(Y^e/K)}{dt} = \frac{\dot{Y}^e K - Y^e \dot{K}}{K^2} = \frac{\dot{Y}^e}{K} - y^e i(\cdot) = \beta_{y^e}(y^d - y^e) + y^e(n - i(\cdot)).$$

In essentially the same way one obtains equation (16.50).

The law of motion of the aggregate expectation of equity price inflation given by equation (16.51) results from taking the time derivative of π_e,

$$\dot{\pi}_e = \alpha_{\pi ec}\dot{\pi}_{ec} + (1 - \alpha_{\pi ec})\dot{\pi}_{ef},$$

and inserting therein the laws of motion governing the expectations about the equity prices given by equations (16.14) and (16.15).

Finally, the laws of motion for real balances and real bonds per unit of capital have to be derived. Based on the knowledge of the laws for inflation $\hat{p}$ and investment $i(\cdot)$ we can derive the differential equation for bonds per unit of capital shown in equation (16.52) from

$$\dot{b} = \frac{d(B/pK)}{dt} = \frac{\dot{B}}{pK} - b(\hat{p} + i(\cdot)),$$

where $\dot{B}$ is given by equation (16.37). The same idea is used for the changes in the money supply.

Notes

1 Representative households or principal-agent capitalism?

1 The reader is referred to vol. 38 of the journal *History of Political Economy* (2006) for a series of articles that discuss the implications of this theorem.
2 Assuming a given positive natural rate of growth n or exogenous and disembodied Harrod neutral change at the rate m would only marginally augment the presentation of the laws of motion of the model; see Chapter 15 in this regard.
3 Here ω_0 is the steady-state real wage rate; see the next section for details.
4 See the above remarks on the assumed family structure.
5 Note again that we have assumed that labor is supplied inelastically.
6 This two-class Pasinetti model is considered in Greiner (2001) with life cycle utility functions in place of the simple utility functions used here to get Pasinetti type capital stock dynamics (with bequest) in the simplest possible way. Also, including the stock magnitude K into the utility functions of workers and capitalists would not alter the model significantly.
7 Assuming a given positive natural rate of growth n or exogenous and disembodied Harrod neutral technical change at the rate m would only marginally augment the presentation of the laws of motion of the model.
8 The distribution of wealth may be different between workers, due to fluctuating real wages and bequest, but this does not matter on the macrolevel, since they will be shown to save all with the same rate out of their current income.
9 Note that we here assume a partial extended family, since employed and unemployed worker households share their income in their consumption and saving decision. A next step may therefore be to discriminate also between worker households, for example by introducing a high-skill labor market that clears and a labor market for the unskilled workers who do not save.
10 Assuming smooth factor substitution would not change the results very much, but would of course deliver a more complicated determination of the employment rate of the model. See Chiarella and Flaschel (2000a, ch. 5) on this point.
11 In this subsection lower-case letters (including w and p) indicate logarithms.

2 The two-class Pasinetti model from a neoclassical perspective

1 For a more detailed survey of this line of research, see Bénabou (1996) or Perotti (1994).
2 This chapter is based on Greiner (2001), "Distribution and endogenous growth: the two-class Pasinetti model," *Jahrbücher für Nationalökonomie und Statistik*, **221**, 309–321. We thank the editors of that journal for allowing us to reprint this article (with some

cosmetic changes and some formal adjustments, mainly to align with the notation of the book).

3 We suppress the time argument if no ambiguity arises.

4 The assumption $g < \rho_p$ is also sufficient for (2.4) to take on a finite value.

5 As to the economic meaning of determinate and indeterminate growth paths, see e.g. Benhabib and Farmer (1994).

6 Recall that an increase in $g^\star$, brought about by a higher u, implies a decline in $k^\star$ and vice versa.

3 Expectations and the (un-)importance of the real wage feedback channel

1 This chapter is partly based on the results achieved in Flaschel *et al.* (2008a), "On equilibrium determinacy in new Keynesian models with staggered wage and price setting," *The B.E. Journal of Macroeconomics*, **8**(1), Art. 31, 1–10, available at www.degruyter.com, doi:10.2202/1935-1690.1802; see also Asada *et al.* (2010a, ch. 5).

2 Here I is the identity matrix.

3 Considering in particular negative eigenvalues that are smaller than -2, it would be strange from a macroeconomic point of view to obtain from such a situation period model instability as compared to the very strong asymptotic stability implied in the continuous-time case.

4 For two analyses of the consequences of such a discrepancy for the resulting dynamics of macroeconomic models, see Aadland and Huang (2004) as well as Flaschel and Proaño (2009).

5 We refer the reader the Flaschel *et al.* (2008a) for the proofs of Propositions 3.1 and 3.2.

6 For counterfactual examples where the determinacy properties of the rational expectations equilibrium in an economy do depend on the decision frequency assumed, see Hintermaier (2005).

7 See also Asada *et al.* (2010a, ch. 5) on these matters.

8 See comments by J. Fuhrer on "Empirical and policy performance of a forward-looking monetary model" by A. Onatstu and N. Williams, presented at the FRB San Francisco conference on "Interest rates and monetary policy," March 19–20, 2004. http://www.frbsf.org/economics/conferences/0403/jeff_fuhrer.pdf.

9 See http://www.frbsf.org/economics/conferences/0403/jeff_fuhrer.pdf.

10 In a plenary lecture at the "Computing in Economics and Finance" conference in 2007, Volker Wieland has compared as two possible approaches simple traditional Keynesian (TK) models with new Keynesian models. In view of this lecture, the present chapter can be considered as an attempt toward the formulation of more advanced models of the TK type.

11 Note that we use, as in the new Keynesian models, the log of the output level as quantity variable and a zero target rate of inflation of the central bank.

12 Note that the model considered in this section is close in spirit to the ones considered in Asada *et al.* (2006) and Chen *et al.* (2006). The reader is referred to these works for more details on such dynamical systems and further empirical investigations of this model prototype (for the US economy in the cited papers).

13 Here z denotes labor productivity (in hours).

14 See Flaschel *et al.* (2008c, ch. 1).

4 Viability and corridor stability in Keynesian supply driven growth

1 This chapter is based on Flaschel (2001b), "Viability and corridor stability in Keynesian supply driven growth," *Metroeconomica*, **52**(1), 26–48, with permission of John Wiley & Sons Ltd.

2 See Orphanides and Solow (1990) for a brief presentation of the literature on Keynes–Wicksell models of monetary growth and Chiarella and Flaschel (2000a, ch. 3) for

a coherent reformulation and generalization of this model type (from three to four dimensions).

3 This is in contradiction to what is implied by the formula (3′) in Perko (1991, p. 317) and (A2) in Lux (1995a, p. 367); see Section 4.2 for corrections of the formula used by these two authors.

4 A further side condition for economic viability, namely $V \leq 1$, is fulfilled when appropriate nonlinearities (in one of the isoclines of the dynamics) are assumed; see Figure 4.4 for an example.

5 Rose (1967) and Goodwin (1967) type models are investigated in detail in Flaschel *et al.* (1997) and Chiarella and Flaschel (2000a).

6 A much more general case which includes interest rates, real balances and inflationary expectations and which leads to a five-dimensional (5D) dynamical system is considered in Flaschel (2001a).

7 Lux (1995a), who makes use of the Perko formula in order to get corridor stability in the Dendrinos model of regional factor movements, contains two further misprints of this type: the term $b_{20}x_2^2$ should be replaced by $b_{02}x_2^2$ in formula (A1), and $a_{20}a_{20}$ by $a_{20}a_{02}$ and $b_{20}b_{20}$ by $b_{20}b_{02}$ in formula (A2) in Lux (1995a, p. 367). Note here however that Lux (1995a) does not consider a linear growth rate model and thus may obtain corridor stability despite the printing error in the Perko formula in the case he considers.

8 The output expansion function may be further modified from the economic point of view to include nonlinear reactions of output expansion for rates of employment close to 1.

9 The same observation also holds for the case where $g_1(0) < 0$, but not $g_2(0) < 0$, holds.

10 This value of y is indicated as "saddle" in Figure 4.2.

11 In the case of local explosiveness around the interior steady state there is therefore a positive threshold value for the output/capital ratio y below which the dynamics (4.1) and (4.2), and more importantly its modification in the present section, give rise to a monotonic decline of both the rate of employment and the output/capital ratio toward $(0, 0)$.

12 This viability domain shrinks to zero if the parameter $\bar{y}_1$ is made larger and larger, as numerical simulations have shown. An analytical discussion of assertion 3 in Proposition 4.3 calls for the investigation of the separatrix leading into the saddle as shown in Figure 4.2.

13 The other parameter values for this simulation of the model are: $y_2 = 1$, $n = 0.05$, $\bar{V} = 0.95$, $\bar{U} = 0.9$, $s_c = 0.8$, $i_1 = 0.2$, $i_2 = 0.2$, $y^p = 1$.

14 The extrinsic nonlinearity is modeled by $\exp[-\alpha(y - y_0)/(y^p - y)]$ for $y \geq y_0$ in the considered simulation.

15 See Solow and Stiglitz (1968) for an early use of such adjustment rules and Rose (1990) for a different application of these.

16 See Chiarella and Flaschel (2000a, ch. 3) for general approaches of this kind that include the treatment of medium-run inflationary expectations.

17 See Chiarella and Flaschel (2000a, ch. 3) for the details of the derivation.

18 As in non-Walrasian disequilibrium theory, here however without any regime switches, since investment demand is purely notional and only serves to determine the inflation rate of the model.

19 These are not necessarily lower turning points, since u, $\rho = y(1 - u)$ can both approach zero.

20 The base parameter set for this simulation of the model is: $\bar{y}_1 = 10$, $\bar{y}_2 = 0.3$, $n = 0.1$, $\bar{V} = 0.95$, $\bar{U} = 0.9$, $s_c = 0.8$, $i_1 = 0.5$, $i_2 = 0.3$, $y^p = 0.5$, $x = 2$, $\beta_w = 0.7$, $\beta_p = 0.5$, $\kappa_w = \kappa_p = 0.5$.

5 Wicksellian inflation pressure in Keynesian models of monetary growth

1 This chapter is based on Chiarella and Flaschel (2000a), "Keynes–Wicksell models of monetary growth: synthesizing Keynes into the classics," in *The Dynamics of Keynesian Monetary Growth: Macrofoundations*, chapter 3, reproduced with permission of Cambridge University Press.

2 See also Chiarella and Flaschel (1996b) for a discussion of this model type where more stress is laid on a consideration of the government budget restraint and the occurrence of complex dynamics.

3 These may also be called models of "supply-side Keynesianism."

4 That is, we attempt to represent models of "demand-side Keynesianism" despite the presence of an elaborate wage–price module (representing "aggregate supply" as this is often called in the literature).

5 Such an extension simply adds two further equations ($\omega = f'(l^d)$ and $y = f(l^d)$) to the model and two further unknowns (l^d, y), which in general leads to an increase in the stability of the model.

6 The parameter τ has to be removed from all equations of the following model if the second alternative in equation (5.12) is chosen as the tax collection rule, in which case $\tau = (t^n + rb)/(\rho + rb)$. Note here also that the money demand function which we employ in (all of) the following represents an appropriate linearization of the general form $M^d = M^d(pY, -\pi, (1-\tau)r - \pi, pK)$, where the term pK is used for the time being as a proxy – for reasons of mathematical simplification – of the influence of nominal wealth pW on money demand. Note finally that the magnitude $\dot{E} = \dot{E}^d$ in the following model can also be negative – in the case in which the supply of new money and new bonds exceeds private savings. In this extreme case, firms sell so much from their inventories that they can finance investment from these "windfall profits."

7 Note here that the expected inflation rate π used in the calculation of the real rate of interest represents an average over the medium run in our interpretation of the wage–price dynamics of module 7 of the model. In principle, this also requires that the expected rate of return and the nominal rate of interest are to be considered as representing such averages. This is easily done by assuming certain dynamic feedback rules for these average concepts in view of their short-run equivalents; see Flaschel *et al.* (1998) and Chiarella *et al.* (2005). One might also argue on empirical grounds that investment depends negatively on expected inflation π as faster inflation may create an uncertain environment for investors. The role that inflationary expectations will play in the following is thereby reversed. We do not go into this topic here any further, but will adhere to the traditional way in which the investment function has been formulated in models of Keynes–Wicksell type. The topics discussed in this note are left for future research.

8 Note that we here follow Sargent (1987, p. 18) and assume that the expected change in the price of equities is zero.

9 The expression δK represents that part of production that is kept by firms for capital replacement purposes and for voluntary inventory changes.

10 Note that both are financed by issuing new equities, since firms have no earnings from current production.

11 Note that this also covers the case of an excessive new bond and money supply ($\dot{M} + \dot{B} > pS_p$) by the government in which case we can have negative aggregate savings S and a reduction in the stock of equities financed by excessive sales of firms from inventories. A constraint of the type $pS = p_e\dot{E} > 0$ is therefore not really necessary in the present formulation of the model. Note also that in such a case it is not only investment demand, but also other demand (here implicitly assumed to be satisfied before investment demand is considered) that is (completely) met by appropriate inventory changes. Also in such a situation it is therefore only investment demand that can be rationed in the present model.

12 Note here again that this "simple" assumption bears strong consequences with respect to the ability of the government to influence the pace of capital accumulation. Nevertheless, we shall not dispense with this standard assumption of continuous-time macrodynamic theory here, but shall leave its detailed reconsideration for future investigations.

13 Note that the system in fact exhibits two further laws of motion for the variables $\nu = N/K$ and $e = E/K$ which however do not feed back to the other laws of motion of the model. These two laws read

$$\dot{\nu} = \delta_2 + \beta_k(s(\cdot) - i(\cdot) - n) - n\nu + \hat{l}\nu \quad [\nu_0 = \delta_2/n],$$

$$\hat{e} = \frac{(1-\tau)r - \pi}{(1-\tau)\rho} s(\cdot) - n + \hat{l} \quad [e_0 \text{ indeterminate}].$$

It is of course necessary to check that both ν and e remain nonnegative and finite in the course of the dynamic evolution of the above dynamics. Note that the second law implies that the number of equities grows at the rate n in the steady state, while bonds B and money M both grow at the rate μ.

14 The following presentation of this steady state of the dynamics immediately implies that money is not superneutral in this model, i.e. the rate of growth of the money supply exercises an influence on the real side of the steady state of the model.

15 It is easy to calculate for the additional dynamic variables N/K, $p_eE/(pK)$ the steady-state values of δ_2/n and $(1-\tau)\rho_0/((1-\tau)r_0 - \pi_0)$, respectively.

16 Note that we have ($\bar{U}, \bar{V} = 1$)

$$y_0 = y^p, \quad l_0^d = y_0/x, \quad l_0 = l_0^d,$$

$$\pi_0 = \mu_0 - n, \quad m_0 = h_1 y_0,$$

$$\omega_0 = (y_0 - \delta - \rho_0)/l_0^d, \quad r_0 = \rho_0 + \mu_0 - n.$$

Sargent (1987, ch. V) obtains the superneutrality of this steady state by assuming $g =$ const. and $\mu_2 = 0$ in addition to the above assumption t^nconst.

17 See Flaschel (1984, 1993), Flaschel and Sethi (1996) and Flaschel *et al.* (1997) for various representations and investigations of the Goodwin growth cycle model and its extensions, and Flaschel and Groh (1995) for some empirical observations on this model type that extend Solow's (1990) reappraisal of this very fundamental model of cyclical growth.

18 See Hirsch and Smale (1974, p. 192ff.) and Brock and Malliaris (1989, p. 94ff.).

19 The function $\beta_w(\cdot)$ may be nonlinear and is assumed to fulfill $\beta_w(V) \in (0, 1)$, $\beta_w' > 0$. Note that the expression $x = y/l^d$ in this new Phillips curve represents labor productivity Y/L^d.

20 Note here that we have used 1 in the 4D dynamics (5.36)–(5.39) to denote that level of employment where there is no money wage drift from the side of the labor market, which is here assumed to be a magnitude significantly below full employment.

21 This would lead to regimes of absolute goods supply shortages or absolute labor supply shortages.

22 Note here however that the equations (5.11) and (5.23) are not without problems, problems which are discussed and removed in Chiarella and Flaschel (2000a, ch. 4) when going from the Keynes–Wicksell prototype model to the Keynesian one.

23 See also Akerlof and Stiglitz (1969, p. 272) in this regard.

24 This is provided $\omega < x = Y/L^d$, in other words as long as profits remain positive.

25 See Flaschel (1993), Flaschel and Sethi (1996) and Flaschel *et al.* (1997) for various representations and investigations of the Rose employment cycle model and its extensions.

26 Together with $\kappa_p < 1$, of course.
27 The dynamics are of Goodwinian type if $i = s_c$ holds.
28 See also Akerlof and Stiglitz (1969, p. 278) on this sort of a Phillips curve.
29 This law replaces the linear function $\beta_w(V - 1)$.
30 The $\dot{\omega}$ isocline is given by

$$\frac{l^d}{b} < l = \frac{l^d}{\beta_w^{-1}\{[(1-\kappa_w)/(1-\kappa_p)]\beta_p(i(\cdot)+n-s(\cdot))\}}$$
$$= \frac{l^d}{\beta_w^{-1}\{[(1-\kappa_w)/(1-\kappa_p)]\beta_p(s_c-i)l^d\omega+\text{const.}\}} < \frac{l^d}{a}$$

and is thus a strictly increasing function of ω for $i < s_c$.
31 Note here that the true upper bound on the variable ω is given by $(y - \delta - t^n)/yx$ and not by x as in the above figure.
32 The isocline $\dot{\omega} = 0$ is horizontal if $\kappa_w = 1$ holds.
33 Note the formal similarity to the Kaldor (1940) trade cycle model.
34 Note that the cycle is clockwise – and between the limits a, b – when the variables u, V are used in place of ω, l.
35 This is the sets of all limit points of the considered trajectories.
36 See Hirsch and Smale (1974, p. 248).
37 Rose (1967) assumes for the following monetary extension of his model of the employment cycle the relationship $r = r(y)$ (with a variable ratio y due to the existence of neoclassical factor substitution) which allows – as in his chapter – a reduction of the dynamics again to dimension two in the two real variables ω, l. In the context of the present dynamical model, this does not represent, however, a convincing simplification.
38 See Chiarella (1990a, ch. 7) and Turnovsky (1995, ch. 3).
39 See Flaschel (1993, ch. 6) for investigations of a related situation.
40 Alternatively set $\beta_p = \infty$; see the following analysis.
41 Such a situation is investigated in Sargent (1987, ch. V) for the case of a constant value of g and $\mu_2 = 0$ by means of the saddle-path methodology introduced in Sargent and Wallace (1973). See the following for further discussion of this methodology.
42 See Groth (1988) for further details on the discussion and analysis of such a combined mechanism.
43 This is generally assumed in such "Keynesian" IS–LM growth models.
44 Note that the rate of profit is constant in the present context.
45 It is easy to show in the case of the above 2D dynamical system that the conditions for the Hopf bifurcation theorem will apply with respect to the parameter β_{π_1}. The following demonstration of the conditions that imply the validity of the Poincaré–Bendixson theorem, however, gives rise to a situation that is much more general than that of a Hopf limit cycle (or that of a Hopf closed orbit structure).
46 This is so as long as m lies below the value $\bar{m}$ at which $r = r(m)$ is zero.
47 This coupled growth cycle model can be usefully compared with Hicks's (1974) analysis of the real and monetary factors in economic fluctuations.

6 Interacting two-country business fluctuations

1 This chapter is based on Chiarella *et al.* (2006b), "Interacting business cycle fluctuations: a two-country model," *Singapore Economic Review*, **51**(3), 365–394. Copyright © 2006 World Scientific Publishing Co. With the kind permission of Springer Science + Business Media, the figures in this chapter are reproduced from Asada *et al.* (2003a), "Two-country business cycle models: Euroland and the USA," in *Open Economy Macrodynamics: An Integrated Disequilibrium Approach*, chapter 10, pp. 451–523. Springer-Verlag, Berlin, Heidelberg.

2 The two labels chosen distinguish the so-called Keynes–Metzler–Goodwin (KMG) approach from the simpler Keynes–Wicksell–Goodwin (KWG) approach where there is no quantity adjustment in the market for goods and where therefore primarily an IS-driven inflation dynamics is the focus of interest. These two model types were established in Chiarella and Flaschel (1996a, b) and reconsidered in a larger context in Chiarella and Flaschel (2000a) as well as Chiarella *et al.* (2000b).

3 The theory of coupled oscillators represents a topic with many interesting features. Owing to space constraints the proper application of this theory to the questions treated here remains a subject for future research; see however Haxholdt (1995) and Brenner *et al.* (2002) on these matters.

4 See also Chiarella and Flaschel (1996b) with respect the first presentation of the KWG model type, based on the literature on the Keynes–Wicksell monetary growth dynamics of the 1960s and 1970s.

5 Note that for workers $s_w = \tau_w = 0$.

6 However equation (6.27) excludes the possibility that inventories N grow even in a non-growing economy ($K =$const.). Let $\hat{\delta}_2$ denote the desired ratio of inventories and output, $\hat{\delta}_2 Y = \hat{\delta}_2 y K = N$. Differentiating with respect to time and noting that the steady state is characterized by $\dot{K} = nK$, the following definition of δ_2 seems appropriate: $\delta_2 = \hat{\delta}_2 y n K$. In a stationary economy, $n = 0$, the equilibrium is then characterized by a constant stock of inventories.

7 We do not yet consider foreign market operations by the central banks.

8 For $\dot{M} = \dot{M}^d$, $\dot{E} = \dot{E}^d$, $\dot{M}^* = \dot{M}^{d*}$, $\dot{E}^* = \dot{E}^{d*}$, equations (6.11), (6.19), (6.47) and (6.51) lead to the following set of four equations in the four unknowns $\dot{B}_1^d$, $\dot{B}_2^d$, $\dot{B}_1^{d*}$ and $\dot{B}_2^{d*}$:

$$\begin{bmatrix} 1 & e & 0 & 0 \\ 0 & 0 & 1/e & 1 \\ 1 & 0 & 1 & 0 \\ 0 & 1 & 0 & 1 \end{bmatrix} \begin{bmatrix} \dot{B}_1^d \\ \dot{B}_2^d \\ \dot{B}_1^{d*} \\ \dot{B}_2^{d*} \end{bmatrix} = \begin{bmatrix} pS_g - \dot{M} - p_e\dot{E} \\ p^*S_g^* - \dot{M}^* - p_e^*\dot{E}^* \\ \dot{B} \\ \dot{B}^* \end{bmatrix}.$$

As can easily be verified, the rank of the 4×4 matrix on the left-hand side is three, yielding one degree of freedom. Hence, once the division of new domestic bonds between domestic residents and foreigners is chosen, the division of foreign bonds is determined as well.

9 Whereas the first line in (6.54) follows directly from inserting the use of private and government savings from (6.11) and (6.36), the derivation of the second line is slightly more complicated. Using the definitions of private and government savings,

$$S = S_p + S_g = \omega L^d + Y_c^D - C + T - rB/p - G,$$

and inserting expressions for Y_c^D, C and T according to (6.8), (6.12) and (6.34) yields

$$S = \omega L^d + \rho K - C_1 - (ep^*/p)C_2 - G - rB_1/p + e(1 - \tau_c^*)r^*B_2/p.$$

Making use of the definition of ρ in (6.1) and noting that from (6.24) and (6.25) that $Y - \delta K - G - C_1 = \Delta Y + I + C_1^* = I^a + C_1^*$, one finally obtains the desired expression

$$S = I^a + \{C_1^* - (ep^*/p)C_2\} + \{e(1 - \tau_c^*)r^*B_2/p - (1 - \tau_c)rB_1^*/p\}.$$

10 We thus allow here for imperfect capital mobility – in contrast to the approach assumed for domestically traded bonds and equities.

11 For simplicity, only asymptotically rational expectations are assumed here.

12 The assumptions we make for the foreign economy are the same as the ones here for the domestic economy and are therefore not made explicit in this section.

13 Note that the parameter τ_c has thus to be removed from the model's equations, since taxes are now lump sum.

14 Rigorous stability proofs for the propositions of this section are provided in Asada *et al.* (2003a, ch. 10).

15 Note again that y and l^d are given magnitudes in the KWG dynamics.

16 In particular we have

$$c_2^* = \omega^* y^*/x^* + \gamma_c^*(\eta)(1 - s_c^*)(\rho^* - t_c^*),$$
$$c_2 = (l^*/l)(1 - \gamma_c(\eta))(1 - s_c)(\rho - t_c)\eta.$$

Note also that X^p can be rewritten as $X^p = \omega y/x + (1 - s_c)(\rho - t_c) + i(\cdot) + n + \delta + g + nx(\cdot) - y$.

17 The first two parametric assumptions imply that trade does not influence the price–quantity dynamics in the two countries considered. The other two imply that both e and ϵ can be frozen at their steady-state values.

18 Note here that the parameter β does not represent a speed of adjustment condition, but characterizes the degree of capital mobility. Setting this parameter to a small value has the convenient effect that the law of motion for the exchange rate is basically dependent on trade and can thus be used to eliminate the net export term $nx(\cdot)$ from the laws of motion for the domestic and the foreign economy as far as the calculation of determinants is concerned. We conjecture however that the obtained result on determinants also holds for large values of β, though row operations are considerably more difficult then.

19 In which case $r^* - r$ can be reduced to $\omega - \omega^*$, but in this form remains as a new item in the fifth row of the considered Jacobian.

20 The simulations that follow were performed using the SND software package described in Chiarella *et al.* (2002), which can be downloaded together with the project files for the simulations of this chapter from Carl Chiarella's homepage at http://www.business.uts.edu.au/finance/.

21 The parameters of this simulation run are as follows (the modifications (1) in trade and (2) in financial links are shown in brackets): $s_c = 0.8,\ \delta = 0.1,\ t_c = 0.35,\ g = 0.35,\ n = 0.05,\ \mu = 0.05,\ h_1 = 0.1,\ h_2 = 0.2,\ y^p = 1.0,\ x = 2.0,\ \beta_w = 2,\ \beta_p = 5,\ \kappa_w = 0.5,\ \kappa_p = 0.5,\ \beta_\pi = 3,\ \alpha_\pi = 0.5,\ i = 0.5,\ \beta_k = 1.0,\ \bar{V} = 0.8,\ s_c^* = 0.8,\ \delta^* = 0.1,\ t_c^* = 0.35,\ g^* = 0.35,\ n^* = 0.05,\ \mu^* = 0.05,\ h_1^* = 0.1,\ h_2^* = 0.2,\ y^{p*} = 1.0,\ x^* = 2.0,\ \beta_w^* = 2.0,\ \beta_p^* = 1.0,\ \kappa_w^* = 0.5,\ \kappa_p^* = 0.5,\ \beta_\pi^* = 3,\ \alpha_\pi^* = 0.5,\ i^* = 0.5,\ \beta_k^* = 1.0,\ \bar{V}^* = 0.8,\ \beta_e = 0\ (\beta_e = 1),\ \beta = 0\ (\beta = 2.5),\ \beta_\epsilon = 0\ (\beta_\epsilon = 1),\ \alpha_\epsilon = 0.5,\ \gamma_c = 0.99\ (\gamma_c = 0.5),\ \gamma = 0\ (\gamma = 1),\ \gamma_c^* = 0.99\ (\gamma_c^* = 0.5),\ \gamma^* = 0\ (\gamma_2 = 1),\ m_{\text{shock}} = 1.1$.

22 The parameters of this simulation run are as follows (with $\beta_e = 0,\ 2,\ 2.2$ in the top time series): $s_c = 0.8,\ \delta = 0.1,\ t_c = 0.35,\ g = 0.35,\ n = 0.05,\ \mu = 0.05,\ h_1 = 0.1,\ h_2 = 0.2,\ y^p = 1.0,\ x = 2.0,\ \beta_w = 2,\ \beta_p = 1,\ \kappa_w = 0.5,\ \kappa_p = 0.5,\ \beta_\pi = 3,\ \alpha_\pi = 0.5,\ i = 0.5,\ \beta_k = 1.0,\ \bar{V} = 0.8,\ s_c^* = 0.8,\ \delta^* = 0.1,\ t_c^* = 0.35,\ g^* = 0.35,\ n^* = 0.05,\ \mu^* = 0.05,\ h_1^* = 0.1,\ h_2^* = 0.2,\ y^{p*} = 1.0,\ x^* = 2.0,\ \beta_w^* = 2.0,\ \beta_p^* = 1.0,\ \kappa_w^* = 0.5,\ \kappa_p^* = 0.5,\ \beta_\pi^* = 3,\ \alpha_\pi^* = 0.5,\ i^* = 0.5,\ \beta_k^* = 1.0,\ \bar{V}^* = 0.8,\ \beta_e = 0,\ \beta = 1.0,\ \beta_\epsilon = 1.0,\ \alpha_\epsilon = 0.5,\ \gamma_c = 0.5,\ \gamma = 1.0,\ \gamma_c^* = 0.5,\ \gamma^* = 1.0,\ m_{\text{shock}} = 1.02$.

23 Note that the shown fluctuations are obtained by shocking the economy out of the steady state via a 10% increase in the money supply. This is a large shock and one which shocks the economy the more the further from the unstable steady state is the unstable limit cycle surrounding it.

24 The parameters of this simulation run are as follows (with $\beta_e = 0$ and thus a fixed exchange rate throughout): $s_c = 0.8,\ \delta = 0.1,\ t_c = 0.35,\ g = 0.35,\ n = 0.05,\ \mu =$

$0.05,\ h_1=0.1,\ h_2=0.2,\ y^p=1.0,\ x=2.0,\ \beta_w=5,\ \beta_p=1,\ \kappa_w=0.5,\ \kappa_p=0.5,\ \beta_\pi=3,\ \alpha_\pi=0.5,\ i=0.5,\ \beta_k=1.0,\ \bar{V}=0.8,\ s_c^*=0.8,\ \delta^*=0.1,\ t_c^*=0.35,\ g^*=0.35,\ n^*=0.05,\ \mu^*=0.05,\ h_1^*=0.1,\ h_2^*=0.2,\ y^{p*}=1.0,\ x^*=2.0,\ \beta_w^*=5,\ \beta_p^*=1.0,\ \kappa_w^*=0.5,\ \kappa_p^*=0.5,\ \beta_\pi^*=3,\ \alpha_\pi^*=0.5,\ i^*=0.5,\ \beta_k^*=1.0,\ \bar{V}^*=0.8,\ \beta_e=0,\ \beta=0,\ \beta_\epsilon=0,\ \alpha_\epsilon=0.5,\ \gamma_c=0.7,\ \gamma=1,\ \gamma_c^*=0.7,\ \gamma^*=1,\ m_{\text{shock}}=1.1.$

25 The parameters of this simulation run are as follows: $s_c=0.8,\ \delta=0.1,\ t_c=0.35,\ g=0.35,\ n=0.05,\ \mu=0.057,\ h_1=0.1,\ h_2=0.2,\ y^p=1.0,\ x=2.0,\ \beta_w=2,\ \beta_p=3,\ \kappa_w=0.5,\ \kappa_p=0.5,\ \beta_\pi=3,\ \alpha_\pi=0.5,\ i=0.5,\ \beta_k=1.0,\ \bar{V}=0.8,\ s_c^*=0.8,\ \delta^*=0.1,\ t_c^*=0.35,\ g^*=0.35,\ n^*=0.05,\ \mu^*=0.05,\ h_1^*=0.1,\ h_2^*=0.2,\ y^{p*}=1.0,\ x^*=2.0,\ \beta_w^*=1.95,\ \beta_p^*=0.5,\ \kappa_w^*=0.5,\ \kappa_p^*=0.5,\ \beta_\pi^*=3,\ \alpha_\pi^*=0.5,\ i^*=0.5,\ \beta_k^*=1.0,\ \bar{V}^*=0.8,\ \beta_e=0,\ \beta=0,\ \beta_\epsilon=0,\ \alpha_\epsilon=0.5,\ \gamma_c=0.5,\ \gamma=1,\ \gamma_c^*=0.5,\ \gamma^*=1,\ m_{\text{shock}}=1.1.$

26 The parameters of this simulation run are as follows: $s_c=0.8,\ \delta=0.1,\ t_c=0.35,\ g=0.35,\ n=0.05,\ \mu=0.06,\ h_1=0.1,\ h_2=0.2,\ y^p=1.0,\ x=2.0,\ \beta_w=2.5,\ \beta_p=1,\ \kappa_w=0.5,\ \kappa_p=0.5,\ \beta_\pi=3,\ \alpha_\pi=0.5,\ i=0.5,\ \beta_k=1.0,\ \bar{V}=0.8,\ s_c^*=0.8,\ \delta^*=0.1,\ t_c^*=0.35,\ g^*=0.35,\ n^*=0.05,\ \mu^*=0.06,\ h_1^*=0.1,\ h_2^*=0.2,\ y^{p*}=1.0,\ x^*=2.0,\ \beta_w^*=0.6,\ \beta_p^*=1,\ \kappa_w^*=0.5,\ \kappa_p^*=0.5,\ \beta_\pi^*=3,\ \alpha_\pi^*=0.5,\ i^*=0.5,\ \beta_k^*=1.0,\ \bar{V}^*=0.8,\ \beta_e=0,\ \beta=0,\ \beta_\epsilon=0,\ \alpha_\epsilon=0.5,\ \gamma_c=0.5,\ \gamma=1.5,\ \gamma_c^*=0.5,\ \gamma^*=1.5,\ m_{\text{shock}}=1.1.$

27 Fixed and flexible exchange rate regimes are compared in Baxter and Stockman (1989), Gerlach (1988) and Greenwood and Williamson (1989). A two-country analysis for a fixed exchange rate regime that is very much in the spirit of the model used here is provided in Asada *et al.* (2003b). There the case of fixed exchange rates is considered on its own level and not just by setting a certain parameter in a flexible exchange rate regime equal to one.

28 The parameters of this simulation run are as follows: $s_c=0.8,\ \delta=0.1,\ t_c=0.35,\ g=0.35,\ n=0.05,\ \mu=0.057,\ h_1=0.1,\ h_2=0.2,\ y^p=1.0,\ x=2.0,\ \beta_w=2,\ \beta_p=3,\ \kappa_w=0.5,\ \kappa_p=0.5,\ \beta_\pi=3,\ \alpha_\pi=0.5,\ i=0.5,\ \beta_k=1.0,\ \bar{V}=0.8,\ s_c^*=0.8,\ \delta_2=0.1,\ t_c^*=0.35,\ g^*=0.35,\ n^*=0.05,\ \mu^*=0.05,\ h_1^*=0.1,\ h_2^*=0.2,\ y^{p*}=1.0,\ x^*=2.0,\ \beta_w^*=1.95,\ \beta_p^*=0.5,\ \kappa_w^*=0.5,\ \kappa_p^*=0.5,\ \beta_\pi^*=3,\ \alpha_\pi^*=0.5,\ i^*=0.5,\ \beta_k^*=1.0,\ \bar{V}^*=0.8,\ \beta_e=0,\ \beta=0,\ \beta_\epsilon=0,\ \alpha_\epsilon=0.5,\ \gamma_c=0.5,\ \gamma=1,\ \gamma_c^*=0.5,\ \gamma^*=1,\ m_{\text{shock}}=1.1.$

29 The parameters of this simulation run are as follows: $s_c=0.8,\ \delta=0.1,\ t_c=0.35,\ g=0.35,\ n=0.05,\ \mu=0.057,\ h_1=0.1,\ h_2=0.2,\ y^p=1.0,\ x=2.0,\ \beta_w=2,\ \beta_p=3,\ \kappa_w=0.5,\ \kappa_p=0.5,\ \beta_\pi=3,\ \alpha_\pi=0.5,\ i=0.5,\ \beta_k=1.0,\ \bar{V}=0.8,\ s_c^*=0.8,\ \delta^*=0.1,\ t_c^*=0.35,\ g^*=0.35,\ n^*=0.05,\ \mu^*=0.05,\ h_1^*=0.1,\ h_2^*=0.2,\ y^{p*}=1.0,\ x^*=2.0,\ \beta_w^*=1.95,\ \beta_p^*=0.5,\ \kappa_w^*=0.5,\ \kappa_p^*=0.5,\ \beta_\pi^*=3,\ \alpha_\pi^*=0.5,\ i^*=0.5,\ \beta_k^*=1.0,\ \bar{V}^*=0.8,\ \beta_e=2,\ \beta=1,\ \beta_\epsilon=1,\ \alpha_\epsilon=0.5,\ \gamma_c=0.5,\ \gamma=1,\ \gamma_c^*=0.5,\ \gamma^*=1,\ m_{\text{shock}}=1.1.$

30 The parameters of this simulation run are as follows: $s_c=0.8,\ \delta=0.1,\ t_c=0.35,\ g=0.35,\ n=0.05,\ \mu=0.05,\ h_1=0.1,\ h_2=0.2,\ y^p=1.0,\ x=2.0,\ \beta_w=3,\ \beta_p=3,\ \kappa_w=0.5,\ \kappa_p=0.5,\ \beta_\pi=3,\ \alpha_\pi=0.5,\ i=0.5,\ \beta_k=1.0,\ \bar{V}=0.8,\ s_c^*=0.8,\ \delta^*=0.1,\ t_c^*=0.35,\ g^*=0.35,\ n^*=0.05,\ \mu^*=0.05,\ h_1^*=0.1,\ h_2^*=0.2,\ y^{p*}=1.0,\ x^*=2.0,\ \beta_w^*=1,\ \beta_p^*=1,\ \kappa_w^*=0.5,\ \kappa_p^*=0.5,\ \beta_\pi^*=3,\ \alpha_\pi^*=0.5,\ i^*=0.5,\ \beta_k^*=1.0,\ \bar{V}^*=0.8,\ \beta_e=2.0,\ \beta=1.2,\ \beta_\epsilon=1.0,\ \alpha_\epsilon=0.5,\ \gamma_c=0.5,\ \gamma=1.0,\ \gamma_c^*=0.5,\ \gamma^*=1.0,\ m_{\text{shock}}=1.1.$

31 The parameters of this simulation run are as follows: $s_c=0.8,\ \delta=0.1,\ t_c=0.35,\ g=0.35,\ n=0.05,\ \mu=0.05,\ h_1=0.1,\ h_2=0.2,\ y^p=1.0,\ x=2.0,\ \beta_w=3,\ \beta_p=3,\ \kappa_w=0.5,\ \kappa_p=0.5,\ \beta_\pi=3,\ \alpha_\pi=0.5,\ i=0.5,\ \beta_k=1.0,\ \bar{V}=0.8,\ s_c^*=0.8,\ \delta^*=0.1,\ t_c^*=0.35,\ g^*=0.35,\ n^*=0.05,\ \mu^*=0.05,\ h_1^*=0.1,\ h_2^*=0.2,\ y^{p*}=1.0,\ x^*=2.0,\ \beta_w^*=1,\ \beta_p^*=1,\ \kappa_w^*=0.5,\ \kappa_p^*=0.5,\ \beta_\pi^*=3,\ \alpha_\pi^*=0.5,\ i^*=0.5,\ \beta_k^*=1.0,\ \bar{V}^*=0.8,\ \beta_e=2.0,\ \beta=1.2,\ \beta_\epsilon=1.0,\ \alpha_\epsilon=0.5,\ \gamma_c=0.5,\ \gamma=1.0,\ \gamma_c^*=0.5,\ \gamma^*=1.0,\ m_{\text{shock}}=0.1.$

32 The parameters of this simulation run are as follows: $s_c=0.8,\ \delta=0.1,\ t_c=0.35,\ g=0.35,\ n=0.05,\ \mu=0.057,\ h_1=0.1,\ h_2=0.2,\ y^p=1.0,\ x=2.0,\ \beta_w=2,\ \beta_p=3,\ \kappa_w=0.5,\ \kappa_p=0.5,\ \beta_\pi=3,\ \alpha_\pi=0.5,\ i=0.5,\ \beta_k=1.0,\ \bar{V}=0.8,\ s_c^*=0.8,\ \delta^*=0.1,\ t_c^*=0.35,\ g^*=0.35,\ n^*=0.05,\ \mu^*=0.05,\ h_1^*=0.1,\ h_2^*=0.2,\ y^{p*}=1.0,\ x^*=2.0,\ \beta_w^*=$

1.95, $\beta_p^* = 0.5$, $\kappa_w^* = 0.5$, $\kappa_p^* = 0.5$, $\beta_\pi^* = 3$, $\alpha_\pi^* = 0.5$, $i^* = 0.5$, $\beta_k^* = 1.0$, $\bar{V}^* = 0.8$, $\beta_e = 2$, $\beta = 1$, $\beta_\epsilon = 1$, $\alpha_\epsilon = 0.5$, $\gamma_c = 0.5$, $\gamma = 1$, $\gamma_c^* = 0.5$, $\gamma^* = 1$, $m_{\text{shock}} = 1.1$.

7 Distributive cycles, business fluctuations and the wage-led/profit-led debate

1 As we will discuss below, the inclusion of a stabilizing monetary policy rule as well as a negative dependence of the real wage dynamics on its own level will qualify this categorization.

2 We believe that it is a great advantage to have at our disposal a pair of dynamic relationships in place of Keynes's (1936) single static one, in order to investigate on this enlarged basis the type of the real wage channel and the role of monetary policy, as will be done in the next section.

3 The qualitative features are not changed by this special assumption, if the multiplier process is sufficiently weak, but the slopes of the isoclines are then no longer as extreme as in the limit case of zero diagonal entries.

4 We will come back to this point below.

5 In actual economies the first situation may be stopped by contractive monetary and fiscal policy, while the remedy in the second case may only be downward wage rigidity, formalized by way of a kinked wage Phillips curve for example (see Chiarella and Flaschel 2000a, Flaschel *et al.* 2007).

6 This seems to be the situation – of the four cases sketched in Figure 7.2 – that is the least plausible.

7 Since the signs in the Jacobians also hold true for all points in the positive orthant of $\Re^2$ (which cannot be left by the trajectories that start in it, since its boundary is an invariant set of the dynamics) the two cyclical patterns also hold true in the large and – if made convergent by adding again the negative diagonal entries – are globally convergent by virtue of Olech's theorem. In the case of the other two figures – the saddles – the unstable separatrices directed toward the boundary of the economic phase space are approaching the axes of the positive orthant, but are not cutting them (or are converging to the origin of the phase space or to infinity). And in the cases where the dynamics switch by parameter changes to one of the other regimes shown in Figure 7.2, this will only occur in general (up to flukes) in the way shown by the black arrows in this figure, but not by a simultaneous change of two market characteristics at the same time.

8 See Flaschel *et al.* (2008d) for a description of this methodology.

9 In a variety of related studies with various co-authors we have investigated both theoretically and empirically the interaction of real wages and economic activity from a dynamical systems perspective – see Flaschel and Krolzig (2006), Franke *et al.* (2006), Chen *et al.* (2006), Flaschel and Proaño (2007) and Proaño *et al.* (2009).

10 For a recent survey on the empirical literature on this topic, see Hein and Vogel (2008).

11 It should be clear that this type of graphical analysis in the case of a profit-led goods demand leads also to an observational profit-led outcome.

12 For a simple inclusion of smooth factor substitution – which makes y^p dependent on the real wage – see Chiarella and Flaschel (2000a, ch. 5) and also Chiarella *et al.* (2005) for the discussion of alternative production technologies.

13 The units here are hours (which is in fact the relevant measure for the labor input of firms and therefore for the aggregate production function in the economy). Nevertheless, due to the lack of available time series of this variable for the Euro area (this series is available only for the USA) and for the sake of comparability of the parameter estimates with the ones obtained in other studies, it will be assumed here that the dynamics of employment in hours and employment (in persons) are quite similar.

14 We have stressed elsewhere (see e.g. Chen *et al.* 2006) the close formal correspondence of this model of a wage–price spiral with the new Keynesian model

of staggered wage and price setting introduced by Erceg *et al.* (2000). Yet we have to stress in this regard that despite the formal similarity in the expressions that describe the wage–price dynamics, the theoretical approach of disequilibrium-led wage and price inflation dynamics pursued here is in direct opposition to the general equilibrium new Keynesian framework that was already introduced by Chiarella and Flaschel (1996b).

15 As pointed out by Sims (1987), such a strategy allows one to circumvent the identification problem which arises in econometric estimations where both wage and price inflation equations have the same explanatory variables.

16 In earlier work, see in particular Chiarella and Flaschel (2000a) and Chiarella *et al.* (2005), inflationary climate expression has been assumed to be updated in an adaptive manner (representing the inertia inherent in the wage–price spiral). For the sake of expositional simplicity and in order to keep the model's dimension as low as possible, we assume here a constant $\bar{\pi}^c$.

17 For a discussion of the microfoundations of the wage Phillips curve in line with Blanchard and Katz (1999), see Flaschel and Krolzig (2006).

18 In the prominent Bhaduri and Marglin (1990) model, long-run growth may be either "wage-led" or "profit-led," depending on the actual parameter values in the savings and investment functions. The outcome of the income distribution conflict, thus, is not *ab initio* and universally given, but rather depends on the concrete characteristics of the different economies.

19 See Flaschel and Krolzig (2006) and Chen and Flaschel (2006) for details.

20 Furthermore, it should be pointed out that this ambiguity in the real wage dynamics is also noticed and discussed by Barbosa-Filho and Taylor (2006).

21 All of the employed gaps are measured relative to the steady state of the model, in order to allow for an interest rate policy that is also consistent with the steady state.

8 DAD–DAS: estimated convergence and the emergence of "complex dynamics"

1 This chapter is based on Chiarella *et al.* (2010), "Keynesian macrodynamics: convergence, roads to instability and the emergence of complex business fluctuations," *AUCO Czech Economic Review*, **4**(3), 236–262, with permission of AUCO.

2 Here we make use of and build on the estimation results achieved in Chen *et al.* (2006, ch. 6).

3 Other quantities are defined in a standard way, thus w is money wages, p price of output y, and ω is real wage ω/p.

4 The corresponding reduced-form expression for the wage inflation Phillips curve reads

$$\widehat{w} = \kappa[\beta_{we}(e-1) - \beta_{w\omega}\ln\omega + \kappa_w(\beta_{pu}(u-1) + \beta_{p\omega}\ln\omega)] + \pi^m,$$

and will be of use later on when nonlinear forms of the wage Phillips curve have to be considered.

5 For the estimates with π^1 and π^6 shown in Figure 8.1, see Chen *et al.* (2006).

9 International linkages in a Keynesian two-country model

1 With the kind permission of Springer Science + Business Media, this chapter is based on Flaschel *et al.* (2008c) "Keynesian dynamics and international linkages in a two-country model," in *Topics in Applied Macrodynamic Theory*, Dynamic Modeling and Econometrics in Economics and Finance, Vol. 10, Part II, chapter 9, pp. 417–454.

2 We will, however, not engage in this debate here but rather adopt the most traditional view according to which $\partial\hat{u}/\partial v$ is unambiguously negative.

3 Despite being largely criticized due to its "lack of microfoundations," in a large number of microfounded, "rational expectations" models such as Taylor (1994), Okun's law is used to link production with employment.
4 Recently, the overly unrealistic assumption in DSGE models such as Erceg *et al.* (2000) of wages set by the households in a monopolistic manner has been replaced through more realistic wage setting schemes based on job search wage bargaining considerations by Trigari (2004) and Gertler and Trigari (2006).
5 As pointed out by Sims (1987), such a strategy allows one to circumvent the identification problem which arises when both wage and price inflation equations have the same explanatory variables.
6 In the empirical applications of this adaptive revision of the CPI inflation we will simply use a moving average of the CPI inflation with linearly declining weights.
7 In the academic literature there is an ongoing and still not solved debate about whether there is indeed an interest smoothing parameter in the monetary policy reaction rule of the central banks or whether the observed high autocorrelation in the nominal interest rate is simply the result of highly correlated shocks or only slowly available information; see e.g. Rudebusch (2002, 2006) for a thorough discussion.
8 All of the employed gaps are measured relative to the steady state of the model, in order to allow for an interest rate policy that is consistent with it.
9 See De Grauwe and Grimaldi (2006, ch. 1) for an extensive discussion of the advantages of the heterogeneous agents approach with respect to the rational expectations approach in the explanation of empirical financial market data.
10 See Samanidou *et al.* (2007) for a comprehensive survey article on this strain of research.
11 As the model is formulated we have no real anchor for the steady-state rate of interest (via investment behavior and the rate of profit it implies in the steady state) and thus have to assume here that it is the monetary authority that enforces a certain steady-state values for the nominal rate of interest.
12 See Proaño *et al.* (2011) for a detailed description of this procedure.
13 The set of instrumental variables in the 3SLS estimation consisted on the same lagged values of the two countries used in the previous estimations.
14 In the dynamic adjustments simulations of the next section we will calibrate this coefficient to be, if not *lower*, at least *equal* to that of the Euro area.
15 The numerical simulation in this section were performed using MATLAB. The simulation code is available upon request.
16 We adopt this specific value from Rabanal and Tuesta (2006).
17 This statement is based on the estimations results previously discussed, which lead to the presumption that, if present, these channels are not statistically important for the dynamics of the capacity utilization in the USA given the dataset used.
18 Downloadable from Carl Chiarella's website at UTS, Sydney, Australia, at http://datasearch.uts.edu.au/business/staff/finance/details.cfm?StaffId=72.

10 Integrating macromodels of employment, price and inventory dynamics

1 This chapter is based on Chiarella and Flaschel (1996a), "An integrative approach to prototype 2D macromodels of growth, price and inventory dynamics," *Chaos, Solitons & Fractals*, **7**(12), 2105–2133. Copyright © 1996, Elsevier.
2 Alternatively, as in the case of Rose (1967), by IS disequilibrium.
3 See Wiggins (1990) for the details and graphical representations of such Hopf bifurcations.
4 The earlier Hopf bifurcation analysis of this chapter still applies.

11 Calibration of an unobservable inflation climate

1 The details of this brief outline are spelled out in Franke (2005).

2 To emphasize the expression "adaptive" beyond the serious scientific paths, we may mention a one-line advertising campaign of *hp-invent* in Germany in autumn 2004, which was directly formulated in English and read "Solutions for the adaptive enterprise." In contrast to ruling theory, the profane business world was apparently less attracted by a slogan like "*The* solution for the *rational* firm."

3 Though it is different from the often rather informal (but also multidimensional) reasoning known from the calibrations of the real business cycle models, where, in particular, no objective function is minimized or maximized.

4 As in Franke (2005), the output gap might also be dated t instead of $t-1$. We have introduced this lag in the present chapter since in subsequent research we want to incorporate our Phillips curve in the standard small-scale models that study monetary policy on the basis of a Phillips curve, an IS-like relationship, and an interest rate reaction function. Here we are particularly interested in comparisons with backward-looking models that employ an accelerationist Phillips curve, a strand of quantitative research that was initiated by Rudebusch and Svensson (1999, p. 207ff.). They estimate a quarterly Phillips curve whose output term likewise enters with date $t-1$.

5 Note that this concept is inherent in Phillips curve estimations with demeaned or detrended inflation rates where the sum of the coefficients on lagged inflation is significantly less than one. This is easily seen by adding target inflation on both sides of such a regression equation, when it is assumed that $\pi^\star$ approximately equals the trend inflation in the data.

6 Though the basic conception of the present approach will be similar as in Franke (2005, secs. 4.2 and 4.3), it leads us here to a fairly different procedure. In particular, the way in which stochastic perturbations are treated will allow us to construct confidence intervals for the parameters. Apart from that, we no longer use CPI inflation but replace it with a broader price concept (see below).

7 Employing the standard smoothing parameter $\lambda = 1600$. The output series as well as the empirical inflation series referred to below are taken from the US Department of Labor, Bureau of Labor Statistics, http://data.bls.gov/lpc/home.htm.

8 With regard to inflation we use the annualized quarterly changes of the implicit price deflator of the nonfinancial corporate business sector, detrended again by HP. For the simulations below, the latter implies that target inflation in (11.13) has to scaled down at zero, $\pi^\star = 0$.

9 Also in subsequent work where, in particular, Rudebusch employed the same Phillips curve specification, this estimate remained essentially unchanged; see, for example, Rudebusch (2001, p. 206).

10 Underlying are the AIC coefficients in row A of Table 11.1 and the shocks $\varepsilon_{\pi,t} = \hat{u}_{\pi,t}$ to the Phillips curve.

11 An estimation of inflation with this RMSD is characterized by $R^2_B = 0.652$, while, in comparison, RMSD = 0.272 from row A in Table 11.1 gives rise to $R^2_A = 0.973$. Besides, R^2_B can be directly inferred from the $R^2 = R^2_{15}$ of the estimation of (11.16), via the relationship $R^2_B = 1 - R^2_{15} = 1 - 0.348 = 0.652$.

12 It would be logical to call these coefficients "calibrates," but this coinage seems too artificial.

13 Based on the Jarque–Bera statistic, the p-values of RMSD, α_c, γ and α_y, respectively, are 0.036, 0.000, 0.000 and 0.063.

14 Incidentally, the deviations of the frequency distributions from normal are also reflected in a certain asymmetry of the feasibility intervals, though this feature may not be overrated.

15 The small bars at the bottom indicate (from left to right) the lower 2.5%, the mean value, and the upper 2.5% of the distribution. The thin solid line depicts (the density of) the normal distribution with the same mean and standard deviation.

16 Or (11.21) itself is not derived but introduced directly, with only one error term $\varepsilon_{\pi,t}$.

17 500 samples suffice if only the mean value of the RMDSs needs to be known.
18 On the basis of a 101 × 101 grid, where at each point the average RMSD across 500 bootstrap samples is computed. The cross indicates its minimal value.
19 The shaded area is the 95% "feasibility" band based on 5000 bootstrap samples from equation (11.18). The bold line depicts the coefficients obtained from the estimated residuals; the other two lines (medium and thin) result from two different bootstrap samples of $\varepsilon_{\pi,t}$ sequences (which are identical for each α_c). The cross indicates the optimal values from part C of Table 11.1.
20 The thin solid line represents the predictions from (11.22) based on $\alpha_c = 0.410$, $\gamma = 0.453$, $\alpha_y = 0.292$, and the dotted line the predictions from $\alpha_c = 0.30$, $\gamma = 0.47$, $\alpha_y = 0.47$ ($\alpha_g = 0$ in both cases).
21 Quarter t depicts inflation during this quarter and the expectations of inflation four quarters ahead as they are formed in quarter t. We are here not interested in forecasting accuracy, for which inflation would be contrasted with the expectations formed four quarters before.
22 It should, however, not be concealed that $\alpha_g \approx 2.9$ is not very robust to estimations over subperiods of the sample.
23 The thin solid line is the estimated impulse–response function and the shaded area represents its confidence band of ±2 standard deviations. The bold line is the model's response to the same shocks.

12 A macroeconometric framework for the analysis of monetary policy

1 A rule of this type, however, can already be found in Fair (1984).
2 See Svensson (1997).
3 This chapter is based on Flaschel *et al.* (1998).
4 For a similar treatment of expectations, see for example recent contributions collected in Taylor (1999).
5 See, for example, Christiano and Gust (1999).
6 For a more detailed study of the following, and further, macroeconomic feedback mechanisms, see Chiarella *et al.* (2000b). Such feedback mechanisms appear to us essential to macroeconomics. They are often neglected in micro-based macroeconomic studies.
7 For a corresponding continuous-time model, see Chiarella and Flaschel (2000a).
8 Assuming consols ($p_{bt} = 1/r_t$) in place of the fixed price bonds assumed by Sargent (1987) does not significantly alter the dynamics of the private sector to be considered below, due to the neglect of interest income and wealth effects in the present formulation of the model.
9 See Chiarella *et al.* (2000b) for a demonstration that the nature of the present approach to disequilibrium growth is not changed very much by the inclusion of, for example, endogenous technical change of Uzawa–Lucas–Romer type.
10 Note that interest rate steering according to this money supply rule is fairly roundabout, since it involves all of the following static and dynamic equations (written for simplicity in continuous time):

$$r = r_0 + (h_1 y - m)/h_2, \quad m = M/(pK),$$
$$\hat{m} = \mu - (\hat{p} + \widehat{K}),$$
$$\dot{\mu} = \beta_{m_1}(\bar{\mu} - \mu) + \beta_{m_2}(\bar{\pi} - \hat{p}) + \beta_{m_3}(\bar{U} - U).$$

The Taylor interest rate policy rule, to be described below, is directly operating on the interest rate in order to steer economic activity and the rate of inflation. This rule however assumes that the supply of money is determined by money demand and thus possibly is fairly volatile if money demand is very interest-sensitive.
11 Svensson (1997) suggests such a formulation of the inflation gap.

12 The rate of change of the money supply μ implied by the Taylor rule reads (in terms of continuous time for simplicity)

$$\mu = \hat{M} = \hat{p} + \frac{h_1\dot{Y} + h_2\dot{K}(r_0 - r) - h_2K\dot{r}}{h_1Y + h_2K(r_0 - r)}.$$

This expression differs considerably from the money supply rule of module 4 of the model. It must be inserted into the government budget constraints (12.22) in order to determine the evolution of government debt in the case of the Taylor interest rate policy rule.

13 This convention conforms with the definition of ρ^e_{t+1} that we use in the determination of share prices below.

14 The above simple money demand function can be obtained as a Taylor approximation of a general money demand function if it is assumed that money demand is homogeneous of degree one in income and wealth and if the variable K_t is used as a proxy for the evolution of real wealth.

15 A related determination of the wage–price dynamics by cost-push and demand-pressure components can be found in Fair (2000).

16 One coefficient less than unity is in fact already sufficient.

17 We adopt the moving-average rules for normal profits and the rate of interest in order to avoid the addition of two further laws of motion of the adaptive expectations type.

18 Note that the reduced-form equation (12.39) defines a Phillips curve of the traditional across-markets type, but one where also the rate of capacity utilization of firms is present besides the rate of employment, both in the form of deviations from their NAIRU levels.

19 Where $l^d_t = x_t L^d_t / K_{t-1}$.

20 With $\kappa = 1/(1 - \kappa_w \kappa_p)$.

21 The steady-state values for the financial assets of our model are

$$b_0 = \frac{g - (t^w + t^c) - \bar{\mu} m_0}{\bar{\mu}}, \quad b^w_0 = \frac{s_w u_0 y_0 - t^w}{\bar{\mu}},$$

$$b^c_0 = b_0 - b^w_0, \quad q_0 = \left(\frac{p_e E}{pK}\right)_0 = 1,$$

but are of no importance here since this part of the model does not yet influence the dynamics of the private sector.

22 Note that $\rho^m_t = \rho_t$ and $r^m_t = r_t$.

23 The subsequent preliminary discussion of the stability properties of our model uses parameters that are based on estimates as undertaken in Section 12.4.

24 In Fair (2000) also the coefficient β_w (see our equation (12.35)) is insignificant so that he has neglected the impact of unemployment on wages in his regression.

25 With $i(\cdot)$ set to 0.

26 Note that in this exercise the fitted line is obtained by simulating not the entire system of equations, but the corresponding behavioral functions using the estimated parameters.

13 The dynamics of "natural" rates of growth and employment

1 This chapter is based on Chiarella and Flaschel (1998), "Dynamics of natural rates of growth and employment," *Macroeconomic Dynamics*, **2**(3), 345–368. Copyright © 1998 Cambridge University Press, reproduced with permission.

2 Extended Metzlerian formulations of the quantity adjustment process are provided in Chiarella and Flaschel (2000a, ch. 7).

3 A sixth state variable, government debt per unit of capital b, is here suppressed by way of suitably chosen policy rules which allow us to neglect the role of the GBR – see Chiarella and Flaschel (2000b) for its explicit treatment.
4 By "hysteresis" we refer to the phenomenon whereby a dynamical system may have a continuum of steady states so that the attractor to which the economy converges is dependent upon the initial conditions of the trajectories – see Franz (1990, ch. 1) for a discussion of hysteresis in economics.
5 See the appendix to this chapter for its extensive form and the employed notation.
6 The full model is provided in the appendix to this chapter, together with a summary of the notation that is used.
7 With $\kappa = 1/[1 - \kappa_p \kappa_w]$.
8 The use of smooth factor substitution in such models does not change their qualitative behavior – see Chiarella and Flaschel (2000a, ch. 5).
9 We disregard wage taxation for reasons of simplicity – see Chiarella and Flaschel (2000a, ch. 6) for its treatment.
10 The rate of savings out of labor income is assumed to be zero.
11 In the special case $n(V, \gamma) = \gamma$ – to be investigated numerically later on – the set of steady states is given by a surface in $\Re^9$.
12 For a more detailed treatment of the following, see also Chiarella and Flaschel (2000a, ch. 8).
13 See Flaschel *et al.* (1997) for related situations in the context of IS–LM growth models.
14 This change in the money wage Phillips curve modifies the laws of motion for ω, m in a straightforward way – see Chiarella and Flaschel (1996a) for details.
15 Note here that $n(V, \gamma)$ is given by $0(V-1) + 1(\gamma - 0.05) + 0.05 = \gamma$ in all of the simulations that follow.
16 Here $\bar{V} = 1$ by way of a simple renormalization.

14 High-order disequilibrium growth dynamics

1 This chapter is based on Chiarella and Flaschel (2000c), "High order disequilibrium growth dynamics: theoretical aspects and numerical features," *Journal of Economic Dynamics and Control*, **24**(5–7), 935–963. Copyright © 2000, Elsevier.
2 Using a neoclassical production function instead does not change the qualitative outcomes of this Keynesian model of monetary growth significantly – see Chiarella and Flaschel (2000a, ch. 5) for the changes that have to be made in the model in such a situation.
3 See Chiarella and Flaschel (1998) for an endogenization of such trend rates of growth.
4 In the present chapter we do not allow for trends in the price and wage level (and in the nominal and real rate of exchange) for reasons of simplicity.
5 See Asada *et al.* (2003a) for more general scenarios.
6 The nominal interest rate abroad, r_0^*, is assumed as given exogenously, as is the foreign price level, p_0^*, for the small open economy under consideration.
7 See again Asada *et al.* (2003a) for more elaborate presentations of this component of expectations formation.
8 See Asada *et al.* (2003a) for the treatment of the general case.
9 In view of the linear structure of the assumed technological and behavioral equations, the above presentation of our model shows that its nonlinearities are, on the one hand, due to the necessity of using growth laws in various cases and, on the other, to multiplicative expressions for some of the state variables of the form uy, y/l and $\hat{l}y$; see also Chiarella and Flaschel (1996a) on this matter. Though therefore having intrinsic nonlinearities of the kind of the Rössler and the Lorenz dynamical system, our 8D dynamics may, however, still be of a simple type, since these nonlinearities do not too often appear in its eight equations.

10 The equation for ω_0 is obtained by solving the goods market equilibrium condition

$$y_0^e = y_0^d = (1-\tau_w)\omega_0 y_0/x + \gamma_c(\eta_0)(1-s_c)(\rho_0^e - t^n) + c_1^*(\eta_0) + \delta + n + g,$$

with respect to ω_0. This is possible since our above assumptions imply that the trade account and the capital account must be balanced in the steady state whereby the expression $\gamma_c(\eta_0)(1-s_c)(\rho_0^e - t^n) + c_1^*(\eta_0)$ can be replaced by the expression $(1-s_c)(\rho_0^e - t^n)$.

11 For a proof of Proposition 14.2 the reader is referred to Asada *et al.* (2003a).

12 This is, for example, the case if β_w, β_p, β_π, β_n and the parameter h_2 are chosen sufficiently small and the parameter β_{y^e} sufficiently large (see Asada *et al.* 2003a, ch. 7). See also Chiarella and Flaschel (1996b) for a model type that is simpler in its feedback mechanisms, but which nevertheless gives rise to similar dynamical investigations.

13 A broad and detailed exposition of the following is provided in Asada *et al.* (2003a).

14 Owing to the size of the capital output ratio the time unit in this simulation run (and in all the following ones) is one year and the chosen step size is 1/100.

15 Note that the change also occurs in the adjustment of inventories.

16 This situation can also be interpreted as international trade that is responding with some time delay to the terms of trade (of the past).

17 Note that now $\beta_\epsilon = 10$ and $\beta = 2$.

18 See also Chiarella and Flaschel (1996a, b, 2000b) for presentations of complex dynamics that can arise via extrinsic nonlinearities in the case of strong local instability of the private sector.

19 The case of an isolated operation of such a nonlinearity is also investigated in Chiarella and Flaschel (2000a).

20 Accompanied by decreases in the nominal rate of interest (due to decreasing price levels) and depreciation of the domestic currency, but also slightly decreasing capacity utilization rates of firms.

21 The length of the overall cycle is approximately 35 years. This phase length depends negatively on β_w and positively on f as computer simulations have shown.

22 The parameters used for this simulation that differ from those of Table 14.1 are $h_2 = 0.1, \beta_w = 0.5, \beta_\pi = 2, \alpha_\pi = 1, \beta_{y^e} = 5, \beta_e = 2$.

23 The parameters that differ from those of Table 14.1 are $s_c = 0.7, h_2 = 0.1, \beta_w = 0.21, \beta_p = 0.7, \beta_\pi = 0.5, \alpha_\pi = 0.5, \beta_{n^d} = 0.2, \beta_{y^e} = 1, \beta_e = 3, \beta_\epsilon = 3, \alpha_\epsilon = 1 (\beta_1 = 0.1)$.

15 AD–AS disequilibrium dynamics and endogenous growth

1 With kind permission of Springer Science + Business Media, this chapter is based on Chiarella *et al.* (2000a), "AS–AD disequilibrium dynamics and economic growth," in *Optimization, Dynamics and Economic Analysis*, eds. E. J. Dockner *et al.*, pp. 101–117. Physica-Verlag GmbH & Co.

2 Note that we use $\hat{x}$ to denote the growth rate of a variable x.

3 See also Chiarella and Flaschel (2000a) for detailed presentations and analyses of such AD–AS disequilibrium growth models.

4 The case of smooth factor substitution is considered in Chiarella and Flaschel (2000a) and found to be of secondary importance with respect to the feedback structures contained in the model (and their implications).

5 Chiarella and Flaschel (2000a, ch. 5) show how such an approach can be extended to the case of smooth factor substitution without much change in its substance.

6 A detailed presentation of the government sector is given in Chiarella and Flaschel (1999).

7 A much more advanced wage–price block is discussed in Chiarella *et al.* (2000b).

8 This represents an augmented target in the wage negotiations of workers.

9 See Chiarella and Flaschel (2000a) for further details on this wage–price block of the model.

10 The proof of this part of the proposition can also be obtained from Chiarella and Flaschel (2000a, 6.2) by setting β_n equal to zero and by applying the proof strategy used there to the then resulting 5D subdynamics. Positive but small β_n combined with the positivity of the determinant of the Jacobian of the full dynamics then again imply the assertion made on the parameter β_{y^e}.

16 Stabilizing an unstable economy and the choice of policy measures

1 This chapter is based on Asada *et al.* (2010b), "Stabilizing an unstable economy: on the choice of proper policy measures," *Economics: The Open-Access, Open-Assessment E-Journal*, **4** (2010–21), available at http://dx.doi.org/10.5018/economics-ejournal.ja.2010-21.

2 In recent work on behavioral finance the interaction of the fundamentalist and behavioral traders is seen as central in creating bubbles and crashes – see Brunnermeier (2008).

3 We do not allow for regime switches as they are discussed in Chiarella *et al.* (2000b).

4 See Chiarella and Flaschel (2000a) for the inclusion of workers' savings into a Keynes–Metzler–Goodwin (KMG) framework.

5 Note that the above discussion of asset markets is focused on stocks and not on stock–flow interactions as they are implied by the budget equations of the considered model, where stock–flow consistency is given as shown in Köper (2003) on the basis of the assumed budget equations.

6 We want to stress here however that all propositions and theorems – with the exception of the policy ineffectiveness theorem – also hold in the case of an interest rate elastic equity demand, a situation that in particular will come about if the interest rate departs by too much from its steady-state position.

7 Note that even though the stock of the financial assets money M, bonds B and equities E is considered as exogenously given at each moment of time, M, B and of course p_e are determined through the above portfolio equations, since the central bank has then to adjust to the demands of households with respect to the two assets M and B, transforming the initially given values $\bar{M}_2 = \bar{M} + \bar{B}$ into the components of $\bar{M}_2$ that are now desired by the asset-holders.

8 Brunnermeier (2008) calls them behavioral and fundamentalist traders.

9 Note that as a result of this equilibrium specification, the evolution of $\hat{p}_e$ cannot be expressed in an explicit manner. Chartist's expectations can however be represented equivalently by means of an integral equation as, for example, Sargent (1987) expresses adaptive inflationary expectations.

10 See Chiarella and Flaschel (2000a) for the treatment of a production function with smooth factor substitution and a discussion as to why this assumption is not as restrictive as might be believed by many economists.

11 See for example Sargent (1987) for the introduction of net of interest taxation rules.

12 See also Rose (1990).

13 It should again be pointed out that the above portfolio structure implies that the central bank's monetary policy can only affect the asset markets significantly through its effects on the rate of profit of firms r or the expectations of capital gains π_e^e ($\bar{E}$, p, K being given magnitudes), since we have assumed that $\partial f_e(\cdot)/\partial i = 0$.

14 See Chiarella and Flaschel (2000a) and Chiarella *et al.* (2000b).

15 Note that while m and b are of course varying over time, for the determination of q and i (the variables that bring the asset markets into equilibrium), m and b are given magnitudes at each point in time.

16 Note with respect to this part of the lemma that the steady-state values used in the above assumption are calculated before this assumption is applied to a determination of the steady-state value of the nominal rate of interest.

17 The Mundell or real rate of interest effect is not so obviously present in the considered dynamics as there is no long real rate of interest involved in the investment (or consumption) behavior. Increasing expected price inflation does not directly increase aggregate demand, economic activity and thus the actual rate of price inflation. This surely implies that the model needs to be extended in order to take account of the role that is generally played by the real rate of interest in macrodynamic models.
18 Note that l may vary, but does not feed back into the presently considered subdynamics.
19 This would correspond to a strong Keynes effect in the corresponding working model of Chiarella and Flaschel (2000a).
20 Furthermore, it should be pointed out that it is in the logic of such a tax system – which may be monitored through a corresponding tax declaration scheme – that it should be in principle applied in a symmetric way so that not only are capital gains taxed, but also capital losses subsidized (so that the implementation of such a tax is entirely to the disadvantage of the asset-holders of the model). The final implementation of such a system in reality, and thus the compromise with the status quo, is however a matter of political debate.
21 Note that we have not introduced here into our model long bonds and yield spreads between bonds of different maturity. To do so might be the subject of future research.
22 This policy was actually anticipated by Bernanke *et al.* (2004).
23 See Charpe *et al.* (2011) for a first attempt in this direction.
24 To include debt issuance of firms would amplify the bubbles and bursts, since the interaction of asset price movements and leveraging is rather destabilizing; see Semmler and Bernard (2009).
25 This makes central bank money now endogenous in a pronounced way. Note however that we do not yet consider commercial banks and the endogeneity of the money supply that they are creating.
26 For details of the calculations involved see Chiarella and Flaschel (2000a) and Köper (2003).

Bibliography

Aadland, D. and Huang, K. (2004), "Consistent high-frequency calibration," *Journal of Economic Dynamics and Control* **28**(11), 2277–2295.

Abreu, D. and Brunnermeyer, M. (2003), "Bubbles and crashes," *Econometrica* **71**, 173–204.

Aghion, P. and Howitt, P. (1998), *Endogenous Growth Theory*, MIT Press, Cambridge, MA.

Akerlof, G. A. and Stiglitz, J. E. (1969), "Capital, wages and structural unemployment," *Economic Journal* **79**(314), 269–281.

Alesina, A. and Rodrick, D. (1994), "Distributive politics and economic growth," *Quarterly Journal of Economics* **109**, 465–490.

Arrow, K. (1962), "The economic implications of learning by doing," *Review of Economic Studies* **29**, 155–173.

Asada, T., Chiarella, C., Flaschel, P. and Franke, R. (2003a), *Open Economy Macrodynamics. An Integrated Disequilibrium Approach*, Springer, Berlin.

Asada, T., Inaba, T. and Misawa, T. (2003b), "An interregional dynamic model. The case of fixed exchange rates," *Studies in Regional Science* **31**(2), 29–41.

Asada, T., Chen, P., Chiarella, C. and Flaschel, P. (2006), "Keynesian dynamics and the wage–price spiral. A baseline disequilibrium model," *Journal of Macroeconomics* **28**, 90–130.

Asada, T., Chiarella, C., Flaschel, P. and Franke, R. (2010a), *Monetary Macrodynamics*, Routledge, London.

Asada, T., Chiarella, C., Flaschel, P., Mouakil, T., Proaño, C. R. and Semmler, W. (2010b), "Stabilizing an unstable economy: on the choice of proper policy measures," *Economics: The Open-Access, Open-Assessment E-Journal* **4** (2010–21). (doi:10.5018/economics-ejournal.ja.2010-21).

Barbosa-Filho, N. and Taylor, L. (2006), "Distributive and demand cycles in the US economy – a structuralist Goodwin model," *Metroeconomica* **57**(3), 389–411.

Barro, R. (1994), "The aggregate supply/aggregate demand model," *Eastern Economic Journal* **20**, 1–6.

Barro, R. J. and Sala-i Martin, X. (1995), *Economic Growth*, McGraw-Hill, New York.

Baxter, M. and Stockman, A. (1989), "Business cycles and the exchange rate regime: some international evidence," *Journal of Monetary Economics* **23**(3), 377–400.

Bénabou, R. (1996), "Inequality and growth," in B. S. Bernanke and J. J. Rotemberg, eds, *NBER Macroeconomics Annual 1996*, Vol. 11, MIT Press, Cambridge, MA, pp. 11–92.

Bénabou, R. (2000), "Unequal societies: income distribution and the social contract," *American Economic Review* **90**(1), 96–129.

Benhabib, J. and Farmer, R. (1994), "Indeterminacy and increasing returns," *Journal of Economic Theory* **63**, 19–41.

Benhabib, J. and Miyao, T. (1981), "Some new results on the dynamics of the generalized Tobin model," *International Economic Review* **22**, 589–596.

Benhabib, J. and Rustichini, A. (1996), "Social conflict and growth," *Journal of Economic Growth* **1**, 129–146.

Bernanke, B. S. and Blinder, A. S. (1992), "The federal funds rate and the channels of monetary transmission," *American Economic Review* **82**(4), 901–921.

Bernanke, B. S. and Mihov, I. (1998), "Measuring monetary policy," *Quarterly Journal of Economics* **113**(3), 869–902.

Bernanke, B. S., Reinhart, V. R. and Sack, B. P. (2004), "Monetary policy alternatives at the zero bound: an empirical assessment," *Brookings Papers on Economic Activity* **2004**(2), 1–78.

Bhaduri, A. and Marglin, S. (1990), "Unemployment and the real wage: the economic basis for contesting political ideologies," *Cambridge Journal of Economics* **14**, 375–393.

Blanchard, O. J. and Katz, L. (1999), "Wage dynamics: reconciling theory and evidence," *American Economic Review* **89**, 69–74.

Blanchard, O. J. and Wolfers, J. (2000), "The role of shocks and institutions in the rise of European unemployment: the aggregate evidence," *Economic Journal* **110**(462), 1–33.

Bluedorn, J. C. and Bowdler, C. (2006), "The open economy consequences of US monetary policy," Unpublished manuscript, Nuffield College.

Bowles, S. and Boyer, R. (1995), "Wages, aggregate demand and employment in an open economy: an empirical investigation," in *Macroeconomic Policy after the Conservative Era*, Cambridge University Press, Cambridge.

Brenner, T., Weidlich, W. and Witt, U. (2002), "International co-movements of business cycles in a 'phase-locking' model," *Metroeconomica* **53**, 113–138.

Brock, W. A. and Malliaris, A. G. (1989), *Differential Equations, Stability, and Chaos in Dynamic Economics*, North-Holland, Amsterdam.

Brunnermeier, M. K. (2008), "Bubbles," in S. N. Durlauf and L. E. Blume, eds, *The New Palgrave Dictionary of Economics*, 2nd edn, Palgrave Macmillan, Basingstoke.

Burns, A. and Mitchell, W. (1946), *Measuring Business Cycles*, NBER Book Series Studies in Business Cycles, NBER, New York.

Calvo, G. (1983), "Staggered prices in a utility maximizing framework," *Journal of Monetary Economics* **12**, 383–398.

Canova, C. and Marrinan, J. (1998), "Sources and propagation of international output cycles: common shocks or transmission," *Journal of International Economics* **46**(1), 133–166.

Charpe, M., Flaschel, P., Hartmann, F. and Proaño, C. (2011), "Stabilizing an unstable economy: fiscal and monetary policy, stocks, and the term structure of interest rates," *Economic Modelling* **28**(5), 2129–2136.

Chen, P. and Flaschel, P. (2006), "Measuring the interaction of wage and price Phillips curves for the US economy," *Studies in Nonlinear Dynamics and Econometrics* **10**, 1–35.

Chen, P., Chiarella, C., Flaschel, P. and Semmler, W. (2006), "Keynesian macrodynamics and the Phillips curve. An estimated baseline macromodel for the US economy," in C. Chiarella, P. Flaschel, R. Franke and W. Semmler, eds, *Quantitative and Empirical Analysis of Nonlinear Dynamic Macromodels*, Elsevier, Amsterdam.

Chiarella, C. (1986), "Perfect foresight models and the dynamic instability problem from a higher viewpoint," *Economic Modelling* **3**(4), 283–292.

Chiarella, C. (1990a), *The Elements of a Nonlinear Theory of Economic Dynamics*, Springer, Berlin.

Chiarella, C. (1990b), "Excessive exchange rate variability: a possible explanation using nonlinear economic dynamics," *European Journal of Political Economy* **6**, 315–352.

Chiarella, C. (1992), "Monetary and fiscal policy under nonlinear exchange rate dynamics," in G. Feichtinger, ed., *Dynamic Economic Models and Optimal Control*, North-Holland, Amsterdam, pp. 527–546.

Chiarella, C. and Flaschel, P. (1995a), "A complete Keynesian model of monetary growth with sluggish price and quantity adjustments," Discussion Paper, University of Bielefeld.

Chiarella, C. and Flaschel, P. (1995b), "Descriptive monetary macrodynamics: foundations and extensions," Draft manuscript, Department of Economics, University of Bielefeld.

Chiarella, C. and Flaschel, P. (1996a), "An integrative approach to prototype 2D-macromodels of growth, price and inventory dynamics," *Chaos, Solitons & Fractals* **7**(12), 2105–2133.

Chiarella, C. and Flaschel, P. (1996b), "Real and monetary cycles in models of Keynes–Wicksell type," *Journal of Economic Behavior and Organization* **30**(3), 327–351.

Chiarella, C. and Flaschel, P. (1998), "Dynamics of natural rates of growth and employment," *Macroeconomic Dynamics* **2**(3), 345–368.

Chiarella, C. and Flaschel, P. (1999), "Towards applied disequilibrium growth theory. I. The starting model," UTS Business Working Paper No. 94.

Chiarella, C. and Flaschel, P. (2000a), *The Dynamics of Keynesian Monetary Growth: Macrofoundations*, Cambridge University Press, Cambridge.

Chiarella, C. and Flaschel, P. (2000b), "The emergence of complex dynamics in a 'naturally' nonlinear integrated Keynesian model of monetary growth," in W. A. Barnett, C. Chiarella, S. Keen, R. Marks and H. Schnabl, eds, *Commerce, Complexity, and Evolution: Topics in Economics, Finance, Marketing, and Management: Proceedings of the Twelfth International Symposium in Economic Theory and Econometrics*, Cambridge University Press, Cambridge.

Chiarella, C. and Flaschel, P. (2000c), "High order disequilibrium growth dynamics: theoretical aspects and numerical features," *Economic Dynamics and Control* **24**(5–7), 935–963.

Chiarella, C., Flaschel, P., Groh, G., Köper, C. and Semmler, W. (1999), "Towards applied disequilibrium growth theory: VI. Substitution, money holdings, wealth-effects and further extensions," UTS Business Working Paper No. 98.

Chiarella, C., Flaschel, P., Groh, G. and Semmler, W. (2000a), "AS–AD disequilibrium dynamics and economic growth," in E. Dockner, ed., *Optimization, Dynamics and Economic Analysis*, Physica-Verlag, Heidelberg, pp. 101–117.

Chiarella, C., Flaschel, P., Groh, G. and Semmler, W. (2000b), *Disequilibrium, Growth and Labor Market Dynamics. Macro Perspectives*, Springer, Heidelberg.

Chiarella, C., Flaschel, P., Khomin, A. and Zhu, P. (2002), *The SND Package. Applications to Keynesian Monetary Growth Dynamics*, Dynamic Economic Theory, Vol. 22, Peter Lang, Frankfurt am Main.

Chiarella, C., Flaschel, P. and Franke, R. (2005), *Foundations for a Disequilibrium Theory of the Business Cycle. Qualitative Analysis and Quantitative Assesment*, Cambridge University Press, Cambridge.

Chiarella, C., Flaschel, P., Franke, R. and Semmler, W. (2006a), "A high-dimensional model of real-financial market interaction: the cascade of stable matrices approach," in C. Chiarella, R. Franke, P. Flaschel and W. Semmler, eds, *Quantitative and Empirical Analysis of Nonlinear Dynamic Macromodels*, Contributions to Economic Analysis, Vol. 277, Elsevier, Heidelberg, pp. 359–384.

Chiarella, C., Flaschel, P. and Hung, H. (2006b), "Interacting business cycle fluctuations: a two-country model," *Singapore Economic Review* **51**(3), 365–394.

Chiarella, C., Flaschel, P. and Hung, H. (2010), "Keynesian macrodynamics: convergence, roads to instability and the emergence of complex business fluctuations," *AUCO Czech Economic Review* **4**(3), 236–262.

Christiano, L. and Eichenbaum, M. (1992), "Current real business cycle theory and aggregate labor market fluctuations," *American Economic Review* **82**, 430–450.

Christiano, L. and Gust, C. (1999), "Taylor rules in a limited participation model," NBER Working Paper 7017.

Christiano, L., Eichenbaum, M. and Evans, C. L. (1994), "The effects of monetary policy shocks: evidence from the flow of funds," Working Paper 94-2, Federal Reserve Bank of Chicago.

Christiano, L., Eichenbaum, M. and Evans, C. (1999), "Monetary policy shocks: What have we learned and to what end?," in J. B. Taylor and M. Woodford, eds, *Handbook of Macroeconomics*, Vol. 1A, Elsevier, Amsterdam, pp. 65–148.

Clarida, R., Gali, J. and Gertler, M. (1998), "Monetary policy rules in practice, some international evidence," *European Economic Review* **42**, 1033–1067.

Cooley, T. F. (1995), *Frontiers of Business Cycle Research*, Princeton University Press, Princeton, NJ.

Davidson, R. and MacKinnon, J. (2004), *Econometric Theory and Methods*, Oxford University Press, New York.

De Grauwe, P. and Grimaldi, M. (2005a), "The exchange rate and its fundamentals in a complex world," *Review of International Economics* **13**(3), 549–575.

De Grauwe, P. and Grimaldi, M. (2005b), "Heterogeneity of agents and the exchange rate: a nonlinear approach," in P. De Grauwe, ed., *Exchange Rate Economics: Where Do We Stand?*, CESifo Seminar Series, MIT Press, Cambridge, MA, pp. 125–168.

De Grauwe, P. and Grimaldi, M. (2006), *The Exchange Rate in a Behavioral Finance Framework*, Princeton University Press, Princeton, NJ.

Debreu, G. (1974), "Excess demand functions," *Journal of Mathematical Economics* **1**(1), 15–21.

Dore, M. (1993), *The Macrodynamics of Business Cycles: A Comparative Evaluation*, Blackwell, Oxford.

Dornbusch, R. (1976), "Expectations and exchange rate dynamics," *Journal of Political Economy* **84**(6), 1161–1176.

Durlauf, S. (1996), "A theory of persistent income inequality," *Journal of Economic Growth* **1**, 75–94.

Ehrmann, M. and Fratzscher, M. (2005), "Exchange rates and fundamentals: new evidence from real-time data," *Journal of International Money and Finance* **24**(2), 317–341.

Eichenbaum, M. and Evans, C. L. (1995), "Some empirical evidence on the effects of shocks to monetary policy on exchange rates," *Quarterly Journal of Economics* **110**(4), 975–1009.

Eickmeier, S. (2007), "Business cycle transmission from the US to Germany – a structural factor approach," *European Economic Review* **51**(3), 521–551.

Erceg, C. J., Henderson, D. W. and Levin, A. T. (2000), "Optimal monetary policy with staggered wages and prices," *Journal of Monetary Economics* **46**, 281–313.

Estrella, A. and Fuhrer, J. (2002), "Dynamical inconsistencies: counterfactual implications of a class of rational expectations models," *American Economic Review* **92**, 1013–1028.

Fair, R. (1984), *Specification, Estimation and Analysis of Macroeconometric Models*, Harvard University Press, Cambridge, MA.

Fair, R. (2000), "Testing the NAIRU model for the United States," *Review of Economics and Statistics* **82**, 64–71.

Farmer, R. E. A. (2010), "How to reduce unemployment: a new policy proposal," *Journal of Monetary Economics* **57**(5), 557–572.

Fernandez, R. and Rogerson, R. (1996), "Income distribution, communities and the quality of public education," *Quarterly Journal of Economics* **111**, 135–164.

Ferri, P. and Greenberg, E. (1989), *The Labor Market and Business Cycle Theories*, Springer, Heidelberg.

Filardo, A. (1998), "New evidence on the output cost of fighting inflation," *Economic Review. Federal Reserve Bank of Kansas City* **64**(9/Q3), 33–61.

Flaschel, P. (1984), "Some stability properties of Goodwin's growth cycle. A critical elaboration," *Journal of Economics* **44**, 63–69.

Flaschel, P. (1993), *Macrodynamics. Income Distribution, Effective Demand, and Cyclical Growth*, Peter Lang, Frankfurt am Main.

Flaschel, P. (2001a), "Disequilibrium growth in monetary economies: basic components and the KMG working model," in L. Punzo, ed., *Cycles, Growth and Structural Change*, Routledge, London, pp. 128–168.

Flaschel, P. (2001b), "Viability and corridor stability in Keynesian supply-driven growth," *Metroeconomica* **52**(1), 26–48.

Flaschel, P. and Groh, G. (1995), "The classical growth cycle: reformulation, simulation and some facts," *Economic Notes* **24**, 293–326.

Flaschel, P. and Krolzig, H.-M. (2006), "Wage–price Phillips curves and macroeconomic stability. Basic structural form, estimation and analysis," in C. Chiarella, P. Flaschel, R. Franke and W. Semmler, eds, *Quantitative and Empirical Analysis of Nonlinear Dynamic Macromodels*, Elsevier, Amsterdam.

Flaschel, P. and Proaño, C. R. (2007), "AS–AD disequilibrium dynamics and the Taylor interest rate policy rule: Euro area-based simulation and estimation," in P. Arestis, E. Hein and E. Le Heron, eds, *Aspects of Modern Monetary and Macroeconomic Policies*, Palgrave Macmillan, New York, pp. 172–197.

Flaschel, P. and Proaño, C. (2009), "The J2 status of 'chaos' in macroeconomic period models," *Studies in Nonlinear Dynamics and Econometrics* **13**(2), Art. 2.

Flaschel, P. and Sethi, R. (1996), "Classical dynamics in a general model of the Keynes–Wicksell type," *Structural Change and Economic Dynamics* **7**(4), 401–428.

Flaschel, P. and Sethi, R. (1999), "Stability in models of money and perfect foresight: implications of non-linearity," *Economic Modelling* **16**(2), 221–233.

Flaschel, P., Franke, R. and Semmler, W. (1997), *Dynamic Macroeconomics. Instability, Fluctuations and Growth in Monetary Economies*, MIT Press, Cambridge, MA.

Flaschel, P., Gong, G. and Semmler, W. (1998), "A Keynesian based econometric framework for studying monetary policy rules," SCEPA Working Paper, Schwartz Center for Economic Policy Analysis, New School University, New York.

Flaschel, P., Groh, G. and Semmler, W. (1999), "Investment of firms in capital and productivity growth. A macrodynamic analysis," Discussion Paper, University of Bielefeld.

Flaschel, P., Tavani, D., Taylor, L. and Teuber, T. (2007), "A structuralist model of the wage–price spiral with non-linear demand pressure terms," SCEPA Working Paper, Schwarz Center for Economic Policy Analysis, New School University, New York.

Flaschel, P., Franke, R. and Proaño, C. R. (2008a), "On equilibrium determinacy in new Keynesian models with staggered wage and price setting," *The B.E. Journal of Macroeconomics* **8**(1), Art. 31, 1–10. (doi:10.2202/1935-1690.1802).

Flaschel, P., Franke, R. and Semmler, W. (2008b), "Kaleckian investment and employment cycles in postwar industrialized economies," in P. Flaschel and M. Landesmann, eds, *Mathematical Economics and the Dynamics of Capitalism: Goodwin's Legacy Continued*, Routledge, London.

Flaschel, P., Groh, G., Proaño, C. and Semmler, W. (2008c), *Topics in Applied Macrodynamic Theory*, Dynamic Modeling and Econometrics in Economics and Finance, Vol. 10, Springer, Berlin.

Flaschel, P., Kauermann, G. and Teuber, T. (2008d), "Long cycles in employment, inflation and real wage costs. Qualitative analysis and quantitative assessment," *American Journal of Applied Sciences* **5** (Special Issue), 69–77.

Foley, D. (1975), "On two specifications of asset equilibrium in macro-economic models," *Journal of Political Economy* **83**, 303–324.

Franke, R. (1996), "A Metzlerian model of inventory growth cycles," *Structural Change and Economic Dynamics* **2**, 243–262.

Franke, R. (2005), "Sophisticatedly simple expectations in the Phillips curve," Mimeo, Institute for Monetary Economics, Technical University Vienna.

Franke, R. and Lux, T. (1993), "Adaptive expectations and perfect foresight in a nonlinear metzlerian model of the inventory cycle," *Scandinavian Journal of Economics* **95**(3), 355–363.

Franke, R. and Semmler, W. (1999), "Bond rate, loan rate and Tobin's q in a temporary equilibrium model of the financial sector," *Metroeconomica* **50**(3), 351–385.

Franke, R., Flaschel, P. and Proaño, C. R. (2006), "Wage–price dynamics and income distribution in a semi-structural Keynes–Goodwin model," *Structural Change and Economic Dynamics* **17**(4), 452–465.

Frankel, J. A. and Froot, K. A. (1990), "Chartists, fundamentalists, and trading in the foreign exchange market," *American Economic Review* **80**(2), 181–185.

Franz, W. (1990), *Hysteresis Effects in Economic Models*, Physica-Verlag, Heidelberg.

Frauenthal, J. C. (1980), *Introduction to Population Modeling*, Birkhäuser, Stuttgart.

Freedman, C. (1996), "What operating procedures should be adopted to maintain price stability?," in *Achieving Price Stability: A Symposium*, Federal Reserve Bank of Kansas City, pp. 241–285. (www.kc.frb.org/publicat/sympos/1996/pdf/s96freed.pdf).

Fuhrer, J. (1997), "The (un)importance of forward-looking behavior in price specifications," *Journal of Money, Credit, and Banking* **29**, 338–350.

Galí, J. (2008), *Monetary Policy, Inflation and the Business Cycle*, Princeton University Press, Princton, NJ.

Galí, J. and Gertler, M. (1999), "Inflation dynamics: a structural econometric analysis," *Journal of Monetary Economics* **44**, 195–222.

Galí, J., Gertler, M. and López-Salido, J. D. (2001), "European inflation dynamics," *European Economic Review* **45**, 1237–1270.

Galí, J., Gertler, M. and López-Salido, J. (2005), "Robustness of the estimates of the hybrid new Keynesian Phillips curve," *Journal of Monetary Economics* **52**(6), 1107–1118.

Gandolfo, G. (2010), *Economic Dynamics*, 4th edn, Springer, Berlin.

Gantmacher, F. R. (1998), *The Theory of Matrices*, American Mathematical Society, Providence, RI.

Gerlach, H. (1988), "World business cycles under fixed and flexible exchange rates," *Journal of Money, Credit, and Banking* **20**, 621–632.

Gertler, M. and Trigari, A. (2006), "Unemployment fluctuations with staggered Nash wage bargaining," Unpublished manuscript, New York University.

Goodwin, R. (1967), "A growth cycle," in C. Feinstein, ed., *Socialism, Capitalism and Economic Growth*, Cambridge University Press, Cambridge, pp. 54–58.

Gordon, D. (1995), "Growth, distribution, and the rules of the game: social structuralist macro foundations for a democratic economic policy," in G. Epstein and H. Gintis, eds, *Macroeconomic Policy after the Conservative Era*, Cambridge University Press, Cambridge, pp. 335–383.

Greenwood, J. and Williamson, S. D. (1989), "International financial intermediation and aggregate fluctuations under alternative exchange rate regimes," *Journal of Monetary Economics* **23**, 401–431.

Gregory, A., Head, A. and Raynauld, J. (1997), "Measuring world business cycles," *International Economic Review* **38**(3), 677–701.

Greiner, A. (2001), "Distribution and endogenous growth: the two-class Pasinetti model," *Jahrbücher für Nationalökonomie und Statistik* **22**, 309–321.

Groth, C. (1988), "IS–LM dynamics and the hypothesis of combined adaptive–forward looking expectations," in P. Flaschel and M. Krüger, eds, *Recent Approaches to Economic Dynamics*, Peter Lang, Frankfurt am Main, pp. 251–265.

Haxholdt, C. (1995), "Nonlinear dynamical phenomena in economic oscillations," PhD Thesis, PhD Series 10.95, Handelshøjskolen i København.

Hein, E. and Vogel, L. (2008), "Distribution and growth reconsidered – empirical results for six OECD countries," *Cambridge Journal of Economics* **32**, 479–511.

Hibbs, D. (1973), *Mass Political Violence: A Cross-Sectional Analysis*, John Wiley, New York.

Hicks, J. R. (1974), "Real and monetary factors in economic fluctuations," *Scottish Journal of Political Economy* **21**(3), 205–214.

Hintermaier, T. (2005), "A sunspot paradox," *Economic Letters* **87**, 285–290.

Hirsch, M. and Smale, S. (1974), *Differential Equations, Dynamical Systems and Linear Algebra*, Academic Press, New York.

Hoogenveen, V. and Kuipers, S. (2000), "The long-run effects of low inflation rates," *Banca Nazionale del Lavoro Quarterly Review* **53**, 267–286.

Ito, T. (1980), "Disequilibrium growth theory," *Journal of Economic Theory* **23**(3), 380–409.

Judd, K. R. (1998), *Numerical Methods in Economics*, MIT Press, Cambridge, MA.

Judge, G., Hill, R., Griffiths, W., Lütkepohl, H. and Lee, T.-C. L. (1998), *Introduction to the Theory and Practice of Econometrics*, John Wiley, New York.

Kaldor, N. (1940), "A model of the trade cycle," *Economic Journal* **50**, 78–92.

Kaldor, N. (1966), "Marginal productivity and macroeconomic theories of distribution," *Review of Economic Studies* **11**, 143–156.

Kalyvitis, S. and Michaelides, A. (2001), "New evidence on the effects of US monetary policy on exchange rates," *Economic Letters* **71**, 255–263.

Keynes, J. M. (1936), *The General Theory of Employment, Interest and Money*, Macmillan, New York.

Kim, S. (1999), "Do monetary policy shocks matter in the G-7 countries? Using common identifying assumptions about monetary policy across countries," *Journal of International Economics* **48**, 367–412.

Kim, S. (2001), "International transmission mechanism of US monetary policy shocks: evidence from VARs," *Journal of Monetary Economics* **48**, 339–372.

Kim, S. and Roubini, N. (2000), "Exchange rate anomalies in the industrial countries: a solution with a structural VAR approach," *Journal of Monetary Economics* **45**, 561–586.

Kirman, A. (1993), "Ants, rationality, and recruitment," *Quarterly Journal of Economics* **108**(1), 137–156.

Köper, C. (2003), *Real-Financial Interaction in Contemporary Models of AS–AD Growth*, Peter Lang, Bern.

Köper, C. and Flaschel, P. (1999), "Real-financial interaction. A Keynes–Metzler–Goodwin portfolio approach," Discussion Paper, Bielefeld University.

Kuh, E. (1967), "A productivity theory of wage levels – an alternative to the Phillips curve," *Review of Economic Studies* **34**(4), 333–360.

Layard, R., Nickell, S. and Jackman, R. (1991), *Unemployment: Macroeconomic Performance and the Labor Market*, Oxford University Press, Oxford.

Levhari, D. (1966), "Extensions of Arrow's learning by doing," *Review of Economic Studies* **33**, 117–131.

Ljungqvist, L. and Sargent, T. J. (1998), "The European unemployment dilemma," *Journal of Political Economy* **106**(3), 514–550.

Loury, G. (1981), "Intergenerational transfers and the distribution of earnings," *Econometrica* **61**, 251–272.

Lucas, R. (1988), "On the mechanics of economic development," *Journal of Monetary Economics* **22**, 3–42.

Lux, T. (1992), "A note on the stability of endogenous cycles in Diamond's model of search and barter," *Journal of Economics* **56**, 185–196.

Lux, T. (1995a), "Corridor stability in the Dendrinos model of regional factor movements," *Geographical Analysis* **27**, 360–368.

Lux, T. (1995b), "Herd behaviour, bubbles and crashes," *Economic Journal* **105**, 881–896.

Malinvaud, E. (1980), *Profitability and Unemployment*, Cambridge University Press, Cambridge.

Mantel, R. R. (1977), "Implications of microeconomic theory for community excess demand functions," in M. Intriligator, ed., *Frontiers of Quantitative Economics*, Vol. III, North-Holland, Amsterdam, pp. 111–126.

Mas-Colell, A., Whinston, M. D. and Green, J. R. (1995), *Microeconomic Theory*, Oxford University Press, New York.

Metzler, L. A. (1941), "The nature and stability of inventory cycles," *Review of Economic Statistics* **23**, 113–129.

Minsky, H. P. (1982), *Stabilizing an Unstable Economy*, 2nd edn, McGraw-Hill, New York.

Naastepad, C. and Storm, S. (2007), "OECD demand regimes (1960–2000)," *Journal of Post-Keynesian Economics* **29**(2), 211–246.

Obstfeld, M. and Rogoff, K. (1995), "Exchange rate dynamics redux," *Journal of Political Economy* **103**(3), 624–660.

OECD (2002), "The ins and outs of long-term unemployment," in *OECD Employment Outlook 2002*, OECD, Paris, pp. 189–239.

Okun, A. M. (1970), *The Political Economy of Prosperity*, Brookings Institution, Washington, DC.

Orphanides, A. and Solow, R. M. (1990), "Money, inflation, and growth," in B. M. Friedman and F. H. Hahn, eds, *Handbook of Monetary Economics*, Vol. 1, North-Holland, Amsterdam, ch. 6, pp. 223–261.

Parker, T. S. and Chua, L. O. (1989), *Practical Numerical Algorithms for Chaotic Systems*, Springer, Berlin.

Pasinetti, L. L. (1962), "Rate of profit and income distribution in relation to the rate of economic growth," *Review of Economic Studies* **29**, 267–279.

Patinkin, D. (1965), *Money, Interest, and Prices*, 2nd edn, Harper & Row, New York.

Peersman, G. and Smets, F. (2003), "The monetary transmission mechanism in the Euro area: evidence from VAR analysis," in I. Angeloni, A. Kashyap and B. Mojon, eds, *Monetary Policy Transmission in the Euro Area*, Cambridge University Press, Cambridge, pp. 36–56.

Perko, L. (1991), *Differential Equations and Dynamical Systems*, Springer, Heidelberg.

Perotti, R. (1994), "Income distribution and investment," *European Economic Review* **38**, 827–835.

Persson, T. and Tabellini, G. (1996), "Is inequality harmful for economic growth?," *American Economic Review* **84**, 600–621.

Pohjola, M. (1981), "Stable, cyclic and chaotic growth: the dynamics of a discrete-time version of Goodwin's growth cycle model," *Journal of Economics* **41**(1–2), 27–38.

Powell, A. A. and Murphy, C. W. (1997), *Inside a Modern Macroeconometric Model: A Guide to the Murphy Model*, 2nd edn, Springer, Berlin.

Press, W. H., Flannery, B. P., Teukolsky, S. A. and Vetterling, W. T. (1986), *Numerical Recipes: The Art of Scientific Computing*, Cambridge University Press, Cambridge.

Proaño, C. (2008), "Heterogeneous expectations, FX fluctuations and dynamic macroeconomic stability," Unpublished manuscript, Bielefeld University.

Proaño, C., Flaschel, P., Ernst, E. and Semmler, W. (2007), "Gradual wage–price adjustments in Keynesian macrodynamics. Evidence from the US and the Euro area," SCEPA Working Paper, Schwartz Center for Economic Policy Analysis, New School University, New York.

Proaño, C. R., Flaschel, P., Ernst, E. and Semmler, W. (2009), "Disequilibrium macroeconomic dynamics, income distribution and wage–price Phillips curves: evidence from the US and the Euro area," in P. Flaschel, ed., *The Macrodynamics of Capitalism. Elements for a Synthesis of Marx, Keynes and Schumpeter*, Springer, Berlin, pp. 305–333.

Proaño, C. R., Flaschel, P., Krolzig, H.-M. and Diallo, M. B. (2011), "Monetary policy and macroeconomic stability under alternative demand regimes," *Cambridge Journal of Economics* **35**(3), 569–585.

Rabanal, P. and Tuesta, V. (2006), "Euro–dollar real exchange rate dynamics in an estimated two-country model: What is important and what is not," Working Paper 06/177, IMF.

Rizvi, S. A. T. (2006), "The Sonnenschein–Mantel–Debreu results after thirty years," *History of Political Economy* **38**(Suppl. 1), 228–245.

Rødseth, A. (2000), *Open Economy Macroeconomics*, Cambridge University Press, Cambridge.

Romer, P. M. (1986), "Increasing returns and long-run growth," *Journal of Political Economy* **94**(5), 1002–1037.

Rose, H. (1967), "On the non-linear theory of the employment cycle," *Review of Economic Studies* **34**, 153–173.

Rose, H. (1990), *Macroeconomic Dynamics: A Marshallian Synthesis*, Basil Blackwell, Cambridge, MA.

Rosser, J. B. (1999), "On the complexities of complex economic dynamics," *Journal of Economic Perspectives* **13**, 169–192.

Rosser, J. B. (2000), *From Catastrophe to Chaos: A General Theory of Economic Discontinuities*, 2nd edn, Mathematics, Microeconomics, Macroeconomics, and Finance, Vol. I, Kluwer Academic, Norwell, MA.

Rotemberg, J. and Woodford, M. (1999), "Interest rate rules in an estimated sticky price model," in J. Taylor, ed., *Monetary Policy Rules*, University of Chicago Press, Chicago.

Rudd, J. and Whelan, K. (2005), "New tests of the new Keynesian Phillips curve," *Journal of Monetary Economics* **52**(6), 1167–1181.

Rudebusch, G. (2001), "Is the Fed too timid? Monetary policy in an uncertain world," *Review of Economics and Statistics* **83**, 203–217.

Rudebusch, G. D. (2002), "Term structure evidence on interest rate smoothing and monetary policy inertia," *Journal of Monetary Economics* **49**, 1161–1187.

Rudebusch, G. D. (2006), "Monetary policy inertia: Fact or fiction?," *International Journal of Central Banking* **2**(4), 85–135.

Rudebusch, G. D. and Svensson, L. E. (1999), "Policy rules for inflation targeting," in J. B. Taylor, ed., *Monetary Policy Rules*, University of Chicago Press, Chicago, ch. 15, pp. 203–246.

Saint-Paul, G. and Verdier, T. (1993), "Education, democracy and growth," *Journal of Development Economics* **42**, 399–407.

Samanidou, E., Zschischang, E., Stauffer, D. and Lux, T. (2007), "Agent-based models of financial markets," *Reports on Progress in Physics* **70**, 409–450.

Samuelson, P. A. and Modigliani, F. (1966), "The Pasinetti paradox in neo-classical and more general models," *Review of Economic Studies* **33**, 269–303.

Sargent, T. (1987), *Macroeconomic Theory*, 2nd edn, Academic Press, New York.

Sargent, T. and Wallace, N. (1973), "The stability of models of money and growth with perfect foresight," *Econometrica* **41**, 1043–1048.

Schneider, J. and Ziesemer, T. (1994), "What's new and what's old in new growth theory: endogenous technology, microfoundation and growth rate predictions – a critical overview," Discussion Paper, Maastricht.

Schumpeter, J. A. (1939), *Business Cycles. A Theoretical, Historical and Statistical Analysis of the Capitalist Process*, Vols. I, II, Porcupine Press, Philadelphia.

Semmler, W. and Bernard, L. (2009), "Boom–bust cycles: leveraging, complex securities and asset prices," Technical Report, New School University, New York. (http://www.newschool.edu/nssr/cem/papers/wp/financial/SemmlerBernardNewversion Sept2709_mrLucas_4.pdf)

Sims, C. (1980), "Macroeconomics and reality," *Econometrica* **48**(1), 1–48.

Sims, C. (1987), Comments and discussion on O. J. Blanchard *et al.*, "Aggregate and individual price adjustment," *Brookings Papers on Economic Activity* **1987**(1), 117–120.

Sims, C. (1992), "Interpreting the macroeconomic time series facts: the effects of monetary policy," *European Economic Review* **36**, 975–1011.

Sims, C. (1998), "Stickiness," *Carnegie–Rochester Conference Series on Public Policy* **49**(December), 317–356.

Sims, C. (2000), "Vector autoregression models of economic time series," in J. Taylor and M. Woodford, eds, *Handbook of Macroeconomics*, Elsevier, New York.

Skott, P. (1989a), *Conflict and Effective Demand in Economic Growth*, Cambridge University Press, Cambridge.

Skott, P. (1989b), "Effective demand, class struggle and cyclical growth," *International Economic Review* **30**(1), 231–247.

Skott, P. (1991), "Cyclical growth in a Kaldorian model," in *Nicholas Kaldor and Mainstream Economics*, Macmillan, London, pp. 379–394.

Smets, F. and Wouters, R. (2003), "An estimated dynamic stochastic general equilibrium model for the Euro area," *Journal of the European Economic Association* **1**(5), 1123–1175.

Solow, R. (1956), "A contribution to the theory of economic growth," *Quarterly Journal of Economics* **70**(1), 65–94.

Solow, R. (1990), "Goodwin's growth cycle: reminiscence and rumination," in *Nonlinear and Multisectoral Macrodynamics*, Macmillan, London, pp. 31–41.

Solow, R. and Stiglitz, J. (1968), "Output, employment and wages in the short-run," *Quarterly Journal of Economics* **82**, 537–560.

Sonnenschein, H. (1973), "Do Walras' identity and continuity characterize the class of community excess demand functions?," *Journal of Economic Theory* **6**(4), 345–354.

Sontag, E. (1998), *Mathematical Control Theory: Deterministic Finite Dimensional Systems*, 2nd edn, Springer, New York.

Stockhammer, E. and Onaran, O. (2004), "Accumulation, distribution and employment: a structural VAR approach to a Kaleckian macro model," *Structural Change and Economic Dynamics* **15**(4), 421–447.

Stockhammer, E., Onaran, O. and Ederer, S. (2009), "Functional income distribution and aggregate demand in the Euro area," *Cambridge Journal of Economics* **33**(1), 139–159.

Strogatz, S. (1994), *Nonlinear Dynamics and Chaos*, Addison-Wesley, Reading, MA.

Svensson, L. E. (1997), "Inflation forecast targeting: implementation and monetaring inflation targets," *European Economic Review* **41**, 1111–1146.

Svensson, L. E. (1999), "Inflation targeting as a monetary policy rule," *Journal of Monetary Economics* **43**(3), 607–654.

Tavani, D., Flaschel, P. and Taylor, L. (2011), "Estimated non-linearities and multiple equilibria in a model of distributive-demand cycles," *International Review of Applied Economics* **25**(5), 519–538.

Taylor, J. (1993), "Discretion versus policy rules in practice," *Carnegie–Rochester Conference Series on Public Policy*, **39**(December), 195–214.

Taylor, J. B. (1994), *Macroeconomic Policy in a World Economy: From Econometric Design to Practical Operation*, W. W. Norton, New York.

Taylor, J. (1999), *Monetary Policy Rules*, University of Chicago Press, Chicago.

Tobin, J. (1969), "A general equilibrium approach to monetary theory," *Journal of Money, Credit, and Banking* **1**, 15–29.

Tobin, J. (1975), "Keynesian models of recession and depression," *American Economic Review* **65**, 195–202.

Trigari, A. (2004), "Equilibrium unemployment, job flows and inflation dynamics," Working Paper 304, European Central Bank.

Turnovsky, S. J. (1977), *Macroeconomic Analyis and Stabilization Policies*, Cambridge University Press, Cambridge.

Turnovsky, S. J. (1995), *Methods of Macroeconomic Dynamics*, MIT Press, Cambridge, MA.

Uzawa, H. (1965), "Optimum technical change in an aggregative model of economic growth," *International Economic Review* **6**, 18–31.

Veniers, Y. and Gupta, D. (1986), "Income distribution and socio-political instability as determinants of savings: a cross-sectional model," *Journal of Political Economy* **96**, 873–833.

Walsh, C. E. (2003), "Labor market search and monetary shocks," in S. Altug, J. Chadha and C. Nolan, eds, *Elements of Dynamic Macroeconomic Analysis*, Cambridge University Press, Cambridge, pp. 451–486.

Wiggins, S. (1990), *Introduction to Applied Nonlinear Dynamical Systems and Chaos*, Springer, Berlin.

Woodford, M. (2003), *Interest and Prices. Foundations of a Theory of Monetary Policy*, Princeton University Press, Princeton, NJ.

Zellner, A. (1992), "Statistics, science and public policy," *Journal of the American Statistical Association* **87**, 1–6.

Zellner, A. (2002), "My experience with nonlinear dynamics models in economics," *Studies in Nonlinear Dynamics and Econometrics* **6**(2), 1–18.

Index

www.ingramcontent.com/pod-product-compliance
Ingram Content Group UK Ltd.
Pitfield, Milton Keynes, MK11 3LW, UK
UKHW022006180926
475701UK00003B/214
9781138901339